WOMEN

A Global Anthology of Women's Resistance

IMAGINE

From 600 B.C.E. to Present

CHANGE

WOMEN IMAGINE CHANGE

A Global Anthology of Women's Resistance

From 600 B.C.E. to Present

Edited by

Eugenia C. DeLamotte,

Natania Meeker,

and Jean F. O'Barr

ROUTLEDGE: NEW YORK AND LONDON

Published in 1997 by
Routledge
29 West 35th Street
New York, NY 10001

Published in Great Britain by
Routledge
11 New Fetter Lane
London EC4P 4EE

Printed in the United States of America on acid-free paper.

We are grateful to the authors and publishers acknowledged in these pages for their permission to reprint copyrighted material. We have made every reasonable effort to identify and locate copyright owners of the included material. If any information is found to be incomplete, we will gladly make whatever additional acknowledgment might be necessary.

Cover and text design by Mark Abrams.

Library of Congress Cataloging-in-Publication Data

Women imagine change: a global anthology of women's resistance from
600 B.C.E. to present / edited by Eugenia Delamotte, Natania Meeker,
and Jean O'Barr.—1st ed.
p. cm.
ISBN 0-415-91530-9.—ISBN 0-415-91531-7 (pbk.)
1. Literature—Women authors. 2. Women and literature.
3. Feminism and literature. I. DeLamotte, Eugenia C. II. Meeker,
Natania. III. O'Barr, Jean F.
PN6069.W65W623 1997 97-18037
CIP

To the students of Duke and Arizona State Universities
and to the Duke alumnae/i
whose enthusiasm, insight, and resources
enable us to tell the stories of women's resistance

TABLE OF CONTENTS

GEOGRAPHICAL/CULTURAL TABLE OF CONTENTS

Here the excerpts are organized by geographic origin, arranged by continent or region and subdivided by nation, using the contemporary name of the nation in that area. In addition, the United States selections are subdivided by ethnic origin. Excerpts are arranged chronologically within each subcategory. (A few authors are listed within more than one category.)

Please note that these geographic names and divisions often differ from the political and cultural organization of the time in which an excerpt was written. More precise accounts of the historical background of authors and their writings are provided in the headnotes to the excerpts.

AFRICA (SUB-SAHARAN)

ASIA

Bangladesh

China

India

Japan

Russia

NORTH AMERICA

Canada

CHRONOLOGICAL TABLE OF CONTENTS

600 BCE TO 1299 CE

1300 TO 1799

1800 TO 1899

1900–1960

1961–1995

ACKNOWLEDGMENTS

Every book has an origin story. Our origins illustrate the way academic feminism and women's activism can inform and reinforce one another. The story begins in Jean O'Barr's and Eugenia DeLamotte's many years' experience teaching Women's Studies, feminist theory, and women's literature. We had long sought material for courses that expanded student understandings of how women have found ways to resist oppression and exercise power in their lives. Semester after semester, we ended up with too much reading, not enough contextual material, and skyrocketing book costs. We dreamt of an up-to-date anthology that would be global in its scope and historical in its perspective.

This dream was realized through the commitment of a group of women activists among the alumnae of Duke University. These women had come together over the years under the aegis of the

Women's Studies Program to take part in the growing scholarship on women, gender, and feminist theories. The group made a tenth birthday present to the program in 1993: the funds to undertake the anthology project.

With money to hire assistants, pay bills, buy equipment, and afford released time, our story shifted back to campus. In 1994, Brenda Denzler and Elizabeth Waters, both graduate students at Duke, joined the project as research assistants. They located authors and found sources for the ideas. We scoured the library. We found fragments in our files and on our own bookshelves. We talked to colleagues. We remembered essays we and our students had found inspiring. Those early days of collecting material were supported by the steady help of the Women's Studies staff at Duke—Sarah Hill, Nancy Rosebaugh, and Vivian Robinson. And Cynthia Banks-Glover spent many hours entering the material, delighting in the ideas that these foremothers offered.

In 1995, Natania Meeker became our research assistant. As we accumulated more materials, we sorted and conceptualized, resorted and reconceptualized. We taught drafts of the manuscript in classes at both Duke and Arizona State; we presented selections before public audiences around the country. Our narrative emerged from these encounters and from the conversations among the three of us. It quickly became apparent that Natania Meeker was more peer than assistant and she joined the editorial team early in 1996. We found ourselves drawing on our own experiences in living in many parts of the world and our individual scholarly backgrounds. Eugenia DeLamotte reflected on her two years of teaching in Denmark, her own scholarly work on the nineteenth-century novel, and her investigations into the work of African-American authors. Natania Meeker has a strong interest in Islamic cultures, derived from her many years spent in Turkey, that she brought together with her specialization in the literature and philosophy of eighteenth-century France and the Enlightenment. Jean O'Barr's first research on African women proved a strong resource. Her examinations of academic culture and her work with women students added yet other dimensions. Despite these varied backgrounds, we were ever mindful of the fact that we were products of intellectual and cultural contexts that demanded constant challenging.

We wanted something theoretically accessible, but also theoretically nuanced. We wanted selections organized around students' concerns but also presented in historical context, with information different readers could use in different ways, to unlock for themselves a door into each writer's world. Students' questions over the years became the shaping principle of the anthology, beginning with the most basic and urgent: What should change for women, and what are the best strategies for effecting that change? The activism of our students from every venue fueled our scholarship.

During the 1996–7 academic year, Jennifer Parchesky joined us as editorial assistant. In this capacity she helped oversee the final editing of the manuscript, the composition of the index, and the creation of the alternate tables of contents. Her dedication, energy, and skills made the final stages of a complex process not only possible but enjoyable.

Many colleagues contributed guidance. In particular, we would like to thank Dawn Bates, John Berninghausen, Mary T. Boatwright, Dorothy Broom, Kathleen Ferraro, David Foster, Jehanne Gheith, Monica Green, Nancy Gutierrez, Annis Hopkins, Elizabeth

Horan, Katsuko T. Hotelling, Micaela Janan, Tris Laughter, Asunción Lavrin, Deborah Losse, Stephen R. MacKinnon, Mary Melcher, Carol Meyers, Kristen Neuschel, Chia-lin Pao Tao, Jewell Parker Rhodes, Laurel Rodd, Kathleen Ross, Mary Rothschild, M. Kathy Rudy, Kathleen Sands, Stephanie Sieburth, Irene Silverblatt, K. Lynn Stoner, Hoyt Tillman, and Laura Tohe.

The staff at Routledge embraced the project and made our story theirs. We thank each of them for their many contributions—Abigail Baxter, our copyeditor, who taught us the value of the simple sentence and the precise word, Ande Ciecierski, Heidi Freund, Ilene Kalish, Carolyn Mork, Alex Mummery, Laura-Ann Robb, and Sarita Sahni.

This is an ambitious project, emboldened by students hungry for knowledge, and made possible by a group of alumnae determined that this knowledge should be available. The collection models a relationship between academic feminism and women activists. It challenges us to broaden our ideas about women and feminism, resistance and power, now and into the future.

ECD, NM, and *JFO*

CONTRIBUTORS

In addition to the range of women's voices represented in the excerpts themselves, the headnotes and section introductions also reflect the unique perspectives, voices, and areas of expertise of their individual authors. (Headnote authors are identified by their initials at the end of each headnote.) A number of those who contributed headnotes were students in women's studies courses taught in 1995 and 1996 by Eugenia DeLamotte at Arizona State University and Jean O'Barr at Duke University.

At Arizona State University, Michelle A. Holling *[MAH]* is a Chicana feminist doctoral student in Communication. Her work uses rhetorical and feminist theories to illuminate contemporary debates surrounding Proposition 187, AIDS, and representations of Chicanas and Latinas in film. Robin Menefee's *[RM]* field as a feminist scholar is the interrelationship between women and technology. A graduate of Arizona State University, she is pursuing a master's degree while teaching computer programming at Kilgore Community College. Patricia J. Novelli *[PJN]* earned a B.A. in Women's Studies and Art History in 1996 and plans to pursue a doctorate. Her goal is to further integrate feminist theory into the teaching and writing of art history and criticism. Kevin Quashie *[KQ]* is a graduate student in English who works on gender and race in nineteenth- and twentieth-century American narrative. His current project develops a theory of African-American literature that looks at how silence, "singing," and sound speak the interior voice.

At Duke University, Kathryn K. Fenn *[KKF]* is a graduate student in history. She studies nineteenth- and twentieth-century U.S. cultural history, specializing in the intersection of popular culture and gender relations. Joe Spinazzola *[JS]* is a graduate student in clinical psychology, where his current research focuses on adolescent girls' self-representations, gender role socialization, and female identity development. His clinical work specializes in the treatment of survivors of familial and relationship abuse. Katrin Volkner *[KV]* is a doctoral student in German Studies, where she works on literature and culture of the nineteenth and twentieth centuries. Her research interests include popular scientific discourses, women's history, and the development of "middlebrow culture" in turn-of-the-century Germany. Jennifer Parchesky *[JP]* is a doctoral candidate in the Literature Program at Duke University, where she works on American literature, film, and cultural studies. Her interests include popular fiction and early women filmmakers. She is currently completing a dissertation on melodrama, gender, and the middle class in the 1920s and 1930s.

Eugenia C. DeLamotte *[ECD]* is Associate Professor of English at Arizona State University. Her areas of specialization include women's literature, African-American literature, and feminist theory. Her publications include *Perils of the Night: A Feminist Study of Nineteenth-Century Gothic* (1990) and a study of writer Paule Marshall, *Places of Silence, Journeys of Freedom* (forthcoming, 1998). Her next book will examine rhetorics of self-decolonization in women's writing at the turn of the twentieth century, with a focus on some of the writers included in this anthology: Anna Julia Cooper, Luisa Capetillo, Voltairine de Cleyre, and Bonita Wa Wa Calachaw Nuñez.

Natania Meeker *[NM]* is a doctoral candidate in the Literature Program at Duke University with a strong interest in feminist theory and women's history. Her concern with Islamic women's issues began when she lived and studied in Turkey. Her current field of specialization is French literature and philosophy of the eighteenth century, and her research interests include Enlightenment materialist philosophy, theories of reading, and representations of the imagination. Her article, "Rethinking the Universal, Reworking the Political: Postmodern Feminism and the Enlightenment," appeared in *Women in French Studies* 3 (1995). She is currently spending a year in Paris researching her dissertation.

Jean F. O'Barr *[JFO]* is the Director of Women's Studies at Duke University. Her primary research interests are in women and education with an emphasis on how cultural practices and institutional arrangements affect gender relations. She has published numerous books that explore the relationships among students' classroom experiences, faculty development, and power dynamics in higher education, including *Feminism in Action: Building Institutions and Community through Women's Studies* (1994). Dr. O'Barr did fieldwork in Tanzania and has published books and articles on African women. A campus and community activist, Jean O'Barr is recognized as a leader in the field of women's studies.

A NOTE ON THE TEXT

The excerpts in this volume generally follow the style and format of the sources given in the copyright line. All additions, emphasis, and bracketed comments are those of the source so identified, with two exceptions.

- We have inserted ellipses to indicate omitted text.
- We have added our own footnotes while retaining some of those from the original sources. The author of each footnote is indicated in brackets at the end of the note.

WOMEN

A Global Anthology of Women's Resistance

IMAGINE

From 600 B.C.E to Present

CHANGE

INTRODUCTION

Eugenia C. DeLamotte, Natania Meeker, Jean F. O'Barr

Women Imagine Change: A Global Anthology of Women's Resistance is a worldwide and multicultural anthology of women's narratives. It draws material from the lives of women at many points in time and from many positions in their lives. We present their ideas under the rubrics of five themes: Sexuality, Spirituality, and Power; Work and Education; Representing Women, Writing the Body Politic; Identifying Sources of Resistance; and Vision and Transformation. These themes appear to us to be central to women's experiences of resistance, an idea we elaborate below. Each selection is preceded by a headnote, written by one of the editors or by one of our students. In addition, each of the five sections begins with an introduction that discusses how the theme of that section reverberates in women's lives.

Our goal in compiling this anthology is to lay

some groundwork for bringing together what appear to us to be at least four separate strands of thought in conversations about women and men, gender relations, and feminism.[1] The strands are rarely explicit in such conversations, but present nonetheless, whether the conversations are held within the academy or outside it. One strand emphasizes differences between the sexes and assumes that being male or female is a primary determinant of experience. A second strand emphasizes the similarities between women and men and puts the accent on the human condition of each individual's experiences or on experiences of oppression that cross gender lines. A third strand acknowledges the multiple determinants of oppression and connects them in the lives of women while disputing the significance of gender in systems of oppression. And the fourth strand questions the stability of the categories of woman and man. In the language of the academy, those in this fourth conversation "deconstruct" the very concepts of maleness and femaleness. These four strands are readily observable in many contexts, the connections among them less so. Moreover, the multiple relationships among these strands are not usually recognized in contemporary conversations. Each strand emerges at a particular moment, claims explanatory power for the question at hand, and fades into the background as another strand emerges. Any combination of these strands may be present at one time, but explicit discussions of the interrelatedness of all four are much more difficult to achieve.

We do not claim to have created a single conversation from these multiple strands; that remains a distant goal. We do claim that by focusing on women's resistance we are fostering a broader conversation among the separate strands, and that this conversation arises out of the nexus between women's writing about themselves and the representations of women that circulate in scholarly work and popular culture. The words of hundreds of women illustrate for us the infinite variety of ways in which women have reflected upon, reacted to, and initiated social change by resisting the gendered conditions of their lives as they understand them. Furthermore, reading these words reveals the ways that gender works in women's lives, sometimes claiming center stage, at other times receding in importance. It is this need to think from a both/and, rather than an either/or, perspective on women and resistance that informs our project.

How then do we think about gender as a conceptual category? We recognize that gender may not be the most salient category for every woman in every excerpt. But in every instance gender is there. We see gender, race, class, ethnicity, ability, sexual orientation—and all the other such categories that are used to justify hierarchies of power—as actually and conceptually inseparable. We have come to think of them (with the help of theorists such as Gloria Anzaldúa, bell hooks, Gerda Lerner, Audre Lorde, Barbara Smith, and Patricia Williams) as "interlocking" (hooks) and "mutually constitutive" (Lerner) of each other, with each category being used by systems of dominance to construct all the other categories. We focus on gender because our goal in this project is to be part of a larger endeavor for feminist social change.

Although we have used ideas about gender to provide the primary analytic and conceptual framework for this anthology, we have not chosen to promote a particular theory of gender but rather to emphasize common themes we see emerging from women's lived experiences. We recognize that many feminist scholars have criticized the drive to define "women" by their essential difference from men, and have challenged the notion that "experience" is an unproblematic vehicle of truth.[2] Nonetheless, we believe that the category of "women's experiences" remains a meaningful explanatory tool. We are not advocating an emphasis on "women's experience" as a way of escaping the power of ideology or the significance of social context.[3] We emphasize that ideas about the social role of gender are historically and culturally specific and that the way in which a whole set of ideologies functions to define and to limit women's activities differs markedly according to time and place. Indeed, one of the tasks of this anthology has been to demonstrate this fact.

Therefore, although the salience of the concepts of "women" and "gender" varies widely in the excerpts presented here, we maintain that the commonalities (and differences) evident among the women in this anthology have contemporary relevance. We believe that, by bringing together many women's thoughts on the relation between gender and social change, we can encourage readers to reflect on how gender has mattered—and continues to matter—politically. Along with many of the writers collected in this volume, we would like to envision a future when such "interlocking" categories as gender, race, class, and sexual orientation are no longer mechanisms of oppression.

OUR CRITERIA FOR SELECTING THE EXCERPTS

Our premise about the need for connective conversations determines who we think the audience for the anthology is, how we have selected our material, and how we have framed the material selected. Because we direct our attention toward the possibilities for social change—both the possibilities for transformations in individual women's lives and those for alterations of cultural ideas and structures—we think the audience for this anthology is broad. Undergraduate students in women's studies and the liberal arts will have in hand a storehouse of material to inform their questions and debates. Graduate students and faculty who plan to teach and research subjects related to feminism will discover a variety of new voices to pursue in their scholarly endeavors. And general readers with an interest in women's issues will find inspiration and resources for their own struggles. We hope all of our readers will find in our work ways to move these conversations forward.

Our emphasis on women's lived experience explains our decision to limit the excerpts, with few exceptions, to first-person narratives. This choice helped solve the problem of how to select from the vast amount of contemporary feminist writing. We applaud the burgeoning of research literature about women in every field and have drawn on it extensively in thinking through what we wanted to present. The detailed recovery by historians and literary critics of women's records and writings, analyses by social scientists of women's work and family patterns, accounts of women's leadership in civic and religious institutions, discoveries about women's physical and mental health, and research being carried out in many other fields of scholarship have all worked their way into our thinking. We believe that such feminist scholarship, in its efforts to connect theory and practice, can only be enhanced by dialogue with other forms—letters, autobiographies, personal essays, oral histories—in which women have articulated the knowledge they have gained through personal experiences of oppression and resistance.

Working with the category of first-person narratives, we kept four criteria before us as we made selections. First, we strove to maintain the international focus of this anthology by including the writings of women from some forty countries, past and present. Feminism has always been an international protest movement[4]—as we discuss in the section **Identifying Sources of Resistance**—and we want to introduce global foremothers to our readers.

Second, we committed ourselves to portraying the multiplicity of women's voices. Readers will find an array of women here, many of them rarely anthologized outside specialist circles. Since our primary goal was to present multiple perspectives on several themes (which we discuss later in this introduction), we sought to organize the anthology around writings on resistance by women from a wide variety of cultures, classes, races, and regions. The thirty U.S. women whose works are presented here come from a wide variety of ethnic, racial, and regional backgrounds, while the remaining seventy selections represent voices from more than thirty countries around the world. While this is certainly not a representative sample of women around the world (if such a thing were possible), and while the selections necessarily reflect the editors' interests and expertise, we believe that, in reading across the tables of contents, readers will be struck by both the global and the multicultural perspectives available to them.

In order to understand how resistance develops and is brought to bear on the social systems and cultural ideologies of a particular time and place, our emphasis has been on the way women's knowledge about themselves and their circumstances changes, how they develop their knowledge and transmit it. We think that bringing together these texts, many of which appear here in translation, is part of this transmission of knowledge in which women have always engaged. Translations are a key part of the feminist project represented by this anthology. For this reason, we do not see these translations as deformations of (supposedly pure) original texts. Instead, we see them as an important part of the transformation and transmission of knowledge by and about women. While we hope that these excerpts will inspire readers to seek out the full and original texts, we also hope that they will consider the translations that appear here as contributions to the dynamic process of interpretation.[5]

Our third criterion arose out of student inquiries, as well as the readings and conversations in our daily lives, about what some call the "presentism" of much discussion about women, men, and gender. In making our selections, we endeavored to find women's writings from other times, fully cognizant of the dangers of reading "then" (whenever that may be) from the point of view of "now." Yet it seems essential to us, if we are to analyze contemporary questions, that we have access to perspectives from the past. Feminist wisdom often repeats the dictum that without a past we cannot create a future. Yet the marginalization of women, and of the questions they consider important, from the production of knowledge means that women's wisdom is more frequently lost than remembered. Thus, our third criterion led to the decision to begin each excerpt with a headnote that not only gives biographical information about the author but also locates her in her historical context, presents some key issues of that time, and anticipates some of the questions today's readers may bring to the excerpt.

Fourth, and finally, we limited ourselves to the written words (occasionally recorded by others) of women. Our focus is on how women have voiced their own experiences and what they report doing with those experiences; it is not on what men say about women. We have had to exclude the many other forms—material objects, visual images, songs and oral traditions—in which women give voice to their resistance, simply because any one publication must set limits to become internally consistent and useful as a point of departure for analysis.

CONTEMPORARY QUESTIONS

Most importantly, our choice of excerpts reflects our understanding of the questions women are posing today about the relationships among their personal power to resist, the powers of various groups to which they belong, and the larger systems of power they confront. As we hear them, these questions arrange themselves in four clusters. One cluster has to do with social change and an individual's role in it. What is the locus of power for social change? Is it better to advocate change from inside an institution, or to go outside and invent alternatives? Which is more effective, and under what conditions? A second cluster examines power from another vantage point: What kinds of power do I want for myself and/or the social groups to which I belong? A third cluster involves gender. Why is gender such an important organizing principle of social life? How did it come about that the categorization as female or male determines so many aspects of individual lives? Should it be this way? Should (and could) it be changed? The fourth cluster centers on the future: What should the world be like for women in all their diversity?

Underlying these four clusters of questions is the issue of social responsibility to self, to others, and to philosophical, religious, and ethical principles. There are many ways of posing the questions that cluster around this most basic issue, depending on how a woman interprets the organization of her society, whether she belongs to groups whose interests appear to conflict, and whether her philosophy assigns a positive value to individualism (a concept that has been important to many feminists in the West but is by no means universal).[6] For many, perhaps most, women, the question of social responsibility has to do primarily with how to interpret their multiple responsibilities to the family, racial, religious, ethnic, national, class, and political units to which they belong. How are these responsibilities intertwined? What happens when they conflict with each other, or with the systems of power in which they are embedded?

PERSPECTIVES ON RESISTANCE

As we ourselves pondered these questions, we came to see the need for an anthology that shows how women have reflected on the conditions of their lives and often acted to change them. We chose to define this process of reflecting upon, reacting to, and initiating change as a process of *resistance*. Rather than attempting to develop a global theory of feminist social change, we have been guided by a vision of this book as a set of observations about how women have *lived* resistance. We believe that any theory of resistance must come to grips with the fact that resistance is lived in culturally and historically specific ways. While we see resistance as an important part, and an ongoing process, of living in society, we believe in the necessity to ground our understanding of resistance in a historical perspective.

In presenting this set of observations about women, the following assumptions have directed our thinking:

1. Our focus on the process of resistance stems from our interest in systems of power. For some time scholars have emphasized the role power plays in organizing social life; women's studies scholars in particular have viewed ideas about power structures and the circulation of power as fundamental to an understanding of gender roles and women's place in the power structures of society. We believe that individual women's lives need to be read in terms of the *interlocking* systems of power within which all human beings live; analyses of women must take into account all of the sociocultural institutions that shape women's experiences. We need to look at individual efforts in the context of larger systems of social organization.

   We do not mean to suggest that the circulation of power is the only process that explains human social organization.[7] Rather, we suggest that a close look at the ways in which specific political and material circumstances shape the writings included here will bring readers to an understanding of the specific—and multiple—forces that may shape women's lives.

2. We believe that systems of power are almost always informed by some set of categories based on gender. These categorizations may work and be understood in very different ways, and they always interrelate with other ways of structuring power such as those based on age, race, or control of material resources. At least from the time written history begins, however, we see some women acting to change the way ideas about gender shape social practices. It is this continuity in women's resistance to gendered oppression that inspired this anthology.

3. Although we see continuity in the history of women's resistance, we see specific moments of resistance as very different from one another. A typology of women's resistance should vary along with the factors that make gender carry different meanings and work in different ways for different women. In most cultures, the social fact of being a woman can be partially erased—or emphasized—by virtue of being other things (for example, wealthy). Women's sites of resistance vary accordingly. In some cultures, women are excluded by virtue of their gender from participation in those activities which are thought to define what it means to be fully human (for example, rational debate or sacred practices). This experience might be described as paradoxical: in such a system, women are both human and less than human.[8] Whether or not women are thought to be essentially inferior to men in these cultures, they are nevertheless systematically denied access to a range of experiences that are seen in those cultures as making up the fullness of life. Many readers are familiar with the negative impact this kind of exclusion has on women's direct political participation. Gendering society in this way also implies a host of other factors, from the cultural to the religious, that shape women's general participation in the social order.

In Europe and the United States, feminist scholarship, seeking to understand women's situation globally, has often generalized from the (recent) experience of women in Western cultures, where the widespread belief in women's innate and natural inferiority to men has motivated feminist struggle at least since the eighteenth century. While Western patriarchy is by no means a universal paradigm, it is nonetheless true that, since the beginnings of Western imperialist expansion in the late fifteenth century, Western ways of gendering the world and its inhabitants have had material, political, and ideological impacts on other cultural systems. Even before Western imperialism began, many ancient societies considered gender an important category in determining the allocation of power and resources. In recent times, the spread of Western notions about what it means to be human—notions that claim to have universal relevance—have affected women's experience of themselves, their access to resources, and the priority they are assigned in policymaking the world over. In this context, women's resistance may involve an attempt to gain access to the universal categories that are thought to define human nature; this has been one of the central preoccupations behind the concern with education characteristic of Western bourgeois feminism, for example. Feminists worldwide, however, continue to draw attention to the way in which the material and political conditions of women's lives are at issue in different cultures' definitions of what it means to be human. Recent feminist writing, especially that by women of color, has begun to focus attention away from the class- and culture-specific problem of access to the universal, and has emphasized the variety and interrelatedness of multiple forms of oppression.[9]

In sum, while we see women's resistance as part of the dynamic of social life, we do not view those who resist and those who compel as two monolithic social groups. As revealed in this anthology, women's resistance is fluid and mobile, complex and polyvalent. Those activities that might be said to constitute women's resistance adapt to shifts in material conditions, ideologies, and social systems. In addition, our present circumstances inevitably influence our readings of past resistance. Some of the excerpts we have included might be interpreted by contemporary readers as describing a kind of unconscious resistance. Yet the readers themselves, of any text, are always engaged in a process of unconscious interpretation. The danger of reading resistance into women's writings is an ever-present one. This collection, rather than imposing a prefabricated definition of "women's resistance" onto a diverse company of texts by women, expands our ideas of what women's resistance might mean by allowing us to read and learn from reports of experience from the women themselves.

Our analysis of resistance raises the question: Does women's resistance work? In order to think about possible answers, readers should keep in mind that the story of women's resistance is not a linear one. Nor can the narrative of feminist struggle globally be recounted as a progressive history. The writings collected here demonstrate that women in the past were different from their contemporaries in ways that are difficult to comprehend. Some of the excerpts that we have included emerge from sociocultural systems whose subtle workings may not be fully understood by any contemporary reader. We ask the readers of this anthology to imagine as they read, how, in the past, men and women thought about individuals and groups, the sexual and the social, "in ways our culture has all but forgotten" (Williamson 132).

We believe that it is possible to learn from these differences. Every reader brings something of herself or himself to a text. We see the desires and expectations that readers bring to these excerpts as part of a shifting, developing conversation between past and present. The more than one hundred women whose experiences and ideas we record do not offer readers direct answers to the questions their own life situations raise about the best way to think about social responsibility, to conceptualize power, to understand the meaning of gender, to imagine an ideal world, or to effect social change. Instead, these authors suggest ways of getting at answers by offering their varied experiences as a resource for other women. By showing that women have always resisted obstacles, that many of those obstacles have been overcome, and that the insights of ancestors are one important set of analytic tools to employ against new obstacles, they strengthen our resolve.

SECTION OVERVIEW

Having described the concept of resistance and the questions readers may bring to this anthology, we now turn to a discussion of the themes developed in this anthology and conclude this introduction with an overview of the progression implied by the placement of each section.

We have arranged the excerpts in five thematic sections that became apparent to us as we worked on these materials. This thematic organization reflects our sense of the connections among the many aspects of women's experiences, connections that might not be readily apparent, but that seem to us enlightening. (Alternate tables of contents, organized chronologically and geographically/culturally, are also provided for readers who find these axes of connection useful.)

For example, we were surprised to discover how frequently women's reflections on their experiences connect the issues of sexuality and spirituality. Thus in the first section, **Sexuality, Spirituality, and Power**, we look at women's spiritual lives, sometimes lived within organized religions, sometimes outside. We look at the ways in which women's spiritual experiences are linked to their ideas about their bodies and their experiences of desire, particularly their erotic and sexual yearnings. This section suggests that, despite the extensive attention given to each of these aspects of women's experience in recent feminist scholarship, the ties between them invite greater exploration.

In the second section, **Work and Education**, we explore women's experiences as laborers and learners. Women's work and education are familiar themes in contemporary conversations as well as standard topics in feminist research. The excerpts presented here, however, suggest that these two themes are integrated in women's lives in many ways that have yet to be fully analyzed. We emphasize not only the ways in which women have sought access to, and control over, these resources, but also the ways in which laboring and learning fit into a larger system of social relations and cultural ideology that simultaneously enables and restricts women.

Our third section, **Representing Women, Writing the Body Politic**, examines women's thinking about cultural representations of gender. In this section, women both critique such representations and participate actively in reshaping them. These excerpts point to the link between the ways in which women are represented culturally—in literature and the arts, through dress and fashion, as sexual and social beings—and the ways in which the material and political circumstances of women's lives are defined and restricted by such representations. The writers in this section investigate how representations of women become part of larger cultural systems. We see such investigations as part of, and made possible by, feminist activism.

As women come to understand their lives through experience and reflection, what needs to change? The authors in the last two sections, **Identifying Sources of Resistance** and **Vision and Transformation**, suggest ways of translating the knowledge that women gain into power that will alter both their own circumstances and the social systems within which they live. **Identifying Sources of Resistance** focuses on specific modes and acts of resistance described by women who have reached a level of understanding of their own circumstances and been moved to act upon them. The authors of the last section, **Vision and Transformation**, elaborate their ideas about resistance and social change on an even broader scale, using their experiences and observations as the basis for analyses of social systems. They call for us to think about the imbrication of gender with other systems of oppression. And they require us to understand how resisters live within the systems they seek to alter.

The sections that begin the anthology, **Sexuality, Spirituality, and Power** and **Work and Education**, open the discussion of the book's fundamental issue: the complicated relationship between important aspects of women's lives—sexual, spiritual, creative, and intellectual—and the power structures that constitute various authority systems—religious, social, cultural, political, intellectual, economic. In Section One, for example, sexuality and spirituality (fused in various ways through a third concept, the erotic), are sources of power for women's resistance to authority. As we will see, if they have been important sites of control by patriarchal authority systems, they are also potential sites of liberation. What connects the writers represented here is their conscious search for, and shaping of, a space in which to exercise their powers, whether defined collectively or individually or both, in ways that resist dominant gender norms related to women's spiritual and sexual lives.

At the ideological level, authority systems have a great deal to do with the way women experience and evaluate their powers, through the same oppressive processes by which authority systems work more generally to shape women's sense of their potential. This dynamic operates in the context of women's lives as we consider them in Section Two, **Work and Education**. Here we see women fighting for control of the uses to which their potential is put. Relatedly, we see their struggles for control over the kinds of learning required of them, and offered to them, in response to their perceived potential as producers and reproducers. We consider the many sources of learning in women's lives, as well as the way those sources foster resistance and/or transmit kinds of knowledge that may be sources of oppression. This section suggests that women's resistance inevitably involves a search for control over ways of knowing and doing.

Section Three, **Representing Women, Writing the Body Politic**, is a pivot-point in our argument as it turns from resistance in specific domains of women's lives into the larger arenas of the transforming power of women's knowledge. Section Three reflects on the way women represent themselves in the world and to the world; it concentrates in particular on the relationship between women's writing and women's place in society. We regard all representation as operating to some degree inside ideology, and we discuss misrepresentation as one of the modes through which systems of domination work. We see the texts included here as lying on a continuum from misrepresentation to representation. Along this continuum the authors perform one or more kinds of sociocultural work: creating new social definitions of "woman" or "womanhood," drawing on socially defined notions about women that are already in place, struggling against the constraints such definitions place upon them as writers. Their efforts to combat and create representation lead, almost inevitably, to a need for representation as political subjects. The question of representation from these last two standpoints, written representation and political representation, involves the two fundamental issues of knowledge and power, whose interrelationship we explore in Sections Four and Five when we return to the themes of the first three sections from two different angles.

Section Four, **Identifying Sources of Resistance**, asks how women learn ways of transforming particular circumstances of their lives. From what sources do what kinds of knowledge enable them to resist and to gain some measure of power over their circumstances? The emphasis here is on childhood experiences, on the forms of support women receive from others, and on the sites where they have sought influence and control.

Section Five moves out into the broader question of **Vision and Transformation**, and asks how women have created and transmitted the kinds of knowledge that can provide a basis for *systemic* social change. Some of the women in this last section speak from what might be termed a visionary perspective. Two of them, Mary Wollstonecraft and Luisa Capetillo, explicitly raise the question of the "utopian" quality of their work. But what the diverse writings collected in this anthology reveal is that, throughout history, many women, acting on the courage of their imaginations, have significantly transformed their lives and the lives of others. Much of what Wollstonecraft wanted—the vision she knew her contemporaries would see as impossible—has come to pass in at least some women's lives. It could come to pass in others. As Capetillo concludes, everything in the future is utopian, for it exists nowhere yet: "The essential thing is to put it into practice. To begin!"

NOTES

[1] We are aware of the difficulty of using the term "feminist" to describe *all* women's efforts to work for political change in social systems that discriminate on the basis of gender. "Feminism" as a term has strong historical associations with women's movements that were overwhelmingly white, bourgeois, and of Western origin. The term was first coined in France (*feminisme*) in the 1880s by Hubertine Auclert, a key figure in the French woman suffrage movement of the time and founder of the first French woman suffrage society (Cott 14). In her discussion of the word's history, Nancy Cott suggests that "feminism" first appeared in the United States in the context of an article written in 1906 discussing the European socialist and woman suffrage advocate Madeleine Pelletier (14–15). Cott continues, "Feminism burst into clear view a few years later because it answered a need to represent in language a series of intentions and a constituency just cohering, a new moment in the long history of struggles for women's rights and freedoms. In part it was a semantic claim to female mod-

ernism. . ." (15). We had the particular history of the term in mind when, rather than attempting to construct a problematic history of global feminist social change, we chose to focus on narratives of women's resistance.

[2] For further discussion of the debates over the "essentialist" category of "woman," see Denise Riley, *"Am I That Name?"* and Diana Fuss, *Essentially Speaking.*

[3] Here we agree with Diana Fuss that "While experience can never be a reliable guide to the real"—since it is always filtered through the eyes of the beholder—"this is not to preclude any role at all for experience in the realm of knowledge production. . . . What I mean by this is simply that experience is not the raw material knowledge seeks to understand, but rather knowledge is the active process which produces its own objects of investigation, including empirical facts" (Fuss 118).

[4] See Ellen Carol DuBois's description of international feminism in her article "Woman Suffrage Around the World: Three Phases of Suffragist Internationalism," in *Suffrage and Beyond: International Feminist Perspectives.*

[5] Translations share with anthologies an important role in the development of literary canons. See Kristiaan Aercke's argument for the importance of translations in her discussion of literary canon formation in the introduction to *Women Writing in Dutch.* "Dynamic interaction is very important for a literary system, for without it, the system ceases to develop. . . . Hence the importance of literary translation as a theoretical and practical activity: since translated texts do influence the creation of new texts in the host language, they do contribute to the dynamics of the host canon. Translations, in other words, are functional products in the literary economy—just like anthologies" (Aercke 9). The reconfiguration of a literary system by means of translations also has political implications, of course, some of which we have tried to develop above.

[6] The Native-American feminist Paula Gunn Allen points out that in Euro-American culture individualism is seen as positive, and much Western literature praises those (often men) who define themselves in opposition to all groups. In Native-American literature by both women and men, however, being separated from the group is the great pain, the great evil (*Spider Women's Granddaughters* 4–9). In contrast, the Englishwoman Mary Wollstonecraft based her feminist manifesto in the late eighteenth century on the idea that woman's "first duty is to herself," to develop her individual potential, and on the argument that only then can the greatest amount of "virtue" accrue to society as a whole.

[7] As Fredric Jameson points out in his article "On 'Cultural Studies'" in the journal *Social Text*: "My sense is that interpretations in terms of power must come as punctual demystifications. . . . But if everything is power, then we neither require that reminder, nor can it retain any of its demystificatory force" (44–45).

[8] See Joan Wallach Scott's discussion of universalism in *Only Paradoxes to Offer: French Feminists and the Rights of Man.*

[9] See for example, Rose Brewer on the specific contributions of African-American feminists to this perspective; see also the essays in Gloria Anzaldúa's *Making Face, Making Soul, Haciendo Caras.*

WORKS CONSULTED

Aercke, Kristiaan. Introduction. *Women Writing in Dutch*. Ed. Kristiaan Aercke. Women Writers of the World 1. New York: Garland, 1994.

Allen, Paula Gunn. Introduction. *Spider Woman's Granddaughters: Traditional Tales and Contemporary Writing by Native American Women*. Ed. Paula Gunn Allen. Boston: Beacon, 1989.

Anzaldúa, Gloria, ed. *Making Face, Making Soul, Haciendo Caras: Creative and Critical Perspectives by Women of Color*. San Francisco: Aunt Lute Foundation Books, 1990.

Brewer, Rose M. "Theorizing Race, Class and Gender: The New Scholarship of Black Feminist Intellectuals and Black Women's Labor." *Theorizing Black Feminisms: The Visionary Pragmatism of Black Women*. Eds. Stanlie M. James and Abena P. A. Busia. London: Routledge, 1993.

Cott, Nancy F. *The Grounding of Modern Feminism*. New Haven: Yale UP, 1987.

DuBois, Ellen Carol. "Woman Suffrage Around the World: Three Phases of Suffragist Internationalism." *Suffrage and Beyond: International Feminist Perspectives*. Eds. Caroline Daley and Melanie Nolan. New York: New York UP, 1994.

Fuss, Diana. *Essentially Speaking: Feminism, Nature and Difference*. New York: Routledge, 1989.

hooks, bell. *Black Looks: Race and Representation*. Boston: South End, 1992.

—. *Feminist Theory from Margin to Center*. Boston: South End, 1984.

—. *Talking Back: Thinking Feminist, Thinking Black*. Boston: South End, 1989.

Jameson, Fredric. "On 'Cultural Studies.'" *Social Text* 34 (1993): 17–52.

Lerner, Gerda. "Reconceptualizing Differences Among Women." *Journal of Women's History* (Winter 1990): 106–122.

Riley, Denise. *"Am I That Name?" Feminism and the Category of "Women" in History*. Minneapolis: U Minnesota Press, 1988.

Scott, Joan Wallach. *Only Paradoxes to Offer: French Feminists and the Rights of Man*. Cambridge: Harvard UP, 1996.

Smith, Barbara. *Home Girls: A Black Feminist Anthology*. New York: Kitchen Table: Women of Color Press, 1983.

Williams, Patricia J. *The Alchemy of Race and Rights: Diary of a Law Professor*. Cambridge: Harvard UP, 1991.

Williamson, Margaret. *Sappho's Immortal Daughters*. Cambridge: Harvard UP, 1995.

SEXUALITY, SPIRITUALITY, AND POWER

Eugenia C. DeLamotte

When we first began collecting excerpts for this anthology, two categories emerged as obviously important. We termed one of them Religion; the other, Sexuality and the Body. While marking each excerpt for possible inclusion in as many of our categories as seemed to apply, we noticed that each of us, independently, had found a surprisingly large number of excerpts that seemed appropriate for either the Religion section or the Sexuality and Body section. At the same time, none of these excerpts seemed to fit in one section without reference to the other. Then a passage from Cherríe Moraga gave us the idea of considering the two categories together.

> Women of color have always known, although we have not always wanted to look at it, that our sexuality is not merely a physical response or drive, but

> holds a crucial relationship to our entire spiritual capacity. Patriarchal religions—whether brought to us by the colonizer's cross and gun or emerging from our own people—have always known this. Why else would the female body be so associated with sin and disobedience? Simply put, if the spirit and sex have been linked in our oppression, then they must also be linked in the strategy toward our liberation.
>
> To date, no liberation movement has been willing to take on the task. To walk a freedom road that is both material and metaphysical. Sexual and spiritual. Third World feminism is about feeding people in all their hungers. (*Loving in the War Years* 132)

This passage was valuable because it located a source of oppression in women's lives at the very disjunction we were struggling to sustain. Moraga's analysis modeled a way to move beyond sorting women's experience into binary oppositions of soul and body, spiritual and sexual desire, religious life and erotic life. Her work modeled ways of moving beyond other false dichotomies as well. For example, her analysis of women's "hungers" and the ways in which religious authority systems shape their responses to those hungers illuminates the connections and tensions often obscured by conventional distinctions between the "public" and "private." Furthermore, when she speaks of religious authority systems she holds in the same line of sight material and spiritual needs, indigenous and colonial religions, and Third World and Western patriarchies. Finally, when she looks at patriarchal religion in the West, she refuses to take at face value its traditional opposition of body and soul. Instead she raises questions about something those distinctions obscure: the role played by women's bodies in patriarchal concepts of spirituality.

How does the double territory of body and spirit become a site of oppression in women's lives? And how, in resistance, have women been able to transform that colonized territory into a site of freedom? In this introduction we provide two lenses through which to view these issues. The first lens focuses on the question of where each writer positions her resistance—from within a religious authority system or from outside. The second lens focuses on the relationship between that resistance and the erotic. What connects these two focal points is the issue of power. Who controls a woman's sexual experience, her sexual expression, her sense of connection to whatever spiritual dimension she believes to exist beyond and/or within her, and her impulse toward transcendence whether of the body or through the body? Who controls her spiritual/bodily sense of herself, particularly as a physical/spiritual force in the world?

By looking at religious institutions we find a way of examining the power exercised over women—or, the power made available to them by an external source of control. By looking at the erotic we find a way of recognizing women as themselves agents of power. The erotic is an especially useful category because it fuses mind and body, sex and spirit, passion and thought, desire and the energy for change. It thus allows us to look at a woman's internal power in the context of the whole range of who she is—her body, her desires, her sexuality, her intellect, and her passions. Within any religious authority system, there is a complicated interplay between this internal power and the opportunities the system affords or does not afford for exercising it. That is why the question of whether to resist from within or from outside is problematic for women in the first place.

DEFINITIONS

The term "erotic" is usually taken to mean "of, devoted to, or tending to arouse sexual love or desire." Thus it involves feeling, perception, and ideas as well as physical sensation. In this conventional definition from *Webster's New World Dictionary,* however, the "erotic" is imagined as an external force acting on the desiring subject. Our definition, in contrast, follows such theorists as Ana Castillo, Audre Lorde, and Cherríe Moraga in regarding the erotic as a creative, transformative power *of* the desiring subject.[1]

The related term "sexuality" is susceptible to an equally wide variety of interpretations, most particularly because any discussion of sexuality must be situated geographically and historically. Ideas about sexuality relate to ideas about race, class, and gender in a certain place at a certain time. The concept of sexual *identities,* for example, as opposed to sexual *practices,* appears to be quite recent in the West (Foucault). Indeed, the concept derives from the same nineteenth-century European intellectual matrix that gave rise to modern ideas of race and racial identity—ideas that linked inherent moral, spiritual, and intellectual qualities to biological characteristics shared exclusively by members of the race in question (Appiah 276). Together with similar concepts of class and gender, these ideas about racial and sexual identity were in turn bound up together in ideologies of imperialism—the effects of which continue to unfold globally in women's lives today. Because of these links, it is particularly important to ask how the authors represented here conceptualize sexuality—as an identity, an expression of identity, a state of mind, a set of practices? Do they see sexuality as intrinsic to the body, or as something the body *does?* Do they regard the experience and expressions of sexual desire as innate or as socially constructed? And what do they see as the relation between the power of sexuality and women's power to shape their own lives?

Similarly, concepts of "spirituality" differ across the many religious and philosophical traditions in which women have been situated. In much traditional African thought and practice, for example, spirituality is a force or energy that both infuses the physical world and, in certain senses, remains apart from it. Thus it is seen as "a dynamic energy that allows the self to merge (extend) into the totality of phenomenal experience" (Baldwin 180), or as "an all pervasive 'energy' that is the source, sustainer, and essence of all phenomenon [sic] . . . that pervasive essence that is known in an extrasensory fashion (i.e., the fastest moving energy, consciousness, God)" (Myers 75).[2] Buddhism began as a religion that identified the highest state of spiritual enlightenment with freedom from desire, a release achieved through detachment, including detachment from sense pleasures (Rahula 18–19), whereas in Islamic thought, sexuality is seen as an aspect of spiritual well-being (Mernissi 44). Even within a specific tradition, concepts of spirituality differ over time. For medieval European Catholic writers such as Margery Kempe, "spirituality" would have denoted a category of experience set apart from material reality. In contrast, contemporary liberation theologians such as María Clara Bingemer see spirituality as conceptually inseparable from liberatory action that addresses the material conditions of people's lives.

Finally, we have chosen to distinguish the term "spirituality" from the term "religion" because "spirituality," in its contemporary connotations, need not be expressed through an organized religious institution. We acknowledge, however, that the choice to conceptualize "spirituality" as something that can be radically distinct from institutionalized religion, or might exist as an oppositional force within but apart from that institution, may be quite a modern one—one that many of the writers included here would not have recognized. For these reasons it is important to keep questioning these terms even as we use them to help organize our thinking about women's resistance.

What follows is a discussion of that resistance as it appears in the excerpts that make up this chapter. We group the writers first in terms of their relation to religious authority systems and the particular kinds of resistance they represent. We then look back at those same groups and ask how the erotic relates to their modes of resistance.

BODY/SPIRIT AS A SITE OF RESISTANCE: RELIGIOUS AUTHORITY SYSTEMS

In order to look at the position of these writers' resistance inside or outside of religious authority systems, we need first to ask what roles such systems play in creating and sustaining the oppression of women. For millennia, religious authority systems have been a major force shaping people's daily experience of their world: how they obtain and prepare food, bear and raise children, organize time. Women engaged in resistance to oppressive circumstances of their lives have inevitably done so in such religious contexts, a fact that explains why so few of the excerpts we present are situated altogether outside any religious authority system.

Because in most cultures religious doctrine and ritual are bound up with daily life, the first intersection of religion and gender subordination that most women experience is in the family, around which so many of women's daily activities revolve. Patriarchal families have traditionally been infused with religious doctrines and rituals that define women's roles as feeding other people's hungers. Many religious rituals, for example, take place in the home and revolve around women's preparation of food or care for others' health; most religious traditions have some way of regulating, for the benefit of the society as a whole but most particularly for the benefit of men, women's experience of menarche, menstruation, childbirth, and sexuality. In such traditions, the patriarchal organization of family is linked to the patriarchal organization of the religious authority system, whose hierarchy reinforces the gender subordination implicit in many religious rituals and doctrines.

The structural and ideological procedures by which such hierarchies have appropriated women's spirituality have been the same procedures by which they have appropriated women's bodies. For example, the exaltation of men through images of the highest spiritual reality as male (images of a male God or saviour, for example), or of the highest state of spiritual enlightenment as embodied by a man (the Buddha, for example), together with the corresponding implication that women are spiritually inferior, is part and parcel of the denigration of women as *bodily* inferior. Bound up with this denigration is the denigration of women's spiritual and physical functions within patriarchal religious hierarchies. Often special limits are placed on what spiritual power women may represent (embody) in ritual; what sacred objects they may touch; what sacred thresholds they may cross; what sacred mountains they may climb; which spaces they may occupy in places of worship. Physical strictures on women in holy places reflect not only men's position above them in a spiritual hierarchy but men's bodily domination of women more generally. Thus it is logical that within such patriarchal religious hierarchies, men's "spiritual" authority over women includes, in particular, various kinds of authority to regulate their bodies, especially their reproductive practices and their expressions of sexuality.

The arrogation to men of "spiritual" authority to regulate women's bodies—predicated on, reflected in, and reinforced by depictions of the highest spiritual states of being as male—is linked in complex ways with the arrogation to men of "authority" over women's bodies more generally. In economic and social terms, women's bodies tend to be valued or devalued in relation to their function as signs of men's status. Thus it is not surprising that religious authorities, as in the case of Grazida Lizier, have often made women's bodies a sort of spiritual battleground, a turf on which they and the state authorities allied with or opposed to them play out their own power struggles.

Within this broad framework, the story of women's relation to religious institutions is characteristically a story of alternations between periods in which women have had more or less power, greater or lesser roles to play, depending on the economic resources controlled by the religious institutions and the closeness of connection between the particular religion and the dominant political system. Mahayana Buddhism in Japan is a typical example. Feminist historian Haruko Okano recounts that the first Buddhist temple in sixth-century Japan was built for nuns, who conducted religious rituals and were seen as having special, almost mythical powers. After monasteries were built, monks and nuns were for some time accorded similar status in their religious functions. By the eighth century, however, monasteries and nunneries came in pairs, with monasteries in financial control of nunneries. By the ninth century, nuns did so much menial labor for monks that their nunneries were seen as the monasteries' "laundry rooms." This degradation of nuns' roles coincided with a process during which monks became "functionaries of the state" and the public religious functions of nuns became restricted (Okano 18–22).

Such shifts in women's institutional religious power relative to men—paralleled in many other times and places—tend to coincide with the elaboration of religious ideologies that denigrate women. Thus, corresponding to these institutional shifts in Japanese Buddhism was the development of an ideology that regarded women as incapable of attaining buddhahood without a spiritual metamorphosis into a man. Views of women's bodies as inferior then led back around to restrictions on women's physical participation in certain rituals, such as prohibitions based on women's association with "impurity" (for example, blood) against their presence in certain holy places—especially the temples most closely associated with state control (19–22). "What must be done—what changes must be undertaken," Haruko Okano asks, "in order that women can be truly liberated *as* women, rather than *from* being a woman?" (26).

Despite the ways in which patriarchal religious institutions have opposed such liberation, many women have moved within such institutions to create space, or use what space they found, for transcending patriarchal authority and gender conventions. In the first group of selections we present (those of Vibia Perpetua, Margery Kempe, Rebecca Cox Jackson, Sumangalamata, Nanduttara, and Vimala), we see women transcending authority through a spirit-centered life that they view as a triumph over mere bodily needs—in the case of Vibia Perpetua, the need for life itself. Even in those excerpts that seem in some ways to deny the body, however, the site of resistance to the circumstances of the authors' lives is a conjunction of body and spirit. Perpetua and Rebecca Cox Jackson envision spiritual conflict in physical, bodily terms that pit them against male aggressors; Margery Kempe's spirituality expresses itself dramatically, and bodily, in fits of weeping and groaning that disrupt male-centered religious rituals; Sumangalamata's religious victory frees her from the "cooking pot," hunger, her husband, "greed and hate," just as Nanduttara's and Vimala's bring release from sensual obsession with the body and "passion." In the case of Jackson, Kempe, and Sumangalamata, the writer uses religion not only as a source of spiritual transcendence but as a means of rejecting or renegotiating oppressive physical conditions in her life. Just as Sumangalamata escaped an oppressive marriage by becoming a Buddhist nun, Margery Kempe and Rebecca Cox Jackson renegotiated the terms of their marriages by insisting on their spiritual calls to celibacy.

Kempe's and Jackson's resistance in the area of sexuality makes them an interesting bridge to the next group of selections, those by Anne Lister, Grazida Lizier, and Carolyn Mobley, all of which involve some sort of mediation between a woman's religion and her sexuality. In these selections the authority of a particular religious system, bound up in each case with class and racial hierarchies, is pitted against a woman's creative freedom to reinvent herself and her "powers of desire."[3] Thus the nineteenth-century Lister, an upper-class Englishwoman, queers the authority of biblical texts by using them to talk about birth control and lesbianism; Lizier, a thirteenth-century French peasant, defends her extramarital sexual relationship with a priest solely on the authority of her own ideas and insights. In contrast, Mobley, a contemporary African-American Christian, recounts her painful struggle to reconcile her religious beliefs with her lesbianism without renouncing either her feelings or the authority of the Bible. Mobley finally resolves her dilemma through a daring reinterpretation of a holy text that enables her to use religion itself as a means of freedom from normative sexual behaviors.

The writers in the next group create space for themselves as women—albeit still from within religious authority systems—in a different way. Despite their wide diversity chronologically and geographically, Laura Geller, Marguerite d'Oingt, María Clara Bingemer, Glückel of Hameln, Chung Hyun Kyung, and Ghada Samman[4] all enact their resistance by consciously reshaping religious hierarchies, ritual, or doctrine to empower rather than marginalize women. Once again, what is at stake is the double territory of spirit and body.

Of these women, Laura Geller, by virtue of being one of the first three women to be ordained as rabbis, is perhaps the most striking example of resistance from within patriarchal religious hierarchies. As a rabbi, Geller has in turn worked to develop new rituals for moments in women's physical lives that Jewish ritual has not "blessed" before: menarche, miscarriage, stillbirth, abortion, and menopause.

Such resistance at the level of organizational hierarchy and ritual inevitably involves resisting certain aspects of religious doctrine. Marguerite d'Oingt, María Clara Bingemer, and Glückel of Hameln exemplify resistance to masculine images of a deity or a community of believers. In her use of an indigenous female deity to counter such imagery, Chung Hyun Kyung also exemplifies another form of doctrinal resistance that is widespread today: woman-centered decolonizations of colonial religions. Ghada Samman, in a related move, calls Islamic women to affirm their place of "honor" at the center of their religion, and resist marginalization not only by men but by their own interpretations of Islam.

Of the writers in this group, Marguerite, Bingemer, and Chung are responding most directly to an almost universal aspect of monotheistic religions for millennia: the anthropomorphizing of the highest spiritual reality in the shape of a man. The problem they confront is posed succinctly in Alice Walker's novel *The Color Purple.* Like many women throughout history, Walker's character Shug experiences the male embodying of God as an imposition on *her* body. You have to get man "off your eyeball," she tells Celie: "Man corrupt everything. . . . He on your box of grits, in your head, and all over the radio. He try to make you think he everywhere. Soon as you think he everywhere, you think he God. But he ain't" (179).

Against such images of the male body of God, Marguerite and Bingemer assert counterimages of the female body as holy metaphor. During the Medieval period in Europe both male and female Christian writers imagined Jesus as a mother, but Marguerite invested this kind of imagery with particular intensity. Her image of Jesus enduring a kind of physical suffering only women endure makes an interesting comparison to the selection from contemporary Brazilian theologian Bingemer, who pictures Latin American women's bodies broken and shared like the body of Christ in Catholic ritual. Unlike Marguerite and Bingemer, whose traditions imagine deity only as male, Chung is able to draw on a Korean religious tradition in which deity is already conceptualized as female.

While these three writers create images that destabilize doctrines of the divine as masculine, Glückel of Hameln's excerpt destabilizes an image that has perhaps been equally problematic for women. How often, in religions all over the world, do holy texts portray the whole community of believers as masculine—sons of a father deity, fathers of future generations, brothers? Glückel instead imagines her whole Jewish community as a woman squatting on the birthing stool. Ghada Samman addresses the question of women's place in the community of believers by insisting that "Islam is women's honour" and that women be true to that fact. Like many feminists who situate themselves within a religious tradition but call for its reform, she appeals to precedents in a holy text. Referring to a woman known for her learning and independent spirit, the favorite wife of the Prophet Muhammad after the death of his first wife Khadijah, Samman says, "God honoured Aisha with a verse that revealed her innocence and that of all women who dare to be human in a society that insists that women remain colourful mummy/slaves."

All of the writers discussed thus far have worked within a religious authority system to create space for transcending patriarchal authority and gender conventions. Their works invite us to think about the interplay in their lives between religion as a source of power for women and religion as a means of control over women. Women throughout history have used religious authority systems creatively to gain control over their bodies; to argue for political reform or revolution; to break silences; to exercise their talents as healers, writers, teachers, speakers, counsellors. Yet many women all over the world have seen their indigenous religions, or the religions imposed by colonizing powers, as sources of oppression and injustice. In such cases, a particular organized religion has itself become the target of their resistance, often by those working from within who have used certain aspects of the religion as justification for resisting others, but also sometimes from the outside, by women who reject religious institutions completely.

Outside the context of organized religions, women have worked to decolonize the double territory of body/spirit in a number of ways. One such method is the explicit rejection of male control—exerted through religious authority systems—over the double territory of women's bodies and souls. The next group of writers presented in this chapter—Bonita WaWa Calachaw Nuñez, Fatima Mernissi, and Voltairine de Cleyre—denounce a particular religious institution for its denigration of women. They seek to reclaim women's bodies from appropriation by "spiritual" authorities, sometimes assigning the role of demon either to themselves as rebels or to the religious institutions they deplore. All of them seek to demystify religious authority systems by revealing the roles those systems play in supporting political hegemony.

BODY/SPIRIT AS A SITE OF RESISTANCE: THE EROTIC

Even in their rejection of religious traditions, in many ways all of these writers keep a religious institution at the center of their discourse. In contrast, Sei Shōnagon and Audre Lorde discuss women's bodies/spirituality as completely set apart from religious institutions. Sei Shōnagon writes lightheartedly about the rituals of sexual love, from a position at the imperial court—a position that she represents as quite outside the constraints of ordinary women's lives.

Often the position of speaking "outside"—especially outside of and apart from institutionalized religions—directs particular attention toward reclaiming women's sexuality and the power of the erotic. Audre Lorde forcefully articulates this position by linking the erotic not only to spiritual power but to political activism—to all the energies on which women draw to effect change in their worlds. Kwok Pui-lan's response to Lorde underscores the immensity of the problems women face as they seek to effect such change.

The problems Kwok Pui-lan discusses involve the ways in which the sexual objectification of women's bodies works against women's ability to use the erotic as a source of power in their lives or see it as part of their spiritual capacity. Her call for readers to be aware of these problems opens an interesting path back through the readings we have grouped according to their forms of resistance within or outside religious authority systems. If, with Audre Lorde, we see the erotic as an inner source of transformative power that fuses mind and body, sex and spirit, thought and feeling, desire and energy, we can use the erotic itself as a lens to look back from a different angle at the interplay in each of these excerpts between a woman's internal power and the external structures working to control her power.

We should look, for example, at the nature of the tremendous energies on which Perpetua, Margery Kempe, Rebecca Cox Jackson, Sumangalamata, Nanduttara, and Vimala were drawing in their rejection of all kinds of social, cultural, and religious expectations about their proper roles as women. Perpetua could be seen in one sense as transcending the body entirely, through spiritual martyrdom. But her refusal to yield to her father or the state religion in order to save her body from destruction is presented in a set of dream-images of bodily fulfillment and satisfaction. What do Perpetua's dreams of being a naked man anointed with oil by handsome young men, or her dream of her brother Dinocrates sating his desperate thirst, splashing "full of happiness" in a pool of water that will never run dry, have to do with her spiritual strength? Similarly, Kempe's and Jackson's vigorous choice of celibacy should be considered alongside Kempe's erotic dreams of making love with Christ and Jackson's religious vision of her friend Rebecca Perot bathing in a beautiful river in her undergarment, plunging under and emerging again and again—"Like an Angel, oh, how bright!" Both Kempe and Nanduttara speak of escaping sensuous desire; Perpetua denied her body completely in death; as part of religious devotion Jackson often went for long periods without eating and joined a sect that forbade sexual relations. If we are to think about the role of the erotic in their extraordinary expressions of personal power, we must also seek to understand exactly what role each of them thought the body played in spiritual life.

The next group of selections addresses this question much more directly because the writers focus overtly on sexuality. Lister, Lizier, and Mobley negotiate ways to validate their own experiences of sexual desire in opposition to a religious institution's attempt to regulate or deny them. In thinking about this group of writers, however, it is important to remember that the erotic involves sexuality but is not limited to it, just as the erotic is a dimension of the spiritual but does not comprise the whole of it. Thus, even though these writers talk overtly about sexuality, we must look as well for the broader role the erotic plays in their expression of internal power through resistance. What is the full range of desire, for example, that gives them such force and tenacity in asserting their claims to be different as women? What other kinds of desire are fused with sexuality in the energy these women use to oppose social, cultural, and religious institutions?

The following group of writers poses a different kind of challenge, encapsulated in Geller's intriguing final line comparing her feminist reading of sacred texts to love-making. "Wrestling with Torah is like making love," she says. "I get close enough to be wounded. . . . But I've gotten close enough to be blessed. . . ." The ways in which the double territory of body/spirit is at stake for these women in their efforts to reform religion mean that the erotic must play a range of complex roles in their resistance. All of these women think in some way or another about the embodiment of spirit in the flesh. To reclaim women's bodies from denigration in the realms of hierarchy, ritual, and doctrine is not only to reclaim women's bodily desires but to express those desires through the act of reclaiming. We might think in this context about the sense of women's bodily selves all these writers evoke, so explicitly and intensely, against the grain of religious traditions that have denied women so many forms of bodily expression and been silent about so much of their bodily experience. Chung, in fact, brings women's bodies physically into the space of her religion by rendering her speech not just in words but in dance.

Among the writers whose discourse of sexuality, desire, and spirituality is positioned outside a religious tradition, it is not surprising to see angrier attacks on the appropriation of women's sexuality by religious authority systems (Calachaw and Mernissi), on the complicity of such systems in the fulfillment of men's sexuality at the expense of women's erotic life (de Cleyre), and on the distortion of the whole range of women's erotic powers by oppressive external systems (Lorde). In these writers who affirm the body most explicitly, as with the first group of writers who deny it most explicitly, it is again crucial to ask how the body is being conceptualized—in opposition to, or fused with what other concepts of God, the soul, the spirit, and so on. Voltairine de Cleyre is a good example of how complicated the answers may be. "God is deaf," she says, "and his church is our worst enemy." And, "The question of souls is old. We demand our bodies now." At the same time she seeks to reclaim—one might even say resanctify—woman's body as a genuine "temple of the spirit," inhabited by the full range of her powers.

Women's freedom to exercise these powers, as we have said, is what links the two focal points of this introduction. Whatever the writer's position within or outside a religious authority system, whatever her relation to the external forces that work to control her life, we see the erotic as a source of power on which she has drawn to write or speak or dream in the first place. In that sense each of these excerpts is itself an act that helps liberate the double territory of body and spirit.

NOTES

[1] See Castillo's chapter, "Toward an Erotic Whole Self," in *Massacre of the Dreamers* (121–144); Lorde's essay, "Uses of the Erotic," in this section; and the Moraga passage cited above.

[2] Explanations quoted in Pettis 18–19.

[3] A phrase we borrow from Ann Snitow, Christine Stansell, and Sharon Thompson.

[4] Ghada Samman appears later in the section, contrasted with Fatima Mernissi in a headnote on feminist approaches to Islam. For the purposes of this general introduction, however, we group her with other women who resist from within a religious tradition.

WORKS CONSULTED

Appiah, Kwame Anthony. "Race." *Critical Terms for Literary Study.* Eds. Frank Lentricchia and Thomas McLaughlin. Chicago: U of Chicago P, 1990.

Baldwin, Joseph A. "African Self Consciousness and the Mental Health of African Americans." *Journal of Black Studies* 15 (1984): 177–94.

Castillo, Ana. *Massacre of the Dreamers: Essays on Xicanisma.* New York: Plume, 1994.

Foucault, Michel. *The History of Sexuality.* Vol. 1: Introduction. Trans. Robert Hurley. New York: Vintage Books, 1980.

Lorde, Audre. "Uses of the Erotic: The Erotic as Power." 1978. *Sister Outsider: Essays and Speeches By Audre Lorde.* Freedom, CA: Crossing Press, 1984. 53–59.

Mernissi, Fatima. *Beyond the Veil: Male-Female Dynamics in Modern Muslim Society.* Revised ed. Bloomington: Indiana UP 1987.

Moraga, Cherríe. *Loving in the War Years.* Boston: South End, 1983.

Myers, Linda James. "The Deep Structure of Culture: Relevance of Traditional African Culture in Contemporary Life." *Journal of Black Studies* 18 (1987): 72–85.

Okano, Haruko. "Women's Image and Place in Japanese Buddhism." Trans. Kumiko Fujimura-Fanselow and Yoko Tsuruta. *Japanese Women: New Feminist Perspectives on the Past, Present, and Future.* Ed. Kumiko Fujimura-Fanselow and Atsuko Kameda. New York: Feminist Press, 1995.

Pettis, Joyce. *Toward Wholeness in Paule Marshall's Fiction.* Charlottesville: UP of Virginia, 1995.

Rahula, Walpola Sri. *What the Buddha Taught.* Rev. ed. New York: Grove, 1959.

Snitow, Ann, Christine Stansell, and Sharon Thompson, eds. *Powers of Desire: The Politics of Sexuality.* New York: Monthly Review Press, 1983.

Walker, Alice. *The Color Purple: A Novel.* New York: Harcourt Brace Jovanovich, 1982.

Webster's New World Dictionary of the American Language. Second College Edition. Ed. David B. Guralnik. New York: Prentice-Hall, 1980.

VIBIA PERPETUA *(c. 181–203 CE)*

A Martyr's Vision

Vibia Perpetua was one of the early North African Christian martyrs, condemned to death in Carthage in 203 CE for her refusal to perform a sacrifice honoring the Roman emperor. While in prison she kept a record of her experiences and her dreams—a record that was widely read by early Christians, including such writers as Augustine, and then eventually forgotten until its rediscovery in the seventeenth century (Rader 11, von Franz 4). Her experiences included her dramatic encounters with her father, who opposed her decision to resist, and her concern for her baby, who was still breast-feeding at the time Perpetua was arrested. Her dreams, which she regarded as divine revelations, recorded her thoughts and feelings as she came nearer and nearer to the day when she would be thrown to wild animals as entertainment for the crowd looking down at the arena.

Perpetua is one of the very few women of her day whose writings have been preserved, perhaps because they were copied into the middle of another narrative, *The Passions of Saints Perpetua and Felicitas,* by a man. This narrator, or more properly, redactor, is often identified as Tertullian, who was one of the early Christian Church Fathers and Bishop of Carthage at the time of Perpetua's death (von Franz 5). The authenticity of Perpetua's authorship of the interior narrative has been debated, but a number of scholars have demonstrated that her style differs distinctly from that of the writer in whose narrative hers, together with another martyr's narrative in yet a third style, is enclosed (see Dronke 1, Rader 13).

From these writings we learn that Perpetua was a catechumen, being instructed in her newly chosen religion, when she was arrested; she was baptized (anointed with water to affirm her new birth as a Christian) while in prison. She was of a noble family and well-educated. Although she was married and had a young son, she never mentions her husband in the narrative, for reasons that are not known. All of her family except her father were either Christians or sympathetic to Christianity, and one of her father's worries was that her refusal to abjure her new religion would place them all under surveillance (Dronke 10). Felicitas, the other woman in the group of six Christians put to death on 7 March 203 CE, was Perpetua's slave.

Of these two women's deaths we have the record provided in the framing narrative, which recounts that on the day of their death the men were mauled in the arena by a leopard, a bear, and a boar. The women were stripped and brought in nets into the arena, then dressed in gowns when the crowd was disturbed by the sight of one so young and another, Felicitas, whose breasts were dripping with milk (she had given birth in prison). The women were gored by a mad cow, an animal selected as a more appropriate match for them. Perpetua's gown was torn and, "more concerned with her sense of modesty than with her pain," the redactor says, she covered her thighs, then pinned back her dishevelled hair to avoid giving the appearance "that she was mourning in her hour of triumph." At the end of the entertainment the victims were put to death by the sword; the narrator reports that Perpetua, stabbed in the ribs, guided the gladiator's hand to her throat ("Martyrdom," trans. in Rader 29).

There is good reason to believe, from the style and immediacy of Perpetua's narrative, that it is a genuine record of her inner and outer experiences in prison (Dronke 1–17). There is perhaps less reason to trust the redactor's framework, which recorded Perpetua's martyrdom for the spiritual benefit of a Christian community, and presumably emphasized details consistent with its vision of the world—including the male writer's understanding of gender. Dronke points out, for example, that the redactor's "picture . . . of Perpetua in the arena, covering her legs and tidying her hair after being gored, consorts ill with the dream of the woman who strips naked and is anointed for combat: one who is unafraid to write like that will hardly have gone to her death in a fit of prudery" (15).

Beginning with the insights she herself offered in her narrative, Perpetua's dreams have been the subject of many interpretations. Her dream of her brother's thirst, for example, was interpreted by early Christians as a dream about the Christian ritual of baptism; her dream of an old man milking sheep and offering her cheese has been seen as referring to the Christian ritual of eucharist. More recently scholars have pointed to the pre-Christian religious and literary symbols that infuse the dreams. Marie Louise von Franz has offered a Jungian reading; Mary R. Lefkowitz reads the dreams in terms of Perpetua's motivation for martyrdom; Peter Dronke links the dreams with the outer experiences Perpetua records, in an attempt to provide a "fuller understanding of her self-awareness" (1–17).

Whatever the significance of her dreams and their relation to the events of her final days, Perpetua's narrative provides extraordinary access into the inner world of a woman determined to keep faith with her spiritual convictions to the point of death. But resistance from within organized religions, with their patriarchal structures, is complex. Keeping faith with this new religion involved resisting two other versions of patriarchy. We see Perpetua resisting the imperial patriarchy of the Roman Empire by refusing the sacrifice for the emperor; more intimately, we see her resisting her father's insistence that she submit to state authority. Like many women after her, she appealed to the highest authority of a father God to refute these other fathers. In the excerpts included here, we see these conflicts played out in a visionary realm whose symbolic resolutions—presented in strikingly physical imagery—serve as a source and an expression of spiritual power.

ECD

FROM *THE PASSION OF PERPETUA*[§]

III When we were as yet only under legal surveillance, and my father, out of love for me, kept trying to refute me by argument and to break my resolve, I said: 'Father, do you see that container over there, for instance—a jug or something?' And he said: 'Yes, I do.' And

[§] Reprinted with the permission of Cambridge University Press from *Women Writers of the Middle Ages: A Critical Study of Texts from Perpetua (†203) to Marguerite Porete (†1310)* by Peter Dronké. Copyright © 1984 by Cambridge University Press. Material excerpted from pages 2–4.

I said to him: 'It can't be called anything other than it is, can it?' And he said: 'No.' 'So too, I can't call myself anything other than what I am: a Christian.'

Then my father, angry at this word, bore down on me as if he would pluck out my eyes. But he only fumed, and went away, defeated, along with the devil's sophistries. Then, for the few days that I was without my father, I gave thanks to God—I felt relieved at his not being there. In that short space of time we were baptized. But the Spirit enjoined me not to seek from that water any favour except physical endurance. After a few days we were taken to prison, and I grew frightened, for I had never known such darkness. Oh grim day!—intense heat, because of the crowds, extortions by soldiers. Above all, I was tormented with anxiety there, on account of my child.

Then Tertius and Pomponius, the consecrated deacons who were looking after us, arranged by a bribe that they let us out into the better, cooler part of the prison for a few hours. Coming out of the dungeon, everyone began to move freely; I breast-fed my child, who was already weak with hunger. Anxiously I spoke to my mother about him, I consoled my brother, I gave them charge of my son. I was worn out, seeing them so worn because of me. Such were my fearful thoughts for many days. Then I managed to have the child allowed to stay with me in prison. And at once I grew well again, relieved of the strain and anguish for him. And suddenly the prison became a palace to me, where I would rather be than anywhere. . . .

VI Another day, whilst we were eating our midday meal, we were suddenly taken away to the hearing, and arrived at the forum. At once the rumor swept the neighborhood, and an immense crowd formed. We mounted the tribunal. The others, when interrogated, confessed. Then my turn came. And my father appeared there with my son, and pulled me off the step, saying: 'Perform the sacrifice! Have pity on your child!' So too the governor, Hilarianus, who had been given judiciary power in place of the late proconsul Minucius Timinianus: 'Spare your father's old age, spare your little boy's infancy! Perform the ritual for the Emperor's welfare.' And I answered: 'I will not perform it.' Hilarianus: 'You are a Christian then?' And I answered: 'I am a Christian.' And as my father still hovered, trying to deflect me, Hilarianus ordered him to be thrown out, and he was struck with a rod. And I grieved for my father's downfall as if I'd been struck myself: that's how I mourned for his pitiful old age.

Then the governor sentenced us all and condemned us to the beasts of the arena. And joyful we went back to prison.

Then, as the baby was used to breast-feeding and staying in the prison with me, I at once sent the deacon Pomponius to my father, imploring to have it back. But my father did not want to let it go. And somehow, through God's will, it no longer needed the breast, nor did my breasts become inflamed—so I was not tormented with worry for the child, or with soreness.

VII A few days later, while we were all praying, suddenly in the middle of my prayer I let slip a word: the name, Dinocrates. And I was amazed, for he had never entered my thoughts except just then. And I grieved, remembering his plight. Then at once I realized that I was entitled to ask for a vision about him, and that I ought to; and I began to pray for him a lot, and plaintively, to God. That very night, this is what I was shown: I saw Dinocrates coming out of a dark place, where there were many people. He was very hot and thirsty, his clothes dirty and his looks pallid—he still had on his face the same wound as when he died. When alive he had been my brother, who at the age of seven died wretchedly, of a cancer of the face, in such a way that everyone saw his death with revulsion. So I prayed for him, and between me and him there was a great gap, such that we could not come near each other. Beside Dinocrates was a pool of water, with a rim that was higher than he. And Dinocrates stretched up as if to drink. I was full of sorrow that, even though the pool had water, the rim was so high that he could not drink. And I awoke, and realized that my brother was struggling. Yet I was confident that I could help him in his struggle, and I prayed for him everyday, till we moved to the military prison—for we were destined to fight in the garrison-games: they were on Emperor Geta's birthday. Day and night I prayed for Dinocrates, groaning and weeping that my prayer be granted.

VIII On a day when we remained in fetters, I was shown this: I saw the place I'd seen before, and there was Dinocrates, clean, well-dressed, refreshed; and where the wound had been I saw a scar; and the pool I'd seen previously had its rim lowered; it was down to the boy's navel. And he was drinking from the pool incessantly. Above the rim was a golden bowl full of water. Dinocrates came near it and began to drink from that, and the bowl never ran dry. And when he had drunk his fill, he began to play with the water, as children do, full of happiness. And I awoke: I realized then that he'd been freed from pain. . . .

X The day before our fight, this is what I saw in vision: Pomponius the deacon was coming to the prison gate and knocking urgently. And I went out to him and opened for him. He was wearing a loose, gleaming white tunic, and damasked sandals, and he said: 'Perpetua, we are waiting for you: come!' He took my hand and we began to go over rough, winding ways. We had hardly reached the amphitheatre, breathless, when he took me into the middle of the arena, and said: 'Don't be afraid; here I am, beside you, sharing your toil.' And he vanished. And I saw the immense, astonished crowd. And as I knew I had been condemned to the wild beasts, I was amazed they did not send them out at me. Out against me came an Egyptian, foul of aspect, with his seconds: he was to fight with me. And some handsome young men came up beside me: my own seconds and supporters. And I was stripped naked, and became a man. And my supporters began to rub me with oil, as they do for a wrestling match; and on the other side I saw the Egyptian rubbing himself in dust. And a man of amazing size came out—he towered even over the vault of the amphitheatre. He was wearing the purple, loosely, with two stripes crossing his chest, and patterned sandals made of gold and silver, carrying a baton like a fencing-master and a green bough laden with golden apples. He asked for silence, and said: 'This Egyptian, if he defeats her, will kill her with his sword; she, if she defeats him, will receive his bough.' And he drew back.

And we joined combat, and fists began to fly. He tried to grab my feet, but I struck him in the face with my heels. And I felt airborne, and began to strike him as if I were not touching ground. But when I saw there was a lull, I locked my hands, clenching my fingers together, and so caught hold of his head; and he fell on his face, and I trod upon his head.

The populace began to shout, and my supporters to sing jubilantly. And I went to the fencing-master and received the bough. He kissed me and said: 'Daughter, peace be with you!' And triumphantly I began to walk towards the Gate of the Living. And I awoke. And I knew I should have to fight not against wild beasts but against the Fiend; but I knew the victory would be mine.

This is what I have done till the day before the contest; if anyone wants to write of its outcome, let them do so.

WORKS CONSULTED

Dronke, Peter. *Women Writers of the Middle Ages: A Critical Study of Texts from Perpetua (†203) to Marguerite Porete (†1310).* Cambridge: Cambridge UP, 1984.

Lefkowitz, Mary R. "The Motivation for St. Perpetua's Martyrdom." *Journal of the American Academy of Religion* 44 (Sept. 1976): 417–21.

Rader, Rosemary. "The *Martyrdom of Perpetua:* A Protest Account of Third-Century Christianity."*A Lost Tradition: Women Writers of the Early Church.* By Patricia Wilson-Kastner, G. Ronald Kastner, Ann Millin, Rosemary Rader, and Jeremiah Reedy. Washington, DC: Univ. Press of America, 1981.

von Franz, Marie-Louise. *The Passion of Perpetua.* Trans. Elizabeth Welsh. Rpt. Jungian Classics Series 3. Irving, TX: Spring Publications, 1980.

MARGERY KEMPE *(c. 1373–1438)*

Chastity and Spiritual Desire

The two excerpts below come from a work that is unusual on several levels. Begun in 1436, the manuscript is not only the first extant English autobiography (Windeatt 9), but unlike most early autobiographies, it recounts the life of a middle-class woman—one who led a remarkably unconventional life (Atkinson 13). Finally, although there are a number of visionary writings by women mystics in the Middle Ages, this work provides in extraordinary detail an insight into the relationships among its author's experiences of spirituality, gender, sexuality, and class.

Herself illiterate, Margery told her story, twenty years after the first events it describes, to a man who, according to a priest to whom she later showed it, wrote in a nearly illegible mixture of German and English. This priest, after some delay and soul-searching about her controversial reputation, copied the book while reading it aloud to Margery. Although opinions differ about the role he might have played in shaping certain aspects of the narrative, especially its rendering of various theological ideas, most analyses conclude that the work is primarily Margery's and not that of her scribes.

Margery was the daughter of a prominent burgess (a full citizen of the city), who had been at various times mayor, member of Parliament, alderman of an influential guild, a justice of the peace, and a chamberlain. She married a less prominent burgess, John Kempe, probably a brewer, and for a time, Margery herself went into business as a brewer. Her spiritual journey began with what would appear to have been a post-partum depression after the birth of her first child, when she was "out of her mind" for over half a year, tormented by "devils opening their mouths all alight with burning flames of fire," pawing her, dragging her about, and opening their mouths to swallow her (41–42). A vision of Christ sitting beside her bed and reassuring her brought her out of this tumult, but, she explains, she continued in her old sinful ways after her recovery, until business failures led her to think God was punishing her.

After a spiritual epiphany she changed her life in a series of dramatic moves that made her a controversial figure from that time forward. She began to argue with her husband, to whom she had already borne fourteen children, over what she regarded as her calling to celibacy (the subject of the first excerpt). She insisted on wearing white and on gaining the approval of church authorities for what amounted to a self-invented nun's habit. She visited Jerusalem and began manifesting her spiritual state through copious weeping and loud groaning, manifestations that were variously regarded as bizarre, insane, signs of heresy, or a spiritual gift.

Of interest within the themes of this section is the way in which Margery used her body as an expression of her oppositional spirituality, often sobbing and groaning so loudly that she undermined the authority of priests attempting to conduct religious services. In such moments her body became a site of authority—an alternative authority, stronger than that of the priests, and invested in her by God. Margery, who refers to herself as "this creature" (that is, God's creation), represents her body as a vessel for the spiritual power poured into it by a higher source. An interesting comparison, in the section **Identifying Sources of Resistance**, is Hildegard of Bingen's reliance on the authority of her visions to assert her positions on issues of ecclesiastical authority, including authority over material resources.

Of interest as well for gender issues is the precedence God takes over family in Kempe's narrative. Kempe's spiritual calling, which required long pilgrimages and celibacy, enables her to redefine her temporal roles as wife, daughter, and mother. Her erotic visions of a union with Christ (our second excerpt) transform all three of these relationships, but she defines herself most importantly as a wife to Christ. In another vision (not reprinted here), Margery envisions herself taking care of the baby Jesus. Jesus' mother Mary is there, and Margery is serving Mary; still, Margery's motherly offices for the child place him in the role of her son. In such visions she believes herself elevated to higher relationships that take precedence over earthly ones.

Margery Kempe's book and life have been the subject of much historical and literary analysis, especially in recent years. Some of these are summarized in chapter 7 of Clarissa W. Atkinson's *Mystic and Pilgrim* (195–220), which focuses on questions of sexuality, mysticism, gender, individuality, and mercantilism. The difference between Lynn Staley Johnson's interpretation and Nancy Partner's indicates the variety of recent approaches to Kempe. Johnson reads Kempe as a social critic, and draws a useful distinction between "Kempe" the author and "Margery" the character; she sees Kempe as quite artful in her use of Margery. Nancy Partner focuses on love and desire, and revises an old interpretation of Kempe's experiences as "hysterical in origin" (267), by interpreting the supposed hysteria in the light of medieval women's experiences of gender subordination. Ruth Shklar reads Kempe as creating a "model of dissent and reform [that functions] as a critique of the prevailing discourses that would define heresy" (279). Gerda Lerner, noting that Kempe's spirituality was "rooted in ordinary dailyness" (84), reads her in the light of the "history of feminist consciousness," as someone whose unusual life pointed "toward other choices for women in the future" (87).

However one defines Margery—as social critic, religious dissenter, hysteric, or pioneer—what emerges from such readings, and from Margery Kempe's book itself, is a portrait of a woman who was a resister in almost every domain of her life. She resisted her husband and redefined their relationship according to her new inspiration; she resisted the authority of the church even as she actively sought its blessing; she resisted many of the conventional gender arrangements determined by her class and marital standing. In sum, Margery's experience of spirituality redrew the circumference of her social world. In this, her work has much in common with the work of Rebecca Cox Jackson, another religious visionary for whom a sense of God's power was a sustaining force in withstanding mere earthly powers.

ECD

FROM *THE BOOK OF MARGERY KEMPE*[5]

Chapter 11

It happened one Friday, Midsummer Eve, in very hot weather—as this creature was coming from York carrying a bottle of beer in her hand, and her husband a cake tucked inside his clothes against his chest—that her husband asked his wife this question: 'Margery, if there came a man with a sword who would strike off my head unless I made love with you as I used to do before, tell me on your conscience—for you say you will not lie—whether you would allow my head to be cut off, or else allow me to make love with you again, as I did at one time?'

'Alas, sir,' she said, 'why are you raising this matter, when we have been chaste for these past eight weeks?'

'Because I want to know the truth of your heart.'

And then she said with great sorrow, 'Truly, I would rather see you being killed, than that we should turn back to our uncleanness.'

And he replied, 'You are no good wife.'

And then she asked her husband what was the reason that he had not made love to her for the last eight weeks, since she lay with him every night in his bed. And he said that he was made so afraid when he would have touched her, that he dared do no more.

'Now, good sir, mend your ways and ask God's mercy, for I told you nearly three years ago that you[r desire for sex] would suddenly be slain—and this is now the third year, and I hope yet that I shall have my wish. Good sir, I pray you to grant what I shall ask, and I shall pray for you to be saved through the mercy of our Lord Jesus Christ, and you shall have more reward in heaven than if you wore a hair-shirt or wore a coat of mail as a penance. I pray you, allow me to make a vow of chastity at whichever bishop's hand that God wills.'

'No,' he said, 'I won't allow you to do that, because now I can make love to you without mortal sin, and then I wouldn't be able to.'

Then she replied, 'If it be the will of the Holy Ghost to fulfill what I have said, I pray God that you may consent to this; and if it be not the will of the Holy Ghost, I pray God that you never consent.'

Then they went on towards Bridlington and the weather was extremely hot, this creature all the time having great sorrow and great fear for her chastity. And as they came by a cross her husband sat down under the cross, calling his wife to him and saying these words to her: 'Margery, grant me my desire, and I shall grant you your desire. My first desire is that we shall still lie together in one bed as we have done before; the second, that you shall pay my debts before you go to Jerusalem; and the third, that you shall eat and drink with me on Fridays as you used to do.'

'No sir,' she said, 'I will never agree to break my Friday fast as long as I live.'

---

[5] Reprinted from *The Book of Margery Kempe,* translated by B.A. Windeatt (Penguin Classics, 1985). Copyright © 1985 by B.A. Windeatt. Reproduced by permission of Penguin Books, Ltd. Material excerpted from pages 58–60, 126–127.

'Well,' he said, 'then I'm going to have sex with you again.'

She begged him to allow her to say her prayers, and he kindly allowed it. Then she knelt down beside a cross in the field and prayed in this way, with a great abundance of tears: 'Lord God, you know all things. You know what sorrow I have had to be chaste for you in my body all these three years, and now I might have my will and I dare not, for love of you. For if I were to break that custom of fasting from meat and drink on Fridays which you commanded me, I should now have my desire. But, blessed Lord, you know I will not go against your will, and great is my sorrow now unless I find comfort in you. Now, blessed Jesus, make your will known to my unworthy self, so that I may afterwards follow and fulfill it with all my might.'

And then our Lord Jesus Christ with great sweetness spoke to this creature, commanding her to go again to her husband and pray him to grant her what she desired: 'And he shall have what he desires. For, my beloved daughter, this was the reason why I ordered you to fast, so that you should the sooner obtain your desire, and now it is granted to you. I no longer wish you to fast, and therefore I command you in the name of Jesus to eat and drink as your husband does.'

Then this creature thanked our Lord Jesus Christ for his grace and his goodness, and afterwards got up and went to her husband, saying to him, 'Sir, if you please, you shall grant me my desire, and you shall have your desire. Grant me that you will not come into my bed, and I grant you that I will pay your debts before I go to Jerusalem.[1] And make my body free to God, so that you never make any claim on me requesting any conjugal debt after this day as long as you live—and I shall eat and drink on Fridays at your bidding.'

Then her husband replied to her, 'May your body be as freely available to God as it has been to me.'

This creature thanked God greatly, rejoicing that she had her desire, praying her husband that they should say three paternosters in worship of Trinity for the great grace that he had been granted them. And so they did, kneeling under a cross, and afterwards they ate and drank together in great gladness of spirit. This was on Friday, on Midsummer's Eve.

Chapter 36, Jesus Speaks To Margery In A Vision [Eds.]

'And if I were on earth as bodily as I was before I died on the cross, I would not be ashamed of you, as many other people are, for I would take you by the hand amongst the people and greet you warmly, so that they would certainly know that I loved you dearly.

'For it is appropriate for the wife to be on homely terms with her husband. Be he ever so great a lord and she ever so poor a woman when he weds her, yet they must lie together and rest together in joy and peace. Just so must it be between you and me, for I take no heed of what you have been but what you would be, and I have often told you that I have clean forgiven you all your sins.

'Therefore I must be intimate with you, and lie in your bed. Daughter, you greatly desire to see me, and you may boldly, when you are in bed, take me to you as your wedded husband, and your dear darling, and as your sweet son, for I want to be loved as a son should be loved by a mother, and I want you to love me, daughter, as a good wife ought to love her husband. Therefore you can boldly take me in the arms of your soul and kiss my mouth, my head, and my feet as sweetly as you want. And as often as you think of me or would do any good deed to me, you shall have the same reward in heaven as if you did it to my own precious body which is in heaven, for I ask no more of you but your heart, to love me who loves you, for my love is always ready for you.'

Then she gave thanks and praise to our Lord Jesus Christ for the high grace and mercy that he showed to her, unworthy wretch.

This creature had various tokens in her hearing. One was a kind of sound as if it were a pair of bellows blowing in her ear. She—being dismayed at this—was warned in her soul to have no fear, for it was the sound of the Holy Ghost. And then our Lord turned that sound into the voice of a dove, and afterwards he turned it into the voice of a little bird which is called the redbreast, that often sang very merrily in her right ear. And then she would always have great grace after she heard such a token. She had been used to such tokens to about twenty-five years at the time of writing this book.

Then our Lord Jesus Christ said to this creature, 'By these tokens you may well know that I love you, for you are to me a true mother and to all the world, because of that great charity which is in you; and yet I am cause of that charity myself, and you shall have great reward for it in heaven.'

NOTE

[1] Surviving Lynn records refer to Margery's father, John Brunham, as alive but in ill health on 19 December 1412, and on 16 October 1413 as deceased. Inheritance of a legacy may have helped Margery to strike this bargain with her husband [Windeatt].

WORKS CONSULTED

Atkinson, Clarissa W. *Mystic and Pilgrim: The Book and the World of Margery Kempe.* Ithaca: Cornell UP, 1983.

Johnson, Lynn Staley. "Margery Kempe: Social Critic." *Journal of Medieval and Renaissance Studies* 22.2 (Spring 1992): 159–184.

Kempe, Margery. *The Book of Margery Kempe.* Trans. Barry Windeatt. London: Penguin, 1985.

Lerner, Gerda. *The Creation of Feminist Consciousness: From the Middle Ages to Eighteen-seventy.* New York: Oxford University Press, 1993.

Partner, Nancy. "'And Most of All for Inordinate Love': Desire and Denial in *The Book of Margery Kempe.*" *Thought* 64 (Sept. 1989): 254–267.

Shklar, Ruth. "Cobham's Daughter: *The Book of Margery Kempe* and the Power of Heterodox Thinking." *Modern Language Quarterly* 56.3 (Sept. 1995): 277–304.

Windeatt, Barry. Introduction. *The Book of Margery Kempe.* Trans. Barry Windeatt. London: Penguin, 1985.

REBECCA COX JACKSON *(1795–1871)*

Three Visions

Rebecca Cox Jackson was born in Philadelphia in 1795 to a family of free African Americans. The most influential relationship of her early years was with her older brother Joseph, whom she respected and revered as a father. Joseph was a pillar of the Bethel African Methodist Episcopal Church of Philadelphia (AME), one of the most powerful institutions within one of the largest free African-American communities of the time. Jackson lived in Joseph's home for many years, was a seamstress, and probably controlled her own income. Thus, her situation was one of relative security for an African-American woman in the early nineteenth century (Humez 10–13). Security, however, was not to be Jackson's chosen lot.

In 1831, Jackson experienced a private conversion during a violent thunderstorm, and six months later publicly experienced sanctification during a neighborhood revival. This public event established her as a leader in a "Covenant Meeting" of AME members who sought to live a life of Christian perfection. As she began to preach and develop her own theology, irreconcilable conflicts with her family and community began to emerge.

Intertwined in Jackson's developing theology were the extreme physical imagery of many of her spiritual visions (most explicit in the first excerpt we include here, her "Dream of Slaughter") and her decisive turn to celibacy. Jackson's prophetic gift developed as she began to hear and obey perfectly an inner voice that provided guidance and comfort. In one of her writings, Jackson describes a profound occurrence when she physically and spiritually experienced unity with a visionary female spiritual mentor: "And as soon as I was under [the water], this woman entered into me . . . And as she entered me, the heavenly influence of her divine spirit overcame my soul and body and I can't tell the heavenly feeling I had" (Humez 133).

Jackson's inner voice (often strengthened through rituals of bodily mortification such as fasting and weeping [Humez 93]) allowed her to endure extreme fatigue and pain. She was able to hold her hand on a red-hot stove to convince her husband that her body belonged to God—neither to her nor to him (Humez 18)—and to work at such a non-stop pace that her family believed her to be "agoing crazy" (qtd. in Humez 87). She came to dedicate herself fully to celibacy after a revelation that carnality was "of all things the most filthy in the sight of God" (qtd. in Humez 17). Jean Humez argues that her celibacy is most clearly understood as evidencing "her need to gain complete control over the use of her body" (17). This synthesis of physical and spiritual power allowed Jackson to transcend "sinfulness" and to see herself on a solitary mission to save the souls of others: "Therefore the world, the flesh, and the devil were all against me, and I stood alone in the earth. And of the people, there were none with me, even as there were none with Christ when He stood in the Judgement" (qtd. in Humez 142).

Jackson thus sought first to convince people of the darkness of their sins, and then to purify their way of living (she advocated celibacy) in order to follow the example of Christ. As her reputation grew, Jackson began to preach on the itinerant circuit of the northeast. While touring, she did not spare the AME church in her disclosures of sinfulness, but openly criticized its carnality. Her criticism led to attempts by the AME hierarchy to suppress her preaching and leadership of prayer meetings, by charging that she was trying to split the church (a very real concern for the first separate African-American Methodist church, which was under attack by Euro-American Methodists throughout this period).

Even during the evangelical and egalitarian fervor of the second Great Awakening, which began in the United States in the 1790s, to be a female preacher was enough to cause controversy among all but the most radical of communities and incite repressive action by church officials (Hardesty 12–13, 24, 57, 72). Just as the itinerant preacher Jarena Lee had to prove her holiness and disobey church restrictions (see excerpt in **Work and Education**), Jackson also had to struggle to make a path for herself. In contrast however to Lee, who eventually received official sanction, the hostility of Jackson's relations with the AME church meant not only that she was spiritually alone when she traveled, and had to rely on a community's kindness and interest in her message, but also that she had to deal with the active attempts by the church to stop her preaching. Nonetheless, Jackson became an extremely popular figure, and her notoriety perhaps as much as her charismatic style drew large crowds and touched off several waves of evangelical fervor.

In 1840, Jackson's travels led her to a predominantly Euro-American group of "Perfectionists" living near Albany, New York. There she found a community who shared her ideals for purity of living, and for the first time she was no longer alone, struggling against sinners. In 1843 this group, including Jackson, decided to join a Shaker sisterhood (again predominantly Euro-American) in the neighboring community of Watervliet. In the Shaker community, Jackson found an even more advanced perfectionist project which derived from a more established and egalitarian theology that was remarkably similar to the beliefs she had developed through her own experiences.

Of the nineteenth-century evangelical sects, the Shakers were perhaps the most egalitarian about race and gender. Shakers had strong sympathies with abolitionists, were involved in the Underground Railroad, and welcomed the occasional African-American worshipper or fugitive into their community. The Shakers' version of perfectionism committed them to celibacy. They believed in divine revelation through human beings and encouraged ecstatic experience in worship. Theologically, they believed in a four-in-one Godhead: Father, Mother, Son, and Daughter, all coeternal partners. This belief led them to their separate their community into male and female parts, each with its own crucial roles and autonomous authority. They also believed that the Second Coming had already occurred, but that this time, God had taken the form of a woman—the founder of Shakerism, Ann Lee. Under the influence of these ideas, Jackson had her first vision of the God Mother.

Yet along with this radical egalitarianism, the Shakers were also insular, convinced that any contact between "believers" and the outside world of sin was highly dangerous and should be tightly controlled. Again Jackson found herself in conflict with a religious hierarchy—a conflict that stemmed from her belief that the Shakers were keeping their light under a bushel. She was especially troubled by what she perceived as the Shakers' neglect of the plight of the African-American community. Conflicts between Jackson and the head mother of Watervliet eventually led to Jackson's departure to pursue her mission of preaching to the fallen children of God. But Jackson never abandoned her Shaker beliefs, and continued to study Shaker works and refine her own philosophy. She also never surrendered her ideal of a perfectionist community. With her companion, Rebecca Perot, she founded her own Shaker sisterhood in Philadelphia in 1859.

Rebecca Cox Jackson combined in her prophetic career a number of often conflicting ideas and traditions—the Protestant ideals of evangelical outreach and reform, a focus on charismatic worship, vocal and spontaneous confession of sin and testimony about the alighting of the Holy Spirit, a physical and spiritual relationship with a complex deity, and Shaker ideals of perfectionism and a complete holiness in living. In certain ways this unique combination made Jackson a bridge between African-American and Euro-American religious and spiritual traditions of the nineteenth century, even as her experience of spiritual power bridged differences of class, race, and gender in her life inside and outside the church. A central question addresses the connection between Jackson's experience of oppression in both religious communities—and more broadly, the relation between those experiences and her experiences of oppression in society at large. How did Jackson's struggle with her brother Joseph (whom she took as her religious authority for the first thirty years of her life) and the rest of the male AME leadership affect her conception of God the Father, and later, God the Mother? How did the intersections of the spiritual and the physical in her visions relate to her experiences as an African-American woman in the church and in the world?

The historical context for Jackson's conversion, Humez has pointed out, was a period of growing racism, including racial violence, in Philadelphia—a city many free African Americans had chosen for its relatively progressive laws on slavery, education, and suffrage (Humez 15). In a world where the threat of physical violence was a part of African-American women's lives, spiritual power provided a crucial element of self-defense. As Humez says, "That the joyful sense of complete personal security, of attaining to sanctification in life, could be of great psychological value for a woman who had to deal daily with white racism is suggested by Amanda Smith's comment, 'I think some people would understand the quintessence of sanctifying grace if they could be black about twenty-four hours' " (6). In addition, Jackson chose to resist the patriarchal structure of the AME Church, and the "Dream of Slaughter" suggests that Jackson experienced that conflict with visceral force, as yet another threat of violence. Against such threats, Jackson's spiritual powers gave her not only a certain security, but a certain authority—over members of her own race as well as over Euro-Americans who, in other contexts, would have had physical, legal, and economic power over her. The "Dream of the Cakes" and its real-life sequel (the second and third excerpts included here) provide an interesting perspective on the interplay between race, class, and gender in Jackson's life, and on her understanding of spiritual authority.

Finally, there is the question of sexuality and its relation to Jackson's experience of gender relations inside and outside her religious communities. Unlike other itinerant African-American female preachers of her day, Jackson lived and traveled for many years with the woman companion, Rebecca Perot, described in such glowing physical/spiritual imagery in the last vision excerpted below. Her joy in this woman companion resonates with her joyful vision of a Mother God in 1842:

> Her face was round like a full moon, with the glory of the sun reflecting from her head . . . And she was beautiful to look upon . . . She being in the center, she extended her golden wings across the room over the children, with her face toward me and said, "These are all mine," though she spoke not a word. And what a Mother's look she gave me. And at that look, my soul was filled with love and a motion was in my body, like one moving in the waves of the sea. I was happy. And I felt to embrace all her children in the arms of my soul. I understood by one of the discerners that there was sixteen angels in the room that night. I only saw our Blessed Mother, and that was as much as I was able to bear. (168)

ECD and *KKF*

FROM *THE WRITINGS OF REBECCA COX JACKSON*[§]

"A Dream of Slaughter"

In a night or two after I had this dream, I also dreamed I was in a house, entered in at the south door. I heard a footstep quick behind me and looked at the east window and saw a man coming. I run upstairs, told the child's nurse a robber was in the house. She fled. I went to the east window, then to the west, to jump out. I found in so doing I should kill myself, so I sat down on a chair by the west window with my face to the north. He came up and came right to me. He took a lance and laid my nose open and then he cut my head on the right side, from the back to the front above my nose, and pulled the skin down over that side. Then he cut the left, did the same way, and pulled the skin down. The skin and blood covered me like a veil from my head to my lap. All my body was covered with blood. Then he took a long knife and cut my chest open in the form of the cross and took all my bowels out and laid them on the floor by my right side, and then went in search of all the rest of the family. This was a family that I sewed in. When the lance was going through my nose it felt like a feather was going over my nose. I sat in silent prayer all the time saying these words in my mind, "Lord Jesus, receive my spirit."

After I found he was gone I thought I would make my escape before he returned. I was afraid if he found me alive he would want to treat me more cruel. But a voice above my head told me to sit still, as though I was dead, for that was the only thing that would save

[§] Reprinted from *Gifts of Power: The Writings of Rebecca Jackson, Black Visionary, Shaker Eldress.* Edited by Jean McMahon Humez. Copyright © 1981 by The University of Massachusetts Press. Material excerpted from pages 94–96, 99–100, 126–127. Literary rights owned by The Berkshire Atheneum, Pittsfield, Massachusetts. Used by permission.

me. And this was the way I sat all the time he was amangling my body—as though I was dead. So in a moment after those words were spoken to me, he came in and came to me as if he was agoing to do something else to me, and I was afraid. I thought I would implore his mercy to save my life, but the same voice spoke to me and said, "He can show no mercy." And in the same moment, the same voice from above spoke to him and asked, "What is your occupation?" (and also the man that was with him). He said the man rid[1] the entrails but he opened the heart. And He commanded him not to touch me again. And they both fled from before me by the power of that voice. And then I found what it was that keep me alive. He had not as yet taken out my heart, but my entrails were laying all this time by my right side on the floor.

And then I awoke and my dream troubled me. I was so faint when I woke I could not get up for some time. And when I did I cried, "I shall die! I shall die!" Samuel said, "What is the matter?" "Oh my dream! My dream!" And I was all in a tremble. And these words were spoken to me, "Thy life is hid in Christ. Thy life is hid in Christ. Thy life is hid in Christ." Three times these words were spoken to me. And I was strengthened and my soul filled with the love of God. And I began to walk the floor back and forth apraising the Lord as though nothing had been.

This man was a Methodist preacher and about four years after I had this dream he persecuted me in as cruel a manner as he treated my body in the dream. And he tried to hedge up my way and stop my spiritual useful influence among the people and destroy my spirit life. But my life was hid in Christ. And in 1840, God from above spoke to him in Albany and he troubled me no more. He had packed his trunk at night to start for Philadelphia in the morning, and in the morning, he was dead. So he was not allowed to take out my heart. It was the garden of the Lord, where He sowed His seed, which is Christ in which my life is hid, on which my life depended for to be brought to light by the Resurrection of Jesus Christ. And this depended on my perfect obedience to all His divine will as it is made known to me. This is the way I am to find eternal light and life in my soul.

And here I was showed also, in this dream, how I would have to suffer while I was adoing His holy will. And I was not to rest nor emplore mercy at the hand of a persecutor, for the spirit of persecutors could show no mercy. For it is the Devil, and he knows no mercy. So with God there is nothing impossible. In and with His wisdom, He saw fit to call and raise me up in this city as a living witness for Him and His work, the work of the latter day of glory. And although there was no mortal that I could go to and gain instruction, so it pleased God in His love and mercy to teach me in dreams and visions and revelation and gifts. Herein my faith was often put to the test.

"The Dream of the Cakes"

A dream. I thought I was going to bake some cakes. A sister come in that belonged to the Covenant. I said, "I am glad you have come!" "Why?" "Because I am going to bake some cakes." I sat down on a low stool before a griddle. It laid on two bricks, the fire under it. It stood in the northeast corner of the room on the floor. The fireplace was on the west side of the room. However, I greased the griddle, put on a little batter, about a tablespoonful.

It run all over the griddle, a beautiful brown on both sides, though I did not turn it. And in a moment the people ate it all up—they were all white.[2] I did not see them before I saw them eating my cake. I knowed not where they came from—I looked at the sister. "Did you see that? Well, I will try it again."

I poured on another. It run all over, under, and into the fire. They ate it out of the fire and off the griddle. And the people increased as the cake enlarged. I put on the third. It ran all over the griddle, on the fire, under it, on the ashes, under it, and spread about one yard around. The people ate it off the griddle, off the fire, from under it, off the ashes, under the ashes. They ate it all, except a little piece about one inch in length, a half an inch in width. This little piece lay before my right foot in the ashes. It was all I seen. I picked it up and said, "Let us taste it. They ate it so good." I broke it and put the piece in my mouth. It was the sweetest I ever tasted. I gave her the other, said, "Here, taste. No wonder they ate it up!"

So the people increased at the baking of the third cake to a large multitude. I don't think I put on more than a spoonful each time—it is my manner in baking any kind of batter cakes to try the griddle with batter enough to make a cake the size of a half a dollar, so that if it sticks, then there is not much batter wasted.

And I woke in the morning, I told my dream. My dreams became a burden to my family. I shall only mention a few of them in this writing in order to show how it pleased God in His wisdom to lead a poor unlearned ignorant woman, without the aid of mortal.

. . . So I went, and when I got there the house was full, and all around the door, and they were nearly all white people. And when I saw the table, book, and candle, I like to fall, my knees smote together. I cried out aloud, "Lord Jesus, if Thou hast sent me here to preach, clothe me with Thy power! And if Thou hast not, make me a public example before this people!" And in a moment, as it were, I was wrapped up in a mantle and clothed with power. And while I was speaking, I saw that this was the people that ate my cakes off the griddle and out of the fire and out of the ashes in 1831. There were two women that fell down and cried aloud. One of them was the wife of a mate of a vessel, and her brother was present. He stood near me, and when he saw his sister fall, he was taken with a shaking, and he made his way out the best he could.

There was some wicked men that was down there at that time. When they heard that a woman was going to speak, they came to prevent it. So it seemed they had placed theirselves before the table, before I got there. The one that was the leader stood nearest the table. I was told he didn't stand long before he was glad to sit down. When I first saw him sitting arocking, I thought he sat there because he had no seat. Just before I got through the spirit of prophecy rested upon me. I spoke as the spirit gave utterance. The head officer of that village stood just inside of the door. He had been under an exercise of mind about a duty which he had not done. When I closed, he made his way to the table with tears and said, "The Lord has sent this woman here to search me out." And he made an open confession with tears before all the people. When he was doing this, the man sitting on the floor said, "My name is Aswearing Jack. I am the wickedest man in this place. But this woman has told me the truth, and I want you to please to pray for me." He wept freely and told what he came to do. "But I won't touch this woman, nor nobody shan't. I han't got much money, but all I have I will give to this woman, that she may go and tell everybody and do all the good she can."

. . . March 27, 1851, I dreamt that Rebecca and me lived together. The door opened west, and there was a river that came from the west and it ran eastward, passing our house on the south side and one part came front on the west—a beautiful white water. I stood in the west door looking westward on the beautiful river. I saw Rebecca Perot coming in the river, her face to the east, and she aplunging in the water every few steps, head foremost, abathing herself. She only had on her undergarment. She was pure and clean, even as the water in which she was abathing. She came facing me out of the water. I wondered she was not afraid. Sometimes she would be hid, for a moment, and then she would rise again. She looked like an Angel, oh, how bright!

NOTES

[1] To remove or clear away, as a butcher would an animal's entrails in a slaughterhouse [Humez].

[2] This dream account apparently aims to justify the fact that RJ's early congregations were often white or predominantly white. It may even reflect her retrospective uneasiness with the fact that the Shakers, "God's true people on earth," were predominantly white [Humez].

WORKS CONSULTED

Humez, Jean McMahon ed. *Gifts of Power: The Writings of Rebecca Jackson, Black Visionary, Shaker Eldress.* Amherst: U of Massachusetts P, 1981.

Hardesty, Nancy A. *Your Daughters Shall Prophecy: Revivalism and Feminism in the Age of Finney.* Brooklyn, New York: Carlson, 1991.

SUMANGALAMATA, NANDUTTARA, AND VIMALA *(6th century BCE)*

"I Am Free"

The poems written by these three Buddhist nuns come from an ancient collection that has no parallel in any other religion of the world. Dating from the origins of Buddhism in India in the sixth century BCE, the *Therigatha,* "Songs of the Women Elders," record not only these women's spiritual experiences but details of their lives, glimpses of the gender arrangements they were leaving behind to become nuns. Because these songs circulated orally for some five hundred years before being committed to writing in 80 BCE, it is impossible to know what changes might have been made in the original verses, or the exact accuracy of the biographical information written in the fifth century CE to accompany them (Tharu and Lalita 65). Even so, they provide a unique primary source for contemporary Buddhist women in search of their collective spiritual history (Gross 18).

In the literature of Buddhism over the last two thousand years, recorded accounts of the Buddha's views on women vary, but there is agreement on two points. First, he stated unequivocally that women as well as men could attain the highest state of enlightenment—nirvana. This state promises a release from all desire and the suffering it causes. Tharu and Lalita describe an "epiphanic experience in which the painful constrictions of secular life fall away and the torment of feelings subsides as the peace and freedom of nirvana are attained" (67). The poems in the *Therigatha* express the freedom that comes from such an epiphany.

Second, although the Buddha may have initially resisted women's requests to found an order of nuns who would, like monks, renounce the world of their households, families, and material possessions, he did establish such an order. But dominant tradition has it that he set forth eight rules regulating nuns, all clearly directed toward subordinating nuns to monks in matters of discipline, daily interaction, and ritual. Whatever a nun's seniority, she had to defer to any monk of any rank. This rigorous gender subordination, as well as an apparent preference for women in the role of lay supporters of Buddhism rather than world-renunciants, reflected gender norms in the society as a whole (Chakravarti 31–34). Although men's families often opposed their abandonment of household responsibilities, in general such renunciation was probably easier for them than for women (Gross 36, Falk 164).[1] Still, the absence of gender distinctions in spiritual achievement meant that the nun's life offered significant liberation from the totality of women's subordination in the outside world.

This seems to have been true across the wide range of class backgrounds represented by the writers of the *Therigatha,* and by the three excerpts we have included here. Sumangalamata came from an unprivileged class. Her father and husband worked in the rushes (Tharu and Lalita 68), and most translations describe the husband as a "weaver of sunshades." As her poem tells us, she worked in her husband's kitchen. Sumangalamata rejoiced in becoming a homeless world-renunciant and escaping the pestle and cooking pots of the "householder."

Nandutarra belonged to the highest ("Brahman") caste in Hindu society. The beginning of the poem describes her participation in the religious rituals appropriate to her class; the second stanza, the rituals of beauty appropriate to her gender. In the end, she rejects both forms of devotion as "two aspects of the same misunderstanding" (Murcott 48), and attains her insight into "things as they are"—a key concept of Buddhism (Gross 8)—by "seeing the body as it really is."

Vimala was a prostitute before becoming a nun. The traditional story of her decision to join the ascetic community dramatically illustrates the role played by release from bodily desire in all of these poems. When Vimala encountered the renowned Buddhist monk, Moggallana (the same monk, in fact, who converted Nanduttara), she attempted to seduce him. He responded, "You bag of dung, tied up with skin. You demonness with lumps on your breast . . . A monk desiring purity avoids your body as one avoids dung" (qtd. in Murcott 124). Why such words inspired Vimala may puzzle some modern readers, but loathsome body imagery was typical in the mental exercises used by both monks and nuns to wean themselves from desire (Gross 47), and this encounter marked the spiritual turning-point of Vimala's life. While it may be the case that, as Murcott argues, the form of Buddhism in question here "inadvertently sets sexuality in opposition to religious accomplishment" (124), an important distinction can be made between Western ascetic traditions and those of Buddhism. The latter regards neither sexuality nor the body as evil in itself, but considers sexual desire, like all desire, as a source of suffering (Gross 31). The renunciant attempts to see things rightly by seeing the ephemeral nature of all things, including the mortality of the body. "For the Buddhist world-renouncer, the body, wealth, family ties, or sense pleasures are not to be avoided because of their intrinsically evil nature, for these things are not viewed as evil. Rather, the attachment and confusion that they tend to breed must be overcome to achieve spiritual liberation" (Gross 31).

This distinction is crucial in thinking about the ways women's powers relate to the control and power religious authorities attempt to exercise. For hundreds of years, a dominant strain of Western Christianity saw the male and female body as evil and debased. Thus, as women came to personify the body, as opposed to the spirit or intellect, it became possible to identify women most especially in their bodily selves as particularly negative and depraved. By the time Christian orders of nuns were being established, this view was firmly in place. In contrast, the early Buddhist poets represented here believed that it was not a woman's body that was evil; plainly, bodily desires of all kinds were impediments to the highest spiritual state that both women and men could attain. This is not to minimize the function that ideas about women's bodies have played in keeping women from full participation in Mahayana Buddhism (see the introduction to this section), nor to minimize the impact of patriarchal religious structures on women's spiritual lives in any religion. It is only to call attention to the fact that, while control of women's bodies—their sexual and reproductive capacities—has been a central issue in almost every major religious system, the particular ways in which individual religions view women's bodies may differ profoundly. Within those religions, women's spiritual and physical experiences of themselves, and the ways they resist a religion's control, differ as well.

ECD

FROM THE *THERIGATHA*[§]

Sumangalamata

Free, I am free!
How glad I am to be free
from my pestle.
My cooking pot seems
worthless to me.
And I can't even bear
to look at his sun-umbrella—
my husband disgusts me!

So I destroy greed and hate
with a sizzle.
And I am the same woman
who goes to the foot of a tree
and says to herself,
"Ah, happiness,"
and meditates with happiness.

Nanduttara

I used to worship fire,
the moon, the sun,
and the gods.
I bathed at fjords,
took many vows,
I shaved half my head,
slept on the ground,
and did not eat after dark.

Other times
I loved make-up and jewelry,
baths and perfumes,
just serving my body
obsessed with sensuality.

Then faith came.
I took up the homeless life.

[§] Reprinted from *The First Buddhist Women: Translations and Commentary on the Therigatha* by Susan Murcott © 1991 with permission of Parallax Press, Berkeley, California. Material excerpted from pages 106, 48, 126–127.

Seeing the body as it really is,
desires have been rooted out.

Coming to birth is ended
and my cravings as well,
Untied from all that binds
my heart is at peace.

Vimala

Young
intoxicated by my own
lovely skin,
my figure,
my gorgeous looks,
and famous too,
I despised other women.

Dressed to kill
at the whorehouse door,
I was a hunter
and spread my snare for fools.

And when I stripped for them
I was the woman of their dreams;
I laughed as I teased them.

Today,
head shaved,
robed,
alms-wanderer,
I, my same self,
sit at the tree's foot;
no thought.[2]

All ties
untied,
I have cut men and gods
out of my life,

I have quenched the fires.

NOTES

[1] On the other hand, the Buddha required that certain categories of men as well as women get permission from kin before being ordained (Chakravarti 31).

[2] *avitakka,* literally "free from conceptual thinking." The mediator achieves this degree of concentration and realization in the second jhana [Murcott].

WORKS CONSULTED

Barnes, Nancy Schuster. "Buddhism." *Women in World Religions.* Ed. Arvind Sharma. Albany, NY: State U of New York P, 1987.

Chakravarti, Uma. *The Social Dimensions of Early Buddhism.* Delhi: Oxford UP, 1987.

Falk, Nancy Auer. "The Case of the Vanishing Nuns: The Fruits of Ambivalence in Ancient Indian Buddhism." *Unspoken Worlds: Women's Religious Lives.* Ed. Nancy Auer Falk and Rita M. Gross. Belmont, CA: Wadsworth, 1989.

Gross, Rita M. *Buddhism After Patriarchy: A Feminist History, Analysis, and Reconstruction of Buddhism.* Albany, New York: State U of New York P, 1993.

Murcott, Susan. *The First Buddhist Women: Translations and Commentary on the Therigatha.* Berkeley: Parallax, 1991.

Tharu, Susie, and K. Lalita, eds. *Women Writing in India 600 B.C. to the Present.* Vol. 1. New York: Feminist Press at CUNY, 1991.

Therigatha, Translations in English

Norman, K.R., trans. *The Elders' Verses: II Therigatha.* London: Pali Text Society, 1971.

Rhys-Davids, Mrs. C.A.F., trans. *Psalms of the Early Buddhists.* London: Pali Text Society, 1909.

Norman and Rhys-Davids, trans. *Poems of Early Buddhist Nuns (Therigatha).* London: Pali Text Society, 1989. (Includes the translations in both volumes listed above, minus notes and introductions.)

ANNE LISTER *(1791–1840)*

"No Priest But Love"

Of the many women's diaries that have come down to us from the nineteenth century, Anne Lister's is unique. In a secret code it provides a meticulous record of a lesbian's experience of love, sexuality, and courtship in the conservative upper-class world of northern England. In many ways she belonged to that world: she read sermons aloud with her aunt on Sundays, expressed shock at someone's Unitarian tendencies, and refused to visit neighbors she considered vulgar, despite her attraction to their daughter. What sets Anne Lister apart from that world, however, is not only her feelings toward women—since many women must have experienced similar feelings—but the openness with which she recognizes their sexual components, and the importance she gives them in her self-analysis. Lister's nickname, "Gentleman Jack" (Whitbread ix), points to her inside/outside status. Wealthy, self-cultivated, pursuing private study in all the subjects an educated man of her class would know, she had many of the markings of a "gentleman," and her upper-class standing seems to have cleared some space for pursuits that transgressed gender boundaries—including the pursuit of women.

One of Lister's primary attachments was with Mariana Lawton, whose decision to marry for convenience put significant strain on their ongoing affair. In the diary, Anne despairs of a permanent union with Mariana (whom she refers to as M___) because it depends upon Mariana's husband dying in the near future. Although both she and Mariana hope for that improbable event, Lister concludes that, in the meantime, she needs a woman's company. The excerpts presented here recount Lister's attempt to begin a new relationship with Mrs. Maria Barlow, a woman whom she met in Paris. After living and traveling with Barlow and her daughter, however, Lister ended the relationship out of loyalty to her married lover. Eventually she found another "emotional and financial partnership" with Ann Walker, a wealthy neighbor (Whitbread xi)—a partnership they privately "confirmed for ever" with a gold ring (diary 27 Feb. 1834, qtd. in Liddington, "Inheritance" 268). It lasted until Lister's death of fever on a trip with Ann to Russia. Her partner inherited life tenancy of Lister's estate, where they had lived together for almost six years despite the gossip occasioned by Walker's puzzling decision to leave her own house (Liddington, "Inheritance").

Despite the need for secrecy that Lister's diary amply records, not only her class but her gender provided an opportunity for sexual freedom. Before the late nineteenth century, views on women's sexuality often led to disbelief in lesbian sexual activity. In 1811, for example, two British schoolmistresses accused of "improper and criminal conduct" won a libel case on the grounds that, as the House of Lords ruled, the "crime here alleged has no existence" (Faderman 147–52). In addition, the first volume of Lister's diary reveals that her class made it possible to pursue a lesbian relationship across racial lines; the "Eliza" referred to in the excerpt below was "'a girl of colour', Eliza Raine, wealthy daughter of an East India Company surgeon" and a boarding-school roommate of Lister's (Liddington, "Anne").

Jill Liddington has chronicled what she calls the inaccurate "filtering," a prudish screening, of the details of Lister's life by succeeding generations of historians and even one novel of 1872, *The Mistress of Langdale Hall: A Romance of the West Riding.* The code in which Lister wrote "roughly a sixth" of her twenty-seven volume diary was first deciphered in 1885, by an antiquarian friend of the family who expressed horror at the "unpublishable" nature of the material and suggested burning the whole diary ("Anne" 47 and 52). Some years later, however, he privately revealed the code to a librarian who kept the secret. The family member in possession of the letters, probably homosexual himself, also kept silent about the diary's coded contents. A later historian who referred publicly to the coded sections as "excruciatingly tedious . . . of no historical interest whatever" (56) seems to have destroyed her own transcript of them. It was not until the 1980s that Helena Whitbread became the first historian to publish large portions of the coded material and to discuss Lister's lesbianism explicitly. The following excerpts suggest the clarity with which Lister and her lovers were able to discuss their sexual desires, despite the indirectness of the language they used. In the first, Lister feigns naiveté about sexual practices early in her flirtation with the older woman; in the second, their discussions become more explicit. Both passages suggest how these women appropriated the socially sanctioned discourses of heterosexual love, marriage, and biblical authority as a means of expressing desires that resisted religious and social prohibitions.

ECD and *JP*

FROM *THE DIARIES OF ANNE LISTER* §

Friday 15 Oct. [1824. Eds.] French Contraceptive Methods Give Pleasure Without Danger

Walked with Mrs. Barlow 3/4 hour along the boulevard. . . she did not seem ennuyée with my company & we sat quietly in her room till 1–3/4 when luncheon was announced. . . I asked her for her bible. [I] said I knew what she alluded to as the French way of preventing children. Shewed her Genesis 36, the verse about Onan.[1] I was right, so therefore the French husbands spill their seed just before going to their wives which, being done, they take the pleasure without the danger. I wonder the women like it. It must spend the men before they begin. 'I must shew you the other passage,' said Mrs. Barlow, 'because I know you wish to know.' I asked the chapter. She said Romans. 'Yes,' said I, 'the first chapter' & pointed to that verse about women forgetting the natural use, etc.[2] 'But,' said I, 'I do not believe it.' 'Oh,' said she, 'it might be taken in another way, with men.' I agreed but without saying anything to betray how well I understood her. 'Yes,' she said, 'as men do with

§ Reprinted by permission of publisher from *I Know My Own Heart: The Diaries of Anne Lister, 1791–1840,* edited by Helena Whitbread. Copyright © 1988. Published by Smith Settle Publishers, Otley, England. Material excerpted from pages 32–33, 49 in the New York University Press edition, published 1992 under the title *No Priest But Love.*

men.' Thought I to myself, she is a deep one. . . . I should like to be instructed in the other (between two women) . . .

Saturday 13 Nov. Anne Explains Her Sexuality To Mrs. Barlow

At 2–20 went down to Mrs. Barlow, meaning to go out. She thought it would be too much for her. I therefore sat with her till 4–35. Lovemaking, vindicating style of conversation respecting myself. A great pickle. 'Scaped my maid & got away among the work-people. My father was one year in the Militia.[3] When my mother thought I was safe I was running out in an evening. Saw curious scenes, bad women, etc. Then went to the Manor school & became attracted to Eliza Raine. Said how it [Anne's preference for, or sexual attraction to, women] was all nature. Had it not been genuine the thing would have been different. [I] said I had thought much, studied anatomy, etc. Could not find it out. Could not understand myself. It was all the effect of the mind. No exterior formation accounted for it. Alluded to their being an internal correspondence or likeness of some of the male or female organs of generation. Alluded to the stones not slipping thro' the ring till after birth, etc.[4] She took all this very well. . . . Got on the subject of Saffic [sic] regard. [I] said there was artifice in it. It was very different from mine & would be no pleasure to me.[5] I liked to have those I loved near me as possible, etc. Asked if she understood. She said no. [I] told her I knew by her eyes she did & she did not deny it, therefore I know she understands all about the use of a ——— [The word is not entered in the journal]. Alluded to self-pollution, how much it was practised. Thought my connection with the ladies more excusable than this. . . . Said if a man loved his wife as he ought, he could say anything to her & indelicacy depended on their own minds. Many things might pass between them without indelicacy that might otherwise be shocking. She agreed, tho' I hinted at things—sometimes having no night-shift at all for a little while. She said if I wore men's clothes she should feel differently. She could not then sit on my knee. If my father had brought me up as a son she would have married me as I am, had I stated my case to her alone, even tho' she had had rank & fortune & been nineteen & at that age she was well worth having. I thanked her. Happening to say I often told my uncle & aunt how I longed to have someone with me, she wondered what they would think of the person. . . . Then, expressing my wish to have her, she answered, "But, we have had no priest but love. Do you not know the quotation?" I did not yet I said yes. Kissed her repeatedly, rather warmly. We get on gradually. Perhaps I shall have her yet before I go. . .

NOTES

[1] Lister is probably referring to *Genesis* 38:

> And Judah said unto Ō'năn, Go into thy brother's wife, and marry her, and raise up seed to thy brother.
>
> And Ō'năn knew that the seed should not be his; and it came to pass, when he went unto his brother's wife, that he spilled *it* on the ground, lest that he should give seed to his brother.

And the thing which he did displeased the lord; wherefore he slew him also. (*Genesis* 38.8–10, King James Version) [Eds.; emphasis added.]

[2] "For this cause God gave them up unto vile affections; for even their women did change the natural use into that which is against nature:

And likewise also the men, leaving the natural use of the woman, burned in their lust one toward another; men with men working that which is unseemly, and receiving in themselves that recompense of their error which was meet." (*Romans* 1.26–27, King James Version)

See also the Carolyn Mobley excerpt in this section for another interpretation of this passage. [Eds.]

[3] In fact, the army career of Anne's father spanned some thirty-six years. He obtained a commission as an ensign in the 10th Regiment of Foot in 1770 and was still serving, as a recruiting officer, in 1805–6 [Whitbread].

[4] Anne seems to be trying to present a rather garbled account of her idea of how the development or non-development of the genital organs can cause a confusion of sexual identity in a person. Her ideas appear to derive from reading the Classical works of the Ancients on anatomy rather than nineteenth-century anatomists. Thomas Lacquer, in his article entitled "La Difference: Bodies, Gender and History" (published in *The Threepenny Review*, spring 1988) states:

"For several thousand years it had been a commonplace that women have the same genitals as men, except that, as Nemesius (bishop of Emesa in the sixth century) put it: '. . . Theirs are inside the body and not outside it. . . .' Galen . . . in the second century AD . . . could already cite the anatomist, Herophilus (third century BC) in support of his claim that a woman has testes with accompanying seminal ducts very much like the man's, one on each side of the uterus—the only difference being that the males' are contained in the scrotum and the females' are not . . . Indeed, doggerel verse of the nineteenth century still sings of these hoary homologues after they have disappeared from learned texts:

. . . though they of different sexes be,
Yet, on the whole, they are the same as we.
For those that have the strictest searchers been,
Find women are but men turned outside in.'" [Whitbread]

[5] Anne believed Sapphic love between women to be learned behaviour rather than natural. She says: "The one [i.e. Sapphic love] was artificial and inconsistent [presumably because Sappho married], the other [her own sexuality] was the effect of nature. . . ." See p. 273 of *I Know My Own Heart.* [Whitbread]

WORKS CONSULTED

Faderman, Lillian. *Surpassing the Love of Men: Romantic Friendship and Love between Women from the Renaissance to the Present.* London: Junction, 1981.

Liddington, Jill. "Anne Lister of Shibden Hall, Halifax (1791–1840): Her Diaries and the Historians." *History Workshop Journal* 35.1 (Spring 1993): 45–77.

—. "Beating the Inheritance Bounds: Anne Lister (1791–1840) and Her Dynastic Identity." *Gender and History* 7.2 (1 Aug. 1995): 260–274.

Lister, Anne. *No Priest But Love.* Ed. Helena Whitbread. New York: NYU Press, 1992.

Whitbread, Helena, ed. *I Know My Own Heart: The Diaries of Anne Lister, 1791–1840.* Otley, England: Smith Settle Publishers, 1988.

GRAZIDA LIZIER *(1297/8–?)*

Is Making Love a Sin?

It is unusual to have a written record of a medieval peasant woman's views; it is even more unusual to come upon a frank account of a peasant woman's views on religion and sexuality. Such an account, reprinted below, exists because of the meticulous records kept by a fourteenth-century Catholic bishop, Jacques Fournier (later Pope Benedict XII), in his efforts to stamp out the heresy of Catharism (also known as Albigensianism and discussed below) in Southern France. His methods included imprisonment, inquisition, only occasional torture because he was known for his brilliant questioning, and such penalties as death, fines, or the wearing of a yellow cross to denote heresy (Ladurie xiii-xvii). From his records we know that Grazida Lizier was a twenty-one-year-old widow, a resident of the village of Montaillou, the last stronghold of Cathars after a century-long persecution. Her father, an iron-willed patriarch, forced her mother out of their house because she was not sympathetic enough to Catharism, after which she supported herself as a "tavern-keeper," that is, by selling wine from house to house (Ladurie 34, 6).

In questioning Grazida, Fournier hoped to condemn her as a heretic and implicate, as well, the local priest Pierre Clergue, who had been her lover from the time she was fourteen or fifteen until about a year before Fournier's inquisition. Disappointed after the first interview (excerpted below), Fournier imprisoned her for more than seven weeks and tried again. Though she had presented her unorthodox ideas about sin and sex as hers alone in the first interview, this time she attributed to her lover the idea that "to lie with a woman was no sin as long as it gave her pleasure" (qtd. in Dronke 205). She accounted for her earlier testimony by saying she had been warned against telling the truth—that ruining Pierre's reputation might endanger her life. Clergue was from the wealthiest family of Montaillou, and, as Emmanuel Le Roy Ladurie concludes, "It was not a good thing to resist the Clergue clan" (159).

Aside from the question of what kind of duress elicited Grazida's change in her testimony, Peter Dronke has pointed out that the second interview does not substantially contradict the first. Even allowing for the fact that a well-practiced libertine in his late thirties must inevitably have had some influence on a young girl in their discussions of sin and sex, a significant difference exists between Pierre's reasoning and Lizier's. "If at the beginning of their affair Pierre had relaxed her traditional beliefs, he was too shallow ever to arrive at Grazida's own" (206).

The divergence between Grazida's views and those of either Catharism or Catholicism (Dronke 203–204) suggests that, as she forcefully asserts, her ideas were indeed her own—self-invented within the context of accepted notions about the moral nature of sexual activity. One of these notions was that, as Lizier says, "all such coupling of men and women gives displeasure to God"—whether within or outside of marriage—although procreation mitigates the sinfulness of married sex (Dronke 206, 316). Extramarital acts displease Him "more," presumably because their intent is other than producing children. (Indeed, another of Pierre's twelve lovers recorded in detail the form of birth-control he used, a special herb hung around the woman's neck and placed "at the opening of [her] stomach" at the time of intercourse [Ladurie 172–73]). But God's displeasure is not, in Lizier's view, what constitutes sin; the determining factor for her is the presence or absence of "mutual joy."

Lizier's ideas are especially interesting in the context of the Western dichotomizing of soul and body, referred to in the headnote on Sumangalamata, Nanduttara, and Vimala in this section. The heresy for which Lizier was being investigated, Catharism, originated as a rigorously dualistic religion that saw the material world, including the human body, as evil, a creation of the devil. Orthodox Catholic doctrine saw all creation as God's, although both Catharism and Catholicism shared an emphasis on "the antinomy between the flesh and spirit" (Leff 423). By the time Grazida was born there was a new version of Catharism that saw material beings as evil "only in their actual physical state" and God as the creator of their ideal forms or archetypes (Leff 423). The "perfect" among Cathars thus renounced the material world, including sexual pleasure; mere "believers" did so only at the end of their lives, indeed as close to the end as possible. It is worth asking exactly in what ways Grazida shared or rejected the dualisms of both religious systems to which she was exposed. In her view of an afterlife that includes Paradise but not Hell, for example, Dronke sees "a quest for an integrated world-view, for the complete overcoming of dualism" (209). We might think, as well, about how the dualism of gender in Grazida's testimony intersects with the dualisms that separated her from her male lover and inquisitor: dualisms of age and youth, wealth and poverty, formal education and other ways of knowing.

Finally, Grazida's testimony raises the question of what kinds of religious authority systems have attracted women in search of space for their own expressions of spirituality. More than fifty years before Grazida's birth, Pope Innocent III's war on Cathars in Southern France, the "Albigensian crusade," ended with victory when two hundred people were burned at the stake. What threat did they pose that was great enough to incite this persecution almost to extinction? Gordon Leff suggests that the danger of all medieval heresies was their common attempt to approach God without the mediation of the Church (424). Throughout history, religious movements that emphasize the experiential, the active, and the unmediated role of the believer have been especially fertile grounds for women's resistance. Whatever Lizier's relation to Catharism, she seems to have chosen such an unmediated role by working out her own theology, including a self-created doctrine of free love.

ECD

GRAZIDA LIZIER'S TESTIMONY: THE FIRST INTERVIEW[§]

Seven years ago, or thereabouts, in summer, Pierre Clergue came to my mother's house—she was out reaping—and incited me to let him make love with me. I consented; I was still a virgin then, fourteen years old I think, or perhaps fifteen. He took me in the barn where

§ Reprinted with the permission of Cambridge University Press from *Women Writers of the Middle Ages: A Critical Study of Texts from Perpetua (†203) to Marguerite Porete (†1310)* by Peter Dronke. Copyright © 1984 by Cambridge University Press. Material excerpted from pages 204–205.

the straw is kept, but not at all violently. Afterwards he made love with me often, till the next January, and this always in my mother's house. She knew, and tolerated it. It was mostly in the daytime.

Then in January, he gave me in marriage to Pierre Lizier, my late husband. And after that he still often lay with me, in the four years my husband was alive: my husband knew about it, and did not put up resistance. When he asked me about our love-making, I said yes, it was true, and he told me to take care it should be with no other man. But Pierre and I never made love when he was at home, only when he was out.

I didn't know Pierre Clergue was, or was said to be, a cousin of my mother, Fabrisse: I had never heard anyone to say so. I didn't know she was related to him by blood in any way. Had I known she was a cousin of his—though an illegitimate one—I would not have let Pierre near me. Because it gave me joy and him also when we made love, I did not think that with him I was sinning.

At the time we made love together, both before I was married and after, as our love-making in all that time gave joy to us both, I did not think I sinned, nor does it seem so to me now. But now there'd be no joy in it for me—so, if I were to make love with him now, I believe it would be a sin.

When I was married and made love with the priest Pierre, it did not seem more proper to make love with my husband—all the same it seemed to me, and I still believe, it was as little sin with Pierre as with my husband. Did I have any qualms at the time, or think that such deeds might displease God? No I had none, and did not think my lying with Pierre should displease any living being, since it gave joy to us both.

If my husband had forbidden it? Supposing he had—even though he never did—I still would not have thought it a sin, because of the shared joy of love. If any man whatever lies with any woman (unless she is related to him by blood), whether she's a virgin or has been seduced, whether in marriage or outside it—all such coupling of men and women gives displeasure to God, and yet I still do not think the partners sin, insofar as their joy is mutual. Does it displease God more when the partners are married than when they are not? I think it displeases him more when they are unmarried lovers.

I don't know, but I've heard it said there is a paradise, and I believe it; I've also heard there is a hell, but that I don't believe, though I won't urge it is untrue. I believe there is a paradise, for it is something good, as I've heard tell; I don't believe in hell (though I don't argue against it), for that is something evil, as people say. I've often heard that we shall rise again after death—I don't believe that, though I don't discredit it.

I still believe it is no sin when love-making brings joy to both partners. I have believed that ever since Pierre first knew me. No one taught me these ideas except myself. I haven't taught them to others—no one has ever asked me about them.

I believe God made those things that are helpful to man, and useful too for the created world—such as human beings, the animals men eat, or are carried about on—for instance oxen, sheep, goats, horses, mules—and the edible fruits of the earth and of trees. But I don't think God made wolves, flies, mosquitoes, and such things as are harmful to man; nor do I think he made the devil, for that is something evil, and God made nothing evil.

WORKS CONSULTED

Dronke, Peter. *Women Writers of the Middle Ages: A Critical Study of Texts from Perpetua (†203) to Marguerite Porete (†1310)*. Cambridge: Cambridge UP, 1984.

Leff, Gordon. "Heresy in the Middle Ages." *Dictionary of the History of Ideas: Studies of Selected Pivotal Ideas*. Ed. Philip P. Wiener. Vol. 2. New York: Scribner's, 1973.

Le Roy Ladurie, Emmanuel. *Montaillou: The Promised Land of Error.* Paris, 1975. Trans. Barbara Bray. New York: George Braziller, 1978.

CAROLYN MOBLEY *(late 20th century)*

St. Paul and Lesbian Sexuality

As an African-American child growing up in a small, segregated, Florida town, Carolyn Mobley was raised a devout Christian in the Baptist church. When an adult she set out to fulfill her calling as a Christian educator, despite her knowledge that the church hierarchy would not condone her lesbian sexuality. Indeed she was eventually fired for being a lesbian, whereupon she devoted herself openly to gay activism, and became the first woman cochair of the African-American Lesbian/Gay Alliance. Eventually she succeeded in returning to church work in a way that did not conflict with her experience of her sexuality, by serving as assistant pastor for the Metropolitan Community Church of the Resurrection in Houston, Texas, one of the more than 250 MCC congregations worldwide whose members are predominantly lesbians and gay men. Here, she is free to work actively for gay and lesbian rights as part of her religious vocation.[1]

In the excerpt reprinted here, Mobley describes an experience shared by many adolescents raised in religious traditions that do not condone gay or lesbian sexualities. Mobley's religious convictions led her to the Christian Bible as a source of authority; her own feelings asserted a different kind of authority; her mother, intervening against her lesbianism in a way that also contradicted her religious teachings, added a third dimension to her conflict. In this passage we see Mobley, with the moral support gained from her admiration of Martin Luther King, privately engaging in a creative interaction with the scriptures of her religious tradition—an interaction that in many ways parallels the kind of reading we see in María Clara Bingemer (see excerpt in this section) and Margaret Fell (see **Vision and Transformation**). In each case, the authority of the scripture and women's experiential relation to it serve as a source of strength in resisting other kinds of patriarchal authority. In Mobley's case, the experience of resisting racism, which she describes in sections of the narrative not reprinted here, was perhaps a source of strength in learning how to resist authority within her own religious community. In this sense her narrative should be compared with those of Rebecca Cox Jackson (see this section) and Jarena Lee (in the **Work and Education** section). In addition, her readings of St. Paul are an interesting contrast to those of Anne Lister (see this section), who also found the references to "unnatural" sexuality important, but with a very different emphasis.

ECD

FROM "THE CHRISTIAN EDUCATOR"[§]

At the age of ten I became a Christian. In black Protestant churches, kids, for the most part, aren't automatically taken in the church when they're born. Unlike the Catholics, you have to make your own decision and say, "Yes, I want to be baptized and I want to be a part of the church." . . . It's been a firm faith for me. I've never wavered from it, even when I began to feel some tensions between my belonging to Christ and my being a lesbian. . . .

The older I got, the more conflict I felt about my feelings. It was a religious thing for me. I knew that what I was feeling was wrong according to the church. But I managed to use my convictions about being in the church to get out of dating boys. As a Baptist, I really wanted to be all that I thought God wanted me to be, which meant no drinking, no smoking, and no dancing. That reasoning worked well as an excuse for not going to the sock hops after the high school football games. Even in eighth grade, when we had a prom-type event, I didn't dance. There was a dinner, but after that I went out to sit in the car. My mother came and got me and made me go back inside. She said my behavior was very anti-social.

In high school, my mother gave up and didn't make me go to the proms, but she told me that she thought I should go. So I did, even though I didn't want to get all dressed up, put on the makeup, or dance with boys. I told the boy who took me that I didn't want to dance, that he could dance with other people. It was just trauma city for me, but I endured it.

You know, it wasn't that I didn't like to dance. I just didn't want to be held close by these guys. It just felt real awkward, very unnatural and uneasy. Later on, when I realized I could dance with women, I found out I loved dancing.

Besides going to the proms, I also dated, even though I didn't like it. I was praying God would change my feelings and take away my desire to be with females, to let me be more open to having a boyfriend. This boy walked me home from school most days and sometimes he would come over on weekends, and we'd sit and watch TV. He would always end up wanting to neck and stuff. I would say, "Oh, no. I know God didn't want me to do this. It's one thing for me to sit here and watch TV with you, but no, no, no.". . .

Dr. King's commitment to disobeying unjust laws had a profound impact on my thinking. I began to question the things that I was told to do: "Are they really right? Are they right if I'm told they're right by a person in a position of authority?" I began to realize that parents could steer you wrong. Teachers could steer you wrong. Preachers, God knows, could steer you wrong. They were all fallible human beings. That really changed my way of looking at myself and the world. And it certainly helped me reevaluate the message I was getting from the church about homosexuality. It made me examine more closely what scripture had to say about it.

As a college student, I continuously read scripture on my own. I especially reread Ro-

[§] Reprinted from *Making History: The Struggle for Gay and Lesbian Rights, 1945–1990,* edited by Eric Marcus. Copyright © 1992 by Eric Marcus. Reprinted by permission of HarperCollins, Publishers, Inc. Material excerpted from pages 320–324.

mans numerous times. I finally got the picture that God wasn't against homosexuals and that even Paul, who wrote that passage in Romans about homosexuality and was against homosexuals[2] was a human being subject to error, just like me. So I thought the man was wrong, period. What he was espousing was inaccurate, and it needed to be challenged. That was what Dr. King was about, challenging error wherever it was found.

With that understanding, I decided to live my own life. By the time I finished college, I was ready to become a sexually active adult. I began to come out to myself and I came out to my mom the very first year I was home after college. That was 1971. I had my first sexual experience shortly thereafter with a woman I had met in college.

When I told my mother that I was a lesbian, she didn't say a whole lot. She kind of got teary eyed and then said, "Maybe you should see a psychiatrist." Then she said, "Maybe you ought to take birth control pills. Then you'd feel freer to experiment with men and you might discover you're not this way after all." I said, "I really can't knock it until I've tried." I thought that maybe I owed it to her or the universe to try.

So I got on birth control pills and decided I would have sex with a man. I really thought that I would try this several times and see if it made a difference. I tried it once—with the boy who was my boyfriend throughout high school. Every summer when I came home he was constantly asking me to go to bed with him, and I never would. So I picked him and set up a time and spent the night with him at his apartment. It was like, this is a joke. I couldn't believe I was doing it. It was totally unsatisfying. I thought, *Well, so much for that. I don't think I need to do this again.* That was not a way to solve this "problem" at all.

I gave up on having sex with men and I got off the pill. I also began to reinterpret further that whole Romans scripture about giving up what was natural for something unnatural. A light went off in my head. Paul had a point. His argument about doing what was natural really did make sense, but you had to know what was natural for you. It was unnatural for me to screw a man, so I decided that I wouldn't do that again. The only natural thing was for me to do what I'd been feeling since day one in the world. Why would I try to change that? How foolish I'd been. I thought to myself, *Thank you, Paul. I got your message, brother. We're okay.*

When that light went on in my head, I knew it was from God, that it was my deliverance. God didn't deliver me from my sexuality. God delivered me from guilt and shame and gave me a sense of pride and wholeness that I really needed. My sexuality was a gift from God, and so is everyone's sexuality, no matter how it's oriented. It's a gift to be able to love.

NOTES

[1] Biographical information in this paragraph comes from Eric Marcus' introduction (319) to the essay by Mobley that is excerpted here.

[2] *Romans* 1.26–27. See Anne Lister excerpt in this section, footnote 2. [Eds.]

WORKS CONSULTED

Marcus, Eric. Introduction. "The Christian Educator." By Carolyn Mobley. *Making History: The Struggle for Gay and Lesbian Rights, 1945–1990*. Ed. Eric Marcus. New York: HarperCollins, 1992.

Mobley, Carolyn. "The Christian Educator." *Making History: The Struggle for Gay and Lesbian Equal Rights, 1945–1990*. Ed. Eric Marcus. New York: HarperCollins, 1992.

LAURA GELLER *(1950–)*

"Encountering the Divine Presence"

When Laura Geller was ordained as a rabbi at Hebrew Union College in 1975 she became one of the first three women ever to hold that position. At the time she entered rabbinical school, however, her intent was not to break new ground, but "to study Judaism in an intense way." Only after she had begun study did she discover, first, that she wanted to become a rabbi, and second, that there were no women rabbis. Refusing the choice "between being a feminist or being a Jew," Geller focused on the space she found in Judaism that allowed for interpretation. She concluded that "although Judaism is patriarchal it is not monolithic" (Interview 1).

For a portion of her student years Geller served as the student rabbi at Vassar College. Subsequently she was the first woman rabbi to become Hillel director at the University of Southern California in Los Angeles, a position she held for fourteen years before becoming Director of the American Jewish Congress, Pacific Southwest Region. Currently she is Senior Rabbi in the Temple Emmanuel in Beverly Hills, California. Her goals there are to transform worship, to work for social justice, and to create "a community of learners who actively participate in their lifelong spiritual journey" (Interview 2).

Early in her career, Geller found that her role as a rabbi had a different impact on people's experience of worship than the role of male rabbis. Because men are perceived as having more "power and prestige," she says, women rabbis are perceived as less distant from the congregation. The result is a "breakdown of hierarchy" that changes congregations from "passive consumers of the rabbi's wisdom" into "active participants in their own Jewish lives" (Reactions 211–212). Furthermore, Geller believes that the presence of a woman rabbi challenges Jews to creatively reconceive God. Although Jewish tradition asserts that God encompasses and transcends both masculinity and femininity, at a subjective level the fact that a rabbi is male reinforces images of God as male. A woman rabbi disrupts this process, provoking new questions that end not only in new images of God but in new images of humanity "created in God's image." The result is new images "of men's and women's roles within our tradition and our world" (Reactions 212–213).

Geller's writing and work, particularly her creation and revision of ritual, are centered on this reconceptualization. As she has said, "Gender is the subtext of everything I do" (Interview 1). During her single college days, in 1976, Geller wrote, with Elizabeth Koltun, "Single and Jewish: Toward a New Definition of Completeness." This article questions the Jewish ideal of marriage and family as necessary components for completeness and "the good life." Geller and Koltun go on to redefine the "three components of completeness" as "commitment to Jewish survival, fulfilling human relationships, and moral sexual activity (or avoidance of immoral sexual activity)." Singles, she and Koltun protest, "do not fit into the Jewish community" and "find themselves in limbo." Even those who are single by virtue of widowhood or divorce find little within the faith community to support or hold them to the community. The creation of a ritual celebrating singlehood helps members of the community continue to feel like valuable participants (43–45). Although Geller has said in an interview that rituals for being single involve some problematic questions ("Why is the person single? Is he/she going to stay that way? What are we celebrating?"), she notes that she "has celebrated the single state with one person who had come to realize she was always going to be single" (Interview 2).

Much of Geller's rethinking of ritual is directed toward the celebration of uniquely female moments. In each case, the new ritual connects a previously hidden or taboo aspect of a woman's life to her faith, her community, and God. Following women's lives more intimately and closely than male rabbis could, Geller creates rituals to note and celebrate moments of women's lives that men cannot fully understand or appreciate. Some examples of these have been the ritualized marking of the onset of menses or menopause, the birth or death of a child, and the weaning of a child. Some rituals were designed to give space for grief to other uniquely female moments such as miscarriage, abortion, hysterectomy, breast cancer, and a husband's death or divorce. As Harold Kushner writes, "Our prayer and ritual do not affect the rainfall, but they affect the way we see the rainfall" (36). It is necessary to affect the way we see girls and women. By creating ritual recognizing the sacredness of such moments in women's lives, Geller helps to reclaim women's dignity, re-imagining women in the image of a re-imagined God.

At the beginning of her article on new naming ceremonies for girls, Geller quotes from Monique Wittig: "You say there are no words to describe this time, you say it does not exist. But remember. Make an effort to remember. Or, failing that, invent" (247). Geller's inventions of ritual for Jewish women affirm their spirituality in new ways. They also create a support system for women and a sense of value for their lives and experiences. In this, Geller is one of the architects of a new tradition. Failing to remember we invent, and part of what we invent are new forms of remembering. "Someday," Geller says, "a mother will look into the eyes of her baby girl at her child's Brit and see her own mother looking into her own eyes. And when that chain goes back for generations, we will know we have succeeded" ("Brit" 67).

RM and *ECD*

FROM "ENCOUNTERING THE DIVINE PRESENCE"[§]

What drew me to Judaism had little to do with encountering the Divine Presence. Raised in the Reform Judaism of the 1950s and early 1960s, I learned that being Jewish meant being concerned with *tikkun olam,*[1] although I didn't learn the Hebrew expression until much later. My earliest Jewish memory is not of candle lighting or *kiddush* or even the Four Questions. It is, rather, a memory of sneaking down to the living room after I had

[§] "Encountering the Divine Presence" by Laura Geller. Reprinted from *Four Centuries of Jewish Women's Spirituality: A Sourcebook,* edited by Ellen M. Umansky and Diane Ashton. Copyright © by Laura Geller. Reprinted by permission of Laura Geller. Published 1992 Boston: Beacon Press. Material excerpted from pages 242–247.

been put to bed and overhearing my mother and father discuss with members of our Temple's Social Action Committee the propriety of buying a house as a "straw." I was five or six. To me, a "straw" was something you drank chocolate milk with. The next morning my parents explained to me about racism and segregation, that black families couldn't buy houses in certain neighborhoods. "Buying a house as a straw" meant buying a house in a segregated neighborhood in order to sell it to a black family. We should do this, they explained, because we are Jewish. Being Jewish meant being involved with *tikkun olam.*

Years later, when I was already in rabbinical school and was struggling to learn the most basic Jewish skills, I became friendly with Jews who had grown up in traditional homes, Jews who knew how to *daven* [pray] and *lain* [sing the verses of the Torah] and were fluent in Hebrew. I was jealous of their comfort with the tradition, angry at how little I had learned in my Reform Jewish upbringing. But I had learned one thing that many of them had not learned—that being Jewish meant being involved with *tikkun olam.* One shouldn't have to choose between Jewish skills and Jewish values, but I realized through my jealousy that as an adult one can learn how to *daven* and *lain* and speak Hebrew, but it is much harder as an adult to learn that being Jewish means being involved with *tikkun olam.* Still, it had nothing to do with encountering the Divine Presence. . . .

I knew it was important to be involved in *tikkun olam* and I sensed *tikkun olam* had something theoretically to do with God. And all this inchoate thought had something to do with being Jewish.

So I went to rabbinical school to learn to be Jewish.

The first year of the program, the year in Israel, was not an easy year for me. For the first time I encountered traditional Judaism and its attitude toward women. I went with my classmates to Mea She'arim [an ultraorthodox section of Jerusalem] on Simchat Torah and watched *them* dance. I wrestled with a Torah that was on the one hand exhilarating and on the other hand excruciating, texts of liberation and texts of terror. I felt like I was sinking in quicksand, and that I would have to choose between my heart and my liver, my sense of self as a woman and my evolving Jewish commitment.

In my second year at [Hebrew Union College], in a wonderful old classroom overlooking 68th Street [in New York city], we learned *Berachot* with our teacher Rabbi Julius Kravitz. I had never learned about all the occasions for a blessing—new clothes, new fruit, seeing the ocean, seeing a rainbow, being in the presence of a scholar, on hearing good news or even bad news—I was exhilarated! God is present at every moment; it is up to us to acknowledge God's presence. We do it through saying blessings. Rabbi Kravitz said, "There is no important moment in the lifetime of a Jew for which there is no blessing." I remember thinking, "Yes! There is no important moment in the lifetime of a Jew for which there is no blessing." And then I realized that it was not true. There had been important moments in my lifetime for which there was no blessing . . . like when I first got my period. There in the classroom overlooking 68th Street I again became the thirteen-year-old girl running to tell her mother she had just got her period. And I heard again my mother tell me that when she got her first period my grandmother slapped her. I could almost feel the force of my grandmother's hand on my mother's face, the shame, the confusion, the anger.

I remembered my grandmother's explanation when I asked her why; she answered, "Your mother was losing blood, she was pale, she needed color in her cheek, the evil eye, poo poo poo." And, as I thought back to that time, I understood that there should have been a blessing—*sh'asani eisha, she'hechianu* [Thank you, God, for having made me a woman]—because holiness was present at that moment.

God had been present all along but I had never noticed. Perhaps I wasn't looking, or perhaps I was looking in the wrong places. If I had been looking I would have looked to a great and powerful wind to tear the mountain and shatter the rocks, to the earthquake or to the fire . . . but instead, I needed to listen to the gentle whisper, the still small voice, the Presence one encounters by diving deep and surfacing. As the playwright Ntozake Shange wrote: "I found god in myself / & i loved her / i loved her fiercely" (Ntozake Shange, from *for colored girls who have considered suicide/when the rainbow is enuf*).

A blessing would have gently taught me what it means to be a woman, would have invisibly instructed me how miraculous the human body is, would have drawn me closer to my mother, my grandmothers and all the women whose lives made mine possible. A blessing would have named the divinity present in this moment of transformation, this moment of connection. On 68th Street I suddenly realized that my experience is Jewish experience. There is a Torah of our lives as well as the Torah that was written down. Both need to be listened to and wrestled with: both unfold through interactive commentary.

I have come to believe that all theology is autobiography, that to be a Jew means to tell my story within the Jewish story. I had understood on some level even as a child that the Jewish story had shaped my story, the story of *Yetziat Mitzrayim* [the going out of Egypt], *matan Torah* [the giving of the Torah], and *tikkun olam* had formed the core of my sense of my self and my purpose in the world. But now I believe that my story also shapes the Jewish story. My experience propels me to ask different questions of Torah, to uncover different voices that more closely resemble my own. . . .

Prayer remains very difficult for me. I make the mistake of taking literally what should be taken seriously. I feel alienated from the Father, the King.

I try to remember that when the tradition speaks of God as father, it doesn't mean that God is really a father. It means that there is something in my relationship with my father that opens me up to God and that there is something about my encounter with God that opens me up to my father. But I learn something different about God through my connection to my mother, my husband, my son, my teachers, my students, my friends. God is the Thou I discover through my encounter with the human thous in my life, people of whom I can say "for seeing your face is like seeing the face of God." I ache to find prayers that speak toward the totality of divinity, words I can use that can bind me to other Jews as they connect me with God. . . .

Rabbi Eugene Borowitz taught me that study is a form of prayer. Study is easier for me, especially study in *chevrusa*. In wrestling with texts I feel less lonely. Wrestling with Torah is like making love. I get close enough to be wounded—and the texts often hurt. But I've gotten close enough to be blessed—the astonishing moment of blinding insight when the world suddenly looks forever different, when we discover wholeness in what seemed to be disparate and unconnected. Divinity is clearly present in those moments. And so, like my teacher Rabbi Borowitz, I always say a blessing before I learn. . . .

NOTE

[1] *tikkun olam:* "obligation to improve the world" (Gail Berkeley, "A Convert's Road to Prayer" in Umansky, *Four Centuries of Jewish Women's Spirituality* 224) [Eds.].

WORKS CONSULTED

Geller, Laura. *"Brit Milah"* and *"Brit Banot." Lifecycles: Jewish Women on Life Passages and Personal Milestones.* Ed. Rabbi Debra Orenstein. Vermont: Jewish Lights Publishing, 1994. 57–67.

—. "Encountering the Divine Presence." *Four Centuries of Jewish Women's Spirituality: A Sourcebook.* Ed. Ellen M. Umansky and Diane Ashton. Boston: Beacon, 1992. 242–247.

—. Interview of Laura Geller by Robin Menefee. (Unpublished), April 22, 1996, and April 24, 1996.

—. "Reactions to a Woman Rabbi." *On Being a Jewish Feminist: A Reader.* Ed. Susannah Heschel. New York, Schocken, 1983. 210–213.

—, and Elizabeth Koltun. "Single and Jewish: Toward a New Definition of Completeness." *The Jewish Woman: New Perspectives.* Ed. Elizabeth Koltun. New York: Schocken, 1976. 43–49.

Kushner, Rabbi Harold. *Who Needs God.* New York: Pocket Books, 1989.

MARGUERITE D'OINGT *(?–1310)* AND MARÍA CLARA BINGEMER *(late 20th century)*

Jesus as Woman, Woman as Jesus

Some religious traditions are able to fuse notions of feminine and masculine, or female and male, in ideations of God; in some, the question of gender does not arise because of the nature of a particular language. The Indonesian theologian Marianne Katoppo has said, for example, that the pronoun for God was not a problem for her until she began theologizing in English, Dutch, and German. In her language, the same word means both "she" and "he" (65–66), and the word for God, "Lord," has no gender without being qualified (88). Nor do Eastern religions, she says, have such a "fierce dichotomy" between male and female as in the Christian West (66, 72). In recent years, the nature of this dichotomy has become an equally fierce topic of debate among Christian theologians. Most Western languages seem to force a choice of pronouns, and there are no well-remembered traditions in the West of female embodiments of divinity such as Shakti in Hinduism. Even so, contemporary theologians such as María Clara Bingemer work to expand conceptions of the Christian God to include the female—and to include women. The excerpt from Marguerite d'Oingt, almost seven hundred years before, cautions us against believing there are no precedents.

The medieval Catholic mystic Marguerite d'Oingt (sometimes referred to erroneously as Marguerite de Duyn) grew up in one of the most powerful noble families of Lyon, France, in the latter part of the thirteenth century (Gardette 9–12). She became a nun at a nearby Carthusian monastery, by her own choice (Gaillard 341), attaining the position of prioress by 1288. Here she wrote the three works for which she is known. One is in Latin, the *Pagina meditationum (Page of meditations),* begun in 1286. Two are in her native language of Francoprovençal: a life of the prioress Beatrice of Ornacieux, and a visionary work to which her superiors assigned the title of *Speculum* when it received their approval in 1294. Although other Carthusian nuns might well have kept notebooks of their private meditations, this official recognition makes Marguerite's unusual (Gardette 16–18).

Marguerite described the act of writing as a healing process, a release from the fullness of heart brought about by what God had written there in a mystical vision. Speaking of herself in the third person, Marguerite explained to a male cleric who had criticized her, "She thought that if she put these things in writing, as Our Lord had put them in her heart, her heart would be lighter. I firmly believe that, if she had not put it in writing, she would have died or become crazy. . . . And that is why I believe that it was written by the will of Our Lord" (qtd. in Paulsell 257). As Stephanie Paulsell points out, this image is a way of authorizing Marguerite's writing: God writes in her heart, she writes what God wrote (257). And too, Marguerite authorizes herself by testifying, in an objective, first-person analysis, to the validity of "her" own evidence.

In the excerpt below, Marguerite presents an image that would today be unfamiliar to most Christians—the image of Jesus as Mother. As Caroline Bynum has shown, however, this image was not uncommon in Marguerite's day, nor did it express a particularly female viewpoint; indeed it seems to have been developed first by twelfth-century Benedictine and Cistercian monks (111–112). Bynum sees the rise of the image in both men's and women's writing from the twelfth to the fourteenth centuries as "part of a new sense of God, which stresses his creative power, his love, and his presence in the physical body of Christ and in the flesh and blood of the eucharist" (135).

When knowledge of this medieval image resurfaced in the twentieth century, it was initially greeted with distress—as something, according to the 1969 *Dictionnaire de Spiritualité* (Dictionary of Spirituality), that "makes theologians wince" (qtd. in Bynum 110). No doubt the distress continues, but alongside it there now exist many positive associations (for example, McLaughlin and Pagels) that make the medieval image part of a modern feminist search for ways to resist imagining God as solely male. Particularly important in this search have been the figures of Hildegard of Bingen (see excerpt) and the fourteenth/fifteenth-century English mystic Julian of Norwich, "whose vision of God as mother," Bynum says, is "one of the greatest reformulations in the history of theology" (136).

María Clara Bingemer, a Brazilian theology professor, writes from the perspective of another great spiritual reformulation, that of feminist liberation theology. The emergence of liberation theology in the late 1960s is often associated with Catholic Latin America, but it took place as well in Africa, Asia, and the African-American U.S. (Musto xxvi). Rooted in the political turmoil of developing countries in the 1960s and in the racial struggles of the U.S. and South Africa, liberation theology is a version of Christianity that takes as its starting point the perspective of the poor. It interprets Jesus as the liberator of the poor and critiques oppressive systems in society and in the church, while calling for personal, social, and political transformations that will help bring about the kingdom of God in this world (Berryman 4–6, Musto xxi-xxii). As Bingemer expresses it, God is a source of "liberation—socioeconomic, political, cultural, racial, ethnic, sexual—from every type of death" (310).

At the beginning many male liberation theologians did not think of Bingemer's last term, "sexual," as belonging to the list. In a revealing incident at a 1981 conference of the Ecumenical Association of Third World Theologians (an organization of which Bingemer has been regional coordinator for Latin America), when Marianne Katoppo called on participants to consider the gendering of language about God, some thought her remarks were a joke (Oduyoye 25). Many feminist theologians saw this incident as women's concerns breaking into the larger irruption of Third-World theology into First-World theology. Women's "irruption into the rational male theological world of the past," Bingemer says, is like that of the woman who disturbed the ritual order of a meal by pouring a box of perfume over Jesus' feet (310–11). She sees this action as symbolic of "the female way of doing theology," a new method that springs "from the impulse of desire that dwells at the deepest level of human existence" (311).

Bingemer's "female way of doing theology" rests on a consciousness of herself as merely a spokeswoman for the oppressed. Thus her work speaks in a collective, not just an individual voice (309–10). She sees God as a Divine Mystery that at once integrates, affirms, and transcends the "enriching differences" of the two sexes; she sees woman as created in the image of God not only "in her rational soul" but "in her sexed female body" (314). Bingemer looks to the Bible for female images of God, emphasizing the many Old Testament references to God as *rahamin* (Hebrew for womb) and calling attention to maternal images of Jesus and the Holy Spirit. With Ivone Gebara she has written a work entitled *Mary: Mother of God, Mother of the Poor* (1987) as part of the feminist effort "to recover the figure of Mary in its liberating and prophetic potential" for women of Latin America (313).

The excerpt reprinted here epitomizes Bingemer's theological commitments and method in its interpretation of the eucharist, the central religious ritual of Catholicism. Arising out of the last meal Jesus is said to have shared with his disciples, the symbol of the eucharist involves bread and wine which are regarded as transubstantiated —changed in form—into his body and blood. In Bingemer's use of the eucharistic image are the sacrifices of the many women who have literally given their flesh and blood in struggles for Latin American liberation—such women as Domitila Barrios de Chungara and Amada Pineda, who appear later in this anthology.

ECD

MARGUERITE D'OINGT

From *Page of meditations* [§]

(addressed to Jesus [Eds.])

Are you not my mother and more than mother? The mother who bore me labored at my birth for one day or one night, but you, my sweet and lovely Lord, were in pain for me not just one day, but you were in labor for more than thirty years. Oh, sweet and lovely Lord, how bitterly were you in labor for me all through your life! But when the time approached where you had to give birth, the labor was such that your holy sweat was like drops of blood which poured out of your body onto the ground.

MARÍA CLARA BINGEMER

"Woman's body, eucharistically given" [§§]

There is another dimension of the Eucharist in which women find themselves. This is the strict significance of the sacrament as the transubstantiation and real presence of the body and blood of the Lord which is given to the faithful as food. Feeding others with one's own body is the supreme way God chose to be definitively and sensibly present in the midst of

§ Reprinted from *The Writings of Margaret of Oingt: Medieval Prioress and Mystic,* edited by Renate Blumenfeld Kosinski. Published 1990 by Focus Information Group, Newburyport, MA. Material excerpted from page 31.

§§ Reprinted from "Women in the Future of the Theology of Liberation" by María Clara Bingemer, in *Feminist Theology from the Third World, A Reader,* edited by Ursula King. Published 1994 by Orbis Books. Material excerpted from pages 316–317. Originally published in *SEDOS* Bulletin (Rome, Italy) Vol. 22 No. 2, February 1990. Copyright © *SEDOS,* reprinted by permission.

the people. The bread that we break and eat refers us back to the greater mystery of Jesus' incarnation, death, and resurrection. It is his person given as food; it is his very life made bodily a source of life for Christians. It is women who possess in their bodiliness the physical possibility of performing the divine eucharistic action. In the whole process of gestation, childbirth, protection, and nourishing of a new life, the sacrament of the Eucharist, the divine act, happens anew.

Throughout Latin America, in the rural areas and the poor districts on the edges of cities, there are millions of women conceiving, bearing, and suckling new children of the common people. Sometimes they do it with difficulty, pain, and suffering, sometimes with the last trickle of life left in them. The female body, which multiplies in other lives, which gives itself as food and nourishes with its flesh and blood the lives it has conceived, is the same body that wastes away and dies tilling the earth, working in factories and homes, stirring pots and sweeping floors, spinning thread and washing clothes, organizing and chairing meetings, leading struggles, and starting the singing at liturgical celebrations. Woman's body, eucharistically given to the struggle for liberation, is really and physically distributed, eaten, and drunk by those who will—as men and women of tomorrow—continue the same struggle. Breaking the bread and distributing it, having communion in the body and blood of the Lord, means for women today reproducing in the community the divine act of surrender and love so that the people may grow and victory may come.

Women who do theology in Latin America and who share the same sacramental vocation, the same eucharistic destiny with their sisters from the poorest environments, are called to open a new path, a possible future so that this sacramental act may become more present, recognized, and believed in Latin American's journey toward liberation.

WORKS CONSULTED

Berryman, Phillip. *Liberation Theology: Essential Facts About the Revolutionary Movement in Latin America—And Beyond.* Philadelphia: Temple UP, 1987.

Bingemer, María Clara. "Women in the Future of the Theology of Liberation." *LADOC* (Latin America Documentation) 20.6 (1990): 7–15. Rpt. in King 308–317.

Bynum, Caroline. *Jesus as Mother: Studies in the Spirituality of the High Middle Ages.* Berkeley: U of California P, 1982.

Gaillard, Bernard. "Marguerite D'Oingt." *Dictionnaire de spiritualitité ascétique et mystique: doctrine et histoire.* Ed. M. Villier, F. Cavallera, et al. Vol. 10. Paris: Beauchesne, 1980.

Gardette, Pierre. Introduction. *Les Oeuvres de Marguerite d'Oingt.* Ed. Antonin Duraffour, Pierre Gardette, and Paulette Durdilly. Publications de l'institut de linguistique roman de Lyon 21. Paris: Société d'édition "Les belles lettres," 1965.

Gebara, Ivone, and María Clara Bingemer. *Mary: Mother of God, Mother of the Poor.* Trans. Phillip Berryman. Maryknoll, NY: Orbis, 1989.

Katoppo, Marianne. *Compassionate and Free: An Asian Woman's Theology.* Risk Book Series 6. Maryknoll, NY: Orbis, 1979.

King, Ursula, ed. *Feminist Theology from the Third World: A Reader.* Maryknoll, NY: Orbis, 1994.

Kosinski, Renate Blumenfeld, ed. *The Writings of Margaret of Oingt: Medieval Prioress and Mystic.* Newburyport, MA: Focus Information Group, 1990.

Marguerite d'Oingt. *Les Oeuvres de Marguerite d' Oingt.* Antonin Duraffour, Pierre Gardette, and Paulette Durdilly, eds. Publications de l'institut de linguistique roman de Lyon 21. Paris: Société d'édition "Les belles lettres," 1965.

McLaughlin, Eleanor C. "Women, Power and the Pursuit of Holiness in Medieval Christianity." *Women of Spirit: Female Leadership in the Jewish and Christian Traditions.* Eds. Rosemary Ruether and Eleanor C. McLaughlin. New York: n.p., 1979.

Musto, Ronald G. *Liberation Theologies: A Research Guide.* New York: Garland, 1991.

Oduyoye, Mercy Amba. "Reflections from a Third World Woman's Perspective: Women's Experience and Liberation Theologies." Ed. V. Fabella and S. Torres. *Irruption of the Third World: Challenge to Theology.* Maryknoll, NY: Orbis, 1983. Rpt. in King 23–43.

Pagels, Elaine H. "What Became of God the Mother? Conflicting Images of God in Early Christianity." *Signs* 2 (1976): 293–303.

Paulsell, Stephanie. "Writing and Mystical Experience in Marguerite d'Oingt and Virginia Woolf." *Comparative Literature* 44.3 (Summer 1992): 249–267.

GLÜCKEL OF HAMELN *(1646–1724)*

Israel: "A Woman in Travail"

See also **Vision and Transformation**

Glückel of Hameln began writing her memoir after her husband died, "to drive away the melancholy that comes with the long nights." It is the only complete autobiography of a Jewish woman to come down to us from before 1800 (Umansky 35). Written in Jüdisch-Deutsch between 1690 and 1719, it records for her children her outward life experiences as well as much of her inner life in the form of moral and spiritual reflections and prayer.

The setting for all her experience was the tight-knit, mutually supportive world of the Jewish community in a predominantly Christian culture. The religious art of that culture included derogatory and scatological images of Jews as demonic and bestial, Christ-killers, murderers of children; its religious history included the massacre of thousands of Jews during the Crusades (Lerner, "Jewish History"). Glückel herself experienced pogroms—violent attacks on Jewish communities—and anti-semitic persecutions (Lerner, *Rise* 131). She also experienced her religious faith as a source of strength in every area of her life. Inside the community, as Beth-Zion Abrahams says, "in those close quarters [Jews] could live their own life to the very utmost within the four ells of the Torah, with none to mock or say them nay" (ix).

Glückel was engaged at age twelve and married at fourteen to the son of a merchant who soon set up his own business. Like many women of her time, she joined her husband in this business. Also like many of them, she took it over when he died, and supported her large family through vigorous enterprise in trade both at home and throughout Europe. Her second marriage, undertaken late in life in the hope that her second husband's wealth would provide for her and her children, was a disappointment; within a year she had been impoverished by his bankruptcy. Upon his death her son and daughter-in-law welcomed her into their home.

In the selection that follows, Glückel meditates on the wave of excitement generated between 1665 and 1667 by Shabbatai Zevi, the "false Messiah." Many Jews were hopeful that recent persecutions in Poland were "the long-foretold 'birthpangs of the Messiah'"; indeed, Glückel's parents-in-law prepared two parcels of food and clothing for the anticipated journey home to the Holy Land (Abrahams xi-xii). In the following account, Glückel uses physical experiences particular to women—pregnancy and childbirth—to describe this incident in the spiritual experience of her whole religious community.

ECD

FROM THE AUTOBIOGRAPHY OF GLÜCKEL OF HAMELN[§]

During this time I was brought to bed with my daughter Mattie; she was a beautiful child. And also, at about this time, people began to talk of Sabbatai Zevi,[1] but *woe unto us, for we have sinned,* for we did not live to see that which we had heard and hoped to see. When I remember the penance done by young and old—it is indescribable, though it is well enough known in the whole world. O Lord of the Universe, at that time we hoped that you, O merciful God, would have mercy on your people Israel and redeem us from our exile. We were like a woman in travail, a woman on the labour-stool who, after great labour and sore pains, expects to rejoice in the birth of a child, but finds it is nothing but wind. This, my great God and King, happened to us. All your servants and children did much penance, recited many prayers, gave away much in charity, throughout the world. For two or three years your people Israel sat on the labour-stool—but nothing came save wind.

NOTE

[1] The advent of Sabbatai Zevi and his rise to pseudo-messiahship in the years 1665–7 provided a romantic and colourful interval in the life of the Jewries in most parts of the world. In many countries Jews were wrought up to a fervor of faith which made them ready to believe that redemption was at hand and that the sons of Israel were now to prepare for the second exodus. In many communities whole families liquidated their possessions and waited only for the trumpet of Messiah before setting forth on their journey to the Holy Land. There is no doubt that Glückel's sidelight is by no means an exaggeration, but an interesting personal picture of the effect of the messianic delusion upon her immediate surroundings. The excitement spread also to the non-Jews. The Fifth Monarchy literature of Puritan England was not unconnected. In Pepys's diary reference is made to these Jewish messianic expectations [Abrahams].

WORKS CONSULTED

Abrahams, Beth-Zion. Introduction. *The Life of Glückel of Hameln: 1646–1724; written by herself.* Trans. and ed. Beth-Zion Abrahams. New York: Thomas Yoseloff, 1963.

Glückel of Hameln. *The Memoirs of Glückel of Hameln.* Trans. Marvin Lowenthal. New York: Schocken, 1977.

Lerner, Gerda. "Jewish History in the Middle Ages." Lecture at Arizona State University, May 1996.

—. *The Rise of Feminist Consciousness from the Middle Ages to Eighteen-seventy.* New York: Oxford UP, 1993.

Umansky, Ellen M. and Dianne Ashton. *Four Centuries of Jewish Women's Spirituality: A Sourcebook.* Boston: Beacon, 1992.

[§] Reprinted from *The Life of Glückel of Hameln: 1646–1724; written by herself.* Translated and edited by Beth-Zion Abrahams. Published 1963 by Thomas Yoseloff Publishers, New York. Material excerpted from page 45.

CHUNG HYUN KYUNG *(late 20th century)*

The Bodhisattva and the Holy Spirit

"We Asian women no longer are passive soil for the Christian seed of truth (the imagery so often used to describe Christian missions in Asia). Rather, we will be mothers who will actively participate in the birth of the new spirituality and theology . . ." (*Struggle* 114). Behind these words written by Chung Hyun Kyung is a long spiritual, personal, and political journey that began with her family's sudden plunge into poverty when she was a child. Her father went bankrupt, and she spent the rest of her childhood longing for her old "clean," affluent neighborhood, and working hard for the education that could return her from the ghetto to the lost "paradise" of wealth. Her efforts won her a scholarship to the most prestigious school in South Korea, a school attended primarily by wealthy students. Having never identified with the other children in the ghetto, Chung now had the shattering experience of realizing that there was also an "unbridgeable gap" between her and the privileged students, of which she was most painfully aware each day when they opened their lunch boxes. She wondered why God had created this gap, giving her family and others so little and these rich children so much. At university she found her first "salvation experience" in the student movement, a world-wide political and cultural movement that opposed first world militarism and imperialism and supported the liberation, including the psychological liberation, of subjugated peoples. In this movement, analyses of colonialism and neo-colonialism taught Chung to reformulate her question about the gap between herself and the wealthy students so that it became a question about "unequal power relationships among people, institutions, and nations" (*Struggle* 1–2).

In terms of Chung's future lifework, the impact of the student movement on her religious views was most important. Realizing that she had been subjected to a "theological imperialism" that taught her only European theology but never her own people's "theological reflections" on their cultural and historical situation, she resolved to resist that imperialism by deconstructing it. She went to Union Theological Seminary in New York City to work on a doctorate, choosing a thesis topic on Asian women. Then, on a research trip back to Korea in 1987, she had an experience that made her realize that her project had been *only* deconstructive—that "reacting against the oppressive system would not necessarily lead me to constructing a liberating reality" (*Struggle* 3).

This revelation came from her discovery of her biological mother, of whom she had never heard—an impoverished single woman whom her father had persuaded to bear a child for him when it became clear his wife could not conceive. The day after the child's first birthday, he and his wife took her away against the wishes of the mother, who suffered a nervous breakdown. Throughout Chung's childhood, this mother who had promised never to see her until she had married and had her first child, followed her life from a distance, keeping an album of photographs sent by the father and gleaning information wherever she could, without ever revealing she was the child's mother. "She had watched me and prayed for me for thirty years," Chung says. "They were prayers offered from the shadow of history" ("Following" 59).

When Chung, with the help of a cousin, met her mother and heard her story, she experienced a kind of "baptism . . . something in my deepest being was broken open . . . something was washed away and I felt truly free. Through this ill, seventy-two-year old woman, my mother, I felt that I was encountering the power of the despised in my people's history" (*Struggle* 4). She resolved "to do theology in solidarity with and in love for [her] mother so as to resurrect crucified persons—like her—by giving voice to their hurts and pains, especially those Asian women who are located on the 'underside of the underside of history'[1] in a white, capitalist, male-dominated world" (*Struggle* 5).

Out of this dedication, Chung wrote *Struggle to be the Sun Again,* a study of Asian women's theology that takes its title from the Japanese feminist manifesto of 1911 by Hiratsuka Raicho (see excerpt in **Representing Women**). Hiratsuka's poem begins, "Originally, woman was the sun. She was an authentic person. But now woman is the moon." In her linking of Asian women's spirituality to their struggle against dependency on men for their self-definition, Chung makes four critical points. First, she argues that "Asian women theologians should realize that *we are the text,* and the Bible and tradition of the Christian church are the context of our theology" (111). She argues against giving the kind of authority to the Bible and Western Christian tradition that perpetuates Asian Christians' "cultural dependency . . . upon the so-called Mother Church in the West" (111). Second, she calls for a shift in focus away from institutionalized religion and toward "Asian women's popular religiosity" (112); she points to popular veneration of the Buddhist goddess Kwan Yin or the Filipino mother-God Ina as evidence "of women's resistance to patriarchal religions" (112). Third, she calls for a rejection of "the doctrinal purity of Christian theology" (113) in favor of a liberatory "syncretism"—that is, a method of finding spiritual resources in multiple religious systems. Much more than a lazy pluralism that respects religious diversity, Chung describes this syncretism as an active "religious solidarity" that draws on many religious traditions to change unjust social, political, religious, and cultural systems. Finally, she points out that what Asian women care about is not a pure religious "orthodoxy" (the concern of many male church leaders), but their own and their people's liberation. "What matters for them is not Jesus, Sakyamumi, Mohammed, Confucius, Kwan Yin, or Ina, but rather the life force which empowers them to claim their humanity" (113).

In her essay "Following Naked Dancing and Long Dreaming," Chung cites both her "mothers" as examples of this kind of "survival-liberation-centered syncretism" (67) in a world where it must have been difficult for either of them, she says, to sustain their sanity. Her adoptive mother was "officially" a Christian. This religion gave her a public role outside the house, inside of which she prepared feasts for the ancestor worship associated with her husband's Confucianism. In her private crises she consulted not her church ministers but female fortune-tellers whose predictions were based on Taoist, Shamanist, and Buddhist philosophy; she also celebrated Buddha's birth every year, an opportunity for dancing and drinking with women friends that the women's mission society did not provide. Similarly, Chung's birthmother, pregnant against Korean religious prohibitions, dreamed nonetheless of Buddha's blessing on the birth and of a propitious shamanistic symbol, a mountain of salt. Later she became a deacon in a Pentecostal church. As Chung concludes, her mothers' spirituality centered on no single religious tradition. Various traditions were important at different stages of their lives, "but none dominated their inner life. The real center for their spirituality was life itself" (66).

The excerpt that follows shows Chung in the process of reconstructing theology from this same center, participating in the liberatory syncretism invented by many women like her mothers. It comes from her invocation at the Seventh Assembly of the World Council of Churches in 1991 (King 390). She began the invocation by inviting participants to take off their shoes and dance with her on holy ground. She ends with an image of female deity.

ECD

"BREAK DOWN THE WALL WITH WISDOM AND COMPASSION."[§]

I want to close my reflection on the Holy Spirit by sharing with you my image of the Holy Spirit from my cultural background . . . The image does not come from my academic training as a systematic theologian, but from my gut feeling, deep in my people's collective unconsciousness that comes from thousands of years of spirituality.

For me the image of the Holy Spirit comes from the image of Kwan Yin. She is venerated as the goddess of compassion and wisdom by East Asian women's popular religiosity. She is a bodhisattva, enlightened being. She can go into nirvana any time she wants to, but refuses to go into nirvana by herself. Her compassion for all suffering beings makes her stay in this world, enabling other living beings to achieve enlightenment. Her compassionate wisdom heals all forms of life and empowers them to swim to the shore of nirvana. She waits and waits until the whole universe, people, trees, birds, mountains, air, water, become enlightened. They can then go to nirvana together, where they can live collectively in eternal wisdom and compassion. Perhaps this might also be a feminine image of the Christ who is the first-born among us, one who goes before and brings others with her.

Dear sisters and brothers, with the energy of the Holy Spirit let us tear apart all walls of division and the "culture of death" that separate us. And let us participate in the Holy Spirit's political economy of life, fighting for our life on this earth in solidarity with all living beings, and building communities for justice, peace, and the integrity of creation. Wild wind of the Holy Spirit, blow to us. Let us welcome her, letting ourselves go in her wild rhythm of life. Come Holy Spirit, Renew the Whole Creation. Amen!

[§] Reprinted from "Come Holy Spirit—Renew the Whole Creation." Invocation given by Chung Hyun Kyung at the Seventh Assembly of the World Council of Churches, in Canberra, Australia, February 1991. Full text in Assembly Report, *Signs of the Spirit,* edited by Michael Kinnamon. Copyright © World Council of Churches Publications, 1991. Used by permission. Also included in *Feminist Theology from the Third World: A Reader,* edited by Ursula King, published 1994 by Orbis Books. Material excerpted from pages 392–394.

NOTE

[1] Quotation from Nantawan Boonprasat Lewis, "Asian Women Theology: A Historical and Theological Analysis." *East Asian Journal of Theology* 4.2 (Oct. 1986): 18.

WORKS CONSULTED

Chung, Hyun Kyung. "Come Holy Spirit—Renew the Whole Creation." Invocation, Seventh Assembly of the World Council of Churches, Canberra, Australia, Feb. 1991. Full text in Assembly Report. *Signs of the Spirit.* Ed. Michael Kinnamon. Geneva: WCC Publications, 1991.

—. "Following Naked Dancing and Long Dreaming." *Inheriting Our Mothers' Gardens: Feminist Theology in Third World Perspective.* Ed. Letty M. Russell, Kwok Pui-lan, Ada María Isasi-Díaz, and Katie Geneva Cannon. Louisville: Westminster Press, 1988.

—. *Struggle to Be the Sun Again: Introducing Asian Women's Theology.* Maryknoll, NY: Orbis, 1990.

King, Ursula, ed. *Feminist Theology from the Third World: A Reader.* Maryknoll, NY: Orbis, 1994.

BONITA WA WA CALACHAW NUÑEZ *(1888–1972)*

"Fighting the White Man's Gods"

The place of Bonita Wa Wa Calachaw Nuñez's birth, a desert hut in Southern California, suggests that she belonged to the Rincon Band of the Luiseño people (Steiner xii). She was never to know for certain, because as soon as she was born she was taken to New York City by a white woman, Mary Duggan. As Calachaw explained, Duggan had been delayed on her trip home from California and was passing the time by wandering along the roads. She "stopped at a wooden *shack*. And in that *shack* was My real Mother Indian having *labor pains*. Mother Mary *Duggan* took things into her hands and in a few minutes I was born. Mother gave Me to her" (1).

An ardent feminist and activist on behalf of Native American rights, Duggan, who was single, raised the child with the help of her brother in the affluent world of Riverside Drive. Dressed in clothes they thought expressed her identity as a Native American, lovingly shielded from shocks to what they saw as her nervous susceptibility, Calachaw grew up in a strange combination of isolation and stimulating contact with the scientific, political, and artistic movements of her day. In this world she was sometimes reviled, sometimes admired as a celebrity, always a curiosity. For the most part, her adoptive parents educated her at home. They especially encouraged her to develop her precocious artistic talents, which flowered in a distinctive style of bold black lines; a palette dominated by reds, yellows, brown, and whites; and a concentration on Native American figures. These figures are sometimes alone, sometimes gathered in warm unities of kinship, community, and friendship with animals. In childhood she gained much of her artistic training as a medical illustrator of her adopted father's specimens—cancerous bones, for example—with which she seems to have felt a kind of mystical unity, perceiving them first as beautiful before she knew they involved disease, and producing drawings he found astonishing in their apparent insight into aspects of cellular structure she could not have seen with the naked eye. Later in life, Calachaw became well-known for her illustrations in medical journals (Ronnow 189).

"Mother Duggan" tried to get Calachaw into Barnard College, but she was refused admission on racial grounds. When she found Duggan crying over the rejection letter, Calachaw reassured her, "I will make good *regardless*." But she wrote years later, "I have not forgotten I was denied the Right of a college education" (90). She married a Puerto Rican labor organizer, Manuel Carmonia-Nuñez, at the extremely ambivalent encouragement of her "Mother" and the Doctor; she herself was almost debilitatingly apprehensive and her Mother, she says, conducted the wedding as if it were a funeral. She expresses a wide range of emotions in writing of her husband, from tenderness to passion to ambivalence; eventually they separated. She had at least one child, who died at age three.

After Mary Duggan's death, Calachaw became impoverished. She sold "Indian Liniment" on the streets; then, in the 1920s she began selling her oil paintings on the sidewalks of

Greenwich Village. While most Native Americans lived on reservations, as an "urban Indian" she encountered painful displays of racism. A white woman who saw her peddling liniment exclaimed, "An Indian! Why, are there any Indians now alive? I thought they were all dead" (234). Other potential customers stood in front of her and discussed her appearance: was she Chinese? Japanese? A mother told her little girl to stop looking at her art: "Why look at rubbish? She's a wild Indian. Come on and look at real painting" (88). Her journals show her skillfully confronting the objectifying gaze of the passersby, as well as withstanding the many overt pressures to allow herself to be co-opted and and her work appropriated. She refused to become an actress on "exhibition" as an Indian; she refused to portray Native Americans with feathers; she refused to let the need for money compromise her vision of the culture she painted.

In her adult life Calachaw, raised for the most part away from other Native Americans, expanded her connections to such an extent that thousands of people knew and loved her (Steiner xiv). Beginning around the time of World War I, she became active in the Native American rights movement, and worked tirelessly in the cause. Her work included sending letters and money from her welfare checks to Native Americans who wrote her from all over the country. She traveled to California in search of her mother and lived for a time with the Luiseño, as well as with Native Americans in a number of urban centers. After she died, Stan Steiner found in her East Harlem apartment "thousands of odd pieces of paper covered with scribbled messages and poetry," a diary in thirty-eight notebooks, many scrapbooks, and a room full of frescoes and paintings. Most of what is known about her comes from his organization of these materials into the book *Spirit Woman.*

Near the end of the book is a sketch of Carlos Montezuma, also a tireless agitator for Native American rights. Across the top Calachaw copied his advice to her: "Keep talking Freedom, Wa-Wa. Let no one stop you" (225). Bonita Wa Wa Calachaw Nuñez kept talking Freedom to the end of her life, and her last writings reveal her faith that a younger generation would carry on her work. "The past has been sold on false Ideas that have not been properly investigated," she wrote. "I am not worried. I know the youth, everywhere, will Question the Authority of all Lands. God cannot hide or hinder the youthful Mind" (229). Thus it is fitting that when she died, the children from the ghetto where she lived took possession of her paintings. Steiner was alarmed to see them happily carrying away whole armfuls, but a neighbor corrected him: "They were her students. She teached them to paint. And she give them her paintings, always" (xvi).

ECD

FROM THE DIARY OF BONITA WA WA CALACHAW NUÑEZ

"The Girls Of Mourning"[§]

I do not Know whether what the Priest teaches is a law of the Catholic church. All I do Know [is] what I have learned by talking to Indians who are *members.* I want to tell you what three Indian girls told me. I will call these girls the Girls of *Mourning.*

§ Reprinted from *Spirit Woman: The Diaries and Paintings of Bonita Wa Wa Calachaw Nuñez,* edited by Stan Steiner. Copyright © 1980 by Stan Steiner. Reprinted by permission of HarperCollins Publishers, Inc. Material excerpted from pages 178–180, 184–185.

Their Confession was they had committed a sexual *Crime, adultery.* I saw three very young Indian girls dressed in deep *Black,* half their Faces were *covered.* Knowing *my* people like bright *colors,* I was *shocked.* I just could not think why this terrible looking *masquerade.* Well let [Me] tell you *why.* They went to *Confession,* and their Priest told them they will have to *go* into *mourning* for one *year.*

On hearing this I began to ask more *Questions.* I) What happens to the *Men?* Do they too go into *mourning? No,* they must pay Money to the saint of the *church.* 2) What happens if there is a *baby?* The *church* takes it away was the *Answer.* It seems the church *becomes* an *adoption center.*

There is more to this than meets the Eye. I will do My best to explain what was told Me by an Indian *who owned some* very fine *Land,* about what the Indians called the *church*-baby. This *churchism* seems to play a very strange part in certain legal Rights to deprive an illegitimate child of its Rights of *real estate,* or property.

When all of the original family has passed away I was told the church steps in and takes over. I hope some day *someone* will look into this legal Right of the church who seeks to control My People.

Simple-minded misery [is] placed on the shoulders of these poor Indians by their church, and faith. This law is pure *infanticide,* characterized by the Pale Face God of goodness in their insincere religious activeness. This is how My feeling took shape when I saw Indian Women gowned in Black. And an 11 year old, who was to *be* gowned in Black.

The old Woman took Me to a *home* where an 11 year old girl was to *become* a *parent.*

I had asked the Old Woman in Black rags if this little girl will have to wear *black.* Her answer was—If we take her to the Man in the *church.* I told her to keep the little girl *hidden.* I said, "Don't let her *go and tell what had* happened."

Voltaire Awaken, I Need Your Help

A dear little girl of the Catholic faith went to Confession. She asked her Confessor, a Priest, whether it was a good example to have an Indian lady as a friend. She told the Priest I was a painter of wonderful pictures, and I seemed to understand her. The Priest told the child I was a good Indian.

Time changes everything. So I learned. Think of it: an atheist being considered as a good person by a Catholic Priest.

Voltaire awaken, I need your help!

Voltaire was interested in the Truth. He discovered Truth was in the image of Man. And the laws of Life were Natural. Even Voltaire's Character was one with his writing . . .

Victor Hugo, in his writing, exposed the Priests and their hypocrisy.

These diabolical Minds have made the God-fearing Minds think.

Satan is rather an interesting character. His Ideas rather instruct, than Kill, the right thinking personality. Ah, a few more satanic masters and the World would be rid of ignorance.

The Strange White Gods

It seems I meet many people. I never have met a so-called saint.

The Indians *discovered* they would not only *have to* fight for the Freedom, for a Right to Live, but to *fight* the strange White Man's *Gods*. The *reaction* was to train the *Indian* for the *church*. And the *confusion* is *now* a mountain in height.

If there is one of us who may show signs of leadership he must be clothed into a Black robe of a hypocrite.

What do they mean by a "good Christian?" Rich Men are called Christians and they impose the faults that produce such widespread poverty in the World.

I once stopped and heard a Man say, "Blessed it is to be poor." I [could not] imagine any Human Being having a desire of wanting to be *poor.*

My People are not deprived of their sanity. They cannot solve the mystery because they are told that *God* is the Cause of said condition. We want to Know why God is so unaware of their plight.

How can they talk God to people or teach *children* with empty stomachs?

If a God designed the Indian to the forces of existence, and horror of poverty, then God is a willful Criminal.

My religion is My service to My People.

WORKS CONSULTED

Nuñez, Bonita Wa Wa Calachaw. *Spirit Woman: The Diaries and Paintings of Bonita Wa Wa Calachaw Nuñez.* Ed. Stan Steiner. New York: Harper and Row, 1980.

Ronnow, Gretchen. "Bonita Wa Wa Calachaw Nuñez." *Native American Women: A Biographical Dictionary.* Ed. Gretchen M. Bataille. New York: Garland, 1993.

Steiner, Stan. Introduction. *Spirit Woman: The Diaries and Paintings of Bonita Wa Wa Calachaw Nuñez.* By Nuñez. New York: Harper and Row, 1980.

FATIMA MERNISSI *(1941–)* **AND GHADA SAMMAN** *(1942–)*

Islam and Feminism: Changing Interpretations

In her introduction to *Women, Islam and the State,* a collection of essays on women and the formation of modern Muslim nations, Deniz Kandiyoti argues that research on the role of women in Muslim societies has long been dominated by two competing—and equally problematic—paradigms (Kandiyoti 1–3). The first model appears in the works of those scholars who have used readings of the Quran and early Islamic history as the analytic base for their explanations of the conditions of women's lives throughout the Islamic world. This position has been adopted by critics working from feminist as well as fundamentalist perspectives. While Muslim feminists might interpret the Quran progressively in order to call for political change, fundamentalists tend to use this sacred text to legitimate separation of the sexes and to stress the importance of women's domestic work. Kandiyoti critiques the ahistorical nature of such methods when she affirms, "Whatever the strategic merits of engaging with conservative ideologues on their own terrain, this approach is ultimately unable to account for the important variations encountered in women's conditions both within and across Muslim societies. Nor is it able to conceptualize the possible connections between other features of society such as political systems, kinship systems or the economy" (1).

The second paradigm characterizes an ever-growing body of scholarship that examines the specific conditions of Muslim women's lives in different places and at different times. Although this kind of research sheds valuable light on individual cultural practices, it often does not make broader arguments about the particular role played by Islamic ideology in women's oppression. Kandiyoti's conclusion in another article is that, "This leads to a paradoxical situation whereby Islam sometimes appears to be all there is to know, and at other times to be of little consequence in understanding the condition of women, or more broadly, gender relations in Muslim societies" ("Islam and Patriarchy" 24). While these perspectives remain visible in scholarship on Muslim women, more and more Muslim feminists and scholars align with Kandiyoti to stress the importance of analyzing the relations between women and Islam "both within and across Muslim societies."

The history of Muslim feminism is of course a long and complex one; it is also closely linked to the history of Western colonialism in the Muslim world.[1] In many Muslim societies, the struggle for women's emancipation has been seen as connected to a desire on the part of members of the middle and upper classes to become more "Westernized." For this reason ". . . change concerning women was felt by Muslim men to be a final invasion in the last sphere they could control against aggressive infidels, once sovereignty and much of the economy had been taken over by the West" (Keddie 13). Thus, from the beginning, the "woman question" was marked by national and class divisions; those in favor of the emancipation of women tended to be part of an educated progressivist elite, while those against such changes were more likely to be members of the petit bourgeois classes who were in competition with Western trade. An additional strain of Muslim feminism was closely linked to new nationalist and anti-imperialist projects; around the turn of the century Muslim feminists (including the Iranian Taj Al-Saltana whose work is excerpted in **Representing Women**) increasingly presented women "as a wasted national resource" (Kandiyoti, Introduction 10). In any case, readers need to keep in mind that Muslim societies were not simply reacting to Western influences in the formation of feminist and nationalist movements; they were—and continue to be—engaged in initiating specific and distinct processes of social change.

We present here two excerpts from different perspectives on the relationship between Islam and the position of women in the Muslim world. It is true that both of these excerpts could be criticized, from Kandiyoti's point of view, for their tendency to view Islam as a unique and fundamental category of analysis from which to examine Muslim women's lives. Fatima Mernissi uses her reading of the Quran and the writings of Muslim religious scholars to develop a complicated theory about the ways in which relationships between men and women are regulated in the Islamic world. While she links this reading to a "case study" of Moroccan social practices, the theoretical underpinnings of her argument depend on generalizations across different Muslim societies as well as a belief in a direct link between the dictates of the Quran and Muslim social organization. Ghada Samman addresses a different point about the relationship between the coming of Islam and the emancipation of women; nevertheless, she also argues for a progressive reading of the Quran as the basis of feminist social change. We have included these two pieces here to give readers a sense of the diversity and richness of Muslim feminist writing on the role of religion in women's lives. In this headnote, we have tried to place these two perspectives in the context of current research and identify other ways of conceptualizing the role that Islam has played in determining the circumstances of women's lives in the world-wide variety of Muslim societies.

We would like to encourage those readers interested in women's roles in Muslim societies to seek out analyses of specific time periods and geographical locations. Scholars and students of Muslim women have often tended to let abstract notions of "Islam" or "the Muslim world" organize their thinking from the beginning, rather than investigating particular social formations in diverse Muslim cultures. Scholarship on Muslim women too often concentrates on their religious beliefs, veiling, and female genital mutilation (usually in that order) as if such practices were necessarily central to an understanding of all women's lives in all Muslim societies. In fact, "the Muslim world" encompasses an amazing array of populations and nations and includes a significant number of the inhabitants of such areas of the world as the Philippines, Yugoslavia, Indonesia, and East Africa as well as the Middle East and India. In this anthology, we have tried to give readers a sense of this diversity as well as an understanding of some of the debates which have shaped Muslim feminist criticism and politics in the past and present.

As both Samman and Mernissi demonstrate, women's relationships to Islam defy easy explanation. Western feminist writers have too often tried to argue against "Muslim patriarchy" as a monolithic and consistently oppressive system; contemporary Muslim feminists have in turn often had to stress the weakness of this notion as a category for understanding Muslim women's lives. Neither the ongoing process of "Westernization" nor the more recent fundamentalist "reforms" have had uniform effects. Keddie reminds readers that ". . . some poorer women have suffered from modernization's economic effects, becoming more, rather than less, restricted; having to work in unhealthful and poorly paid positions; and often removed from the community security of rural life" (14). Moreover, Islamist reforms could be perceived as providing benefits for some women even while they restrict the activities of others. For non-elite women, Islamism may provide a kind of protection and access to respect that they were formerly denied. It is also true that Islamists encourage women's participation in many aspects of social life, including women's organizations and discussion groups; "[g]irls and women whose parents or husbands do not normally let them out allow them to go to mosque meetings" (Keddie 18). In addition, Western feminists and critics need to keep in mind that the oft-repeated discourse about the marginalization and oppression of Muslim women in particular, and Third World women in general, serves to reinforce notions about the Western nature of progress and the "uncivilized" state of non-Western peoples.[2]

Fatima Mernissi is an eminent Muslim feminist scholar who has published books which include *Women in Public Space in a Muslim Society: Morocco* (1983), *Le Maroc raconté par ses femmes* (1984; published in English as *Doing Daily Battle: Interviews with Moroccan Women* [1989]), and *Le Harem politique* (1987; published in English as *The Veil and the Male Elite: A Feminist Interpretation of Women's Rights in Islam* [1991]) as well as numerous articles.[3] She was born into a traditional family in Fez, Morocco. She studied at Muhammad V University in Rabat and the Sorbonne in Paris, and went on to receive a Ph.D. in sociology from Brandeis University. More recently, she has been a professor of sociology at Muhammad V University as well as a visiting professor at the University of California at Berkeley and Harvard University. She is the holder of a research appointment at the Institut Universitaire de Recherche Scientifique in Rabat. Her scholarly and feminist work has paved the way for much of the research currently being done on Muslim women, and the text which we have excerpted here, *Beyond the Veil: Male-Female Dynamics in Modern Muslim Society,* continues to be an important source for students of feminism, women, and Islam.

Ghada Samman is a well-known writer whose fiction and political commentary examine the difficulties faced by women in the Arab world. Born in al-Shamiya, Syria, she was educated at the American University in Beirut and at the University of London, where she earned her MA. She has published collections of short stories—including *Your Eyes are my Destiny* (1962), *There's No Sea in Beirut* (1965) and *The Night of Strangers* (1966)—as well as novels and collections of essays. She has also established her own publishing house in order to be able to publish more freely. The article reprinted below is partly in reaction to a pamphlet condemning Muslim feminism distributed by a religious group of which Shaikh Ali al-Tantawi was the president. At the time this article was written, Samman was working and living alone in order to establish her independence as an author and as a woman.

NM

FATIMA MERNISSI

From Beyond the Veil: Male-Female Dynamics in Modern Muslim Society[§]

"Women and the Sacred Threshold: Allah's Boundaries and Men's Obedience"

Beyond the Veil is a book about sexual space boundaries. It tries to grasp sex as it materializes, as it melts into space and freezes it in an architecture. It started from a harmless question: Why can't I stroll peacefully in the alleys of the Medina that I like and enjoy so much? I came to wonder how Muslim society designs sexual space, how it projects into space a specific vision of female sexuality.

The book illustrates an important dimension of religion that is often ignored, since religion is usually confused with and reduced to spirituality: Islam is, among other things, an overwhelmingly materialistic vision of the world. Its field is not the heavens so much as terrestrial space and terrestrial power and access to all kinds of plain worldly pleasures, including wealth, sex, and power. That is the reason, I guess, why *Beyond the Veil,* in spite of dozens of other books treating the same topic of women and Islam, still makes sense to students and other readers. It does not treat Islam and women from a factual point of view, but rather it identifies one of the key components of the system—namely, the way Islam uses space as a device for sexual control.

Beyond the Veil does not seem to age, because it is not so much about facts as data as it is about an ageless problem: the way societies manage space to construct hierarchies and allot privileges. One can easily trace, through the concept of the threshold, of boundaries, of limits, the hidden hierarchies determining the use of space, as well as the laws and mechanisms of control that underlie Islam as a sexual philosophy, as a vision of both virility and femininity as sacred architecture . . .

. . . Different social orders have integrated the tensions between religion and sexuality in different ways. In the Western Christian experience sexuality itself was attacked, degraded as animality and condemned as anti-civilization. The individual was split into two antithetical selves: the spirit and the flesh, the ego and the id. The triumph of civilization implied the triumph of soul over flesh, of ego over id, of the controlled over the uncontrolled, of spirit over sex.

Islam took a substantially different path. What is attacked and debased is not sexuality but women, as the embodiment of destruction, the symbol of disorder. The woman is *fitna,* the epitome of the uncontrollable, a living representative of the dangers of sexuality and its rampant destructive potential. We have seen that Muslim theory considers raw instinct as energy which is likely to be used constructively for the benefit of Allah and His society if people live according to His laws. Sexuality *per se* is not a danger. On the contrary, it has three positive, vital functions. It allows the believers to perpetuate themselves

[§] Reprinted by permisssion of publisher from *Beyond the Veil: Male-Female Dynamics in Modern Muslim Society,* Revised Edition, by Fatima Mernissi. Copyright © 1987. Published by Indiana University Press. Material excerpted from pages xv-xvi, 44–45, 175–177.

on earth, an indispensable condition if the social order is to exist at all. It serves as a 'foretaste of the delights secured for men in Paradise,'[4] thus encouraging men to strive for paradise and to obey Allah's rule on earth. Finally, sexual satisfaction is necessary to intellectual effort.

The Muslim theory of sublimation is entirely different from the Western Christian tradition as represented by Freudian psychoanalytic theory. Freud viewed civilization as a war against sexuality.[5] Civilization is sexual energy 'turned aside from its sexual goal and diverted towards other ends, no longer sexual and socially more valuable.'[6] The Muslim theory views civilization as the outcome of satisfied sexual energy. Work is the result not of sexual frustration but of a contented and harmoniously lived sexuality.

> The soul is usually reluctant to carry out its duty because duty [work] is against its nature. If one puts pressures on the soul in order to make it do what it loathes, the soul rebels. But if the soul is allowed to relax for some moments by the means of some pleasures, it fortifies itself and becomes after that alert and ready for work again. And in the woman's company, the relaxation drives out sadness and pacifies the heart. It is advisable for pious souls to divert themselves by means which are religiously lawful.[7]

According to Ghazali, the most precious gift God gave humans is reason. Its best use is the search for knowledge. To know the human environment, to know the earth and galaxies, is to know God. Knowledge (science) is the best form of prayer for a Muslim believer. But to be able to devote his energies to knowledge, man has to reduce the tensions within and without his body, avoid being distracted by external elements, and avoid indulging in earthly pleasures. Women are a dangerous distraction that must be used for the specific purpose of providing the Muslim nation with offspring and quenching the tensions of the sexual instinct. But in no way should women be an object of emotional investment or the focus of attention, which should be devoted to Allah alone in the form of knowledge-seeking, meditation, and prayer.

Ghazali's conception of the individual's task on earth is illuminating in that it reveals that the Muslim message, in spite of its beauty, considers humanity to be constituted by males only. Women are considered not only outside of humanity but a threat to it as well. Muslim wariness of heterosexual involvement is embodied in sexual segregation and its corollaries: arranged marriage, the important role of the mother in the son's life, and the fragility of the marital bond (as revealed by the institutions of repudiation and polygamy). The entire Muslim social structure can be seen as an attack on, and a defence against, the disruptive power of female sexuality. . . .

. . . What modern Muslim societies ought to strive towards is a family based on the unfragmented wholeness of the woman. Sex with an unfragmented human female is a glorious, not a soiling and degrading act. It implies and generates tenderness and love. Allegiance and involvement with an unfragmented woman do not distract men from their social duties, because the woman is not a marginal tabooed individual; rather, she is the centre, the source, the generator of order and life.

Islam's basically positive attitude toward sexuality is more conducive to healthy perspectives of a self-realizing sexuality, harmoniously integrated in social life, than the West's basically negative attitude toward sexuality. Serious changes in male-female conditioning in Western countries imply revolutionary changes in society which these reformist countries are determined to avoid at any cost. Muslim societies cannot afford to be reformist; they do not have sufficient resources to be able to offer palliatives. A superficial replastering of the system is not a possible solution for them.

At a deeper level than laws and official policy, the Muslim social order views the female as a potent aggressive individual whose power can, if not tamed and curbed, corrode the social order. It is very likely that in the long run such a view will facilitate women's integration into the networks of the decision-making and power. One of the main obstacles Western women have been dealing with is the society's view of women as passive inferior beings. The fact that generations of university-educated women in both Europe and America failed to win access to decision-making posts is due in part to this deeply ingrained image of women as inferior. The Muslim image of women as a source of power is likely to make Muslim women set higher and broader goals than just equality with men. The most recent studies on the aspirations of both men and women seem to come to the same conclusion: the goal is not to achieve equality with men. Women have seen that what men have is not worth getting. Women's goals are already being phrased in terms of a global rejection of established sexual patterns, frustrating for males and degrading for females. This implies a revolutionary reorganization of the entire society, starting from its economic structure and ending with its grammar. . . .

One may speculate that women's liberation in an Arab context is likely to take a faster and more radical path than in Western countries. The Arab ruling classes are beginning to realize that they are charged with building a sovereign future, which necessarily revolves around the location and adequate utilization of all human and natural resources for the benefit of the entire population. The Arab woman is a central element in any sovereign future. Those who have not realized this fact are misleading themselves and their countries.

GHADA SAMMAN

"Our Constitution—We the Liberated Women" [§]

It's a Crime for the Slave to Love her Bonds
Let us pray
For the slave who loves her bonds
For the slave who is whipped

[§] Reprinted by permission of the authors from *Opening the Gates: A Century of Arab Feminist Writing*, edited by Margot Badran and Miriam Cooke. Copyright © 1990 by Margot Badran and Miriam Cooke. Published by Indiana University Press and Virago Press. Material excerpted from pages 139–140.

We don't know in which cave she got used to being whipped, but we hear her tearful, moaning submission. We threw her ropes on which she spat. She melted her chains. She re-united them for a master to re-tie her because she's afraid to live, because she is too cowardly to bear the responsibility of living. We gave her our voting rights, the right to participate in the running of the country and decide its future, the right to struggle in the path of God and country, the right to toil and to bear responsibility.

Yesterday I read a protest in some newspaper signed by some sisters in Hama (these women had refused suffrage). They were protesting the acquisition of the right to live and to fight and the honour of responsibility and struggle. What can I say?

Millions of women have moaned, aeons of sadness have settled in our hearts like a heavy fog. Generations have longed to participate in humanity along with men. Now the authorities honour us and invite us to practice our humanity. They grant us the honour of duties and responsibilities. So, shall we refuse? What can I say? Only the coward refuses to live. Some sisters from Hama are refusing the call of the country so as to escape responsibility while shouting 'Islam'.

Islam is women's honour. They escape from our country's battles out of weakness and resignation, shouting 'Islam'. Aisha fought when it became necessary. They are afraid of mixing with men and of what people will suspect. Aisha was suspected once. God honoured Aisha with a verse that revealed her innocence and that of all women who dare to be human in a society that insists that women remain colourful mummy/slaves whose existence revolves around the household, make-up and stupid stories.

I shall not respond to Professor Ali Tantawi (a shaikh and president of a religious group who published a pamphlet against the feminist revolution). He has the right to his personal opinion as long as he remains true to himself. Some day we may convince him that his fears are unfounded and that women, these sweet gentle creatures whom no one has described as exquisitely as our great Shaikh, are also strong human beings capable of sharing men's responsibilities. Professor Ali Tantawi's opposition to us is not treachery. It is a noble challenge that increases the violence of the noble response.

As for our Hama sisters and the treachery among the ranks of us, women of this country, this is the treachery of the eyelashes to the eye, of the fingernail to the finger, of the hand to the arm. What can I say? What can half of me say if I choose for the other half to be paralyzed when the enemy is all around?

Let us pray.

For the cancer which is us. Let us pray because we shall amputate the arm if it betrays.

Palestine is moaning while we twist in the cocoons of our time and our defeat. Algeria is crucified every dawn and there are still some of our women who do not know who Jamila [Bouhired, an Algerian heroine] is. The world is in competition to get to the moon and they are drawing a veil over their hearts and chains over their existence. All Jewish women are fighters, why not also Muslim women as in the past?

Let us pray.

For those who accuse Islam of denigrating them, whereas it is Islam that delivered us from the deserts where we were being buried like cadavers. Our heads only touched the clouds when eagles snatched us up and flew with us to the caves of terror and disgrace.

Islam forbade us to be dolls decorating tables and playthings for the god of Petrol, and butterflies around the coloured lamps of vanities.

Let us pray.

For the butterflies who refuse to break out of their cocoons and to confront the storm. They have become used to being jailed worms.

Let us pray.

For those who refuse winter's toil and summer's harvest. They have condemned themselves to the suicide of silence and defeatism. Today suicide is the ultimate cowardice because our lives are not ours alone they belong to our past, to our destiny and to the future of our country and we are compelled to live. . . .

NOTES

[1] The connection between imperialist and feminist ideology is an important one for many women whose cultures have been subjected to colonization by Western nations. See, for example, the discussion of Stiwanism in the excerpt by Mọlara Ogundipẹ-Leslie in **Vision and Transformation.**

[2] Mernissi makes this point in the introduction to the revised edition of *Beyond the Veil* when she says, "We often hear and read about women's marginalization, women's deprivation, and women's exclusion from modernity in the Third World. This kind of leftist self-serving, hasty analysis, which could be called the 'Cassandra syndrome,' has led to simplistic generalizations about how bad the state is and how neglected women are" (xxix).

[3] Biographical information about Mernissi is taken from *Beyond the Veil.* Information about Samman is taken from the introduction to her article printed in *Opening the Gates: A Century of Arab Feminist Writing.*

[4] Al-Ghazali, *Revivification,* p. 28. [Mernissi]

[5] Sigmund Freud, *Civilization and Its Discontents,* New York 1962. [Mernissi]

[6] Sigmund Freud, *A General Introduction to Psychoanalysis,* New York, 1952, p. 27. [Mernissi]

[7] Al-Ghazali, *Revivification,* p. 32. [Mernissi]

WORKS CONSULTED

Badran, Margot and Miriam Cooke, eds. *Opening the Gates: A Century of Arab Feminist Writing.* Bloomington: Indiana UP, 1990.

Kandiyoti, Deniz. "Islam and Patriarchy: A Comparative Perspective." *Women in Middle Eastern History: Shifting Boundaries in Sex and Gender.* Ed. Nikki R. Keddie and Beth Baron. New Haven: Yale UP, 1991.

—. Introduction. *Women, Islam and the State.* Ed. Deniz Kandiyoti. Women in the Political Economy series. Ed. Ronnie J. Steinberg. Philadelphia: Temple UP, 1991.

Keddie, Nikki R. Introduction. *Women in Middle Eastern History: Shifting Boundaries in Sex and Gender.* Ed. Nikki R. Keddie and Beth Baron. New Haven: Yale UP, 1991.

Mernissi, Fatima. *Beyond the Veil: Male-Female Dynamics in Modern Muslim Society.* Revised ed. Bloomington: Indiana UP, 1987.

VOLTAIRINE DE CLEYRE *(1866–1912)*

"Sex Slavery"

"Her life was a protest against all sham, a challenge to all hypocrisy, and an inspiration for social rebellion." Alexander Berkman's eulogy in 1912 recalls the intensity with which Voltairine de Cleyre battled—through poverty, illness, depression, and doubt—for a cause she saw as the key to human freedom. She and her contemporaries referred to that cause as Anarchism, a term that has been subject to such widespread misinterpretation that we must take care to understand what it meant for those who claimed it at the turn of the twentieth century. Most specifically de Cleyre, like Emma Goldman, was an anarchist *feminist* whose analysis of power relations in general was allied to an analysis of women's subjugation to sexual control by men through the coercive authority of church and state.

During de Cleyre's lifetime "Anarchism" applied to a variety of views centered around a commitment to individual liberty and a rejection of all authority, especially governmental, that impinged on that liberty. Emma Goldman called it, "The philosophy of a new social order based on liberty unrestricted by man-made law; the theory that all forms of government rest on violence, and are therefore wrong and harmful, as well as unnecessary." In place of government, anarchists proposed "a condition of society regulated by voluntary agreement" (*Mother Earth* 7.1, March 1912: 155). Exactly what kind of "condition" this might be, was a source of debate; de Cleyre envisioned "thousands of small communities stretching along the lines of transportation, each producing very largely for its own needs, able to rely upon itself, and therefore able to be independent" like the free individuals comprising it (*Selected Works* 134).

De Cleyre traced her anarchism to the intellectual legacy of her father, a "freethinking" socialist who named her for the French Enlightenment philosopher Voltaire, and to the convent school to which he nonetheless sent her at age fourteen in the hope of curing her "impertinence and impudence."[1] Her experience there was not unmitigatedly painful; she admired at least one teacher and briefly considered becoming a nun herself. But her struggles against the school's authoritarian regime, she said, left "white scars" on her soul and led her "Will" inexorably "in one direction, the knowledge and assertion of its own liberty" (*Selected Works* 156).

Her formal schooling over at age seventeen, de Cleyre began another kind of education among various groups of political activists, culminating in her affiliation with the group who took Liberty as a defining concept. Barely sustaining herself in the "desperate struggle with hunger"[2] by giving private lessons in subjects she had learned at the convent, she began writing and lecturing, first as an atheist "freethinker," and then as a socialist. The turning point in her life came in 1886, when five Anarchists were unjustly condemned to death after a bomb exploded at a workers' rally near Haymarket Square in Chicago. At first swept along with public opinion that they should be hanged, de Cleyre came to see that they were being victimized for their ideas, to which she was then drawn herself.

In her description of the reasons for her turn to anarchism, however, de Cleyre cited, "above all," her outrage at the subordination of women, including "a bitter, passionate sense of personal injustice" at the "subordinated cramped circle prescribed for women in daily life, whether in the field of material production, or in domestic arrangement, or in educational work; or in the ideals held up to her . . ." ("Why I Am an Anarchist," *Mother Earth* [1908]: 20–21). Her political analysis of governments as inherently oppressive institutions was thus bound up at its core with her experience of oppression as a woman and her analysis of gender relations. It is her analysis of the role of gender at the heart of oppressive systems in general, and her thoroughgoing rejection of all the institutions bound up with women's subordination, that give her work its contemporary ring.

The nature of de Cleyre's feminism is evident in the titles of her writings and lectures dealing most specifically with women's issues: "Sex Slavery" (around 1890), "The Gates of Freedom" (1891), "The Case of Woman vs. Orthodoxy" (1896), "Why I Am an Anarchist" (1897), "They Who Marry Do Ill" (1907), "Love in Freedom," "The Woman Question" (published 1913), and a number of essays, poems, and lectures on Mary Wollstonecraft, whom she admired as a "great pioneer" (Avrich 158). An emphasis on individual liberty formed the crux of her feminism and that of her anarchism. She saw women deprived of liberty "by socialization, by the institution of marriage, and by the social pressure to reproduce" (Palczewski 146); the remedy lay in economic, emotional, and sexual independence. "Young girls!" she cried at the beginning of her lecture on "The Gates of Freedom" in 1891. "If any one of you is contemplating marriage remember . . . what the contract means. The sale and control of your person in return for 'protection' and support" (qtd. in Marsh 132).

Throughout her adult life she rejected such a "sale" of herself. As Margaret Marsh says, de Cleyre's insistence on living out her feminist ideals "forced those who came in contact with her to confront her philosophy in the particular as well as in the abstract" (146). The confrontations were not easy. Just as de Cleyre led a stormy political life, she led a stormy personal life, including a long estrangement from her friend Emma Goldman and a number of difficult sexual and emotional relationships with men. One of these involved an argument after which both she and her lover took poison (Avrich 83–84); another resulted in a child whom she referred to as exclusively the father's and consigned to him to raise; at least one ended with her rejection of her lover's pressure on her to live with him in an arrangement she regarded as marriage.

A letter she wrote to Samuel H. Gordon in 1897 provides a glimpse of the conflicts involved in her personal struggles for liberty: "If you want me back I shall come all the sooner if you treat me as a free woman and not as a slave. Last summer I wanted to enslave you—at least so much that my days and nights were tears because you preferred other people to me, though theoretically I know I was wrong. I will never, *never* live that life again. It is not worth while *living* at that price. I would rather die here in England and never see your beautiful face again than live to be the slave of my own affection for you. I will never, let come what will, accept the condition of married slavery again. I will not do things for you; I will not *live* with you, for if I do I suffer the tortures of owning and being owned" (qtd. in Avrich 84). Rejection of conventional motherhood and marriage—by which she meant any "permanent dependent relationship," whether sanctioned by the state or not[3]—was fundamental to de Cleyre's definition of liberty for herself. This freedom included her right to pursue her chosen work of lecturing, writing, and agitating for a cause that she saw as the key to ensuring liberty for all.

For that work de Cleyre took no money, contrary to the practice of some Anarchist activists; instead she barely supported herself as an English teacher. Her clients were impoverished immigrants in the predominantly Jewish neighborhood of Philadelphia where she lived most of her adult life. Here she not only taught English but worked at learning Yiddish, putting down deep political and emotional roots in the Jewish Anarchist community.

Her refusal of payment for her tireless schedule of writing and lecturing reflected the rigor with which she lived out her principles. She renounced the quest for "things," which she saw as the "Dominant Idea" of her age, and applied herself to her political work with so austere a commitment that contemporaries and subsequent writers compared her to an anchorite, a nun, or a saint.[4] One of the most severe personal tests of her beliefs occurred in December, 1902, when a former student, suffering sickness and delusion, shot her point-blank as she was getting onto a streetcar (Avrich 171). In accordance with her belief that it is governments and their institutions that create criminals, she refused to identify or prosecute her assailant, but raised money on his behalf. "I have no resentment towards the man," she said. "If society were so constituted as to allow every man, woman and child to lead a normal life there would be no violence in this world. It fills me with horror to think of the brutal acts done in the name of government. Every act of violence finds its echo in another act of violence. The policeman's club breeds criminals" (Philadelphia *North American* [24 Dec.1902], qtd. in Avrich 174–75).

Her attitude toward her assailant reflects the views she held on violence throughout most of her career. Although some anarchists in de Cleyre's day advocated violence and all of them were depicted in the popular press as doing so, in fact, a range of anarchist positions surrounded the issue, from Christian pacifism to calls for armed battle against repressive authority. Influenced early on by the pacifism of Tolstoy, de Cleyre was personally opposed to violence as a means of realizing anarchist goals, but saw individual instances of violence as inevitable and natural responses—to be understood rather than judged—to the systematic violence of the state. Inspired by the Mexican Revolution toward the end of her life, however, she turned more definitively toward support of violent forms of "direct action" as a means of ending coercive authority.

The news of revolution in Mexico brought de Cleyre, then extremely ill and weak, out of a grimly depressed period of physical and emotional exhaustion during which she lost faith in the ideals for which she had so strenuously fought. The prospect of at least one immediate victory in what she had come to see as a long and possibly futile battle inspired her to a renewed dedication that ended only with her death in 1912 at the age of forty-five. But throughout her brief career she must have inspired many women to commit themselves to that same long battle as "revolutionists . . . *being* what we teach . . . Better the war of freedom than the peace of slavery" ("Gates of Freedom," qtd. in Marsh 133).

From the Haymarket Anarchists, de Cleyre said she learned an important lesson: that "little dreams are folly. That not in demanding little . . . not in mountain labor to bring forth mice, can any lasting alleviation come; but in demanding, much,—all . . ." (*Selected Works* 167). The context was workers' control of their labor, but the insight animated her approach to every social and political issue. At the core of that philosophy was her complete rejection of the life prescribed for her as a woman, her insistence on living out her own individual freedom and defining her own work. "I never expect men to *give* us liberty," she said. "No, women we are not *worth* it, until we *take* it."

ECD

FROM "SEX SLAVERY"[§]

. . . Yes, for that is adultery where woman submits herself sexually to man, without desire on her part, for the sake of "keeping him virtuous," "keeping him at home," the women say. (Well, if a man did not love me and respect himself enough to be "virtuous" without prostituting me, he might go, and welcome. He has no virtue to keep.) And that is rape, where a man forces himself sexually upon a woman whether he is licensed by the marriage law to do it or not. And that is the vilest of all tyranny where a man compels the woman he says he loves, to endure the agony of bearing children that she does not want, and for whom, as is the rule rather than the exception, they cannot properly provide. It is worse than any other human oppression; it is fairly *God*-like! To the sexual tyrant there is no parallel upon earth; one must go to the skies to find a fiend who thrusts life upon his children only to starve and curse and outcast and damn them! And only through the marriage law is such tyranny possible. The man who deceives a woman outside of marriage (and mind you, such a man will deceive in marriage too) may deny his own child, if he is mean enough. He cannot tear it from her arms—he cannot touch it! The girl he wronged, thanks to your very pure and tender morality-standard, may die in the street for want of food. *He* cannot force his hated presence upon her again. But his wife, gentlemen, his wife, the woman he respects so much that he consents to let her merge her individuality into his, lose her identity and become his chattel, his wife he may not only force unwelcome children upon, outrage at his own good pleasure, and keep as a general cheap and convenient piece of furniture, but if she does not get a divorce (and she cannot for such cause) he can follow her wherever she goes, come into her house, eat her food, force her into the cell, *kill* her by virtue of his sexual authority! And she has no redress unless he is indiscreet enough to abuse her in some less brutal but unlicensed manner. I know a case in your city where a woman was followed so for ten years by her husband. I believe he finally developed grace enough to die; please applaud him for the only decent thing he ever did.

Oh, is it not rare, all this talk about the preservation of morality by marriage law! O splendid carefulness to preserve that which you have not got! O height and depth of purity,

---

[§] Reprinted from *Selected Works of Voltairine de Cleyre* edited by Alexander Berkman. Published 1914 by Mother Earth, New York. Material excerpted from pages 345–347, 350–352.

which fears so much that the children will not know who their fathers are, because, forsooth, they must rely upon their mother's word instead of the hired certification of some priest of the Church, or the Law! I wonder if the children would be improved to know what their fathers have done. I would rather, much rather, not know who my father was than know he had been a tyrant to my mother. I would rather, much rather, be illegitimate according to the statutes of men, than illegitimate according to the unchanging law of Nature. For what is it to be legitimate, born "according to law"? It is to be, nine cases out of ten, the child of a man who acknowledges his fatherhood simply because he is forced to do so, and whose conception of virtue is realized by the statement that "a woman's duty is to keep her husband at home"; to be a child of a woman who cares more for the benediction of Mrs. Grundy than the simple honor of her lover's word, and conceives prostitution to be purity and duty when exacted of her by her husband. It is to have Tyranny as your progenitor, and slavery as your prenatal cradle. It is to run the risk of unwelcome birth, "legal" constitutional weakness, morals corrupted before birth, possibly a murder instinct, the inheritance of excessive sexuality or no sexuality, either of which is disease. It is to have the value of a piece of paper, a rag from the tattered garments of the "Social Contract," set above health, beauty, talent or goodness; for I never yet had difficulty in obtaining the admission that illegitimate children are nearly always prettier and brighter than others, even from conservative women. And how supremely disgusting it is to see them look from their own puny, sickly, lust-born children, upon whom lie the chain-traces of their terrible servitude, look from these to some healthy, beautiful, "natural" child, and say, "What a pity its *mother* wasn't virtuous!" Never a word about *their* children's fathers' virtue, they know too much! Virtue! Disease, stupidity, criminality! What an *obscene* thing "virtue" is! . . .

. . . The question of souls is old—we demand our bodies, now. We are tired of promises, God is deaf, and his church is our worst enemy. Against it we bring the charge of being the moral (or immoral) force which lies behind the tyranny of the State. And the State has divided the loaves and fishes with the Church, the magistrates, like the priests take marriage fees; the two fetters of Authority have gone into partnership in the business of granting patent-rights to parents for the privilege of reproducing themselves, and the State cries as the Church cried of old, and cries now: "See how we protect women!" The State has done more. It has often been said to me, by women with decent masters, who had no idea of the outrages practiced on their less fortunate sisters, "Why don't the wives leave?"

Why don't you run, when your feet are chained together? Why don't you cry when a gag is on your lips? Why don't you raise your hands above your head when they are pinned fast to your sides? Why don't you spend thousands of dollars when you haven't a cent in your pocket? Why don't you go to the seashore or the mountains, you fools scorching with city heat? If there is one thing more than another in this whole accursed tissue of false society, which makes me angry, it is the asinine stupidity which with the true phlegm of impenetrable dullness says, "Why don't the women leave!" Will you tell me where they will go and what they shall do? . . .

. . . When America passed the fugitive slave law compelling men to catch their fellows more brutally than runaway dogs, Canada, aristocratic, unrepublican Canada, still stretched her arms to those who might reach her. But there is no refuge upon earth for the enslaved sex. Right where we are, there we must dig our trenches, and win or die. . . .

NOTES

[1] As he explained to his wife in a letter Sept. 17, 1880 (Marsh 126–27).

[2] As she described it in an autobiographical sketch (Avrich 38).

[3] Her definition in "Those who Marry Do Ill" (qtd. in Palcezwski 147).

[4] On this canonizing, see Marsh's comments (123–24 and passim).

WORKS CONSULTED

Avrich, Paul. *An American Anarchist: The Life of Voltairine de Cleyre.* Princeton: Princeton UP, 1978.

Berkman, Alexander. Tribute to de Cleyre in "Voltairine de Cleyre: A Tribute," by Harry Kelly, George Brown, Mary Hansen, and Alexander Berkman. *Mother Earth* 7.5 (July 1912): 146–153.

de Cleyre, Voltairine. *Selected Works of Voltairine de Cleyre.* Ed. Alexander Berkman. New York: Mother Earth, 1914.

—. *The First Mayday: The Haymarket Speeches, 1895–1910.* Ed. Paul Avrich. Orkney, NY: Cienfuegos Press, Libertarian Book Club, and Soil of Liberty, 1980.

Marsh, Margaret S. *Anarchist Women, 1870–1920.* Philadelphia: Temple UP, 1981.

Palczewski, Catherine Helen. "Voltairine de Cleyre." *Women Public Speakers in the United States, 1800–1925: A Bio-Critical Sourcebook.* Ed. Karlyn Kohrs Campbell. Westport, CT: Greenwood, 1993.

SEI SHŌNAGON *(c. 966–?)*

The Good Lover

See also **Work and Education**

Sei Shōnagon completed *The Pillow Book* when she was around thirty-seven, an age that was considered to be particularly unlucky among Japanese women during the Heian period.[1] Accordingly, the end of this work might be seen to signal a major transition in the author's life as she enters old age. In the epilogue to the book, Sei Shōnagon writes, "It is getting so dark that I can scarcely go on writing; and my brush is all worn out. Yet I should like to add a few things before I end." These references to "darkness" and "worn-out brushes" have been viewed as suggestive of the author's anxiety concerning this transitional period in her life.[2] In fact, it is just this sort of restrained yet evocative description which gives *The Pillow Book* much of its contemporary resonance.

Sei Shōnagon wrote *The Pillow Book* during the period lasting from around 996 until around 1002, when she was in service at the court of the empress Teishi. The author and the empress grew to be great friends during this time, and Sei Shōnagon devotes many lines in her work to praise of this beloved royal personage. While a decision to begin writing may have been influenced by the fact that her father had made a career as an imperial poet and author, it is very likely that Sei Shōnagon did not intend to circulate *The Pillow Book* publicly. Her work might best be described as a "private document . . . made public" (Konishi 386).

In the excerpted passage, Sei Shōnagon describes some of the social—and sexual—rituals which were an accepted part of courtly life. Interestingly, Sei Shōnagon was married two or three times and took a number of lovers, although she was not considered by contemporaries to be a "notorious" or promiscuous woman in any way. The sexual practices which she depicts here suggest that aristocratic women's erotic desire could and did find a socially acceptable means of expression within a series of ritualized behaviors. This vision of female sexuality can seem remarkably worldly in contrast to the other, more consciously spiritual depictions of women's desire which are included in this section; in fact, we have placed it here in order to give a sense of the multiple ways in which women's erotic practices become structured by the societies in which they live. The women Sei Shōnagon describes are free to take one or many lovers, albeit in a highly ritualized and aristocratic setting. These women may even consider such ritual practices, which might seem stultifying to a modern reader, as a source of collective validation and power.

Even though Heian court ladies spent much of their time protected by silken curtains from the gaze of male visitors, Sei Shōnagon seems to have considered men her intellectual and social equals. (She develops a critique of the way in which an ideology of gender difference can function to limit women's achievements in a second excerpt from *The Pillow Book* in the **Work and Education** section.) The passage here serves as an example of a ritualized culture in which female sexuality, rather than being the primary locus of religious and secular anxiety, instead offers opportunities for women to assert themselves as agents. While Sei Shōnagon speaks of "depressing" and "hateful things" in this passage, she also provides her reader with a forthright description of the way in which Japanese women of the Heian court experienced a variety of sensual and sexual pleasures.

NM

FROM *THE PILLOW BOOK OF SEI SHŌNAGON*[§]

Depressing Things

. . . It is quite late at night and a woman has been expecting a visitor. Hearing finally a stealthy tapping, she sends her maid to open the gate and lies waiting excitedly. But the name announced by the maid is that of someone with whom she has absolutely no connexion. Of all the depressing things this is by far the worst.

Hateful Things

. . . A good lover will behave as elegantly at dawn as at any other time. He drags himself out of bed with a look of dismay on his face. The lady urges him on: 'Come, my friend, it's getting light. You don't want anyone to find you here.' He gives a deep sigh, as if to say that the night has not been nearly long enough and that it is agony to leave. Once up, he does not instantly pull on his trousers. Instead he comes close to the lady and whispers whatever was left unsaid during the night. Even when he is dressed, he still lingers, vaguely pretending to be fastening his sash.

Presently he raises the lattice, and the two lovers stand together by the side door while he tells her how he dreads the coming day, which will keep them apart; then he slips away. The lady watches him go, and this moment of parting will remain among her most charming memories.

Indeed, one's attachment to a man depends largely on the elegance of his leave-taking. When he jumps out of bed, scurries about the room, tightly fastens his trouser-sash, rolls up the sleeves of his Court cloak, over-robe, or hunting costume, stuffs his belongings into the breast of his robe and then briskly secures the outer sash—one really begins to hate him.

The Women's Apartments along the Gallery

. . . Throughout the night one hears the sound of footsteps in the corridor outside. Every now and then the sound will stop, and someone will tap on a door with just a single finger. It is pleasant to think that the woman inside can instantly recognize her visitor. Sometimes the tapping will continue for quite a while without the woman's responding in any way. The man finally gives up, thinking that she must be asleep; but this does not please the woman, who makes a few cautious movements, with a rustle of silk clothes, so that her

---

[§] Reprinted by permission of Oxford University Press from *The Pillow Book of Sei Shōnagon,* by Sei Shōnagon. Ivan Morris, translator and editor. Copyright © 1967 by Ivan Morris. Published 1967 by Oxford University Press. Material excerpted from pages 41, 49–50, 84 in the Penguin edition.

visitor will know she is really there. Then she hears him fanning himself as he remains standing outside the door.

In the winter one sometimes catches the sound of a woman gently stirring the embers in her brazier. Though she does her best to be quiet, the man who is waiting outside hears her; he knocks louder and louder, asking her to let him in. Then the woman slips furtively towards the door where she can listen to him.

On other occasions one may hear several voices reciting Chinese or Japanese poems. One of the women opens her door, though in fact no one has knocked. Seeing this, several of the men, who had no particular intention of visiting this woman, stop on their way through the gallery. Since there is no room for them all to come in, many of them spend the rest of the night out in the garden—most charming.

NOTES

[1] "Shōnagon wrote during the great mid-Heian period of feminine vernacular literature that produced not only the world's first psychological novel, *The Tale of Genji,* but vast quantities of poetry and a series of diaries, mostly by Court ladies, which enable us to imagine what life was like for upper-class Japanese women a thousand years ago" (Morris 10).

[2] This interpretation of passages from the epilogue is advanced in Donald Keene's *Seeds in the Heart: Japanese Literature from Earliest Times to the Late Sixteenth Century.*

WORKS CONSULTED

Keene, Donald. *Seeds in the Heart: Japanese Literature from Earliest Times to the Late Sixteenth Century.* New York: Henry Holt, 1993.

Konishi, Jin'ichi. *A History of Japanese Literature.* Vol 2. Ed. Aileen Gatten. Princeton: Princeton UP, 1986.

Morris, Ivan, Trans. *The Pillow Book of Sei Shōnagon.* Baltimore: Penguin, 1971.

AUDRE LORDE *(1934–1992)*

"The Erotic as Power"

Barbara Christian recalls that when Audre Lorde published her first poem about lesbian sexual love, she tacked it up "on her office door for all to see," like Martin Luther at Wittenberg nailing his Ninety-Five Theses to the door of the church. "I heard the reverberations from coast to coast," Christian says, when Lorde's "insistence on speaking, whatever the consequences, became a model for many women" (2). Throughout the 1970s and 80s, Audre Lorde was one of the boldest and most eminent voices for feminist change in the U.S. She called for not only a social and political transformation through women's organized resistance, but a transformation of feminist resistance itself. Rather than allowing differences among women to undermine collective efforts, Lorde argued such differences should be seen as productive sources of power. Her many volumes of poetry explore her love for women, her erotic experience, and the sources of power that enable women—especially women who experience difference as oppression—to survive. She records her own experiences in *Zami* (1982), a "biomythography" describing her life through the 1950s, and *The Cancer Journals* (1980), which recount her battle against breast cancer. Her life, poetry, essays, and speeches were all dedicated to what she termed "the transformation of silence into language and action."

Audre Lorde grew up in Harlem, the daughter of Grenadian immigrants who started out in 1924 as a laborer and chambermaid. Later her father owned a small real estate office in which her mother did much of the work, including management. This mother was a formidable influence on Lorde's life: a strong, outspoken, highly competent woman who "knew how to pretend that the only food left in the house was actually a meal of choice, carefully planned" (*Zami* 11). She worked hard, Lorde later decided, to appear powerful, hiding her vulnerabilities as a Black woman and trying to shield her children from as much knowledge of racism as she could. Lorde remembered her wiping the spit off their clothes while complaining of crude people who spit carelessly into the wind, never revealing it had been aimed at them. She also remembered her mother's helpless fury at her heartbreak when, to her bafflement, she lost an election at her racist elementary school: "Fair, fair, what's fair, you think? Is fair you want, look in god's face" (*Zami* 65).

Lorde's childhood was bounded by this fortifying but also domineering influence of her mother. She experienced her early childhood through a haze of visual impairment and a silence that was either an inability to speak or a sense of having nothing to say that would not be punished. When Lorde was four, Augusta Baker, a children's librarian in Harlem, inspired her to say something: "I want to read" (*Zami* 21–23). "And it went from there," she recounted later. "I learned how to read, I learned how to talk, I learned how to write. Later I became a librarian" (Winter interview 75).

Lorde said that her earliest memories were "of war between Me and Them," with

"Them" being the rest of her family (Winter 74). In adolescence this war intensified as she was drawn increasingly into progressive political friendships and a bohemian high-school crowd, a world the rest of her family could not understand. After a period of excruciating conflict, especially with her mother, she left home. In the succeeding years she finished high school, attended Hunter College, and worked as a commercial x-ray technician, a job that may have caused the cancer from which she died. She graduated from Hunter in 1959 and received a Master's in Library Science in 1961 from Columbia University. After several years of work as a librarian, she became a lecturer in creative writing at City University of New York (1968), then poet-in-residence at Tougaloo College, where she discovered that she wanted teaching and writing for her lifework (Tate interview 110). In the same year she published her first book of poetry, *The First Cities*.

After teaching at Herbert Lehman College, John Jay College of Criminal Justice, and Hunter College, Lorde became a distinguished professor at Atlanta University and English professor at Hunter College. In the 1980s she became an eminent speaker and writer, winning many awards for her creative writing and public service. Her books of poetry include *The First Cities* (1968), *Coal* (1968), *Cables to Rage* (1970), *From a Land Where Other People Live* (1973), *The New York Head Shop and Museum* (1974), *Black Unicorn* (1978), *Our Dead Behind Us* (1986), and *The Marvelous Arithmetic of Distance* (1993). Her nonfiction includes two collections of essays, *Sister Outsider* (1984) and *Burst of Light* (1988), as well as *The Cancer Journals* (1980) and *Zami* (1982).

Lorde discovered her love for women during young adulthood, entering into a complicated negotiation of differences in the world of "gay-girls." Most of the lesbians she met were white, and many who identified themselves as progressive insisted that their lesbianism made them as much an "outsider" as she. In this, she felt, they were wrong; her white friends could pass as straight by dressing in a certain way, but nothing could change her experience of racism. At the same time she found in her lesbian community a creative, transformative process generated by the bonding of women—a process that was to emerge many years later as a goal of the women's movement, and in which she felt she and her friends had pioneered.

Her accounts of these experiences of sisterhood and difference, redemptive closeness and destructive rifts, reveal the personal experience out of which she forged her influential feminist theory of the 1970s and 80s. Lorde created stark, vivid expositions of racism in the women's movement and sexism in African-American activist movements, believed in the power of women's connections with each other, and argued that the erotic is not only part of our spiritual power but a source of political power. Kate Rushin remembers her asking a group of Oberlin graduates, "Are you willing to use the power that you have in the service of what you say you believe?" Throughout her vibrant career, Lorde was a striking example of someone who did just that. As Rushin says, "How wonderful that Audre who was once a little girl who could not speak and who could not see well, born in Harlem during the Depression, determined herself to become one of the most visionary, outspoken, and eloquent writers of our time" (85).

ECD

FROM "USES OF THE EROTIC: THE EROTIC AS POWER"[§]

There are many kinds of power, used and unused, acknowledged or otherwise. The erotic is a resource within each of us that lies in a deeply female and spiritual plane, firmly rooted in the power of our unexpressed or unrecognized feeling. In order to perpetuate itself, every oppression must corrupt or distort those various sources of power within the culture of the oppressed that can provide energy for change. For women, this has meant a suppression of the erotic as a considered source of power and information within our lives.

We have been taught to suspect this resource, vilified, abused, and devalued within western society. On the one hand, the superficially erotic has been encouraged as a sign of female inferiority; on the other hand, women have been made to suffer and to feel both contemptible and suspect by virtue of its existence.

It is a short step from there to the false belief that only by the suppression of the erotic within our lives and consciousness can women be truly strong. But that strength is illusory, for it is fashioned within the context of male models of power.

As women, we have come to distrust that power which rises from our deepest and non-rational knowledge. We have been warned against it all our lives by the male world, which values this depth of feeling enough to keep women around in order to exercise it in the service of men, but which fears the same depth too much to examine the possibilities of it within themselves. So women are maintained at a distant/inferior position to be psychically milked, much the same way ants maintain colonies of aphids to provide a life-giving substance for their masters.

But the erotic offers a well of replenishing and provocative force to the woman who does not fear its revelation, nor succumb to the belief that sensation is enough.

The erotic has often been misnamed by men and used against women. It has been made into the confused, the trivial, the psychotic, the plasticized sensation. For this reason, we have often turned away from the exploration and consideration of the erotic as a source of power and information, confusing it with its opposite, the pornographic. But pornography is a direct denial of the power of the erotic, for it represents the suppression of true feeling. Pornography emphasizes sensation without feeling.

The erotic is a measure between the beginnings of our sense of self and the chaos of our strongest feelings. It is an internal sense of satisfaction to which, once we have experienced it, we know we can aspire. For having experienced the fullness of this depth of feeling and recognizing its power, in honor and self-respect we can require no less of ourselves.

It is never easy to demand the most from ourselves, from our lives, from our work. To encourage excellence is to go beyond the encouraged mediocrity of our society is to encourage excellence. But giving in to the fear of feeling and working to capacity is a luxury

[§] Reprinted with permission from "Uses of the Erotic: The Erotic as Power" in *Sister Outsider: Essays and Speeches by Audre Lorde*. Copyright © 1984. Published by The Crossing Press: Freedom, CA. Material excerpted from pages 53–58.

only the unintentional can afford, and the unintentional are those who do not wish to guide their own destinies.

This internal requirement toward excellence which we learn from the erotic must not be misconstrued as demanding the impossible from ourselves nor from others. Such a demand incapacitates everyone in the process. For the erotic is not a question only of what we do; it is a question of how acutely and fully we can feel in the doing. Once we know the extent to which we are capable of feeling that sense of satisfaction and completion, we can then observe which of our various life endeavors bring us closest to that fullness.

The aim of each thing we do is to make our lives and the lives of our children richer and more possible. Within the celebration of the erotic in all our endeavors, my work becomes a conscious decision—a longed-for bed which I enter gratefully and from which I rise up empowered.

Of course, women so empowered are dangerous. So we are taught to separate the erotic demand from most vital areas of our lives other than sex. And the lack of concern for the erotic root and satisfactions of our work is felt in our disaffection from so much of what we do. For instance, how often do we truly love our work even at its most difficult?

The principle horror of any system which defines the good in terms of profit rather than in terms of human need, or which defines human need to the exclusion of the psychic and emotional components of that need—the principle horror of such a system is that it robs our work of its erotic value, its erotic power and life appeal and fulfillment. Such a system reduces work to a travesty of necessities, a duty by which we earn bread or oblivion for ourselves and those we love. But this is tantamount to blinding a painter and then telling her to improve her work, and to enjoy the act of painting. It is not only next to impossible, it is also profoundly cruel.

As women, we need to examine the ways in which our world can be truly different. I am speaking here of the necessity for reassessing the quality of all the aspects of our lives and of our work, and how we move toward and through them.

The very word *erotic* comes from the Greek word *eros,* the personification of love in all its aspects—born of Chaos, and personifying creative power and harmony. When I speak of the erotic, then, I speak of it as an assertion of the lifeforce of women; of that creative energy empowered, the knowledge and use of which we are now reclaiming in our language, our history, our dancing, our loving, our work, our lives.

There are frequent attempts to equate pornography and eroticism, two diametrically opposed uses of the sexual. Because of these attempts, it has become fashionable to separate the spiritual (psychic and emotional) from the political, to see them as contradictory or antithetical. "What do you mean, a poetic revolutionary, a meditating gunrunner?" In the same way, we have attempted to separate the spiritual and the erotic, thereby reducing the spiritual to a world of flattened affect, a world of the ascetic who aspires to feel nothing. But nothing is farther from the truth. For the ascetic position is one of the highest fear, the gravest immobility. The severe abstinence of the ascetic becomes the ruling obsession. And it is one not of self-discipline but of self-abnegation.

The dichotomy between the spiritual and the political is also false, resulting from an incomplete attention to our erotic knowledge. For the bridge which connects them is formed by the erotic—the sensual—those physical, emotional, and psychic expressions of what is deepest and strongest and richest within each of us, being shared: the passions of love, in its deepest meanings.

Beyond the superficial, the considered phrase, "It feels right to me," acknowledges the strength of the erotic into a true knowledge, for what that means is the first and most powerful guiding light toward any understanding. And understanding is a hand-maiden which can only wait upon, or clarify, that knowledge, deeply born. The erotic is the nurturer or nursemaid of all our deepest knowledge. . . .

During World War II, we bought sealed plastic packets of white, uncolored margarine, with a tiny, intense pellet of yellow coloring perched like a topaz just inside the clear skin of the bag. We would leave the margarine out for awhile to soften, and then we would pinch the little pellet to break it inside the bag, releasing the rich yellowness into the soft pale mass of margarine. Then taking it carefully between our fingers, we would knead it gently back and forth, over and over, until the color had spread throughout the whole pound bag of margarine, thoroughly coloring it.

I find the erotic such a kernel within myself. When released from its intense and constrained pellet, it flows through and colors my life with a kind of energy that heightens and sensitizes and strengthens all my experience.

We have been raised to fear the *yes* within ourselves, our deepest cravings. But, once recognized, those which do not enhance our future lose their power and can be altered. The fear of our desires keeps them suspect and indiscriminately powerful, for to suppress any truth is to give it strength beyond endurance. The fear that we cannot grow beyond whatever distortions we may find within ourselves keeps us docile and loyal and obedient, externally defined, and leads us to accept many facets of our oppression as women.

When we live outside ourselves, and by that I mean on external directives only rather than from our internal knowledge and needs, when we live away from those erotic guides from within ourselves, then our lives are limited by external and alien forms, and we conform to the needs of a structure that is not based on human need, let alone an individual's. But when we begin to live from within outward, in touch with the power of the erotic within ourselves, and allowing that power to inform and illuminate our actions upon the world around us, then we begin to be responsible to ourselves in the deepest sense. For as we begin to recognize our deepest feelings, we begin to give up, of necessity, being dissatisfied with suffering and self-negation, and with the numbness which so often seems like their only alternative in our society. Our acts against oppression become integral with self, motivated and empowered from within.

In touch with the erotic, I become less willing to accept powerlessness, or those other supplied states of being which are not native to me, such as resignation, despair, self-effacement, depression, self-denial.

WORKS CONSULTED

Christian, Barbara. "Your Silence will Not Protect You: A Tribute to Audre Lorde." *Berkeley Women's Law Journal* 8 (1933): 1–5.

Lorde, Audre. "Uses of the Erotic: The Erotic as Power." Paper delivered at the Fourth Berkshire Conference on the History of Women, Mount Holyoke College, 25 Aug. 1978. Rpt. in *Sister Outsider: Essays and Speeches by Audre Lorde.* Freedom, CA: Crossing Press, 1984.

—. Interview with Claudia Tate. *Black Women Writers at Work.* Ed. Claudia Tate. New York: Continuum, 1990. 100–116.

—. "I'm Angry about the Pretenses of America." Interview with William Steif. *Progressive* 55.1 (1 Jan. 1991): 32–33.

—. Interview with Nina Winter. *Interview with the Muse: Remarkable Women Speak on Creativity and Power.* Ed. Nina Winter. Berkeley, CA: Moon Books, 1978.

—. *Zami: A New Spelling of My Name: A Biomythography by Audre Lorde.* Freedom, CA: Crossing Press, 1982.

Plummer, Betty. "Audre Lorde." *African American Women: A Biographical Dictionary.* Ed. Dorothy C. Salem. New York and London: Garland, 1993.

Rushin, Kate. "Clearing Space for Us: A Tribute to Audre Lorde." *Radical America* 24.4 (1 Sept. 1990): 85–88.

KWOK PUI-LAN *(late 20th century)*

Feminist Theology and Female Sexuality

Kwok Pui-lan was raised in a Buddhist family but converted to Christianity at age twelve, under the influence of Huang Xianyun, one of the first two women in the world to be ordained as an Anglican priest. What does it mean to be Christian and Chinese, when Christianity came to Hong Kong as part of the transaction that ceded the island to the British? What does it mean to be a feminist Chinese Christian when both the Confucian tradition and the Christian tradition have been exposed as androcentric and patriarchal? ("Mothers" 21–24). Kwok Pui-lan's answer involves the kind of multi-faith dialogue advocated by many Asian feminist Christian theologians who reject the either/or dichotomies of the Christianity brought by the missionaries. As Kwok argues in "The Future of Feminist Theology," Asians "have always believed that truth is more than a few propositional statements. In Western symbolic logic, the opposite of 'A' is 'negation A,' and the two must be mutually exclusive. The yin-yang philosophy in oriental thinking understands that 'A' and 'negation A' are correlated, interdependent, and interpenetrating. The Buddhist logic is even more radical for it insists that all reality is neither one nor many but is not-two (non-duality), in the attempt to overcome dichotomy in our thinking" (69).

In keeping with these views, Kwok Pui-lan draws on a combination of indigenous and Christian traditions in her work, calling on all women "trying to transform the world religions for the sake of our own salvation" to "empower each other by sharing what lies beyond patriarchy in our own traditions" (70). As part of her contribution to this effort she has written a study of Chinese women and Christianity from 1860 to 1927. In this work she emphasizes how Chinese women resisted the Church patriarchy of the new religion and transformed it from within—and how they then used a transformed Christianity to resist traditional Chinese patriarchy.

Like María Clara Bingemer and Chung Hyun Kyung, Kwok Pui-lan is a liberation theologian who stresses the difference spirituality should make in all the conditions of people's lives, including their material conditions. In this excerpt she responds specifically to Audre Lorde's vision of the erotic as part of women's total spiritual capacity. Kwok Pui-lan calls attention to the ways in which, under a system of sexual exploitation, the conditions of women's lives deny access to the language of the erotic as a source of spiritual power and a tool for thinking about women's spirituality.

ECD

FROM "THE FUTURE OF FEMINIST THEOLOGY: AN ASIAN PERSPECTIVE."[§]

The language of the erotic

Ever since the African-American poet and writer Audre Lorde published the classic article "The Uses of the Erotic: The Erotic as Power," feminist theologians such as Rita Nakashima Brock and Carter Heyward have been excited about the possibility of talking about God and the power of the erotic. But strangely enough, the language of the erotic is noticeably missing in the theological construction of African-American women, and feminist theologians from other parts of the world also find it difficult to speak about the power of female sexuality.

In the fall of 1991, the American public had a chance to see on television how Professor Anita F. Hill, a law professor at the University of Oklahoma, made allegations with vivid details that Judge Clarence Thomas, nominee for Associate Justice of the Supreme Court, had sexually harassed her when she worked for him some ten years ago. Professor Hill said that she was deeply embarrassed, humiliated, and hurt when those incidents occurred. African-American women theologians and ethicists are not inclined to use the language of the erotic in their religious imagination because their bodies were sold and their sexuality institutionally controlled during slavery. As Delores Williams has said, during the period of slavocracy, "many white males turned to slave women for sexual pleasure and forced these women to fulfill needs which, according to racist ideology concerning male-female relations, should have been fulfilled by white women." When their bodies were defiled and used for the lust of the white oppressors, the language of the erotic had also been stolen from them for a long time.

Asian women find it embarrassing to talk about sex and the erotic not only because decent women are not supposed to raise those issues in public, but also because many of our sisters are working as prostitutes in the hotels, nightclubs, bars, disco joints, and cocktail lounges in the big cities like Manila, Bangkok, Taipei, Hong Kong, and Seoul. The international human flesh trade as a result of sex tourism has brought in much needed foreign cash for so-called economic "development." On the other hand, it has led to the degradation of women, venereal diseases, exploitation by pimps, bribery of the police, and a host of other social problems. In the Philippines, some 7,000 registered hospitality girls used to service the airmen at the American Clark Air Base, and there were more than 20,000 prostitutes, waitresses, street walkers catering to the sexual appetites of American servicemen at the naval bases in Olongapo City. According to a recent report by the United Nations, among the 400,000 prostitutes in Thailand, more than 60%, or 250,000, are HIV positive. Behind each of these figures is a human body mutilated, defiled, and transgressed.

The tragic situation of prostitutes in Asia calls for responses from women's organizations, civic groups, and churches. In the Philippines, GABRIELA, a national organization

---

[§] Reprinted, by permission of the author and publisher, from "The Future of Feminist Theology: An Asian Perspective" by Kwok Pui-lan, published by the Auburn Theological Seminary, New York, NY, in *The Auburn News* Fall 1992. Copyright © 1992 by Kwok Pui-lan. Also included in *Feminist Theology from the Third World: A Reader*, edited by Ursula King, published 1994 by Orbis Books. Material excerpted from pages 72–75.

of women's groups, has worked for the provision of alternative jobs for prostitutes, the punishment of users of, and traffickers of, women and children, and more stringent laws against vice establishments involved in the flesh trade. In Thailand, women's groups established New Life Centers for prostitutes and several organizations, such as the Foundation for Women, Empower, and the Association for Promotion of the Status of Women, have demanded changes of existing laws relating to prostitution. Women in Japan have also worked in solidarity with Korean and Filipino women to demonstrate against Japanese involvement in sex tourism. The magnitude of the international flesh trade and the courageous action of these women's groups challenge us to rethink the connection between the language of the erotic, the control of the female body, and power over women in its naked and symbolic forms. . . .

Many of us today would not be comfortable discussing sexuality and few would try to imagine what the gospel according to the prostitutes would be. While the French feminists are talking about *jouissance,* and some lesbians are trying to break the taboo to talk about passionate love and relationships among women, many women have yet to find a language to speak about the pleasure of the body, female sexuality, and the power of the erotic because the yoke of "compulsory heterosexuality" is still heavy upon us. But many of the metaphors of Christianity come out of the familial context and sexual relationships between persons, such as the Father and the Son, the Church as the bride of Christ, and Adam and Eve as the first couple. The experiences of women, whose sexuality has been controlled and who suffer violence to their bodies, challenge some of these "beloved" images and should be taken up as a serious theological issue in our feminist reconstruction.

When I look back to the twenty years since the publication of *Beyond God the Father,*[1] I rejoice that we have such a plurality of voices and multiplicity of images and symbols. Feminist theology will continue to have a future if the kind of work that we are doing stimulates, encourages, and motivates women and men to struggle against all forms of oppression, to seek justice, and to love ourselves and others. Feminist theology will not have a future if we hear only the white women's voices which try to prescribe a "universal feminism" for everybody. More awareness of the contextual and embodied nature of God-talk will help us value various formulations and approaches from different historical and cultural contexts. . . .

NOTE

[1] One of the founding texts of feminist theology, Mary Daly's *Beyond God the Father: Toward a Philosophy of Women's Liberation* was first published in 1973 [Eds.].

WORKS CONSULTED

Kwok Pui-lan. *Chinese Women and Christianity: 1860–1927.* American Academy of Religion Academy Series 75. Atlanta, GA: Scholars Press, 1992.

—. "The Future of Feminist Theology: An Asian Perspective." *Feminist Theology from the Third World: A Reader.* Ed. Ursula King. Maryknoll, NY: Orbis, 1994.

WORK AND EDUCATION

Jean F. O'Barr

This section combines writings on work and on education, two topics that are closely intertwined in the lives of most women. We want to suggest the multiple and complex relationships between work and education, and the socio-cultural systems in which they are embedded. Labor and learning are processes that human beings pursue over long periods of time, that do not necessarily culminate in a single end product, and that can be considered social institutions: arrangements of people, material resources, ideas, and patterns of social interaction that are culturally recognized as belonging together.

In these selections, *work* is much more than something done for monetary compensation in a place separate from one's residence. Likewise, *education* has antecedents and consequences far beyond the training young people receive from formal institutions. Work and education are the means by which societies reproduce themselves at the most basic level: by providing food, material goods, services, care for children, and the training necessary to enable future generations to do the same. Work and education are also the means by which societies reproduce the hierarchical structures that control access to power.

Thus, both work and education can become tools for socio-political advancement, just as they are often tools of oppression. By the same token, resistance within these areas may profoundly challenge the power structures of a society, or—sometimes even simultaneously—may drive them to entrench themselves more deeply. Resistance in these areas may be enacted from a position of almost no privilege, or it may be enabled by the privileges a woman already has within power structures—privileges that she both relies on and challenges. For all these reasons, we pay particular attention to the way privilege and resistance are imbricated.

LABOR AND LEARNING IN CULTURAL CONTEXTS

Work incorporates all the activities that people engage in to feed, clothe, and sustain themselves. Sometimes the work that women have done is the work traditionally associated with families, be it their own or others—the provision of foodstuffs through gathering and hunting, the tending of gardens and the care of animals, the processing of food and goods, the construction of clothing, the maintenance of living space, and, in some cases, the management of workers, whether kin or nonkin (and including other women), in households large and small. Sometimes the work that women have done remains unrecorded and, therefore, less recognized—the first steps in processing raw materials for guilds or factories; trade and commerce that have been termed petty; the production of items, such as candles or clay pots, for sale and barter outside of the household; curing and healing; or sharing the labor of a family business, such as publishing a newspaper or running a commercial shop. Women also work as creators of knowledge, whether as agriculturalists, artisans, healers, inventors, essayists, or artists. And sometimes the work of women is decried, especially when they are seen to be challenging the moral order—for example, by engaging in sex work outside culturally established sites. However a socio-cultural system has defined women's work, some women have challenged the boundaries and sought to enlarge the domain of women's work itself.

This record of activities indicates how central are the roles—albeit unrecorded, undervalued, or even unacceptable—that women have played in the economies of the societies where they lived. The list of places in which women have labored is long: in farms, in shops, in cottage industries, in factories and their forerunners, in marketplaces, in mansions, in streets and courtyards, in the homes of others, in schools and convents and hospitals, in their own gardens, kitchens, and barns. Sometimes women have been compensated with goods or currency; under slavery, they have not been compensated at all. Women working as housewives rarely receive monetary recognition. Often women have been forced to turn the fruits of their labors over to kin, slave owners, feudal lords, or the state. At the same time, women of privileged classes have often profited from the labor of other women.

The variety of work women do throughout the life cycle is staggering in its complexity. Women not only plant, harvest, process, preserve, cook, and construct; they provide moral teaching, physical care giving, historical memory, community building, and, in the twentieth century, they provide for the psychological well-being of family and friends. And always that work is done within the context of the work that other women do. Women of greater privilege in many times have been relatively more free to engage in political, economic, and artistic work from which women of lesser rank have been restricted, their energies drained by the rigors of daily life. Most often these rigors have supported that wider range of activities enjoyed by elite women. Alternatively, elite and middle-class women of some eras have been more physically restricted than the women who worked for them, women who may have more freely navigated markets and communities on behalf of those who employed them.

It is important to pause here in this listing of women's labors and take note that in many cultures, women are assumed to be the primary providers of emotional work as wives, mothers, daughters, maintainers of kin networks, and providers of sexual services. This emotional work—work that makes other forms of labor possible for both men and women—is often taken for granted in analyses of women and men, and becomes something that one gender naturally does for the other. It is critical to read *work* as incorporating both the production of things and the reproduction—both biological and social—of those who produce the things. Indeed, women's work illustrates how often misleading it is to divide work into separate and distinct domains.

At the most basic level, the kind of labor women are expected to do in a given culture has shaped what they are expected to learn and how they are expected to learn it. Women in all cultures engage in learning, and what they learn is determined by the kind of labor allocated to them. From within their cultures, women resist the limits of learning allotted to them by seeking other kinds of learning that they understand may lead to other kinds of work, and hope will relieve their toils while offering greater rewards.

The story of what women learn begins long before the story of literacy and formal education. A whole body of knowledge is transmitted to girls, whoever they are, about what work girls and women do: from the most basic agricultural and household tasks to the most sophisticated types of professional training or the most stylized social behaviors that contribute to the maintenance of systems of power. In this context, girls are most often educated by women who teach them the roles that those in power expect, and the values that sustain the status quo. Occasionally, as we shall see, girls and women confront those demands; other times mothers serve as teachers for the existing power system, and transmit the knowledge that shapes daughters into women who will perpetuate the gender system that is in place. This teaching of daughters is a large part of mothers' and women's work, one of the many ignored and often elided connections between work and education that we explore in this section.

At the same time, much of the knowledge that women generate and transmit to girls runs in a kind of resistant counterpoint to the knowledge prescribed by power systems in which they live. Women teach women how to manage men, how to use systems of power; they transmit knowledge of healing, childbirth, faith, and ritual; they explore cracks in the systems of control and invent and model ways to circumvent its excesses. And, of course, some women, sometimes, refuse to share this knowledge, using it instead to their own advantage in the power struggles instigated by patriarchy.

Women created systems of knowledge about women long before literacy and education were available to them. Even when women do gain access to formal education, they often must struggle to integrate multiple sources of knowledge: what they know from their own experiences, the inherited rules of the patriarchal systems in which they live, and the explanations put forth by formal systems of education, as well as the new knowledge they may gain by exploring and reading subversively. Women who resist are seeking yet another way of knowing—their own construction of knowledge, drawing on the other streams, but moving beyond them.

In cultures in which political and economic power requires access to literacy, women have not come by reading and writing easily. From earliest times in literate societies, women have sought the pen as a means of describing themselves and resisting inaccurate descriptions by others. Historically, those women of elite classes who have been literate gained education through the men of their families—indulgent fathers, cooperating husbands, brothers and sons who shared their skills, and sometimes their tutors. In these households there was sympathy for their individual pursuits if not support for the goal of educating women. In general, for women of less advantaged positions, the struggle for literacy, education, and knowledge has been fraught with more difficulty, inevitably longer, and subject to greater limitations. Not least is the limitation imposed on women who must do productive work at the same time as they are learning, either because they must finance their own educations or because they must contribute to family income.

Sometimes women have encouraged other women in their quest for learning, exchanging books and letters, creating gatherings for the exchange of ideas based on reading, teaching one another to read and write. Gaining literacy, learning languages, studying texts, owning books, writing letters, engaging in argumentation, composing essays, and giving speeches are some of the means by which women sought to gather the tools that would enable them to understand their world and influence others. Whether the goal was the grasp of natural phenomena, a study of the nature of the divine, participation in political systems, an impassioned retort to bias against women, or simply relief from situations they found intolerable, women in literate cultures sought access to languages and literatures so that they might study texts and gain access to authority. In later centuries, many such women sought education via tutors, the emergent universities, and scientific societies so that they might contribute to the debates of the time, on science and medicine, on politics and philosophy, on economics and family life, on international affairs, and the future of the human condition.

In Europe, from the 17th century on, women began creating secular schools for girls. The curriculum of those schools was a source of great debate among teachers, community leaders, and the public at large: were women to be taught the subjects that men studied, thereby placing them in competition with men? were they to confine themselves to subjects thought culturally suitable for those destined to be young wives? were they to be taught trades so that they might contribute to the family and local economies? What was the point of education for women? Were they to be educated to be helpmates to the men in their lives? Did they seek knowledge for its own sake? Was education a means to greater spiritual fulfillment? Or was education the vehicle through which mothers created citizens? Was education a source of self-development or a source of service to the community and its members? Behind all these questions lies the basic premise that formal education was not designed for women. Those women who embarked on such an adventure required a justification that could be sanctioned by the socio-cultural system at hand. And justification was difficult, because systems of education, work, and social privilege are functionally intertwined.

Three ideas underlie our thinking about the themes in this section. First, we address the invisibility of much of the work women do. Work is more than the creation of goods and services; it is also the making of the conditions that make the work itself possible. Women frequently are socially assigned to the invisible roles of reproducing the conditions through which more visible work by men is done. And that maintenance includes a substantial amount of emotional work, work that builds relationships among people, work that again is seen as natural and inevitable but rarely called "work."

Likewise, while formal education has opened to women students, it has kept them invisible as subjects of study. Until very recently, all formal education denied both men and women knowledge about women's lives. Feminist theorists have investigated the ways in which knowledge is constructed and the role that women play in that construction. They have found that much that passes for objective knowledge is only a partial account of human activity, one that excludes women's contributions to that activity. In particular, working-class women and women of color from all classes—women who have intricate knowledge of the conditions of their own lives—have found it difficult to disseminate that knowledge in the face of an educational curriculum limited by those in power. Furthermore, for more than 200 years, feminists have argued that the education offered women reproduces assumptions about women rather than challenging and expanding ideas of womanhood. In this sense both work and education can be seen as social institutions that reproduce and reinforce gender patterns, which are also aspects of race and class systems, even as women seek different kinds of work and education in the name of equality.

Second, economic systems vary tremendously with time, place, and hierarchies of race and class. The fact that race, class, and gender are not separate but aspects of one another is nowhere more apparent than in the organization of labor. And the ways that women and men experience that organization are profoundly different. For example, women often can control the labor of men of subordinate groups, but they rarely have equal power over men of their own group. There is a further important complication: women are not an homogeneous group in the workplace. Some perform physical labor for the benefit of others, who do little. Still others perform the work of control and leadership, with or without a consciousness of gender. Yet whatever their location in whatever system, many women writing here resist the relegation of women to specific domains and the prohibitions against their entry into others. It is this complex working out of the ways in which women try to gain more control over the conditions, scope, and kinds of work they do, often through the mechanism of education, that renders these accounts inspiring. For example, working-class women may not need more access to work: they may need control over their working conditions and access to other kinds of work. Likewise, part-time workers may not need more access to work but access to full-time jobs with their concomitant benefits. Furthermore, as women assume positions as workers, they may seek to alter the definitions of that work so that it matches more closely the characteristics they bring to it as female workers.

Third, history plays an important role in our understandings of the relationships among women, work, and education. The demand for access to education has been the driving polemic of mainstream Western feminism from the 17th to the 20th century. Western feminist narratives about work and education signal an important shift in the way in which women's social roles are conceptualized. Prior to the 17th century and the period we know as the Enlightenment, most cultures valued the knowledge women gained from their everyday roles: knowledge of agriculture and husbandry, of religion and ritual, of cooking and healing, of economics and household management, of trade and commerce. The importance of this knowledge diminished as institutions of formal education arose and claimed a superior understanding of phenomena, natural and supernatural. The emergence of mass literacy, culminating in widespread formal education, had two important effects. It marginalized women's experiential knowledge, and it favored the abstract knowledge of men that was being transmitted from the ancient world. Thus, women's struggle for access to education must be understood on several levels. It is an effort to avail themselves of the new systems of power. It is a conflict with the systems of knowledge that predate and are ignored by these new institutions. And it is the source of new ideas about women that, in their publication, create women as a category to control.

Thus, the question of adequate representation for women in educational institutions is far from simple. The larger question of how education works to reproduce the social order is at issue. Access to literacy—reading and writing as well as the knowledge obtained thereby—was for women a power struggle, as we shall explore further. Access to the professions presented another level of struggle. There women sought knowledge as a resource that would provide them with the cultural tools they needed to create and influence ideas. But knowledge about the social world is one of the ways in which the social world itself comes into existence.Thus, knowledge reflects and reproduces forms of social organization. The contemporary efforts of feminist scholarship to transform the production of knowledge into a more holistic enterprise is a current phase of this very struggle.

ACTING AGAINST AND WITHIN SYSTEMS OF POWER

We present twenty-one writers here, each acting against and within complex social forces. These women are enmeshed in a variety of traditions and societies that are acting upon and shaping each one of them. While work and education go hand in hand in defining social orders, as we have argued, each woman must negotiate the various social narratives of "work" and "education" at any given historical moment. Social arrangements are never stable. One of the reasons that resistance is possible at all is that various kinds of social knowledge and different institutional forces are acting upon and available to women simultaneously.

We begin with two excerpts from Domitila Barrios de Chungara, speaking in 1978 from her perspective as a woman from a Bolivian mining community. In one, she links her struggles for education with the working conditions of her family. In a second, she explains her daily rounds as a wife in the same community. Her sobering account of the imbrication of work and education grounds the selections that follow by articulating the complicated intertwining of women, work, and education, and by suggesting how resistance is undertaken even in the most overwhelmingly oppressive social contexts.

The role of class is perhaps the most profound of our supporting themes. Women's belief in their abilities or inabilities, influenced by the cultural rhetoric surrounding them, demonstrates the pervasive workings of class as it relates to work and education. Thus, Atukuri Molla, a member of a lower-class, artisan caste in sixteenth-century India, claims that she does not have the skills necessary to translate the vast religious epic that she in fact translates. The selection by Hipparchia, writing in third century BCE Greece, stands in direct contrast to that of Atukuri Molla. As an elite woman trained in argumentation, she successfully refutes the charge that the profession of philosopher makes her unwomanly. Similarly, Laura Cereta, writing in the 15th century, scornfully attacks the male critics who claim that intellectual women are the exception to the rule. She argues in sharp prose in favor of women's learning and against the arguments that men use to disparage women's accomplishments. Sei Shōnagon, writing in tenth-century Japan, defends herself against the charge that her work is indecorous for a woman by combining a claim to class privilege with an appraisal of work for the self-satisfaction it provides. Mary Collier's narrative complicates the relationship of class to women, work, and education even further, for she argues from a working-class position for access to the knowledge she knows is associated with the upper classes. This eighteenth-century English woman was a washerwoman and agricultural laborer among other things. But she also conceived of herself as a poet, working to impart to her male readers knowledge of the gendered conditions of her life and the reasons those conditions needed change.

Class is not the only aspect of social identity that shapes the relationship of women to work and education. Politics, ideology, ethnicity, and sexuality all condition the terms under which women labor and learn. A poignant example of just how extensive the impact of politics can be on women's work comes from East Germany in the 1980s. The role of the state in setting the conditions of women's work and education is a complicated one. Many women have looked to the state to guarantee access to work and education. But it does not always do so, as the case of Maria Curter illustrates. As the East German socialist government was dismantled to reunify a single German nation, the conditions that had operated to encourage women's work were eliminated. The socially mandated forms of work women had known fell away. Older structures of gendered work and education resurfaced and were coupled with new ideas introduced by international businessmen about appropriate behavior and tasks for women. The result was that women were left without access to work as they had known it—in spite of having extensive formal education. Maria Curter's account of how what the state gives can be taken away is a clear account of how fundamentally work is embedded in socio-cultural systems.

The next three selections, by Rokeya Hossain, Zitkala-Ša, and Mab Segrest, provide perspectives on further subtleties of this network. These women enact their resistance by working within educational institutions that are themselves designed to reproduce hierarchies which define women as subordinate. Hossain's story of how she succeeded in setting up a school for girls only to find that it was virtually impossible to simultaneously meet the conditions of purdah and the requirements of formal education is sobering. Zitkala-Ša recounts her experiences as a student and teacher in schools designed to promote Native American assimilation. And Mab Segrest writes as a closeted lesbian teacher in a conservative Baptist college. All three authors provide a critical window on the educational process and its limitations for women. The last two elaborate not just on what education leaves undone for women, but on the additional demands that such education places on women who work within them and who are challenging them. In particular, they explore the extra, emotional work that positions in education entail for women who resist. Their critiques go beyond an argument about extra burdens, to the heart of the nature of the educational enterprise as it serves women. They confront earlier reformers' hopes that once education embraced women students, women would be empowered. Taking issue with these ideas, they suggest that until education expands to include knowledge of women's lives and is woven into the surrounding culture, it remains only a partial solution to women's search for social power. They echo the convictions of Mary Collier: to achieve fundamental change in how women of every social position lead their lives and express themselves, their life experiences need to be put at the center of educational discourse.

Occasionally, women have held positions of political power and authority. These office holders pose intriguing questions about women's work as leaders. Later in the anthology, we present women who reflect on the contributions of women in leadership positions. Here we want to demonstrate that there have been women who were exceptions to the rule and who gained political authority. Nzinga of Angola, a ruler who successfully negotiated with the Portuguese in the seventeenth century, offers one example of a woman in such an authoritative position. While we must rely on reports of her activities rather than her own words, we have in Nzinga an account of an extraordinary woman who assumed the highest leadership position in her society and successfully employed her skills and experiences to exercise power in a fashion distinctive to her. Was Nzinga particularly conscious of the dynamics we now label as gender? Was her elite status more important than her sex as a key to her triumphs? What were the conditions in her society that enabled her to assume a position of authority and use it? What had she experienced that enabled her to think of herself as doing the work of a political leader? While we can probably never obtain the answers to these questions in her case, Nzinga's story encourages us to ask these same questions throughout the anthology.

Thus far our discussion of women's resistance to restrictions placed on their work and education has centered around the efforts to justify women's transgression of boundaries that limited what they were entitled to learn and to do. Our second group of selections shifts the focus somewhat to women who have transgressed boundaries in another way: by maintaining a sense of agency, control, and dignity even while those boundaries constrain, objectify, and subordinate them. In these selections, women express agency by gaining the knowledge and positions necessary to do work that only men are supposed to do. These selections focus on the professions and the ways in which women have had to overcome not only cultural mores and individual obstacles, but organized efforts to circumscribe the work women do and the education they receive.

Three selections center on the struggles of women for self-expression in the arts. Artemisia Gentileschi, an artist in seventeenth-century Italy, urges her patron to pay her as he would pay a male artist. Fanny Mendelssohn Hensel in nineteenth-century Germany is born to privilege and early given a professional education as a musician. But her natal family insists that she place the duties of wife and mother before her professional interests. Nonetheless, she composes musical pieces throughout her life while struggling with her famous brother, Felix, over her role as creator. Binodini Dasi achieves fame in the theater as an actress in nineteenth-century Bengal and must fight to use the money she has earned to build her own theater in the face of opposition that says women should not control artistic production. Separated by time, space, and social location, these three accounts drive home for us as readers the strength of cultural mores opposed to women working as artistic creators, the resistance individual women had to mount to overcome those mores, and the negative attitudes toward women that were part of the daily practices of the artistic communities they sought to enter. Clearly, there is no satisfactory way to compare the burden of the restrictions felt by each of these women, for each labored under the conditions of her circumstances and, for each, those circumstances were inhibiting and painful. Yet for each woman, the determination to have their way at some level by finding and taking advantage of the cracks in their social surroundings comes through clearly.

While participation in the arts has long been a goal for many women, the struggles surrounding entrance into industrial work and the professions of law, medicine, the church, and politics have shown themselves to be even more formidable. As each of these work sites developed into a specialized branch of knowledge, became supported by educational programs, workers' organizations, and professional societies, and acquired cultural prestige, women were blocked from participation at several points. They had to struggle to get the education that would allow them to practice their professions. They had to struggle to gain permission, legally or informally, to set themselves up as professionals. They had to compete with male colleagues for the business that would enable them to survive as working professionals. They had to argue for their right to speak for their professions. And at each stage, the difficulties for women without connections and resources were greater than for those who could count on the help of others.

Catherine Waugh's narrative account of her attempts to secure a position as a lawyer stands as a clear example of professional foreclosure. The gender assumptions that prohibit her entrance into the legal profession have been repeated for thousands of women who followed her. Jarena Lee's experiences as an African-American woman seeking to make the ministry her calling a century earlier are strikingly parallel. She offers us a detailed and personal narrative of her encounters with opposition over time. Although Waugh and Lee have different experiences arising from their racial and class backgrounds, the arguments used against them as women wanting to be professionals and leaders are remarkably similar. Carmen Lucia's work as a "woman organizer" in the U. S. labor movement produced similar responses. She was successful as a professional organizer, and dedicated to seeing problems from workers' points of view; nevertheless, her fellow leaders put her in a category of her own.

The picture in medicine is much the same. Nongenile Masithathu Zenani, a twentieth-century South African woman, recounts her entrance into traditional medicine as fraught with familiar professional and familial restrictions. Rosalie Slaughter tells of her yearning to be a doctor and of the role of her family in making that possible in nineteenth-century America. Mrs. M. D., a nurse in Australia in the 1920s, pleads with her government to allow her to continue her work as midwife. And finally Elsie Riddick's short diary entry sums up the situation of many professional women. Working in the newly emergent bureaucracy of state government at the turn of the century, Elsie's "payday" paragraph describes what women in similar situations have long experienced: their work receives less monetary compensation than that of their male counterparts. Setting Riddick's calculations beside Collier's observations and comparing them with Gentileschi's argument enables us to analyze the relationship of women to work and education over several centuries and to demonstrate the persistence of women in responding to restrictions and reconfiguring boundaries.

Many women have long recognized the gap between the distorted beliefs about their capabilities for education and work and the actual experiences they have had as women who labor and learn. Our selections suggest the vast range of strategies women have employed to gain control over what they learn and do. The women we read here are attempting to increase their knowledge, through their work and through their education, for they see such processes as one way in which to transform their lives.

DOMITILA BARRIOS DE CHUNGARA *(1937–)*

"I Had to Combine Everything"

See also **Vision and Transformation**

Domitila Barrios de Chungara was born in a tin-mining district of Bolivia. She describes her Indian father as having been "educated first in the countryside and then in the mines" (48), meaning that, in both places, he learned the necessity for political resistance. By the time she was three he had been blacklisted by the mining companies for union organizing and revolutionary activities and "deported" to Pulacayo, the Andean village where she grew up in extreme poverty. This experience taught her the same lessons her father had learned. Obtaining a formal academic education was more difficult. The struggles she describes in the excerpt below continue to be typical for girls all over the world; the report of the 1995 UN Fourth World Conference on Women in Beijing (see **Vision and Transformation**) cites pressure to work in the home, instead of going to school, as the major impediment to girls' education. Barrios de Chungara's story shows how complicated this pressure—both direct and indirect, external and psychological—can be.

In 1957 Barrios de Chungara married and moved to Siglo XX, the mining village where she was living in a two-room house with her husband and seven children at the time these excerpts were written. Here, in 1961, in response to their total deprivation of food, medicine, healthcare, and three months' wages, she and the other miners' wives formed the Housewives' Committee. With this began the relentless political work that shaped Barrios de Chungara's life for the next decades: work for which she was harassed, imprisoned, tortured, and terrorized by threats to her children.

Some background is required to understand the magnitude of the struggle in which she was engaged. In 1952 the Bolivian Revolution brought about limited land reform and universal suffrage—but also a number of repressive measures directed against miners by U.S. and West German investors (68n). Bolivian unions nevertheless remained strong until the mining industry collapsed in 1985. Much of their strength, as Barrios de Chungara's autobiography makes clear, came from the aggressive work of the miners' wives' committees, which "played a decisive role" in political resistance to the military dictatorship that had taken power in 1964 (Küppers 16).

Although Barrios de Chungara obtained some basic skills in the school she describes below, her education came, for the most part, from her work in this resistance—work that included analyzing, together with other activists, the reasons for their intolerable living conditions. She learned also from reading and researching those intellectuals who were able to share their ideas effectively; she studied Marxist analysis under the direction of a tutor who sent her books and marked passages with questions and comments specifically for her.

A number of episodes in *Let Me Speak* picture Barrios de Chungara using this knowledge to hold her ground during intimidating confrontations with more formally educated people. At one meeting, for example, she demolished a government commissioner's lecture with a scathing speech from the floor, beginning with an attack on him for "reading from your book and putting your numbers on the blackboard." Having been laughingly invited to give a woman's perspective, she took up the challenge: "right from the start we're going to tell you, señor, that we don't live off of numbers. We live from reality." Then, refuting his charge of "anti-military psychosis" and translating it into ordinary language, she called his attention to "what the people know": a long, terse list of facts and incidents that contradicted his arguments. At the end of her tirade she asked the government representatives to respond. "But none of them wanted to" (187–190).

ECD

FROM *LET ME SPEAK! TESTIMONY OF DOMITILA, A WOMAN OF THE BOLIVIAN MINES*[§]

Well, in 1954 it was hard for me to return to school after the vacation, because we had a house that was just a little room where we didn't even have a yard and we didn't have anyplace to leave the kids or anyone to leave them with. So we talked with the principal of the school and he gave me permission to take my little sisters with me. Classes were in the afternoon and in the morning. And I had to combine everything: house and school. So I'd carry the littlest one and the other one hung onto my hand, and Marina carried the bottles, and my sister, the other little one, carried the notebooks. And that's how all of us would go to school. In a corner we had a little crate where we'd leave the baby while we studied. When she cried, we'd give her her bottle. And my other little sisters wandered around from bench to bench. I'd get out of school, I had to carry the baby, we'd go home and I had to cook, wash, iron, take care of the kids. All that seemed very hard to me. I wanted so badly to play! And there were so many other things I wanted to do, like any other little girl.

Two years later, the teacher wouldn't let me take my sisters because they made too much noise. My father couldn't pay for a maid, since his wage wasn't enough for the food and clothing we needed. For example, at home I always went barefoot; I only used my shoes to go to school. And there were so many things I had to do and it was so cold in Pulacayo that my hands would split open and a lot of blood would come out of my hands and feet. My mouth too, my lips would crack. And my face would also bleed. That's because we didn't have enough warm clothing.

Well, since the teacher had laid down the law, I began to go to school alone. I'd lock up the house and the kids had to stay in the street, because the house was dark. It didn't have a window, and they were terrified if I locked them in. It was like a jail, with just one door.

---

§ Reprinted from *Let Me Speak! Testimony Of Domitila, A Woman of the Bolivian Mines,* by Domitila Barrios de Chungara with Moema Viezzer. Translated by Victoria Ortiz. Copyright © 1978 by Monthly Review Press. Reprinted by permission of Monthly Review Press. Material excerpted from pages 53–57 and 35–36.

And there wasn't any place to leave the kids, because at that time we lived in a neighborhood where there weren't any families. Only single men lived there.

Then my father told me to leave school, because I already knew how to read and I could learn other things by reading on my own. But I didn't obey him and I continued going to my classes.

Then one day the little one ate carbide ashes that were in the garbage pail, the carbide that's used to light the lamps. They'd thrown food on top of the ashes and my little sister, who I think was hungry, went to eat out of the can. She got a terrible intestinal infection and then she died. She was three years old.

I felt guilty about my little sister's death and I was very, very depressed. And even my father would say that it happened because I hadn't wanted to stay home with the kids. I'd brought up that sister since she was born, so her death made me suffer a lot.

From then on I began to take much more care of my little sisters. Much more. When it was very cold and we didn't have anything to cover ourselves with, I'd grab my father's old rags and cover them with those, I'd wrap up their feet, their bellies. I'd carry them, try to entertain them. I devoted myself completely to the girls. . . .

In the sixth grade I had a great teacher who knew how to understand me. He was a pretty strict teacher and on the first day that I didn't bring in all the supplies, he punished me very severely. One day he pulled me by the hair, slapped me, and, in the end, threw me out of school. I had to go home, crying. But the next day I went back, and through the window I watched what the kids were doing.

At one point the teacher called me:

"I suppose you haven't brought your supplies," he said.

I couldn't answer and started to cry.

"Come in. Go ahead, take your seat. And stay behind when school's over."

By that time one of the girls had told him that I didn't have a mother, that I cooked for my little sisters and all that.

At the end of school I stayed and then he said to me:

"Look, I want to be your friend, but you've got to tell me what's wrong. Is it true that you don't have a mother?"

"Yes, sir."

"When did she die?"

"When I was still in first grade."

"And your father, where does he work?"

"With the mine police, he's a tailor."

"Okay, what's the matter? Look, I want to help you, but you've got to be honest. What's the matter?"

I didn't want to talk, because I thought he was going to call my father in, like some teachers did when they were angry. And I didn't want him called in, because that's what the deal had been with him: I wasn't supposed to bother him or ask him for anything. But the teacher asked me more questions and then I told him everything. I also told him that I could do my homework, but that I didn't have notebooks, because we were very poor and my daddy couldn't buy them, and that years ago my father had wanted to take me out of school because he couldn't pay for it anymore. And that with a lot of sacrifice and effort I'd been able to get to the sixth grade. But it wasn't because my father didn't want to, it was because he couldn't. Because, in spite of all the belief there was in Pulacayo that a woman shouldn't be taught to read, my father always wanted us to know at least how to do that.

It's true, my father was always concerned about our education. When my mother died, people would look at us and say: "Oh, the poor little things, five women, not one man . . . what good are they? They'd be better off dead." But my daddy would say proudly: "No, let my girls alone, they're going to live." And when people tried to make us feel bad because we were women and weren't much good for anything, he'd tell us that all women had the same rights as men. And he'd say that we could do the same things men do. He always raised us with those ideas. Yes, it was a very special discipline. And all that was very positive in terms of our future. So that's why we never considered ourselves useless women.

The teacher understood all that, because I told him about it. And we made a deal that I'd ask him for all the school supplies I needed. And from that day on we got on very well. And the teacher would give me and my little sisters all the supplies we needed. And that's how I was able to finish my last year in school, in 1952. . . .

But in spite of everything we do, there's still the idea that women don't work, because they don't contribute economically to the home, that only the husband works because he gets a wage. We've often come across that difficulty.

One day I got the idea of making a chart. We put as an example the price of washing clothes per dozen pieces and we figured out how many dozens of items we washed a month. Then the cook's wage, the babysitter's, the servant's. We figured out everything that we miners' wives do every day. Adding it all up, the wage needed to pay us for what we do in the home, compared to the wages of a cook, a washerwoman, a babysitter, a servant, was much higher than what the men earned in the mine for a month. So that way we made our compañeros understand that we really work, and even more than they do in a certain sense. And that we even contribute more to the household with what we save. So, even though the state doesn't recognize what we do in the home, the country benefits from it, because we don't receive a single penny for this work.

And as long as we continue in the present system, things will always be like this. That's why I think it's so important for us revolutionaries to win that first battle in the home. And the first battle to be won is to let the woman, the man, the children participate in the struggle of the working class, so that the home can become a stronghold that the enemy can't overcome. Because if you have the enemy inside your own house, then it's just one more weapon that our common enemy can use toward a dangerous end. That's why it's really necessary that we have very clear ideas about the whole situation and that we throw out forever that bourgeois idea that the woman should stay home and not get involved in other things, in union or political matters, for example. Because, even if she's only at home, she's part of the whole system of exploitation that her compañero lives in anyway, working in the mine or in the factory or wherever—isn't that true? . . .

WORKS CONSULTED

Barrios de Chungara, Domitila. *Let Me Speak! Testimony of Domitila, a Woman of the Bolivian Mines.* With Moema Viezzer. Trans. Victoria Ortiz. New York: Monthly Review, 1978.

Küppers, Gaby, ed. *Compañeras: Voices from the Latin American Women's Movement.* London: Latin American Bureau, 1994.

ATUKURI MOLLA *(early 16th century)*

"I Am No Scholar"

Atukuri Molla, a sixteenth-century Indian woman from the potter caste, wrote a new version of the *Ramayana,* one of the major epic poems of the Hindu faith. Her achievement is extraordinary on several counts. Women, particularly women outside the brahmin caste, rarely wrote. Furthermore, Atukuri Molla wrote in Telugu, not classical Sanskrit, a fact that made her version of this popular epic more widely available. Finally, legend says that she accomplished the work in a mere few days (Tharu and Lalita 95). We include her here in the section on work and education to illustrate the fact that, in all cultural traditions, some women find ways to participate in the creation of knowledge and, when they do, they often do so in distinctive ways (Morgan 302).

Our information on Atukuri Molla's life is scant. Along with her father, to whom she pays tribute in the poem, she was a member of the Virasaivas movement, one of the many religious reform movements called bhakti, or "devotion" movements, that arose in medieval India. According to Susie Tharu and K. Lalita, such movements were led by artisan groups resisting the domination of the upper classes. These resistance groups encouraged participation in ritual regardless of caste or sex, wrote in regional languages to maximize their accessibility to many people, and used everyday imagery. The poetry from these movements circulated for hundreds of years before being written down, and new oral and written versions appeared continuously. While the political origins and impact of the bhakti poets are a matter of debate among contemporary scholars, there is little question that many of them were female. The movements opened space for women to combine their learning with their religious vocation, but their unorthodox views sparked retaliation (56–61).

Oral tradition reports that Atukuri Molla was a rebel, a woman whose mother died early and who was very close to her father. Atukuri is her parental family name and suggests that she did not marry. She dedicated her epic to the god Rama, rather than to a king or other powerful person as was customary. She "also seems to have been consciously arguing for a new poetic diction that would appeal to the immediacy of the senses as much as to the learning of scholars" (Tharu and Lalita 95). In the excerpt we include here, she follows the convention of diminishing her own abilities (adhered to by men as well as women but often more pronounced among women writers), yet goes on to produce a much-acclaimed work. Her rhetorical self-deprecation, echoed by many women writers in many places, represents one avenue by which women justified transgressing boundaries, a subject we take up at length in the third section of this anthology.

JFO

FROM *MOLLA RAMAYANAM*[§]

I am no scholar
distinguishing the loanwords
from the native stock.
I know no rules of combination
no large vocabulary.

I am no expert
in composition and illocution,
semantics and style.

Nor do I know
phonetics, case relations,
roots of verbs and figures of speech,
meter and prosody, either.

Untrained though,
in composing poems and epics
in mastering lexicons and rules
I do write poems
by the grace of the famous Lord
Sri Kantha Malles.

WORKS CONSULTED

Morgan, Robin, ed. *Sisterhood Is Global: The International Women's Movement Anthology.* New York: Anchor Press, 1984.

Tharu, Susie, and K. Lalita, eds. *Women Writing in India: 600 B.C. to the Early Twentieth Century.* Vol. 1. New York: Feminist Press at CUNY, 1991.

[§] Atukuri Molla. From *Molla Ramayanam,* translated by B. V. L. Narayanarow. Reprinted by permission of The Feminist Press at the City University of New York, from *Women Writing in India: Volume I: 600 B.C. to the Early Twentieth Century,* edited by Susie Tharu and K. Lalita. Copyright © 1991 by Susie Tharu and K. Lalita. Material excerpted from pages 96–97.

HIPPARCHIA *(3rd century BCE)*

"My Wisdom Is Better"

This excerpt was written by Diogenes Laertius, a historian who wrote the multi-volume *Lives and Opinions of Eminent Philosophers* during the late 3rd century CE. Laertius preserved the ideas, beliefs, biographies and personal documents (such as wills) of the most famous Athenian philosophers of the Classical (411 to early 280s BCE) and Hellenistic (270 to 30 BCE) periods. Thus it is significant that he included the story of Hipparchia in his larger account of the intellectual milieu of Athens from the fifth to the third century—the "golden age" of Athenian philosophy. Laertius' account emphasizes the rarity of Hipparchia's actions, and indicates how integral to the philosophical thought of this period was the concern with women and gender relations.

Hipparchia lived six centuries before Laertius wrote his account of her choice to become a philosopher. Of aristocratic birth, Hipparchia married Crates, a member of the Cynic philosophical school, despite her parents' disapproval. In the Hellenistic period the Cynic and Epicurean schools were unusual in their deviation from the prevailing conservative views on women's roles and marriage inherited from Plato and Aristotle, the dominant thinkers of the Classical period. Epicurus admitted women into his school on the same terms as men, and both schools argued that the fulfillment and happiness of the individual were far more important than the well-being of the family and state (Pomeroy 131–137). They generally discouraged marriage, but accepted it if both the man and woman were in mutual agreement. As proponents of Cynic beliefs, Hipparchia and Crates had a relationship that diverged significantly from the sexual conventions associated with upholding the Athenian family and state.

Before the age of thirty, male Athenian citizens typically engaged in three general categories of sexual relationships: heterosexual relations with *hetairai,* prostitutes, and slaves; homosexual unions between an older teacher and a younger pupil; and marriage to a respectable female citizen. These categories embodied the emotional division of labor in ancient Athenian society, and provided for the social, intellectual, and sexual needs of its most favored members—male citizens (Just 143).

The class of prostitutes known as *hetairai* denoted a higher class of intellectually and artistically accomplished women who would serve men as pleasant and entertaining companions at parties and gatherings, as well as provide sexual services. It was thus only disreputable women who could gain access to the male realm of intellectual gatherings and discussions. The ideal homosexual relationship was between a mentor and a pupil; the mentor, often older by at least five to ten years, assumed the role of moral and intellectual advisor, as well as active sexual partner, while the younger man (likely in his mid- to late teens) emulated the older, admired his wisdom, and learned from it. Built into the erotic relationship was a commonality of interests and ideals into which the pupil was being initiated. By contrast, a respectable wife filled a well-defined role as the producer of a legitimate heir for her husband; (both father and mother had to be citizens for a child to be an Athenian citizen). The wife was not expected to provide either sexual pleasure or social and intellectual companionship—indicated by the fact that, at her first marriage, an Athenian wife was usually around the age of fourteen and her husband thirty (Just 149–152).

In a fascinating rejection of these divisions, Hipparchia drew freely upon the first two dominant models in her relationship with Crates—the educated prostitute and the younger, homosexual student who emulated the older teacher. This crossing of boundaries is made explicit in our first selection that describes how Theodorus pulls off Hipparchia's cloak (an action that symbolically consigns her to a brothel). This gesture invokes the dominant belief among Athenians that any woman present at a gathering of men, eating, drinking, or talking amongst them, was a prostitute (Just 347–348). In the second selection we present, Hipparchia defends her own lifestyle by claiming that she has what she needs to be a philosopher—indeed, that her wisdom is her superior talent. Through his detailed descriptions of Hipparchia's interactions with male philosophers, Laertius captures the social and intellectual tensions generated between the traditional mores and philosophical ideals of gender in classical Athens.

KKF

FROM *LIVES AND OPINIONS OF EMINENT PHILOSOPHERS* BY DIOGENES LAERTIUS [§]

A female philosopher.

Hipparchia fell in love with both Crates' discourses and his way of life. She paid no attention to any of her suitors, their money, their high birth or their good looks. To her Crates was everything. And in fact she threatened her parents that she would kill herself, if they didn't let her marry him. Her parents begged Crates to dissuade her. He did everything he could, but finally when he couldn't persuade her, he stood up and took off his clothes in front of her and said: 'This is your bridegroom; these are his possessions; plan accordingly!' He didn't think she would be able to be his partner unless she could share in the same pursuits.

But the girl chose him. She adopted the same dress and went about with him; she made love to him in public; she went to dinner parties with him. Once, when she went to a dinner party at Lysimachus' house, she put down Theodorus called the Atheist by using the following trick of logic: if an action could not be called wrong when done by Theodorus it could not be called wrong when done by Hipparchia. Therefore, if Theodorus does nothing wrong when he hits himself, Hipparchia does nothing wrong if she hits Theodorus. He had no defense against her logic, and started to pull off her cloak.

[§] Reprinted from *Women's Life in Greece and Rome: A Source Book in Translation,* by Mary R. Lefkowitz and Maureen B. Fant. Copyright © 1992 by Johns Hopkins University Press. Reprinted by permission of Johns Hopkins University Press. Material excerpted from pages 167–168.

But Hipparchia did not get upset or excited as other women would. Then when he said to her: 'Here I am, Agave, who left behind my shuttles beside my loom.'[1] 'Indeed it is I,' said Hipparchia: 'Theodorus—you don't think that I have arranged my life so badly, do you, if I have used the time I would have wasted on weaving for my education?' These and many other stories are told about the woman philosopher.

Epigram on Hipparchia

I, Hipparchia, have no use for the works of deep-robed women; I have chosen the Cynics' virile life. I don't need capes with brooches or deep-soled slippers; I don't like glossy nets for my hair. My wallet is my staff's traveling companion, and the double cloak that goes with them, the cover for my bed on the ground. I'm much stronger than Atalanta from Maenalus, because my wisdom is better than racing over the mountain.

NOTE

[1] Agave's boast to her father in Euripides, Bacchae 1326, when she returns from the hunt, thinking she has caught a lion; but the head she is carrying turns out to be her son's [Lefkowitz and Fant].

WORKS CONSULTED

Just, Roger. *Women in Athenian Law and Life.* London: Routledge, 1989.

Pomeroy, Sarah B. *Goddesses, Whores, Wives, and Slaves: Women in Classical Antiquity.* New York: Schocken, 1975.

LAURA CERETA *(1469–1499)*

"Wearied by Your Carping"

One of the first challenges that historians of women put to their profession was the question of periodization: did the conventional ways of defining historical periods (using the dates of discoveries, military events, and the life and death of kings and popes) hold the same explanatory power when women were written into history? The answer was a resounding no. A clear example came from the European Renaissance, the period between 1300 and 1600 when texts from the classical world were rediscovered. The Renaissance has been characterized as a period of explosive learning for the scholar who roved easily and knowledgeably among all the arts and sciences. The contemporary term "renaissance man," rooted in this period of history, still refers to a well-rounded person. And "renaissance woman"? What that term entailed is less clear. The research of some of those in the first generation of feminist historians focused on this question. From this corpus of scholarly texts, we have learned that most women were excluded from the new opportunities for learning, although a few elite women named the exclusion and resisted the new ideas about gender that were beginning to circulate.[1] Laura Cereta is an example of this kind of resistance.

Laura Cereta was born of a noble Italian family and learned to write in Latin and Greek at an early age. Her brief, and childless, marriage lasted less than two years because of the death of her husband. In 1488, she compiled her letters, and thus left none of her writing from the last eleven years of her life. Her letters cover her life with both her family and her husband, her interests in mathematics, history, moral philosophy, and ideas about religion. Five letters are about the relationship between learning and gender. She writes in the tradition of an intellectual humanist, in epistles that were often intended for public reading (Rabil 24). Historians have located the works of some thirty women who wrote in Europe during this period. Engaging in and initiating debates, these women wrote to one another, as well as to the leading male scholarly figures and theologians of their time.

In the period following her husband's death, Cereta immersed herself even more deeply in her literary studies. "These efforts, in turn, brought forth critics, both male and female, who jealous of her accomplishments, belittled her work. Two principal charges were brought against her: that a woman could not be learned and that her father had written her letters for her. She turned against her critics with a ferocity at least equal to theirs" (King and Rabil 81). In our selection here, she makes a distinctive argument: singling out women for praise is another means of marginalizing them. She goes on to suggest that since women have been conditioned to value their bodies over their minds, "they need to be encouraged rather than opposed or falsely praised" (Rabil 14).

JFO

FROM "LETTER TO BIBULUS SEMPRONIUS"§[2]

My ears are wearied by your carping. You brashly and publicly not merely wonder but indeed lament that I am said to possess as fine a mind as nature ever bestowed upon the most learned man. You seem to think that so learned a woman has scarcely before been seen in the world. You are wrong on both counts, Sempronius, and have clearly strayed from the path of truth and disseminate falsehood. I agree that you should be grieved; indeed, you should be ashamed, for you have ceased to be a living man, but have become an animated stone; having rejected the studies which make men wise, you rot in torpid leisure. Not nature but your own soul has betrayed you, deserting virtue for the easy path of sin.

You pretend to admire me as a female prodigy, but there lurks sugared deceit in your adulation. You wait perpetually in ambush to entrap my lovely sex, and overcome by your hatred seek to trample me underfoot and dash me to the earth. It is a crafty ploy, but only a low and vulgar mind would think to halt Medusa with honey.[3] You would better have crept up on a mole than on a wolf. For a mole with its dark vision can see nothing around it, while a wolf's eyes glow in the dark. For the wise person sees by [force of] mind, and anticipating what lies ahead, proceeds by the light of reason. For by foreknowledge the thinker scatters with knowing feet the evils which litter her path.

I would have been silent, believe me, if that savage old enmity of yours had attacked me alone. For the light of Phoebus cannot be befouled even in the mud.[4] But I cannot tolerate your having attacked my entire sex. For this reason my thirsty soul seeks revenge, my sleeping pen is aroused to literary struggle, raging anger stirs mental passions long chained by silence. With just cause I am moved to demonstrate how great a reputation for learning and virtue women have won by their inborn excellence, manifested in every age of knowledge, the [purveyor] of honor. Certain, indeed, and legitimate is our possession of this inheritance, come to us from a long eternity of ages past. . . .

Only the question of the rarity of outstanding women remains to be addressed. The explanation is clear: women have been able by nature to be exceptional, but have chosen lesser goals. For some women are concerned with parting their hair correctly, adorning themselves with lovely dresses, or decorating their fingers with pearls and other gems. Others delight in mouthing carefully composed phrases, indulging in dancing, or managing spoiled puppies. Still others wish to gaze at lavish banquet tables, to rest in sleep, or, standing at mirrors, to smear their lovely faces. But those in whom a deeper integrity yearns for virtue, restrain from the start their youthful souls, reflect on higher things, harden the body with sobriety and trials, and curb their tongues, open their ears, compose their thoughts in wakeful hours, their minds in contemplation, to letters bonded to righteousness. For knowledge is not given as a gift, but [is gained] with diligence. The free mind, not shirking effort, always soars zealously toward the good, and the desire to know grows ever more

§ Reprinted from *Her Immaculate Hand: Selected Works By and About the Women Humanists of Quattrocento Italy*, edited by Margaret L. King and Albert Rabil, Jr. Copyright ©1983 by the Center for Medieval and Early Renaissance Studies at the State University of New York at Binghamton. Reprinted by permission of the Center for Medieval and Early Renaissance Studies. Material excerpted from pages 81–84.

wide and deep. It is because of no special holiness, therefore, that we [women] are rewarded by God the Giver with the gift of exceptional talent. Nature has generously lavished its gifts upon all people, opening to all the doors of choice through which reason sends envoys to the will, from which they learn and convey its desires. The will must choose to exercise the gift of reason.

[But] where we [women] should be forceful we are [too often] devious; where we should be confident we are insecure. [Even worse], we are content with our condition. But you, a foolish and angry dog, have gone to earth as though frightened by wolves. Victory does not come to those who take flight. Nor does he remain safe who makes peace with the enemy; rather, when pressed, he should arm himself all the more with weapons and courage. How nauseating to see strong men pursue a weakling at bay. Hold on! Does my name alone terrify you? As I am not a barbarian in intellect and do not fight like one, what fear drives you? You flee in vain, for traps craftily-laid rout you out of every hiding place. Do you think that by hiding, a deserter [from the field of battle], you can remain undiscovered? A penitent, do you seek the only path of salvation in flight? [If you do] you should be ashamed.

I have been praised too much; showing your contempt for women, you pretend that I alone am admirable because of the good fortune of my intellect. But I, compared to other women who have won splendid renown, am but a little mousling. You disguise your envy in dissimulation, but cloak yourself in apologetic words in vain. The lie buried, the truth, dear to God, always emerges. You stumble half-blind with envy on a wrongful path that leads you from your manhood, from your duty, from God. Who, do you think, will be surprised, Bibulus, if the stricken heart of an angry girl, whom your mindless scorn has painfully wounded, will after this more violently assault your bitter words? Do you suppose, O most contemptible man on earth, that I think myself sprung [like Athena] from the head of Jove? I am a school girl, possessed of the sleeping embers of an ordinary mind. Indeed I am too hurt, and my mind, offended, too swayed by passions, sighs, tormenting itself, conscious of the obligation to defend my sex. For absolutely everything—that which is within us and that which is without—is made weak by association with my sex.

I, therefore, who have always prized virtue, having put my private concerns aside, will polish and weary my pen against chatterboxes swelled with false glory. Trained in the arts, I shall block the paths of ambush. And I shall endeavor, by avenging arms, to sweep away the abusive infamies of noisemakers with which some disreputable and impudent men furiously, violently, and nastily rave against a woman and a republic worthy of reverence. January 13 [1488]

NOTES

[1] For a discussion of these issues see DuBois (1985) and Schiebinger (1989).

[2] Scholars have been unable to identify Bibulus Sempronius and suggest that the name, which means "drunkard," is probably Cereta's invention (King and Rabil 81). [Eds.]

[3] Literally the text reads: "blind Medusa by dropping oil [into her eyes]." [King and Rabil]

[4] Phoebus Apollo, i.e., the Sun. [King and Rabil]

WORKS CONSULTED

DuBois, Ellen C. et al. *Feminist Scholarship: Kindling in the Groves of Academe.* Urbana: U of Illinois P, 1985.

King, Margaret L., and Albert Rabil, Jr., eds. *Her Immaculate Hand: Selected Works By and About the Women Humanists of Quattrocento Italy.* Binghamton: Medieval and Renaissance Texts and Studies, 1983.

Rabil, Albert, Jr. *Laura Cereta: Quattrocento Humanist.* Binghamton: Center for Medieval and Renaissance Texts and Studies, 1981.

Schiebinger, Londa. *The Mind Has No Sex? Women in the Origins of Modern Science.* Cambridge: Harvard UP, 1989.

SEI SHŌNAGON *(c. 966–?)*

"Women Serving in the Palace"

See also **Sexuality, Spirituality, and Power**

In this passage from *The Pillow Book,* Sei Shōnagon develops an account of the way in which gender functions to structure courtly rituals and practices. Initially, she depicts the life of a Court lady as one of relative freedom. Her dismissal of women who remain at home with their husbands is an affirmation of the relative social power available to women at Court—a kind of power perhaps only too scarce in less rarefied milieux. In this context, the statement, "When I make myself imagine what it is like to be one of those women who live at home, faithfully serving their husbands . . . I am filled with scorn" becomes both an expression of aristocratic privilege and an indication of the way in which the status of women remained linked to social class in Heian culture. Nevertheless, Sei Shōnagon sees clearly the means by which women are excluded—even at the aristocratic level—from opportunities for social advancement. While a man might better his social status through professional promotions, she explains, a woman can only "attain such honours" as a result of marriage. The social organization of gender differences serves here to restrict all women's class mobility and to limit their social options.

Sei Shōnagon wrote *The Pillow Book* as a woman who worked not only as a Court Attendant but also as a writer.[1] In fact, these two seemingly disparate roles have much in common with one another. Sei Shōnagon's performance of court duties served to perpetuate the cultural rituals of courtly society; her writing helps to construct (on a theoretical level) and to sustain (in a practical way) the aristocratic audience familiar with the way of life she describes in *The Pillow Book*. In her literary work, Sei Shōnagon refers again and again to the cultural institutions and practices which help connect her readers to one another. Similarly, her participation in the daily life of the court serves on a practical level to maintain this tradition of aristocratic display. She labors both as an observer of, and a participant in, the empress Teishi's retinue.

This excerpt from *The Pillow Book* might well be compared with the works of other women of the elite classes (such as Hildegard of Bingen) who were in many ways exempt from subservient social roles by virtue of their aristocratic status. To a contemporary audience, such writings emphasize the means by which highly ritualized societies make room for, and in some cases even facilitate, women's critique of traditional gender roles.

NM

FROM *THE PILLOW BOOK OF SEI SHŌNAGON*[§]

When I Make Myself Imagine

When I make myself imagine what it is like to be one of those women who live at home, faithfully serving their husbands—women who have not a single exciting prospect in life yet who believe that they are perfectly happy—I am filled with scorn. Often they are of quite good birth, yet have had no opportunity to find out what the world is like. I wish they could live for a while in our society, even if it should mean taking service as Attendants,[2] so that they might come to know the delights it has to offer.

I cannot bear men who believe that women serving in the Palace are bound to be frivolous and wicked. Yet I suppose their prejudice is understandable. After all, women at Court do not spend their time hiding modestly behind fans and screens, but walk about, looking openly at people they chance to meet. Yes, they see everyone face to face, not only ladies-in-waiting like themselves, but even Their Imperial Majesties (whose august names I hardly dare mention), High Court Nobles, senior courtiers, and other gentlemen of high rank. In the presence of such exalted personages the women in the Palace are all equally brazen, whether they be the maids of ladies-in-waiting, or the relations of Court ladies who have come to visit them, or house-keepers, or latrine-cleaners, or women who are of no more value than a roof-tile or a pebble. Small wonder that the young men regard them as immodest! Yet are the gentlemen themselves any less so? They are not exactly bashful when it comes to looking at the great people in the Palace. No, everyone at Court is much the same in this respect.

Women who have served in the Palace, but who later get married and live at home, are called Madam and receive the most respectful treatment. To be sure, people often consider that these women, who have displayed their faces to all and sundry during their years at Court, are lacking in feminine grace. How proud they must be, nevertheless, when they are styled Assistant Attendants, or summoned to the Palace for occasional duty, or ordered to serve as Imperial envoys during the Kamo Festival! Even those who stay at home lose nothing by having served at Court. In fact they make very good wives. For example, if they are married to a provincial governor and their daughter is chosen to take part in the Gosechi[3] dances, they do not have to disgrace themselves by acting like provincials and asking other people about procedure. They themselves are well versed in the formalities, which is just as it should be.

People Who Look Pleased with Themselves

. . . High office is, after all, a most splendid thing. A man who holds the Fifth Rank or who serves as Gentleman-in-Waiting is liable to be despised; but when this same man becomes a Major Counsellor, Great Minister, or the like, one is overawed by him and feels that nothing in the world could be as impressive. Of course even a provincial governor has a position that should impress one; for after serving in several provinces, he may be ap-

---

[§] Reprinted by permission of Oxford University Press from *The Pillow Book of Sei Shōnagon*, by Sei Shōnagon. Ivan Morris, translator and editor. Copyright © 1967 by Ivan Morris. Published 1967 by Oxford University Press (Penguin edition 1971). Material excerpted from pages 39–40 and 192–193 in the Penguin edition.

pointed Senior Assistant Governor-General and promoted to the Fourth Rank, and when this happens the High Court Nobles themselves appear to regard him with respect.

After all, women really have the worse time of it. There are, to be sure, cases where the nurse of an Emperor is appointed Assistant Attendant or given the Third Rank and thus acquires great dignity. Yet it does her little good since she is already an old woman. Besides, how many women ever attain such honours? Those who are reasonably well born consider themselves lucky if they can marry a governor and go down to the provinces. Of course it does sometimes happen that the daughter of a commoner becomes the principal consort of a High Court Noble and that the daughter of a High Court Noble becomes an Empress.[4] Yet even this is not as splendid as when a man rises by means of promotions. How pleased such a man looks with himself! . . .

NOTES

[1] We would like to note that *The Pillow Book* was not written for publication, although its author does seem to have expected that her work would circulate informally (Keene 420–421, Konishi 384–386). Sei Shōnagon did use her writing to reflect on aristocratic social practices, however, and this activity was an important part of her daily routine at court.

[2] Attendant: the following three ranks of women officials served in the Naishi no Tsukasa (Palace Attendants' Office): (i) two Chief Attendants, (ii) four Assistant Attendants, (iii) four Attendants. Under them came one hundred women. In Shōnagon's time the two top posts were occupied by concubines of the Emperor; in the present passage she refers to the third category of official. [Morris]

[3] Gosechi: Court Dances performed in the Eleventh Month by young girls of good family. Of the four girls who participated in the dances, three were the daughters of High Court Nobles and one (as in the present passage) the daughter of a provincial governor. [Morris]

[4] Empresses were usually chosen from the Imperial family itself or from among the daughters of the Chancellor, the Regent, or one of the Great Ministers. When Shōnagon writes about a High Court Noble's daughter who has been appointed to the rank of Empress, she may be thinking of Fujiwara no Takeko, the daughter of Naritoki, who was appointed First Empress to Emperor Sanjō though her father during his lifetime never advanced beyond the rank of Major Counsellor. [Morris]

WORKS CONSULTED

Keene, Donald. *Seeds in the Heart: Japanese Literature from Earliest Times to the Late Sixteenth Century.* New York: Holt, 1993.

Konishi, Jin'ichi. *A History of Japanese Literature.* Vol. 2. Trans. Aileen Gatten and Nicholas Teele. Princeton: Princeton UP, 1986.

Morris, Ivan. Introduction. *The Pillow Book of Sei Shōnagon.* By Sei Shōnagon. Trans. and ed. Ivan Morris. Baltimore, MD: Penguin, 1971.

MARY COLLIER *(c. 1690–c. 1762)*

"The Constant Action of Our Lab'ring Hands"

Mary Collier, a washerwoman and agricultural laborer, wrote her poem *The Woman's Labour* during a period when it was not unusual for working-class women in England literally to starve to death. Merchant and manufacturing capitalists had begun to rise to economic and political power, and, by their expansion, had increased the separation of public and private spheres. Many women found themselves unable to engage in traditional forms of work, for example, domestic spinning. In addition, the kind of labor that working-class women did perform (Collier gives the examples of harvesting and char, or domestic servant, work), became increasingly devalued and underpaid. *The Woman's Labour* provides a striking description of the unrelenting round of labor that working-class women faced daily. "But to rehearse all Labour is in vain/" she comments, "Of which we very justly might complain:/For us, you see, but little Rest is found;/Our toil increases as the Year runs round." In addition, Collier documents a refusal on the part of upper-class men and women to acknowledge laboring women's work as productive and socially important.

In *The Woman's Labour,* Collier depicts the double and even triple workloads that define the quality of working-class women's existence. According to Collier, not only must these women labor all day in their various occupations (as men do), but they come home to incessant "domestick Toils": husband and children to be fed and tended to, clothing to be mended, dishes to be done, even domestic animals to be cared for. As Collier perceptively remarks, "Our Toil and Labour's daily so extreme,/That we have hardly ever Time to Dream." Here, Collier makes the link between her existence as a laboring woman and her vocation as a poet. She is acutely aware that, for working-class women, access to some form of education (relatively rare) in no way guarantees access to leisure time. For Collier, her writing as well as her daily life are defined not only by her gender but by the way in which her status as a woman of the working class restricts her social and literary options. In this poem, she describes and resists both gender and class-based forms of discrimination and oppression.

Although Collier worked as a washerwoman until the age of 63 (and ran a farmhouse until "the infirmities of Age" drove her to retire), her situation was somewhat exceptional in light of the fact that she neither married nor had children. She herself attributes her ability to engage in the writing of poetry to her relative abundance of leisure time. "Oft have I thought as on my Bed I lay," she begins *The Woman's Labour,* "Eas'd from the tiresome Labours of the Day." She was taught to read by her parents, although she did not attend school, and became the first known working-class woman in England to publish literary work. Nevertheless, her writing never provided her the relief from the burden of wage labor for which she had hoped.

The Woman's Labour, published in 1739, is perhaps her best-known work; it is a response to a poem by the author Stephen Duck, also of working-class origins, which belittles the nature of the work performed by female agricultural laborers. It is noteworthy that, while Duck went on to enjoy aristocratic patronage and some literary standing as a poet, Collier never achieved this kind of status.

Finally, *The Woman's Labour* reminds modern readers of the way in which notions of gender and class serve to define each other (the excerpt by Jo Carrillo in **Representing Women** speaks eloquently of the role played by race in this nexus). Carrying the triple burdens of wage labor, child-care, and housework, working-class women are shut out from what is perceived as real, material production (the socially significant work of men), as well as from so-called true, literary work. Collier resists these limitations. She manipulates a conventional poetic form (the georgic) in her depiction of women's "Toil" and argues convincingly for the real social importance of working-class daily work.

NM

FROM *THE WOMAN'S LABOUR*[§]

. . . No Learning ever was bestow'd on me;
My Life was always spent in Drudgery:
And not alone; alas! with Grief I find,
It is the Portion of poor Woman-kind.
Oft have I thought as on my Bed I lay,
Eas'd from the tiresome Labours of the Day,
Our first Extraction from a Mass refin'd,
Could never be for Slavery design'd;
Till Time and Custom by Degrees destroy'd
That happy State our Sex at first enjoy'd.
When Men had us'd their utmost Care and Toil,
Their Recompense was but a Female Smile;
When they by Arts or Arms were render'd Great,
They laid their Trophies at a Woman's Feet;
They, in those Days, unto our Sex did bring
Their Hearts, their All, a Free-will Offering;
And as from us their Being they derive,
They back again should all due Homage give . . .

WHEN Ev'ning does approach, we homeward hi
And our domestick Toils incessant ply:
Against your coming Home prepare to get

[§] Reprinted from *First Feminists: British Women Writers 1578–1799*. Edited by Moira Ferguson. Copyright ©1985 by Indiana University Press. Reprinted by permission of Indiana University Press. Material excerpted from pages 258–263.

Our Work all done, Our House in order set;
Bacon and Dumpling in the Pot we boil,
Our Beds we make, our Swine we feed the while;
Then wait at Door to see you coming Home,
And set the Table out against you come:
Early next Morning we on you attend,
Our Children dress and feed, their Cloaths we mend;
And in the Field our daily Task renew;
Soon as the rising Sun has dry'd the dew.

WHEN Harvest comes, into the Field we go,
And help to reap the Wheat as well as you;
Or else we go the Ears of Corn to glean;
No Labour scorning, be it e'er so mean;
But in the Work we freely bear a Part,
And what we can, perform with all our Heart.
To get a Living we so willing are,
Our tender Babes unto the Field we bear,
And wrap them in our Cloaths to keep them warm,
While round about we gather up the Corn;
And often unto them our Course do bend,
To keep them save, that nothing them offend:
Our Children that are able bear a share,
In gleaning corn, such is our frugal Care.
When Night comes on, unto our Home we go,
Our Corn we carry, and our Infant too;
Weary indeed! but 'tis not worth our while
Once to complain, or rest at ev'ry Stile;
We must make haste, for when we home are come,
We find again our Work but just begun;
So many Things for our Attendance call,
Had we ten Hands, we could employ them all.
Our Children put to Bed, with greatest Care
We all Things for your coming home prepare:
You sup, and go to Bed without Delay,
And rest yourselves till the ensuing Day;
While we, alas! but little Sleep can have,
Because our froward Children cry and rave;
Yet, without fail, soon as Daylight doth spring,
We in the Field again our work begin,
And there, with all our Strength, our Toil renew,
Till Titan's golden Rays have dry'd the Dew;
Then home we go unto our Children dear,

Dress, feed, and bring them to the Field with care.
Were this your Case, you justly might complain
That Day or Night you are secure from Pain;
Those mighty Troubles which perplex your Mind,
(Thistles before, and Females come behind)
Would vanish soon, and quickly disappear,
Were you, like us, encumber'd thus with Care.
What you would have of us we do not know:
We oft take up the Corn that you do mow;
We cut the Peas, and always ready are
In every Work to take our proper Share;
And from the Time that Harvest doth begin,
Until the Corn be cut and carry'd in,
Our Toil and Labour's daily so extreme,
That we have hardly ever time to Dream.

THE Harvest ended, Respite none we find;
The hardest of our Toil is still behind:
Hard Labour we most chearfully pursue,
And out, abroad, a Chairing often go: . . .

WHEN bright Orion glitters in the Skies
In Winter Nights, then early we must rise;
The Weather ne'er so bad, Wind, Rain, or Snow,
Our Work appointed, we must rise and go;
While you on easy Beds may lie and sleep,
Till Light does thro' your Chamber Windows peep: . . .
But when from Wind and Weather we get in,
Briskly with Courage we our Work begin;
Heaps of fine Linnen we before us view,
Whereon to lay our Strength and Patience too;
Cambricks and Muslins which our ladies wear,
Laces and Edgings, costly, fine, and rare,
Which must be wash'd with utmost Skill and Care;
With Holland Shirts, Ruffles and Fringes too,
Fashions, which our Fore-fathers never knew.
For several Hours here we work and slave,
Before we can one Glimpse of Day-light have;
We labour hard before the Morning's past,
Because we fear the Time runs on too fast.

AT length bright Sol illuminates the Skies,
And summons drowsy Mortals to arise;

Then comes our Mistress to us without fail,
And in her Hand, perhaps, a Mug of Ale
To cheer our Hearts, and also to inform
Herself what Work is done that very Morn;
Lays her Commands upon us, that we mind
Her Linnen Well, nor leave the Dirt behind:
Nor this alone, but also to take Care
We don't her Cambricks nor her Ruffles tear;
And these most strictly does of us require,
To save her Soap, and sparing be of Fire;
Tells us her Charge is great, nay furthermore,
Her Cloaths are fewer than the Time before:
Now we drive on, resolv'd our Strength to try,
And what we can we do most willingly;
Untill with Heat and Work, 'tis often known,
Not only Sweat, but Blood runs trickling down
Our Wrists and Fingers; still our Work demands
The constant Action of our lab'ring Hands . . .

BUT to rehearse all Labour is in vain,
Of which we very justly might complain:
For us, you see, but little Rest is found;
Our Toil increases as the Year runs round . . .

So the industrious Bees do hourly strive
To bring their Loads of Honey to the Hive;
Their sordid Owners always reap the Gains,
And Poorly recompense their Toil and Pains.

WORKS CONSULTED

Ferguson, Moira, ed. *First Feminists: British Women Writers 1578–1799*. Bloomington: Indiana UP, 1985.

Greene, Richard. *Mary Leapor: A Study in Eighteenth-Century Women's Poetry*. Oxford: Clarendon Press, 1993.

Landry, Donna. *The Muses of Resistance: Labouring-Class Woman's Poetry in Britain, 1739–1796*. Cambridge: Cambridge UP, 1990.

Lonsdale, Roger, ed. *Eighteenth-Century Women Poets: An Oxford Anthology*. Oxford: Oxford UP, 1989.

MARIA CURTER *(1946–)*

"My Job Disappeared When the Wall Opened"

The euphoria felt by many Germans at the fall of the Berlin Wall in 1989 quickly yielded to a state of sobriety in both East and West Germany. The collapse of the socialist system in the German Democratic Republic (GDR) was followed by a hasty unification process in which the West German order—especially its market economy—was transposed upon the former GDR. Overnight, on October 3, 1990, East Germans became citizens of the Federal Republic of Germany (FRG). For people in the former East, this transition, often referred to as the *Wende* (turn), demanded the ability to adapt to a new system within a brief period of time. They gained new liberties, but also had to struggle with the loss of familiar structures. More than six years after the *Wende,* the people in the two parts of Germany still speak of each other as "us" and "them." Existing tensions are exacerbated by the much higher unemployment rate in the East. Women have been particularly affected by recent waves of lay-offs since they were often the first ones to be fired from their jobs. Many analysts of the current situation regard East German women as the losers of the unification. Along with job security, they lost a number of social benefits and the right to legal abortion.

Maria Curter's narrative, recorded by an American professor in 1991, illustrates the contradictory situation in which many women from the East found themselves. The inconsistencies that appear in her evaluation, both of her life in the GDR and the events after the *Wende,* wind through Curter's text and can be read as symptoms of the enormous effort required to cope with the new situation. Curter, a research biologist, gives us a sense of how crucial it is for her to keep a sense of control over her life.

Maria Curter weighs the advantages of living in the GDR against the disadvantages. Some of the benefits for women included inexpensive day care, generous financial support for the birth of children, one-year maternity leave, one day off a month for "household chores," and around twenty days a year in paid time-off to care for sick children (Dodds and Allen-Thompson 1–21). The GDR praised itself for establishing gender equality. Closer examination reveals that many of its policies reinscribed more traditional gender roles. In this excerpt, Curter uncovers some of these contradictions. While most women in the GDR were economically independent, traditional role expectations still prevailed. Many women felt they had to be self-styled superwomen, juggling the demands of work, household, and childcare (Merkel 372). In hindsight, they appreciated the job security and the availability of positions where 90% of the women were employed—as opposed to 50% in West Germany. Still, while the GDR constitutionally guaranteed a job (Gerhard 395), work did not necessarily translate into influence in other domains or positions in politics, business, or culture.

Key elements of gender inequality both in the GDR and the FRG come to light in this excerpt. Single mothers were more prevalent in East than in West Germany, but married women continued to be the norm. Curter's experiences as a single mother were also linked to a confrontation with racism on a regular basis, since her daughter's father was African. The GDR never felt obliged to address race issues, and racism directed against a small population of students and workers from foreign countries existed in many parts of society.

Maria Curter continues to struggle for a self-determined life in which she can fulfill her aspirations. By 1995, Maria Curter had written 150 job applications, but had not received a single positive answer. When she last talked to the interviewer she wondered about the possibility of a lecture tour through the U.S.; perhaps she would even sign up for a crash course in English. . . .

KV

FROM *THE WALL IN MY BACKYARD*[§]

. . . My job disappeared when the Wall opened. The entire academy of Sciences has been dissolved. So I'm now in a retraining program to learn to become an environmental consultant. With this training I could get a job in industry, whether in East or West, I don't care.

The state took a lot off your shoulders, but it demanded something in return: the right to tell you what you could do. They told us where and when we could travel, how we could invest our money—to the extent that any of us had any money to invest—and told us what we could buy. Having the state take over many things in your life meant you had to accept the other things that came along with it.

Now the citizens of the GDR have chosen the CDU[1] and along with it certain inconveniences: now they have to take care of their own taxes and insurance policies. They no longer have a secure job, they no longer have inexpensive day care, and they can't plan for the next five years. But they have the freedom to travel and to the extent that they have any money, they can invest it as they choose. I don't know what this all means. For me personally it's nothing but negative. I've lost my job, and I don't know what lies ahead.

The ideal social system has yet to be found: each one we've come up with so far has advantages and disadvantages in the GDR. I could have left if the conditions here had been intolerable. I could have married outside the GDR, for example. There were always ways to get out. But I chose to stay. I was in the Party and was even asked to attend a school for Party functionaries, but I declined. I didn't want to get involved to that extent.

The socialist ideology always espoused equality for women in all areas of their development. When I was eighteen or nineteen I took this notion very seriously, and it was valid to a certain extent. Women could go to college if they wanted and were encouraged to go

[§] Reprinted by permission of the publisher from *The Wall In My Backyard: East German Women In Transition,* edited by Dinah Dodds and Pam Allen-Thompson (Amherst: The University of Massachusetts Press, 1994), copyright © 1994 by The University of Massachusetts Press. Material excerpted from pages 121–128.

into typically male jobs, like construction. Women in fact went into engineering in large numbers. Women could work on equal footing with men and felt they could contribute equally, up to a certain point, that is. When women wanted to be more than just basic workers, things got more complicated. Then we heard such things as, "Yes, but your child gets sick so often." . . .

I was always very independent. I knew what I was capable of, and I never had to depend on anyone. That's how things were here. Women were economically independent. They never had the economic pressure to get married, and it was easy to get divorced. Men had no responsibilities after the divorce except to support their children. They didn't have to pay alimony. After the divorce men paid a certain percentage of their salary for child support, and that was the end of it.

The other side of the coin was that men took advantage of women's independence. They said, "If she's so independent, let her carry the coal up from the basement." A lot of the nice things that had to do with men's and women's roles disappeared. Women didn't get bouquets of flowers. Although lots of policies for women were very progressive, many of the attitudes remained traditional and middle class: women should really stay at home. No one admitted how widespread this attitude was. . . .

I wanted a husband and a family, but I didn't want a husband just so that I could say I had a husband who earned well. I wanted a real partner, and since I hadn't found one by the time I was twenty-five, and since my biological clock was ticking, I decided to have Peggy then. I could always continue to look for a partner. The fact that I had a child without being married was simply not an issue. I only really became aware of the difference recently when I had to fill out my income tax forms. For us, a child was a child, and it didn't matter whether the child was born to a single woman or a married one. It was only important when it came to inheritance matters. All educational opportunities were the same. As a single mother, I never felt any discrimination.

However after the *Wende,* I was one of the first to be fired from my job at the Academy, I think because I was a single woman with a child. Two other women with the same degree that I have, whose husbands earn a good salary and who have no children, were not fired, nor were two women who threatened to go to court. I am suing them to rehire me. As long as I am in my retraining program, I will continue to get my salary. So if I don't get my job back, I'll at least get a salary. I don't want to harp on this business of single women with children, but it's true that men do try to get women like me—self-confident, competent women—out of the way. Maybe it's a kind of complex. They expect single women to come flying to them, and when that doesn't happen, they have to show that they're a man. It's macho. Of course, it depends on the individual people, on what kind of work you're talking about, what level of society. I wouldn't want to generalize about it.

My daughter's father was an African. I wanted to have a child, but the relationship didn't work out. I knew I could support one child, and I already had an apartment. . . .

I sent Peggy to *Kinderkrippe*[2] and of course she went to day care. Some people thought I was a bad mother because I didn't keep her at home when she was tiny, but I was traveling a lot then, about ten days a month, not ten consecutive days, but two days here, three days there. Peggy was able to spend the night at day care and that saved me from having to go begging to friends for a favor of a night or two. She didn't have the advantage of two parents, but if I had it to do over again, I would do it exactly the same way.

Even though almost all women worked outside the home, services weren't set up to help them. There were no precooked meat dishes, for example, which you just had to heat up at home. When I finished work at 5:45 there was no time to take clothes to the laundry. It could have been centrally regulated with working women in mind. Another example which I noticed as a single woman: whenever I had to go to a government agency to take care of some small matter, the offices all closed at 6:00, and you had to get special permission from your boss to leave work early. On the other hand we had so-called household day, the paid day of leave to take care of things like this, but if you had more than one thing to take care of, you couldn't do it in a day. And then the household day was only given to married women or women with children or women older than forty. Men didn't have it unless they had to take care of a child, but the people at work didn't much like it. They said to him, "Get yourself a girlfriend; she'll get a household day."

The *Wende* has been very good. I can now make my own decisions about where to live or what job to take. If I weren't so angry about how the unification has come about I could rejoice about all the possibilities. But I didn't choose the Federal Republic; I didn't voluntarily give up my job. These things were determined for me by others, and that makes me mad. I like to make my own decisions.

NOTES

[1] CDU: the conservative ruling party in Germany. [Eds.]

[2] *Kinderkrippe:* day care facility for very young children. [Eds.]

WORKS CONSULTED

Dodds, Dinah, and Pam Allen-Thompson. Introduction. *The Wall in My Backyard: East German Women in Transition.* Ed. Dinah Dodds and Pam Allen-Thompson. Amherst: U of Massachusetts P, 1994.

Gerhard, Ute. "Die Staatlich institutionalisierte 'Lösung' der Frauenfrage: Zur Geschichte der Geschlechterverhältnisse in der DDR." *Sozialgeschichte der DDR.* Ed. Hartnut Kaelble, Järgen Kocka, and Hartmut Zwahr. Stuttgart: Klett-Cotta, 1994.

Merkel, Ina. "Leitbilder und Lebensweisen von Frauen in der DDR." *Sozialgeschichte der DDR.* Hartmut Kaelble, Järgen Kocka and Hartmut Zwahr, eds. Stuttgart: Klett-Cotta, 1994.

ROKEYA SAKHAWAT HOSSAIN *(1880–1932)*

The Purdah Bus

Rokeya Sakhawat Hossain was born in 1880 into a conservative upper-class Muslim family with an estate in Pairaband, a village in the north of what is now Bangladesh. Although Rokeya's father enforced a strict observance of purdah among his female relatives (the system of female seclusion that is the object of Rokeya's scathing critique in her book, *The Secluded Ones*), Rokeya was nonetheless taught to read and write both Bengali[1] and English by her eldest brother, who tutored her late at night after the rest of the family had retired to sleep. In addition, the encouragement of her older sister, Karimunnessa, who was married off before the age of fifteen when her literary interests and love of Bengali literature were discovered, helped motivate Rokeya to develop her intellectual bent. As a young girl, Rokeya was deeply marked by the confinement and arranged marriage of her sister, of whom she later said, "If society had not been so oppressive, Karimunnessa would have been one of the brightest jewels of this country" (qtd. in Tharu and Lalita 341).

Rokeya's husband, Syed Sakhawat Hossain, to whom she was married in her late teens, was proud of his wife's unconventional concern with issues of women's education and social advancement. He encouraged Rokeya to write and publish her views,[2] and, when he died in 1909—some thirteen years after his marriage to Rokeya—she established a school for girls in Bhagalpur with money he had left her. She was forced to abandon this venture and move to Calcutta, however, because of an on-going quarrel with the husband of Sakhawat's daughter (by his first wife) over Rokeya's right to inherit her husband's money. In 1911 she opened the Sakhawat Memorial Girls' School in Calcutta which is still functioning; she had eight students initially, a number which increased to eighty-four after four years of hard work and endless patience. In a letter to her cousin describing her efforts on behalf of her students, Rokeya wrote, "By the Grace of Allah, we have 70 students studying in the five classes . . . two horse drawn carriages. I have to keep an eye on everything. I even have to make sure that the horses are regularly massaged in the evening . . ." (qtd. in Jahan, "Rokeya" 41).

Some of the hostility and difficulties Rokeya faced in her work as an educator are described in the piece we have reprinted here from *The Secluded Ones,* a series of articles published between 1928 and 1930. While Rokeya concentrates her critical attentions in this collection on the unjust—and sometimes ridiculous—aspects of the Muslim purdah system, "she was too well-informed to remain unaware of the fact that women of other societies were also exploited and oppressed" (Jahan, "Introduction" 18). According to Rokeya, the betterment of woman's lot was possible only as a result of comprehensive social change. While she has been criticized for the elitist and Western aspects of her writing, her work through the Muslim Women's Association (*Anjumane-Khawatin-e Islam*), which she founded in 1916, included the formation of a literacy program for slum women. Moreover, although she was considered to be a political radical by contemporaries, she advocated observance of a kind of attenuated purdah and used the *burqa* (a cloak which covered the body and head) when appearing in public. She died of heart failure in 1932 at the age of fifty-three.

The history of Muslim writing about women in turn-of-the-century India is a complex one and is deeply imbricated with the history of British colonialism as it was variously manifested among different ethnic populations. Barbara D. Metcalf describes what she calls "the old colonial historical narrative" in the following terms:

> That story goes like this: the British came; they recognised the depravity of purdah, widow burning, child marriage and female infanticide; sensible Indians immediately recognized a superior culture when they saw one, and, thanks to British tutelage, they began the "regeneration" their society needed. (1)

It is important to keep in mind not only that the practice of customs like purdah varied widely across and within the Muslim populations of India (Papanek 60), but that the British used a superficial criticism of the alleged oppression of Indian women as a way of maintaining their own authority over gender roles (Metcalf). While the emancipation of women in India took place alongside a growing nationalist movement in which women were becoming more active participants, writers like Rokeya were also criticized for promoting antinationalist rhetoric that reflected a negative view of traditional Muslim cultural practices.

During the nineteenth century, the movement for women's emancipation in India focused particularly on the oppressive conditions of the lives of Hindu—rather than Muslim—women. Muslim power in India had severely eroded during the eighteenth and early nineteenth centuries (Shahida Lateef refers to Muslims at this time as "a dispossessed power group" [19]) and many Muslim communities were facing a period of economic and political crisis. Bengali Muslims responded to systematic dispossession by attempting to solidify previously diverse Muslim populations into a unified community of believers, and by trying to gain access to systems of formal education for Bengali Muslim men. Bengali Muslim women, as a group, tended to benefit less from these reformist impulses because of cultural and religious prohibitions against interaction between the sexes.

Nevertheless, discourse concerning the behavior and education of Muslim women emerged as an important part of the social criticism of late nineteenth-century India. Writers and social reformers who worked around this time to further the education of women included men like Sayyid Mumtaz Ali and Sayyid Ahmad Khan. Rokeya Sakhawat Hossain remains perhaps the most noteworthy female social activist of this period. Rokeya's critique of purdah may have stemmed partly from her recognition of the advantages gained by Hindu women who participated in the new reformist culture of their husbands. Nonetheless, her writings and activism played a significant role in the gradual changing of Muslim attitudes towards female seclusion.

NM

REPORT FORTY-SEVEN FROM *THE SECLUDED ONES*[§]

In the words of a poet:

> Not fiction, not poetry, this is life.
> Not theatre this, but my real house.

Only three years ago, we had our school bus. The day before the bus came, one of our teachers, an English woman, had gone to the auto depot to inspect the bus. Her comment was, "This bus is horribly dark inside. Oh, no! I'll never ride that bus!" When the bus arrived, it was found that there was a narrow lattice on top of the back door and the front door. Excepting these two pieces of latticework, three inches wide and eighteen inches long, the bus could be called completely "airtight"!

The bus took the girls to their homes that first afternoon. The maid, accompanying the girls, reported after she came back that it was terribly hot inside the bus. The girls were very uncomfortable. Some of them vomited. Some of the little girls were whimpering in the dark.

Before the bus went to fetch the girls on the next day, the English woman who taught in our school opened the shutter of the back-door. She hung colored curtains on the open shutters. Even then it was found that a few of the girls fainted away, a few of them vomited on the way, and most of them had headaches, etc. In the afternoon, the aforementioned teacher opened the shutters on the side of the bus and hung curtains there also.

That evening, a Hindu friend, Mrs. Mukherjee, came to see me. She was glad to know about the progress the school was making. Suddenly she said, "Incidentally, what a fine bus you have! The first time I saw it, I thought a huge chest was being drawn on wheels. My nephew ran out and said, "Oh, aunty! Look! The moving black hole of Calcutta is passing by! Really! How can the girls possibly ride that bus?"

On the afternoon of the third day, several of the mothers came to complain. They said, "Your bus is certainly God's punishment. You are burying the girls alive!" I said, helplessly, "What can I do? If the bus was not such, you would have been the ones to criticize the bus as "purdahless." They said angrily, "What? Do you want to maintain purdah at the expense of our children's lives? We are not going to send our daughters to your school anymore!" That evening the maid reported that every guardian complained about the bus and warned that the girls would not ride this sort of bus.

The next evening, I had four letters. The writer of the letter written in English had signed himself, "Brother-in-Islam." The other three were in Urdu. Two of these letters were anonymous. The third one had five signatures. The import of all four letters was the same—all of them were from well-wishers. For the continuing welfare of my school they were informing me that the two curtains hanging by the side of the bus moved in the

---

[§] Reprinted by permission of The Feminist Press at the City University of New York, from *Sultana's Dream and Selections from The Secluded Ones,* by Rokeya Sakhawat Hossain, translated and edited by Roushan Jahan. Copyright ©1988 by The Feminist Press at the City University of New York. Material excerpted from pages 33–35.

breeze and made the bus purdahless. If something better was not arranged by tomorrow, they would be compelled, for the benefit of the school, to write in the various Urdu newspapers about this purdahlessness and would stop the girls from riding in such a purdahless bus.

What a dilemma I was in—

> If I don't catch the cobra
> The king will have my head—
> If caught carelessly
> Surely the cobra'd bite me!

I do not think anyone else had tried to catch such a cobra [the irate critics] to satisfy the whims of such a king [the equally irate guardians]. On behalf of the women imprisoned in seclusion, I wish to say—

> Oh, why did I come to this miserable world,
> Why was I born in a purdah country!

NOTES

[1] According to Roushan Jahan, "girls were not usually encouraged to read and write in Bangla. Defying custom, and valuing their Bengali identity over their religious one, Rokeya and her gifted elder sister, Karimunnessa, persisted in learning Bangla" (38). Bengali was not often taught to children in families like Rokeya's because of its extensive use by non-Muslim populations.

[2] One of her earliest and best-known fiction works, a short story entitled *Sultana's Dream* (1905), is an utopian fantasy of a world of "reverse purdah" where men are secluded and women are in charge of political and intellectual affairs.

WORKS CONSULTED

Jahan, Roushan. Introduction. *Inside Seclusion: The Avarodhbasini of Rokeya Sakhawat Hossain.* Trans. and ed. Roushan Jahan. Dacca, Bangladesh: Women for Women, 1981.

—. "Rokeya: An Introduction to Her Life." *Sultana's Dream and Selections from The Secluded Ones.* Trans. and ed. Roushan Jahan. New York: Feminist Press at CUNY, 1988.

Lateef, Shahida. *Muslim Women in India—Political and Private Realities: 1890s-1908.* New Delhi: Kali for Women, 1990.

Metcalf, Barbara D. "Reading and Writing about Muslim Women in British India." *Forging Identities: Gender, Communities and the State in India.* Ed. Zoya Hasan. Boulder, CO: Westview Press, 1994.

Papanek, Hanna. "Afterword—Caging the Lion: A Fable for Our Time." *Sultana's Dream and Selections from The Secluded Ones.* Trans. and ed. Roushan Jahan. New York: Feminist Press at CUNY, 1988.

Tharu, Susie, and K. Lalita. *Women Writing in India: 600 B.C. to the Early Twentieth Century.* Vol. 1. New York: Feminist Press at CUNY, 1993.

ZITKALA-ŠA (RED BIRD, GERTRUDE [SIMMONS] BONNIN) *(1876–1938)*

Planted in a Strange Earth

See also **Representing Women, Writing the Body Politic**

In Zitkala-Ša's name lies much of the history of her life, her motivations, and the kinds of problems that beset her as an activist and writer during a critical period of transition in Native American history. When her mother was pregnant with Gertrude, her father deserted the family; she was therefore given the name of her stepfather and retained it for some time even after he and her mother separated. When she went away to a school run by whites, however, the wife of her half-brother said angrily that she had "deserted home" and should give up the name Simmons too. She described the incident in a letter to her fiancé Carlos Montezuma in 1901, when she had already achieved an international reputation as a writer: "Well, you can guess how queer I felt, away from my own people—homeless—penniless—and even without a name! Then I chose to make a name for myself—and I guess I have made 'Zitkala-Ša' known—for even Italy writes it in her language" (Fisher *x*).

In choosing a Native American name for herself, Zitkala-Ša simultaneously reaffirmed the "cultural ties" her relatives accused her of forsaking, and asserted her "independence" as an individual with the right to define her own identity (Fisher *x*). In the end the name she made for herself in the U.S. and abroad was based on the same paradox. At a time when many Native Americans were worried about the loss of their oral traditions, she was one of the first to write them down in English. Educated in Euro-American culture, she made her stories and essays a means of educating Euro-Americans about her people. She preserved the oral traditions for the sake of her Native American culture, and created an art that would bear her own individual stamp.

Raised in South Dakota, Zitkala-Ša received her formal schooling at White's Indiana Manual Labor Institute (the school described in the excerpt presented here), attended Earlham College between 1895 and 97, and taught at Carlisle Indian School for the next two years—until the stress associated with the contradictions of her position led her to resign. In their educational philosophy, White's and Carlisle rigorously pursued the assimilation of Native Americans which was intended to remove them psychologically and intellectually from their own culture. A standard policy among white educators, Native American literature and oral histories are replete with descriptions of the humiliating methods that were often used to attain it. At their mildest, these methods were demeaning, such as forcing children to cross-dress as punishment for speaking their native languages; at worst, they amounted to torture.

In the years that followed her anguished departure from Carlisle, Zitaka-Ša increasingly turned her energies to Native American rights activism. For two years she studied violin at New England Conservatory, then determined to return to her homeland for a time. Breaking her engagement to Carlos Montezuma when he would not agree to practice medicine on a reservation, she eventually married another Sioux, Raymond T. Bonnin, with whom she lived in Utah until 1916. In that year, her election to office in the Society of the American Indian, the first Native American rights organization run solely by Native Americans, took her and her husband to Washington. Here she organized the National Council of American Indians in 1920 and became an active lobbyist on issues such as citizenship, governmental reforms to facilitate Native American claims against the United States, opening jobs in the Indian Service to Native Americans, and abolishing the Bureau of Indian Affairs (Young 199).

One of her major efforts was to persuade the General Federation of Women's Clubs to undertake work on behalf of Native Americans. Her work as an activist, to which the majority of her adult life was devoted, is well-illustrated in the title of a study she wrote with Charles N. Fabens and Matthew K. Sniffen: *Oklahoma's Poor Rich Indians: An Orgy of Graft and Exploitation of the Five Civilized Tribes—Legalized Robbery.* The major effects of this study on government policy toward Native Americans support historians' evaluation of Zitkala-Ša as one of the major forces in the Pan-Indian movement of the 1920s.[1]

ECD

FROM *AMERICAN INDIAN STORIES*[§]

. . . Late in the morning, my friend Judéwin gave me a terrible warning. Judéwin knew a few words of English; and she had overheard the paleface woman talk about cutting our long, heavy hair. Our mothers had taught us that only unskilled warriors who were captured had their hair shingled by the enemy. Among our people, short hair was worn by the mourners, and shingled hair by cowards!

We discussed our fate some moments, and when Judéwin said, "We have to submit, because they are strong," I rebelled.

"No, I will not submit! I will struggle first!" I answered.

I watched my chance, and when no one noticed I disappeared. I crept up the stairs as quietly as I could in my squeaking shoes, —my moccasins had been exchanged for shoes. Along the hall I passed, without knowing whither I was going. Turning aside to an open door, I found a large room with three white beds in it. The windows were covered with dark green curtains, which made the room very dim. Thankful that no one was there, I directed my steps toward the corner farthest from the door. On my hands and knees I crawled under the bed, and cuddled myself in the dark corner.

From my hiding place I peered out, shuddering with fear whenever I heard footsteps near by. Though in the hall loud voices were calling my name, and I knew that even Judéwin was searching for me, I did not open my mouth to answer. Then the steps were quickened and the voices became excited. The sounds came nearer and nearer. Women and girls entered the room. I held my breath and watched them open closet doors and peep behind large trunks. Some one threw up the curtains, and the room was filled with sudden

[§] Reprinted from *American Indian Stories* by Zitkala-Ša, Foreword by Dexter Fisher. Published 1985 by the University of Nebraska Press. Material excerpted from pages 52–61.

light. What caused them to stoop and look under the bed I do not know. I remember being dragged out, though I resisted by kicking and scratching wildly. In spite of myself, I was carried downstairs and tied fast in a chair.

I cried aloud, shaking my head all the while until I felt the cold blades of the scissors against my neck, and heard them gnaw off one of my thick braids. Then I lost my spirit. Since the day I was taken from my mother I had suffered extreme indignities. People had stared at me. I had been tossed about in the air like a wooden puppet. And now my long hair was shingled like a coward's! In my anguish I moaned for my mother, but no one came to comfort me. Not a soul reasoned quietly with me, as my own mother used to do; for now I was only one of many little animals driven by a herder . . .

Within a year I was able to express myself somewhat in broken English. As soon as I comprehended a part of what was said and done, a mischievous spirit of revenge possessed me. One day I was called in from my play for some misconduct. I had disregarded a rule which seemed to me very needlessly binding. I was sent into the kitchen to mash the turnips for dinner. It was noon, and steaming dishes were hastily carried into the dining-room. I hated turnips, and their odor which came from the brown jar was offensive to me. With fire in my heart, I took the wooden tool that the paleface woman held out to me. I stood upon a step, and, grasping the handle with both hands, I bent in hot rage over the turnips. I worked my vengeance upon them. All were so busily occupied that no one noticed me. I saw that the turnips were in a pulp, and that further beating could not improve them; but the order was, "Mash these turnips," and mash them I would! I renewed my energy; and as I sent the masher into the bottom of the jar, I felt a satisfying sensation that the weight of my body had gone into it.

Just here a paleface woman came up to my table. As she looked into the jar, she shoved my hands roughly aside. I stood fearless and angry. She placed her red hands upon the rim of the jar. Then she gave one lift and stride away from the table. But lo! the pulpy contents fell through the crumbled bottom to the floor! She spared me no scolding phrases that I had earned. I did not heed them. I felt triumphant in my revenge, though deep within me I was a wee bit sorry to have broken the jar.

As I sat eating my dinner, and I saw that no turnips were served, I whooped in my heart for having once asserted the rebellion within me.

NOTE

[1] See for example Udall 31. For an annotated bibliography of secondary works on Zitkala-Ša up to 1991, see Bataille and Sands.

WORKS CONSULTED

Bataille, Gretchen M. and Kathleen M. Sands, eds. Editorial Assistant Catherine Udall. *American Indian Women: A Guide to Research*. New York: Garland, 1991.

Fisher, Dexter. Foreword. *American Indian Stories.* By Zitkala-Ša. Lincoln: U of Nebraska P, 1985.

Udall, Catherine. "Bonnin, Gertrude Simmons." *Native American Women: A Biographical Dictionary.* Ed. Gretchen M. Bataille. New York: Garland, 1993.

Young, Mary E. "Bonnin, Gertrude Simmons." *Notable American Women 1607–1950: A Biographical Dictionary.* Ed. Edward T. James, Janet Wilson James, Paul S. Boyer. Vol 1 . Cambridge, MA: Belknap Press of Harvard UP, 1971.

Zitkala-Ša. *American Indian Stories.* Lincoln: U of Nebraska P, 1985.

MAB SEGREST *(1949–)*

"Confessions of a Closet Baptist"

See also Vision and Transformation

"I listen with fascination to friends who grew up as 'red diaper babies' during the McCarthy era, brought up by leftist parents. I was a 'white diaper baby,'" Mab Segrest says (Memoir 16). Raised in an Alabama family proud of their white Christian Southern heritage, she received an education full of mixed messages from her mother, who made much of her personal relationships with African Americans and occasionally supported their political actions against racism, but also, with her husband, worked to establish a system of segregated schools. As an adult, Segrest became a political organizer against hate groups in North Carolina, inspired in part by her realization that she was a lesbian and that "people who said 'nigger' also said 'queer.'" In the process she found herself becoming something the Ku Klux Klan calls a "race traitor," the term from which she takes the title of her recent personal and political autobiography.

After receiving her Ph.D. from Duke University in 1979, Segrest taught at Campbell College until 1983, and, at the same time, worked with a group of lesbian writers who pushed each other to confront their submerged racism. Since then she has been active both as a writer and organizer, for six years as coordinator of North Carolinians Against Racist and Religious Violence, and, most recently, with the Urban Rural Mission of the World Council of Churches which unites community organizers and liberation theologians around the world. She lives in Durham, North Carolina, with her partner and daughter. Her most recent work is a co-edited anthology, *The Third Wave: Feminist Essays on Racism,* published with Kitchen Table: Women of Color Press.

ECD

FROM "CONFESSIONS OF A CLOSET BAPTIST"[§]

I lead a double life. By day I'm a relatively mild-mannered English teacher at a Southern Baptist college. By night—and on Tuesdays and Thursdays and weekends—I am a lesbian writer and editor, a collective member of *Feminary,* a lesbian-feminist journal for the South. My employers do not know about my other life. When they find out, I assume I will be fired, maybe prayed to death. For the past four years my life has moved rapidly in opposite directions.

When I started teaching English at my present school five years ago, I knew I was a

[§] Reprinted from *My Mama's Dead Squirrel: Lesbian Essays On Southern Culture,* by Mab Segrest. Copyright © 1985 by Mab Segrest. Reprinted by permission of Firebrand Books, Ithaca, New York. Material excerpted from pages 72–77.

lesbian. I was living with P, my first woman lover. I wasn't out politically. I had not yet discovered the lesbian culture and lesbian community that is now such an important part of my life. The first time I had let myself realize I was in love with P, I sat under a willow tree by the lake at the Girl Scout camp where we both worked and said aloud to myself in the New York darkness: "I am a lesbian." I had to see how it sounded, and after I'd said that, gradually, I felt I could say anything. When, three years ago, P left to live with a man, I knew my life had changed. I read lesbian books and journals with great excitement. I joined the collective of *Feminary,* then a local feminist journal, and helped turn it into a journal for Southern lesbians. I started writing. I did all this while working for the Baptists, feeling myself making decisions that were somehow as frightening as they were inevitable. Early issues of *Feminary* record the process. First there is a poem by "Mabel." Then an article by "Mab." Then the whole leap: "Mab Segrest." I knew if I could not write my name, I couldn't write anything. I also knew: if I can't be myself and teach, I won't teach. . . .

. . . Teaching is the work I love best. I can bring much of myself to it and much of it to myself. But as a lesbian teacher in a society that hates homosexuals—especially homosexual teachers—I have learned a caution towards my students and my school that saddens me. The things my life has taught me best I cannot teach directly. I do not believe that I am the only one that suffers.

The first time homosexuality came up in my classroom it was a shock to my system. It was in freshman composition, and I was letting a class choose debate topics. They picked gay rights, but nobody wanted to argue the gay side. Finally, three of my more vociferous students volunteered. I went home shaken. I dreamed that night I was in class, my back to my students, writing on the board (I always feel most vulnerable then), and students were taunting me from the desks—"lesbian! queer!"

The day of the debate I took a seat in the back row, afraid that if I stood up in front *IT* would show. I would give myself away: develop a tic, tremble, stutter, throw up, then faint dead away. I kept quiet as my three pro-gay students held off the Bible with the Bill of Rights, to everyone's amazement, including my own. (I certainly knew it could be done; I just didn't expect them to do it. No one else in the class had figured any legitimate arguments were possible.) Then the anti-gay side rallied and hit on a winning tactic. They implied that if the opponents really believed their own arguments, they were pretty "funny." I called an end to the debate, and the pro-gay side quickly explained how they didn't mean anything they had said. Then one of my female students wanted to discuss how Christians should love people even when they were sick and sinful. I said the discussion was over and dismissed the class. The only time I had spoken during the entire debate was in response to a male student behind me who had reacted defensively to a mention of homosexuality in the army with, "Yes, and where *my* father works, they castrate people like that." I turned to him with quiet fury. "Are you advocating it?" All in all I survived the day, but without much self-respect.

The next year, on a theme, a freshman explained to me how you could tell gay people "by the bandannas they wear in their pockets and around their necks." She concluded, "I think homosexuals are a menace to society. *What do you think?*" A pregnant question, indeed. I pondered for awhile, then wrote back in the margin, "I think society is a menace to homosexuals." I resisted wearing a red bandanna the day I handed back the papers. . . .

I see the unease of most college students over sexuality—whether they express it in swaggering and hollow laughter over queer jokes, or in timidity, or in the half-proud confession of a preacher at how he knocked his wife's teeth out—and how it is part of a larger dis-ease with sexuality and the definitions of *men* and *women* in this society. I see how they, and most of us, have been taught to fear all of our feelings. And I understand all too well when I realize I am afraid to write—to even know—what I think and feel for fear of losing my job; how money buys conformity; how subtly we are terrorized into staying in line.

The closest I ever came to saying what I wanted to was in an American literature class last year. Gay rights came up again—I think I may have even steered the discussion in that direction. And a student finally said to me, "But what about teachers? We can't have homosexuals teaching students!" I resisted leaping up on the podium and flashing the big *L* emblazoned on a leotard beneath my blouse. Instead, I took a deep breath and began slowly. "Well, in my opinion, you don't learn sexual preference in the classroom. I mean, that's not what we are doing here. *If* you had a gay or lesbian teacher, he or she would not teach you about preference." I paused to catch my breath. They were all listening. "What he or she would say, *if you had* a gay teacher, is this . . ." (by now I was lightly beating on the podium) " ' . . . don't let them make you afraid to be who you are. To know who you are.' She would tell you, 'Don't let them get you. Don't let them make you afraid.' " I stopped abruptly and in the silence turned to think of something to write on the board.

If they ever *do* have a lesbian teacher, that is exactly what she will say.

1980

WORKS CONSULTED

Alarçon, Norma, Lisa Albrecht, Jacqui Alexander, Sharon Day, Mab Segrest, and Barbara Smith, eds. *The Third Wave: Feminist Essays on Racism.* New York: Kitchen Table: Women of Color Press, forthcoming.

Segrest, Mab. *Memoir of a Race Traitor.* Boston: South End, 1994.

—. *My Mama's Dead Squirrel: Lesbian Essays on Southern Culture.* New York: Firebrand, 1983.

NZINGA OF ANGOLA *(c. 1581–1663)*

"Portrait of an African Queen"

The idea that women in the distant past held positions of formal authority has long captured imaginations. Historians in many eras have sought examples of women who ruled; feminists have compiled lists of women who held political power; cultural stories, dwelling as they do on the unusual, have found women in positions of power to fill that criterion. Recent empirical scholarship has tempered our understanding of many of these figures and enabled us to know not only more about who these women actually were, but also what the stories told about them have represented over time. Nzinga of Angola provides such a story.

In the seventeenth century, Nzinga was the monarch of a kingdom in the area that is now part of Angola. Records kept by slave traders, priests, and Portuguese and Dutch officials chronicle her story. While we do not have her own words, a consensus arises among all reporters on certain facets of her life.

At the time Nzinga gained the position of monarch, her ethnic group, the Mbundu, as well as many others in the area, were entwined in complex relationships with the Portuguese and the Dutch, two colonial powers attempting to control African territories. Nzinga and other African leaders dealt with the constantly shifting agents of those powers, military leaders, political governors, Jesuit priests, and slave merchants among others. During Nzinga's lifetime of some eighty years, the relationships moved from war to truce and back again many times. The portraits of Nzinga, in colonial sources, in the work of African historians, and in popular folklore, range among portrayals of her as "a proto-nationalist resistance leader, . . . the consummate Mbundu politician, . . . the devout Christian and Portuguese ally" (Miller 201).

While we cannot know precisely what she did and why she did it, we do know that she was a talented military strategist who inflicted numerous defeats on the colonial powers attempting to overtake the territories she sought to control. We do know that she was able to assume the title of monarch, although she was not herself in the direct line of succession, and that, much of the time, she retained the political allegiance of lineages. Furthermore, we know that while some neighboring areas had traditions of female queens, the Mbundu did not; yet through military and political skills, Nzinga was able to create and maintain a new tradition. We know that she understood power dynamics at a very fundamental level and was able to maneuver first the Portuguese and then the Dutch into bargains that benefitted her own agenda. We know that she worked with female supporters as well as with her sisters (a term that refers in her culture to a wider set of kin than simply the children born from the same mother) in her political exercises. And finally, we know that her personality and accomplishments were sufficiently strong and intriguing to merit many pages of commentary in the reports, letters, and diaries of the Europeans who came into contact with her (Henderson 89). It is from these sources that both the facts and the interpretations about her have grown. We reprint here excerpts from one account, compiled by British author David Sweetman in a series for young people.

The excerpt we have selected tells of a famous meeting between the Portuguese governor and Nzinga as she was gaining power as the *ngola,* the term colonial powers loosely applied to the highest political office among the Mbundu. The excerpt goes on to interpret her conversion to Christianity as a political act and, in the third part, mentions the fact that she organized her supporters into a band similar to contemporary guerilla fighters. The last part illustrates her powerful military presence among her followers. The legends that have grown up around her, multiplied over the years, by many sources, are evident in this selection.

If the historical records enable us to outline her life and accomplishments, and if the stories surrounding her give us some sense of the meanings that have been attached to that record, the questions contemporary readers bring to Nzinga's story are numerous. What conditions enable women to assume positions of power and authority? Do women who hold positions of power act differently from men of similar backgrounds or like positions? What is the relationship between a female ruler and the women under her? What makes one female leader a precedent and another merely an exception? Contemporary research on women and leadership in a number of domains from politics and local activism to corporate settings, tells us that women in positions of power and authority do make some difference in how organizations run, in the outcomes the organizations produce and the practices they change. Nzinga, an ancestor to this discussion, continues to capture the imagination of those who think about women and political power—both for what we can know and for what is left unknown.

JFO

A FAMOUS MEETING[§]

Nzinga's position was extremely delicate: her brother had surrendered everything (the Portuguese had even appointed a puppet *ngola*) and yet she was expected to negotiate a settlement. But she was a natural diplomat and realized that her only hope was to brave it out. Her meeting with the new governor, João Correa de Souza, has become a legend in the history of Africa's confrontations with Europe. Nzinga organized her arrival at the governor's residence in such a way that no one could be in any doubt that this was a 'royal' occasion and not the humble arrival of a conquered messenger. Musicians heralded her approach as she entered the audience chamber escorted by her serving women. Now occurred the event that was to make her so famous, an event happily recorded by a Dutch artist a little while later. There was only one chair, the governor's throne. Nzinga was de-

[§] Reprinted by permission of the publisher from *Women Leaders in African History* by David Sweetman, published by Heinemann Educational Books. Copyright © 1984 by Heinemann Educational Publishers. Material excerpted from pages 40–46.

termined not to be placed at a disadvantage. Summoning one of her women, who came forward and fell to her hands and knees, the haughty princess sat down on this human seat. When Governor de Souza entered, he found himself already outmanoeuvred. During the following interview he was not allowed to regain the upper hand.

Over the years of fighting, the Mbundu had taken a number of Portuguese prisoners. When de Souza asked for their return, however, Nzinga smilingly agreed, provided all the Mbundu who had been carried off to Brazil and elsewhere were brought back in exchange. It was clearly an impossible condition and after much discussion the solution was a treaty whereby Portugal would recognize the Ngola Mbandi as ruler of an independent Ndongo kingdom and would withdraw its army. In return, the Mbundu would return the Portuguese prisoners, help the Europeans with the slave trade and take part in joint efforts to resist the Jaga. . . .

CONVERSION

Probably as part of a private agreement intended to reinforce the treaty, Nzinga stayed on in Luanda in order to receive instruction in the Christian faith. Such a move was more political than religious. Indeed the Jesuit priests concerned were deeply implicated in the slave trade. They officiated at daily mass baptisms in the docks, where lines of captives shuffling into the ships were first sprinkled with holy water and given a new name. But Nzinga knew that her status as a 'Christian' ally of Portugal would entitle her people to favoured treatment. Her baptism in the cathedral at Luanda would have been attended by a good deal of public ceremonial. She chose as her Christian name Dona Anna de Souza in order to strengthen her links with the governor. . . .

MILITARY STRATEGIES [EDS.]

Her tactics for resisting the outnumbered but better-armed Portuguese have been much admired and even imitated successfully in this century. She formed her people into a guerrilla army. By keeping them on the move she was able to avoid a disastrous battle while harassing her enemies wherever they least expected it. She used the island Cuanza as a base whenever she could, though occasionally the Portuguese would force her to move. In late 1629 and early 1630 she promised to marry the Jaga chief and with this strengthened alliance moved east to Matamba where she defeated the ruling queen and created a new land for herself and her people. Between 1630 and 1635 she built up her new country. It was free of tribalism in the sense that it was not dominated by one people, for she merged her Mbundu with any Jaga who wished to settle, along with slaves escaping from the Portuguese. . . .

We know something of the details of Nzinga's life at this time from the dispatches of Captain Füller, the Dutch military attaché who accompanied her. He described how everyone fell to their knees and kissed the ground at her approach, a strange sight for women did not usually hold power. She was obliged to dress as a man and kept a 'harem' of young men dressed as women who were her 'wives'. Although she was advised by a council of elders, Füller makes it clear that she was the military strategist and although past sixty led her warriors herself. . . .

WORKS CONSULTED

Henderson, Lawrence W. *Angola: Five Centuries of Conflict.* Ithaca: Cornell UP, 1979.

Miller, Joseph C. "Nzinga of Matamba in a New Perspective." *Journal of African History* 16 (1975): 201–216.

Sweetman, David. *Women Leaders in African History.* London: Heinemann, 1984.

ARTEMISIA GENTILESCHI *(1593–1652)*

"The Spirit of Caesar in the Soul of a Woman"

Artemisia Gentileschi was an Italian Baroque painter who worked in the major cities of Italy—Rome, Naples, Venice, Florence, and probably Genoa—as well as in London, England. She painted in oil on canvas and fresco, enjoyed great popularity in her time, and is recognized today as having had a remarkable facility as an artist. Her paintings can be found in museums and personal collections from the Pommerfelden in Schloss Weissenstein, Germany, to the Uffizi in Florence, Italy, and the Institute of Art in Detroit, Michigan.

Like the majority of the women visual artists of the Baroque era whose works are known to scholars, Artemisia Gentileschi was the daughter of an established painter. She was trained by her father, Orazio, and worked as an assistant in his studio. There is some speculation that he changed the date on at least one of her paintings to capitalize on the popularity of her work and suggest that her talents were evident at a younger age. It was in her father's studio that Artemisia met Caravaggio, a painter as well-known for his unruly social behavior as for his unconventional artistic style. Caravaggio was an important influence on Artemisia's painting, which shares a similar juxtaposition of deep colors and a sensational use of highly contrasting dark and light values. They painted similar subjects, such as the Apocryphal stories of Judith and Holofernes and Susannah and the Elders. (Her extant works also include *Cleopatra,* a *Self-Portrait as an Allegory of Painting,* and an allegory of *Fame.*)

A very public passage in Gentileschi's life often serves as a highly gendered lens for the interpretation of her art by historians. When she was seventeen, her father filed suit against one of his studio assistants, Agostino Tassi, for repeatedly raping her. Gentileschi survived this experience, and the public humiliation it entailed, with her artistic ambitions undeterred, but many critics have interpreted her art as a personal response to this violence. They cite her graphic depictions of the decapitation of men (Holofernes), the vulnerability of unjustly accused women (Susannah), and the heroism of potentially victimized women (Judith). While some critics have dismissed her work for this reason, we might also use the same biographical evidence to interpret her art as a very powerful act of resistance, or view this event as only one of many factors affecting Gentileschi's work as an artist.

Gentileschi's work was well-respected by her contemporaries, and she was generously compensated by her patrons, who included Cosimo II of the Medici family in Florence, and King Charles I of England. Some artists of this era, including a limited number of women, were supported solely by one patron for the length of their career, but Gentileschi was not included in this elite class. She garnered individual commissions for her paintings, and the following letters document the arduous work of securing fair payment. Her deferential tone was necessitated by her social station as much as by her gender, and does not negate the conviction of her confidence. These letters are a testament to her understanding of the system within which she must operate to receive just compensation.

Despite her success, it was not until recently that Gentileschi's work became the subject of extensive study, beginning with Mary Garrard's 1989 monograph *Artemisia Gentileschi: The Image of the Female Hero in Italian Baroque Art.* Garrard effectively tackles a key area of contention for feminist art historians: the attribution to men of works that, very likely, were produced by women artists. In addition to stylistic analyses, which Garrard uses to reassign works to Gentileschi, accurate attribution is greatly facilitated by the discovery of historical records such as the letters reprinted here. This kind of primary documentation is an invaluable scholarly tool. Not only does it authenticate the authorship of particular works, it allows a rare glimpse at the sensibility of the practitioner and her views on the way gender influenced her career.

PJN

LETTERS TO DON ANTONIO RUFFO FROM ARTEMISIA GENTILESCHI[§]

Naples, November 13, 1649

My Most Illustrious Sir,

I prefer not to discuss our business in this letter in case that gentleman [the bearer] will read it. With regard to your request that I reduce the price of the paintings, I will tell Your Most Illustrious Lordship that I can take a little from the amount that I asked, but the price must not be less than four hundred ducats, and you must send me a deposit as all other gentlemen do. However, I can tell you for certain that the higher the price, the harder I will strive to make a painting that will please Your Most Illustrious Lordship and that will conform to my taste and yours. With regard to the painting which I have already finished for Your Most Illustrious Lordship, I cannot give it to you for less than I asked, as I have already overextended myself to give the lowest price. I swear, as your servant, that I would not have given it even to my father for the price that I gave you. Don Antonio, my Lord, I beg you, for God's sake, not to reduce the price because I am sure that when you see it, you will say that I was not presumptuous. Your nephew, the Duke, thinks that I must have great affection for you to charge you such a price. I only wish to remind you that there are eight [figures], two dogs and landscape and water. Your Most Illustrious Lordship will understand that the expense for models is staggering.

[§] Reprinted by permission of the *New York Literary Forum* from *The Female Autograph,* edited by Domna C. Stanton, in a special issue of *New York Literary Forum* 12–13. Copyright © 1984 by *New York Literary Forum.* Material excerpted from pages 103–105.

I am going to say no more except what I have in my mind, that I think Your Most Illustrious Lordship will not suffer any loss with me and that you will find the spirit of Caesar in the soul of a woman.

And thus I most humbly bow to you.

Your Most Illustrious Lordship's most
humble servant *Artemisia Gentileschi*

From Naples, November 13, 1649

My Most Illustrious Sir,

I received a letter of 26th October which I greatly appreciated, particularly noting how my Master always concerns himself with favoring me despite my unworthiness. In it, you tell me about that gentleman who wishes to have some paintings by me, that he would like a Galatea and a Judgment of Paris, and that Galatea should be different from the one that Your Most Illustrious Lordship owns. There was no need for you to suggest this to me, since, by the grace of God and of the Most Holy Virgin, it would occur to a woman with my kind of talent to vary the subjects in my paintings; never has anyone found in my pictures any repetition of invention, not even of one hand.

As for the fact that this gentleman wishes to know the price before the work is done, believe me, as I am your servant, that I do it most unwillingly since it is very important to me not to err and thus burden my conscience, which I value more than all the gold in the world. I know that by erring I will offend my Lord God and I thus fear that God will not bestow his grace on me. Therefore, I never quote a price for my works until they are done. However, since Your Most Illustrious Lordship would like me to do it, I will do what you command. Tell this gentleman that I want five hundred ducats for both; he can show them to the whole world and, should he find anyone who does not think that the paintings are worth two hundred scudi more, I do not want him to pay me the agreed price. I assure Your Most Illustrious Lordship that these are paintings with nude figures requiring very expensive female models, which is a big headache. When I find good ones they fleece me and at other times, one must suffer their trivialities with the patience of Job.

As for my doing a drawing and sending it, I have made a solemn vow never to send my drawings because people swindled me. In particular I just today found out that, in order to spend less, the Bishop of St. Gata, for whom I did a drawing of souls in Purgatory, commissioned another painter to do the painting using my work. If I were a man I cannot imagine it would turn out this way, because when the concept [*inventione*] has been realized and defined with lights and darks, and established by means of planes, the rest is a trifle. I think that this gentleman is wrong to ask for drawings since he can see the design and the composition of the Galatea.

I don't know what else to say except that I kiss Your Most Illustrious Lordship's hands and most humbly bow to you, praying for the greatest happiness from Heaven.

Your Most Illustrious Lordship's most
humble servant *Artemisia Gentileschi*

I advise Your Most Illustrious Lordship that when I ask a price I don't do as they do in Naples, where they ask thirty and then give it to you for four. I am Roman and thus I want to act in the Roman manner.

WORKS CONSULTED

Chadwick, Whitney. *Women, Art, and Society.* Thames and Hudson: London, 1990.

Garrard, Mary D. *Artemisia Gentileschi: The Image of the Female Hero in Italian Baroque Art.* Princeton: Princeton UP, 1989.

Pollock, Griselda. "Artemisia Gentileschi." Book Review. *Art Bulletin* 72.3 (1988): 499–505.

—. "Theory, Ideology, Politics: Art History and Its Myths." *Art Bulletin* 78.1 (1996): 16–22.

—. *Vision and Difference: Femininity, Feminism and Histories of Art.* Routledge: London and New York, 1988.

Silvers, Anita. "Has Her(oine's) Time Now Come?" *Journal of Aesthetics and Art Criticism* 48 (Fall 1990): 365–379.

FANNY MENDELSSOHN HENSEL *(1805–1847)*

"I'm Beginning to Publish"

Letter from Felix Mendelssohn to his mother

June 2nd, 1837

> . . . I maintain that no one should publish, unless they are resolved to appear as an author for the rest of their life . . . and from my knowledge of Fanny I should say she has neither inclination nor vocation for authorship. She is too much all that a woman ought to be for this. She regulates her house, and neither thinks of the public nor of the musical world, nor even of music at all, until her first duties are fulfilled. Publishing would only disturb her in these, and I cannot say that I approve of it. I will not, therefore, persuade her to this step . . .[1]

Fanny Mendelssohn Hensel grew up in a musical family. Her mother, who gave Fanny and her younger brother Felix their first piano lessons, had trained with a student of Bach. A precocious student, Fanny was described as having "Bach fingers." Although musical interactions provided the substance of Fanny's existence, she, unlike her brother, was not to be groomed for a professional career in music.

Whereas Fanny's mother introduced the family to music, her father dictated their values and beliefs. The Mendelssohn household was steeped in the views of Fanny's grandfather, the philosopher Moses Mendelssohn, who introduced the central ideas of the French Revolution to Germany with his translations of Rousseau. Rousseau's works, vigorously asserting the equality of men in civic discourse, reinforced with equal vigor women's subordination in the family. In this context, it is not surprising to read Fanny's father's stern reminder on her twenty-third birthday: "You must become more steady and collected, and prepare more earnestly and eagerly for your real calling, the *only* calling of a young woman—I mean the state of a housewife" (qtd. in Sebastian Hensel 84).

Felix was to become an international musician while Fanny would remain at home, directing the Mendelssohn family's musical soirees and Sunday matinees. Over the years, Fanny engaged in an intense correspondence with her brother. Their voluminous letters served as a means for her to maintain her close personal ties with Felix, share vicariously in his achievements, and influence the shape of some of his compositions. For most of her life, however, Fanny herself would not publish, despite encouragement to do so from her husband, the court painter Wilhelm Hensel. Instead, her compositions would be exposed to musical circles almost exclusively through the home-based salon.

It is clear that Felix, not her husband, wielded the authoritative voice on the issue of publishing, as Fanny reveals in an unsuccessful attempt to win Felix's support: "I would of course comply totally with the wishes of my husband on any other matter, yet on these issues alone it's crucial I have your consent, for without it I might not undertake anything of the kind" (*The Letters of Fanny Hensel to Felix Mendelssohn* 222). While it is interesting to consider this dynamic from a contemporary perspective, one should keep in mind not only Felix's stature in the musical profession, but also the primary importance, during this historical period, of intense familial ties in the fulfillment of intimacy.

Felix's refusal to offer his encouragement exerted a powerful influence on Fanny. Until the last year and a half of her life, Fanny published only two pieces on her own.[2] The first such effort occurred in 1837, the year in which her father died and Felix was estranged from the family. He did not return home for well over a year, having married without his family's meeting his bride until eight months after the wedding. Fanny harbored resentment about Felix's behavior. It was also during this time that Felix distanced himself from further collaborations with Fanny by composing and performing major pieces to which she had no exposure. It would appear that the increased distance between Fanny and Felix in the next decade served to "free" Fanny: in the absence of his influence, and with the encouragement of her husband, Fanny finally began publishing her compositions in 1846 at the age of forty-one.

This need for male allies and support in order to engage in traditionally male forms of work foreshadows the struggles of modern women to enter the professions (see Catherine Waugh), and invites comparison with the reliance of many women on male benefactors for the financial assistance to maintain their work (see Binodini Dasi). The experiences of each of these women reveal the various mechanisms of access to public forms of power—in these cases, an access that was contingent upon private power relationships with men. In Fanny Hensel, we see the critical importance of private male authorization. Her brother's refusal to persuade her to publish functioned as a prohibitive factor that virtually stifled her efforts.

Fanny Hensel's life was characterized by a constant tension between her absolute persistence in the creative work of a professional musician and her denial of this identity, at times even to herself. If, as Felix suggested, Fanny had truly been content with her role as housewife, why would she have composed over 450 pieces in her lifetime? At the end of our selection Fanny reflects upon the immense joy of going each day, unhindered, to her own work. When Fanny died, on May 14 of that year, her unexpected stroke occurred in the midst of rehearsing one of Felix's pieces with her choir, her Bach fingers silenced on the keys of her piano. One cannot help but reflect upon the irony of this moment, and wonder about the relation between the joy and stress of living one's life's work under a brother's shadow.

JS

LETTER TO FELIX MENDELSSOHN FROM FANNY MENDELSSOHN HENSEL[§]

Berlin, July 9, 1846

My dear Felice, thank you for your letter with the nicest news that positioned your mention of the rice pudding at the top, naturally. I could have tolerated more news, for if you imagine that Cecile wrote a great deal, you are, as they say here, under a false illusion. Cecile is too stolid to write details. I gratefully acknowledge, however, that I was the idiot upon whom you bestowed a half hour [of your time]. And why not? Am I to imagine that I'm not as worthy in your eyes as Spohr?[3] I definitely won't be such a modest rogue. In fact, we could conclude a contract with each other stating that you would write a long letter after every music festival and every important event so that one could find out about them. Whenever we get together after a long separation, too many of the details are lost, and, as Gans said, it is better to hear some things twice than not at all. Now an entire oratorio of yours is being introduced to the world again, and I don't know a note of it. When will we hear it? Actually I wouldn't expect you to read this rubbish now, busy as you are, if I didn't have to tell you something. But since I know from the start that you won't like it, it's a bit awkward to get under way. So laugh at me or not, as you wish: I'm afraid of my brothers at age 40, as I was of father at age 14. —Or, more aptly expressed, desirous of pleasing you and everyone I've loved throughout my life. And when I now know in advance that it won't be the case, I thus feel rather uncomfortable. In a word, I'm beginning to publish. I have Herr Bock's sincere offer for my lieder and have finally turned a receptive ear to his favorable terms. And if I've done it of my own free will and cannot blame anyone in my family if aggravation results from it (friends and acquaintances have indeed been urging me for a long time), then I can console myself, on the other hand, with the knowledge that I in no way sought out or induced the type of musical reputation that might have elicited such offers. I hope I won't disgrace all of you through my publishing, as I'm no *femme libre* and unfortunately not even an adherent of the *Young* Germany movement. I trust *you* will in no way be bothered by it, since, as you can see, I've proceeded completely on my own in order to spare you any possible unpleasant moment. I hope you won't think badly of me. If it succeeds—that is, if the pieces are well liked and I receive additional offers—I know it will be a great stimulus to me, something I've always needed in order to create. If not, I'll be as indifferent as I've always been and not be upset, and then if I work less or stop completely, nothing will have

[§] Reprinted by permission of the *New York Literary Forum* from *The Female Autograph*, edited by Domna C. Stanton, in a special issue of *New York Literary Forum* 12–13. Copyright © 1984 by *New York Literary Forum.* Material excerpted from pages 177–178.

been lost by that either. "That is the true basis of our existence and salvation."...

Farewell, you dear ones. Say hello to dear Cecile and all five children. Hensel also sends his best.

Your Fanny

FROM FANNY'S DIARY, APRIL, 1847[§]

Yesterday the first breath of spring was in the air. It has been a long winter, with much frost and snow, universal dearth and distress, indeed a winter full of suffering. What have we done to deserve being among the few happy ones in the world? My inmost heart is at any rate full of thankfulness, and when in the morning after breakfasting with Wilhelm we each go to our own work, with a pleasant day to look back upon, and another to look forward to, I am quite overcome with my own happiness.

NOTES

[1] Felix Mendelssohn. *Mendelssohn's Letters from 1833–1847.* Trans. Lady Wallace. London: Longman, Green, 1878. 115–116.

[2] Six of Fanny's pieces had previously been published under Felix's name in two of his early opuses.

[3] The composer and violinist Louis Spohr was a guest of Felix's in Leipzig. [Stanton]

WORKS CONSULTED

Hensel, Sebastian. *The Mendelssohn Family: 1729–1847. From Letters and Journals. Vols. 1 and 2.* New York: Harper and Brothers, 1882.

Kuperferberg, Herbert. *The Mendelssohns: Three Generations of Genius.* New York: Scribner, 1972.

Hensel, Fanny Mendelssohn. *The Letters of Fanny Hensel to Felix Mendelssohn.* Ed. and trans. Marcia Citron. Pendragon Press, 1987.

Mendelssohn, Felix. *Mendelssohn's Letters from 1833–1847.* Trans. Lady Wallace. London: Longman, Green, 1878.

Quin, Carol. *Fanny Mendelssohn Hensel: Her Contributions to Nineteenth-Century Musical Life.* Doctoral Thesis, University of Kentucky, 1981.

Sirota, Victoria Resseyer. *The Life and Works of Fanny Mendelssohn Hensel.* Doctoral Thesis, Boston University School of Music, 1981.

[§] Reprinted from Sebastian Hensel, *The Mendelssohn Family: 1729–1847: From Letters and Journals.* Volume 2. Published 1882 by Harper and Brothers. Material excerpted from page 334.

BINODINI DASI *(1863–1941)*

My Story

By the time eleven-year-old Binodini Dasi became a theatrical superstar in Bengal in 1874, the notion of the professional female performance artist had been synonymous with that of the prostitute for over 2,000 years in India. Her accomplishments as an actress, poet, essayist, and autobiographer conflicted with rigid cultural ideology that defined such activity as fit only for women of ill-repute.

Known as "dancing girls," a designation evocative of their characteristically dual role as entertainers and courtesans, prostitutes held contradictory positions of privilege and condemnation in Indian society. They were the only group of women exempt from purdah—the system that severely restricted women's participation in public life and interaction with men by imposing veils and seclusion on married Indian women. The purdah system was adopted by select Hindu elite beginning in the twelfth century following the Muslim conquest of India.[1] As the minimum age of marriage for Hindu women was progressively and systematically reduced from the mid-teens to well before puberty, Hindu women faced an increasingly narrow window of opportunity to receive education or training in the arts before their seclusion. For centuries this situation enforced a condition of illiteracy among almost all Hindu women.

Explanations for the adoption of the Muslim purdah system are many, including its function as a system of control over women's sexuality. In Hindu ideology women were associated with the unbridled forces of nature and were nearly always considered to be dangerous; the seat of their power rested in their sexual relationships with their husbands. Benevolent women were expected to turn over control of their sexuality to their husbands. A respectable woman's temptation to break purdah was equated with the desire to become a prostitute.

Able to roam unveiled throughout the cities, prostitutes and dancing girls remained free from the restrictions that respectable women endured over dress, behavior, sexual expression, and education. Interestingly, over time, courtesans in Hindu India became the custodians of the arts. Men frequently sought their company not only to gratify their sexual desires but to enjoy their singing, dancing, and poetry, pleasures they could not share with their wives. Protected, and often in the service of the state or the temple, prostitutes and dancing girls were viewed as sources of revenue for these institutions as well as preservers of the "sanctity and permanence" of the marital relationship.[2] The so-called freedom of these women to exercise their sexuality needs to be examined within this context.

Born in Calcutta to a family of actors and prostitutes, Binodini was to face many forms of unveiled oppression in her life. Her theatrical career began at the age of 11, at the time in India when prostitutes began to be used in theater productions for female roles that for centuries had been performed by men. While practice of the arts on a professional level had never been permissible for respectable Indian women, prior to Muslim rule in India the involvement of women in informal theatrical productions, which were comparable to the salons of the West, was socially permissible. Over time women's participation in and exposure to the fine arts declined; by the early nineteenth century, singing, dancing, and writing were denigrated to activities suitable only for the dancing girls.

Binodini first performed in a small role in the Great National Theater and within months she was touring with the company as the lead female actress, performing in over 50 plays in twelve years. Her brief career ended in 1884 not long after the Star Theater was sold to colleagues who refused to give her a share in the new ownership. Had her celebrated beauty already waned by the age of twenty-four? Had her refusal at this point in her life to seek assistance from another male supporter erased what leverage she had in the theater? This was neither the first nor the final door closed to her because she was a prostitute.

Following her retirement from the theater, Binodini again turned to a man for financial support, a married lover who provided for her and set her up in a house until his death in 1912, at which point she returned to the world of her childhood—the downtrodden parts of the city where the prostitutes lived. Little is known about the last 30 years of her life. One cannot help but speculate on her angle of vision as she watched the dramatic improvements for early twentieth-century Indian women in their access to public life. Was Binodini Dasi a victim in a historical drama, entering the scene mere decades too early to benefit from and participate in the growing social and educational opportunities for women? Or was she a ghost of a much earlier time, when some women were free to dance and sing and roam the streets without threat of condemnation or control? Or was Binodini a catalyst of this change, a woman who fought to participate in the career she loved and refused to accept her culture's reductive definition of her character? Perhaps she was all these things.

JS

FROM *MY STORY*[§]

I decided to set up a theater. Why should I not? . . . When my mind was quite made up, I got Gurmukh Rai to support my scheme. I know this has been an age-old custom with us, to abandon one man's protection, only to fall back on another's; but it disturbed and pained me at the time. People might laugh at the very idea of our type displaying any sense of guilt or distress at playing false. Careful thought would bring home to them that we are women too. When the Almighty sent us to this world, he did not deny us the tender emotions of a womanly heart. He gave us all, and we lost all, by ill fate! But does the social order not bear any responsibility for this? The tenderness that our hearts were full with once

[§] Binodini Dasi. *My Story.* Reprinted by permission of The Feminist Press at the City University of New York, from Susie Tharu and K. Lalita, *Women Writing in India: Volume I: 600 B.C. to the Early Twentieth Century,* edited by Susie Tharu and K. Lalita. Copyright © 1991 by Susie Tharu and K. Lalita. Material excerpted from pages 292–296.

can never be fully destroyed. As proof, take the way we rear our children. We too desire a husband's love, but where do we find it? Who is willing to give us heart for heart? There is no shortage of men who come in lust, and charm us with their talk of romance; but which of them would give his heart to test whether we have hearts too? Were we the ones who first played false, or did we learn to only after we ourselves had been deceived? Has anyone ever investigated that? . . . Money cannot buy anyone's love. We too cannot sell our love for money. That is what the world holds against us. The playwright Girishbabu in his poem "Barangana" (Harlot) portrays these unfortunate women very accurately. "She had a lotus heart like any other woman," he says. In many regions water turns rock-hard! That is how it is with us! Falling helpless victims of oppression again and again, our hearts grow hardened one day.

Let us not go into that now, however. To adjust to the changed situation I have described earlier, I and the rest of the theater people had to struggle greatly. Because when the aforesaid young gentleman came to know that I was planning permanent links with a theater under someone else's patronage, he tried putting all manner of obstacles in our way, whether in anger or through sheer cussedness I do not know. . .

At one point, there was even a threat on my life! One day, after rehearsals, I was asleep in my room—it was about six in the morning—when I woke up suddenly at a crashing sound and the heavy trudge of boots! There stood a young gentleman in military uniform, sword at his side, right in the middle of my room, saying, "Meni, why sleep so much?" I sat up startled, and he went on, "Look, Binod, you have to quit their company. Whatever money they have spent on you so far, I'll pay back. Here's ten thousand now; if it comes to more, I'll give that too.". . . Well, his high-handed manner made me so angry I said, "No, never! I have given them my word; I cannot go back on it now." He said, "If it's for the money, I'll give you another ten thousand." His words inflamed me even more! I stood up and said, "Here, keep your money! It is I who have earned money, rather than money having earned me! Fate willing, your ten or twenty thousand will come to me again several times over. You can leave now!" When he heard that, he went blazing mad, put his hand on his sword, and said, "Is that so? You think I'll let you off that easy? I'll cut you to pieces first! The twenty thousand I was going to give you I'll spend on something else, and let's see then." And he took his sword out from its sheath and aimed it straight at my head. My eyes had been on that sword of his, so the minute he swung out, I crouched down behind a table harmonium. The sword struck the top of the harmonium and knocked three inches off the wood! He lifted it off and hit out again, but luck favored him, and I was not destined to die, so this time the blow fell on the music stool. I rose up at once and caught his raised hand, and said, "What exactly are you up to? If you want to slay me, leave it for later; think what you will face in the end. How does it matter whether this tainted life of mine remains or ends? What will become of you? Think of your family, think of leaving this world marked and burdened forever, all for the sake of a despised harlot. For shame! Listen to me. Calm down. Tell me what you want me to do, but cool off now."

I had heard that when the first surge of fury subsides, people come to their senses. That is exactly what happened. He flung away the sword and sat down on the spot with his face in his hands. I was filled with pity at his distress! I thought, to hell with everything; let me go back to him again. But I was so thoroughly enmeshed by then with the theater people and Girishbabu that it was impossible for me to escape. Well anyway, I survived that day. He walked out without a word! . . .

. . . With great enthusiasm, and with a lot of expense, the theater was finally ready. It must have taken just under a year. But along with this there is one thing I feel I just must mention. While the theater was coming up, they had all said, "This theater will have your name linked with it. So even after you die, your name will live on. In other words, 'B' Theater will be its name." That had made me happier still. But ultimately they did not keep their word—why I do not know. Right up to the point when the theater was to be registered, I thought it was to be named after me. But the day they went and registered it—all arrangements were complete by then, the theater was to open a week from that day—I asked them eagerly about the name they had given. Dashubabu cheerfully answered, "Star." When I heard this, I was so deeply hurt inside that I flopped down on the spot and couldn't utter a word for two full minutes. After a while I controlled myself and said, "Good!" I thought about it later. Had their show of love and affection been just empty words to serve their own interests? But what could I have done. I was helpless! I was totally in their hands by then! And I had never dreamed they could trick me like this, act in such bad faith. The time I refused the offer of all that money did not hurt me half so much as their behavior did. Though I never said a word about it to anyone, I couldn't forget it either. I remembered it all my life. Besides, I loved the theater so much, thought it so much my own, and a new hall put up, no matter how, was such a great happening that the matter could have received no importance in any case. But in later times too, after the theater was ready, I was not treated well! They tried to quote all kinds of rules to prevent me from staying there, even as a salaried actress. And they succeeded, so for two months I was forced to sit at home. After that I was back again, thanks to Girishbabu's efforts, and my own insistence on my proprietary rights.

NOTES

[1] Less stringent manifestations of the seclusion of women occurred prior to the twelfth century among certain royal families as a means of shielding female royalty from the eyes of the lower castes. It should be noted that even once purdah was the rule among the Hindu people, its practice was hardly absolute among the lower castes; peasant and working-class women, especially those that lived in rural areas, did not remain in seclusion but continued to work in the fields alongside their male family members.

[2] Compare this discussion to that of courtesans in the ancient Greek world in the headnote on Hipparchia in this section.

WORKS CONSULTED

Altekar, A.S. *The Position of Women in Hindu Civilization: From Prehistoric Times to the Present Day.* Delhi: Motilal Banarsidass, 1978.

Joardar, Biswanath. *Prostitution: In Historical and Modern Perspectives.* New Delhi: Inter-India Publications, 1984.

Gupta, Kamala. *Social Status of Hindu Women in Northern India: 1206–1707 A.D.* New Delhi: Inter-India Publications, 1987.

Tharu, Susie, and K. Lalita, eds. *Women Writing in India: 600 B.C. to the Early Twentieth Century.* Vol. 1. New York: Feminist Press at CUNY, 1991.

Wadley, Susan S. "Women and the Hindu Tradition." *Women in India: Two Perspectives.* Ed. Doranne Jacobson and Susan S. Wadley. New Delhi: Manohar, 1992.

CATHERINE G. WAUGH *(1862–?)*

"Women as Law Clerks"

In 1905 the American psychologist G. Stanley Hall presented a treatise on differences in the male and the female brain—a treatise in which he formalized, and lent scientific authority to, common notions about the mental inferiority of women. By contrasting the male and female brain, Hall claimed that the male brain was ideally suited to specialization and expertise, considered defining characteristics of the professional, while the female brain had limited capacity for these functions. According to this theory, the notion of the professional woman was a contradiction in terms. It was in this social milieu that Catherine Waugh, recently graduated from Illinois' Union College of Law in 1886 as one of approximately 100 women lawyers in the country, found that no law firm would hire her.

Like the physician Rosalie Slaughter (see excerpt in this section), Catherine Waugh was one of a handful of turn-of-the-century U.S. women who, without the assistance of a husband, father, or brother already in the field, attempted to enter traditionally male-dominated professions. Law, however, constituted one of the strongest bastions of male domination. Armed with folklore about women who died of overwork, traditional notions of the sanctity of women's domestic role, and the Supreme Court's 1873 ruling that the practice of law was unfit for women and a "threat to femininity," the legal profession fought to prohibit the inclusion of women. When the first woman was admitted to the bar in 1869, women were still generally excluded from courtroom litigation and relegated to office work, typically as assistants to male relatives.

The relative absence of women in the legal profession presents a distinct contrast to the presence of women in the medical profession; by 1910, there were 9,000 licensed women physicians in the United States and only 1,500 women lawyers. Women's traditional participation in folk medicine, and their culturally recognized knowledge about childbirth and menstruation, had provided precedents for their entry into the medical profession. Law, by contrast, had its origins in trade and philosophy and thus belonged to traditionally male spheres of politics, business, and finance. Moreover, law played a critical role in the construction and maintenance of modern values and systems of regulation, a role not to be overlooked when questioning the rationale for men's more vigorous efforts to restrict women's access to this profession.

It was not until Catherine Waugh married a law-school colleague, three years after the composition of the essay included here, that she was finally accepted as a partner in her husband's law firm. In Waugh's eventual entry into the legal profession, we see an example of women's private associations with male allies functioning as the principal avenue into male-dominated public spheres. This avenue recalls the earliest recorded efforts by women to enter traditional male domains of work and education (see Hipparchia in this section).

What is most striking about Waugh, a suffragist who worked on women's issues for 50 years, was not her eventual admittance to the bar. Her path was almost without exception the one taken by the privileged minority of women with access to education. Rather, what distinguishes Waugh is the manner in which, through her writing, she resists this system of gendered oppression. With a keenness of vision and biting wit, Waugh exposes, categorizes, and dismantles the arguments upon which barriers against the inclusion of women into the legal profession were constructed.

JS

FROM "WOMEN AS LAW CLERKS"[§]

Law Office of Catherine G. Waugh
107 East State Street,
Rockford, Ill. . . . . . 188[7]

In the Union College of Law in Chicago from which I graduated in 1886, sex seemed no hindrance to our gaining the full benefit of all instructions. At first it certainly was quite a trial to recite before all those young men who would pause in the midst of throwing paper wads and slinging overshoes to see if either of the women knew enough to answer questions. This critical scrutiny soon changed to kindly approval and while they fought us vigorously in debate and moot court, their manly courtesy toward us made what might have been an uncomfortable place to a solitary girl so fraternally pleasant, that the Law College brings back only happy memories.

Many friends advised me to settle in Chicago and capture my share of the large fees floating about. So I decided to get a clerkship in some first class law firm and from the first support myself and most important learn the practice. Other classmates were doing the same already and why not I?

Miss Marten gave me a list of good men and firms and wrote me personal letters to several. Armed with these and letters and recommendations from two Judges friends of mine and the College of Professors I sallied forth to seek my fortune. I sailed out inflated with enthusiasm and confidence in my own abilities. I dragged myself back collapsed with chagrin and failure, and it took many days of rebuff to so quench my indomitable spirit.

Mr. F. whose sister was a friend of mine said he would have been delighted with my assistance but he already had more clerks than he knew what to do with.

Mr. W. was glad to make my acquaintance but that was the wrong season of the year to look for such a place. But on account of his father-in-law [sic]

[§] Reprinted by permission of *New York Literary Forum,* from "Women as Law Clerks: Catherine G. Waugh" by Nancy F. Cott, from *The Female Autograph,* edited by Domna C. Stanton. Special issue of *New York Literary Forum* 12–13. Copyright © 1984. Material excerpted from pages 185–189.

the Judge's kind letter he would make diligent inquiry, and carefully took my name and address so he could write me as soon as he found the place. So out I went thanking him for those exertions I imagined he would be making in my behalf, poor deluded creature that I was.

Mr. J. preferred the help of his two sons and must also confess he disapproved of women stepping out of their true sphere the home. This of course led to some discussion the nature of which you can no doubt imagine.

Pompous Judge J. never knew of anyone who needed a clerk and a dozen young men would be ready for a place as soon as vacant. This was delivered with his eyes still clinging to his newspaper and coupled with some sage reflections about the difficulty of any young person ever succeeding.

Bristly, bullet headed little Mr. B. exclaimed vehemently, "I don't approve of women at the bar, they can't stand the racket. I would prefer to find a place for my daughter in someone's kitchen and I advise you to rather go home and take in sewing. I am opposed to women practicing law." I assured him it was not in default of having opportunities to enter kitchens that I wished to do law work. That though it greived [sic] me not to be able to please everyone in my choice of a profession it seemed more properly a matter for my own decision, inwardly reflecting that only when I had defeated that pettifoger [sic] in some illustrious lawsuit would he be fully answered. Take in sewing at 60 cents a dozen for fine shirts? No thank you. He can make shirts himself. I'd never make shirts for him if he had to wrap himself in burlap instead.

Two others had advertised for law clerks and when I applied in person were dumfounded. No objections were made to my qualifications but they wanted a man and as I was not a man and never would be they were ready to wish me a good day. I argued with them that in law school I had done everything any other student had and why not here, that any place suitable for a decent man to go on legal business would not be shunned by me. But tho [sic] I defeated them on every argument they beat me on the main point, no woman law clerk.

Kindly old gentlemen would tell me I did not look very strong and that I must not forget Miss Hulett, Miss Perry and another girl lawyer in St. Louis who died of overwork. It is amazing how many times the ghosts of those girls were resurrected to scare me away from the thought of practice.

I answered by letter every advertisement for a law clerk but a troublesome conscience always forced me to write my full name and that of course disclosed the distressing fact that I was no man.

One man said, "I want a clerk who is a regular bulldozer and can blow people up hill and down and you don't look equal to it." Whether any legal knowledge would have been necessary he did not state.

But one man wrote to me stating he needed just such help. He agreed to all my modest demands, told of the large law business he would gradually turn over to me, enthused on women in the law, asked about my financial backing, whether I was engaged to be married, what my education had been and would I agree to stay five years when once he had let me into all his business. He waived all my various testimonials declaring he could read in my countenance that I would suit exactly. He was a fine looking gray-haired gentleman and I was elated at having found such a safe place, with prospect of learning so much from my fatherly employer. Confiding my success to a friend also a friend of his I was alarmed by his advice "Don't you go near him. His law business is non est. He has been twice divorced and probably intends to raise you to the eminence of No. 3 as he has proposed to several during the past month." So I did not go even tho' he wrote several times to try it "hoping we might make arrangements that would suit *permanently* all around." So farewell to my gray haired patron.

One of my classmates who now adorns the woolsack in one of Chicago's justice courts said "Go to my old gent the Judge I have told him about you and he will help you." So I sought Judge B. and Mrs. B. who were very kind and encouraging and the first thing I knew there was a bit of an item in the Legal News telling about my qualifications.

But I have reason to suppose that every reader deliberately skipped that portion of the paper as I never heard of it except through fellow students who joked me on having a free ad.

Then I sought an influential lady who professed vast admiration for me through hearing the Professor's praises. She kissed me at a meeting and parting, called me "Dear," "My Love" and "Sweet Child" all in the first interview and knew she would find me a place at once but as I never heard of any one to whom she spoke on the subject her efforts were probably limited to the said demonstrations of affection.

Then my dear cousin the manufacturer would speak to his attorney if he could ever think of it, but alas he never thought of it.

Numbers of attorneys were very polite and hoped I would succeed but could not tell if they would need a clerk but took my name and address. Others again told me plainly they objected to having a woman.

For the smiles and kind words which perhaps they would not have wasted on a man applicant of course I felt thankful but would gladly have dispensed with them and received the clerkship they were daily giving young men classmates of mine.

When at last I gave up the search it seemed as if there was no place on earth for a young woman just graduated from law school. If she had ten or twenty years of successful practice to back her, then the world would make an exception in her favor and condescendingly allow her to continue but who would help her to begin?

It was a dreary prospect to think of.

But my fit of melancholy did not last forever, so I came back to my home in Rockford Illinois with its less than twenty five thousand inhabitants and hung out my shingle here alone. My rebuffs and discouragement in Chicago made the kind words and helpful deeds of those who had known me all my life so much of a consolation that I am again nerved up to the struggle and tho it seems like bragging to say it I beleive [sic] I will succeed. . . .

WORKS CONSULTED

Cott, Nancy F. "Women as Law Clerks: Catherine G. Waugh." *The Female Autograph.* Ed. Domna C. Stanton. Spec. issue of *New York Literary Forum* 12–13 (1984): 181–84.

Woloch, Nancy. *Women and the American Experience.* New York: Knopf, 1984.

JARENA LEE *(1783?)*

The Life and Religious Experience of Jarena Lee

Jarena Lee's presence as a member and supporter of women's rights within the structure of the African Methodist Episcopal (AME) Church was crucial to the gains made by Blackwomen[1] in the oldest church in Black America. Historically the church was the center of Black social and political activity, and indeed, prior to the mass integration of Black Americans into white areas, the church had become a powerful base for Black people advocating liberation theology and political change. The AME church was founded in 1787 in Philadelphia by Richard Allen in response to discrimination (in such practices as seating and ordination) and a disenchantment with the political agenda of white Methodists. The AME church became the most powerful among Black churches. Along with Rebecca Cox Jackson and Maria Stewart, Jarena Lee was a forerunner for later Methodist women, such as Amanda Berry Smith, Julia Foote, and Zilpha Elaw, who would advocate a woman's right to preach the Word (see Angel).

Lee's account of her life and her religious experience forms part of the central canon of narrative writing by Blackwomen in America. The fact that the first narratives by Blackwomen in America were spiritual only reinforces the role that religion played in the volatile and evolving politics of race and gender in the nineteenth century (and in turn, the roles that race and gender politics played in the evolution of the church in Black America). Furthermore, the presence of these spiritual narratives reflects the recognition (in particular by Blackwomen) that religion was both an important tool, and, in its patriarchal and racist aspects, a crucial impediment to be resisted in the struggle for liberation on race and gender fronts.

Born in 1783 in Cape May, New Jersey, Lee had her first conversion experience in 1804 during a Presbyterian service. One year later, she began working as a domestic near Philadelphia, and it was there that she heard a sermon by Allen and became a Methodist. Lee felt the call to preach early on and in 1809 petitioned Allen for that right; she was denied on the basis that "[the church] did not call for women preachers." Instead, she was allowed to give religious advice at particular functions and when directed by religious leaders (Lee 324). In 1811 she married Joseph Lee, who was a pastor in Snow Hill. During the six years of their marriage, Lee was very ill and experienced many deaths in her family. After the death of her husband in 1817, she was left with two small children and her undying passion to preach (Davidson 135–137; see also DeCosta-Willis).

Lee wrote and published at her own expense two accounts of her autobiography. The first, *The Life and Religious Experience of Jarena Lee, a Coloured Lady, Giving an Account of her Call to Preach the Gospel*, was published in 1836; the second was published in 1849 with the amended title *Religious Life and Journal of Mrs. Jarena Lee, Giving an Account* . . . . The second narrative is about seventy-five pages longer and provides a more detailed look at her life and thoughts; for example, it is in the 1849 version of her narrative that she gives her thoughts on slavery (Davidson 138; Humez 321).

Lee's narrative uses the familiar spiritual trope of being called, or inspired, to do the work of God. Certainly Lee believed she heard an instruction to preach, yet the way she narrates her experience reflects a definite rhetorical motive—an argument used in similar narratives by Blackwomen. Realistically, to pose as being *merely* "called," this invoking of a higher power to buttress an inner drive, may have been the only way that she and other women preachers could assert their right to preach in their effort to attain their rightful place in the AME hierarchy. Furthermore, Jean McMahon Humez argues that the writings of religious women of this time all emphasize similar concerns: ". . . a concern with attaining a special level of holiness, a kind of salvation in life; the experience of gradually developing religious leadership skills within small prayer groups, predominantly or entirely female in membership; the struggle, as women, with male opposition to their ministry within the black independent churches; and the reliance on supernatural gifts as a source of power, wisdom, and authority not only in daily life but in attaining to a career as a religious leader" (4). These themes are all represented in Lee's life and work.

To this end, Lee uses careful and effective rhetoric to claim the woman's place in the gospel. In answer to Allen's response to her first petition to preach, she wrote, "And why should it be thought impossible, heterodox, or improper for a woman to preach? seeing the Saviour died for the woman as well as for the man . . . Is he *not a whole Saviour instead of a half one? as those who hold it wrong for a woman to preach would seem to make it appear*" (Lee 324, emphasis added). She argues that Mary was "the first to preach the risen Saviour," and begins an argument that uses Biblical examples of women who preached, a tradition that Elaw and Foote followed almost verbatim. Lee is aware of her audience—Black religious people of the North, especially Black men in the AME church—and anticipates, lists, and refutes their arguments in her narrative.

In 1918, she returned to Philadelphia and again petitioned Allen, who had been promoted to bishop of the AME church, for the right to hold prayer meetings in her home. Her petition was granted. A year or so later, she powerfully asserted her right to preach: during a sermon by an uninspired male preacher, she took over the pulpit and proclaimed herself to be "like Jonah; for it had been then nearly eight years since the Lord had called me to preach . . . but that I had lingered . . . and delayed to go at the bidding of the Lord" (Lee 325). Her enactment of the Biblical text was not only a declaration to male religious leaders (Allen was amongst those present in the congregation) of her right to preach, but was also a self-assertion that this was what she was called to do. In this example, Lee proposes that both she and male religious leaders have defied the will of God. The eight-plus year battle had been fought against exterior restrictions and interior reservations. But her bold and potentially dangerous coup was fruitful. First, it solidified her right to hold prayer meetings. Second, it paved the way for her to become a revival preacher, for though she was never officially ordained as a minister of the church, she did travel to Canada, Maryland, and the frontier settlement of Cincinnati as an itinerant preacher (Davidson 138).

In her use of the Bible to support her claims, it is clear that Lee is also aware of the ways that the Bible had been used against her; in the complete narrative, she contends with the scriptures of the Apostle Paul. Additionally, she is aware of the ways gender and notions of motherhood affected her—a free Blackwoman in the North in nineteenth-century America—and recognizes how they hampered her claims for the right to preach. Near the end of her narrative, she skillfully cites an example of having left her sick child in order to fulfill a missionary commitment. She describes being "made able to preach without one worry for her child," who she finds is healthy when she returns. This description challenges the essentialist and limited notions of womanhood/motherhood in two ways: first, her ability to focus on work even when her child is sick overcomes the potential distraction of "natural" motherliness; and second, other people (perhaps men?) are able to care for a sick child as well as its own mother can.

Lee's narrative—like those of other women who were advocating a place for women in the church—did not directly employ the feminist rhetoric of the time; yet it is clear in the stances that she took on marriage (limiting to a woman's potential), work, and motherhood that, in her life and writing, she intended to challenge ideas of who Blackwomen were and what it was they were supposed to do. Lee blazed a Black feminist theological tradition—one developed by Jackson, Stewart, and the other women who followed—a tradition with locations in Black liberation theology and in feminist rhetoric, and in still another place all of its own.

KQ

FROM *THE LIFE AND RELIGIOUS EXPERIENCE OF JARENA LEE*[§]

Between four and five years after my sanctification, on a certain time, an impressive silence fell upon me, and I stood as if someone was about to speak to me, yet I had no such thought in my heart. But to my utter surprise there seemed to be a voice which I thought I distinctly heard, and most certainly understood, which said to me, "Go preach the Gospel!" I immediately replied aloud, "No one will believe me." Again I listened, and again the same voice seemed to say—"Preach the Gospel; I will put words in your mouth and will turn your enemies to become your friends."

At first I supposed that Satan had spoken to me, for I had read that he could transform himself into an angel of light for the purpose of deception. Immediately I went into a secret place, and called upon the Lord to know if he had called me to preach, and whether I was deceived or not, when there appeared to my view the form and figure of a pulpit, with a Bible lying thereon, the back of which was presented to me as plainly as if it had been a literal fact.

[§] *The Life and Religious Experience of Jarena Lee, a Coloured Lady, Giving an Account of her Call to Preach the Gospel,* by Jarena Lee. Used by permission of The Western Reserve Historical Society, Cleveland, Ohio. Reprinted from *Religious Experience and Journal of Mrs. Jarena Lee, Giving an Account of her Call to Preach the Gospel* (1849), as it appears in *Gifts of Power: The Writing of Rebecca Cox Jackson, Black Visionary, Shaker Eldress,* edited by Jean McMahon Humez, published 1981 by The University of Massachusetts Press. Material excerpted from pages 323–326.

In consequence of this, my mind became so excited, that during the night following, I took a text and preached in my sleep. I thought there stood before me a great multitude, while I expounded to them the things of religion. So violent were my exertions and so loud were my exclamations, that I awoke from the sound of my own voice, which also awoke the family of the house where I resided. Two days after I went to see the preacher in charge of the African Society, who was the Rev. Richard Allen . . . to tell him that I felt it my duty to preach the Gospel . . . Several times on my way there, I turned back again; but as often as I felt my strength again renewed, and I soon found that the nearer I approached to the house of the minister, the less was my fear. Accordingly, as soon as I came to the door, my fears subsided, . . . I was tranquil.

I now told him, that the Lord had revealed to me, that [I] must preach the Gospel. He replied, by asking in what sphere I wished to move in? I said, among the Methodists. He then replied that a Mrs. Cook, a Methodist lady, had also some time before requested the same privilege; who, it was believed, had done much good in the way of exhortation, and holding prayer meetings; and who had been permitted to do so by the verbal license of the preacher in charge at that time. But as to women preaching, he said that our Discipline knew nothing at all about it—that it did not call for women preachers. This I was glad to hear, because it removed the fear of the cross—but no sooner did this fear cross my mind, than I found that a love of souls had in a measure departed from me; that holy energy which burned within me, as a fire, began to be smothered. This I soon perceived.

O how careful ought we to be, lest through our by-laws of church government and discipline, we bring into disrepute even the words of life. For as unseemly as it may appear now-a-days for a woman to preach, it should be remembered that nothing is impossible with God. And why should it be thought impossible, heterodox, or improper for a woman to preach? seeing the Saviour died for the woman as well as for the man . . . . Is he not a whole Saviour, instead of a half one? as those who hold it wrong for a woman to preach, would seem to make it appear.

Did not Mary *first* preach the risen Saviour, and is not the doctrine of the resurrection the very climax of Christianity—hangs not all our hope on this, as argued by St. Paul? . . .

But some will say that Mary did not expound the Scripture, therefore she did not preach, in the proper sense of the term. To this I reply, it may be that the term preach in those primitive times, did not mean exactly what it is now *made* to mean; perhaps it was a great deal more simple then, than it is now—if it were not, the unlearned fisherman could not have preached the gospel at all. . . .

To this it may be replied, by those who are determined not to believe that it is right for a woman to preach, that the disciples, though they were fisherman and ignorant of letters too, were inspired to do so. . . . If then, to preach the Gospel, by the gift of heaven, comes by inspiration solely, is God straitened: must he take the man exclusively? May he not, did he not, and can he not inspire a female to preach the simple story of the birth, life, death and resurrection of our Lord, and accompany it too with power to the sinner's heart? As for me, I am fully persuaded that the Lord called me to labor according to what I have received, in his vineyard. . . .

In my wanderings up and down among men, preaching according to my ability, I have frequently found families who told me that they had not for several years been to a meeting, and yet, while listening to hear what God would say by his poor female instrument, have believed with trembling—tears rolling down their cheeks, the signs of contrition and repentance towards God. I firmly believe that I have sown seed, in the name of the Lord, which shall appear with its increase at the great day of accounts, when Christ shall come to make up his jewels. . . .

It was now eight years since I had made application to be permitted to preach the Gospel, during which time I had only been allowed to exhort, and even this privilege but seldom. This subject was now renewed afresh in my mind; it was as a fire shut up in my bones. During this time, I had solicited of the Rev. Bishop, Richard Allen, who at this time had become Bishop of the African Episcopal Methodists in America, to be permitted the liberty of holding prayer meetings in my own hired house, and of exhorting as I found liberty, which was granted to me. By this means, my mind was relieved, as the house soon filled when the hour appointed for prayer had arrived. . . .

Soon after this . . . the Rev. Richard Williams was to preach at Bethel Church, where I with others were assembled. He entered the pulpit, gave out the hymn, which was sung, then addressed the throne of grace; took his text, passed through the exordium, and commenced to expound it. The text he took is in Jonah, 2d chap., 9th verse—"Salvation is of the Lord." But as he proceeded to explain, he seemed to have lost the spirit; when in the same instant, I sprang, as by altogether supernatural impulse, to my feet, when I was aided from above to give an exhortation on the very text which my brother Williams had taken.

I told them I was like Jonah; for it had been then nearly eight years since the Lord had called me to preach his Gospel to the fallen sons and daughters of Adam's race, but that I had lingered like him, and delayed to go at the bidding of the Lord, and warn those who are as deeply guilty as were the people of Nineveh.

During the exhortation, God made manifest his power in a manner sufficient to show the world that I was called to labor according to my ability, and the grace given unto me, in the vineyard of the good husbandman.

I now sat down, scarcely knowing what I had done, being frightened. I imagined, that for this indecorum, as I feared it might be called, I should be expelled from the church. But instead of this, the Bishop rose up in the assembly, and related that I had called upon him eight years before, asking to be permitted to preach, and that he had put me off; but that he now as much believed that I was called to do that work, as any of the preachers present. These remarks greatly strengthened me, so that my fears of having given an offense, and made myself liable as an offender, subsided, giving place to a sweet serenity, a holy joy of a peculiar kind, untasted in my bosom until then. . . .

NOTE

[1] Following Joan Martin, I use the terms "Blackwoman" and Blackwomen" to indicate a particular location of experience that is collective and individual. See headnote on Cornelia in the section **Identifying Sources of Resistance** for further discussion of the term.

WORKS CONSULTED

Angel, Stephen W. "Religion." *Reference Library of Black America*. Ed. Kenneth Estell. 10 vols. Detroit: Afro-American Press, 1994. 771–792.

Davidson, Phebe. "Jarena Lee." *Legacy* 10:2 (1993): 135–141.

DeCosta-Willis, Miriam. "Jarena Lee." *Notable Black American Women*. Ed. Jessie Carney Smith. Detroit: Gale Research, 1992. 662–3.

Humez, Jean McMahon. Introduction. *The Writings of Rebecca Jackson, Black Visionary, Shaker Eldress*. Ed. Humez. Amherst: U of Massachusetts P, 1981. 1–64.

Lee, Jarena. *Religious Experience and Journal of Mrs. Jarena Lee, Giving an Account of her Call to Preach the Gospel* (1849). In *The Writings of Rebecca Jackson, Black Visionary, Shaker Eldress*. Ed. Jean McMahon Humez. Amherst: U of Massachusetts P, 1981. 321–327.

Martin, Joan. "The Notion of Difference for Emerging Womanist Ethics: The Writings of Audre Lorde and bell hooks." *Journal of Feminist Studies in Religion* 9 (1993): 39–52.

CARMEN LUCIA *(1902–1985)*

"The Employers Were Afraid of Me"

> Trade unions are still, in our kind of society, the only social organization that can lift women immediately out of poverty and give them some measure of control over their lives.
>
> *Ah Quon McElrath*[1]

Scholars of U.S. women's history have tended to focus on the ideological concerns of white feminists of the middle and upper classes. For example, the debates outlined in the headnote for Ednah Dow Littlehale and Caroline Wells Healy (in **Vision and Transformation**) provided both the terms and underlying beliefs that have structured the writing of women's history for many years. In the past decade or so, however, attempts have been made to broaden the base of women's history, to include the views and actions of working-class women as well as those of women of color.[2] These efforts have revealed that "sisterhood" has rarely transcended the boundaries of race and class, and that non-elite women have developed systems of belief, and strategies for improving their lives, that are distinct from those of more privileged groups.

Carmen Lucia was born in Calabria, Italy, two years before her family emigrated to Rochester, New York. There they began working in various clothing trades and became active in the factories' unions. Lucia herself began working in a clothing factory at the age of fourteen, and from the outset distinguished herself as an outspoken critic of the many varieties of inefficiency and unfairness that she found in both factories and unions. She soon caught the attention of union leadership, and was asked to start working as a union organizer—the beginning of a lifelong career. She worked for a number of the major clothing and millinery unions (perhaps the most unionized trades of those in which women predominated), traveled throughout the country, and eventually settled in Atlanta. Through her work she gained access to a number of unusual educational experiences, and also cultivated a talent for writing poetry. Her creativity, imagination, and wide-ranging knowledge of social psychology come across repeatedly in her autobiographical interview, excerpted in the selection which follows.

As both a factory worker and organizer, and as a single (divorced) mother of an only daughter, Lucia experienced, firsthand, unequal pay scales and discrimination against unmarried women—both of which she fought throughout her life. But first and foremost, Carmen Lucia was a union organizer. Like many other women interviewed for the "Twentieth Century Trade Union Woman"—an oral history project—Lucia's primary identification was with the working class.[3] In contrast to middle- and upper-class feminists, who favored reforms centered on the individual woman, and like many of the working-class women in this anthology, female union activists focused on the collective action of all working people as the best means of achieving equality for women. These activists placed great value on their ability to apply theory to practice, to be realistic and knowledgeable, and to produce concrete gains for working people.

KKF

FROM AN INTERVIEW WITH CARMEN LUCIA[§]

I wanted to dramatize things and make it like theater, but also present the facts. For some strike activities we would always choose the prettiest girls, the most slender girls, because it was just like an advertisement. I'd hurriedly make dresses and have the girls in white dresses with red sashes. They always looked so striking. Now when I was at City Hall in Philadelphia, there's a curving stairway that goes up to another floor. As I watched at the bottom while the girls went up I thought what a beautiful picture that was, to see those young girls imbued with the spirit of doing something, really catching the spirit of democracy in action. We had moments like that on picket lines that I treasure so much.

From Philadelphia I was sent to Chicago. I had to go wherever the union sent me in spite of the fact that I had this little child. In Chicago, when I went on the picket line, the pickets were standing in a corner with their signs, but not picketing. I went over there and asked, "What's the matter? Why aren't you picketing?" They said, "That cop over there, he's a mean bastard." "Oh, come on," I said. "You have a legal right to picket, as long as you picket and you don't bother anybody, he can't do anything to hurt you." They said, "That's what you think." "All right," I said, "give me the sign and I'll go."

I thought, if I take the picket sign and chant union slogans they'll follow me. They didn't. They knew better than I did. When the scabs came out, now what could one woman do with a sign? There were police all over. They had formed a cordon for the scabs to come through. I thought, they're not going to keep me from going through there. I said, "Excuse me. I've got to picket." So I did that. I was foolish then. I put my hand on a woman and I said, "Listen, honey, I want to talk to you." I would never have attacked her.

As soon as my hand touched her shoulder, I don't know what happened. A ton of bricks fell on me. I was severely beaten by the cop. Taken into an alley. If I hadn't had a big fur collar on my coat, he'd have bashed my brains out. He was that mean, and he got mad when I defied him. What I found out was that the other union organizer had forgotten to pay the cops that day. In those days, you had to grease their palms in order for them to leave you alone. Especially in Chicago. So they really beat me. When I got to the police station, it was the first time that I really began to feel the pain. The cop had pulled my arm out of my socket. I was bleeding from several places. I was too angry to feel pain at the time, but when I cooled off a little bit, I found that I was hurt.

Finally the union found what police station I was in, and they came and got me to the

---

[§] Reprinted from *Rocking the Boat: Union Women's Voices, 1915–1975*, edited by Brigid O'Farrell and Joyce L. Kornbluh. Copyright © 1996 by Brigid O'Farrell and Joyce L. Kornbluh. Reprinted by permission of Rutgers University Press. Material excerpted from pages 45–46, 57.

hospital. The doctor yanked the arm to put it back in the socket. I've never forgotten that pain as long as I've lived. The girl whose arm I had laid the hand on felt very badly. She saw the beating I got. I understood that she went the next day and got the girls to go and join the union. She said, "Anybody that could be beaten up like that for the sake of trying to help us should be rewarded." The beating was worthwhile. We got the shop in the union. . . .

I did have a reputation. The employers were afraid of me. I don't know why, but my name used to strike terror. I didn't mean it that way, but that's what used to actually happen. People that don't have a definite point of view go with the wind. They change so quickly. That doesn't mean that you can't sometimes change for the better. But some people changed from one day to another depending on who was speaking or who was leading or whatever was a more favorable position to take. I have never been that way. The union knew who to call when they wanted the job done.

Years ago, Harry Bridges thought I wanted to take over the Retail Clerks Union, but I had no such aspirations. I never wanted that kind of top job, and I'll tell you why: I was afraid I'd lose my contact with the people and I'd become greedy. I'd become totally unaware of the workers' problems. I saw too much of that going on when they got jobs that went to their heads. They weren't the same people, and I didn't want to become one of them.

I was called upon by a lot of universities to speak. I remember one time I was introduced and the chairman said, "We have three speakers: a lady, a gentleman, and a woman organizer." I turned that into a joke and I had everybody laughing. Yes, I'm still an organizer!

NOTES

[1] Quoted in Brigid O'Farrell and Joyce L. Kornbluh, *Rocking the Boat.*

[2] This issue is addressed explicitly in Nancy A. Hewitt's "Beyond the Search for Sisterhood: American Women's History in the 1980s," and Nancy Cott's "What's in a Name? The Limits of 'Social Feminism'; or, Expanding the Vocabulary of Women's History."

[3] See the introduction to *Rocking the Boat.*

WORKS CONSULTED

Cott, Nancy. "What's in a Name? The Limits of 'Social Feminism'; or, Expanding the Vocabulary of Women's History." *Journal of American History* 76 (December 1989).

Hewitt, Nancy A. "Beyond the Search for Sisterhood: American Women's History in the 1980s." *Social History* 10.3 (1985).

O'Farrell, Brigid, and Joyce L. Kornbluh, eds. *Rocking the Boat: Union Women's Voice, 1915–1975.* New Brunswick: Rutgers UP, 1996.

NONGENILE MASITHATHU ZENANI *(c. 1906–)*

"When a Doctor Is Called, She Must Go"

The advance of modern and scientific medicine has often led to a suppression of a rich body of knowledge held by female healers and a variety of medical practices that are considered unscientific. In recent years, modern medicine has slowly acknowledged the wealth of information and experience contained in alternative healing practices. In many parts of the world, these methods have always played a central role in the treatment of the sick. Frequently, women are the primary keepers of healing traditions, and hold respected positions in their societies. Nongenile Zenani's narrative enables us to gain insight into the life and development of a healer in South Africa. She told her story to an American researcher who recorded and translated it in the 1980's.

As a child, Nongenile, a member of the Xhosa tribe, was sent to live with her grandparents. She grew up among traditionalists, that is, among people who observe old tribal customs. Her parents had converted to Christianity and had accepted many Western values. Tensions between Xhosa traditions and Western influences weave through Nongenile's life and are crucial for an understanding of her situation. Nongenile did not receive any formal schooling, which, according to her, "was not valued in any way" by the traditionalists (Scheub 13). Her days were filled with activities closely related to Xhosa customs. During puberty, for example, she participated in various rituals for the initiation of young women. She left her grandparents' home and returned to her parents to escape an arranged marriage. She strongly opposed the compulsory nature of the marital practices that left no space for women to choose their partners. But, despite her resistance, her father forced her to marry. Since Xhosa women were mainly defined through their status as wives and mothers, it was impossible for her father to imagine his daughter not complying with his will (Green 196f, Hammond-Tooke 118f., *Standard Encyclopaedia of Southern Africa* 550–58).

In the excerpt here, we meet Nongenile as a newly-wed wife. It is the first time in her narrative that she mentions her calling as a doctor. The contrast with Rosalie Slaughter's account (also in this section) is instructive. The process of initiation into the profession of medicine that Nongenile recounts is typical for a certain kind of South African healer—a group of diviners (*igqira*), healers who are called to the profession through the promptings of their ancestors (Hammond-Tooke 104). Diviners learn about their vocation through dreams and visions and an ancestor-sent illness that can only be cured if the afflicted follows the calling (Green 188). Older doctors then diagnose the chronic illness as a call to diviner-mediumship and take in the future healer as an apprentice. Nongenile's story allows us to witness her apprenticeship and her initiation into the profession, including ritual dancing and treatment of her own patients.

After about a year, Nongenile is told by the older doctor to set up her own practice. How she cures her patients is not revealed. Does she follow the Xhosa tradition to call on ancestors' spirits to heal patients (Janzen 37)? The majority of diviners in Southern Africa are women; they are highly respected and usually have a relatively lucrative income. Why is this profession mainly controlled by women in a patriarchal society where women are leaders in few areas of life?

Nongenile experiences conflicts when she becomes a doctor. Her husband demands that she not allow her obligations as a healer to interfere with her duties as a wife. How does she evaluate these two roles? How does she resolve the different sets of demands? Her argumentation does not address whether there might be a connection between her dissatisfaction with the role that Xhosa society assigns to most women and her calling as a healer. Does she ever see her position as a Xhosa doctor as a way to gain respect and power beyond marriage and motherhood?

KV

FROM "AND SO I GREW UP"[§]

. . . Then difficulties arose. The subject regarding my vocation to be a doctor came up again, it became more persistent as my nervousness and chest troubles intensified. Now, whenever a person who had done something came into my sight—if this person had done something bad—my body would itch, I would become uncomfortable; I would become excitable, nervous, I would experience intense pains in my chest. I could not stay with a person who had done something bad.

This became more and more evident in me, and caused my husband considerable anxiety. He wanted to send me to more doctors then, to determine what was wrong with me. And he did take me to the doctors, he took me by night. We went to a doctor, and my husband had me examined there. The doctor explained that my body pores were those of 'white death.' My blood was repelled by anything evil or dirty. I am therefore a 'white' person. The doctor advised that I be treated to ensure my strength against the things that trouble the blood.

My husband said, 'Well, I give her to you, Doctor. Treat her, because this is painful to me too.'

The doctor then charged a fee for pounding herbs, but he did not charge for the diagnosis. I was to do the pounding.

My husband produced the money, a pound, and left me with the doctor, saying that he would come to visit me frequently, but that I would be under the care of this doctor.

I stayed with that doctor then, and time passed for me there. He treated me in every way, purging me, washing me, feeding me a medicine that pained my body. And my trouble ceased.

The pains in my chest ended, my anxieties were calmed. He made me dance, also a part of the treatment—he did everything.

[§] Reprinted from "And So I Grew Up: The Autobiography of Nongenile Masithathu Zenani," researched and translated by Harold Scheub, in *Life Histories of African Women,* edited by Patricia W. Romero. Published by Ashfield Press, London, 1988. Material excerpted from pages 43–45.

Then, during the year, as his place was visited by sick people who had come to be treated, this doctor told me to go and take care of a person who had come to be examined. I was sent to another house; I went and examined that person. I finished that, and the doctor asked me to prepare some medicine for this patient. I did that. I treated him, and he became well. The doctor then rewarded me with doctor's white beads, a string of beads that was tied to my head, on the cranium—the first string of beads, beads of initiation. These were tied on.

The second time I completed an examination, a set of doctor's beads was put around my neck. Then my husband came again, he arrived to find me wearing these sets of beads. During his presence, a sick person came; I went to examine him, and I finished the job while my husband was still there.

Time passed, we went on like that—until I was treating my own patients. I would diagnose some of their diseases, they would come to me and I would treat them, and they would get well. And some of them would also become doctors, those with symptoms similar to mine. Various kinds of people came to me—a person with one kind of ache, a person who was barren, a person burdened by some illness. There were all kinds of people, all sorts and 'Well, it's about time that she should go and set up her own practice, at her own house. She should treat her own people, because she's now got quite a clientele here.'

That was the decision of the doctor. I returned then, and remained at my own house.

There were some difficulties, which might have caused great confusion had they not changed in time: while I was establishing my practice, traveling all over the countryside treating people, my husband became very angry. Why did I not come home anymore? I seem to be going to so many homesteads to treat patients, and I don't return to my own home! I might be gone as long as a week, even *two* weeks. That bothered him, we were annoying each other now, and it began to seem like a bad situation for our marriage. Eventually, it became clear that I wanted my husband to return the *lobola*.[1] I could no longer be his wife, because I would not be able to treat people as a white doctor does—people come to European doctor's offices to be treated, but the Xhosa doctor goes to the people, and thus must travel throughout the area. We are fetched, and go all over the countryside. When a doctor is called, she must go to treat people wherever they happen to be. Now if my husband demands that I operate in a manner that is unnatural, in a way that is not the way I have been created, then it is better if I depart from him for a period of ten years.

I did leave him, then I returned. He was suffering because of my absence. He begged me, saying that he had done a childish thing, not realizing what he had been doing. He feared that his wife would be carried away from him by certain people.

So I did come back, and from that time there were no misunderstandings in our relationship . . . though another difficulty might have arisen.

NOTE

[1] *lobola* This is the complex contractual arrangement made between the bride and groom and their families. Here, Mrs. Zenani is referring to the *lobola* cattle, a symbolic part of the exchange. [Scheub]

WORKS CONSULTED

Green, Edward. "Mystical Black Power: The Calling to Deviner-Mediumship in Southern Africa." *Women as Healers: Cross Cultural Perspectives.* New Brunswick: Rutgers UP, 1989. 196f.

Hammond-Tooke, David. *Rituals and Medicines: Indigenous Healing in South Africa.* Houghton: A.D. Donker, 1989.

Janzen, John M. *Ngoma: Disclosures of Healing in Central and Southern Africa.* Berkeley: U of California P, 1992.

Scheub, Harold. "And So I Grew Up: The Autobiography of Nongenile Masithathu Zenani." *Life Histories of African Women.* Ed. Patricia W. Romeo. London: Ashfield, 1988.

Standard Encyclopaedia of Southern Africa. Vol. 11. Cape Town: NASOU, 1970.

ROSALIE SLAUGHTER MORTON *(1876–?)*

"Seeking New Paths"

"I will love, honor, cherish—but not obey" (Slaughter 145). Rosalie Slaughter's wedding vow illustrates the independence that guided her life—beginning with an adamant determination, in the face of vehement family opposition, to follow male ancestors and relatives in the "footsteps of Aesculapius," mythic Roman guardian of physicians and healers (Slaughter 13). This selection from her writings shows how she energetically resisted attempts by her father, a well-established lawyer in Lynchburg, Virginia, to bind her to the domestic duties of a future upper-class wife and mother. At seventeen, instead of entertaining suitors chosen by her father, she enrolled in the Female Medical College of Pennsylvania to pursue a career as a doctor. The excerpt, taken from her autobiography *A Woman Surgeon,* allows us to explore some of the reasons behind her firm resolve.

Rosalie Slaughter sees in her mother's Quakerism a source of strength that enabled her to strive toward self-expression and self-fulfillment. The Religious Society of Friends, a Protestant denomination that emphasizes each individual's ability to feel God without the intermediary assistance of a church, priest, sacrament, or sacred book, regards the following principles as the pillars of faith: community, harmony, equality, simplicity, and sincerity (Brinton 3–13). Throughout her memoirs, Slaughter refers to Quakerism and the five tenets to which she felt a direct connection, one that informed her life-long commitment to social justice.

Even though Slaughter was "seeking new paths" as a woman in medicine and science, she saw her career as part of a larger tradition of women healers in the United States. From early colonial days, women had fulfilled important roles as medical practitioners, particularly in their function as midwives (Ehrenreich and English 40ff). With the rise of male obstetricians and medical professionalism in the eighteenth century, midwives lost much of their influence, yet remained important for their assistance with childbirth in rural areas and among the working classes (Morantz 4ff). In the second half of the nineteenth century, women demanded entrance into the male world of modern medicine. The first female doctor to earn a medical degree in the United States was Elizabeth Blackwell; she graduated from Geneva College in New York in 1849 (Morantz-Sanchez 49). By the end of the nineteenth century, the percentage of female doctors had climbed to around 5 percent, a figure that would not significantly change until the 1960s (Morantz-Sanchez 49).

Upon their entrance into the profession, women faced the opposition of many of their male colleagues. Although Slaughter's difficulties differ from those encountered by Catherine Waugh in her attempts to join the ranks of lawyers (see excerpt in this section), Slaughter often had to struggle with male suspicion about women's scientific abilities. But the energy and resistance that she displays here toward her father's plans stayed with her throughout her life and enabled her to be a successful surgeon and researcher.

KV

FROM *A WOMAN SURGEON*[§]

. . . At first, partly because I felt I would thus prepare for bigger things, and partly because I thought my parents would be less scandalized, I told my mother I would like to become a nurse. She neither argued nor discouraged, merely observing dispassionately that I ought first to ascertain the requirements. She knew that no hospital would be likely to accept a girl of sixteen.

I suspect that I appeared inadequate to a critical eye; certainly, having to send my photograph handicapped my ambition. I was not pampered nor frivolous, but all my photographs, taken in party dress, made me look like a fragile gardenia. Having been educated in Quaker honesty, I was too scrupulous to detour the matter of age. However, I penned earnest notes, emphasizing my serious-mindedness and asking for application blanks; these I duly filled in and sent, accompanied by a letter from my pastor, to the superintendents of schools of nursing far and wide. Whenever I eagerly tore open a long envelope with a hospital address in the corner and then remarked nonchalantly that it contained nothing of importance, a quiet Quaker smile circled my mother's lips.

Unvanquished, I kept on trying, until I finally confessed to my mother that I really did not want to make a life-work of nursing. What relief showed in her eyes!

"That would be just to get started," I added. "I really intend to be a doctor, like the boys."

Dismay blanched her face. Her placidity about my nursing notion had not prepared me for the distressed voice and anxious eyes with which she rejected my choice of a career. . .

Then we had a heart-to-heart, will-to-will talk. All the family, she warned, would oppose the idea. Most of all, my father. Well, I would ask him. She suggested that I wait a few days, since he was far from well. But I wished to have the matter out.

He blinked at me, then scowled and tapped the arm of his chair. He spoke kindly as my mother had. . .

"I do not want my daughter to earn money," he said firmly. "It is not right that you should go into competition with those who need to support themselves. A gentleman's daughter does not work for money; your field of service is to keep on making us happy, and later to marry a man of your own class. It is essential that society's standards be maintained. You will bring up your children with the highest ideals; your home will be a center of culture, helpfulness, and happiness, as this one is; your highest duty is to become a good wife and mother.". . .

We stood on opposite sides of a chasm. I realized that the gap would widen. He would

---

[§] Reprinted from *A Woman Surgeon: The Life and Work of Rosalie Slaughter Morton,* by Rosalie Slaughter Morton. Published 1937 by Frederick A. Stokes Co.

not comprehend my surging desire to plunge forward, putting all that was best in me into the swiftly progressing stream of science. How could he know that my feet were seeking new paths? . . .

WORKS CONSULTED

Brinton, Howard H. *The Nature of Quakerism.* Pendle Hill Pamphlets no. 47. Wallingford: Pendle Hill, 1949.

Ehrenreich, Barbara, and Deidre English. *For Her Own Good: 150 Years of Experts' Advice to Women.* New York: Doubleday, 1978.

Morantz, Regina Markell. Introduction. *In Her Own Words: Oral Histories of Women Physicians.* Ed. Regina Markell Morantz, Cynthia Sodola Pomerleau, and Carol Hansen Fenichel. Westport: Greenwood, 1982.

Morantz-Sanchez, Regina Markell. *Sympathy and Science: Women Physicians in American Medicine.* New York: Oxford UP, 1985.

Morton, Rosalie Slaughter. *A Woman Surgeon: The Life and Work of Rosalie Slaughter Morton.* New York: Stokes, 1937.

Moynihan, Ruth Barnes, Cynthia Russett, and Laurie Crumpacker, eds. *Second to None: A Documentary History of American Women.* Vol. 2. Lincoln: U of Nebraska P, 1993.

MRS. M. D. *(early 20th century)*

"Capable of Nursing"

Midwives, women who assist at birth and who care for the health of women, have been practicing their craft for as long as we have records of human communities. And for just as long, we have accounts of attacks on midwives, from ancient Greek prohibitions to accusations of witchcraft—to laws that stipulate that without formal medical training a woman cannot practice midwifery (Mulligan 172–173). The practice of assisting at births grows out of women's own experiences as wives, mothers, and kinswomen, as well as their roles as producers of food and sustenance, and their participation in religious rituals throughout the life cycle (Zimmerman 453). While every community has always had midwives, the status accorded midwives varies tremendously as a byproduct of the interplay of technology, social structure, and culture (DeVries 133).

Midwives traditionally served apprenticeships with experienced colleagues outside the formal schools for medicine and nursing. Rich in experience and focused on assessing the total circumstances of the woman they were assisting, they did not necessarily employ new tools and technologies. As DeVries points out, "New (and successful) technology challenges the legitimacy and authority of midwifery. As technology replaces tradition, patterns of recruitment are changed and doubts about existing techniques, definitions, and sources of knowledge that surround birth are created" (133–134). The widespread professionalization of medicine beginning during the eighteenth century in the West, and the arrival of international health care providers around the globe in the nineteenth century, all affected the practice of midwifery.

Rather than being "called," midwives came under pressure to be "trained," to grant preeminence to the knowledge that science prescribed over the information that their clients offered. Complex social structures and cultural ideas about modernity likewise redefined the practice of midwifery, and tied it to licensing, payment, and a network of other professionals. Urban industrial culture, with its emphasis on specialization, has diminished the status of midwives in most western societies. The renaissance midwifery experienced in these countries in the middle of the twentieth century, and the renewed attention to midwives in traditional societies, came about partially as a result of the women's health movement, a grassroots movement that challenged the idea that scientific knowledge alone formed a sufficient base from which to achieve well-being.

The letter included here from Mrs. M.D. to the authorities in an Australian town in 1928 captures one such shift in women's health care. Mrs. M.D. was apparently a midwife with a successful practice. The Australian government, like other governments around the world during the progressive era, imposed licensing requirements in an attempt to standardize—and they believed improve—the quality of medical services. Yet the government's aspirations exceeded its abilities. There were no services in the rural areas and the traditional medical practices, such as that of midwifery, were all that were available. The possibility that the government would be able to provide modern services appeared remote. In this letter, Mrs. M.D. does not attack the theory behind the professionalization of nursing, its attendant training and licensing procedures, or the relationship of midwifery to nursing (Melosh 15–35). Rather, she points out its impracticability. Her clients cannot afford the expense of travel. She herself is dependent on the income provided by her profession. She asks that her expertise be recognized and that she be allowed to continue her practice. Apparently her neighbors agreed with her, for she refers to the fact that she is writing not just for herself but for all those who come to her believing she is "capable of nursing." The documents do not tell us the outcome of her petition. The history of women's health care suggests that if her petition was denied, she would have continued without official sanction to find ways to help the women of her area with their birthing and health needs.

JFO

A LETTER FROM MRS. M.D. TO THE INSPECTOR-GENERAL OF HOSPITALS[§]

Dear Sir,

Having received notice from the Secretary of Children's Welfare . . . warning me against taking in maternity cases as I am not a Registered Nurse I am writing you to explain the state of affairs in Wallaroo at the present time. There is only one registered Nurse here, a woman 66 years of age and too old to attend cases, she has a small house and only takes in one or 2 cases per month, there is no one here that goes out nursing, so what are these women to do. I thought that as there was no convenience for them that I would open a place as I have had a lot of experience in nursing and my home is 3 doors from each of the Doctors and enables them to visit oftener and render more attention to patients and both of these Drs know that I am capable of looking after them. I have had more experience in nursing that even Mrs [B———], the registered nurse here, and Mrs [H———] also, who was the other woman to be warned of same, although her home is only a small skillion house and I pity the women that were laid up in Summer time there, so what are the women here to do, where are they to go, they must be attended to and I am not going out to nurse anyone. I have gone to a good deal of expense to make everything as it would be and I am relying on this to keep myself and little boy 12 yrs of age. All day today I have had women calling and asking me, whatever are we doing to do, whatever is wrong. I can

[§] Reprinted by permission of the University of Queensland Press, from *Australia's Women: A Documentary History,* edited by Kay Daniels and Mary Murname. Copyright © 1980 by the University of Queensland Press. Material excerpted from page 253.

assure you it is putting them to a lot of worry and it is unreasonable to think of them going to Moonta or Kadina as the Lady Inspector suggested they could do, it is 8 & 12 miles and would cost 10 & 14/- each way and double at night and mean risking their lives besides, if I were not capable of nursing maternity cases I would not undertake the work.

Will you please grant me a License and let me have a reply as soon as possible.

Mrs. M.D., Wallaroo, 5 June 1928.

WORKS CONSULTED

DeVries, Raymond G. "A cross-national view of the status of midwives." *Gender, Work and Medicine: Women and the Medical Division of Labour.* Elianne Riska and Katarina Wegar, eds. London: SAGE Studies in International Sociology 44 (1993): 131–146.

Melosh, Barbara. *'The Physician's Hand': Work, Culture and Conflict in American Nursing.* Philadelphia: Temple UP, 1982.

Mulligan, Joan E. "Nursing and Feminism: Caring and Curing." *The Knowledge Explosion: Generations of Feminist Scholarship.* Ed. Cheris Kramarae and Dale Spender. New York: Teachers College P, 1992.

Zimmerman, Mary K. "The Women's Health Movement: A Critique of Medical Enterprise and the Position of Women." *Analyzing Gender: A Handbook of Social Science Research.* Ed. Beth B. Hess and Myra Marx Ferree. London: SAGE Publications, 1987.

ELSIE RIDDICK *(1876–1959)*

"I Did the Work and They Drew the Pay"

> I wonder how many women of today have ever stopped to think and wonder how we got the vote. Who did it?
>
> *Elsie Riddick*

It is generally recognized that the national woman suffrage movement in the United States was initiated at the Seneca Falls convention of 1848 by Susan B. Anthony, Carrie Chapman Catt, and others. Their actions have been increasingly well-documented by scholars of U. S. women's history.[1] But in other areas of the country, the suffrage movement developed differently, though always in relation to the national movement and its debates. Since local movements have their own unique chronologies, and since local practices and systems of power can often differ from those in the urban centers of the Northeast, such stories can shed light on the different ways in which the attainment of suffrage has affected women's lives.

In North Carolina, the first suffrage league was not formed until the late nineteenth century, in Buncombe County. North Carolina's first woman suffrage bill was introduced by a Republican from Yancey County in 1897, and was sent to a committee on insane asylums, where it quickly and quietly died. This put a damper on the already tenuous movement for the next fifteen years. It was not until 1912 that the movement again gained momentum, spurred by concern for the quality of North Carolina schools. Members of women's groups had run for positions on local school boards, but the state's Attorney General short-circuited their efforts. Referring to the Constitution, he issued an interpretation that prevented those individuals who did not have the right to vote from running for elective office. North Carolina women came to realize how very limited was their influence on government affairs, and how deeply opposed the law was to women exercising power or influence in any officially sanctioned form. The growing interest of these women in issues such as education, prison reform, and health care led them to understand how the lack of suffrage acutely and directly affected their lives. This fact was especially noticeable because the unofficial influence that women of the Progressive movement exercised in the Northeast in the late nineteenth and early twentieth centuries was not reproduced in contemporary North Carolina.

Elsie Riddick played an interesting role in the history of woman suffrage in North Carolina. Never married, Riddick worked as an accountant for the state of North Carolina for 52 years. She was born in 1876 in Gatesville, NC, daughter of the Gates County sheriff.[2] The excerpt reprinted here covers her experiences after she left her hometown for the first time, at the age of 21, to go to Raleigh in 1897 (the same year the first suffrage bill was born and died). Through her father's connections in Raleigh, she obtained a job as an accountant for the State Commissioner of Agriculture. One of only three women who held a job in government at the time, Riddick quickly came to realize how unequal women's treatment was in the distribution of office work and the allocation of salaries (Chafe 66–78, 233).

Riddick also learned that among the middle classes throughout the nineteenth and into the twentieth centuries, especially in the South, a woman who worked outside the home signified dishonor. The reality of sexual harassment was such a prominent part of many types of work, especially clerical work, that many assumed only "cheap" women would take such jobs. This attitude would only begin to change in the 1950s, when a large number of middle-class women, the majority of whom were married and over the age of 35, began to enter a job market in great need of clerical and retail workers (Chafe 135–153). Riddick's relatively early experience with on-the-job discrimination made her receptive to the renewed interest in suffrage generated by the Attorney General's 1912 ruling. She saw in the suffrage movement the key not only to changing women's lack of access to positions of political power, but also to attaining well-paid and well-respected positions in the work-force.

By 1917, Riddick was president of the Raleigh Women's Suffrage League. Encountering bitter opposition from both men and women in her home state, Riddick and her fellow suffragists spent a great deal of energy promoting a special session of the state legislature dedicated to considering woman suffrage in 1920. At the same time, in the United States Congress, only one more state was needed to pass the 19th Amendment that would give women the vote. On the very day when the North Carolina legislature was convening to consider the issue, the state of Tennessee beat them to the punch. Still, Riddick pushed the state legislature to finish their special session; despite the national decision, North Carolina persisted in rejecting the measure. It would not be until 1971, twelve years after Riddick's death, that, in a symbolic gesture, North Carolina would ratify the 19th Amendment.

Riddick soon became acutely aware that suffrage itself would not transform women's political or economic situations. Many women would not take advantage of the 19th Amendment, and Riddick and her fellow activists redirected their efforts toward getting women to register—a task that for a long time yielded few results. Although Riddick was the first woman elected to head her Democratic precinct and was active for many years in the International Business and Professional Women's Association, she never received equal remuneration for her work in North Carolina state government. For years she was also denied her goal of becoming the chief clerk of the Utilities Commission. Although she would eventually become the first woman to hold that post, she would hold it for only three months before her retirement in 1949. Thus, while Riddick's life reflects much that was ground-breaking for women in the twentieth century, it also provides evidence of the constant obstacles they faced in the realms of work and politics.

KKF

FROM "MISS ELSIE RIDDICK."[§]

In those days when [a woman] said she was a stenographer you could see noses turn up, sneers on the face—in fact, no real nice girl had any business in an office all day with no

[§] Reprinted from "Miss Elsie Riddick," by Carmine Prioli, in *Speaking For Ourselves: Women Of The South* edited by Maxine Alexander. Copyright © 1977, 1981, 1983, 1984 by the Institute for Southern Studies. Reprinted by permission of Pantheon Books, a division of Random House, Inc. Material excerpted from pages 158–159.

one but a man, so they said. All who did were considered cheap and not proper ladies. At the time there were only three women in the government departments: the one in the governor's office, an elderly lady whom he took to Raleigh with him, then one in the chemistry department. . . [then me].

My career began when I walked into the [commissioner of agriculture's] office in July 1897. I went in the office with this old man who was a Republican, but at heart he was the kindest and most considerate human being possible. The secretary was a stout, red-haired, freckle-faced gentleman. I have forgotten, but I believe he was a bachelor. After the introduction he took me to the office of the stenographer next to the commissioner's office and introduced me to the files.

The secretary sat back in his swivel chair, with a cigar, to meet the visitors. Of course, he opened the mail, and more and more of it was turned over to me each day to answer. As I sat every day and watched him in his big chair I began to think I knew just as much about the office and, in addition, there were things I could do that he could not. It seemed I was there to do all the work, as in all offices, and he was there to meet and shake hands with the people (but I cannot say to look pretty because he was anything but that). Then when "payday" came I grew more restless and dissatisfied as I wrote my paycheck for $30, the secretary's for $125, and the commissioner's for around $200. I did the work and they drew the pay. This went on for several months, and I was allowed $40 and finally $50 from the budget.

NOTES

[1] A few of the classic works are Eleanor Flexner's *Century of Struggle* and Ellen Carol DuBois' *Feminism and Suffrage: The Emergence of an Independent Women's Movement in America, 1848–1860*. This area is also covered in more theoretical terms by Nancy Cott in *The Grounding of Modern Feminism*.

[2] Biographical information is taken from Ruth Sheehan's article "Winning Vote Just the Start of Long Fight for Women" that appeared in the *Raleigh News and Observer*.

WORKS CONSULTED

Chafe, William H. *The Paradox of Change: American Women in the 20th Century*. New York: Oxford UP, 1991.

Cott, Nancy. *The Grounding of Modern Feminism*. New Haven: Yale UP, 1987.

DuBois, Ellen Carol. *Feminism and Suffrage: The Emergence of an Independent Women's Movement in America, 1848–1860*. Ithaca: Cornell UP, 1978.

Flexner, Eleanor. *Century of Struggle*. Cambridge: Cambridge UP, 1975.

Sheehan, Ruth. "Winning Vote Just the Start of Long Fight for Women." *Raleigh News and Observer*. August 26, 1995.

REPRESENTING WOMEN, WRITING THE BODY POLITIC

Natania Meeker

How do women represent themselves? What does being a woman represent? The women whose letters, manifestos, poems, and diary excerpts appear in this section have in common the use of written texts as part of their attempts to think about themselves as women, and about the way in which they relate to the world around them through their writing. The concept of representation, in this context, takes on diverse yet related meanings. Women may represent themselves as a group or as individuals in written or oral texts; they may also be represented by others. Moreover, representation connotes a specific political act; women's struggles for the right to participate directly in political systems (as voters, for example) have also been struggles for the right to represent and be represented politically. This section is thus meant to constitute a reflection on the social nature of women's representations, of themselves and their experiences, to the world and in the world. The idea of *representation* is meant first of all to include the many forms that women's thoughts about themselves and their communities may take. More specifically, this section is concerned with those female-authored texts[1] in which women reflect, individually and collectively, on the way they may represent themselves to the social world, and on the ways in which they in turn are represented by society.

As rubric then, representation deals with the relationship between women's writing and women's place in society. Any discussion of representation contains its opposite—the misrepresentations to which women have been subjected and in which they have participated. Accordingly, we examine here the means by which representations of women also inevitably misrepresent that which they portray. All representations function within certain socially defined limits, and acts of misrepresentation are an inherent part of any given representational system because systems are always partial and always subject to interpretation. Notions of representation and misrepresentation might productively be thought to coexist on a kind of continuum. We are thus not seeking to discover the truth about women, but rather to examine the ways in which women have written about—and read about—themselves and their experiences.

Therefore, while the excerpts in **Representing Women, Writing the Body Politic** often function to resist misrepresentation by pointing out and defining its painful and damaging consequences, no excerpt can be seen as definitively representative. In fact, for many of the women writing from within oppressed positions in a sexist, racist, and classist framework, the possibility of self-representation has offered only another opportunity to be misrepresented. Misrepresentation is thus one of the ways in which systems of domination can work most effectively. Ideas about what is and is not representative in a given society, often prevent women of color from engaging in the kind of self-representational writing that may be permitted from middle- and upper-class white women.[2] The writings of the women in this section, then, might be perceived as struggling to explain and resist the ideologies that allow such systems of misrepresentation to perpetuate themselves. These texts, however, also make clear that no act of representation can ever take place entirely outside of ideology. We emphasize that these excerpts must be seen as products of the social contexts that they are actively attempting to shape.

It follows that our interest in the relationship between forms of female resistance and women's ways of representing themselves does not necessarily mean that women's writing (and political participation) is automatically liberating. Only some of the world's women have access to a means of textual production. Access to literacy, often a privilege of the upper classes, is carefully controlled by these classes. We might see literacy's status as a society's estimate of its value, a privilege many are denied the right to possess. The notion that literacy is a path to enlightenment, emancipation, or social success could be considered as one of the means by which the dominant groups or classes in a society maintain their position of superiority. Thus, we would like to distinguish between two groups of women, one with the ability to read and write, and a much larger group with the ability to resist actively.

Nevertheless, we examine the production of texts here as one of the many means by which women analyze and change their circumstances. Female literacy is not a necessary prerequisite for women's resistance and does not constitute a kind of resistance in and of itself. Print technology may be used for different purposes in different societies. Writing may be one of the ways in which women maintain a sense of intellectual or even spiritual community with one another. It may also serve to perpetuate hierarchies and social distinctions.[3] Because this anthology is made up of written texts, we focus in this section on the importance writing holds as a means by which women represent and are represented. Accordingly, the rubric *representations* emphasizes the interplay between individual acts of textual production and the social contexts in which these acts take place.

The title **Representing Women, Writing the Body Politic** refers to the ways in which texts produced by women may do the following kinds of socio-cultural work, often simultaneously: 1) these texts create unique and particular social definitions of woman or womanhood; 2) they make use of socially defined notions about women that are already in place; and 3) they may enact a struggle against the limits that such social definitions place upon women as writers and as political subjects. As suggested earlier, these writings, these textual acts, all exist on a kind of representational continuum; they represent and misrepresent to varying degrees. In the documents collected here, women attempt to define themselves and their communities through writing; they struggle to create and shape themselves both as women and as human beings through their texts. Nevertheless, these writings also work *within* accepted definitions of woman; the texts reshape and resist *and* strengthen certain kinds of political, literary, and social traditions. The question of how women's representations of themselves are related to specific acts of resistance is thus an important focus of many of the excerpts presented here.

WOMEN'S WRITING

The first group of selections reflects specifically on issues relating to the nature of female authorship, the existence of a literary tradition by, and, or for women, and the problems surrounding women's access to literacy. On the one hand, this category will examine women's expressions of resistance through textual productions that are either consciously literary or that reveal an awareness of the difficulties faced by female authors of various kinds. On the other, the excerpts in this category also examine the way in which the construction of a literary field and restricted access to literacy exclude and categorize various forms of representation.

Women have had a long history of engagement with different kinds of literary and artistic production. Sometimes female authors have been a part of a cultural tradition which is explicitly identified with women. For example, in ancient Greece, music and poetry composed by women played an important role in constituting and perpetuating a female community. Young girls were initiated into womanhood by means of singing, dancing, and the playing of music. Poetry and dance were also key parts of women's religious rituals.[4] In more contemporary times, women have maintained a sense of literary or intellectual community with one another through different means. Letter-writing has often been one of the ways in which women both experiment with literary forms and build connections with one another. Female scholars have sought support from each other in their struggles for access to knowledge. Women have also used literature and poetry to construct and strengthen a female literary tradition with deep historical roots.[5] In this section we begin with the figure of Sappho, who wrote around the seventh century BCE, as one of the ancestors to whom women writing in the West have looked for inspiration and legitimation of their own literary efforts. Women writers may also invoke images of such literary foremothers in order to emphasize how they have been denied access to literacy and how their literary contributions have been devalued.

The cultural production of texts—both written and oral—has never been an exclusively masculine domain. Women have long struggled for access to literacy and have produced countless reflections on the act of creative representation. Textual production might be seen as a unique avenue for women's exploration of a variety of ways to define themselves as members of communities and as individuals. Sappho, for example, writes passionate and erotic poetry which can be read as a commentary on different kinds of gendered social relationships. Sappho's poetry may be read as helping to legitimate images of active female desire and of women as loving sexual subjects.

While women have often turned to textual production as a way of asserting their own authority and experience within a certain cultural context, they have also used their writings to criticize the exclusionary nature of formal literary institutions (in a broad sense) as well as the various ways in which access to literacy is socially determined. Sometimes literary production may be seen as an arena for women's analyses of a variety of forms of self-representation; at other times women have launched devastating critiques of the very notion of authorship. Anne Bradstreet's poem "The Prologue" appeared in an edition of her collected poetry entitled *The Tenth Muse*. Bradstreet expresses conflicting notions about women's literary production, and her own, claiming that her poetry is inferior to that of men at the same time as she asserts herself as an author and a literary scholar. She struggles to define her place as a female author within a society in which the very idea of women's writing was fraught with paradoxes.

Contemporary authors continue to explore the ideological contradictions that surround women's attempts to produce literary representations of themselves and their experiences. In her poem entitled "The Journey," Eavan Boland examines her own relationship to poetry through a portrayal of her mythical voyage to the underworld accompanied by Sappho, who appears here as the prototypical female author of the Western poetic tradition. In a complicated way for Boland, the figure of Sappho gives authority to the intensely personal connection between female poet and poem. The paradoxes that are lived by the female author are portrayed by Boland as a source of strength and poetic inspiration. We have chosen to group the excerpts by Sappho, Bradstreet, and Boland together in order to show the complex relationship between women's ideas about their own writing and the existence of a long-standing tradition female authors have at once shaped and been excluded from.

In the next two excerpts by Mariama Bâ and Louise Labé we look at the attempts by two very different women to use writing to establish a sense of community for themselves as women. Bâ's letter to a female friend is taken from her autobiographical novel, *So Long a Letter.* In its last pages she explains how her "heart rejoices each time a woman emerges from the shadows" to engage in feminist work. Through her novel/letter—which praises the connections developed between women over time—Bâ opens up a new kind of literary space in which relationships among women provide a framework for an analysis of "the decisions that decide our future."

Louise Labé's dedicatory letter to a young woman functions something like an introduction to her book of love sonnets. In one sense, Labé's letter is an expression of humanist ideas which were typical of seventeenth-century France. She speaks of the ways in which scholarly knowledge can contribute to what she calls "the general good." On the other hand, Labé concentrates on the importance of women's contributions to "learning" for both a specific intellectual community and the greater public. In addition, she makes the claim that knowledge, unlike "chains, rings, and sumptuous clothes," is something which women can possess that "will be entirely our own." This dedicatory epistle is both an encouragement to a fellow woman writer and an implicitly feminist polemic.

The excerpt by Michèle Le Doeuff also investigates the relationship between a widespread community of thinkers—or, as Le Doeuff describes it, the "philosophical" community—and the feminist vision as she interprets it. In her work, Le Doeuff identifies "thinking philosophically" with "self-assertion through thought." For her, "'thinking philosophically' and 'being a feminist' appear as one and the same attitude: a desire to judge by and for oneself, which may manifest itself in relation to different questions." Le Doeuff takes seriously a feminist philosophical project that emphasizes rational critical thought. According to Le Doeuff, women's right to think critically and philosophically about the world is an intrinsic part of their right to resist dominant systems of authority, both intellectual and political.

GENDERING REPRESENTATIONS

In the second group of selections, we examine the ways in which representations of gender help structure cultural perceptions of women. This focus on the social function of gendered representational systems serves as the link between the more literary concerns of the previous group of selections and the explicitly political orientation of the subsequent excerpts. We broaden our focus here to look at how women define themselves (and are defined) as women within various systems of representation. The writers whose selections are included here do not locate themselves in an explicitly political or public sphere (even though their writings are always politicized to one degree or another); they analyze cultural representations of women—sometimes in order to come to a better understanding of what being female could mean, and sometimes in order to resist such categorizing. They are often concerned with notions of a woman's so-called nature, both as the supposed source of representations of women generally, and as a limitation on women's ability to represent themselves.

The cultural production of texts has often been associated with a masculine public sphere that restricts access to elite men. For instance, in pre-Islamic and early Islamic societies, women were allowed to engage in the composition of specific forms of oral poetry, namely elegies mourning the death of kinsmen slain in battle. Because the recitation of poetry was a public activity, women poets were limited to certain genres that reflected a marginal—albeit sacral—state; their appearance in public under other circumstances might be linked to sexual degradation and defilement.[6] In Western European societies, it was often considered unnatural for a woman to participate in scholarly activities. Women who did attempt to enter into intellectual and literary communities that were dominated by men were often portrayed as monstrous; their desire to have access to certain privileged forms of knowledge was often linked to sexual promiscuity.

Nevertheless, many women did act to resist the oppressive way in which representations of gender functioned. Some women have relentlessly pursued learning and knowledge despite cultural penalties for such activities. Others have struggled to recreate themselves as representing subjects, rather than objects of representation. Around the world, women have fought to have some control over the way in which they clothe and decorate their bodies. The female body is often thought to function as a cultural sign, a blank slate upon which culture may write. Rokeya Sakhawat Hossain, for instance, whose critique of purdah appears in the section on **Work and Education**, asked women, "Why don't you decorate your pet dog with your necklace? . . You could use your bangles and bracelets as curtain rings in your drawing room . . . If men want their wealth displayed, do it in the manner I have suggested. But why display their wealth on your body? That is nothing but a symbol of your slavery" (qtd. in Tharu and Lalita 341–342).

Accordingly, this category also examines the ways in which women's bodies are textually presented and represented. To begin with, we affirm that women's recorded experience of their physical bodies contributes to general social representations of women. Ideas about women's clothing and fashion become important from this perspective, as do the various forms which written representations of women's bodies are allowed to take in any given social context. Here, it is necessary to keep in mind the many different ways in which bodies are represented and function socially. By "bodies" we do not mean only women's libidinal, desiring, or sexual bodies, but also women's laboring, resistant, and political bodies.

Finally, this section emphasizes the way in which women work with and struggle against cultural representations of gender in order to come to an understanding of themselves and their social contexts. The women included here use their analyses of the way in which gendered systems are represented and reproduced to assess and change their own circumstances. Their writings focus on issues ranging from the cultural policing of women's bodies to female authors' relationships to specific representations of gender. We begin this section with an excerpt from Abigail Abbot Bailey, an eighteenth-century American woman who presents a harrowing description of her life with an abusive husband. In this text, Bailey's notions of what it means to exist within the confines of her marriage—as well as of what resistance might entail—invite her to see her situation as a kind of Biblical allegory. Her reactions to her husband's abuse of their daughter reveal the profound effect such a narrative has not only on Bailey's life but on the lives of those around her.

Halidé Edib Adivar's account of her experience as a female colonel in the Turkish army, on the other hand, is a reflection on the way in which both gender and class privileges are perpetuated through a complicated series of cultural representations. When the men in her regiment hire a female dancer—a prostitute—to dance for them, the woman also performs for Halidé Edib. Edib's description of the intense curiosity of the village women concerning the "slut," as well as her subsequent analysis of the effects of prostitution on women, reveal how ideas about class, and assumptions about their sexual availability, structure women's existence as gendered bodies.

Florence Nightingale's analysis of the way in which nineteenth-century society stifled women's creative and imaginative powers is a meditation on how oppression is perpetuated through cultural images. She angrily exposes the system of patriarchal domination that prevents elite and middle-class women from pursuing social and intellectual fulfillment. "Passion, intellect, moral activity—these three have never been satisfied in a woman," she asserts.

Sor Juana Inés de la Cruz's examination of her career as a self-taught, seventeenth-century female scholar is also something of a reflection on the relationship between women's "natural"[7] inclinations and the social roles they are given to fulfill. In the letter reprinted here, Sor Juana embraces her extraordinary intellectual gift as a kind of personal vocation (she states, "my inclination to letters was marked by . . . passion and vehemence"), even as she claims that her "writing has never proceeded from any dictate of my own, but a force beyond me. . . ." In her writing and her scholarship, she challenges social expectations of women. Sor Juana's justification of her right to acquire scholarly knowledge is also a defense of her right to know and to understand her circumstances. Her writing is an enactment and an emblem of her resistance.

Alexandra Kollontai's work on *The Social Basis of the Woman Question* represents a very different attempt to create a paradigm to help understand the basis of human experience. Kollontai discusses a notion of social class as the foundation of political and cultural analysis. She sets herself up in opposition to "the feminists"—a phrase she uses to refer to a certain brand of bourgeois feminism rather than to a broader concept of feminist activism—since, from her point of view, "For the majority of women of the proletariat, equal rights with men would mean only an equal share in inequality." For Kollontai, class analysis is an essential part of any understanding of the forms of oppression women may experience. She presents a powerful reading of the way in which the history of Western feminism has been heavily determined by class issues and, in doing so, reconceptualizes the relationships between and among mutually constitutive systems of power.

The excerpt by Laila of Shaibân-Bakr included here plays several roles in this section. First, it is a sample of a ritual tradition of women's oral poetry. Second, it is a selection written by a woman who, as a member of an Islamic sect known for a history of political and religious resistance, went on to lead her tribe in battle against imperial Baghdad. Third, it may serve to challenge readers' assumptions about the way in which women's writing can be read as resisting social norms. Does Laila's work represent resistance—either individual or tribal—to political domination? This question cannot be answered with conviction. Nevertheless, we hope to show with this poem that the relationship of women's lives to their writings is never a simple or direct one.

THE POLITICS OF REPRESENTATION

Finally, we deal directly with the relationship between women's place in socio-political systems and women's ability to represent themselves individually or as a group in texts. The excerpts here investigate women's writing as both a form of intervention in a political arena and a way of constituting a wide variety of female identities. Women have often used written and oral forms of representation to demand, argue for, and justify their political rights. In this context, female authors show the gesture of self-representation to be a highly politicized act; by using their texts to define and redefine the meaning of womanhood itself, these women engage in a struggle to resist the way in which access to political representation and the public sphere itself has often been limited to men. The women whose texts appear here may be seen as exercising a kind of right to represent themselves. They show explicitly how this act of self-representation, while it may take the most literary of forms, is always a political, social act. This is true even of such quintessentially private forms of writing as entries in a diary; a woman writing in a journal may continue to shape, reflect on, and even resist various socially-defined categories or systems. In this sense, writing is a public act which takes place in a social arena. Women's representation in texts is closely linked to the way in which women represent themselves as social entities. The excerpts reprinted here clarify this connection by examining the relationship between political representation and written self-determination.

In addition, the right to represent and be represented politically, as it is depicted here, may also be thought of as related to forms of misrepresentation, which, while textual, always have social effects. The excerpts in this third category also emphasize the pernicious political consequences of systems of representation that implicitly perpetuate oppressive and violent forms of misrepresentation. According to this perspective, in order to understand why women are writing, we must also ask which women are writing, what writing means in a given social context, and how women may come to consciousness as women through writing. These final selections demand that we take a closer look at the assumptions and the silences that determine how women are written about. They reveal the social and political "facts" which systems of representation serve to create and maintain.

Because women's struggle for political representation has taken on a specific cast with the development of Western notions of universalism and the public sphere, this final group of selections has a more contemporary focus. In the liberal democratic tradition, the idea of universal human rights rests on a concept of autonomous political subjects who are all equal in the eyes of the state. This ideological system has often served to deny the privileges of rights to those individuals or groups who, for one reason or another, are seen to exist outside of the universal (that is, they do not share in those qualifications that make up autonomous and rational human subjects). Thus, women have often had to argue for their right to be represented as political subjects. They have had to struggle on two levels. First, they have had to resist cultural representations of women as natural rather than cultural beings. Secondly, they have had to struggle for access to political systems of representation. Their efforts in this latter domain are a focal point of this third group of excerpts.

The French eighteenth-century feminist and playwright Olympe de Gouges, in her rewriting of the "Declaration of the Rights of Man and Citizen," demonstrates the complex ways in which women's written forms of political resistance can operate. The body of this document follows closely the original wording of the "Declaration," and in so doing affirms that a discussion of women as political citizens necessitates a redefinition of notions of citizenship, national identity, and natural rights. Moreover, de Gouges' text questions the validity of the sex/gender distinction itself. "Search, seek out and single out," she writes, "if you can, sexes in the conduct of nature. Everywhere you will find them intermingled, everywhere working harmoniously together in this immortal masterpiece."

Hiratsuka Raicho, in an excerpt from the first issue of the Japanese feminist magazine *Bluestocking* in 1911, deals explicitly with the connection between representations of gender and the organization of political power. For Hiratsuka, it is the "new woman" of Japan who, by transforming herself, will succeed in transforming the world around her.

Soumay Tcheng, according to her autobiographical account, also represents something of a "new woman," although in a different social context from Hiratsuka. In the excerpt we present here, she tells of her mother's response to her daughter's political activism. "You must help the Chinese woman . . ." her mother says. "Show what one Chinese woman is able to do. You will be helping your sisters for all future time." In this excerpt, a mother endorses her daughter's political practices because of their potentially feminist implications. She also emphasizes the representative functions of Soumay Tcheng's actions as "one Chinese woman" with the power to influence political events.

Taj Al-Saltana's writing on the social functions of the practice of veiling in turn-of-the-century Iran clearly links this form of representing women's bodies to class dynamics in her society. Moreover, in addition to showing that this practice, far from being universal, is related to class status, she also makes a connection between emerging nationalist and feminist discourse in early twentieth-century Iran. She argues that women's voices can and should play an essential part in political "progress" even as she outlines her own program for national advancement.

Olympe de Gouges, Hiratsuka Raicho, Soumay Tcheng, and Taj Al-Saltana explore the relationship among systems of political representation (and forms of political participation) and women's struggle to represent themselves in writing and as citizens of the modern state. The last three writers presented here—Jo Carrillo, Christine de Pizan, and Zitkala-Ša—focus particularly on how representations of women can reproduce systemic forms of oppression. In her poem "And When You Leave, Take Your Pictures With You," Jo Carrillo describes a contemporary manifestation of the way in which such representations serve to perpetuate race- and class-based hierarchies. Her writing examines how white feminists' (mis)representations of women of color serve to maintain the former's economic and racial privileges.

Christine de Pizan's letter to Jean de Montreuil, written in 1402, deals with the systematic misrepresentation of women by men as integral to the functioning of patriarchal society. She understands the misrepresentation of women as an injustice with real social effects. In her letter, she attempts to redress this wrong by speaking passionately about women who are, for her, representative because they are "honorable" and "virtuous." Her letter focuses on how men's representations of women help to perpetuate women's oppression.

By contrast, Zitkala-Ša shows how certain forms of misrepresentation can serve directly to intimidate and silence women in their efforts to represent themselves publicly. She describes an oratorical competition at which several "college rowdies" hold up a white banner displaying a drawing of a Native American labeled "squaw" as Zitkala-Ša delivers her prize-winning speech. Zitkala-Ša is able to resist these attempts to silence and humiliate her. Nevertheless, her experience testifies to the power of representation as well as to the courage and perseverance of those women who have continued to speak and represent themselves despite the hostility, anger, or incomprehension of their audiences.

The struggles described above do not depend on gender alone for their explanation. Feminist theory and writings—particularly in the U.S.—are beginning to focus on the ways in which race, class, and sexuality are represented and misrepresented politically. "The Politics of Representation" is not just about women's attempts to change the way in which political systems of representation work, it is also about the dependence of such systems on the multi-layered acts of misrepresentation as described above. We would like to reiterate here that cultural representations have multiple functions. They reconfigure, reshape, and repeat previously established ideological patterns. Yet, at the same time as these representations act to structure the systems of which they are products, they also work to exclude and deny certain possibilities. From this perspective, social change is not an issue of establishing the truth about things; rather, it is a product of constantly shifting political and cultural patterns that represent and misrepresent simultaneously.

NOTES

[1] We would like to draw attention here briefly to the ways in which authorship can become a gendered notion. Authors are generally granted authority from within a specific network of power relations; in many patriarchal cultures, authority is a male prerogative. Female authors, for instance, have often experienced a very real conflict between their desire to write and their subordinate social positions as women.

[2] In the introduction to *Third World Women and the Politics of Feminism,* Chandra Mohanty writes, "Momsen and Townsend (1987) state that in fact fertility is the most studied aspect of women's lives in the third world. This particular fact speaks volumes about the predominant representation of third-world women in social-scientific knowledge production" (6).

[3] Michael Warner, in his book discussing the development of print culture in eighteenth-century America, makes a similar point. He writes: "Both print and writing could only be alien to the entirely or even partially illiterate, including almost all Native Americans and the enslaved blacks. And saying that letters were 'alien' to the illiterate is more than a tautology, since it is to these groups that writing and print may have appeared most clearly as technologies of power" (11). Women have experienced print and writing as deeply alienating but also as signs of elite status and potentially empowering. In addition, writing might theoreti-

cally give some women access to a public sphere which would otherwise remain closed to them.

[4] For a consideration of women's cultural production in ancient Greece, see Margaret Williamson, *Sappho's Immortal Daughters.*

[5] The scholarly debate on the role of the female author and women's experience in literature has been an intense one. As Laurie A. Finke points out in *Feminist Theory, Women's Writing,* "During the 1980s, feminist literary criticism was marked by an often contentious split between those pragmatically committed to the recovery of the woman writer and, with her, something usually called women's experience . . . and those concerned to explore the implications for feminism of postmodern theories that question the legitimacy of such constructs as the author and experience" (1). In this section, we do not attempt to argue on behalf of a "gynocritics" (Showalter) based on an appeal to women's experience; we would also like to note that discussions of what it means to be a "woman writer" have often been founded solely on analysis of Western European texts. We do examine what many different women have had to say about the way in which culturally and historically specific notions of gender and of writing may have interacted to influence women's means of representing themselves.

[6] For a discussion of the ritual function of women's elegiac poetry in the pre-Islamic and early Islamic periods, see Suzanne Pinckney Stetkevych's *The Mute Immortals Speak: Pre-Islamic Poetry and the Poetics of Ritual.*

[7] It is important to keep in mind that Sor Juana writes in a much different context from that of Florence Nightingale (and of much twentieth-century feminist scholarship). Her analysis of the social constraints that limit her ability to pursue her intense desire for philosophical and scientific knowledge is not structured in terms of nature versus culture. She refers to her desire to learn as a God-given rather than a natural trait. Nevertheless, she does describe this gift from God as an essential component of her subjective experience.

WORKS CONSULTED

Finke, Laurie A. *Feminist Theory, Women's Writing.* Ithaca: Cornell UP, 1992.

Mohanty, Chandra, Ann Russo and Lourdes Torres, eds. *Third World Women and the Politics of Feminism.* Bloomington: Indiana UP, 1991.

Showalter, Elaine. "Feminist Criticism in the Wilderness." *Critical Inquiry* 8 (1981): 179–205.

Stetkevych, Suzanne Pinckney. *The Mute Immortals Speak: Pre-Islamic Poetry and the Poetics of Ritual.* Ithaca: Cornell UP, 1993.

Tharu, Susie and K. Lalita. *Women Writing in India: 600 B.C. to the Early Twentieth Century.* Vol. 1. New York: Feminist Press at CUNY, 1991.

Warner, Michael. *Letters of the Republic: Publication and the Public Sphere in Eighteenth-Century America.* Cambridge, Mass.: Harvard UP, 1990.

SAPPHO *(6th century BCE)*, **ANNE BRADSTREET** *(1612–1672)*, **AND EAVAN BOLAND** *(1944–)*

"Remember It, You Will Remember It": Female Poets and Literary Tradition

We have chosen to present these three poems together in order to suggest some of the ways in which women create and participate in a literary heritage of poetic representation. The writings grouped here succeed in evoking the power of such a heritage to shape and authorize women's lived and literary experiences. We are also, however, interested in the possibility (alluded to by all three authors) that this kind of tradition is, to a certain extent, as much based on women's silence (compelled or voluntary) as on the words which have been transmitted to us. Eavan Boland, the contemporary Irish poet, explains this in a passage from her autobiography: "I believe . . . that when a woman poet begins to write, she very quickly becomes conscious of the silences which have preceded her, which still surround her. These silences will become an indefinable part of her purpose as a poet" (245). Accordingly, we see these poems' varying relationships to literary representations of the Greek woman poet Sappho as evoking a history of silence as well as one of speech. In these poems, Sappho is at once an important authorizer of women's poetic experiences in the Western tradition, and a shadowy figure whose work exists only in fragments. Although Sappho is also, in a sense, representative of the privilege often accorded a specifically Western literary heritage by both male and female authors, we have chosen to concentrate on her image here because of the way in which it forcefully expresses the ambiguities and difficulties inherent in "representing women."

SAPPHO

The figure of Sappho does not lend herself well to traditionalist notions of literary biography. While representations of this poet have been a part of Western cultural currency since the sixth century BCE (she lived around the turn of the seventh and sixth centuries), it is almost impossible to ground a discussion of her poetry in knowledge of her life. It is known that she was an aristocratic, educated woman from the island Lesbos and became the most well-known female lyric poet of Greek and Roman antiquity. Originally, her texts were probably presented as songs, perhaps to groups of young women known as *parthenoi*. (*Parthenoi* were unmarried, adolescent girls entering a period of religious and social initiation that would ultimately prepare them for marriage.) While Sappho's poetry might have played a kind of mentoring role in the education of such young women, some of her poems also addressed adult women (*gynaikes*). In any case, her audience seems usually to have been female, which suggests that her poetry was intimately connected to the shared life of communities of women.

Sappho's poetry has also been viewed not only as evocative of women's experience generally but as a powerful expression of lesbian desire. What is important in this context is not the question "Was Sappho a lesbian?"[1] but rather the way in which women's love and desire for one another is represented both in her poems and by her literary descendants who refer to her as a kind of foremother. Many critics have made a convincing case for Sappho as a lover of women. But, as Margaret Williamson says in her recent study of Sappho entitled *Sappho's Immortal Daughters*, "In the end, however, the challenge of reading Sappho is not to separate the individual from the collective, or (especially) the sexual from the social and religious, but to reunite them in ways our culture has all but forgotten" (132).

In the poem reprinted here, the reader can presume that the speaker/singer is a woman, although it is important to note that, in the form that the poem has been transmitted, there is no grammatical indication of the gender of this voice. This poem is remarkable for the way in which it rewrites the legend of Helen of Troy by representing Helen as the center of a narrative of active desire. It also challenges the militaristic values of the male world, by implicitly setting (female) erotic love against "the chariots of Lydia or the armour of men." But "Anactoria and Helen" is perhaps most interesting in its disruption of traditional categories of gender and women's desire. Helen—and, by implication, the speaker/singer—both rejects the militarism of the first stanza and affirms her own brand of heroism when she leaves her husband and family. Moreover, Helen, Anactoria, and the speaker/singer are all linked in what has been described as "a chain of female desire in which each figure is both loved and loving" (Williamson 170). Helen is both desired by the speaker/singer ("the woman who by far surpassed [all oth]ers in her beauty") and herself actively desiring. Thus, the image of Helen might be said to encompass both the beloved (Anactoria) and the lover (the speaker/singer). In this way, this poem manages to evoke a notion of female erotic love which is full of movement and possibility. By rewriting the legend of Helen of Troy, Sappho recreates one of the most famous representations of women as a testament to an active and powerful feminine desire.

ANNE BRADSTREET

Anne Bradstreet, born in England in 1612 into a Puritan family, was the author of the first published collection of poetry written in America. Although the volume, entitled *The Tenth Muse*,[2] had supposedly been printed without Bradstreet's knowledge or permission, it soon became extremely popular in seventeenth-century England. Nevertheless, Bradstreet received harsh criticism for her demonstration of poetic talent and her dedication to writing, both attributes which young European women of the time were not often given the chance, nor encouraged, to display. Little is known of how Bradstreet acquired the excellent literary education which it is clear from her poetry she possessed. Joseph R. McElrath, Jr. and Allan P. Robb, editors of a recent critical edition of her works, emphasize Bradstreet's "startlingly thorough . . . familiarity with the art of the Renaissance" and her "theological and philosophical sophistication" (xi). In addition to being a poet and a scholar, Bradstreet, who married at age sixteen, was also the mother of eight children and a "powerful matron and patroness of the Massachusetts Bay Colony," to which she and her husband emigrated shortly after their marriage (*Norton Anthology* 61). In his preface to *The Tenth Muse*, her brother-in-law inadvertently reveals the difficulties Bradstreet must have experienced in successfully combining her domestic responsibilities with her devotion to intellectual labor. Disingenuously, he says, ". . . [T]hese poems are but the fruit of some few hours, curtailed from her sleep and other refreshments," (qtd. in *Norton Anthology* 60).

Although her focus is not so evident in our selection here, Anne Bradstreet, not unlike

Eavan Boland, often finds a source of inspiration for her work in her experiences as a wife and mother. She also draws a certain inner strength from her religious convictions (Bradstreet was a devout Puritan). These themes, however, are present alongside an acute sense of the strictures placed upon women by a Puritan society and a Western literary tradition that were strongly patriarchal. Bradstreet is ever-conscious of the contradictions involved in her role as a woman writer. In fact, her poem "The Prologue" has become a classic statement of the problems women face—both practical and theoretical—when they gain access to forms of literary representation in a society where such access is one means by which masculine privilege conventionally perpetuates itself.

In "The Prologue," published in 1650 as the introduction to *The Tenth Muse,* Bradstreet's critique of the ways in which women are denied participation in systems of representation ("If what I doe prove well, it wo'nt advance,/They'l say its stolne, or else, it was by chance") slyly subverts her acknowledgement of women's inability to perform as well as men in the literary arena ("This meane and unrefined stuffe of mine/Will make your glistering gold but more to shine"). Bradstreet begins by stating that her skills are not adequate to the task of writing epic or political verse ("To sing of Wars, of Captaines, and of Kings . . . /For my mean Pen, are too superiour things"). She remarks that a great poet like Guillaume du Bartas (author of a Christian epic poem) might write on any subject he chose, while she must take into account her supposedly meager abilities when deciding on a theme. She goes on to extol the "Preheminence" of men, even as she asks the public to acknowledge her on her own terms. Nonetheless, Bradstreet's submissive posture in the face of male literary prowess does not have to be taken at face value. In "The Prologue," she also presents a lucid critique of historically sexist attitudes towards women authors, ("But sure the antick *Greeks* were far more milde") suggesting that perhaps something other than "nature" is at work assigning a "foolish, broken, blemish'd Muse" to female writers. As critic Rosamund Rosenmeier has expressed it:

> At one level, then, the Bradstreet of "The Prologue" declares that women's worth . . . is the way she has reported it. . . . The rest of the poem, however—particularly in its brief reference to history. . . . and its suggestion of a relationship to the future of the world's great poets—invites us to think that this stage in history and in the immature life of the poetic persona will pass. (59)

EAVAN BOLAND

Eavan Boland was born in 1944 in Dublin, Ireland. She moved with her family to London in 1950, and to New York five years later, not returning to Ireland until she was fourteen. Boland's sense of her own distance from the literary and political heritage of her birthplace—as a child and young woman exiled, in a sense, from her home—underpins much of her poetry. Overall, her poems might be described as marked by a struggle to find a place for her writing as a woman poet within a national literary tradition which has, traditionally, depicted women as "metaphors and invocations, similes and muses," rather than as authors (Boland 27). Boland's poetry dramatizes the tension she experiences between writing as a poet (as part of a poetic tradition which has been overwhelmingly masculine) and writing as a woman, and she does so in a way that acknowledges the power and beauty of a poetic heritage which is particularly Irish. For her, the woman poet is possessed of "the unique chance to fold language and history in on itself, to write a political poem which canvasses Irish history by questioning the poetic structures it shadowed. To dismantle, in other words, the rhetorical relationship by dismantling the poetic persona which supported it. And to seek the authority to do this not from a privileged or historic stance within the Irish poem but from the silences it created and sustained" (201). Boland encourages the woman poet to "humanize her femininity" and in doing so to repoliticize and reinvent the poetic tradition from within. Her poetry is deeply concerned with structure and poetic form, as well as with those telling details of a woman's life which have often been seen as undeserving of poetic emphasis.

In "The Journey," Boland depicts a mother's long wait through the night as her children lie sleeping.[3] As the poem begins, the speaker is reflecting on the fact that "'there has never/. . . been a poem to an antibiotic . . .'" Her child's illness thus becomes the catalyst for a meditation on the seeming inability of poetic language to speak to lived experience. As the speaker points out, "'. . . every day the language gets less/for the task and we are less with the language.'" The first four stanzas of the poem provide the reader with a framework for questioning not only certain notions of literary value but the traditional domain of poetic representation.

Before she drifts off to an exhausted sleep, however, the speaker is visited in her half-waking state by a vision of Sappho, who accompanies her on a journey to the classical underworld—a voyage that functions on one level as a rewriting of that made by the hero Aeneas as part of his legendary founding of Rome. What Sappho shows her, in the journey to "what seemed to be an oppressive suburb of the dawn," is the grief of women who have lost their children, just as the speaker fears she will lose hers to meningitis; it is in the "silences" of women's experience, Sappho suggests, that women's poetry finds its voice. Sappho defines this experience as beyond words and speech ("only not beyond love," importantly), but also as somehow an integral part of poetry. "The Journey" is an assertion of relationships between women which are both poetic and familial; Sappho tells the speaker: "you are dear/and stand beside me as my own daughter." In fact, it is this expression of bonds between women which are forged both within and outside of language that resonates through the work of all three authors presented here.

NM

SAPPHO

Anactoria and Helen (Fragment 16)[§]

[So]me an army on horseback, some an army on foot
and some say a fleet of ships i[s] the loveliest sight

[§] Reprinted by permission of the publisher from *Sappho's Immortal Daughters* by Margaret Williamson, Cambridge, Massachusetts: Harvard University Press. Copyright © 1995 by Margaret Williamson. Material reprinted from pages 166–167.

o[n this] da[r]k earth; but I say it is whatever you desire;

and it is [per]fectly possible to make th[is] clear
to [a]ll; for Helen, the woman who by far surpassed
[all oth]ers in her beauty, l[eft] her husband—
t[he b]est [of all men]

[behind] and sailed [far away] to Troy; she did not spare
a [single] thought for her [ch]ild nor for her dear pa[r]ents
but [the goddess of love] led her astray
[to desire]

. . . *for* . . .
. . . *lightly* . . . w[hich
r]emin[ds] me now of Anactori[a]
[although far] away

[who]se [long-]desired footstep, whose radiant, sparkling face
I would rather see [before me] than the chariots
of Lydia or the armour of men
who [f]ight wars [on foot]

. . . *impossible to happen*
. . . *mankind* . . . *but to pray to [s]hare*

(9 lines missing)

unexpecte[dly]

ANNE BRADSTREET

From *The Prologue*[§]

1.

To sing of Wars, of Captaines, and of Kings,
Of Cities founded, Common-wealths begun,
For my mean Pen, are too superiour things,
And how they all, or each, their dates have run:
Let Poets, and Historians set these forth,
My obscure Verse, shal not so dim their worth.

2.

But when my wondring eyes, and envious heart,
Great *Bartas* sugar'd lines doe but read o're;

[§] Reprinted by permission of Joseph R. McElrath from *The Complete Works of Anne Bradstreet* edited by Joseph R. McElrath, Jr., and Allan P. Robb. Boston, Massachusetts: Twayne Publishers. Copyright © 1981 by Joseph R. McElrath. Material excerpted from pages 6–8.

Foole, I doe grudge, the Muses did not part
'Twixt him and me, that over-fluent store;
A *Bartas* can, doe what a *Bartas* wil,
But simple I according to my skill.

3.

From School-boyes tongue, no Rhethorick we expect,
Nor yet a sweet Consort, from broken strings,
Nor perfect beauty, where's a maine defect,
My foolish, broken, blemish'd Muse so sings;
And this to mend, alas, no Art is able,
'Cause Nature made it so irreparable.

4.

Nor can I, like that fluent sweet tongu'd *Greek*
Who lisp'd at first, speake afterwards more plaine
By Art, he gladly found what he did seeke,
A full requitall of his striving paine:
Art can doe much, but this maxime's most sure,
A weake or wounded braine admits no cure.

5.

I am obnoxious to each carping tongue,
Who sayes, my hand a needle better fits,
A Poets Pen, all scorne, I should thus wrong;
For such despight they cast on female wits:
If what I doe prove well, it wo'nt advance,
They'l say its stolne, or else, it was by chance.

6.

But sure the antick *Greeks* were far more milde,
Else of our Sex, why feigned they those nine,
And poesy made, *Calliope's* owne childe,
So 'mongst the rest, they plac'd the Arts divine:
But this weake knot they will full soone untye,
The *Greeks* did nought, but play the foole and lye.

7.

Let *Greeks* be *Greeks*, and Women what they are,
Men have precedency, and still excell,
It is but vaine, unjustly to wage war,
Men can doe best, and Women know it well;
Preheminence in each, and all is yours,
Yet grant some small acknowledgement of ours.

8.

And oh, ye high flown quils, that soare the skies,
And ever with your prey, still catch your praise,
If e'er you daigne these lowly lines, your eyes
Give wholsome Parsley wreath, I aske no Bayes:
This meane and unrefined stuffe of mine,
Will make your glistering gold but more to shine.

EAVAN BOLAND

From *The Journey*[§]

For Elizabeth Ryle

> Immediately cries were heard. These were the loud wailing of infant souls at the very entranceway; never had they had their share of life's sweetness for the dark day had stolen them from their mothers' breasts and plunged them to a death before their time.
>
> *Vergil, The Aeneid, Book VI*

And then the dark fell and "there has never"
I said "been a poem to an antibiotic:
never a word to compare with the odes on
the flower of the raw sloe for fever

"or the devious Africa-seeking tern
or the protein treasures of the sea bed.
Depend on it, somewhere a poet is wasting
his sweet uncluttered meters on the obvious

"emblem instead of the real thing.
Instead of sulpha we shall have hyssop dipped
in the wild blood of the unblemished lamb,
so every day the language gets less

"for the task and we are less with the language."
I finished speaking and the anger faded
and dark fell and the book beside me
lay open at the page Aphrodite

comforts Sappho in her love's duress.
The poplars shifted their music in the garden,
a child startled in a dream,
my room was a mess—

[§] Reprinted by permission of W. W. Norton & Company, Inc. and Carcanet Press Limited from "The Journey" included in *Outside History: Selected Poems 1980–1990 by Eavan Boland*. Copyright © 1990 by Eavan Boland. Material reprinted from pages 93–96.

the usual hardcovers, half-finished cups,
clothes piled up on an old chair—
and I was listening out but in my head was
a loosening and sweetening heaviness,

not sleep, but nearly sleep, not dreaming really
but as ready to believe and still
unfevered, calm and unsurprised
when she came and stood beside me

and I would have known her anywhere
and I would have gone with her anywhere
and she came wordlessly
and without a word I went with her

down down down without so much as
ever touching down but always, always
with a sense of mulch beneath us,
the way of stairs winding down to a river

and as we went on the light went on
failing and I looked sideways to be certain
it was she, misshapen, musical—
Sappho—the scholiast's nightingale

and down we went, again down
until we came to a sudden rest
beside a river in what seemed to be
an oppressive suburb of the dawn.

My eyes got slowly used to the bad light.
At first I saw shadows, only shadows.
Then I could make out women and children
and, in the way they were, the grace of love.

"Cholera, typhus, croup, diptheria,"
she said, "in those days they racketed
in every backstreet and alley of old Europe.
Behold the children of the plague."

Then to my horror I could see to each
nipple some had clipped a limpet shape—
suckling darknesses—while others had their arms
weighed down, making terrible pietas.

She took my sleeve and said to me "be careful.
Do not define these women by their work:
not as washerwomen trussed in dust and sweating,
muscling water into linen by the river's edge

"nor as court ladies brailled in silk
on wool, and woven with an ivory unicorn
and hung, nor as laundresses tossing cotton,
brisking daylight with lavender and gossip.

"But these are women who went out like you
when dusk became a dark sweet with leaves,
recovering the day, stooping, picking up
teddy bears and rag dolls and tricycles and buckets—

"love's archaeology—and they too like you
stood boot deep in flowers once in summer
or saw winter come in with a single magpie
in a caul of haws, a solo harlequin."

I stood fixed. I could not reach or speak to them.
Between us was the melancholy river,
the dream water, the narcotic crossing.
They had passed over it, its cold persuasions.

I whispered, "let me be
let me at least be their witness," but she said
"what you have seen is beyond speech,
beyond song, only not beyond love;

"remember it, you will remember it"
and I heard her say but she was fading fast
as we emerged under the stars of heaven,
"there are not many of us; you are dear

"and stand beside me as my own daughter.
I have brought you here so you will know forever
the silences in which are our beginnings,
in which we have an origin like water,"

and the wind shifted and the window clasp
opened, banged and I woke up to find
my poetry books spread higgledy-piggledy,
my skirt spread out where I had laid it—

nothing was changed; nothing was more clear
but it was wet and the year was late.
The rain was grief in arrears; my children
slept the last dark out safely and I wept.

NOTES

[1] In any case, this question is impossible to answer on its own terms since the social role of constructions of sexuality in the ancient world was almost certainly radically different from that played by modern categorizations of homo- and heterosexual desire.

[2] "The tenth muse" was a phrase often used in reference to Sappho. According to classical tradition, there were nine muses (all female); the designation "the tenth muse" was intended as a complimentary epithet. The image of the muse as a source of inspiration is part of a long history of representations of "women" as the object of poetic writing produced by a male subject. In this section, Anne Bradstreet and Eavan Boland both examine their own participation in such a history; Boland in particular rewrites the muse/author relationship as an interaction between female subjects working together to give voice to a certain vision of women's experience.

[3] She wrote her poem at a time when she feared her child, who was being treated with antibiotics for meningitis, might die.

WORKS CONSULTED

Boland, Eavan. *Object Lessons: The Life of the Woman and the Poet in Our Time.* New York: W.W. Norton, 1995.

Gilbert, Sandra M., and Susan Gubar. *The Norton Anthology of Literature By Women: The Tradition in English.* New York: W.W. Norton, 1985.

McElrath, Joseph R., Jr., and Allan P. Robb, eds. *The Complete Works of Anne Bradstreet.* Boston: Twayne, 1981.

Rosenmeier, Rosamund. *Anne Bradstreet Revisited.* Boston: Twayne, 1991.

Williamson, Margaret. *Sappho's Immortal Daughters.* Cambridge: Harvard UP, 1995.

MARIAMA BÂ *(1929–1981)*

"Till Tomorrow, My Friend"

Mariama Bâ's epistolary novel *So Long a Letter,* from which the following excerpt is taken, cannot, strictly speaking, be termed autobiographical—particularly since the author herself rejected that label. Neither can it be described as a non-fictional first-person account similar to other excerpts included in this section (including poems by Sappho, Laila of Shaibân-Bakr, and Jo Carrillo). Nevertheless, we include Bâ's work in this section not only to demonstrate the permeability of generic categories, but also to point out the ways in which literary representation shapes—and is shaped by—social life. We have chosen Bâ's work for three reasons. First, *So Long a Letter* destabilizes certain generic expectations. It "represents" the fictional nature of autobiographical writing in general and, as critic Christopher L. Miller has pointed out, violates the implicit rules of both the epistolary genre and the predominantly male African francophone corpus. Second, Bâ's work makes possible a discussion of women's representations of themselves and their experiences within contemporary Senagalese literature. According to Miller, "After *Une Si Longue Lettre,* it will be possible for the first time to think the terms 'African,' 'woman,' 'francophone,' 'writer,' and even 'feminist' all together" (284). Third, *So Long a Letter* dramatizes women's sharing and telling of stories as acts with important political and social implications. In the passages that follow, the narrator Ramatoulaye, a widowed mother of twelve children, shows how her long-term friendship with Aissatou—to whom the letter/novel is addressed—functions as a determining force in her life.

Mariama Bâ was born in Dakar, Senegal. After her mother's death, she was sent as a young girl to live with her maternal grandparents, a relatively wealthy Muslim couple. Bâ, who was one of the first Senegalese women to receive a Western education, has spoken positively of her experience with the French colonial educational system. Her father, a civil servant who in 1959 became the first Minister of Health, taught her how to read and arranged for her to begin school; it was at his insistence that her education was not a traditional Muslim one. After attending the French School in Dakar and the École Normale for girls in Rufisque, Bâ began a career as a professional primary-school teacher, at the same time as she became an active participant in the Senegalese and international women's movements. Like Ramatoulaye, Bâ married and had a large family of nine children; she later divorced her husband, a former Minister of Information. In 1980 *So Long a Letter,* her first novel, was awarded the prestigious Noma Prize for the best work published in Africa. Bâ also wrote a second novel, *Scarlet Song,* but died, after a long illness, before its publication. She is considered to be one of Senegal's most noteworthy female authors; *So Long a Letter* has been variously described as "a pioneering work" (Rueschmann 4) and "a testimony of the female condition in Africa . . . giving that condition a true imaginative depth" (Abiola Irele, qtd. in Rueschmann 4).

Bâ's novel is widely thought of as the first female-authored francophone novel published in sub-Saharan Africa to be structured around an explicit and feminist critique of gender issues. While Senegal was the birthplace of African francophone literature by women, Aminata Sow Fall's work *Le Revenant,* the first novel by a woman to appear in Senegal, was published only in 1976. Before this point, African francophone literature—which emerged as a genre around 1920—was strictly a male affair. Mariama Bâ's writing confronts not only the colonialist heritage of the francophone African novel in general, but also a pre-established corpus of francophone African literature by men. As Miller puts it, Bâ must "begin the reappraisal of gender within the African novel while simultaneously confronting her own marginal status as a writer" (247). Partly because of the ways in which African feminism has been demonized as a form of eurocentrist and classist discourse (see Mọlara Ogundipẹ-Leslie), Bâ also had to face accusations of eurocentrism and classism in her work. Nevertheless, it is true that Bâ's emphasis on the transformative and liberating powers of literacy participates in a common French colonialist trope.[1] *So Long a Letter* also confirms, however, the significance of African tradition to Bâ's feminist vision.

In *So Long a Letter,* Bâ develops a forceful critique of polygamy as an oppressive cultural practice; her belief in the primacy of the heterosexual couple and the importance of heterosexual love in social life is evident from the excerpt that appears below. As the novel progresses, however, the narrator Ramatoulaye places more emphasis on the role played by female friendships in the process of self-definition she undertakes after the death of her husband. Indeed, *So Long a Letter* is structured as a letter written by Ramatoulaye to her friend, Aissatou, who has left behind her life in Africa to work as a translator in the United States. This letter "expresses Ramatoulaye's need to reestablish the former closeness with Aissatou, to reaffirm their common struggle toward a new vision of the African female self" (Rueschmann 16). The refashioning of both her own life and Senegalese society that Ramatoulaye envisions at the end of the book entails a valorization of indigenous African female identity. Finally, *So Long a Letter* links women's power to enact social change to their ability to share their reflections and experiences through narrative. "Thus this 'long letter' moves from self-expression and self-reflection to communication with a community and the entire world of women engaged in a common struggle toward a new society" (Rueschmann 16).

NM

FROM *SO LONG A LETTER*[§]

Dear Aissatou,

I have received your letter. By way of reply, I am beginning this diary, my prop in my distress. Our long association has taught me that confiding in others allays pain.

[§] Selections reprinted from *So Long A Letter* by Mariama Bâ. Translated by Modupé Bodé-Thomas, published in English by Heinemann Publishers, London. Original copyright © 1980 as *Une Si Longue Lettre* by Les Nouvelles Editions Africaines du Sénégal, Dakar, Sénégal, reprinted by permission. Material excerpted from pages 1, 71–72, 88–89 in the Heinemann edition.

Your presence in my life is by no means fortuitous. Our grandmothers in their compounds were separated by a fence and would exchange messages daily. Our mothers used to argue over who would look after our uncles and aunts. As for us, we wore out wrappers and sandals on the same stony road to the koranic school; we buried our milk teeth in the same holes and begged our fairy godmothers to restore them to us, more splendid than before.

If over the years, and passing through the realities of life, dreams die, I still keep intact my memories, the salt of remembrance.

I conjure you up. The past is reborn, along with its procession of emotions. I close my eyes. Ebb and tide of feeling: heat and dazzlement, the woodfires, the sharp green mango, bitten into in turns, a delicacy in our greedy mouths. I close my eyes. Ebb and tide of images: drops of sweat beading your mother's ochre-colored face as she emerges from the kitchen, the procession of young wet girls chattering on their way back from the springs.

We walked the same paths from adolescence to maturity, where the past begets the present.

My friend, my friend, my friend. I call on you three times.[2]

Yesterday you were divorced. Today I am a widow. . . .

I feel an immense fatigue. It begins in my soul and weighs down my body.

Ousmane, my last born, holds out your letter to me. Ousmane is six years old. 'It's Aunty Aissatou.'. . .

These caressing words, which relax me, are indeed from you. And you tell me of the 'end'. I calculate. Tomorrow is indeed the end of my seclusion. And you will be there within reach of my hand, my voice, my eyes.

'End or new beginning'? My eyes will discover the slightest change in you. I have already totalled up my own; my seclusion has withered me. Worries have given me wrinkles; my fat has melted away. I often tap against bone where before there was rounded flesh.

When we meet, the signs on our bodies will not be important. The essential thing is the content of our hearts, which animates us; the essential thing is the quality of the sap that flows through us. You have often proved to me the superiority of friendship over love. Time, distance, as well as mutual memories have consolidated our ties and made our children brothers and sisters. Reunited, will we draw up a detailed account of our faded bloom, or will we sow new seeds for new harvests? . . .

Till tomorrow, my friend.

We will then have time to ourselves, especially as I have obtained an extension of my widow's leave.

I reflect. My new turn of mind is hardly surprising to you. I cannot help unburdening myself to you. I might as well sum up now.

I am not indifferent to the irreversible currents of women's liberation that are lashing the world. This commotion that is shaking up every aspect of our lives reveals and illustrates our abilities.

My heart rejoices each time a woman emerges from the shadows. I know that the field of our gains is unstable, the retention of conquests difficult: social constraints are ever-present, and male egoism resists.

Instruments of some, baits for others, respected or despised, often muzzled, all women have almost the same fate, which religions or unjust legislation have sealed.

My reflections determine my attitude to the problems of life. I analyse the decisions that decide our future. I widen my scope by taking an interest in current world affairs.

I remain persuaded of the inevitable and necessary complementarity of man and woman.

Love, imperfect as it may be in its content and expression, remains the natural link between these two beings.

To love one another! If only each partner could move sincerely towards the other! If each could only melt into the other! If each would only accept the other's successes and failures! If each would only praise the other's qualities instead of listing his faults! If each could only correct bad habits without harping on about them! If each could penetrate the other's most secret haunts to forestall failure and be a support while tending to the evils that are repressed!

The success of the family is born of a couple's harmony, as the harmony of multiple instruments creates a pleasant symphony.

The nation is made up of all families, rich or poor, united or separated, aware or unaware. The success of a nation therefore depends inevitably on the family.

* * *

Why aren't your sons coming with you? Ah, their studies. . . .

So, then, will I see you tomorrow in a tailored suit or a long dress? I've taken a bet with Daba: tailored suit. Used to living far away, you will want—again, I have taken a bet with Daba—table, plate, chair, fork.

More convenient, you will say. But I will not let you have your way. I will spread out a mat. On it there will be the big, steaming bowl into which you will have to accept that other hands dip.

Beneath the shell that has hardened you over the years, beneath your sceptical pout, your easy carriage, perhaps I will feel you vibrate. I would so much like to hear you check or encourage my eagerness, just as before, and, as before, to see you take part in the search for a new way.

I warn you already, I have not given up wanting to refashion my life. Despite everything—disappointments and humiliations—hope still lives on within me. It is from the dirty and nauseating humus that the green plant sprouts into life, and I can feel new buds springing up in me.

The word 'happiness' does indeed have meaning, doesn't it? I shall go out in search of it. Too bad for me if once again I have to write you so long a letter. . . .

Ramatoulaye

NOTES

[1] According to Miller, "Francophone literacy is a lever that Mariama Bâ uses to advance the cause of the dispossessed, even if it is only one group of relatively privileged women for whom she speaks" (176).

[2] An invocation that indicates the seriousness of the subject to be discussed [Bodé-Thomas].

WORKS CONSULTED

Busby, Margaret, ed. *Daughters of Africa: An International Anthology of Words and Writings by Women of African Descent from the Ancient Egyptian to the Present.* London: Jonathan Cape, 1992.

Miller, Christopher L. *Theories of Africans: Francophone Literature and Anthropology in Africa.* Chicago: U of Chicago P, 1990.

Rueschmann, Eva. "Female Self-Definition and the African Community in Mariama Bâ's Epistolary Novel *So Long a Letter.*" *International Women's Writing: New Landscapes of Identity.* Ed. Anne E. Brown and Marjanne E. Gooze. Westport, CT: Greenwood, 1995.

LOUISE LABÉ *(1526–1566)*

Forging Intellectual Connections

Louise Labé, the daughter of an illiterate, though well-to-do, merchant, is one of the best-known feminist poets of the French Renaissance. It remains something of a mystery how a woman of her socio-economic background became not only a renowned author but the host to some of the most cultivated inhabitants of Lyon at the frequent salon gatherings in Labé's home. Nevertheless, it was mainly because of her work (along with that of two other poets who were natives of Lyon, Maurice Scève and Pernette du Guillet) that the city of Lyon has become associated with important developments in French poetry during the sixteenth century. Although in the writings of her contemporaries, Louise Labé was the subject of much speculation and hyperbole about alleged sexual activity, she seems to have had a clear sense of her own accomplishments as well as the obstacles faced by women scholars pursuing their devotion to learning. She was one of a number of women of the period who "assumed a leading role in salon life, thereby supporting and encouraging interest in the arts and the evolution of a 'polite' society" (Cameron 8–9).

Lyon during this period was a center of cultural and intellectual activity. Still, few municipal provisions for formal education were made, particularly for young women. Labé was educated by her stepmother (her mother died while she was still an infant) and her father, both of whom seem to have trained her in the traditionally feminine accomplishments of music and needlework as well as in the more masculine pursuits of fencing and jousting. The selection reprinted here displays Labé's familiarity with some of the major intellectual trends of her time; François Rigolot, a well-known scholar of the French Renaissance, has called Labé's letter "an important text in the history of both humanism and feminism" (8). In this dedicatory letter, addressed to a young woman of good family, Labé calls on women to take advantage of their new-found liberty in order to participate in a humanist community of knowledge. In doing so, she contributes to the debate over women's natural and social status, a quarrel which has been described as "a major topic of discussion in a series of [sixteenth-century] works . . . and, probably, wherever people aware of the latest ideas met" (Farrell 6). According to Labé, women must take possession of knowledge (and become knowing subjects) instead of adorning themselves with ornaments in order to exist as the objects of men's desire. By dedicating her book to another woman, Labé forges a literary and intellectual connection that is also a connection between women.

Louise Labé's desire to participate in a learned community which was overwhelmingly male and her role as a "public" intellectual gave her a reputation for scandalous sexual behavior. (See the headnote for Théroigne de Méricourt for another example of the ways in which women who participate in public life are forced into roles that are primarily sexual.)

Her love sonnets, which may draw upon her experience of having fallen deeply in love with a man whose identity remains unknown, have remained the most famous of her writings. She died in February, 1566, after a long illness, leaving her modest fortune to her two nephews and the friend with whom she was living. Her work continues to speak to modern readers of her own resistance to the constraints to which she was subject by virtue of her class and gender.

NM

FROM LOUISE LABÉ'S *COMPLETE WORKS*[§]

T[o] M[ademoiselle] C[lémence] d[e] B[ourges, of] L[yons]

Now that the time has come, Mademoiselle, that men's harsh laws no longer prevent women from devoting themselves to the arts and sciences, it seems to me that those who have the opportunity ought to study them, using the rightful freedom that members of our sex have so ardently desired in the past. In this way we can show men the wrong they have done us by preventing our getting the benefit and recognition that we could have derived from such study. If any one of us reaches the point where she can set down her thoughts in writing, she ought to do so carefully, not shunning the recognition, but rather adorning herself with it instead of with chains, rings, and sumptuous clothes. These things cannot really be considered ours. They are only thought to be ours because we use them. But the honor that our knowledge brings us will be entirely our own. Neither a robber's craft, nor an enemy's force, nor the passage of time can take them away from us.

Had I been blessed with a mind capable of understanding whatever it wanted to, I would set a good example rather than admonishing others. Since I spent part of my youth training myself in music, however, and since I found the time that remained too short for my unsophisticated mind, and since I cannot, by myself, satisfy my desire to see our sex surpass or equal men, not only in beauty, but in knowledge and virtue, I can only urge noble women to raise their minds somewhat above their distaffs and spindles, and to devote themselves to showing the world that our not being fit for command does not mean that we should be looked down upon as partners either in domestic or in public affairs by those who govern and are in a position of authority. Such study will contribute not only to the reputation of our sex, but to the general good, for men will put more effort into all branches of learning, because they

---

[§] Reprinted with permission of Edith R. Farrell from *Louise Labé's Complete Works,* translated and edited by Edith R. Farrell, published by The Whitston Publishing Company, Troy, New York. Copyright © 1986 Edith R. Farrell. Material excerpted from pages 27–29.

would be ashamed to be surpassed by women over whom they have always claimed superiority in almost everything. . . .

Since women hesitate to appear in public alone, I have chosen you to be my guide, by dedicating this little book to you. I do so only to assure you of the good will that I have so long felt toward you and to encourage you, when you have seen my own rough, poorly-constructed work, to bring out one of your own, better polished and more beautiful.

God keep you in good health.
Lyons, July 24, 1555
Your humble friend, *Louise Labé*

WORKS CONSULTED

Cameron, Keith. *Louise Labé: Renaissance Poet and Feminist.* New York: Berg Publishers, 1990.

Farrell, Edith R. *Louise Labé's Complete Works.* Troy, NY: Whitston, 1986.

Labé, Louise. *Oeuvres complètes.* Ed. François Rigolot. Paris: Flammarion, 1986.

MICHÈLE LE DOEUFF *(1948–)*

"An Art of Fighting Fire with Fire and Looks with Looks"

Michèle Le Doeuff is a French feminist philosopher who has written extensively on the role played by gendered images and social constructions in the field of philosophical inquiry. She is also known for her work on British Renaissance thought and the history of science. She has taught at the École Normale Superieure (Fontenay) in France and is currently a researcher at the prestigious Centre National de la Recherche Scientifique in Paris. As a young woman, she studied at the Sorbonne where she became a student of the moral philosopher Vladimir Jankélévitch, who, according to Le Doeuff, "did not want to have disciples, [and was] a man . . . keen on students going their own way" (Mortley 83). In a description of the start of her intellectual career she emphasizes the ways in which she learned early on to think for herself (Mortley). This emphasis is something of a constant in her work; as she puts it, " . . . my idea of rationality certainly does not involve the worship of any hegemony" (Mortley 85).

While Le Doeuff is of roughly the same generation as such well-known French feminist theorists as Julia Kristeva and Luce Irigaray—and has had her work analyzed alongside that of Kristeva and Irigaray in the study by Elizabeth Grosz entitled *Sexual Subversions: Three French Feminists*—her methodological focus and intellectual preoccupations vary significantly from those of the other two writers. As Grosz remarks, "Her major interests do not directly focus on the textuality of texts (as Kristeva does), nor on the position of women or femininity within representational systems (as Irigaray does). More clearly and less ambiguously than either, Le Doeuff's work is located within the discipline of philosophy" (184). If this is true, it is perhaps in part because Le Doeuff continues to see value in the philosophical project of thinking critically and rationally. While much of her work involves an analysis of the ways in which sexism and phallocentrism work implicitly to sustain certain kinds of philosophical discourse, Le Doeuff does not believe that all of what is implied by "rationality," "reason," and "thinking philosophically" should be rejected because of the misogyny that has been such a defining element in the history of Western philosophy.

By the same token, Le Doeuff is sharply critical of the tendency of many philosophers to reaffirm the absolute and preeminent value of their intellectual work. As a feminist and a philosopher herself, she advocates refusing

> . . . to play the game of theoretical domination, by recognizing that rational thought goes through a process of diversification and that the thing to do is to acknowledge this diversity. . . . It is even possible to abandon thinking of the value of philosophical work as an absolute, without deciding that there is nothing of value in the discourses that abound in the public domain or in the

goals that people set themselves. Once the existence of these other discourses and goals is recognized, we might hope that philosophy will mingle with them and they with philosophy. (26)

In this passage from *Hipparchia's Choice: An Essay Concerning Women, Philosophy, etc.,* Le Doeuff demonstrates her firm belief in the continued intellectual and political value of critical, rational, *feminist* thought. In this study, she develops an historically grounded critique of philosophy as a masculinist and exclusionary discipline alongside a conception of a feminist philosophical project that recognizes its contingent nature as well as its potential power. For Le Doeuff, as she explains in the excerpts included here, "Being a feminist is also a way of integrating the fact of being a philosopher" (29).

Le Doeuff has come under a degree of criticism for what Grosz calls "a certain reverence and respect, a propriety in her patient, meticulous, restricted readings" of the Western philosophical corpus (212); Meaghan Morris, in turn, has wondered "to what extent [Le Doeuff's] *L'Imaginaire Philosophique* . . . is . . . merely engaged in a salvage operation to rescue philosophy from the more damaging charges of feminist critics in France" (qtd. in Grosz 212). Le Doeuff, in turn, has criticized "the anti-intellectualist tendency existing in women's studies or even feminist studies in more than one country . . . from some elegant discourses to sweeping statements such as 'reason is a male thing'" ("Women, Reason, etc." 1). She objects to the way in which notions such as "male rationality" objectify and deny the history of the terms that make them up. While sexism has often functioned as a structuring principle of philosophical discourse, Le Doeuff argues that the vision of a feminist philosophical project is both possible and necessary. As Le Doeuff points out, "Rationality, it is true, is a problematic notion, but when, in philosophy, have we ever come across notions which were *not* problematic?" ("Women, Reason, etc." 3).

NM

FROM *HIPPARCHIA'S CHOICE: AN ESSAY CONCERNING WOMEN, PHILOSOPHY, ETC.*[§]

Considering the main aspects of the question, we can state that feminism is the term which makes it possible to integrate the other two—woman and philosopher—into a dialectic, without reducing them to nothing. Because first of all feminism is the simple knowledge that when one is a woman, that fact always matters in social situations and in relationships, including those where you might expect it least, where you would not think it was relevant. The reality of social relations is never what you might think, it is that which we still need to analyse. You might think there would be free or neutral zones, where the fact of being a man or woman would not matter; when, for example, you are

[§] Reprinted by permission of Blackwell Publishers from *Hipparchia's Choice: An Essay Concerning Women, Philosophy, etc.* by Michèle Le Doeuff. Translated by Trista Selous for Blackwell Publishers, Oxford, England, 1989. Copyright © *Les Éditions du Seuil*, Paris, France. Material excerpted from pages 28–31.

dealing with the transmission of knowledge which is supposed to be abstract, you might think that it was not important what your birth certificate says. And in one sense we should indeed continue to think this, knowing however that the facts will do much to undermine such a supposition. From this point of view to be a feminist is to integrate the fact of being a woman into dialectics: it is a way of knowing that sexualization matters and at the same time, but contradictorily, knowing that it would be possible for it not to matter and that the way in which it now matters is neither good nor legitimate. Whether one goes on to think that the fact of being a woman should not matter at all, or that it should matter in a completely different way, is not very important and depends on personal choices or particular situations.

Being a feminist is also a way of integrating the fact of being a philosopher. Because for two centuries a feminist has been a woman who does not leave others to think for her, whether it be a question simply of thinking or, more particularly, thinking about the feminine condition or what it should be. If we make a link (at least as a hypothesis) between thinking philosophically and self-assertion through thought, or the individual withdrawal from generally held beliefs, then 'thinking philosophically' and 'being a feminist' appear as one and the same attitude: a desire to judge by and for oneself, which may manifest itself in relation to different questions. If philosophy particularly consists of questioning what happens in towns, houses and people's daily lives (and, according to Cicero, such is philosophy's task as seen by Socrates), then the issue of women's lives is necessarily on the agenda. But has it really been so, as an issue, in the twenty-five centuries of philosophy that we can observe? Too little or not in the right way, the feminist would say: so here we have an enquiry and a process to be taken further.

For the project of philosophy and that of feminist thinking have a fundamental structure in common, an art of fighting fire with fire and looks with looks, of objectifying and analysing surrounding thought, of regarding beliefs as objects that must be scrutinized, when the supposedly normal attitude is to submit to what social life erects as doctrine. Nothing goes without saying, including what people think about the roles which have come down to men and women. . . .

And yet, although we can argue that there is harmony between philosophy and feminism, although we can maintain that it is entirely in the interests of a woman philosopher that she be a feminist (as I intend to show), we must take the exposition of the difficulty further. We must recognize that to be a feminist and a philosopher may still generate a contradiction whose effect, at least in my case, was to produce a kind of long impossibility of speaking. The feminist seemed constantly to find objections to subjects that the philosopher might have chosen (these texts from the philosophical tradition contain too many dreadful things against women, I can't get enthusiastic about them), while the philosopher was always filled with reservations about the thousand and one theoretical discourses which intersected in the Women's Movement. How then are we to explain the fact that, while there is a kind of pre-established harmony between thinking philosophically and wanting independence for all women, to place oneself on the join between feminism and philosophy still leads to this kind of mutism? . . .

WORKS CONSULTED

Grosz, Elizabeth. *Sexual Subversions: Three French Feminists.* Sydney: Allen and Unwin, 1989.

Le Doeuff, Michèle. "Women, Reason, etc." *Differences: A Journal of Feminist Cultural Studies* 2.3 (1990): 1–13.

Mortley, Raoul. *French Philosophers in Conversation: Levinas, Schneider, Serres, Irigaray, Le Doeuff, Derrida.* London: Routledge, 1991.

ABIGAIL ABBOT BAILEY *(1746–1815)*

Revolt Against the "Habit of Obedience"

> For it was not an enemy that reproached me;
> then I could have borne it. . .
> but it was thou, a man mine equal,
> my guide, and mine acquaintance. . . .
>
> *Psalm 55*

The type of spiritual autobiography known as the conversion narrative was typical of Evangelical Christians writing in the U. S. in the 18th and 19th centuries (see headnote for Rebecca Cox Jackson in **Sexuality, Spirituality, and Power**). Conversion narratives, of course, antedate the colonization of the New World, and they have taken on a variety of different forms as they conformed with the unique traditions and specific social circumstances of the writer. Jackson's narrative is intimately shaped by slavery and the oppression of the African-American community; the memoirs of Abigail Abbot Bailey are shaped by the mythologies of frontier life: the hierarchical organization of a conservative, Calvinist theocracy; and the personal experience of domestic abuse and violence. These factors not only influenced the style, themes, and specific details of Bailey's memoirs, they also shaped the very nature of her conversion.

Abigail Abbot was born in 1746 in the newly settled regions of colonial New Hampshire to devout parents. In 1767, at the age of 22, she married Asa Bailey, a neighboring landholder of moderate wealth and a respected member of the community, active in local politics and military service. Despite Abigail's hopes that she and her husband would be friends who would support and guide each other in marriage while building a happy home, she soon learned that he was a man of "hard, uneven, rash temper" (Taves 57).

Within a month of their marriage, Abigail Bailey refers to her husband's physical abusiveness as well as his anger. The abuse he inflicted on his wife became so harsh at times that Abigail feared he would kill her; their children soon became victims of his physical cruelty as well (between 1768 and 1791, Abigail and Asa had a total of seventeen children). Asa was also adulterous; within three years of their marriage, Asa had an affair with a hired woman, and three years later attempted to rape a second. Abigail apparently suffered these betrayals, along with his physical and emotional abuse, in silence, until the event that would eventually bring an end to her silent suffering: Asa's incestuous relationship, begun in 1788, with their fourth child, Phebe. In the excerpt that follows, Abigail describes the alternating sweetness and cruelty with which Asa threatened Phebe (whom she calls simply "this daughter"). Elsewhere, she describes the fear, shame, and despair that Phebe suffered (Taves 71, 75).

For a few years, Abigail indirectly attempted to interrupt these incestuous activities, which apparently took her a while to fully comprehend, but because of Asa's threats and manipulations, she was unable to form an alliance with her daughter. Abigail also suffered from various health problems (many associated with childbirth), while the despair she felt over her husband's behavior sapped her strength. After the birth of twins in 1790, however, she appears to have undergone a transformation, or a "conversion," as it is portrayed in her narrative. At this time, she began to demand that her husband end this incestuous adultery, or else be prepared for her to petition for divorce and a property settlement—which she eventually did. For perhaps the first time in her marriage, Abigail no longer allowed her husband's threats and anger to silence her, but said, "the business I now had taken in hand, was of too serious a nature . . . to be thus disposed of, or dismissed with a few angry words" (Taves 77). For the next three years, Asa threatened Abigail, promised to reform, begged her to relent, and tricked her into traveling to New York, ostensibly to sell their property. Instead, he kidnapped the children and tried to deny her rights to divorce and property. Still she persisted, and in 1793, with the aid of friends and family, she had Asa arrested and forced him to forfeit her share of the property and custody of their children.

Abigail's tragic yet eventually triumphant story leaves us with the questions of why she remained with her husband through twenty-two years of abuse and adultery, and then, after so long, why she decided to transform her situation. Any attempt at an answer must take into account a number of social and personal factors. Bailey lived in a highly hierarchical society that encouraged the subordination of commoners to the elite, children to parents, and wives to husbands. New England had been dominated by a Calvinist religious belief that saw all events, fortuitous or tragic, as part of God's divine will. The faithful dedicated much of their lives to solitary introspection that would bring an understanding of this will. The hardships of Abigail's time, disease and Indian attack (both perceived by white settlers in this region as formidable threats), had been mythologized in the genre known as captivity narratives, which described all external hardships as God's attempts to test and purify the souls of a fallen humanity.

Abigail continually casts her narrative in the form of a captivity story, in which she is captive to both her own sinfulness and that of her husband (Taves 16–19). Thus for many years, she sees domestic abuse as something to be tolerated (Job-like) as a righteous punishment for her fallen nature, even as she prays for her husband's redemption. Only when her husband's incestuous actions become known can she decisively begin to shift the blame of sin onto Asa, and recognize him not as "mine equal, my guide" but as her enemy. From this shift in perspective came her conversion to an active stance against her husband—a difficult move to make or to justify successfully in a society that treated marriage as a microcosm of both the well-ordered state and the pious congregation, with the husband standing in for civil and divine authority. The same set of religious beliefs that allowed Abigail to rationalize and endure twenty-two years of abuse, also led her to believe that God was directing her to seek a divorce and bring her husband to justice. Bailey's narrative thus leads us to consider the troubling and complex relationship between religion and domestic violence, as well as the different meanings that justify domestic abuse in different cultural contexts.

KKF

FROM *THE MEMOIRS OF ABIGAIL ABBOT BAILEY*[§]

Soon after, Mr. B. laid this his pretended plan before the children; and after a while he obtained their consent to move to the westward. They were not pleased with the idea, but wished to be obedient, and to honor their father. Thus we all consented, at last, to follow our head and guide, wherever he should think best; for our family had ever been in the habit of obedience: and perhaps never were more pains taken to please the head of a family, than had ever been taken in our domestic circle.

But alas! words fail to set forth the things which followed! All this pretended *plan* was but a specious cover to infernal designs. Here I might pause, and wonder, and be silent, humble, and astonished, as long as I live! A family, which God had committed to my head and husband, as well as to me, to protect and train up for God, must now have their peace and honor sacrificed by an inhuman parent, under the most subtle and vile intrigues, to gratify a most contemptible passion! I had before endured sorrowful days and years, on account of the follies, cruelties, and the base incontinency of him who vowed to be my faithful husband. But all past afflictions vanish before those which follow. But how can I relate them? Oh tell it not in Gath! Must I record such grievousness against the husband of my youth?

Oft as I try to tell the doleful tale,
My quivering lips and faltering tongue do fail:
Nor can my trembling hand, or feeble pen,
Equal the follies of this worst of men!

I have already related that Mr. B. said he would take one of our sons, and one daughter, to wait on him in his distant tour, before he would take all the family. After he had talked of this for a few days, he said he had altered his plan; he would leave his son, and take only his daughter: he would hire what men's help he needed: his daughter must go and cook for him. He now commenced a new series of conduct in relation to this daughter, whom he selected to go with him, in order (as he pretended) to render himself pleasing and familiar to her; so that she might be willing to go with him, and feel happy: for though, as a father, he had a right to command her to go, yet (he said) he would so conduct toward her, as to make her cheerful and well pleased to go with him. A great part of the time he now spent in the room where she was spinning; and seemed shy of me, and of the rest of the family. He seemed to have forgotten his age, his honor, and all decency, as well as all virtue. He would spend his time with his daughter, in telling idle stories, and foolish riddles, and singing songs to her, and sometimes before the small children, when they were in that room. He thus pursued a course of conduct, which had the most direct tendency to corrupt young and tender minds, and lead them the greatest distance from every serious subject. He would try to make his daughter tell stories to him; wishing to make her free and socia-

[§] Reprinted by permission of Indiana University Press, from *Religion and Domestic Violence in Early New England: The Memoirs of Abigail Abbot Bailey,* edited by Ann Taves. Copyright © 1989 by Indiana University Press. Material excerpted from pages 69–76.

ble, and to erase from her mind all that fear and reserve, which he had ever taught his children to feel toward him. He had ever been sovereign, severe and hard with his children, and they stood in the greatest fear of him. His whole conduct, toward this daughter especially, was now changed, and became most disagreeable. . . .

After a while Mr. B's conduct toward this daughter was strangely altered. Instead of idle songs, fawning and flattery, he grew very angry with her; and would wish her dead, and buried: and he would correct her very severely. It seems, that when he found his first line of conduct ineffectual, he changed his behaviour, felt his vile indignation moved, and was determined to see what he could effect by tyranny and cruelty. He most cautiously guarded her against having any free conversation with me, or any of the family, at any time; lest she should expose him. He would forbid any of the children going with her to milking. If, at any time, any went with her, it must be a number; so that nothing could be said concerning him. He would not suffer her to go from home: I might not send her abroad on any occasion. Never before had Mr. B. thus confined her, or any of his children. None but an eye witness can conceive of the strangeness of his conduct from day to day and of his plans to conceal his wickedness, and to conceal himself from the light of evidence.[1]

From the commencement of this new series of wickedness, I did all that I thought proper to frustrate those abominable designs. But I had the mortification to find how unavailing my endeavors were to reform so vile a man.

No language could now express the sorrow and grief of my soul. I gave myself up to weeping and mourning. In these I seemed to find a kind of solitary pleasure. I now thought I could truly say, in the language of the prophet, "Behold and see, if there be any sorrow like unto my sorrow." —"O Lord, behold my affliction; for the enemy hath magnified himself against me. —Mine eyes fail with tears. What thing shall I liken to thee, O daughter of Jerusalem? For thy breach is great like the sea. He hath made me desolate. I forgot prosperity. Remember, O Lord, what is come upon us. We are fatherless; our mothers are widows. The joy of our heart is ceased, and turned into mourning."

But O, I thought to myself, who is this cruel oppressor? this grievous rod in the hands of the High and Lofty One, by whom I am thus sorely chastised? It is not an enemy; then I could have borne it. Neither was it he that hated me in days past; for then I would have hid myself from him. But it was the man mine equal, my guide, my friend, my husband! He has put forth his hand against such as were at peace with him. He has broken his covenant. The words of his mouth had often been smoother than oil, while yet they were drawn swords, and war was in his heart.

What then is man? What are all our dearest connexions, and creature comforts? How fading and uncertain! How unwise and unsafe it must be to set our hearts on such enjoyments! God has set me an important lesson upon the emptiness of the creature. This he has taught me, both in his word, providences, and in the school of adversity. But I, a feeble worm, can benefit by divine lessons, only in strength of Christ. But, praised be the God of grace, I think I can say by happy experience, "I can do all things through Christ, who strengtheneth me." I desire to bless God that he prepared me for the trials which he commenced; that he prepared me in some measure, to meet them with resignation of soul to the divine will, and with confidence in God, that he will order all things for his own glory.

I was lead earnestly to pray that when any signal trials should commence, I might be blessed with strength and grace according to my day: and I think I did not pray in vain. God has remarkably sustained me. . . .

Among the many instances of his wickedly correcting her, I shall mention one. One morning Mr. B. rose from bed, while it was yet dark. He immediately called his daughter, and told her to get up. She obeyed. And as she knew her daily business, she made up her fire in her room, and sat down to her work. He sat by the fire in the kitchen. As my door was open, I carefully observed his motions. He sat looking into the fire for some time, as though absorbed in his thoughts. It soon grew light. The small children arose, and came round the fire. He looked round like one disappointed and vexed. He sprang from his chair, and called his daughter, whom he first called. She left her work in her room, and came immediately to him. In great rage, and with a voice of terror, he asked why she did not come to him, when he first called her? She respectfully told him that he called her to get up, which she immediately did, and went to her work. But she said she did not hear him call her to come to him. He seized his horse whip, and said, in a rage, he would make her know that when he called her, she should come to him. He then fell to whipping her without mercy. She cried, and begged, and repeated her assertion, that she did not know he called her to come to him. She had done as he told her. She got up, and went to her work. But he was not in the least appeased. He continued whipping her, as though he was dealing with an ungovernable brute; striking over her head, hands, and back, nor did he spare her face and eyes; while the poor girl appeared as though she must die. No proper account could he ever be prevailed on to give of this conduct.

None can describe the anguish of my heart on the beholding of such scenes. How pitiful must be the case of a young female, to be subjected to such barbarous treatment by her own father; so that she knew of no way of redress!

It may appear surprising that such wickedness was not checked by legal restraints. But great difficulties attend in such a case. While I was fully convinced of the wickedness, yet I knew not that I could make legal proof. I could not prevail upon this daughter to make known to me her troubles; or to testify against the author of them. Fear, shame, youthful inexperience, and the terrible peculiarities of her case, all conspired to close her mouth against affording me, or any one, proper information. My soul was moved with pity for her wretched case: and yet I cannot say I did not feel a degree of resentment, that she would not, as she ought, expose the wickedness of her father, that she might be relieved from him, and he brought to due punishment. But no doubt his intrigues, insinuations, commands, threats, and parental influence, led her to feel that it was in vain for her to seek redress.

My circumstances, and peculiar bodily infirmities, at that time, were such as to entitle a woman to the tenderest affection and sympathies of a companion. On this account, and as Mr. B. was exceeding stern, and angry with me for entertaining hard thoughts of him, I felt unable to do any thing more for the relief of my poor daughter. My hope in God was my only support. And I did abundantly and earnestly commit my cause to him. I felt confident that he would, in his own time, as his infinite wisdom should determine, grant relief . . . .

NOTE

[1] The discreet reader will repeatedly wonder that this pious sufferer did not look abroad for help against so vile a son of Beliel, and avail herself of the law of the land, by swearing the peace against him. Her forbearance does indeed seem to have been carried to excess. But when we consider her delicate situation at this time; her peaceable habits from youth; her native tenderness of mind; her long fears of a tyrannical cruel husband; her having at no time of her sufferings seen all that we now see of his abominable character as a reason why he should have been brought to justice; her wishes and hopes that he might be brought to reformation; her desires not to have the family honor sacrificed; and the difficulty of exhibiting sufficient evidence against a popular, subtle man, to prove such horrid crimes; —these things plead much in her behalf. After all, it will be difficult to resist the conviction which will be excited in the course of these memoirs that Mrs. B. did truly err, in not having her husband brought to juctice. The law is made for the lawless and disobedient [E.S.]. [Ethan Smith, the pastor of the church Abigail joined upon her conversion, edited and published her memoirs in 1815. *Eds.*]

WORK CONSULTED

Taves, Ann, ed. *Religion and Domestic Violence in Early New England: The Memoirs of Abigail Abbot Bailey.* Bloomington: Indiana UP, 1989.

HALIDÉ EDIB ADIVAR *(1883–1964)*

Feminist and National Hero

> "We have to believe that everything in the world is the result, directly or indirectly, of the work of women."
>
> *Mustafa Kemal Atatürk*[1]

Halidé Edib Adivar's life spans a period of extraordinary social change in what was to become contemporary Turkey. In July 1908, the aging Ottoman Empire was declared a constitutional monarchy, bringing to an end thirty years of absolutist government under Sultan Abdülhamid. Geoffrey Lewis, writing in *Turkey*, his classic study of modern Turkish history, asserts that ". . . the majority of [Turkish] people regarded that day in July 1908 as the beginning of a wonderful new era" (45). By the end of World War I, however, Turkey was once again in the midst of a period of extreme social and political crisis. The empire had collapsed, and the Allied Powers—including Great Britain, France, Russia, and Italy—were squabbling over how best to divide the remaining territory amongst themselves. Nevertheless, the nationalist movement, under the leadership of the military hero and long-term Unionist Mustafa Kemal (later given the surname Atatürk—"Father of the Turks"), managed against tremendous odds to organize an effective resistance to foreign occupation. The new Turkish Republic was declared on October 29, 1923.

The Kemalists conceived of the Republic as a secular nation-state built on the foundations of the newly-developed idea of Turkish identity, a concept which had previously been "almost totally non-existent" (Ahmad 77). During this period, a Turkish national consciousness began to redefine Turkey as a nation in contrast to the rest of the Islamic world, a process reflected in the slogan of the Kemalists during the early years of the Republic: "Let's smash the Idols" (qtd. in Ahmad 79). Turkey replaced the Islamic code of law (the *sharia*) with the Swiss Civil Code, adopted the Gregorian calendar and the international clock, and abolished the Arabic script formerly used in writing in favor of the Latin script. Mustafa Kemal Atatürk spearheaded a national campaign to improve literacy and education rates throughout the new Turkish state. The revolutionaries were strongly influenced in their reformist work by their knowledge of the history of the French Revolution (and, to a somewhat lesser extent, of the decline of tsarist Russia). They consequently placed a high value on ideas of bourgeois revolution and innovation. Atatürk expressed some of the spirit of their project with the words: "It is time for us to eradicate root and branch the errors of the past. . . . With its own script and its native intelligence, our nation will take its place by the side of the civilized world" (qtd. in Ahmad 81).

The history of Turkish feminism is deeply intertwined with that of the rise of the contemporary Turkish nation. During the second constitutional period after 1908, there was a flowering of women's writing and feminist activism undertaken mainly by well-educated and middle-class Ottoman women (Tekeli 11). Women also played decisive roles in both the war effort and the growing nationalist movement; as Deniz Kandiyoti puts it, "Women first demanded their rights under the banner of patriotism, as participants in the war effort and the broader goals of national mobilisation" (43). This first stage of activism on behalf of women's emancipation was characterized by the growth of publications for women, the formation of new patriotic "women's associations" across the country, and the rise of a grassroots reform movement (Tekeli 12).

It was during the early years of the Republic that a series of important political gains were first made toward women's emancipation. For the most part women did not participate,[2] as these advances in women's status resulted from reforms mandated by the government. Deniz Kandiyoti describes this period in the following terms:

> There is little doubt that the woman question became one of the pawns in the Kemalist struggle to liquidate the theocratic remnants of the Ottoman state, a struggle in which male protagonists engaged each other while women by and large remained surprisingly passive onlookers. . . . Despite other evidence of women's activism, especially later on the question of suffrage, this suggests that the process of mobilisation and cooptation of women into the ideological struggles of the Republic followed a path that was quite distinct from early feminist movements in the West.

While women in the West had often fought for political changes as a result of transformations in socio-economic circumstances, in Turkey the economic basis of women's lives went unchanged, even as the new idea of citizenship influenced the development of legislation on women's rights. The emancipation of women was seen by the Kemalists as part of the creation of a modern and civilized society. Mustafa Kemal Atatürk's desire to improve literacy and education in the Republic extended to include women as important contributors to national "progress." Polygamy was outlawed in 1926 with the establishment of the Swiss Civil Code, women were legally permitted to unveil in 1925, and suffrage was finally obtained in 1934. The effect of these reforms on women's lives is often difficult to assess since, as Binnaz Toprak has put it, they "were not designed to change sexual roles but rather had a pragmatic political aim" (289). A Turkish feminist movement organized by and on behalf of women only began to come to the forefront of political life during the 1980s, when a symposium was organized in Istanbul at which the concept of feminism was discussed "for the first time since the turn of the century" (Tekeli 14).

During her career as a writer and political activist, Halidé Edib Adivar spoke out frequently on behalf of women's rights.[3] She was also an important participant in the nationalist movement, worked closely with Atatürk, and served in the Turkish army as a noncombatant private and then as a corporal. Halidé Edib's family, part of the traditional aristocratic society of Istanbul, was wealthy enough to have her educated at home and, later on, to send her to the American College for Girls. As a young woman, Halidé Edib wrote both newspaper articles on women's liberation and a number of extremely popular novels; she also began developing a career as a public speaker and prominent nationalist and intellectual. In fact, her writings on women's education were considered to be so inflammatory that she had to flee for her life in 1909 when the reactionary governmental party regained power. In 1912, she was the only female member to be elected to the Ocak, a Turkish nationalist club whose influence was widespread; she later helped amend the constitution of this society so that other women might be included as members. She became a nationalist hero during the early years of the fight for Turkish national independence, when she made a series of public speeches and began working as a writer and translator for the nationalist army. Her literary writing is still read in Turkey today, and she continues to be widely regarded as a national hero and foremost example of the Turkish "new woman"—a figure whose outlines emerge fully with the birth of the Republic.

The selection we have included here from the writings of Halidé Edib Adivar is taken from an episode in her memoirs in which she describes her military service during the War of Independence. In this excerpt, she recalls her experience in a Turkish village when the village prostitute—who normally performed only for men—is brought to dance for her. In this piece, Halidé Edib Adivar depicts what she sees as the "ugly reality" behind male representations of prostitution and female sexuality. Her discussion of the way in which these representations of women function is bounded on the one hand by her anomalous status as a female military officer and on the other by her elite position as an upper-class, well-educated member of the nationalist intelligentsia. As the story progresses, we begin to see the ways in which she might herself be implicated in the systems that she attempts to explain. Halidé Edib Adivar's narrative—as well as the history of her life and political work—gives readers a perspective on the complexities of the representational systems which helped to define this "new woman" and feminist activist of the Turkish Republic.

NM

FROM *THE TURKISH ORDEAL*[§]

"The slut is coming in to dance for you," they said. "The men are going to let her come, since it's for you."

The slut was a hired woman dancer who usually performed only for the men. Although in the village there are more love affairs without the benediction of the clergy than in a town, there is no prostitution. So that a prostitute or "slut," as they called her, was a person to arouse intense curiosity in the peasant women. The sins of the flesh, and in fact sins of all other categories too, gave rise to no outburst of virtuous indignation among the village folk. They regarded all flagrant sinners much as they would a rope dancer, and felt a secret thrill at the thought of any person daring to do that which was forbidden them by custom and fear. Besides, the presence of a slut at weddings and other such celebrations often coincided with knife-drawings and similar outbursts of violence; and although the peasants as good women deprecated these rough events, as mere females they felt a sneaking admiration for any other female who could stir up such violent passions in the male breast.

[§] Reprinted from *The Turkish Ordeal: Being The Further Memoirs Of Halidé Edib*, by Halidé Edib Adivar. Published 1928 London: The Century Co. (Hutchinson). Material excerpted from pages 206–210.

"Where did the men get her from?" I asked.

"From the Street of the Red Lanterns," they answered.

At once all my impressions of that street returned.

Whether there should be such a street where the government can control prostitution and check the spread of venereal disease, or whether morality should be protected and those streets abolished, has been the subject of long discussions between moralists who think in terms of public morals and scientists who think in terms of public health. The triumph of the latter in Angora was marked by the existence of the Street of the Red Lanterns on the outskirts of the town. . . .

It was one evening which I had promised to spend with Didar, who lived at the other side of Angora. As it was late when I left headquarters, two officer friends offered to ride with me to her house, and to reach there of course we had to go down the inevitable street. As we drew near it we heard a woman's shrill voice scolding, pleading, and weeping in turns, while a man's bass voice tried to down it with oaths and curses. The street itself was deserted, its yellow earthen huts dimly lit by the dull red glow of the lanterns. We had to look round everywhere before we could find the owners of the voices. On our left was a raised mound on which a few huts had been built, and in front of one of them stood an old woman, her arms stretched out, her feet planted firmly on the ground, protecting the entrance against a big rough man who with shouts and blows was trying to get through the forbidden door. For an instant there was a embarrassed silence among us, but I knew that one of my companions was thoroughly roused. He had one of those clean and manly hearts which reveres women even when they live in a Street of Red Lanterns, where the very worst and beastliest in both women and men are unloosed. And I knew that he was wanting to protect the old woman, and was only hesitating because I was there; so I drew rein. At once he leaped from his horse and ran up the mound. We saw him pull the man away and heard him address him with unmistakable authority:

"You leave that woman alone at once! And now go away from here!"

The man looked at him for a moment, then at us, and went away.

There was pity and tenderness in his voice when he spoke to the old woman.

"You may go into your house, mother. You need not be afraid."

But the woman walked behind him down the mound, and while he was remounting his horse she looked at me with eyes swimming with tears and said: *"Allah razi olsoun"* (May Allah be pleased with you).

And I have never forgotten that woman. Who was she? What was she? Why did she bar that door, shielding it with her body, heedless of blows and curses? Was she the mother of one of those girls in flame-colored trousers with resentful eyes? The supreme martyrdom of being a mother has always seemed most poignant to me. How many pairs of mothers' arms are stretched out to receive the blows and curses which the world would inflict on their loved ones? And this slut who was coming to dance for me, might not she be just another such girl, and might not her mother too have sacrificed herself to protect her—but in vain?

"Here she is! Here she is!" they whispered still more excitedly. Then the door opened and the slut came in. I would have laughed if something in her eyes had not arrested me.

She was only a tired, shivering, poorly dressed, middle-aged woman. Though the straight black line of the eyebrows denoted some effort to regain her lost youth, the face had no other make-up. But the eyes were extraordinary. Such hatred, bitterness, resentment I have never seen in any woman's eyes. She did not even look at her excited and interested audience, but I was stabbed by her knowledge of sordidness and cruelty.

"It's cold," I said. "Come and sit down by the fire."

"I am to dance for you," she said.

And I knew then that human kindliness was that which would infuriate her most. She did not want any new light on human nature: to her it was filthy and incurably cruel and she had no hope of it. She was strong and proud in her isolation, and she realized without flinching that her life as she had lived it could not be altered now. But I did not want to see her dance. I could imagine that her slim erect body might express more of the life of Red Lantern Street than I had ever known, but it would have hurt me too much.

"I am sorry," I said, rising; "I have to go."

She was not at all humiliated by the fact that some one did not want to see her much-praised dancing. I believe she was triumphant because she had made me feel for a moment the despair to which she was condemned for life. Like a shadow she vanished, closing the door quickly in my face.

The women in the room were disappointed, like children whose toys had been wrenched from their hands. They wanted to see and touch the slut, this vamp who aroused such devils in their men. And they disguised their disappointment by enumerating all the sinful ways which were common among the creatures. But I did not wait to hear the whole list of their misdeeds. I went back to the farm, deep in thought. And I was not thinking only of the Turks or of the revolution. I was brooding over evils which are far more universal. . . .

NOTES

[1] Quoted in *Women in Turkish Society,* Nermin Adadan-Unat, ed., v.

[2] Nermin Abadan-Unat, in her article entitled "The Impact of Legal and Educational Reforms on Turkish Women," explains that it was Atatürk's personal intervention, rather than the protests of Turkish women's groups, that primarily contributed to the political changes taking place in women's status in the 1920s and 30s.

[3] All biographical information taken from "Excerpts from *Memoirs* and *The Turkish Ordeal* by Halidé Edib Adivar, Turkish Nationalist" in *Middle Eastern Muslim Women Speak,* Elizabeth Warnock Fernea and Basima Qattan Bezirgan, eds.

WORKS CONSULTED

Ahmad, Feroz. *The Making of Modern Turkey.* The Making of the Middle East Series. London: Routledge, 1993.

Fernea, Elizabeth Warnock, and Basima Qattan Bezirgan. "Excerpts from *Memoirs* and *The Turkish Ordeal* by Halidé Edib Adivar, Turkish Nationalist." *Middle Eastern Muslim Women Speak*. Austin: U of Texas P, 1977.

Kandiyoti, Deniz. "End of Empire: Islam, Nationalism and Women in Turkey." Women, Islam and the State. Ed. Deniz Kandiyoti. Philadelphia: Temple UP, 1991.

Lewis, Geoffrey. *Turkey.* New York: Frederick A. Praeger, 1955.

Tekeli, Sirin. "Introduction: Women in Turkey in the 1980s." *Women in Modern Turkish Society: A Reader.* Ed. Sirin Tekeli. London: Zed Books, 1995.

Toprak, Binnaz (Sayari). "Religion and Turkish Women." *Women in Turkish Society.* Ed. Nermin Abadan-Unat. Social, Economic and Political Studies of the Middle East 30. Leiden: E.J. Brill, 1981.

FLORENCE NIGHTINGALE *(1820–1910)*

Women, Intellect, and Imagination: "At Large Among the Stars"

Florence Nightingale is perhaps best known for her work in the profession of nursing—work that first gained widespread recognition when she served as a nurse and administrator in the British military hospitals of the Crimea. But the woman who was referred to as an "angel of mercy" in the press of the day was also the author of a three-volume study on religious philosophy entitled *Suggestions for Thought,* and a harsh critic of the social strictures which prevented middle-class women from embarking on lives of professional and intellectual fulfillment. Indeed, the anger with which Nightingale writes of the enforced idleness of these women's existence in volume two of *Suggestions for Thought* stands in striking contrast to the popular image of her as a selfless healer of the sick and wounded. In fact, although aided to a certain extent by her class status and social connections, Nightingale had to struggle persistently in order to gain even limited access to what was to become her life's work. Nursing, around the middle of the nineteenth century, was still widely thought of as a lowly and distinctly disreputable occupation. Nightingale's mother in particular was strongly opposed to her daughter's decision to study nursing.

Nightingale was born in Florence, Italy, into a wealthy English family; although her parents were both brought up as Unitarians, the family converted to Anglicanism—a more established and socially appropriate religion—at the urging of Nightingale's mother. Nevertheless, Florence Nightingale's family still displayed the politically liberal leanings associated with the Unitarians. Nightingale and her older sister, Parthenope, were given intensive training by their father in subjects which included Latin, history, and philosophy; as Florence matured, her interest in intellectual pursuits soon developed into an extreme dissatisfaction with life as an upper-class woman of leisure—a life that both her mother and sister had embraced with apparent enthusiasm. She began writing *Suggestions for Thought* in 1850, when it seemed as if her aspirations for a professional career might forever remain unfulfilled. About a year later, after much inner agonizing and considerable conflict with her mother, Nightingale eventually left England to study nursing in Paris with the Catholic Sisters of Charity. She was then in her early thirties.

Nightingale was awarded a position as the superintendent of the Institution for the Care of Sick Gentlewomen in Distressed Circumstances soon after her return from Paris. She was later selected as part of a group of thirty-eight nurses (whom she had organized) who traveled to the Crimea to care for British troops. In the Crimea, Nightingale became deeply involved in working for the reform of military hospitals—a cause to which she was to dedicate much of her time and energy. She composed several reports on this subject and worked closely with the British government in her efforts to promote reform. Some years after her return from the Crimea (1856), she founded the Nightingale Nursing School in 1860 as part of her attempts to improve the training that was given nurses; as Mary

Poovey points out, "Nightingale was also committed to professionalized training for women and to women working for pay" (xx). This school was opened in the same year that *Suggestions for Thought,* a selection from which appears below, was privately printed. True to her own sense of a personal and religious mission, Nightingale continued her philanthropic and reformist work throughout her life: collaborating with the War Office on improving sanitation in India, acting as a consultant on military nursing during the Franco-Prussian War, and publishing various studies on the quality of medical institutions and the reorganization of medical care. Her ability to engage in this kind of reformist work was certainly conditioned by her social position as an upper-class white woman; however, her contributions to the improvement of the nursing profession cannot be denied.

In the excerpt reprinted below, Nightingale presents a critical analysis of the ideology of domesticity that structured middle-class female existence in nineteenth-century Western culture. Nightingale's position toward this ideological framework is deeply ambivalent. She points out how clearly women are intellectually and spiritually stifled within the confines of the domestic sphere. Yet her notion of women's mission on earth—certainly informed by her religious beliefs—seems to borrow from ideas of women as the ultimate moral agents supervising the social world. As Poovey remarks, "[Her] solution to the problem of women and work could . . . pass as an extension of woman's God-given duties into the larger family of society" (xxi). Nonetheless, in the excerpt we have chosen, Nightingale's emphasis is on the liberation of women's intellect, imagination, and passions from a daily round of purposeless social and familial obligations.

There is some disagreement among feminist critics about the social effects of the ideology of domesticity, the context in which Nightingale writes. Quite recently, work has been done on how what was originally conceived as a "relegation" of middle-class women to the domestic sphere resulted in the creation of a new arena in which women could exercise crucial influence. For example, in her study of the development of the novel in England, Nancy Armstrong emphasizes "the particular power that our culture does give to middle-class women" (255). She sees women's role in regulating the domestic universe as, to a certain extent, a fundamental characteristic of modern society. According to Armstrong, "it is also reasonable to claim that the modern individual was first and foremost a female" (66). Other critics have lent more importance to the means by which "the domestic universe" oppresses and silences the women who live there. In Nightingale's work, we see how both the oppressive and the empowering tendencies of the ideology of domesticity might coexist.

In keeping with the focus of this section, Nightingale's emphasis in this excerpt is on the discrepancies between what she terms "the farce of hypocrisy" that constitutes women's social behavior, and the inner spiritual life that "the female soul" must struggle to repress. She argues from within a framework that is essentially religious—*Suggestions for Thought* is above all an expression of a religious philosophy—for the emancipation of the "female spirit" from the chains of social convention. As Nightingale describes it, " . . . there is no longer unity between the woman as inwardly developed, and as outwardly manifested." While such a vision of a unified female self has been criticized by recent feminist scholars as "essentialist," it is important to recognize Nightingale's profound desire for the union of "imagination" and social training in a vocation, a "sphere of action," as an important force behind her reformist work.

NM

FROM *CASSANDRA*[§]

Why have women passion, intellect, moral activity—these three—and a place in society where no one of the three can be exercised? Men say that God punishes for complaining. No, but men are angry with misery. They are irritated with women for not being happy. They take it as a personal offence. To God alone may women complain without insulting Him!

And women, who are afraid, while in words they acknowledge that God's work is good, to say, Thy will be *not* done (declaring another order of society from that which He has made), go about maudling to each other and teaching to their daughters that "women have no passions." In the conventional society, which men have made for women, and women have accepted, they *must* have none, they *must* act the farce of hypocrisy, the lie that they are without passion—and therefore what else can they say to their daughters, without giving the lie to themselves?

"Suffering, sad" female "humanity"! What are these feelings which they are taught to consider as disgraceful, to deny to themselves? What form do the Chinese feet assume when denied their proper development? If the young girls of the "higher classes," who never commit a false step, whose justly earned reputations were never sullied even by the stain which the fruit of mere "knowledge of good and evil" leaves behind, were to speak, and say what are their thoughts employed upon, their *thoughts,* which alone are free, what would they say?

That, with the phantom companion of their fancy, they talk (not love, they are too innocent, too pure, too full of genius and imagination for that, but) they talk, in fancy, of that which interests them most; they seek a companion for their every thought; the companion they find not in reality they seek in fancy, or, if not that, if not absorbed in endless conversations, they see themselves engaged with him in stirring events, circumstances which call out the interest wanting to them. Yes, fathers, mothers, you who see your daughter proudly rejecting all semblance of flirtation, primly engaged in the duties of the breakfast table, you little think how her fancy compensates itself by endless interviews and sympathies (sympathies either for ideas or events) with the fancy's companion of the hour! And you say, "She is not susceptible. Women have no passion." Mothers, who cradle yourselves in visions about the domestic hearth, how many of your sons and daughters are *there,* do you think, while sitting round under your complacent maternal eye? Were you there yourself during your own (now forgotten) girlhood?

[§] Reprinted by permission of the publisher from *Cassandra and Other Selections from Suggestions For Thought.* Edited by Mary Poovey. London: Pickering & Chatto Publishers Ltd. Copyright © 1991. Material excerpted from pages 205–228.

What are the thoughts of these young girls while one is singing Schubert, another is reading the *Review,* and a third is busy embroidering? Is not one fancying herself the nurse of some new friend in sickness; another engaging in romantic dangers with him, such as call out the character and afford more food for sympathy than the monotonous events of domestic society; another undergoing unheard-of trials under the observation of some one whom she has chosen as the companion of her dreams? another having a loving and loved companion in the life she is living, which many do not want to change?

And is not all this natural, inevitable? Are they, who are too much ashamed of it to confess it even to themselves, to be blamed for that which cannot be otherwise, the causes of which stare one in the face, *if one's eyes were not closed?* Many struggle against this as a "snare." No Trappist ascetic watches or fasts more in the body than these do in the soul! They understand the discipline of the Thebaïd—the life long agonies to which those strong moral Mohicans subjected themselves. How cordially they could do the same, in order to escape the worse torture of wandering "vain imaginations." But the laws of God for moral well-being are not thus to be disobeyed. We fast mentally, scourge ourselves morally, use the intellectual hair-shirt, in order to subdue that perpetual day-dreaming, which is so dangerous! We resolve "this day month I will be free from it;" twice a day with prayer and written record of the times when we have indulged in it, we endeavor to combat it. Never, with the slightest success. By mortifying vanity we do ourselves no good. It is the want of interest in our life which produces it; by filling up that want of interest in our life we can alone remedy it. And, did we even see this, how can we make the difference? How obtain the interest which Society declares *she* does not want, and *we* cannot want? . . .

Women often try one branch of intellect after another in their youth, *e.g.*, mathematics. But that, least of all, is compatible with the life of "society." It is impossible to follow up anything systematically. Women often long to enter some man's profession where they would find direction, competition (or rather opportunity of measuring the intellect with others), and, above all, time.

In those wise institutions, mixed as they are with many follies, which will last as long as the human race lasts, because they are adapted to the wants of the human race; those institutions which we call monasteries, and which, embracing much that is contrary to the laws of nature, are yet better adapted to the union of the life of action and that of thought than any other mode of life with which we are acquainted; in many such, four and a half hours, at least, are daily set aside for thought, rules are given for thought, training and opportunity afforded. Among us, there is no time appointed for this purpose, and the difficulty is that, in our social life, we must be always doubtful whether we ought not to be with somebody else or be doing something else.

Are men better off than women in this?

If one calls upon a friend in London and sees her son in the drawing-room, it strikes one as odd to find a young man sitting idle in his mother's drawing-room in the morning. For men, who are seen much in those haunts, there is no end of the epithets we have; "knights of the carpet," "drawing-room heroes," "ladies' men." But suppose we were to see a number of men in the morning sitting round a table in the drawing-room, looking at prints, doing worsted work, and reading little books, how we should laugh! A member of the House of Commons was once known to do worsted work. Of another man was said, "His only fault is that he is too good; he drives out with his mother every day in the carriage, and if he is asked anywhere he answers that he must dine with his mother, but, if she can spare him, he will come in to tea, and he does not come."

Now, why is it more ridiculous for a man than for a woman to do worsted work and drive out every day in the carriage? Why should we laugh if we were to see a parcel of men sitting round a drawing-room table in the morning, and think it all right if they were women?

Is man's time more valuable than woman's? or is the difference between man and woman this, that woman has confessedly nothing to do? . . .

Women often strive to live by intellect. The clear, brilliant, sharp radiance of intellect's moonlight rising upon such an expanse of snow is dreary, it is true, but some love its solemn desolation, its silence, its solitude—if they are but *allowed* to live in it; if they are not perpetually baulked and disappointed. But a woman cannot live in the light of intellect. Society forbids it. Those conventional frivolities, which are called her "duties," forbid it. Her "domestic duties," high-sounding words, which, for the most part, are bad habits (which she has not the courage to enfranchise herself from, the strength to break through) forbid it. What are these duties (or bad habits)?—Answering a multitude of letters which lead to nothing, from her so-called friends—keeping herself up to the level of the world that she may furnish her quota of amusement at the breakfast-table; driving out her company in the carriage. And all these things are exacted from her by her family which, if she is good and affectionate, will have more influence with her than the world.

What wonder if, wearied out, sick at heart with hope deferred, the springs of will broken, not seeing clearly *where* her duty lies, she abandons intellect as a vocation and takes it only, as we use the moon, by glimpses through her tight-closed window-shutters?

The family? It is too narrow a field for the development of an immortal spirit, be that spirit male or female. The chances are a thousand to one that, in that small sphere, the task for which that immortal spirit is destined by the qualities and the gifts which its Creator has placed within it, will not be found.

The family uses people, *not* for what they are, nor for what they are intended to be, but for what it wants them for—for its own uses. It thinks of them not as what God has made them, but as the something which it has arranged that they shall be. If it wants some one to sit in the drawing-room, *that* some one is to be supplied by the family, though that member may be destined for science, or for education, or for active superintendence by God, *i.e.,* by the gifts within.

This system dooms some minds to incurable infancy, others to silent misery . . .

At present we live to impede each other's satisfactions; competition, domestic life, society, what is it all but this? We go somewhere where we are not wanted and where we don't want to go. What else is conventional life? *Passivity* when we want to be active. So many hours spent every day in passively doing what conventional life tells us, when we would so gladly be at work. . . .

Women dream till they no longer have the strength to dream; those dreams against which they struggle, so honestly, vigorously, and conscientiously, and so in vain, yet which are their life, without which they could not have lived; those dreams go at last. All their plans and visions seem vanished, and they know not where; gone, and they cannot recall them. They do not even remember them. And they are left without the food either of reality or of hope.

Later in life, they neither desire nor dream, neither of activity, nor of love, nor of intellect. The last often survives the longest. They wish, if their experiences would benefit anybody, to give them to someone. But they never find an hour free in which to collect their thoughts, and so discouragement becomes even deeper and deeper, and they less and less capable of undertaking anything.

It seems as if the female spirit of the world were mourning everlastingly over blessings, not *lost,* but which she has never had, and which, in her discouragement, she feels that she never will have, they are so far off.

The more complete a woman's organisation, the more she will feel it, till at last there shall arise a woman, who will resume, in her own soul, all the sufferings of her race, and that woman will be the Saviour of her race.

Jesus Christ raised women above the condition of mere slaves, mere ministers to the passions of the man, raised them by his sympathy, to be ministers of God. He gave them moral activity. But the age, the World, Humanity, must give them the means to exercise this moral activity, must give them intellect cultivation, spheres of action.

There is perhaps no century where the woman shows so meanly as in this.[1] Because her education seems entirely to have parted company with her vocation; there is no longer unity between the woman as inwardly developed, and as outwardly manifested.

In the last century it was not so. In the succeeding one let us hope that it will no longer be so.

But now she is like the Archangel Michael as he stands upon Saint Angelo at Rome. She has an immense provision of wings, which seem as if they would bear her over earth and heaven; but when she tries to use them, she is petrified into stone, her feet are grown into the earth, chained to the bronze pedestal.

Nothing can well be imagined more painful than the present position of woman, unless, on the one hand, she renounces all outward activity and keeps herself within the magic sphere, the bubble of her dreams; or, on the other, surrendering all aspiration, she gives herself to her real life, soul and body. For those to whom it is possible, the latter is best, for out of activity may come thought, out of mere aspiration can come nothing.

But now—when the young imagination is so high and so developed, and reality is so narrow and conventional—there is no more parallelism between life in the thought and life in the actual than between the corpse, which lies motionless in its narrow bed, and the spirit, which, in our imagination, is at large among the stars. . . .

NOTE

[1] At almost every period of social life, we find, as it were, two under currents running different ways. There is the notable woman who dreams the following out her useful vocation; but there is also the selfish dreamer now, who is ever turning to something new, regardless

of the expectations she has voluntarily excited, who is ever talking about "making a life for herself," heedless that she is spoiling another life, undertaken, perhaps, at her own bidding. This is the ugly reverse of the medal. [FN]

WORKS CONSULTED

Armstrong, Nancy. *Desire and Domestic Fiction: A Political History of the Novel.* New York: Oxford UP, 1987.

Poovey, Mary. Introduction and Chronology. *Cassandra and Other Selections from Suggestions For Thought.* By Florence Nightingale. Ed. Mary Poovey. London: Pickering and Chatto, 1991.

SOR JUANA INÉS DE LA CRUZ *(c. 1651–1695)*

"How Great Is the Strength of My Inclination"

Sor Juana Inés de la Cruz (born Juana Ramírez de Asbaje)[1] was the third child of Doña Isabel Ramírez, a woman who never married but preferred instead to manage the hacienda of her father for more than thirty years following his death. Octavio Paz, in his voluminous biography of Sor Juana, asserts that "A notable characteristic of Sor Juana's family [was] the independence, fortitude, and energy of the women" (67). Sor Juana's childhood proclivities confirm this. She was by all accounts an extremely precocious girl who demonstrated great intellectual curiosity from an early age and pored endlessly over the books in her grandfather's library. Perhaps because of her talents, perhaps because her mother had recently borne a fourth child under somewhat straitened financial circumstances, when Sor Juana was around 10 years old she was sent from her birthplace—a small Mexican village—to Mexico City. Here she was presented at court, and entered the service of the Vicereine, Doña Leonor Carreto. The Vicereine and Sor Juana, now known as something of a child prodigy, became extremely close friends; their association soon developed into a loving and supportive relationship, the first in a series of such friendships with women that would mark Sor Juana's life.

Sor Juana resided for five years at court, where, according to one critic, "she was dependent in the last analysis upon her own charm and wits for survival" (Trueblood 4). At the age of twenty, however, she rather abruptly rejected the worldly life of the court and entered a convent. This choice was not as unusual as it may seem to contemporary readers. Alan Trueblood remarks, "Since all education was the prerogative of the Church, the path of an exceptional woman who had the temerity to value cultivation of her mind above all else, including marriage, inevitably led to the convent" (5). In the excerpt which follows, Sor Juana herself describes her choice in the following way: "I took the veil because, although I knew I would find in religious life many things that would be quite opposed to my character . . . it would, given my absolute unwillingness to enter into marriage, be the least unfitting and the most decent state I could choose, with regard to the assurance I desired of my salvation." While Sor Juana's decision to seclude herself may not have been inevitable in the strictest sense, initially she was able to continue her personal intellectual training as well as write profusely. She was also at the center of a *tertulia,* or conversational gathering, that she held personally and to which she invited well-known intellectuals as well as court acquaintances.

The letter reprinted here is dated March 1, 1691; it was written only a year or so before Sor Juana gave up writing completely in order to devote herself to a life of self-castigation.[2] While the piece is termed *A Reply to Sor Philothea,* it was actually penned in response to an admonishing letter composed by the Bishop of Puebla. The latter, a good friend of Sor Juana's, had recently published one of her polemical writings, to which he had appended a reaction under the name of Sor Philothea. In the excerpt we have included Sor Juana is responding to this criticism of the Bishop. The letter in its entirety is made up of three parts: 1) a direct reply to the Bishop himself, 2) an autobiographical account of Sor Juana's intellectual career, and 3) a vigorous criticism of St. Paul's dictum that women should remain silent in church.[3] We have chosen to focus on Sor Juana's description of her own dedication to learning and the obstacles she faced as an intellectual woman in a society where knowledge that did not remain within certain narrowly defined limits was by and large denied to women.

In her letter, Sor Juana describes her desire to learn as at once that which uniquely defines her ("this native impulse that God Himself bestowed on me") and that which is beyond her control ("a force beyond me"). She struggles to reconcile her pursuit of knowledge with her own religious and social convictions. She claims, ". . . I have attempted to entomb my intellect together with my name and to sacrifice it to the One who gave it to me," but what she sometimes describes as a natural desire to know cannot be obscured. Her scholarly inclinations were the source of many conflicts for Sor Juana, but they also provided her with great pleasure. In the final paragraph of this excerpt, she speaks of the philosophical and scientific knowledge she acquired while cooking, work traditionally performed by women and thus not typically associated with scholarly pursuits. Here she evokes a time during which her God-given desire for knowledge and her gender social role might have existed in harmony with one another: "Well, and what then shall I tell you, my Lady, of the secrets of nature that I have learned while cooking? . . . I often say, when I make these little observations, 'Had Aristotle cooked, he would have written a great deal more.'"

NM

FROM *A REPLY TO SOR PHILOTHEA*[§]

My writing has never proceeded from any dictate of my own, but a force beyond me; I can in truth say, "*You have compelled me.*" One thing, however, is true, so that I shall not deny it (first because it is already well known to all, and second because God has shown me His favor in giving me the greatest possible love of truth, even when it might count against me). For ever since the light of reason first dawned in me, my inclination to letters was marked by such passion and vehemence that neither the reprimands of others (for I have received many) nor reflections of my own (there have been more than a few) have sufficed to make me abandon my pursuit of this native impulse that God Himself bestowed on me. His Majesty knows why and to what end He did so, and He knows that I have prayed He snuff out the light of my intellect, leaving only enough to keep His Law. For more than that is too much, some would say, in a woman; and there are even those who say that it is harmful. His Majesty knows too that, not achieving this, I have attempted to entomb my intellect together with my name and to sacrifice it to the One who gave it to me; and that no other motive brought me to the life of Religion, despite the fact that the exercises and companionship of a community were quite opposed to the tranquility and freedom from

§ Reprinted by permission of The Feminist Press at The City University of New York, from *The Answer/La Respuesta,* by Sor Juana Inés de la Cruz, Critical Edition and Translation by Electa Arenal and Amanda Powell. Translation copyright © 1994 by Electa Arenal and Amanda Powell. Material excerpted from pages 47–53, 61, 75.

disturbance required by my studious bent. And once in the community, the Lord knows—and in this world only he who needs must know it, does—what I did to try to conceal my name and renown from the public; he did not, however, allow me to do this, telling me it was temptation, and so it would have been. If I could repay any part of my debt to you, my Lady, I believe I might do so merely by informing you of this, for these words have never left my mouth save to that one to whom they must be said. But having thrown wide the doors of my heart and revealed to you what is there under seal of secrecy, I want you to know that this confidence does not gainsay the respect I owe to your venerable person and excessive favors . . .

I remember that in those days, though I was as greedy for treats as children usually are at that age, I would abstain from eating cheese, because I heard tell that it made people stupid, and the desire to learn was stronger for me than the desire to eat—powerful as this is in children. Later, when I was six or seven years old and already knew how to read and write, along with all the other skills like embroidery and sewing that women learn, I heard that in Mexico City there were a University and Schools where they studied the sciences. As soon as I heard this I began to slay my poor mother with insistent and annoying pleas, begging her to dress me in men's clothes and send me to the capital, to the home of some relatives she had there, so that I could enter the University and study. She refused, and was right in doing so; but I quenched my desire by reading a great variety of books that belonged to my grandfather, and neither punishments nor scoldings could prevent me. And so when I did go to Mexico City, people marveled not so much at my intelligence as at my memory and the facts I knew at an age when it seemed I had scarcely had time to learn to speak.

I began to study Latin, in which I believe I took fewer than twenty lessons. And my interest was so intense, that although in women (and especially in the very bloom of youth) the natural adornment of the hair is so esteemed, I would cut off four to six fingerlengths of my hair, measuring how long it had been before. And I made myself a rule that if by the time it had grown back to the same length I did not know such and such a thing that I intended to study, then I would cut my hair off again to punish my dull-wittedness. And so my hair grew, but I did not yet know what I had resolved to learn, for it grew quickly and I learned slowly. Then I cut my hair right off to punish my dull-wittedness, for I did not think it reasonable that hair should cover a head that was so bare of facts—the more desirable adornment. I took the veil because, although I knew I would find in religious life many things that would be quite opposed to my character (I speak of accessory rather than essential matters), it would, given my absolute unwillingness to enter into marriage, be the least unfitting and most decent state I could choose, with regard to the assurance I desired of my salvation. For before this first concern (which is, at the last, the most important), all the impertinent little follies of my character gave way and bowed to the yoke. These were wanting to live alone and not wanting to have either obligations that would disturb my freedom to study or the noise of a community that would interrupt the tranquil silence of my books. These things made me waver somewhat in my decision until, being enlightened by learned people as to my temptation, I vanquished it with divine favor and took the state I so unworthily hold. I thought I was fleeing myself, but—woe is me!—I brought myself with me, and brought my greatest enemy in my inclination to study, which I know not whether to take as a Heaven-sent favor or as a punishment. For when snuffed out or hindered with every [spiritual] exercise known to Religion, it exploded like gunpowder; and in my case the saying *"privation gives rise to appetite"* was proven true.

I went back (no, I spoke incorrectly, for I never stopped)—I went on, I mean, with my studious task (which to me was peace and rest in every moment left over when my duties were done) of reading and still more reading, study and still more study, with no teacher besides my books themselves. What a hardship it is to learn from those lifeless letters, deprived of the sound of a teacher's voice and explanations; yet I suffered all these trials most gladly for the love of learning. Oh, if only this had been done for the love of God, as was rightful, think what I should have merited! Nevertheless I did my best to elevate these studies and direct them to His service, for the goal to which I aspired was the study of Theology. Being a Catholic, I thought it an abject failing not to know everything that can in this life be achieved, through earthly methods, concerning the divine mysteries. And being a nun and not a laywoman, I thought I should, because I was in religious life, profess the study of letters—the more so as the daughter of such as St. Jerome and St. Paula; for it would be a degeneracy for an idiot daughter to proceed from such learned parents. I argued in this way to myself, and I thought my own argument quite reasonable. However, the fact may have been (and this seems most likely) that I was merely flattering and encouraging my own inclination, by arguing that its own pleasure was an obligation.

I went on in this way, always directing each step of my studies, as I have said, toward the summit of Holy Theology; but it seemed to me necessary to ascend by the ladder of the humane arts and sciences in order to reach it; for who could fathom the style of the Queen of Sciences without knowing that of her handmaidens? Without Logic, how should I know the general and specific methods by which Holy Scripture is written? Without Rhetoric, how should I understand its figures, tropes, and locutions? Or how, without Physics or Natural Science, understand all the questions that naturally arise concerning the varied natures of those animals offered in sacrifice, in which a great many things already made manifest are symbolized, and many more besides? How should I know whether Saul's cure at the sound of David's harp was owing to a virtue and power that is natural in Music or owing, instead, to a supernatural power that God saw fit to bestow on David? How without Arithmetic might one understand all those mysterious reckonings of years and days and months and hours and weeks that are found in Daniel and elsewhere, which can be comprehended only by knowing the natures, concordances, and properties of numbers? Without Geometry, how could we take the measure of the Holy Ark of the Covenant or the Holy City of Jerusalem, each of whose mysterious measurements forms a perfect cube uniting their dimensions, and each displaying that most marvelous distribution of the proportions of every part? . . .

This shows all too well just how great is the strength of my inclination. May God be praised that He inclined me to letters and not some other vice, which would have been, in my case, nearly insurmountable. . . .

Well, and what then shall I tell you, my Lady, of the secrets of nature that I have learned while cooking? I observe that an egg becomes solid and cooks in butter or oil, and on the contrary that it dissolves in sugar syrup. Or again, to ensure that sugar flow freely one need only add the slightest bit of water that has held quince or some other sour fruit. The yolk and white of the very same egg are of such a contrary nature that when eggs are used with sugar, each part separately may be used perfectly well, yet they cannot be mixed together. I shall not weary you with such inanities, which I relate simply to give you a full account of my nature, and I believe this will make you laugh. But in truth, my Lady, what can we women know, save philosophies of the kitchen? It was well put by Lupercio Leonardo [sic] that one can philosophize quite well while preparing supper. I often say, when I make these little observations, "Had Aristotle cooked, he would have written a great deal more."...

NOTES

[1] "Sor" is the Spanish title for a religious sister; Sor Juana took this name when she entered the convent as a young woman.

[2] Sor Juana was led to this decision by many circumstances, including the increasing conservatism of the court, the hostility with which various religious authority figures had come to regard her literary and philosophical accomplishments, and increasing pressure brought to bear upon her by her former spiritual director—among others—to repent for having "lived so many years without religion in a religious community" (cited in Trueblood 10).

[3] This observation is taken from Josefina Ludme, "Tricks of the Weak."

WORKS CONSULTED

Juana Inés de la Cruz, Sor. *A Sor Juana Anthology.* Trans. Alan S. Trueblood. Cambridge, Mass.: Harvard UP, 1988.

Ludmer, Josefina. "Tricks of the Weak." *Feminist Perspectives on Sor Juana Inés de la Cruz.* Ed. Stephanie Merrim. Detroit: Wayne State UP, 1991.

Paz, Octavio. *Sor Juana or, The Traps of Faith.* Trans. Margaret Sayers Peden. Cambridge, Mass.: Harvard UP, 1988.

ALEXANDRA KOLLONTAI *(1872–1952)*

Feminism and the Question of Class

Alexandra Kollontai was one of the leading advocates for women's rights in Bolshevik Russia, where, in its early years, the government attempted to implement more radical changes in women's legal rights, material conditions, and sexual roles, than any nation had attempted before. As a young woman, Kollontai left behind the values of her aristocratic Russian family to join the Marxist workers' movement of St. Petersburg. In 1908, just before she was forced into exile in Western Europe for her socialist activities, she wrote *The Social Basis of the Woman Question* (the book from which the excerpt below is taken) as a commentary on an upcoming congress of Russian feminist organizations. Returning to Russia after the Bolshevik Revolution in 1917, she was appointed by Lenin to head the Comissariat for Social Welfare, where she led efforts to reform marriage laws, improve maternity care, and create state-run day care. She was also an outspoken advocate for women's increased participation and leadership in the Communist Party and, in 1920, became head of the new Woman's Bureau of the Party (Clements x-xi).

Despite her important achievements in the early years of the revolution, Kollontai's outspoken defense of women's emancipation—particularly their sexual freedom—came into conflict with the Party leadership of the 1920s, when the Party began to react against many earlier innovations and retreated to more traditional social values (Clements ix). Her advocacy of freedom of expression and workers' control of industry also proved controversial within an increasingly repressive and militarized state. In 1922, she was reassigned to a diplomatic position in Norway, where she continued her writing on women's issues, including two volumes of short stories, *Woman at the Turning Point* (1923) and *The Love of Worker Bees* (1923). These stories, which explored women's desires and the conflicts they experienced between love and work, were characterized in Russia as advocating promiscuity, and Kollontai was ordered to cease writing on such issues (234–236). Believing she had little choice, she conceded and spent the last two decades of her career as an ambassador to Norway, Mexico, and Sweden, writing only on diplomatic issues and her own memoirs (xiii).

Alexandra Kollontai's works on women's issues were published and widely praised among Western European feminists in Europe in the 1920s, but declined in popularity as support for both feminism and communism waned. Her work and the reforms she advocated were also marginalized in Soviet histories (Clements 236). In part because of U. S. and Western European hostility toward the Soviet Union, the work of Kollontai and other Bolshevik feminists has received little attention in the Western mainstream of feminist tradition. But the views she articulates were shared by many radical women organizers in the early twentieth century, and thus offer an important historical context for more recent efforts to link questions of gender with questions of class.

In *The Social Basis of the Woman Question,* Kollontai discusses the interdependency of class- and gender-based social "subjection," and her writing echoes some of the themes that form a major portion of the theoretical basis for this anthology. Her interest in what she calls "class contradictions," and how they figure in the women's movement of her time, anticipates the contemporary notion that systems of oppression are mutually constitutive. Of course, as seen in her writing, Kollontai viewed bourgeois feminism—and feminists in general—with hostility. She was committed to class activism and, in the face of this commitment the "woman question" not only loses its "special" quality but fades away altogether. Still, Kollontai's desire to reconcile concern for women's subordinate position with the role played by class in social oppression is not only apparent in the selections that follow but becomes the foundation for her re-examination of the history of women's social activism.

From the outset, Kollontai rejects what she refers to as "the weighing of brains and the comparing of the psychological structure of men and women" in favor of a historical analysis of the material factors behind women's oppression, most importantly women's lack of control of conditions and fruits of their own labor, and their status as the "property" of men. In so doing, she becomes part of a history of materialist feminism that might be traced back to the writings of such authors as Friedrich Engels (*Origins of the Family, Private Property, and the State*), and those of Mary Wollstonecraft (see excerpt in **Vision and Transformation**). Contemporary materialist feminism, which to a certain extent has been overshadowed by deconstructionist feminism in American academia, retains this emphasis on historical processes and the material bases of oppression. Theorists like Michèle Barrett, Christine Delphy, and Juliet Mitchell have made important and relatively recent contributions to materialist feminism; Michèle Le Doeuff (see excerpt in this section) also represents what might be termed a materialist approach to philosophical thinking.

Most striking about Kollontai's approach in the excerpt below is her critique of liberal feminism as an essentially bourgeois movement. As she points out, "For the majority of the women of the proletariat, equal rights with men would mean only an equal share in inequality." While it is true that white, middle-class Western feminists are beginning to understand more about how European and U.S. feminist movements perpetuate many of the inequalities produced by class difference, nevertheless, the "class contradictions" Kollontai points to within feminist history are far from resolved and are an often unacknowledged presence in the writings of the other women we have included in this anthology. Kollontai's image of bourgeois feminists harvesting "the fruits of the efforts" of the "blistered hands" of working-class women has retained its resonance. *The Social Basis of the Woman Question* remains a fundamental critique of representations of gender that situate themselves outside of history and fail to take into account the material processes that Kollontai sees as structuring human existence.

NM and *JP*

FROM *THE SOCIAL BASIS OF THE WOMAN QUESTION*[§]

Leaving it to the bourgeois scholars to absorb themselves in discussion of the question of the superiority of one sex over the other, or in the weighing of brains and the comparing of the psychological structure of men and women, the followers of historical materialism fully accept the natural specificities of each sex and demand only that each person, whether man or woman, has a real opportunity for the fullest and freest self-determination, and the widest scope for the development and application of all natural inclinations. The followers of historical materialism reject the existence of a special woman question separate from the general social question of our day. Specific economic factors were behind the subordination of women; natural qualities have been a *secondary* factor in this process. Only the complete disappearance of these factors, only the evolution of those forces which at some point in the past gave rise to the subjection of women, is able in a fundamental way to influence and change their social position. In other words, women can become truly free and equal only in a world organized along new social and productive lines. . . .

The Struggle for Economic Independence

First of all we must ask ourselves whether a single united women's movement is possible in a society based on class contradictions. The fact that the women who take part in the liberation movement do not represent one homogeneous mass is clear to every unbiased observer.

The women's world is divided, just as is the world of men, into two camps; the interests and aspirations of one group of women bring it close to the bourgeois class, while the other group has close connections with the proletariat, and its claims for liberation encompass a full solution to the woman question. Thus although both camps follow the general slogan of the "liberation of women", their aims and interests are different. Each of the groups unconsciously takes its starting point from the interests of its own class, which gives a specific class colouring to the targets and tasks it sets itself. . . .

The proletarian women's final aim does not, of course, prevent them from desiring to improve their status even within the framework of the current bourgeois system, but the realization of these desires is constantly hindered by obstacles that derive from the very nature of capitalism. A woman can possess equal rights and be truly free only in a world of socialized labour, of harmony and justice. The feminists are unwilling and incapable of understanding this; it seems to them that when equality is formally accepted by the letter of the law they will be able to win a comfortable place for themselves in the old world of oppression, enslavement and bondage, of tears and hardship. And this is true up to a certain point. For the majority of women of the proletariat, equal rights with men would mean only an equal share in inequality, but for the "chosen few", for the bourgeois women, it would indeed open doors to new and unprecedented rights and privileges that until now

[§] Reprinted by permission of Chicago Review Press from *Selected Writings of Alexandra Kollontai,* translated by Alix Holt. Copyright © 1977. Published by Lawrence Hill Books, an imprint of Chicago Review Press, Inc., 814 North Franklin Street, Chicago, Illinois 60610. Material excerpted from pages 58–62.

have been enjoyed by men of the bourgeois class alone. But each new concession won by the bourgeois woman would give her yet another weapon for the exploitation of her younger sister and would go on increasing the division between the women of the two opposite social camps. Their interests would be more sharply in conflict, their aspirations more obviously in contradiction. . . .

The woman question assumed importance for women of the bourgeois classes approximately in the middle of the nineteenth century—a considerable time after the proletarian women had arrived in the labour arena. Under the impact of the monstrous successes of capitalism, the middle classes of the population were hit by waves of need. The economic changes had rendered the financial situation of the petty and middle bourgeoisie unstable, and the bourgeois women were faced with a dilemma of menacing proportions; either accept poverty, or achieve the right to work. Wives and daughters of these social groups began to knock at the doors of the universities, the art salons, the editorial houses, the offices, flooding to the professions that were open to them. The desire of bourgeois women to gain access to science and the higher benefits of culture was not the result of a sudden, maturing need but stemmed from that same question of "daily bread".

The women of the bourgeoisie met, from the very first, with stiff resistance from men. A stubborn battle was waged between the professional men, attached to their "cosy little jobs", and the women who were novices in the matter of earning their daily bread. This struggle gave rise to "feminism"—the attempt of bourgeois women to stand together and pit their common strength against the enemy, against men. As they entered the labour arena these women proudly referred to themselves as the "vanguard of the women's movement". They forgot that in this matter of winning economic independence they were, as in other fields, travelling in the footsteps of their younger sisters and reaping the fruits of the efforts of their blistered hands.

Is it then really possible to talk of the feminists pioneering the road to women's work, when in every country hundreds of thousands of proletarian women had flooded the factories and workshops, taking over one branch of industry after another, before the bourgeois women's movement was ever born? Only thanks to the fact that the labour of women workers had received recognition on the world market were the bourgeois women able to occupy the independent position in society in which the feminists take so much pride. . . .

WORKS CONSULTED

Clements, Barbara Evans. *Bolshevik Feminist: The Life of Aleksandra Kollontai.* Bloomington: Indiana UP, 1979.

Engels, Friedrich. *Origins of the Family, Private Property, and the State.* 1884. Ed. E. Leacock. New York: International Publishers, 1972.

Mill, John Stuart. *The Subjection of Women.* 1869. In *On Liberty and Other Writings.* Ed. Stefan Collini. Cambridge: Cambridge UP, 1989.

LAILA OF SHAIBÂN-BAKR *(8th century CE)*

Rewriting Resistance

The following poem by Laila of Shaibân-Bakr, an elegy composed after her brother's death in battle, might seem in some ways a problematic choice for inclusion in this anthology. For readers unfamiliar with classical Arabic poetry, it may be difficult to decipher the explicit role played by gender in the poem's imagery and theme. Laila's expression of her grief and desire for vengeance might also seem overly stylized and difficult to evaluate within the context of the specific concerns of the Representations section. Even those with some knowledge of the poetic tradition out of which this piece emerges might wonder at the highly traditional quality of the poem, and the relative obscurity of the author (the works of renowned poet al-Khansa are often taken as the best examples of this genre of women's elegies). We have chosen to include Laila's elegy here because of the way in which the poem, taken in context, serves to complicate the link between women's writing and women's acts of resistance. In the discussion which follows, we will show how this work suggests the possibility of multi-layered networks of resistance which exist alongside deeply embedded literary and political customs. The poem itself *resists* an analysis which seeks to reduce it to either a clear expression of gendered rebellion or a simple product of long-standing tradition.

Laila of Shaibân-Bakr was part of an eighth-century Khawarij sect, a group of Arab Muslims whose name means "exiters" or "those who go out." The Khawarij, originally followers (primarily nomadic bedouins) of the caliph Ali, came into existence as religious dissenters between 656 and 661 CE. They were known not only for a certain warlike puritanism and unwillingness to compromise, but also for their absolute rejection of centralized state authority in favor of an egalitarian system of government. Bernard Lewis, in his study *The Arabs in History,* asserts that the Khawarij movement "developed into an aggressive anarchist opposition." They are variously described as "noted for steadfastness" (*The Oxford Encyclopedia of the Modern Islamic World* 419) and representing "the democratic bedouin spirit" (*Classical Arabic Poetry* 65). The Khawarij believed in the democratic election—and rejection—of their leaders (the pre-Islamic doctrine of government by consent); they harassed the early imperial Muslim government for several centuries, but were eventually eliminated. (The only Khawarij sect to survive today is the Ibadiyah, who dislike the Khawarij appellation.) Laila of Shaibân-Bakr's tribal history is thus one of ardent ideological and political resistance to imperial control and armed rebellion against government forces. Her brother died in a battle with imperial troops that took place near the river Khabûr in Upper Mesopotamia around 795.

Little is known of Laila's personal history. We do know, however, that after her brother's death, she took command of his army and fought two battles before finally being deposed by her tribe. This was not necessarily an unusual act for a woman in this era. Denise Spellberg, in her article entitled "Political Action and Public Example: 'A'isha and the Battle of the Camel," states that "In pre-Islamic times, women participated in tribal warfare on the Arabian peninsula. With the advent of Islam, women did not relinquish their place on the battlefield" (49). Even though women fought alongside the Prophet Muhammad in many of his battles, the experience of freeborn (non-slave) women in pre-Islamic and early Islamic peoples was also often marked by seclusion and veiling. Laila's status as an early female warrior may at first tempt us to view her poem, with its admonition to "Rise, people, against calamity's tide / and a fate implacably bent on the best!" in the light of later pieces by women like Théroigne de Méricourt who extol the virtues of the "amazon." However, the link between Laila's acts of resistance as a warrior and that of poetic composition is not an obvious one. First and foremost, Laila's work calls into question the adequacy of oral or written representations to reflect reality.

Laila of Shaibân-Bakr's poem is part of a recognizably traditional corpus of early Islamic and pre-Islamic women's poetry. Her oral lamentation of her brother's death is a highly ritualized expression of public mourning; in fact, this kind of public, poetic grief was obligatory for women in mourning and provided a sort of limited, liminal public female space in which women memorialized their dead kinsmen. As Suzanne Pinckney Stetkevych puts it, "In an oral-formulaic poetry in which both the structure and imagery . . . are largely ritually or traditionally prescribed, what we have to look for is not individuality of expression or personal poetic vision but the power, and hence permanence, of the communal expression of a body of verse and of individual poems or voices within that tradition" (167). This poem thus cannot be read as an expression of Laila's individual personality; it must primarily be considered as a performance of a ritual which is part of a collective poetic tradition. A discussion of Laila's elegy, then, exemplifies the difficulty of reading and interpreting such a work according to contemporary notions of individual, gendered resistance.

We have included the elegy here in order to highlight the elusive quality of representation as well as the complexity of any act of resistance. On the one hand, Laila is a member of a sectarian group defined by its active resistance to political control and its commitment to egalitarian notions of political representation. She is also an exceptional (non-representative) woman warrior and tribal leader. On the other, Laila's elegy takes part in a deeply traditional and highly ritualistic form of woman's expression. From this point of view, although the poem cannot be said to represent an individual's reality, it does play an important role in organizing and reflecting real social relationships within the tribal community. Where does the literariness of this poem end and its political work begin? How much of Laila's individual resistance to convention might an elegy like this be said to represent? Such questions are difficult to answer. But a contemporary reader may still find in Laila's elegy a striking example of the intricate relationship between acts of resistance and acts of representation as they are played out in women's lives.

NM

AN ELEGY [§]

On Nubâta's hill is the scar of a grave
that appears on all hills marking the land;
closed on a hand that was open, free,
on the spirit of action, the heart of resolve.
God lighten the burden cast on a man
who never balked at his people's needs.
If Yazîd and his men have unhorsed him now,
how many the squadrons and ranks he outfought!
Rise, people, against calamity's tide
and a fate implacably bent on the best!
Rise for the moon that fell from the stars,
for the sun that for him would darken her face!
O tree by the river Khabûr, how green—
if in truth you grieve for the son of Ṭarîf!
for him who sought no gain but the Faith,
sought no possessions but lance and sword,
nor pride of horses but chargers swift
and steeds that know their footing afield.
We miss you, brother; we miss the spring,
and with thousands gladly would ransom your life.
Be not disconsolate, brothers alive,
for I see death set on the gallant, the great.

WORKS CONSULTED

Esposito, John L., ed. *The Oxford Encyclopedia of the Modern Islamic World.* Vol. 2. New York and Oxford: Oxford UP, 1995.

Lewis, Bernard. *The Arabs in History.* London: Hutchinson's University Library, 1950.

Spellberg, Denise A. "Political Action and Public Example: 'A'isha and the Battle of the Camel." *Women in Middle Eastern History: Shifting Boundaries in Sex and Gender.* Ed. Nikki R. Keddie and Beth Baron. New Haven: Yale UP, 1991.

Stetkevych, Suzanne Pinckney. *The Mute Immortals Speak: Pre-Islamic Poetry and the Poetics of Ritual.* Ithaca: Cornell UP, 1993.

Tuetey, Charles Greville. *Classical Arabic Poetry: 162 Poems from Imrulkais to Macarri.* London: Kegan Paul International Limited, 1985.

[§] Reprinted with permission of the publisher from *Classical Arabic Poetry: 162 Poems from Imrulkais to Macarri,* Charles Greville Tuetey, editor. London and New York: Kegan Paul International Limited, 1985. Material reprinted from page 216.

OLYMPE DE GOUGES *(1745–1793)*

Women's Rights and Revolution

In a pamphlet condemning the French revolutionary Maximilien Robespierre, Olympe de Gouges writes, "I am an extraordinary animal; I am neither man nor woman. I have all the courage of the one, and sometimes all the weaknesses of the other." Olympe de Gouges' life and numerous writings involve a constant questioning of the ideologies and social institutions which work to define—and to police—such concepts as *man* and *woman, public sphere, universal rights, nature,* and *virtue* (to name only a few). Born in Montauban, in Southern France, the daughter of a butcher, Olympe de Gouges was not only entirely self-educated but self-invented. She rejected the names of her father and husband (Gouze and Aubry, respectively), and recreated herself as the aristocratic Olympe (her mother's name), *femme de lettres*. Her attempts—partially successful—at self-definition make a statement about the relationship between the person and the representative quality of the person's name. She is both the female counterpart of the French Revolution's newly self-made man and a figure who challenges the most sacred functions of the patriarchal household as it is reenvisioned within the newly-minted French republic.[1]

Although Olympe de Gouges was a supporter of the monarchy, and allied herself with the more moderate wing of the revolutionaries, the Girondins, she remained an outspoken and radical feminist throughout her political career. She left the South of France at age eighteen, after the death of her husband. While her native language was not French, she became an extremely prolific writer and orator. Moreover, her "Declaration of the Rights of Woman and the Female Citizen" is one of the best-known feminist texts to emerge from the French Revolution, and is often considered to be one of the founding documents of Western liberal feminism. She was guillotined on November 4, 1793, in an act of violent political retribution characteristic of the Terror during this period, for her monarchist sympathies and ardent opposition to the policies of Robespierre. Even during her imprisonment she continued to compose letters and pamphlets critical of revolutionary politics; she also claimed responsibility for her political actions and insisted on her patriotism and good faith. She maintained her right to free speech and political opinion up until her death, and in her will "left her heart to her country, her honesty to men . . . and her soul to women." De Gouges was one of the first feminists during this period to demand equal rights for women. Although her program of reform was not implemented, her dedication to activism and her desire for change remain a striking testimony to an eighteenth-century woman's bold feminist stance.

The French Revolution, in addition to witnessing the abolition of the nobility and the fall of the monarchy in France, was also a period of important constitutional reform in legislation concerning family life. The liberal Constitution of 1791 declared marriage a civil contract; subsequent laws legislated divorce on an equal basis for both partners, lowered the age of marital consent for women to twenty-one, and abolished primogeniture; equal inheritance was mandated for sons and daughters throughout France. The Revolution was also a period of an intense female political activism which, to a certain extent, transcended class boundaries (see entries on Women of the Third Estate and Théroigne de Méricourt). Women were never granted full political rights, however. In 1793, the National Convention outlawed women's political clubs, and in 1795, women were forbidden to attend any political assembly or to gather in public in groups of more than five. Although the French Revolution was a period of upheaval in which women's social roles were destabilized, it is difficult to evaluate the revolutionary period as one of definitive progress for women's rights. This was the moment, however, when the goals of a new liberal feminism were being shaped and promulgated by activists like Olympe de Gouges.

The *ancien régime* (roughly defined as the monarchist and absolutist government which existed before the French Revolution) had seen the development of various forms of social organization that allowed women certain kinds of political and cultural influence. Some feminist scholars have argued that the hierarchical organization of the feudal society of orders characteristic of pre-revolutionary France allowed women of rank both juridical and military freedom (see Natalie Zemon Davis, Joan Kelly, and Joan Landes); this kind of female public power was also in evidence during the seventeenth and eighteenth centuries with the rise of the *salons,* which were presided over by literate women who functioned as "purveyors of culture" (Landes). During the Enlightenment, however, a different way of conceptualizing the composition of the public sphere began to emerge. While this new public was no longer organized around *explicit* class lines, feminist critics of the period have described it as incorporating a distinctly masculinist gender division. Jean-Jacques Rousseau, one of the most well-known theorists of the Enlightenment period, vehemently decried women's participation in political and cultural life. In addition, in the "Declaration of the Rights of Man and Citizen," women were completely barred—for the first time in French history—from voting.

Olympe de Gouges' "Declaration of the Rights of Woman and the Female Citizen" was written in 1791, after the promulgation of the new Constitution (Mary Wollstonecraft was also writing during this period). It is a document which embodies—and, to a certain extent, refuses to resolve—the contradictions of a historical moment: new possibilities for feminist activism were being opened up at the same time as the old ways in which women had exercised political and cultural influence were foreclosed. The "Declaration" is also the creation of a woman who demanded to be recognized as an author at a time when women did not have the rights of authorship (husbands and fathers were considered to be the sole owners of women's intellectual property according to revolutionary legislation). The "Declaration" links women's ability to gain access to a public sphere with their right to represent themselves in print and in politics. In this document, Olympe de Gouges not only asserts her right to represent herself as a woman and as a political subject, but also claims to speak for all French women. She denigrates the private influence that women often exercised in *ancien régime* France and promotes women's right to represent themselves politically.

De Gouges ultimately articulates the tension between the right of the individual to represent herself as an individual and the right of this individual to participate in a universal public sphere by means of such representation. Her "Declaration" is also a fundamental critique of liberal political theory. In exposing the "Declaration of the Rights of Man and Citizen" as exclusionary and in extending the promise of the universal to women, she demonstrates the peculiar bond which links the general to the particular in modern political thought. She also suggests the fundamental inability of the new political system to adequately contain the notion of sexual difference which it has effectively called into being. But in the end, de Gouges both insists on women's difference from men and maintains the possibility of representing that difference within a universalist political system. She has gone on to become a heroic figure for Western feminism, although her life and works, as Joan Scott has argued, remain "marked by paradox" (56).

NM

FROM *THE RIGHTS OF WOMAN*[§]

MAN, are you capable of being just? It is a woman who is asking you this question, and you will not take away her right to do so. Tell me what has given you the sovereign right to oppress my sex—your strength, your talents? Observe the creator in his wisdom; examine all of nature's grandeur—which you seem to want to imitate—and give me, if you dare, an example of such tyrannical authority.[2] Go back to the animals, consult the elements, study the vegetable kingdom, then cast your eyes over all the modifications of organic matter, and yield to the evidence I offer you. Search, seek out and single out, if you can, sexes in the conduct of nature. Everywhere you will find them intermingled, everywhere working harmoniously together in this immortal masterpiece.

Man alone has botched together a principle as an exception to this. Bizarre, blind, bloated with science and degenerate in this century of enlightment and wisdom, he wants to rule despotically and in the most crass ignorance over a sex which has received all the intellectual faculties . . . yet he claims to want revolution, or at the very least to reclaim his rights.

"DECLARATION OF THE RIGHTS OF WOMAN AND FEMALE CITIZEN"

To be enacted by the National Assembly in its last sessions, or in the first sessions of the next legislature.

Preamble

MOTHERS, daughters, sisters, representatives of the nation all, are demanding to be incorporated into the national assembly. Being of the opinion that ignorance, oblivion or mistrust of the rights of women are the sole causes of public misery and of the corruption of governments, they have resolved to expound the natural, inalienable and sacred rights

[§] Reprinted from *The Rights of Woman,* by Olympe de Gouges, translated by Val Stevenson. Published 1989 London: Pythia Press. Material reprinted from pages 4–10.

of women in a solemn declaration so that this declaration, constantly before the body of society, will always remind them of their rights and duties. The actions of women and men will be comparable at all times with the aims of political institutions, thereby becoming more respected, and women's demands, founded henceforth on simple and incontestable principles, shall revolve around upholding the constitution, morality and happiness of all.

First Article

Woman is born free and remains equal to man in rights. Social distinctions can only be founded on common service.

II

The aim of all political associations is to preserve the natural and inalienable rights of Woman and Man: these are the rights to liberty, ownership, safety and, above all, resistance to oppression.

III

The principle of sovereignty resides in essence in the Nation, which is only the coming together of Woman and Man: authority emanating elsewhere can be exercised by no body or individual.

IV

Liberty and justice lie in rendering everything which belongs to others as of right. Thus the exercise of woman's natural rights has no limit other than the perpetual tyranny of man's opposing them: these limits must be reformed by the laws of nature and reason.

V

The laws of nature forbid all actions harmful to society. Whatever is not forbidden by these wise and holy laws cannot be disallowed, and no-one may be forced to do that which is not ordained.

VI

The Law must be the expression of the general will; all citizens, female and male, should concur personally or through their representatives in its formation, and it must be the same for all. All citizens, being equal in its eyes, must be equally eligible to all honours, positions and public posts according to their abilities, and with no other distinction other than those of their virtue and talents.

VII

No woman is an exception; she is accused, arrested and detained as laid down by the law. Women obey this rigorous Law as men do.

VIII

The law must establish only strictly and obviously necessary laws, and no-one may be punished except by virtue of a Law established and promulgated prior to the crime and legally applicable to women.

IX

Any woman found guilty will be dealt with in the full rigour of the Law.

X

No-one should be persecuted for her fundamental opinions. Woman has the right to mount the scaffold; she must equally have the right to mount the rostrum, provided that the manifestation of her feelings does not disturb the public order established by the Law.

XI

Freedom to communicate thoughts and opinions is one of the most precious rights, since freedom ensures a father's legitimacy towards his children. Any Citizen may therefore freely say, 'I am the mother of your child', without any barbarous prejudice forcing her to hide the truth, with the proviso that doing so be not illegal under other laws.

XII

The guarantee of women's rights entails absolute service; it must be established for the advantage of everyone, and not just those in whom it is entrusted.

XIII

The contributions of women and men towards the upkeep of public services and administration costs are equal. Woman shares all the compulsory work and unpleasant tasks, and ought therefore to take the same share in the distributions of appointments, jobs, offices, high positions and trade.

XIV

Citizenesses and Citizens have the right to ascertain directly, or through their representatives, the need for public contributions. Citizenesses will abide by such decisions only if given an equal share not only in judging the amount involved, but also publicly administering and determining the quotas, basis, collection and duration of taxes.

XV

All women, united by their contributions with all men, have the right to demand from any public servant an account of his administration.

XVI

Any society in which rights are not guaranteed and the separation of powers is not determined, has no constitution. The constitution is void if the majority of the individuals composing the Nation have not co-operated in its drafting.

XVII

Properties are shared or divided by both sexes; they belong to each person by an inviolable and sacred right. No-one can be deprived of their natural patrimony unless public necessity, legally enacted, clearly demands it, and then only on condition of just and previously arranged damages.

NOTES

[1] For more on the self-representation of Olympe de Gouges, see Chapter 2, "The Uses of Imagination: Olympe de Gouges in the French Revolution," in Joan Wallach Scott's *Only Paradoxes to Offer.*

[2] *De Paris au Perou, du Japon jusqu' à Rome,*
Le Plus sot animal, à mon avis, c'est l'homme.

From Paris to Peru, from Rome to Japan,
The stupidest creature, I find, is man. [Olympe de Gouges]

WORKS CONSULTED

Desan, Suzanne. "Women's Experience of the French Revolution: An Historical Overview." *Literate Women and the French Revolution of 1789.* Ed. Catherine R. Montfort. Birmingham, Alabama: Summa Publications, 1994.

An Encyclopedia of Continental Women Writers. Ed. Katharina M. Wilson. New York: Garland Publishing, 1991.

Landes, Joan B. *Women and the Public Sphere in the Age of the French Revolution.* Ithaca and London: Cornell UP, 1988.

Scott, Joan Wallach. *Only Paradoxes to Offer: French Feminists and the Rights of Man.* Cambridge: Harvard UP, 1996.

Vanpée, Janie. *"La Déclaration des Droits de la Femme et de la citoyenne:* Olympe De Gouges's Re-Writing of *La Déclaration des Droits de l'homme." Literate Women and the French Revolution of 1789.* Catherine R. Montfort, ed. Birmingham, Alabama: Summa Publications, 1994.

HIRATSUKA RAICHO *(1886–1971)*

Modernity and the "Woman of the New Japan"

Hiratsuka Raicho is an important figure in a long line of Japanese feminists. She is particularly interesting as a resister, for she began her career from an upper-class background and wanted to see that women's creative works were given a venue. She went on to become a political figure who fought for ideological transformations in women's ideas about themselves as well as for practical policy changes in the realms of marriage, employment and poverty, sexuality, and education. The road that she traveled from one position to another, from writer to political figure, as well as the controversies that arose as the feminist movement in Japan was being shaped, parallel a number of the themes of this anthology.

Hiratsuka Raicho came from a well-off Tokyo family. Upon graduation from high school in 1903, she entered Naruse Jinzo's Japan's Women's University. With "the influence and support of her mother, Tsuya, Raicho early developed a consciousness of herself and a dissatisfaction at finding obstacles thrown in her path" (Sievers 165). She found numerous obstacles in the Women's University at the time, particularly the conservative way in which traditional values were incorporated into both the curriculum and the extracurricular activities (Sievers 166). Hiratsuka continued her education after graduation in 1906 by studying languages and religion and by joining with other women in a literary society. It was in this setting that the idea of a literary magazine to showcase women's writings, entitled *Seito* (*Bluestocking* in English), was born.

The first issue was published in 1911, backed financially by Raicho's mother (Reich and Fukuda 281). It opened with Hiratsuka's manifesto, reprinted below. The response to the issue from women across Japan was stunning. Women sought the magazine as an outlet for their writings. Male critics doubted the quality of the endeavor. And the government expressed concern about such ideas being explored publicly. Those who write on Japanese feminism (see list of works consulted below) appear to agree that the young women who began publishing had little sense of this journal's potential impact. They differed from the first generation of Japanese feminists who had rallied around access to political participation, who were likely to have international connections, and who had developed a feminist agenda through these venues. Hiratsuka and her colleagues sought "a literary articulation of women's awareness of themselves and of their social problems" (Reich and Fukuda 280). What began as a personal concern soon turned into much more. The individual leaders and the literary organization they were creating debated goals and strategies as both evolved. Fulfilling the needs for expression among women that the publication had helped, managing internal dissension over how *Seito* was to develop, and dealing with external critics placed extraordinary demands on the members of the literary society as they sought to establish the contours of the magazine.

Many of *Seito's* contributors were graduates of the newly founded women's colleges and members of well-to-do families. They confessed their individual opposition to the family system, but gradually became concerned with the larger social problems of women. "*Seito* introduced in Japanese translation Ibsen's *A Doll's House* and the Swedish feminist Ellen Key's (1849–1926) essays on love. . . . As they became more concerned with social problems and particularly with the plight of the women of Yoshiwara (their city), as they became more eccentric in dress (bobbing their hair and wearing Western clothes) and habits (frequenting cafes and the geisha quarter), government opposition to the journal increased" (Reich and Fukuda 284). Although Hiratsuka left the editorship in 1915, debates on the journal's emphasis on social problems continued even more vigorously. The final issue came out in 1916. During its six years of publication, the government censored five issues, including the one containing the excerpt we reprint here, "To the Women of the World," in 1913.

Leaving *Seito* did not mean that Hiratsuka left her commitment to Japanese women's issues. She went on, with colleagues, to found the New Woman's Society in 1920, an organization which was committed to bringing together Japanese women of different political persuasions to build a women's agenda by gaining political power for women. The Society enjoyed some success, gaining for women the right to organize and attend political meetings, before disbanding in 1922. Woman suffrage, however, had to wait another twenty years (see excerpts by Kusunose Kita and Mitsui Mariko). Sievers summarizes the impact made by this generation of feminists: "Though they began with little consciousness of connections with the Meiji feminists who preceded them, they did manage to break through barriers of class and government control to claim a continuity that stretched back to the 1870s. . . . They discussed sexuality openly and related it to the politics of women's condition. They added to the Meiji feminists' demand for economic independence a call for psychological and emotional independence—from men and from the family system" (188).

In the excerpts by Hiratsuka reprinted here, we can trace her development as a feminist thinker. "We are eager to know the contents of life for ourselves," writes Hiratsuka in her essay "To the Women of the World." This desire to "know" is part of a feminist project that is both literary and political. On the one hand, it is connected to "the birth of a feminine literature" which Hiratsuka describes in her "Manifesto"; on the other, this valorization of women's "self-awareness" allows Hiratsuka to criticize the way gender functions in Japanese society. This critique is grounded in an investigation of the ways in which the notion of woman's "essential nature" serves political ends. Hiratsuka's "feminine literature" and her political writings both explore and redefine what "woman's nature" might mean for Japanese women. The conceptual progression from feminist literary project to feminist political program might be thought of as a gradual process of politicization; it is also an illustration of how women's representations of themselves might both reflect and bring about political change.

There is a haunting familiarity to the story of Japan's literary feminists in the *Seito* group and their evolution from personal protest to political stance. As individuals and as an organization, they took steps very similar to the steps many U. S. feminists and others would take in the late 1960s and early 70s, moving from personal problems to social problems and the intricate political connections between the two. And, like feminists in later decades of the twentieth century around the world, the differing views on what the central issues were, what strategies were most suitable for attacking them, and how to maintain a coalition while pursuing a variety of goals, caused the *Seito* group considerable tension. Internal struggles in feminist organizations are always exacerbated by the complexities of maintaining a united stance in the larger world. Here, too, Hiratsuka and her colleagues experienced much of what would be repeated—albeit in ignorance of their wisdom—fifty years later around the world.

JFO

FROM THE "MANIFESTO"[§]

Our group has as its objective the birth of a feminine literature. We are animated by an ardent sincerity and our ambition is to express and produce feminine genius; we will succeed through a concentration of spirit. That genius, which is of mysterious essence, is an important part of universal genius, which has no sex!

When Japan was born, woman was the sun, the true human being. Now she is the moon! She lives in the light of another star. She is the moon, with a pale face like that of a sickly person.

This is the first cry of the Bluestockings! . . . We are the mind and the hand of the woman of new Japan. We expose ourselves to men's laughter, but know that which is hidden under that mockery. Let us reveal our hidden sun, our unrecognized genius! Let it come from behind the clouds! That is the cry of our faith, of our personality, of our instinct, which is the master of all the instincts. At that moment we will see the shining throne of our divinity.

"YO NO FUJINTACHI NI" [TO THE WOMEN OF THE WORLD]

It is very sad that even now I have to say such things as follow to the women of the world.

I am often asked the following sort of question especially by women: "Are you and the members of the *Seito* group celibates?" Whenever I meet this strange question—right, it is a very strange question!—I have had to answer "No." And I have sometimes added, "I have never advocated celibacy nor insisted upon the idea of the good wife and wise mother, much less have the women of the *Seito* group." Then they merely say, "Is that so? People say, however, that you and the members of the *Seito* group are celibate," and then they have nothing more to ask. So I always back down, finding no courage to give a further

[§] The two excerpts by Hiratsuka Raicho originally appeared in *Seito,* and were translated by Pauline C. Reich from the French version by Albert Maybon in *La Revue Mondiale* (November 1923), p. 405. The "Manifesto" appeared in *Seito,* vol. 1, no. 1 (September 1911; "To the women of the world" appeared in *Seito*, vol. 3, no. 4 (April 1913). Both pieces were included in "Japan's Literary Feminists: The *Seito* Group," by Pauline C. Reich and Atsuko Fukuda, published in *Signs: Journal of Women in Culture and Society* 2.1 (1976). Our material is excerpted from pages 287–291.

answer that might intrude on their private affairs, because in these questions I cannot help but be surprised to see how shallow, how easygoing, and how peaceful are women's inner lives or what they are thinking about such lives in the modern age. It seems to me that these women have no more substantial thoughts than: "Maybe Raicho is celibate since she hasn't married anyone, though she is old enough to do so," or "I guess she is celibate because people say so; besides, there is a rumor that many of the members of the *Seito* group are celibate, so I'll just ask her whether it is true or not." I can also judge from their free and easy manner in asking the question and their derisive tones that they have never had any more thoughts or considerations than these. Otherwise, I suppose that they should have felt scruples about asking me such absurd questions. I wonder why a fundamental doubt about the conventional ideas that women ought to marry once, that marriage is the only way in which women can live, that every woman should be a good wife and wise mother and nothing more doesn't occur to many of the women of this world. And I wonder why they don't try to examine more thoroughly what women should essentially be, apart from long-term history, immediate utility or convenience, and especially the traditional womanly virtues which came into being for the convenience of men.

We don't dare to insist upon celibacy for every woman; we are too busy to dispute noisily on celibacy or the idea of the good wife and wise mother. We are now doubtful of women's conventional way of life from the roots up. We can no longer stand to continue that sort of life. "Should women marry?" This question itself is the one which we ought to have already asked ourselves. We can believe no longer that women should sacrifice themselves throughout their lives on account of the need to preserve the species, or that reproducing offspring is woman's only work, or that marriage is the sole possible way by which women can maintain their lives, or that to be a wife and mother is all women's vocation. I suppose that, outside of marriage, women's way of life should have limitless possibilities arrived at individually, as should women's choice of vocations, outside of being a good wife and wise mother, be without limit. It would go without saying that each woman should have her own choice. We, therefore, require as high a cultural education as possible. We require high spiritual education for the meaningful lives of women as persons independent of men's lives. Of course, I don't intend to solve all the problems from the materialistic point of view of the socialists; however, we also require vocational education to wipe out the uneasiness and the obstacles of all kinds brought about by the lack of economic independence. When women don't depend on marriage, it is the vocational problem that they cannot help confronting immediately. [N.B.: We must remember that this was written at a time when women were expected to receive moral training in order to be good parents, rather than vocational training as was given in Europe and the United States. Both going out to work and being female and unmarried were unheard-of in Japan. (Reich)] . . .

No longer can modern women who have achieved more or less individual self-awareness be sure that so-called womanly virtues, for instance obedience, gentleness, chastity, perseverance, self-sacrifice and so on, which have long been compelled by men or society, are welcome. We have thought them over, tracing back to their origins why these things have been required of women, and questioned why society has come to permit them as womanly virtues and why they have ultimately come to be believed to be our essential nature.

What did we find out? I won't describe the process here, but it finally appears that soon there will be nothing of any value except that which suits the convenience of men's lives. In short, we cannot find anything whatsoever that has well-founded value. If the women of the world, who stand against us [N.B.: the *Seito* group experienced a great deal of ostracism from Japanese female upholders of the status quo. (Reich)] from unreasonable prejudices and conventional antipathies, or are dazzled by the concrete or abstract curses of the public at whatever is new, come to inquire into things a little more deeply, then I guess there would be not a few things that would occur to them. . . .

. . . Once we have been awakened, we cannot possibly fall asleep. We are now living. We are awake. Our lives will not become a reality without exhaling something which is burning within us. Whatever pressure we might be subjected to, our new lives will never cease finding the gateway. We are eagerly groping for the gate to the real life of women. We are at a loss, wondering how we should centralize our energies.

It is not the time to argue peacefully whether the new women are serious. We have very little time to concern ourselves in matters of this kind. It would be useless for us to hear frequent admonitions to lead a "serious, spiritual, noble and respectable life." We have barely finished the elementary school of the spirit. We have never been able to live blindly just on the outline which was preached and taught by other people. We are eager to know the contents of life for ourselves. We are set stepping, doubting, considering, and studying the fundamentals of what women's real life should be with internal insecurity and with external struggle against so much unjustified persecution. . . .

WORKS CONSULTED

Fujieda, Mioko. "Japan's First Phase of Feminism." *Japanese Women: New Feminist Perspectives on the Past, the Present, and the Future.* Kumiko Fujimura-Fanselow and Atsuko Kameda, eds. New York: Feminist Press, 1995.

Reich, Pauline C., and Atsuko Fukuda, "Japan's Literary Feminists: The *Seito* Group." *Signs: Journal of Women in Culture and Society* 2.l (1976): 280–291.

Sievers, Sharon L. *Flowers in Salt: The Beginnings of Feminist Consciousness in Modern Japan.* Stanford: Stanford UP, 1983.

SOUMAY TCHENG *(early 20th century)*

"Show What One Chinese Woman Is Able To Do"

As a young girl growing up in an aristocratic family in Canton, Soumay Tcheng adamantly refused to have her feet bound. "At night I unrolled the bandages which hurt me so fearfully," she relates in an autobiographical account. "In the morning I ran to school on my own free little toes" (20). Fortunately, Soumay was supported in this rebellious act—as in many others—by her mother, a woman who spent most of her life married to a distant and preoccupied husband, but who nevertheless maintained her belief in her daughter's abilities and ethical integrity. When she was fourteen years old, Soumay possessed enough self-confidence to break off her engagement with a government official, even though she "fully realized the extreme gravity of such an audacious move" (71). In an act which she describes as "entirely unheard-of," she herself penned a letter to her prospective husband to inform him of her decision. She considered the inscription of her name at the end of this epistle (a kind of written assumption of personal responsibility) as the event which marked the beginning of her adult life as "a real person" (75).

Soumay went on to become the first Chinese woman to receive a law degree from the Sorbonne, the French university where she traveled to study in 1914. By this point, she had already dedicated several years of her life to what was often dangerous work with the revolutionary Kuomintang Society in China. (It was this society, originally termed the T'ung-meng hui, that helped sponsor the overthrow of the two-thousand-year-old imperial system in China.[1]) Throughout this period, Soumay's mother never ceased to commend her for her bravery and social commitment.

Soumay Tcheng was a participant in a revolution which irrevocably changed the configuration of Chinese society. She not only witnessed but took part in the downfall of the decadent Ch'ing regime (established by the Manchu warriors who had captured Peking in 1644) and was a staunch advocate of a nationalist and republican perspective. (It is important to note that the Chinese Communist Party did not triumph over the Chinese Nationalists until 1949.) The old Confucian social order had begun to weaken towards the late nineteenth century, when urban intellectuals started to attack the the old regime for its inability to deal with such escalating crises as the encroachment of Western imperialist powers, a tremendous rise in population, and the development of new modes of economic production. The social radicalism of the new intellectuals was heavily influenced by Western ideas of political rights and liberal democracy, an influence which is visible in Soumay Tcheng's accounts of both her educational trajectory and political philosophy. This reevaluation of the beliefs and social structures of Confucian society was linked to a critique of the pre-revolutionary family system and a movement towards family reform.

Modern Chinese feminism emerged alongside this developing critique, around the turn of the century. Ideals of "gender equality, mutual love and free choice" became prevalent at this time among the young intellectual elite, of which Soumay Tcheng was one (Johnson 29). Nevertheless, in China as elsewhere, revolutionary political struggle was not necessarily compatible with activist support for women's rights. In her study of Chinese women and peasant revolution, Kay Ann Johnson explains how, in the early twenties, "compelling pressures pushed activist women away from the reformist women's rights movement toward revolutionary struggles based on a class analysis which demanded a radical restructuring of ruling groups and society" (40).

The excerpt which follows describes a conversation which took place between Soumay and her mother around the beginning of 1912, after Soumay had been transporting bombs for the Kuomintang for around three months. Ironically, Soumay had been chosen for this duty because her status as an aristocratic women made her seem an unlikely saboteur and thus an unlikely target of suspicion. It was, nonetheless, dangerous and nerve-wracking work. In this conversation, Soumay's mother ascribes a feminist purpose to her daughter's revolutionary efforts and frames Soumay's political involvement as a woman's issue. (This is in contrast to Soumay's discussion of her work as primarily patriotic and nationalist.) In her remark, "Show what one Chinese woman is able to do," she confers upon her daughter the privilege of representing her countrywomen to the nation. Soumay Tcheng, her mother implies, has it in her power to be both an exceptional woman and a future representative of the abilities and potential of Chinese women in general. Soumay's mother's emphasis is not only on the advantages to which women have access through education and political work, however, but also on the strong familial ties she and her daughter share. With her statement, "My child, do all you can. I will help you!" she reaffirms her commitment both to women's advancement within the new Chinese Republic and to a familial bond between female family members. In so doing, she reenvisions the role played by what Margery Wolf calls the "uterine family" (an informal family grouping centered around the mother) in the formation of a new kind of Chinese state.

NM

FROM *A GIRL FROM CHINA*[§]

In order to recover more completely from the emotions which I had endured while making my final voyage as a bomb and dynamite carrier, I went down to spend two weeks at Tientsin with my mother. She had, of course, noticed that for some time I had not really been myself. Often she had questioned me, but I had never been able to answer her frankly. Now I considered it my duty to tell her exactly what my life was and what I had undertaken and was trying to accomplish.

I confided to her that I had become a member of the Kwo Ming Tang Society, and that I would follow it and be faithful to it, in life and in death.

Without betraying the profound emotion which such an unexpected revelation caused

[§] Reprinted from *A Girl From China (Soumay Tcheng)*, translated by B. van Vorst. Published in 1925 by Frederick A. Stokes Company. Material reprinted from pages 134–136.

her, my mother very gently asked me if I did not believe that, without going to such extremes, I might render great services to my country. I longed to convince her, to win her over to my point of view. So I told her of our hopes and added that if she saw me ailing it was because I had not taken as great a share as I could have wished in this effort we were making. I was ill because I had not sufficiently served my country.

My mother was for a time plunged in thought. Then finally she said to me:

"My child, do all you can. I will help you!"

My precious mother had suffered so much in her life that she comprehended all. She realized that if she had only been given an opportunity to work as her daughter was now working, her husband would not have been so negligent of her, and her mother-in-law would not have treated her with such cruel disdain.

"You are right," she said to me. "You must help the Chinese women. They have been treated by their families, and by their husbands, as though they were playthings. Not only have they been prevented from educating themselves, but it has been supposed that they were incapable of learning anything. Show what one Chinese woman is able to do. You will be helping your sisters for all future time. Your work is good. Your decision is wise."

My mother had grown very pale as she pronounced these words. They seemed to remain with me like a benediction.

NOTE

[1] The revolution which created the Chinese Republic began on October 10, 1911. The last Manchu emperor, Henry Pu-yi, abdicated four months later. He was six years old at the time.

WORKS CONSULTED

Johnson, Kay Ann. *Women, the Family and Peasant Revolution in China.* Chicago: U of Chicago P, 1983.

Moseley, George. *China Since 1911.* New York: Harper and Row, 1968.

Van Vorst, B. *A Girl From China* (Soumay Tcheng). New York: Frederick A. Stokes Company, 1925.

TAJ AL-SALTANA *(1884–1936)*

"Liberating Women": An Iranian Feminist Perspective on National Identity

Taj al-Saltana's memoirs, written in 1914 in the wake of the Iranian Constitutional Revolution, are among the earliest known examples of Iranian women's autobiographical writing.[1] They provide a detailed account of the author's experiences as a young girl growing up in the Qajar royal harem and, later, as an observer and participant in the political upheavals of her time—an account that is notable not only for its forthrightness but also for the fact of its production within a tradition that has been conspicuously lacking, from a Western point of view, in what critic Farzaneh Milani calls "voluntary self-revelation and self-referentiality" (202). Milani asserts: "This reluctance to talk publicly and freely about the self, however, is not confined to women. Iranian men have also shunned self-representation. . . . Modern Persian literature, which has incorporated many Western literary forms, has avoided to a large extent one of the West's most popular genres" (201–2).

In the Persian tradition, the separation of the private and the public is essential to the preservation of both men's and women's honor. The narrative of confession and self-revelation that in the West has often been considered to possess certain therapeutic powers is seen here as a potential source of disorder and unrest. Women's relationship to forms of self-representation such as the autobiography has been the subject of particularly strict social control. Taj al-Saltana's written "public unveiling" in her autobiography might thus be compared with her adoption of Western dress and consequent rejection of the veil in the early part of the century, well before the 1936 unveiling act (Milani 225). Significantly, she writes about herself (particularly towards the end of her memoirs)—and has been written about—as a "fallen" and notorious woman who eventually finds redemption for her past sins of independence and self-indulgence through emotional and physical suffering.

Taj al-Saltana's autobiography must be understood in the context of the decline of the Qajar regime (she was the daughter of the ruler of Iran, Naser al-Din Shah Qajar) and the rise of constitutionalism as an intellectual and political movement in turn-of-the-century Iran. It should also be pointed out that Taj al-Saltana's background of wealth and privilege was in no way typical of Iranian women of the time. Abbas Amanat, in an introduction to Taj al-Saltana's autobiography, describes her as "belonging to a tiny, secularized upper class in a society dominated by traditional Perso-Islamic values" (11). She spent her childhood in the uniquely cloistered environment of the royal harem, protected from the gaze of outsiders by an army of eunuchs. Her account reveals the importance of the role played by the women of the harem in influencing affairs of state, however obliquely; it also dramatizes the increasing sexual permissiveness of Qajar aristocratic society during the years of its decline. Both heterosexual and lesbian affairs, while not part of common practice, were not entirely unknown in the realm of the harem. Nevertheless, Taj's marriage to a thirteen-year-old boy, arranged to solidify political links between the two families involved, did allow her freedom from the complete seclusion of the harem as well as increased sexual and social independence.

Ultimately, however, her marriage (which ended in divorce partly as a result of her frustration with both her husband Hasan's dissipation and his refusal to support her nationalist and feminist sentiments) caused Taj al-Saltana much unhappiness and emotional trauma. In her autobiography, she describes the couple's terrible financial difficulties (typical of aristocratic families during this period), Hasan's venereal disease and homosexual love affairs, and her own decision to resort to an abortion out of fear for the effects of gonorrhea on her unborn child. As a result of these and other factors, Taj al-Saltana asserted her independence from her husband even before the onset of the Revolution, an act that, as Amanat puts it, "permitted her to augment her life of luxury and entertainment with the cultural experiences of study, music, French, painting, and above all socializing" (59). She also unveiled herself publicly and ceased to participate in regular devotional activities around this time. The growth of print-based media and publishing during the revolutionary period was an important factor in Taj al-Saltana's emancipation, influenced as she was by the translations of French, English, Russian, Turkish, and Arabic works that were becoming available.

Taj al-Saltana helped establish the Society for the Emancipation of Women (*Anjoman-e Horriyat-e Nesvan*), founded towards the end of the 1910s, and was one of the most progressive critics of the Qajar monarchy. In the excerpt we have included here, she not only promotes the idea of economic independence for Iran[2] but stresses the importance of women's participation in national life. As Parvin Paidar remarks in her discussion of the discourse surrounding nationalism during this period, "The concept of nation was essential to the theoretical and political standpoint of reformists because it allowed them to create their own political space. . . . The language of nationhood revolved around the notions of national progress as the highest aim and national interest as the paramount objective" (72). Taj al-Saltana's nationalist perspective takes on a feminist cast in that she sees women not just as "biological reproducers of the nation, educators of children, [and] transmitters of culture" (Paidar 73) but as active political participants in the development of Iran. Her account is an early expression of a feminist nationalism that reached its culmination in the 1920s.

In this excerpt, Taj al-Saltana also calls for the unveiling of women as a necessary part of feminist emancipation. She portrays veiling and seclusion as specifically urban practices "whose abolition would release a massive potential work force" (Amanat 95). Her account traces the connections between class dynamics, the significance of the veil as a symbol of women's status, nationalist discourse, and notions of women's rights that were the objects of intense debate at the time. She was part of a larger movement of women's protest that included popular demonstrations, petitioning of government officials, armed insubordination, and the establishment of secret societies. Throughout the twentieth century, the Iranian feminist movement has been of significance not only to the country's political history but also to the general development of feminist criticism and research in and on the Middle East. Taj al-Saltana's striking account of her experiences and reflections clearly establishes her both as forerunner of and participant in the birth of this movement.

NM

FROM THE *MEMOIRS OF A PERSIAN PRINCESS*[§]

Liberating Women

My teacher! If the women in this country were free as in other countries, enjoyed comparable rights, could enter the realm of government and politics, and could advance their lives, then without a doubt I would not seek the path to my progress through a ministerial position, through trampling on the people's rights and usurping the property of fellow Muslims and selling away my beloved homeland. I would choose a legitimate way and a determined plan for my advancement. Never would I spend the people's wealth to buy myself a mansion, a garden, household furniture, carriages and automobiles. These I would obtain through hard work and service.

I am sure you smiled as you read this and chuckled at my opinions and said: the men of our land have found no path to progress but this; you, an uninformed woman—how have you found a lawful way toward advancement?

My dear teacher! Do we not enjoy freedom of thought?

Yes, we do.

Then peruse carefully what I write next. Then, if you have any objections, you may speak up. I would adhere to a conservative position, not for my personal good but for the commonweal. I would make every effort to promote trade within Persia. I would build factories, not like the Rabi'ov soap-making plant, but ones that would make us independent of foreign trade. I would tap the mines, which God has liberally bestowed on Persia. I would seize the rights to the Bakhtiyari oil fields which generate tremendous annual profits, not leave them to the British. I would find the means to facilitate agriculture and provide its necessities. I would build the Mazandaran highway and regulate the transportation of essential commodities. As they do in California, I would hand over barren land to the people and ask them to make it productive. I would dig numerous irrigation wells and create artificial forests. I would divert the Karaj River toward the city and thereby rescue the people from the misery of filthy water. Not neglecting my own overall welfare, I would live in comfort without committing thievery and treason. The people, too, would benefit from my service and efforts, and live in peace. . . .

Traveling along the Tabriz road, I saw men and women everywhere working side by side in the villages, the women unveiled. In no village could a single idle person be found. When I tried to hire one of the peasants as an attendant, none of them was willing to give up his or her life in the wilderness. All these peasants and farmers are honorable, proud people. There are no prostitutes in any of the villages, because so long as a man and woman are not equal in wealth neither will marry the other. Besides, since the women do not cover their faces, mates are able to choose one another for themselves. After they are married, they always work together as partners in their farming and herding. . . .

[§] Reprinted by permission of the publisher from *Crowning Anguish: Memoirs of a Persian Princess from the Harem to Modernity (1884–1914)* by Taj Al-Saltana. Translated by Anna Vanzan and Amin Neshati. Edited by Abbas Amanat. Copyright © 1993 Mage Publishers, Inc. Material excerpted from pages 283–294.

Oh, my teacher! You who are an educated man and recognize the evils of the veil, why do you not take the women of your house, your larger family, your tribe by the hand and lead them outside? How long must you continue to be these poor women's servant, or, to put it more grandiosely, their "lord and master"? Oh, will I have a receptive ear? Undoubtedly, with all the thousands of logical proofs I have used to establish the harmfulness of the veil to you, nonetheless, since you are Persian and perversely rigid in your ideas, and since your mind has always turned to superficial things without any true thinking, you will say: "She is good-looking and weary of sitting at home, or she wishes to move about freely; therefore she pens these opinions which are contrary to general attitudes." You might even curse me in your heart and say, "What illicit proposals she puts forth to the women!"

But I swear to you, my teacher! When the day comes that I see my sex emancipated and my country on the path to progress, I will sacrifice myself in the battlefield of liberty, and freely shed my blood under the feet of my freedom-loving cohorts seeking their rights. . . .

NOTES

[1] The memoirs were not published until 1982, however.

[2] Amanat points out that "Taj's reference to oil exploration is particularly remarkable and should be seen as one of the earliest expressions of concern over British control of the nascent oil industry in southwestern Iran less than a decade after its inception" (88).

WORKS CONSULTED

Amanat, Abbas. Introduction. *Crowning Anguish: Memoirs of a Persian Princess from the Harem to Modernity 1884–1914.* By Taj al-Saltana. Ed. Abbas Amanat. Trans. Anna Vanzan and Amin Neshati. Washington, DC: Mage, 1993.

Milani, Farzaneh. *Veils and Words: The Emerging Voices of Iranian Women Writers.* Syracuse, NY: Syracuse UP, 1992.

Paidar, Parvin. *Women and the Political Process In Twentieth-Century Iran.* Cambridge: Cambridge UP, 1995.

JO CARRILLO *(1959–*

"And When You Leave, Take Your Pictures With You"

Jo Carrillo's poem "And When You Leave, Take Your Pictures With You" first appeared in 1981 in the pathbreaking anthology *This Bridge Called My Back: Writings by Radical Women of Color,* a collection of written work—including essays, poems, and letters—that aimed to "reflect an uncompromised definition of feminism by women of color in the U.S." (Moraga and Anzaldúa xxiii). *This Bridge Called My Back* functioned not only as an expression of solidarity among feminists of color but also as a much-needed critique of the racism inherent in much white feminist writing and political activity. While the editors and writers of this anthology saw their work as participating in the creation of "a broad-based U.S. women of color movement," they remained acutely conscious of the fact that white American feminists have often acted in racist and exclusionary ways. This book, which envisioned a new kind of political coalition between U.S. women of color and Third World women in general, called on white women to recognize the means by which they perpetuate and sustain racist ideologies and actions. "I can't prepare myself a revolutionary packet that makes no sense when I leave the white suburbs of Watertown, Massachusetts and take the T-line to Black Roxbury," writes Cherríe Moraga. She continues: ". . . the deepest political tragedy I have experienced is how with such grace, such blind faith, this commitment to women in the feminist movement grew to be exclusive and reactionary. I call my white sisters on this" (Preface xiv).

Jo Carrillo's poem provides the title for the third section of *This Bridge Called My Back:* "And When You Leave, Take Your Pictures With You: Racism in the Women's Movement." The section as a whole is an exploration of how "white women of economic and educational privilege have used that privilege at the expense of Third World women" (62). In fact, misrepresentation is a primary means by which many white feminists have marginalized women of color and portrayed their concerns as trivial. Carrillo's poem makes this point explicitly. In it, Third World women are objectified and used as subject matter by their "white sisters/radical friends" who "love to own pictures of us." These falsely cheerful images—images which conceal the truth and silence those whom they represent—become signs of the role played by white women in systems of domination. When Carrillo's poem is read alongside the work of a writer like Christine de Pizan, who also attempts to explain how cultural representations are linked to the structure of political power, we begin to see that what is at issue in these writings is not a simple relationship between those who control the "truth" and those who resist this control. The power to (mis)represent, in these excerpts, functions on many levels and with multiple consequences.

Carrillo is now a professor at the University of California Hastings College of the Law. Her most recent work is *Readings in American Indian Law* (Temple UP, 1997).

NM

AND WHEN YOU LEAVE, TAKE YOUR PICTURES WITH YOU[§]

Our white sisters
radical friends
love to own pictures of us
sitting at a factory machine
wielding a machete
in our bright bandanas
holding brown yellow black red children
reading books from literacy campaigns
holding machine guns bayonets bombs knives
our white sisters
radical friends
should think
again.

Our white sisters
radical friends
love to own pictures of us
walking to the fields in hot sun
with straw hat on head if brown
bandana if black
in bright embroidered shirts
holding brown yellow black red children
reading books from literacy campaigns
smiling.
Our white sisters radical friends
should think again.
No one smiles
at the beginning of a day spent
digging for souvenir chunks of uranium
or cleaning up after
our white sisters
radical friends

And when our white sisters
radical friends see us
in the flesh
not as a picture they own,

they are not quite as sure
if
they like us as much.
We're not as happy as we look
on
their
wall.

WORK CONSULTED

Moraga, Cherríe, and Gloria Anzaldúa, eds. *This Bridge Called My Back: Writings By Radical Women of Color.* 2nd ed. New York: Kitchen Table: Women of Color Press, 1981.

CHRISTINE DE PIZAN *(c. 1365–c. 1430)*

"Those Things I Have Here Refuted"

See also **Vision and Transformation.**

Christine de Pizan is often described as France's first professional female author and woman of letters; her work continues to stand as a pre-eminent example of French feminist thought. In addition to being a lyric poet and the author of several works of socio-historical criticism, Christine de Pizan was also the official biographer of King Charles V and the primary participant in the *querelle* (dispute) over the portrayal of women in the French classic *The Romance of the Rose*. Yet this writer, who went on to become one of the most renowned women in French literature and feminist philosophy, was born in Venice, Italy. When her father, Tommaso di Benvenuto da Pizzano (or Thomas de Pizan in France) was awarded the position of court astrologer by the French King Charles V, the family moved to Paris; Christine de Pizan was three years old at the time. Charles V was a progressive, intellectual ruler, and Christine de Pizan spent her youth in an exceptionally cultured and well-educated milieu. Her father, like her grandfather, had benefitted from university training and had held a position as a public official in the Venetian Republic.

In *The Book of the City of Ladies*, one of her best-known works, Christine de Pizan speaks of how she was encouraged by her father, although not by her mother, in her efforts to obtain an education. She was married at the age of fifteen to Estienne de Castel, a well-connected man of twenty-five who was appointed to the post of royal secretary; through her husband Christine de Pizan gained at least partial access to the group of young French humanist intellectuals of which he was a part. Though her father lost favor at court after the death of Charles V and died around 1387 in relative poverty, Christine de Pizan speaks of the ten years following her marriage as happy ones. When Estienne died suddenly during a Black Death epidemic, however, she suddenly became responsible for the fortunes of her three children, her widowed mother, and a niece. Christine de Pizan was eventually to turn to writing in order to support herself; notably, the difficulties and sorrows of widowhood became a significant focus of her work, a theme which Charity Cannon Willard describes as "highly original" ("The Franco-Italian Professional Writer" 336).

Although it is not clear exactly how Christine de Pizan supported herself during the years following her husband's death, it is possible that she worked as a copyist, one of the few profitable professions for women at the time. In fact, she was one of the first authors writing in the vernacular to take an active role in supervising the copying and illuminating of her own books. She first became known as a court poet after a decade of supporting herself and her family; her explicit commitment to and interest in feminist social critique emerged slightly later, between 1401 and 1403, when her letters sparked the *querelle* over *The Romance of the Rose*. In this literary quarrel, Christine de Pizan attacked the views on women expounded by Jean de Meung in his addition to the poem *Roman de la rose* (written around 1225 by Guillaume de Lorris). The themes that she addressed in her commentaries on the *Rose* became the primary focus of two of her most important works, *The Book of the City of Ladies* and *The Book of the Three Virtues*. As Earl Jeffrey Richards has put it, ". . . Christine was a highly respected and widely disseminated voice on the status of women. A large number of Christine's works spring from her deep sense of commitment" (xx).

We have included an excerpt from Christine de Pizan's contributions to the *querelle* below. This dispute is particularly significant since it stands as the initial *querelle* in a series of early-fifteenth-century intellectual debates over the representation of women known as the *Querelle des femmes*. Helen Solterer, in her analysis of Christine de Pizan's critique of the *Rose,* emphasizes the author's conception of the social function of language. According to Solterer:

> Moving away from a purely formalist problem of signification, Christine is concerned with the way significance is determined socially. . . . That women blush while reading the Rose indicates that they recognize the defamatory way the words of sex can signify for them in courtly society. . . . It is a measure of this language's potentially harmful consequences. Such consequences are borne by individual and group alike. In Christine's view, a determining link exists between the injury defamation inflicts on a woman and on her community—the "ordre de pollicie" as a whole. (157)

Christine de Pizan's letters thus constitute a direct reflection on one of the major points of this section: for her, the negative representation of women in the *Rose* takes on significance because of her understanding of the social effects of language in general. By the same token, the participation of women in intellectual and aesthetic life becomes a means by which they may gain some control over the representational systems that govern social life. In this excerpt below, Christine de Pizan asserts her right as a woman to speak not only for herself but on behalf of her gender when she says, "Yet precisely because I am a woman I can bear truer witness in this dispute than someone who had no direct experience. . . ."

NM

FROM *LESSER TREATISE ON THE ROMANCE OF THE ROSE, JUNE–JULY, 1401*[§]

And again—good Lord!—to go on a bit further: how can it be of any value or to any good purpose that he accuse, blame, and defame women so much, so excessively, impetuously, and certainly most falsely, for several extremely grave vices, holding that their behavior is full of all perversity, as if so many speeches, and in some measure all his characters, were not sufficient to slake his thirst? For if I am told that the Jealous Husband speaks out of passion, I cannot see how it is in character for Genius, who so strongly commands and

[§] From *The Writings of Christine de Pizan,* edited by Charity Cannon Willard. Copyright © 1994 by Persea Books, Inc. Reprinted by permission of Persea Books, Inc. Material excerpted from pages 155–157.

advises that women constantly be bedded, without ever interrupting the work he so stringently commands, when he himself, more so than any other character, speaks so strongly in vituperation of them, saying in fact: "Flee, flee, flee the venomous snake"—and then goes on to say that the work should be pursued without interruption. It is a blatantly grievous contradiction to order avoiding what he wants one to follow and following what he wants one to avoid. For if women are so perverse, he should not have ordered them to be approached in the slightest, since those who fear trouble ought to eschew it.

And since he so strongly prohibits telling secrets to wives—who are so avid to learn them, so he says (and I wonder where by all the devils he found all that bilge and all those empty words he assembled in composing that weary indictment)—I beg all those who claim him as their authority and lend him their faith to please inform me how many men they have seen accused, killed, or hanged, or blamed in the streets on accusation by their wives. I think they will find them few and far between. Notwithstanding it were good and praiseworthy advice for everyone to consider it surer to keep one's secret for one's self, for there are corrupt people in every way of life, and I recently heard a man who was accused and then hanged for having confided in one of his fellows who had his trust. Still I believe that before the face of justice there go few complaints or petitions on these horrifying evils, these great betrayals and diabolical acts that women are said to have learned to perpetrate so maliciously and so furtively. (All the same, a secret is a secret when no one knows it.) And as I said on this matter in one of my poems called *The Letter of the God of Love*, where are the lands and countries which were lost through their great misdeeds? To speak dispassionately, can we hear what great crimes can be blamed on even the worst among them, and who have deceived the most? For what can they do? And how can they deceive you? If they ask for money from your purse, then they neither steal it nor carry it off: don't give it to them if that is what you want. And if you say that you are besotted by them, then you need not be so stupid. Do they go looking for you in your homes, begging your favor or taking you by force? It would be nice to know just how it happens you are deceived.

And again, he has spoken quite superfluously and basely of women in marriage—an institution of which he could know nothing from experience, and yet made such sweeping generalizations: what just cause can this serve or what good come of it? I can see none, other than an impediment to peace and harmony, or to make husbands hearing such silliness and bilge, should they take any stock in it, suspicious of their wives and less affectionate to them. And to tell the truth, since he has condemned them all generally, this very reason leads me to believe that he never knew or frequented a virtuous woman, but having consorted with several dissolute women of ill repute—as the lecherous are wont to do—he believed or pretended to have learned that they were all of a kind, since he had no experience of the others. And had he only blamed dishonorable women and recommended that they be shunned, it would have been right and just instruction. But no! Rather he accuses them all without exception. Still if the author, beyond all reasonable limits, took it upon himself to accuse them or judge them with no regard for the truth, it is not to them that any blame should be imputed, but to the one who told such a lie so obviously untrue that none can believe it, for the opposite is manifestly clear. And no matter what he and all his accomplices in this matter may have sworn, and let none take offense, there have been, still are, and will be many more worthy women, more honorable, better bred, and even more learned, who have done more good for the world than he ever did personally, particularly in matters of ordinary civil conduct and the proper exercise of good morals. And there are many who have set aright their husbands' businesses, bearing the weight of their affairs and secrets, gently and discreetly—despite crudeness and lack of love on the part of their husbands. Many illustrations to the point can be found in the Bible and in ancient history: for example, Sarah, Rebecca, Esther, Judith, and many others; and in our time we have seen many worthy women in France: Queen Jeanne, pious and devout; Queen Blanche, the Duchess of Orleans and daughter of the King of France; the Duchess of Anjou who now bears the title of Queen of Sicily, all women of beauty, modesty, honor, and wisdom—and there are many others; among good women of lesser state, there is Lady de la Ferté, wife of Lord Pierre de Craon, much deserving of our praise, —and many others, so that it were too long a tale to say more.

And believe not, my fair lord, nor let any hold the opinion that I have made and put together this defense because, being a woman, I am prejudiced in women's behalf, for indeed my sole intent is to sustain the very truth, since I know by certain knowledge that it is just the opposite of those things I have here refuted. Yet precisely because I am a woman I can bear truer witness in this dispute than someone who had no direct experience, but instead spoke aimlessly and through conjecture. . . .

WORKS CONSULTED

"Christine de Pisan." *Great Women Writers.* Ed. Frank N. Magill. New York: Holt, 1994.

Richards, Earl Jeffrey. Introduction. *The Book of the City of Ladies.* By Christine de Pizan. Trans. Earl Jeffrey Richards. New York: Persea Books, 1982.

Solterer, Helen. *The Master and Minerva: Disputing Women in French Medieval Culture.* Berkeley: U of California P, 1995.

Willard, Charity Cannon. "The Franco-Italian Professional Writer: Christine de Pizan." In *Medieval Women Writers.* Ed. Katharina M. Wilson. Athens: U of Georgia P, 1984. 333–342.

—. Introduction. *The Writings of Christine de Pizan.* New York: Persea Books, 1994.

ZITKALA-ŠA (RED BIRD, GERTRUDE [SIMMONS] BONNIN) *(1876–1938)*

A Little Taste of Victory, A Hunger in the Heart

See also **Work and Education**

The contents of the speech Zitkala-Ša describes herself giving in this excerpt are interesting in the light of her double life as a white-educated Native American, an experience that led her at times, as she said, to "hang in the heart of chaos" (69). Entitled "Side By Side," her speech was in one sense an impassioned plea for sympathy with Native American resistance, even violent resistance: "What if he fought? His forests were felled; his game frightened away. . . . He loved his family and would defend them. He loved the fair land of which he was rightful owner. . . . Do you wonder still that in his breast he should brood revenge, when ruthlessly driven from the temples where he worshipped?. . . Is patriotism a virtue only in Saxon hearts?"[1] At the same time, the title referred to Native Americans' desire to "stand side by side with you in ascribing royal honor to our nation's flag." Applauding the Native-American "patriotism" that led to self-defense against invasion, Zitkala-Ša's speech was thus simultaneously laying claim, through a different patriotism, to "our" flag. Protesting the wrongs done her people, her oratory also enacted a tribute to the "noble institutions" of the invaders, praising the "treasures of knowledge and wisdom" which she used so effectively on behalf of Native American rights throughout her career as an activist.

ECD

FROM *AMERICAN INDIAN STORIES*[§]

Incurring My Mother's Displeasure

In the second journey to the East I had not come without some precautions. I had a secret interview with one of our best medicine men, and when I left his wigwam I carried securely in my sleeve a tiny bunch of magic roots. This possession assured me of friends wherever I should go. So absolutely did I believe in its charms that I wore it through all the school routine for more than a year. Then, before I lost my faith in the dead roots, I lost the little buckskin bag containing all my good luck.

At the close of this second term of three years I was the proud owner of my first diploma. The following autumn I ventured upon a college career against my mother's will.

I had written for her approval, but in her reply I found no encouragement. She called my notice to her neighbors' children, who had completed their education in three years.

§ Reprinted from *American Indian Stories* by Zitkala-Ša. Published 1985 by University of Nebraska Press. Material reprinted from pages 75–80.

They had returned to their homes, and were then talking English with the frontier settlers. Her few words hinted that I had better give up my slow attempt to learn the white man's ways, and be content to roam over the prairies and find my living upon wild roots. I silenced her by deliberate disobedience.

Thus, homeless and heavy-hearted, I began anew my life among strangers.

As I hid myself in my little room in the college dormitory, away from the scornful and yet curious eyes of the students, I pined for sympathy. Often I wept in secret, wishing I had gone West, to be nourished by my mother's love, instead of remaining among a cold race whose hearts were frozen hard with prejudice.

During the fall and winter seasons I scarcely had a real friend, though by that time several of my classmates were courteous to me at a safe distance.

My mother had not yet forgiven my rudeness to her, and I had no moment for letter-writing. By daylight and lamplight, I spun with reeds and thistles, until my hands were tired from their weaving, the magic design which promised me the white man's respect.

At length, in the spring term, I entered an oratorical contest among the various classes. As the day of competition approached, it did not seem possible that the event was so near at hand, but it came. In the chapel the classes assembled together, with their invited guests. The high platform was carpeted, and gayly festooned with college colors. A bright white light illumined the room, and outlined clearly the great polished beams that arched the domed ceiling. The assembled crowds filled the air with pulsating murmurs. When the hour for speaking arrived all were hushed. But on the wall the old clock which pointed out the trying moment ticked calmly on.

One after another I saw and heard the orators. Still, I could not realize that they longed for the favorable decision of the judges as much as I did. Each contestant received a loud burst of applause, and some were cheered heartily. Too soon my turn came, and I paused a moment behind the curtains for a deep breath. After my concluding words, I heard the same applause that the others had called out.

Upon my retreating steps, I was astounded to receive from my fellow-students a large bouquet of roses tied with flowing ribbons. With the lovely flowers I fled from the stage. This friendly token was a rebuke to me for the hard feelings I had borne them.

Later, the decision of the judges awarded me the first place. Then there was a mad uproar in the hall, where my classmates sang and shouted my name at the top of their lungs; and the disappointed students howled and brayed in fearfully dissonant tin trumpets. In this excitement, happy students rushed forward to offer their congratulations. And I could not conceal a smile when they wished to escort me in a procession to the students' parlor, where all were going to calm themselves. Thanking them for the kind spirit which prompted them to make such a proposition, I walked alone with the night to my own little room.

A few weeks afterward, I appeared as the college representative in another contest. This time the competition was among orators from different colleges in our State. It was held at the State capital, in one of the largest opera houses.

Here again was a strong prejudice against my people. In the evening, as the great audience filled the house, the student bodies began warring among themselves. Fortunately, I was spared witnessing any of the noisy wrangling before the contest began. The slurs against the Indian that stained the lips of our opponents were already burning like a dry fever within my breast.

But after the orations were delivered a deeper burn awaited me. There, before that vast ocean of eyes, some college rowdies threw out a large white flag, with a drawing of a most forlorn Indian girl on it. Under this they had printed in bold black letters words that ridiculed the college which was represented by a "squaw." Such worse than barbarian rudeness embittered me. While we waited for the verdict of the judges, I gleamed fiercely upon the throngs of palefaces. My teeth were hard set, as I saw the white flag still floating insolently in the air.

Then anxiously we watched the man carry toward the stage the envelope containing the final decision.

There were two prizes given, that night, and one of them was mine!

The evil spirit laughed within me when the white flag dropped out of sight, and the hands which hurled it hung limp in defeat.

Leaving the crowd as quickly as possible, I was soon in my room. The rest of the night I sat in an armchair and gazed into the crackling fire. I laughed no more in triumph when thus alone. The little taste of victory did not satisfy a hunger in my heart. In my mind I saw my mother far away on the Western plains, and she was holding a charge against me.

NOTE

[1] All quotations are from Fisher's account of the speech and the essay on which it was based (xii).

WORKS CONSULTED

Fisher, Dexter. Foreword. *American Indian Stories.* By Zitkala-Ša. Lincoln: U of Nebraska P, 1985.

Zitkala-Ša. *American Indian Stories.* Lincoln: U of Nebraska P, 1985.

IDENTIFYING SOURCES OF RESISTANCE

Jean F. O'Barr

The argument we have been building in this anthology is that women have been active resisters in every social domain. Some protest the strictures of traditional religions, others demand recognition of the full range of their desires, many argue for access to education, most want their work valued, and still others have turned to the written word to combat their misrepresentation. In this, the fourth section, we travel over similar territory but we do so from yet another perspective. We record the sources of resistance that women identify and draw on throughout their lives. Examining how women learn and enact resistance challenges the distinctions so often invoked between public and private, communal and personal, when women's lives are analyzed. We begin by looking at childhood experiences, move next to explore the multiple communities in which adult women participate, and then analyze women's relationships to political and legal systems. We emphasize that while the writers in the three previous sections have indeed been resisting, here, these authors reflect more explicitly on the models of resistance that serve as the basis for their knowledge and resistant actions.

CHILDHOOD EXPERIENCES AS SOURCES OF RESISTANCE

We start our investigation in this section with the memories of Huda Shaarawi, an Egyptian feminist who gained international recognition in the early twentieth century by discarding her veil and declaring her commitment to the emerging international feminist movement. The excerpt we include from Shaarawi's memoirs encapsulates many of this section's themes. She writes about her painful consciousness as a young girl of the preferential treatment her brother receives in her family. Her childhood awareness acts as a clear reminder of how early cultural ideas about gender are taught in families and how what is learned is much more than an intended lesson. She turns to the women in her extended family network for understanding and support as she begins to perceive unfairness. When Shaarawi hears the culture's lessons about what girls are and can expect, she refuses to accept them. She recalls the strategies she developed to bring attention to herself even while the cultural attention rushed toward her brother. Throughout her life, she would call attention to the ways in which the subtleties of family life exhibit themselves on the larger screen of public life, and expose the links between them in an oppressive system.

Many young women see gender differences and some learn to protest them. The processes by which they learn resistance vary widely and the next three selections illustrate some of these variations. Cornelia, an African-American woman, born in 1844, was interviewed in the late 1920s about her childhood memories of her mother. In the selection we have included, Cornelia describes her mother's explicit instructions in resistance. Her mother taught by combining words with actions, demonstrating to her young daughter that her human dignity transcended the treatment she received as a slave. Throughout her life, her daughter remembers her mother's central admonition: never let anyone abuse you. Childhood models, for Cornelia as for the other women in this section, articulate and transmit how to be the kinds of individuals they seek to be, whatever the particular time, place, or circumstance. Throughout their lives, they draw on the models their mothers made available to them, using what are thought of as private (that is, personal and familial) experiences to generate reflections and actions in the public (that is, social) world.

Fathers, too, play a role in teaching resistance, as Nadezhda Durova's story suggests. Durova found encouragement from her father in this nineteenth-century Russian upper-class family, but her mother maintained the dominant cultural tradition. Despite her mother's persistent pressures to do women's work and act like a girl, Durova resists by riding her horse at breakneck speeds, stealing away during the night to enjoy the forest, planning her life of freedom while sewing under her mother's supervision, and eventually running away to become a soldier. In the end, Durova joins the Russian army and enjoys a successful military career. Durova rejects the model of femininity that she was taught in the privacy of her childhood home for a public career in the imperial military.

Mothers, fathers, grandparents, and others who comfort resisters, who urge resistance, or who forbid resistance, are all part of a complex pattern of family interactions that not only shape family dynamics but also influence the larger world of community, nation, and globe. Itka Frajman Zygmuntowicz carried the lessons learned from her mother and grandmother to Auschwitz and beyond. Her story gives us a glimpse of the enduring impact of lessons that interweave the personal with the political. Itka's mother shared with her the world of books, the possibility that "when you learn to read . . . you will see the whole world, and you will travel through the ages." Itka Zygmuntowicz's grandmother emphasized the importance of *menschlekhkeit,* a word Itka understands in English as "acting humanely." A survivor of the Holocaust and the only member of her family to leave Auschwitz, she reflects on the ways her family taught her to see the world and to live in it successfully. She distinguishes between hurting someone and defending herself, a childhood idea that was central to her ability to survive the concentration camp and continue to pass on the strategies that enable survival. Thus, learning that to be female also includes learning to be political is yet another model of childhood socialization that some women experience. This model underscores the inaccuracy of thinking that private life can be severed from communal life. For Itka Zygmuntowicz, as for others in this section, resistance to gendered norms is more than disagreement with the treatment girls receive at the hands of their culture. Resistance as a girl or a woman creates a vantage point from which to view the whole socio-political system and to act against its parts and its totality.

The lessons girls acquire in childhood from their natal families are but one set of tools for learning and enacting resistance. Other lessons are learned through friendship, through work, through marriage, and through political activities. In the previous sections, we looked at women's defiance in the domains of religion, work, education, and cultural creation. Here we want to focus on a group of selections that explores how, at various points in their lives, women support one another in resistance throughout these domains. We certainly would not argue that women are always supportive of one another. But we would argue that the support of other women has often been a core ingredient in the ability of women to change their circumstances and emerge from oppressive situations into more favorable ones.

WOMEN SUPPORTING WOMEN

Many women appear to derive their strength from their association with other women. These selections highlight the role that these relationships play in supporting women's resistance to prevailing authority systems. The first of these comes from a young girl in nineteenth-century Nigeria. Baba told her life story to anthropologist Mary Smith in the early 1950s, and we have included two selections from this account. In the first, Baba recounts how young girls practiced trading together; in the second, she explains a custom followed by local women to discover if their marriages are going well. In both selections, the reliance of women on one another is the primary theme. For these African women, agency in many areas of life comes from solidarity with other women at the communal level. Solidarity does not preclude competition, as the second excerpt suggests. But it does mean that these women have mechanisms in their daily lives for drawing on the help of other women and for gaining some degree of control over the authority of their predominantly male culture.

The diary of Nannie Stillwell Jackson, written in 1890 in rural Arkansas, further illustrates women's support of one another. She describes her neighborly interactions with her friend Fanny and tells us, in no uncertain terms, that she defies her husband's attempts to limit her contact with—and presumably her support from—her friend. Her brief account allows us to imagine the sustaining exchanges between these two women, covertly resisting male family authority while complying with female domestic responsibilities. Their words of reflection are few; their activities rich in meanings.

Women's support of one another extends beyond the family into economic realms as well. We are not suggesting that there is some essential connective tendency that women feel to reach out to others. Rather, we want to illustrate that some women's lives are characterized by these connections and that, when present, they appear to be a critical factor in sustaining resistance to authority systems oppressive to women. This appears to be the case when we are talking about collective actions and when we are looking at the claims individual women make on behalf of other women. Selections from the Canton area of China and from medieval Germany illustrate this point. The women of the Canton Delta made important economic contributions to their community and were able to build on that economic relationship to alter other relationships in their lives. One of their strategies was to avoid marriage by banding together and buying themselves out of it. How we interpret their activities—whether they were challenging the status quo or simply falling in line with current practices—remains a point of debate. Nevertheless, their action suggests the benefits of economic solidarity among women. The modern global economy, which divides both the steps in production and the sites of managerial control, appears to offer fewer opportunities for resistance.

Six centuries earlier, an elite woman, Hildegard of Bingen, the influential abbess of a German convent, analyzed the systematic links among limited economic prospects, lack of political voice, and cultural restrictions on women's abilities. In the medieval Catholic church where economics and politics were closely fused, her efforts to exercise control on behalf of her community met obstacles. Hildegard's rejection of orders she considers unjust requires her to examine how the system in which she operates controls women. Whether one is looking at women's collective action or at the leadership of a single woman, these two selections suggest how multiple restrictions intertwine and influence women as a group.

Yet another perspective on women who resist authority comes from an account written by Bee Miles, an Australian woman confined for much of her life to mental asylums. As Miles moves in and out of institutions, and as her own capacity for socially acceptable behavior waxes and wanes, she records her interpretations of what she sees. Simultaneously blessed and cursed with a special angle of vision, Miles reminds us of the long history of defining women's social deviance as mental illness, often treated by confining them to controlled spaces within a society. How does a given society define what actions are beyond cultural sanction? What kinds of people are most frequently categorized in that way? In each instance, what is the difference between "being crazy" and "resisting"? What resources do resisters need to move the system toward change rather than be moved, themselves, to society's margins? Is any woman who bucks the normative standards of her time and culture a resister? Miles' commentary on her wanderings reinforces for us the many questions raised by the other narratives appearing here.

ENACTING RESISTANCE WITHIN MARRIAGE

Although the nature of marriage itself and the place of marriage in the larger socio-political system have varied enormously over time and across cultures, women's resistance to the confining nature of some marriages is a continuing theme in women's writings. The resistance is difficult and complex. By challenging prevailing norms of marriage, women face reformulating (and sometimes severing) the relationships with the people to whom they are most closely bound (parents, spouses, family, friends, lovers), and reconfiguring the ways in which they represent themselves, and are supported, outside the family. In the next set of selections, we examine some of the ways in which women have resisted marriage—by refusing to participate in it, by reformulating its boundaries, by looking for alternatives to it. The critical stance women develop toward marriage, whether acted upon or not, represents an important site of resistance in their adult lives. Their success in challenging their marital circumstances is tied, as are other forms of resistance, not only to what they have learned about resistance but also to their individual circumstances; their class positions; and their access to resources, political rights, and the support of women closest to them.

The fifth-century record of Olympias in Constantinople demonstrates one version of resistance to marriage. She marries young, yet her husband dies before the marriage is consummated. The emperor pressures her to marry again, claiming that she is spending her fortune wildly and needs a man's control. She argues back that fate would not have taken her husband so young if she had been meant to marry again. Eventually, she chooses to give all her money to the church rather than submit to a man's control. This act of public resistance satisfies the authorities and she acquires the personal space she demanded. While the resources under her control enable her to choose a form of resistance to marriage open to only a very few women, her story reminds us of the power that economic control wields over personal choices.

Olympias resisted marriage by avoiding it. Héloïse in twelfth-century France was in fact pressured to marry and then, for a variety of reasons, lived apart from her husband Abelard. In the letter to him reprinted here, she argues against marriage as an institution. Throughout her life, Héloïse maintained that sexual love outside marriage was no more immoral than marriage for the sake of stability and financial support. She resisted the idea that the category of wife was superior to that of whore. She acknowledged the fact that marriages of her time were arrangements between families based on finances and politics and asked why that basis for marriage was superior to arrangements based on desire. Her position called into question the cultural conventions of the day on the most intimate of matters, sex, love and marriage, by drawing on classical traditions that she believed were a more reasonable basis for relationships. Acting on her ideas at a time far removed from our own, Héloïse stands as an intriguing foremother for contemporary readers as she questions how the institution of marriage intersects with sexuality and desire.

Refusing heterosexual marriage is clearly one avenue of resistance that women have pursued over time. For women who remain within marriages that restrict them, the development of a critical stance toward that relationship is another form of resistance. Ning Lao T'ai-T'ai is a nineteenth-century woman in China forced to live within the boundaries of marriage. In her account, she tells of the mistreatment her sister suffers at the hands of her husband's family, which she resists by going "crazy" and walking out the gate of the city. Withdrawing from society through acts deemed unacceptable was perhaps the only way in her region of nineteenth-century China to escape the conditions of marriage and the familial and cultural nexus in which it was situated. Understanding that living outside marriage was not possible in her society, Ning Lao T'ai-T'ai turned to the model of her sister's resistance as the keystone for her own critical stance. Her ability to see how marriage worked to confine her arose not only from her own experiences, but from her analysis of the experiences of others.

One picture of how middle-class American marriage is practiced comes from the diaries of Ruby Thompson. Written over a period of forty years, from the turn of the last century until 1936, Ruby juxtaposes her needs and desires with her experience of marriage. While she never contemplates living outside marriage—an option to which she was legally entitled as Ning Lao T'ai-T'ai was not—she also sees no happy solution for women living inside marriages like hers. Through her diaries, Ruby provides a painful yet brilliant portrait of what constrains her, how she resists those constraints, and her daily attempts to change the dynamics of her marriage to find a personal escape from its hollowness. Alternatives to marriage seem beyond Ruby's grasp despite the struggles she experiences within it; she pours her analyses into her diaries, the site of her resistance and independence.

Other women imagine still other possibilities to marriage as it is practiced in their cultures. Susan B. Anthony, a key leader in the women's suffrage movement in the United States, imagined how men might change in order that marriage might change. A life-long single woman, Anthony paid a great deal of attention to the situation of married women, believing women would only achieve their political goals if they altered the condition of marriage as it was practiced in middle-class nineteenth-century America. She wrote a number of pieces on the ideal man, two of which we include here. The idea that men must change if women are to have the changes that they seek is a constant theme in many women's writings. Another Quaker feminist, Elizabeth Watson, commented a hundred years later on her personal experience with this issue:

> Though I believe deeply in women's liberation, I cannot put men down or join in consciousness-raising activities that foster hatred of everything masculine. I have loved the men in my life too deeply for that kind of betrayal. As women gain rights and become whole human beings, men too can grow into wholeness, no longer having to carry the whole burden of responsibility for running the affairs of humankind, but in humility accepting the vast resources, as yet not very drawn on, and the wisdom of women in solving the colossal problems of the world. (qtd. in *Faith and Practice* 34)

Anthony's excerpts reinforce a theme present throughout these selections: resistance must be understood as an internal activity (of men as well as of women) as well as a call for social change.

Imagining alternatives to marriage itself is one of the ways some women have resisted, albeit usually against cultural standards that stymie them at every turn. The eloquent plea of a contemporary Chinese woman for the fair treatment of single women is a case in point. She does not argue against heterosexual marriage; nor does she embrace sexual relationships with other women. Rather, she demands justice for single women. She resists the idea of marriage as normative by arguing for the right of women to choose not to marry, insisting that the tradition of marriage is itself not a natural state for women. In her defense of the single state, she clearly identifies how public policy—reinforced by cultural norms—shapes ideas about appropriate marriage and family relationships.

The selections presented thus far show how much women learn in childhood about what to expect as adults. They suggest that many women learn even more about gender boundaries, their possibilities and their prohibitions, as they struggle with the cultural norms of heterosexual marriage. Support as well as isolation are consistent themes. As women become friends, neighbors, workers, wives, and leaders, many of them undergo key personal transitions as they struggle with socio-political expectations of what women should be and do. Some women turn to politics—to direct confrontation with oppressive authority systems—to enact resistance, sometimes with each others' support, sometimes on behalf of themselves, often on behalf of others.

POLITICAL INSTITUTIONS AS SITES FOR RESISTANCE

The next five selections look at women who are resisting political constraints. The demand for a voice in communal affairs is ancient. Hortensia's speech to the Roman authorities is an early and stirring example of the argument that women's property should not be taxed when women have no say in how those funds are to be spent. Some 2,000 years later, Kusunose Kita makes a similar argument in nineteenth-century Japan. There are, she says, double standards for men and women over taxation, a voice in government, and property matters—and there should not be. Her demands that government attend to women's needs are echoed a century later by a recent member of the Tokyo Metropolitan Assembly, Mitsui Mariko. Referring to a list of women's concerns that had grown over the past one hundred years, Mitsui calls herself an "avowed feminist assemblywoman" and argues for the importance of seeing the connections between what governments encourage or allow and what happens to women who are under the authority of those governments.

Women's resistance to being shut out of political affairs does not stop with protests about taxes, voting, and public policy. We are familiar today with demands that women be allowed to take on all the obligations of citizenship, including military service (even for those who oppose the military endeavors of a government). Théroigne de Méricourt, a revolutionary feminist who was active at the end of the eighteenth century in France, speaks on behalf of women's right to bear arms. For her, the idea of citizenship is grounded in ideas of military power and she urges that women resist their exclusion from this domain as well. The four women mentioned above urge governments to be responsible and inclusive. Our fifth author, Amada Pineda, demands that they stop being repressive. A Nicaraguan revolutionary, born in the 1940s, she tells the horrors of her political struggles under a repressive regime that makes women's bodies the site of terrorism. As in the case of many other revolutionaries, her political resistance is bound up with resistance to oppressive gender arrangements.

LAW, SEXUALITY, AND RESISTANCE

The foregoing selections have emphasized how women learn to resist and how they enact that resistance in different settings. The women whose excerpts we present next turn explicitly to law and demand that legal institutions hear women's voices. For these advocates, the boundaries between women's needs and public activities are not spaces of separation but sites of fusion: in their opinion, only by seeing how gender and power operate together within legal institutions can social change happen. These selections address one of the most fundamental issues for women, the fusion of sexuality, female bodies and social justice—a fusion women have most frequently had little power to construct or modify.

Our first selection is from Ida B. Wells, a journalist and activist who argues that the lynching of African Americans grew out of systemic racism rather than the misdeeds of individuals. Wells illustrates how some women have turned to the law to redress wrongs. She argues that the very same political, economic, cultural system that allowed the lynching of African Americans must reform itself and stop the practice. Her argument in this selection exemplifies two themes we have found repeatedly in the writings of many women. The first is how some women have worked within a system of law and politics while resisting parts of that authority system. A second theme is the connection between a specific social or cultural practice, in this case, the lynching of African Americans, and the larger socio-political system with its controlling ideas about gender, sexuality, morality, and political rights. For Wells, as for other reformers, her particular cause is one instance in a larger and complex repressive system. And while she demands change for one cause, she also demands social change on multiple fronts.

The next three selections all deal directly with the self-determination of women's bodies. They argue that what appears to be private individual behavior can only be altered by confronting and changing public policy and the law. Harriet Martineau, Margaret Sanger, and Angela Davis each examine different aspects of this crucial issue. For Martineau, it is wife beating; for Sanger, it is access to birth control; for Davis, it is reproductive rights. In addressing each of these forms of control over women's bodies, these women share common approaches. Like Wells, all see the issues as manifestations of a larger socio-political context. For them, the issues are not examples of random and individualized violence against women. Rather, their issues represent systematic means by which authority systems subordinate women on the basis of race, gender, class, age, caste, sexual orientation, religion, ethnicity, and many other such factors. Locating women's first-hand accounts of such violence prior to the mid-nineteenth century has proved difficult. Naming the violence done to them and sharing that knowledge in any form is, in and of itself, an act of resistance that rarely makes its way into public discourse. While the diary entries of Abigail Abbot Bailey gave an individual account of living with an abusive husband (included in the section **Representing Women**), these three writers record the widespread violence against women in its multiple forms.

Our first selection in this cluster is an essay by Harriet Martineau. Writing as a British journalist traveling in the U. S. during the nineteenth century, she is considered one of the founders of modern sociology. She wrote extensively about her observations and described the methods by which one might make accurate observations. Here she discusses the violence she sees women experience as a result of the rampant alcoholism of their husbands. In her analysis of drinking and domestic violence, she works toward an explanation that links individual behaviors, civil and religious laws, and cultural standards about marital expectations. She describes what she believes can be done by government and church authorities to alleviate some of the misery women suffer at the hands of abusive husbands.

Margaret Sanger's two selections give us yet another picture of the ways in which women have resisted control of their bodies. Sanger's first selection describes the situations she encountered as a nurse among poor women who wished to prevent future pregnancies. She goes on to record what contemporary feminists have called a "click," that moment when understanding what she is observing and what she can do about it came to her. The second selection is from an essay that analyzes what the availability of birth control meant in a broader socio-economic context. Sanger's combination of first-hand description and social analysis gave the many immigrant and working-class women of her era a way to think about fertility as well as find practical help. For us, Wells, Martineau, and Sanger reinforce our understanding that first-hand experience with an issue, when combined with an analysis of the power relations inherent in that experience, constitutes compelling evidence for the linkages between women's individual experiences of sexuality and the sociocultural system's control of that sexuality.

Angela Davis's essay concludes this cluster. The excerpt begins with Davis's taking issue with the way in which the birth control movement lost its initial radical edge and was used as a weapon in the arsenal of racism. Davis emphasizes the importance for women of control of their bodies and credits the birth control movement with being a critical step in that process. Yet, as she looks at the current situation, she questions its directions and links the early efforts at birth control with the contemporary practices of involuntary sterilization. She builds on the concept that women's desire to sexually experience their bodies directly confronts cultural mandates that women experience their bodies devoid of agency, exclusively as mothers or as objects of men's desire. Davis, like Wells, Martineau, and Sanger, calls on the state for remedies for excesses, at the same time that she understands the state to be one of the sources of those excesses. For these authors, legal systems, political systems, cultural systems all work together, both as the source of control over women's bodies and as the site where women press their demands for change in the conditions of their lives.

CONCLUSION

The section concludes with an exchange of letters written late in the lives of two leaders of the U.S. suffrage movement in the nineteenth century. They reflect on what they have done over the past forty years and how they could not have done it alone. In simple and friendly banter, they illustrate a major theme: agency and resistance, learned and sustained over a lifetime, are gained and enacted more successfully when like-minded women and men act together rather than in isolation.

Strategies for social change lie at the heart of all twenty-five selections in this section. Are there general lessons to be drawn from these women who translated their individual observations into social questions? How did they acquire knowledge of the processes? How did they sustain themselves while doing so? How would they judge their successes? Clearly we cannot ask them. Nor could they offer complete and satisfactory answers to contemporary problems. Yet reading across their accounts of how they learned and enacted resistance, certain ideas appear consistently. Women's confrontations with oppressive authority systems can be carried out even in isolation and still be effective in bringing about certain changes. Whether these changes alter the whole system or only the circumstances of the individuals involved remains open to question. What these women's voices seem clearly to suggest is that confrontations made collectively, whether by groups of women or on behalf of groups of women, are likely to be longer lasting and to have wider impact on the socio-cultural system as well as the individual resisters. Successful resistance to oppressive authority systems appears to stem from some combination of childhood socialization, life-long learning, sustained support, collective activity, and an understanding of the system being confronted.

WORK CONSULTED

North Pacific Yearly Meeting of the Religious Society of Friends. *Faith and Practice.* 1986.

HUDA SHAARAWI *(1879–1947)*

"He Is the Only Boy"

In this excerpt from her childhood memoirs, Huda Shaarawi recounts her fundamental discontent with the gendered conditions of her life from a vantage point much akin to that taken by Nadezhda Durova (see excerpt in this section): they are women near the ends of their lives, able to reflect upon their passionate resistance and relative triumphs. For both of these women, the preservation of their struggles through the act of writing serves as a final and immutable act of resistance.

Shaarawi's family allegiance was complicated by the divisive tensions associated with her parents' contrasting ethnic heritages and social positions. Her resistance to her culture's privileging of males resulted in an ironic idealization of the memory of her father, a wealthy Egyptian noble who died when Huda was five, and a rejection of her mother, whose way of life reinforced the very cultural values Shaarawi despised.[1] Shaarawi, however, was able to form instrumental relationships with older women that functioned not only as sources of support but enabled her to voice troubling questions and to examine in a secure environment the circumstances of her life. Relationships with the first wife in her father's harem—and later with Eugénie Le Brun, a European woman who held the first *salon* for women in Egypt—informed the direction Shaarawi's life would take.

Much of Shaarawi's memoir's describes the first decades of her life—part of which was spent in a harem—prior to her turn to feminist activism in the early twentieth century. The circumstances of Shaarawi's birth into an aristocratic Egyptian family afforded certain privileges and restrictions particular to that class. As women's social status increased in Egypt, their social freedoms decreased. Veiling in Egypt was not universal and had a complex connection to religious beliefs: women were subjected to the veiling system based on social status.[2] Upper-class Jewish, Christian, and Muslim women were all subjected to veiling and seclusion as a means to ensure their sexual purity and maintain family honor.[3] As a child Huda was educated by private tutors alongside her brother, receiving an unusually broad education and learning several languages including Arabic, French, Turkish, and Persian; she was also trained in poetry, calligraphy, painting, and music. It is unlikely that Shaarawi could have attained the same access to the international feminist community that critically influenced her accomplishments in Egypt if she had not been raised in the harem of an aristocrat.

Huda Shaarawi became one of the leading figures in early twentieth-century Egyptian feminism, a revolutionary who developed public lectures for women and established the country's first women's philanthropic society for poor women and children. She served as the leader of the Feminist Union, the first organization of its kind in the Arab world. Awarded the highest decoration by the senate for services rendered to her country, Huda fought for a minimum marriage age, family reform law, restriction of polygamy, education for girls, and Egyptian independence. Nevertheless, when Egypt gained independence in 1922, its constitution denied women the right to vote.

The climactic moment in Huda Shaarawi's political career occurred in March, 1923 when she returned from an international conference of women in Rome. Causing a national scandal, Shaarawi dramatically cast off her veil in a Cairo train station in front of a crowd of women. Shaarawi understood the veiling system's function as a mechanism of political and sexual oppression of women. To a considerable extent, Huda Shaarawi's achievements in feminist reform represent a step in the progressive efforts and partial defeats of countless women spanning cultures, continents, and centuries. It is only fitting, then, that her unveiling followed her return from the International Conference of Women in Rome. Huda Shaarawi returned to Cairo that day on a ship propelled by many hands joined across oceans and mountains and time.

JS

FROM *HAREM YEARS* [§]

I loved *Umm Kabira*[4] immensely, and she returned that love and showed compassion toward me. She, alone, talked frankly with me on a number of matters . . . She knew how I felt when people favoured my brother over me because he was a boy. . . .

The affection my mother showed me often intensified my agonies because her solicitude, I fancied, was merely an effort to cajole me. If my mother saw me growing jealous while she played with my brother she would hasten with him to my side. At such a moment, I feared I was coming between them, and my anguish would redouble. Yet, it was, indeed, kindness and love that inspired her.

I used to imagine that I was not my mother's daughter—that my real mother was a slave girl who had died, and the truth was being withheld from me. Firmly convinced of this, I suffered all the more. I could keep everything suppressed until nightfall but as soon as I laid my head on the pillow, I was overcome by anxieties and frightening thoughts moved me to tears. This inner turbulence provoked nightmares that woke me in terror, with heart beating so hard I feared it would escape from my chest. I dreamed often that huge beasts were pouncing on me, baring their fangs in my face, and that when I sought refuge with my mother I would find that she had taken my brother in her arms and turned her back on me. 'I am not your child!' I would scream, 'You have lied to me! Tell me the truth! I am not your child! I am not your child!'

Childhood perplexities and self-inflicted torments increased my need for warm affection and swelled my love for the father I had barely known. If he were still alive, I knew, he would not withhold his comfort. . . .

In these states of agitation I sometimes confessed my sufferings to *Umm Kabira* and she consoled me. . . . I once asked *Umm Kabira* why everyone paid more attention to my brother than to me. 'Haven't you understood yet?' she asked gently. When I claimed that

---

[§] Reprinted by permission of The Feminist Press at The City University of New York, from *Harem Years: The Memoirs of an Egyptian Feminist,* by Huda Shaarawi, translated and introduced by Margot Badran. Translation copyright © 1986 by Margot Badran. Material excerpted from pages 34–37.

as the elder I should receive more attention she replied, 'But you are a girl and he is a boy. And you are not the only girl, while he is the only boy. One day the support of the family will fall upon him. When you marry you will leave the house and honour your husband's name but he will perpetuate the name of his father and take over his house.' This straightforward answer satisfied me. I began to love my brother all the more because he would occupy the place of my father.

Soon, however, my uneasiness returned. I repeated my question once again, this time to my mother, who said, 'Your brother has a weak constitution and, as he is the only boy, naturally, everyone is solicitous of him. You are in good health and so people do not have the same concern over you.' Although her words restored my tranquillity, I was also saddened because I saw that my anxieties upset her.

I then hoped to become sick in order to claim equal attention from her. It happened that an illness was circulating and so I was delighted to be the first in the house to come down with it. Unaccustomed to seeing me ailing, my mother grew concerned and immediately called the family doctor, Alwi Pasha. At the end of the examination, I remember, he took out a piece of white paper, shaped it into a cone and poured alum powder into it which he blew into my throat. He also prescribed a mineral purgative. That whole night my head burned with fever.

A few days later, when my brother fell ill, the entire household was plunged into turmoil. Doctors entered our room in groups. One by one they examined my brother, afterwards leaving without so much as a glance at me even though my bed was next to his. That upset me profoundly. Until then I had been responding to the treatment but I suddenly began to take a turn for the worse. Although I was seized by fits of trembling which caused the fever to rise, no one appeared concerned. When my condition continued to grow worse, Alwi Pasha was sent for a second time but did not arrive until a day later, when he appeared in the company of the doctors returning to visit my brother. He stayed with them while they examined my brother, conferring about his further treatment, only looking at me as he made his way to the door. I nearly fainted from distress. My convalescence persisted until my brother was out of bed. I began to prefer death to my miserable lot.

After that I withdrew into myself and resented those around me. I began to spend the afternoons in the garden amid the fruit and flower trees, and the birds, fish, and pet animals. I preferred the companionship of these creatures to the company of humans who injured my self-esteem. I grew attached to a gazelle that followed me everywhere. It would climb to our room on the top floor, come over to my bed, and put its head on my pillow to rouse me with its sweet whine before proceeding to my brother's bed. If I was sick, however, it would remain loyally at my side like a cat or dog. This affection consoled me very much. I loved animals and believed they instinctively sensed my condition. . . .

NOTES

[1] Shaarawi's mother, while not a slave herself, was a Circassian, a people from a region between the Black and Caspian Seas whose women were known for their legendary beauty and frequently sold as slaves to Egyptian men to become prized wives and concubines.

[2] The requirement to remain veiled did not follow Egyptian women outside the confines of Egypt: wealthy Egyptian women commonly traveled unveiled throughout Europe with their families, donning their veils only upon their return to Egypt.

[3] See headnote introducing Binodini Dasi (in **Work and Education**) for an historical account of veiling as a system of control over women's sexuality.

[4] Literally, "Big Mother"—the first wife of her deceased father's harem. [Eds.]

WORK CONSULTED

Shaarawi, Huda. *Harem Years: The Memoirs of an Egyptian Feminist (1879–1924)*. Trans. and ed. Margot Badran. New York: Feminist Press at CUNY, 1986.

CORNELIA *(1844–?)*

"My Mother Was the Smartest Black Woman in Eden"

In this narrative by the ex-slave Cornelia, what becomes most evident is the ethic of survival that characterized her mother's life actions. There is much evidence in this narrative—as there is in recordings of slavery—of the Blackwoman as "de mule uh de world" (Hurston 14). Sojourner Truth's claim that she could do as much work as a man and eat as much when given a chance, which is echoed when Cornelia remembers that Master Jennings said that her mother "has her faults, but she can outwork any nigger in the country," reflects the strongly gendered nature of racism and in particular of the slave experience. In some ways, Blackwomen in slavery were treated "like men," and expected to do just as much and work just as hard (in contrast to their white female mistresses). Still, their positioning as Black*women* meant, at the very least, that they were subject to rape, and were used to bear children in order to perpetuate slavery.

The terms "Blackwoman" and "Blackwomen" are intended here to indicate a particular location of experience that is collective and individual, with the hope that these terms may best characterize how interconnected gender and race oppression are for a Black woman and for Black women in America without essentializing their experiences.[1] Even when race seems to be the overlying matrix, the experiences Blackwomen have take on particular constructions to account for gender; likewise, even when gender seems to be the overlying matrix, their experiences take on particular constructions to account for race. Deborah Gray White says, "the black woman's position at the nexus of America's sex and race mythology has made it most difficult for her to escape the mythology. . . If she is rescued from the myth of the Negro, the myth of woman traps her. If she escapes the myth of woman, the myth of the Negro still ensnares her. Since the myth of woman and the myth of the Negro are so similar, to extract her from one gives the appearance of freeing her from both" (28). Similarly, Patricia Hill Collins and Paula Giddings both talk about the space left in between constructions of race and constructions of gender—or, said differently, between Afrocentric thought and feminist thought. This space is part of the world that Blackwomen inhabit. The Combahee River Collective further elucidates the difficulty of privileging any one location of social identity with their observation that the Blackwomen who were raped during American slavery were not raped as a condition of being women or as a condition of being Black—they were raped as a condition of being both Black and women (275).

In the context of socially defined notions of American womanhood which were employed in everyday life in widespread ways long before the nineteenth century, Blackwomen were seen as crazy, dishonest and conniving, licentious, sexually charged, and nurturing. So it is Cornelia's claim early in her narrative that "my mother was the *smartest* Black woman in Eden" (emphasis added) that is striking, for it connects this Blackwoman's ethic of survival with ideas of will, intellect, reason, care, and love—concepts that were not usually linked with Blackwomen and their actions. Cornelia's mother's assertion that she would kill her own child, an assertion made with "tears streaming down her face," not only evokes the experience of the character Sethe in Toni Morrison's novel *Beloved* (1987), but also that of the biblical King Solomon. It is clear that this is an act of enormous love, which is how Sethe's actions are often gendered and characterized. But the act is also both one of wisdom and resistance (Solomon) and one of resistance and rage, a "killing rage," to use bell hooks' term (13), that comes from great love and a passion for justice. The idea of a Blackwoman's calculated response to oppression—her acts of resistance—is further evidenced when Cornelia's mother states that "[I] had brought five children in the world for the Jennings, and that was enough . . . I don't intend to work when [I feel] bad" as well as in her words to her daughter to "fight and if you can't fight, kick; if you can't kick then bite."

Such statements remind readers that this woman was not crazy. She was making and living life as a Blackwoman in slavery, which for her meant asserting her will and demanding the right to love not only her children but herself enough to resist and refuse when and how she could. According to Deborah Gray White, ". . . slave resistance often manifested itself in intransigent behavior. If resistance . . . was seldom politically oriented, consciously collective, or violently revolutionary, it was generally individualistic and aimed at maintaining what the slaves . . . perceived as an acceptable level of work, shelter, food, punishment, and free time" (76). White explains that while the idea of overthrowing the system was there, slave women and men understood that the odds were against them and used moments of resistance to make the system of bondage as livable as possible (77). Additionally, the Blackwoman had to be crafty in her resistance efforts (feigning illness, using poison) because she often had less access to information necessary for successful escape in comparison with Black men (White 76).

What is most triumphant about the story Cornelia tells is not only its evidence of the passing of a Blackwoman-centered survival ethic from mother to daughter, but the resonance of that tradition with other well-known stories of the triumph of the spirit of Blackwomen in and since slavery. It is these women whose survival ethics form the foundation of the Blackwoman's liberation tradition, these ordinary women and their extraordinary ways.

KQ

FROM AN INTERVIEW WITH CORNELIA, CONDUCTED BY A FISK UNIVERSITY SOCIOLOGIST (C. 1929)[§]

My mother was the smartest black woman in Eden. She was as quick as a flash of lightning, and whatever she did could not be done better. She could do anything. She cooked, washed, ironed, spun, nursed and labored in the field. She made as good a field hand as she

[§] Reprinted from *Black Women in Nineteenth-Century American Life: Their Words, Their Thoughts, Their Feelings,* edited by Bert Lowenberg and Ruth Bogin. University Park: The Pennsylvania State University Press, 1976. Copyright © 1976 by The Pennsylvania State University Press. Reproduced by permission of the publisher. Material excerpted from pages 49–52.

did a cook. I have heard Master Jennings say to his wife, "Fannie has her faults, but she can outwork any nigger in the country. I'd bet my life on that."

My mother certainly had her faults as a slave. She was very different in nature from Aunt Caroline. Ma fussed, fought, and kicked all the time. I tell you, she was a demon. She said that she wouldn't be whipped, and when she fussed, all Eden must have known it. She was loud and boisterous, and it seemed to me that you could hear her a mile away. Father was often the prey of her high temper. With all her ability for work, she did not make a good slave. She was too high-spirited and independent. I tell you, she was a captain.

The one doctrine of my mother's teaching which was branded upon my senses was that I should never let anyone abuse me. "I'll kill you, gal, if you don't stand up for yourself," she would say. "Fight, and if you can't fight, kick; if you can't kick, then bite." Ma was generally willing to work, but if she didn't feel like doing something, none could make her do it. At least, the Jennings couldn't make, or didn't make her . . .

One day my mother's temper ran wild. For some reason Mistress Jennings struck her with a stick. Ma struck back and a fight followed. Mr. Jennings was not at home and the children became frightened, and ran upstairs. For half hour they wrestled in the kitchen. Mistress, seeing that she could not get the better of Ma, ran out in the road, with ma right on her heels. In the road, my mother flew into her again. The thought seemed to race across my mother's mind to tear mistress' clothing off her body. She suddenly began to tear Mistress Jennings' clothes off. She caught hold, pulled, ripped and tore. Poor mistress was nearly naked when the store keeper got to them and pulled ma off.

"Why, Fannie, what do you mean by that?" he asked.

"Why, I'll kill her, I'll kill her dead if she ever strikes me again."

I have never been able to find out the why of the whole thing. My mother was in a rage for two days, and when pa asked her about it and told her that she shouldn't have done it, it was all that Aunt Caroline could do to keep her from giving him the same dose of medicine.

"No explaining necessary. You are chicken-livered, and you couldn't understand." This was all ma would say about it.

Pa heard Mr. Jennings say that Fannie would have to be whipped by law. He told ma. Two mornings afterwards, two men came in at the big gate, one with a long lash in his hand. I was in the yard and I hoped they couldn't find ma. To my surprise, I saw her running around the house, straight in the direction of the men. She must have seen them coming. I should have known that she wouldn't hide. She knew what they were coming for, and she intended to meet them halfway. She swooped upon them like a hawk on chickens. I believe they were afraid of her or thought she was crazy. One man had a long beard which she grabbed with one hand, and the lash with the other. Her body was made strong with madness. She was a good match for them. Mr. Jennings came and pulled her away. I don't know what would have happened if he hadn't come at that moment, for one man had already pulled his gun out. Ma did not see the gun until Mr. Jennings came up. On catching sight of it, she said, "Use your gun, use it and blow my brains out if you will."

Master sent her to the cabin and he talked with the man for a long time. I had watched the whole scene with hands calmly clasped in front of me. I felt no urge to do anything but look on.

That evening Mistress Jennings came down to the cabin. She stopped at the door and called my mother. Ma came out.

"Well, Fannie," she said, "I'll have to send you away. You won't be whipped, and I'm afraid you'll get killed. They have to knock you down like a beef."

"I'll go to hell or anywhere else, but I won't be whipped," ma answered.

"You can't take the baby, Fannie, Aunt Mary can keep it with the other children."

Mother said nothing at this. That night, ma and pa sat up late, talking over things, I guess. Pa loved ma, and I heard him say, "I'm going too, Fannie." About a week later, she called me and told me that she and pa were going to leave me the next day, that they were going to Memphis. She didn't know for how long.

"But don't be abused, Puss." She always called me Puss. My right name was Cornelia. I cannot tell in words the feelings I had at that time. My sorrow knew no bound. My very soul seemed to cry out, "Gone, gone, gone forever." I cried until my eyes looked like balls of fire. I felt for the first time in my life that I had been abused. How cruel it was to take my mother and father from me, I thought. My mother had been right. Slavery was cruel, so very cruel.

Thus my mother and father were hired to Tennessee. The next morning they were to leave. I saw ma working around with the baby under her arms as if it had been a bundle of some kind. Pa came up to the cabin with an old mare for ma to ride, and an old mule for himself. Mr Jennings was with him.

"Fannie, leave the baby with Aunt Mary," said Mr. Jennings very quietly.

At this, ma took the baby by its feet, a foot in each hand, and with the baby's head swinging downward, she vowed to smash its brains out before leaving it. Tears were streaming down her face. It was seldom that ma cried, and everyone knew that she meant every word. Ma took her baby with her. . . .

NOTE

[1] Thus, in this essay Blackwoman is one word, with "Black" modifying and completing "woman" and "woman" modifying and completing "Black," and the one word—a noun—reflecting many locations of experience of oppression and empowerment. I thank Joan Martin ("The Notion of Difference for Emerging Womanist Ethics") and Monique Savage, whose conversations introduced this concept to me.

WORKS CONSULTED

Collins, Patricia Hill. *Black Feminist Thought: Knowledge, Consciousness, and the Politics of Empowerment*. New York: Routledge, 1991.

Combahee River Collective. "The Combahee River Collective Statement." Dated April 1977. *Home Girls: A Black Feminist Anthology*. Ed. Barbara Smith. New York: Kitchen Table: Women of Color Press, 1983.

Giddings, Paula. *When and Where I Enter: The Impact of Black Women on Race and Sex in America.* New York: Morrow, 1984.

hooks, bell. *Killing Rage: Ending Racism.* New York: H. Holt and Co., 1995.

Hurston, Zora Neale. *Their Eyes Were Watching God.* New York: Perennial Library, 1990.

Martin, Joan. "The Notion of Difference for Emerging Womanist Ethics: The Writings of Audre Lorde and bell hooks." *Journal of Feminist Studies in Religion* 9 (1993): 39–52.

Morrison, Toni. *Beloved.* New York: Knopf, 1987.

White, Deborah Gray. *Ar'n't I a Woman?: Female Slaves in the Plantation South.* New York: Norton, 1985.

NADEZHDA "ALEXANDROV" DUROVA *(1783–1866)*

"I Have Taken the Freedom That Is Rightfully Mine"

Nadezhda Durova was born the only child of a Hussar[1] captain, who treated her as a son, and a harsh Ukrainian beauty who found in Nadezhda neither the son she desperately wanted nor the image of a daughter she could accept. In her autobiography, Durova reports being thrown out of a moving carriage as an infant by her frustrated mother, then rescued and cradled in the saddle of her distraught father. These early experiences of rejection and adoration by her respective parents created a dynamic that she understands to have informed the course her life would take.

Beginning in childhood, Durova resisted the culturally sanctioned activities of young women, finding pleasure and freedom in invigorating outdoor activities and mastery of traditionally masculine pursuits, particularly those of a martial nature such as riflery and horsemanship. She maintained an adversarial role with her mother, who enforced acceptable roles for women of her time and station. She idealized her father, whose lifestyle represented a means of escape from these narrowly defined female roles. In an attempt to resist gender barriers Durova ultimately discarded her female attire and assumed a male costume and persona. The irony here is pronounced: can a woman truly resist restrictions of gender imposed by male systems of control by renouncing a female identity and adopting the identity of the oppressor?

Durova's motivations for joining the cavalry appear to have been different from those of other historical military women who were more clearly driven by a sense of nationalistic zeal (see Halidé Edip Adivar in **Representing Women**). Whereas the emerging nation-state served as the site of Durova's resistance, her autobiographical account revels in the freedoms and adventures of cavalry life, less so in notions of patriotism and civic duty. Further complicating the question, Durova's "martial Ardor" and her chosen life as a woman warrior may have represented an expression of her internal war over her own identity. Indeed, scholarly sources document the fact that her account omits her seven years of marriage, including the birth of a son (Zirin 15). Nevertheless, she later insisted that her account contains the full truth of her life (Zirin xix). The fact that she left the cultural constraints of marriage and motherhood at the age of 23, not just her parents' home and role as a daughter at 16, suggests that her resistance was even more multifaceted than this account portrays. At the same time, we are reminded that autobiographical accounts can be profoundly shaped by the ways in which authors choose to remember and represent their experiences.[2]

The notion of a woman warrior disguised as a man was not without precedent in Russian history: in a brilliant act of strategy Catherine the Great won over the allegiance of a disgruntled Russian army by appearing before them in full military costume. Tzar Alexander I must certainly have been familiar with this bit of history when the young soldier Nadezhda Durova was brought before him to determine if she was indeed a woman. Praising her as "an example to Russia," Alexander I gave Durova the pseudonym "Alexandrov," making her his namesake, and granted her a commission.[3] Although she continually struggled to win the respect of her fellow officers because of her boyish appearance, "Alexandrov's" imperially sanctioned male persona was never challenged. She served heroically throughout the Napoleonic wars and became the first woman to receive the St. George Cross. Upon her death she was buried with military honors.

Durova's military career ended when she was called home to become the "staff of her father's old age," a responsibility she readily accepted. She later became one of the first Russian women autobiographers, reflecting on her military experiences in two compilations of diaries and several works of prose fiction. In these accounts, her peculiar position as a outsider in the military afforded her a unique, and perhaps surprisingly, feminist lens with which to examine this institution. Throughout her life, Durova retained her masculine dress and mannerisms in an attempt to preserve her disguise and the possibilities it afforded, even as time and age revealed beneath this veil the countenance of a woman increasingly bent on freedom from gender distinctions altogether.

JS

FROM *THE CAVALRY MAIDEN*[§]

From morning to night I sat over work which, I must confess, was the vilest imaginable because, unlike other girls, I could not, would not, and did not want to acquire the skill, but ripped, ruined, and tangled it until before me lay a canvas ball with a repulsive, snarled strip stretching across it—my bobbin-lace. I sat patiently over it all day, patiently because my plan was prepared and my intentions resolute. At nightfall, when the house quieted down, the doors were locked, and the light in Mama's room went out, I got up, dressed stealthily, sneaked out across the back porch, and ran straight to the stable. There I took Alcides, led him through the garden to the cattleyard, mounted him, and rode out down a narrow lane straight to the riverbank and Startsev mountain. Then I dismounted again and led Alcides uphill, holding him by the halter because I didn't know how to bridle him and had no way of getting him to climb the mountain of his own volition. I led him by the halter across the precipitous slope until I reached a level spot, where I looked for a stump or hillock from which to remount. Then I slapped Alcides' neck and clicked my tongue until the good steed broke into a gallop, a run, and even a breakneck dash.

At the first hint of dawn I returned home, put the horse in the stable, and went to sleep without undressing. This was what led at last to the discovery of my nocturnal excursions. . . .

After this affair my mother wanted without fail to rid herself of my presence at any cost and decided to take me to my old grandmother Aleksandrovicheva in Little Russia. I had entered my fourteenth year by then. I was tall, slim, and shapely, but my martial spirit was

[§] Reprinted by permission of the publisher from *The Cavalry Maiden: Journals of a Russian Officer in the Napoleonic Wars* by Nadezhda Durova. Translated by Mary Fleming Zirin. Copyright © 1988 by Angel books and Indiana University Press. Material excerpted from pages 7–18.

sketched on my features and, although I had white skin, bright rosy cheeks, sparkling eyes, and black brows, every day my mirror and Mama told me that I was very ugly. My face was pitted from smallpox, my features irregular, and Mother's continual repression of my freedom, her strict and at times even cruel treatment of me, had marked my countenance with an expression of fear and sadness. Perhaps I would at last have forgotten all my hussar mannerisms and become an ordinary girl like the rest if my mother had not kept depicting woman's lot in such a dismal way. In my presence she would describe the fate of that sex in the most prejudicial terms: woman, in her opinion, must be born, live, and die in slavery; eternal bondage, painful dependence, and repression of every sort were her destiny from the cradle to the grave; she was full of weaknesses, devoid of accomplishments, and capable of nothing. In short, woman was the most unhappy, worthless, and contemptible creature on earth! This description made my head reel. I resolved, even at the cost of my life, to part company from the sex I thought to be under God's curse. Papa, too, often said, "If I had a son instead of Nadezhda, I shouldn't have to worry about my old age; he would be my staff in the evening of my days." I would be ready to weep at these words from the father I loved so extravagantly. These two contradictory emotions—love for my father and aversion to my own sex—troubled my young soul with equal force. With a resolve and constancy rare in one so young I set about working out a plan to escape the sphere prescribed by nature and custom to the female sex. . . .

At last the decisive time came to act according to the plan as I had worked it out. The Cossacks received the order to move out, and they left on September 15, 1806. Their first full day's halt would be some fifty versts from the city. The seventeenth was my name-day, and the day on which, through fate, coincidence of circumstance, or invincible propensity, it was fixed for me to quit my father's house and take up an entirely new way of life.[4] On September 17, I awoke before dawn and sat by my window to await its appearance; it might well be the last I ever saw in my own land. What awaited me in the turbulent world? Would not my mother's curse and my father's grief pursue me? Would they survive? Could they await the realization of my colossal scheme? How horrible it would be if their death took from me the goal of my actions! These thoughts now clustered and now passed one after another through my head. My heart constricted and tears glistened on my lashes. Just then dawn broke. Its scarlet glow quickly flooded the sky, and its beautiful light, flowing into my room, lit up the objects there: my father's saber, hanging on the wall directly opposite the window, seemed to catch fire. My spirits revived. I took the saber off the wall, unsheathed it, and looked at it, deep in thought. This saber had been my toy when I was still in swaddling-cloths, the comfort and exercise of my adolescent years; why should it not now be my defense and glory in the military sphere? "I will wear you with honor," I said, kissed the blade, and returned it to its scabbard. The sun rose. That day Mama presented me with a gold chain, and Papa, three hundred rubles; even my little brother gave me his gold watch. As I accepted my parents' gifts, I thought sorrowfully that they had no idea that they were outfitting me for a distant and dangerous road. . . .

I ordered Efim to take Alcides by the direct road to Startsev mountain and wait for me at the edge of the forest. I ran hastily to the bank of the Kama and dropped my dressing-gown there, leaving it on the sands with all the trappings of female dress. I was not so barbarous as to intend for my father to think that I had drowned, and I was convinced he would not do so. I only wanted to make it possible for him to answer without confusion any embarrassing questions from our short-witted acquaintances. After leaving the clothing on the bank, I took a goat track which led directly uphill. . . .

Alcides galloped at the same rapid pace for four versts but then, since I had to cover fifty versts that night to reach the hamlet where I knew the Cossack regiment had been assigned to halt, I reined in my steed's quick gallop and went at a walk. Soon I came into a dark pine forest some thirty versts across. Wishing to conserve Alcides' strength, I kept him walking and, surrounded by the deathly hush of the forest and the dark of the autumn night, I became absorbed in my own thoughts: And so I'm at liberty. Free! Independent! I have taken the freedom that is rightfully mine—the freedom that is a precious gift from heaven, the inalienable prerogative of every human being! I have found a new way to take it and guard it from all future claims against it; from now to my grave, it will be my portion and my reward! . . .

NOTES

[1] Borrowed from the Hungarian, the designation "Hussar" referred to a division of Cossacks or light horsemen in the Russian military.

[2] The editors would like to thank Kris Finlon for calling our attention to this issue and contributing to the ideas and information in this headnote.

[3] While it was common practice in Russia during this period to give young girls "pet" names that were identical to those of boys with the same root name (for example, Alexander and Alexandra would both be called "Sasha"), for an adult woman to be given a man's name and permitted to maintain a male identity represented a truly unusual circumstance.

[4] The routine on long marches was two or three days on the road, bivouacking at night, for each full day of rest in a populated settlement. Thus Durova's plan was to reach the site of the Cossacks' September 17th halt before they moved on early the following morning [Zirin].

WORKS CONSULTED

Durova, Nadezhda. *The Cavalry Maiden: Journals of a Russian Officer in the Napoleonic Wars.* Trans. Mary Fleming Zirin. Bloomington: Indiana UP, 1989.

Saunders, David. *The Ukrainian Impact on Russian Culture: 1750–1850.* Edmonton: Canadian Institute of Ukrainian Studies, 1985.

Stanton, Domna C., ed. *The Female Autograph.* Spec. issue of *New York Literary Forum* 12–13 (1984).

Zirin, Mary Fleming. Introduction. *The Cavalry Maiden: Journals of a Russian Officer in the Napoleonic Wars.* By Nadezhda Durova. Trans. Mary Fleming Zirin. Bloomington: Indiana UP, 1989.

ITKA FRAJMAN ZYGMUNTOWICZ *(1926–)*

"Acting Humanely"

Itka Frajman Zygmuntowicz's narrative, told to Sara Horowitz, evidences the power of stories and memories to enable resistance. Recounting these lessons herself, Itka found the resources to live through one of the most horrifying experiences of modern times, the Holocaust. The selections in this anthology document that women have long told their stories, and find in their telling both a way to sustain themselves and a vehicle for passing on their wisdom. Women's narratives, autobiographies, biographies, and memoirs increased dramatically in the 1980s as feminist scholarship concentrated on women's writing, and feminist activists and authors encouraged women to break their silences and write. The 1988 publication of Carolyn Heilbrun's *Writing a Woman's Life* marked a joining of these two efforts. In this popular book, a leading literary critic showed how patriarchal culture determined the stories women were allowed to tell, and Heilbrun urged women to transgress those confining boundaries. Itka tells of her survival against incredible odds. Her story illustrates the power of narrative that Heilbrun advocates: the act of narrating is one of resistance for both teller and listener.

Scholar Sara Horowitz recorded Itka Zygmuntowicz's account, contributing to the small but growing number of women's narratives of the Holocaust. The Holocaust was the genocide that grew out of the policies, events, and experiences initiated by the Nazi government of Germany in the 1930s to eliminate the population they defined as "non-German" (that is, gypsies, political dissidents, gays and lesbians, as well as Jews). At first, plans called for forced emigration and confinement in ghettos; eventually, the edict called for the creation of concentration camps and the systematic murder of these populations. The system spread outside Germany to the territories seized by the Nazis during the course of World War II. Born in Poland, Itka Zygmuntowicz and her family were moved to concentration camps in Germany where only she survived. By the war's end in 1945, some six million Jews had been murdered. When the Allied troops entered the concentration camps after Nazi surrender, they found few survivors. Itka Zygmuntowicz, a young woman of nineteen, was one of them. She was taken by the Swedish Red Cross to their country to rebuild a life, now without family, friends, or country. She eventually moved to the United States where she lives today.

Knowledge of the Holocaust and its impact on morality in the contemporary world were slow to build. The empirical evidence for the concentration camps had been published outside Germany, but the scope of the horrors and the inability (some say unwillingness) of other governments to comprehend the scale of the atrocities resulted in massive ignorance (if not denial) for many years. Because of the torture they had undergone, Holocaust survivors were often rendered unable to tell of their experiences. War crimes trials had been held at the end of the war, but it was not until Adolf Eichmann was tried in 1961 that the world began to come to terms with what the Holocaust had been and continued to mean in the lives of its survivors, their descendants, and the world at large. Holocaust scholarship grew as scholars tried to reconstruct and thereby explain a phenomenon difficult even to comprehend in its totality. The children of survivors were determined to know what had happened to their forebears. They fueled the effort to collect life histories, to document events, to publish fictional accounts, and to set up international agencies to trace concentration camp victims. The material poured forth (Berger 1–15).

As Heinemann points out, most of the stories came from male survivors. While their accounts cover the same events as those of female survivors, the themes in women's narratives differ. Heinemann describes a focus on sexuality and fertility as distinctive means of torture for women (1–38). Horowitz claims:

> women remember differently—or they remember different things. In videotaped testimony, for example, many women survivors relate their final conversations with the mother who perished. In Itka's testimony, as in the tapes of other women, her mother's words give Itka permission to survive and rebuild her life. The mother's words contain a moral imperative as well, both collective and personal. On the collective level, the daughter is enjoined to tell the story of the victims who cannot speak for themselves. On the personal level, the daughter is urged to retain her self—neither to imitate the Nazis nor to absorb the image they project of her. (206)

Mothers and grandmothers are primary influences in teaching strategies of resistance. Itka Zygmuntowicz's memories were nurtured initially within the family circle and contained within them a commitment to the larger community. She recalls the explicit lesson of *menschlekhkeit,* an idea she translates as "acting humanely," as the cornerstone of her philosophy of life. This combination of personal strength and communal concern provided an inner source of power as she confronted horrors beyond imagination.

JFO

FROM "SURVIVAL AND MEMORY"[§]

We didn't have built-in closets like we have now. Then we had what we called a French armoire. It was a tall chest that reached from the floor almost to the ceiling, and it had two doors. The right side was used for the wardrobe, and the other side had shelves and was for linen. The very highest had hats laying there. But, for some reason, the part where we had the wardrobe was always locked. When I was a child, still a preschooler, I used to be so curious about what was in the closet. Why was it locked? I never saw it open, and I couldn't imagine what was in it.

§ Reprinted from "Survival and Memory" by Itka Frajman Zygmuntowicz and Sara Horowitz, from *Four Centuries of Jewish Women's Spirituality: A Sourcebook.* Edited by Ellen M. Umansky and Dianne Ashton. Copyright © Itka Frajman Zygmuntowicz and Sara Horowitz. Published 1992 Boston: Beacon Press. Material excerpted from pages 286–290.

I used to play all kinds of games trying to guess. Maybe a treasure, or maybe a skeleton. I even went so far as to think that maybe I was adopted and they locked up the papers because they were afraid that I would find out. One day mother said, "Itka, come, I want to show you something." And I remember I was so excited with anticipation and curiosity and so frightened simultaneously to find out what was in that closet. She took out the key and opened it. "Look my child." It was old leather-bound books—a whole closet of books. My mother was afraid the children might tear the books. She took out a book, and she said, "When you learn to read, you will discover a treasure here. You will be with the greatest minds. You can sit in Ciechanow, Poland, and you will see the whole world, and you will travel through the ages."

She took out a book. She took me on her knee. I can remember today—we sat near the window on a chair, and she started to read stories, and this became a daily ritual. And this gave me so much closeness to my mother. Because when we read she held me on her lap and I felt the warmth of the relationship and the story. I was a very curious child, and my mother always encouraged that curiosity. . . .

Every morning when I got up, my grandmother would say prayers with me, along with grace after every meal, and every evening. From early childhood on, my parents and grandmother stressed the importance of *menschlekhkeit*—which in English means acting humanely. Whenever I did something wrong, my parents or grandmother always used to correct me by saying, "This isn't *menschlekhkeit,* Itka."

What I liked most about my grandmother was that she never took me for granted. I remember that whenever I did a little errand for her she would thank me many times over. Then, when I would say, "Grandmother, it is just a little thing," she would say, "Yes my little child, but kindness and *menschlekhkeit* are not little things."

I remember once I came home crying bitterly because, as I was walking home from school, a group of non-Jewish kids who I did not even know attacked me. When I came home, my mother asked me, "Why are you crying, Itka?" And I told her. She tried to comfort me. Later she looked at me, and she asked me, "What did you do, my child?" And I said, "Nothing." And my mother said with assurance, "Well, then you have nothing to cry about. Your *menschlekhkeit* does not depend on how others treat you but on how you treat others."

That was very comforting to me, but, when I looked back, it was also very confusing. I believed that I must never hurt or shame anyone. Therefore, I was not sure how I should defend myself when somebody hurt me. That was a big conflict. It took many years after the Holocaust to work this out within me. What I didn't realize—what my parents did not make clear but in retrospect I can understand—is that there is a difference between hurting someone and defending yourself. This I found out much later. Whatever I said or did, my family measured our behavior by the yardstick of *menschlekhkeit.* Is it just? Is it correct? Is it the proper, moral way to behave? They always used to say, "It is not *menschlekhkeit,* Itka." I used to cringe when they told me this, but as I grew older, as I realize now, I started to measure myself by this yardstick.

I recall when I was a little girl a poor man came one day to our door and asked my grandmother for alms. My grandmother gave me a few coins and asked me to give them to the man waiting at the door. I looked with curiosity at the money in my hand and asked my grandmother with astonishment, "Grandma, so much money?" My grandmother smiled and said, "My child, you have only what you choose to give away." My grandmother was a very warm, caring, and compassionate woman, and was very religious. When I questioned her proverb, "You only have what you give away," she answered, "My child, I only give away what God and my parents have given me. We are all givers and takers of life."

My grandmother of blessed memory has been dead for many years, but I can still feel her, sweet and loving. Death is only a physical separation, while love and remembrance are a spiritual union. Only the flesh is mortal, but words and deeds like God are immortal. The words and deeds of every person who has walked this earth before us is still influencing our destiny even though we can no longer influence theirs. Since Adam and Eve, people influence each other for both good and evil. . . .

I became aware that there is a destiny that others choose for us and a destiny that we choose for ourselves. We can choose how to live, and we can choose to protect life or destroy it. For nearly six years, chronic hunger, terror, and death were my steady companions. I am one of a handful of Jewish Holocaust survivors of Auschwitz concentration camps and the sole survivor of my murdered family of blessed memory. The only member of our household in Ciechanow, Poland, who was privileged to die of old age and have a proper Jewish burial was my maternal widowed grandmother. I was grief stricken when my beloved grandmother died, but now I am grateful that she was spared all the suffering that I had to endure.

All on earth that I loved and held sacred I lost in the Holocaust, including nearly six precious years of my life. All on earth that I had left after liberation from Malchow, Germany, was my skeletal body, minus my hair, minus my monthly cycle, a tattered concentration camp shift dress without undergarments, a pair of beaten up unmatched wooden clogs, plus my "badge of honor," a large blue number 25673 that the Nazis tattooed on my left forearm on the date of my initiation to Auschwitz inferno. I was homeless, stateless, penniless, jobless, orphaned, and bereaved. I could not speak or understand Swedish, I had no marketable skills and only seven grades of public school and several grades of Hebrew school. Unlike my non-Jewish fellow survivors, I could not go back home to my beloved family, relatives, and friends and resume my former life as they did. Jewish homes, Jewish families, and Jewish communities were destroyed. I was a displaced person, a stranger; alive, but with no home to live in. I had no one to love me, to miss me, to comfort me, or to guide me. My childhood world was gone, but not from my heart and mind. Nothing dies as long as it is remembered and transmitted from person to person, from generation to generation. Or, as my beloved grandmother used to say, "My child, you only have what you choose to give away!"

WORKS CONSULTED

Berger, Ronald J. *Constructing a Collective Memory of the Holocaust: A Life History of Two Brothers' Survival.* Niwot, Colorado: UP of Colorado, 1995.

Heilbrun, Carolyn. *Writing a Woman's Life*. New York: Ballantine Books, 1988.

Heinemann, Marlene E. *Gender and Destiny: Women Writers and the Holocaust*. New York: Greenwood Press, 1986.

Horowitz, Sara. Interview with Itka Frajman Zygmuntowicz in *Four Centuries of Jewish Women's Spirituality: A Sourcebook*. Ed. Ellen M. Umansky and Dianne Ashton. Boston: Beacon Press, 1992.

BABA OF KARO *(c. 1890–1960)*

Girls' Trading Expeditions, Bond-Friends, and Marriage

Baba was a Muslim Hausa woman in her sixties when Mary Smith, a British woman accompanying her anthropologist husband, M. G. Smith, on his fieldwork in northern Nigeria in West Africa, recorded her life story. *Baba of Karo* is the first published account of the daily life of an African peasant woman that was written from the woman's point of view. Such accounts, from any area of the continent about ordinary events before incorporation into the colonial system and later into the new nation-state, are exceedingly rare.

The Hausa are the largest ethnic group in West Africa and have long attracted "the attention of travelers, Islamic scholars, colonial officials, historians, linguists, and anthropologists," for their "culture and society are complex and include many extremes of experience: urban and rural communities, agricultural systems and highly specialized craft production, Muslim and non-Muslim religious and ritual systems, and a highly elaborated status system based upon occupation and birth" (Coles and Mack 4). In Karo, the small town where Baba lived as a child at the end of the nineteenth century, indigenous Hausa culture was more dominant in daily life than either the Islamic culture that had been brought to the area centuries earlier or the new practices and policies laid down under British colonial rule. In these two excerpts, Baba recalls learning trade as a child and explains how Hausa women cooperated to manage their marriages.

Baba and her cohort of young girls learned the art of trading by engaging in small-scale endeavors, modeled after those of their mothers and female relatives and encouraged by the village. The centrality of women's trading activities to the economies of many countries that produce agricultural products and trade in raw materials on the international market has been the focal point of much research on women and development. Contemporary feminist scholars, trained to ask "and what are the women doing?" have insisted that development experts, national governments, and international agencies recognize the fact that more than three-quarters of the agricultural work in Africa is done by women, but that almost none of the resources that go into improving agricultural work has been directed to women. Baba's trading activities build on this female agricultural tradition and place her at the center of the economy of her region.

The economic status of Hausa women, like many women throughout Africa, is one of the factors traditionally associated with their power and authority (Koopman 15). In the second excerpt, Baba recounts how the women of her village monitored their relationships with their husbands. Through a set of indigenous ritual practices, *Kawaye,* women who belonged to an age cohort, shared information about how their husbands treated them. Such practices as the one described here serve multiple functions. Women are observing how they are treated by their husbands. They are sharing that information directly with their peers. They are notifying their husbands of their satisfactions. And they are publicly recording a social practice that is carried on between the two individuals involved, thereby reinforcing the notion that the status of a marriage is a matter of concern to an entire community. The ability to influence others is one of the bases of power; the recognition that such influence rightfully belongs to a particular person is one of the bases of authority. As many researchers have observed, class status, wealth, age, and ritual power are among the attributes that Hausa women use to determine their positions (Coles and Mack 13). Learned in childhood and carried out through a variety of customs, these practices of Hausa women appear to provide one example of the ways in which women express agency in complex social systems.

JFO

FROM *BABA OF KARO* [§]

Girls' Trading Expeditions

The thing I remember best before I was married was our girls' trading expeditions. We took our money and our big calabashes, we went to Doka and bought yams, we went to Fillata and got groundnuts, we went and bought sweet potatoes from our hamlet, Karo, and from Dankusuba, Sundu, Wawaye, Guga. . . . When we had been to a lot of different villages and bought things, we came home and cooked them. When they were ready we took them to market. This had nothing to do with our parents, we went and sold our goods and put by our money. In the dry season we traded like this. When we had been to market in the morning with our mothers' cakes, eight or ten of us, we would meet our friends and come back, twenty of us, all singing, crowds of girls. Then we would put our heads together, we would go on an expedition. 'Are you coming?' 'Yes, I'm coming.' In the morning we got up early and we went along singing, twenty of us, thirty of us. When we arrived at a village we would go to the market and see things for sale. 'Oh, look at that! It's cheap, we'll go and make a profit.' And we bought it. One girl would buy groundnuts, one would buy yams, one sweet potatoes—each one bought her own produce. The little girls came along too with little loads, about three-pennyworth. We older ones took about a shillingsworth. The country people said 'Welcome, daughters of the village, welcome!' We said, 'M-hm.' Then the country people would laugh, 'Ha! ha! ha!', they never laugh softly. We weren't exactly village children, we used to live in the town. They were country bumpkins, they hadn't got much sense, they weren't used to seeing a lot of people.

When we got back home we would cook the food we had bought, and next day we sold it in the market. The third day we returned to the hamlets. We were traders all right!

Bond-Friends and Marriage

We Bare-Bare women have a special custom: if your husband gives you kola-nuts and tobacco-flowers, you know that he desires you. You sit in your hut in the evening, eating

[§] Reprinted from *Baba of Karo: A Woman of the Muslim Hausa* by Baba and Mary F. Smith. Published in New York, 1955, by Philosophical Library. Reproduced by permission. Material excerpted from pages 61–62, 100–101.

kolanuts and rubbing the tobacco-flowers on your teeth, and you feel good. As you finish with the tobacco-flowers you put them in a flat basket and hang it up on your wall. You do this for seven days, you collect them. On the following Friday you send a young girl to your *kawa* with the used tobacco-flowers. If your *kawa's* husband has also been giving her tobacco-flowers and kolanuts, she hangs your little basket on the wall, and for seven days she collects her used flowers. Then when the Friday comes she puts them all together, yours and hers, and sends them back to you. Then you both know that your marriages are going well. After dark the *kawaye* will go to visit each other, they laugh and are glad because each one knows her husband desires her. But if the husband of one of them does not give her kolanuts and tobacco-flowers, and the other one sends her a little basket full of used flowers, then the neglected one will break up her marriage—that is, it is her *kawa* who has caused the marriage to break up. One wants to be treated as well as one's friend. This is a custom of Bornu women.

WORKS CONSULTED

Coles, Catherine, and Beverly Mack, eds. *Hausa Women in the Twentieth Century.* Madison: U of Wisconsin P, 1991.

Koopman, Jeanne. "Women in the Rural Economy: Past, Present, and Future." *African Women South of the Sahara.* Ed. Margaret Jean Hay and Sharon Stichter. 2nd ed. New York: Wiley and Sons, 1995. 3–22.

Smith, Mary F. *Baba of Karo: A Woman of the Muslim Hausa.* New York: Philosophical Library, 1955.

NANNIE STILLWELL JACKSON *(c. 1854–?)*

"I Shall Tell Her"

Nannie Stillwell Jackson lived in the town of Watson, Arkansas, in the Arkansas-Mississippi delta region, during the late nineteenth century.[1] This region suffered from frequent flooding, which rendered it generally incapable of profitable, large-scale agricultural enterprise. Watson itself was isolated from the closest neighboring town by a rough and muddy twenty-mile stretch of road. Most of the residents of this area were small farmers or merchants who procured goods from the nearby Arkansas River port of Red Fork. Money was extremely scarce, especially in the Jackson home, and the couple depended on a combination of mutual support and creative work in order to survive. Nannie Stillwell married her second husband, W. T. Jackson, in 1889, apparently out of economic necessity, for nowhere in her diary does she speak of him with affection or concern.

This perhaps uncharacteristically cold marriage must be understood in terms of the radical differences between husband and wife. Nannie was approximately 35 years old at the time, with two daughters from her previous marriage and an unusual amount of education (she wrote neatly and was an avid reader), while her husband was an illiterate teenager twenty years her junior who earned a meager salary doing odd jobs around the town. He was thus in a subordinate position in their marriage—a fact clearly registered by his recurring jealousy of his wife's intimate relations with the network of approximately twenty neighborhood women (both Euro- and African-American) who supported each other financially and emotionally. Still, the differences between Nannie and her husband only emphasized the independence and influence of women's networks in rural Arkansas. Nannie Stillwell Jackson's diary thus leads us to consider the shifting relations between men and women under varying economic and social conditions.

Nannie Stillwell Jackson's diary is not the only work of its kind. In what is generally considered a remarkable historical reconstruction, Laurel Thatcher Ulrich simultaneously interpreted and analyzed the deceptively simple and repetitive diary of a late eighteenth-century midwife named Martha Ballard from rural Maine. In her introduction, Ulrich notes that scholars who had previously utilized Ballard's diary, traditional political historians as well as feminist social historians, had generally dismissed it as unimportant, "filled with trivia about domestic chores and pastimes" (9). Ulrich corrects this perception by eliciting from Ballard's detailed and regular entries remarkable insights into the cultural, economic, medical, ideological, political and religious history of rural New England in the early Republic; she also recovers crucial information about an otherwise lost (because unrecorded) autonomous world of rural women's work and social influence. Nannie Stillwell Jackson's diary, although it was written a century later than Ballard's, functions similarly as an invaluable source of information about women's lives.

In the communities of both Nannie Stillwell Jackson and Martha Ballard, as in innumerable others throughout America from the colonial period into the twentieth century, women and men lived in two distinct though intertwined worlds: a world of mutual support between men and women, and a world in which each gender in many ways functioned independently of the other. Using the familiar "check" pattern made up of white, blue, and pale blue squares as a metaphor, Ulrich advises us to "Think of the white threads as women's activities, the blue as men's, then imagine the resulting social web. Clearly some activities in an eighteenth-century town brought men and women together. Others defined their separateness" (75–6). Ultimately, the diary of Nannie Stillwell Jackson provides a window through which to view the largely rural traditions of women's social and economic autonomy.

KKF

FROM THE DIARY OF NANNIE STILLWELL JACKSON[§]

Thursday, June 19, 1890

I baked some chicken bread for Fannie & some for myself, & she gave me some dried apples & I baked 2 pies she gave me one & she took the other I made starch for her & me too, & starched my clothes & ironed the plain clothes & got dinner.

Friday, June 27, 1890

I did some patching for Fannie today and took it to her she washed again yesterday & ironed up everything today I also took two boxes of moss & set out in a box for her, when I came back Mr. Jackson got mad at me for going there 3 times this evening said I went to talk about him & said I was working for nothing but to get him & Mr. Morgan in a row, & to make trouble between them & I just talk to Fannie and tell her my troubles because it seems to help me bear it better when she knows about it. I shall tell her whenever I feel like it.

Wednesday, August 6, 1890

I cut and made one of the aprons for Aunt Francis's grandchild & Lizzie & I partly made the basque Aunt Chaney came & washed the dinner dishes. . . . Mrs Chandler, Fannie, Mrs. Watson & Myrtle McEncrow were here a little while this evening, Aunt Jane Osburn was here too, & Aunt Mary Williams she brought me a nice mess of squashes for dinner. Carolina Coalman is sick & sent Rosa to me to send her a piece of beef I sent her a bucket full of cold victuals . . . got no letters today wrote one for Aunt Francis to her mother & she took it to the post office, I gave her 50 cents for the 2 chickens she brought & a peck of meal for a dozen eggs.

[§] Reprinted from *Speaking For Ourselves: Women Of The South* edited by Maxine Alexander. Copyright © 1977, 1981, 1983, 1984 by the Institute for Southern Studies. Reprinted by permission of Pantheon Books, a division of Random House, Inc. Material reprinted from page 79.

NOTE

[1] Biographical information is taken from Margaret Jones Bolsterli's article "It seems to help me better when she knows about it" in *Speaking for Ourselves: Women of the South.*

WORKS CONSULTED

Bolsterli, Margaret Jones. "It seems to help me better when she knows about it." *Speaking for Ourselves: Women of the South*. Ed. Maxine Alexander. New York: Pantheon Books, 1977.

Ulrich, Laurel Thatcher. *A Midwife's Tale: The Life of Martha Ballard, Based on her Diary, 1785–1812*. New York: Vintage, 1990.

CANTON DELTA MARRIAGE RESISTERS *(early 20th century)*

Diverging From Traditional Marriage Customs

This document consists of a combination of first and third person accounts from interviews conducted by Janice Stockard from 1979 to 1981 with elderly women who worked in the silk trades in the Canton Delta throughout the late nineteenth and early twentieth centuries. Stockard documented that in the Canton Delta (in southern China) from approximately 1860 to 1930, a set of marital practices had grown up that significantly diverged from traditional customs. These practices provided alternatives to those aspects of Confucian familial customs most oppressive to women.

Confucianism was the dominant system of philosophy, ethics, and politics in China for a thousand years prior to the start of the twentieth century (Stacey 30). The Confucian conception of the good society was of a harmonious and hierarchical order in which every member of society knew and assumed her or his proper position. The ideal family structure was an extended joint household (patriarchal and patrilocal), wherein all married sons, their wives, and their children lived along with their unmarried siblings under the supervision of a patriarch who was served and assisted by his wife, servants, and any concubines he might have. The main goal of the patriarch was to insure an unbroken lineage, the members of which would reside together forever on his ancestral land. This ideal necessitated the extreme subordination of individual desires to the maintenance of the family. Such subordination can be seen especially in the area of marriage.

Ideally, marriage had nothing to do with the wishes of the individuals to be married, but rather was arranged by the patriarchs of two families in order to best serve their familial interests. An early betrothal and marriage were preferred, and husband and wife had no contact prior to the marriage day. In most parts of China, upon marriage, a woman was suddenly and irrevocably cut off from her natal family, friends, and acquaintances, while all responsibility for and control over the woman was transferred to her husband's family. With differing amounts of preparation, the new wife's main functions were to take care of all the household tasks and cooking, and to bear children. Her performance of these functions was usually under the direct and intensive supervision of her mother-in-law, a figure infamous for finding fault with her new charge and for ungently shaping her to fulfill the expectations which that mother harbored for her son's home. The legal and customary rights of the new wife were nearly nonexistent in comparison with the authority over her granted to her husband's family. She could be divorced, repudiated, beaten, and even killed for disobedience, while she had no recourse against abuse, and there was no official way for her to leave an unhappy or abusive marital home (Stacey 34–43, Stockard 1–3).[1]

Against this hegemonic background, a constellation of alternatives and resistances developed in the Canton Delta region over time, and in a particular order. The first development, from the mid-nineteenth century, was delayed transfer marriage. In this practice, instead of the sudden relocation of a wife to her husband's family, a wife would marry and then would continue to live in her natal home for an average of three to five years before taking up residence in her husband's home—paying a small number of visits during that period, and gradually preparing to join it. However, the delayed transfer would abruptly terminate if a bridedaughter (the term for a married woman who still lived in her natal home) became pregnant, causing a scandal and loss of prestige for her natal family. It was thus in a woman's interests, both in terms of prestige and in terms of prolonging her independence from her marital family for as long as possible, not to have sex and get pregnant too early (Stockard 1–30). As Stockard discovered, delayed transfer marriage was the norm in this region of China and originated less as a form of women's resistance than as a recognition of working daughters' economic value to their natal family. Nonetheless, this practice did allow women unusual opportunities to resist the constraints associated with marriage.

Such opportunities are particularly evident in another practice evolving out of the delayed transfer, called compensation or second marriage. This was a radical transaction in which a bridedaughter could extend the period of her residence in her natal home indefinitely, by purchasing a second wife for her husband to fulfill her wifely duties of housework, childbearing and rearing, in exchange for her freedom combined with the security of a marital home. The bridedaughter negotiated the terms of her marriage with her husband's family directly, and if they were mutually acceptable, she could remain in her natal home until old age or impending death—for it was a strongly held belief that a woman should not die in her natal home but in the home of her husband's ancestors. The bridedaughter would herself pay the compensation out of her own wages and savings and seek out the secondary bride to be married to her husband. This was by far the most unusual marriage custom of the Canton Delta, and the one that raised a great deal of prejudice in the rest of China against this region's unique customs (Stockard 48–69).

As the practice of compensation marriage developed in the late 1890s, an anti-marital bias also evolved along with it, becoming more and more common and apparent among young women. This led to the rise of "sworn spinsterhood," the most direct rejection of patriarchal marriage. Sworn spinsterhood was not just a state one drifted into, but was a highly specific status, conferred by ritual action. The relative ease or difficulty of attaining that status depended on specific local and family attitudes. When families could not be counted upon to give consent, or a girl heard the news that she was to be betrothed, she would indicate her interest in being a spinster by running away from home and leaving certain unmistakable signs behind of her intentions. The girl would stay away from home until her family accepted her decision, and sometimes also to earn money in preparation for her single life. Upon returning home, her decision to become a spinster was acknowledged and made final by a night of banqueting and gift-giving with her family and friends (or sisters). Central to this night was a hairdressing ritual in which the spinster-to-be combed her own hair back into a unique style. After this she served tea to her family who urged her not to bring disgrace to the family by betraying her spinster lifestyle, which she agreed not to do. From then on, a sworn spinster led a self-supporting life, and as long as she maintained her vow of spinsterhood, she would enjoy being recognized as an eminently capable woman by her family and community (Stockard 70–89).

An important component to all of these marriage alternatives and resistances in Canton was a high degree of companionship and solidarity among women, both married and unmarried. This was fostered in childhood and adolescence through "girls' houses," which were abandoned or extra houses in a community, taken up by a group of girls who lived there with no chaperon. The girls would work and eat at their natal homes in the day, and then return to the girls' house in the evening to socialize and to sleep. Here girls taught each other skills, exchanged information (since the still-mobile bridedaughters could bring news of their new lives, and what to expect), sang and played games (Stockard 31–47).

Why did these practices develop in the Canton Delta? The answer lies in the specifics of the sericulture (silk-producing) industry. Sericulture was a highly lucrative industry that was also unusually dependent on female labor, who did the silk-reeling, and on an independent and mobile work force. This made women who worked in the silk industry economically and socially valuable in this region, and put substantial resources at their disposal—although they were never considered rich or of the elite. In fact, in comparison to Cantonese workers, elites from elsewhere in China were far better equipped to seclude and control their women. By contrast, the economic exigencies of peasant life helped to strengthen women's communities in Canton, by requiring them to leave the home to perform work and develop a community support network amongst themselves (Stockard 51–58, Stacey 44–46). This suggests that when women are more valuable to a social or economic system, regardless of their overall wealth, they may have more choices and flexibility in their lives.

KKF

FROM *DAUGHTERS OF THE CANTON DELTA*[§]

"All the girls in my village joined the girls' house.[2] You learned nothing if you did not join the girls' house. In school teachers taught only things in books. They never taught you any girls' secrets like menstruating and marriage. In the girls' house you also learned important things like how to cry for a sister when she got married. This crying was very important and a girl's sisters had to do it; there are special things one must say at a marriage. The girls learn embroidery at the girls' house. No money was required to join.

The girls in the girls' house read the three-character classics, which are books about Confucius, and sang songs. Some of the songs had no words; some were about the problems of being a woman or of being a *sou hei* [sworn spinster]. There was no head of the house. The girls shared the expenses and work.

Sometimes the members of the girls' house would try to prevent the marriage of one of their sisters. They would try to help the bride-to-be escape, but rarely with success. Usually

§ Excerpted from *Daughters Of The Canton Delta: Marriage Patterns And Economic Strategies In South China, 1860–1930* by Janice Stockard. Reprinted with the permission of the publishers, Stanford University Press. Copyright © 1989 by the Board of Trustees of the Leland Stanford Junior University. Material excerpted from pages 39–40, 65–66, 67, 87–88.

the family of the girl to be married would lock her up with her sisters for several days before the wedding and let them all cry and sing together.

I did not have to decide which girls' house to join. Usually there was a group of five or six girls who lived on the same alley and played together. Often they were cousins. One decided to go into the girls' house and soon another followed and the number grew in no time; it was very easy. Unlike Hong Kong, everyone in the village was close. Everybody left their doors open; girls got to know each other very well. Usually the whole village had the same last name. If there were not enough beds in the girls' house, some girls would return to sleep at home around ten; otherwise, everyone spent the night there" (Sankar 1978, 104–5). . . .

A 64-year-old informant from the rich silk center of Yuhng Keih in Sundak gave one account of the practice of body-wrapping. She said that in Yuhng Keih compensation marriages had been more common in the preceding generation. Some of her own parental great-aunts had been compensating wives. Although body-wrapping had not been practiced in her own generation, she had heard at one time how women had been wrapped and stitched into their undergarments "just like dumplings." They were given pills to prevent urination, and on their return from conjugal visits, their "sisters" had checked to see that the seam was intact. The informant said she had heard her great-aunts tell how once a knife was discovered tucked into the cloth wrapping and that as a result the practice of body-wrapping was forbidden. . . .

A Sundak informant recounted the case of her cousin, her mother's brother's elder daughter. Her marriage had been arranged, and the dowry and bridewealth had been exchanged. At the last minute, however, her cousin managed to arrange for a compensation marriage and paid 300 dollars before the wedding. A *muijai* to act as a secondary wife was found, and both first and secondary brides then married on the same day [*yatchai gwo muhn*]. After the wedding, her cousin did not stay overnight but immediately returned home. In this case, the bridedaughter's parents received the dowry back, but the bridewealth was not returned. . . .

"A father cannot allow his spinster daughter to live in her natal home, because after the celibacy ceremony she is considered 'married' and married women are forbidden to die at home. If she dies within her own kin group, then all the bad things that happen to her family will be blamed on her spirit. Instead, she can live only in a spinster house, and that house is the only place for her to die. A spinster must also build her spinster house in a different surname section from that of her family. In my village there were several surname sections.

I built my spinster house together with several sisters. One was my godmother, one was her younger sister, and the other was my *kai neuih* [goddaughter]. It took us a long time to get the spinster house built; it cost us 180 yüan. We bought bricks from a rich man who kept having to sell the bricks from his house to pay his gambling debts. We also got some building materials from another man who needed money and sold us an old building, which we had to pull down ourselves. After we collected enough materials to build a house, we hired a group of builders and paid for a shed so they could rest and eat in the shade. Of course, they paid us rent for the shed. But they were too slow and could not finish the house. We hired another man, but he just ran off with our money. Finally we hired a third group. This time we paid the rent for the shed; it cost us 10 yüan a month. We ran out of money, and I had to borrow many yüan from my mother. . . . When we moved in, we had a joyful ceremony. All our friends came to help us move our possessions in" (Sankar 1984, 58–59). . . .

NOTES

[1] Unofficial strategies for leaving home are discussed in the Ning Lao T'ai-T'ai headnote.

[2] The first and last selections here are first-person narratives by women of the Canton Delta. The other accounts are in Stockard's words. [Eds.]

WORKS CONSULTED

Stacey, Judith. *Patriarchy and Socialist Revolution in China.* Berkeley: U of California P, 1983.

Stockard, Janice. *Daughters of the Canton Delta: Marriage Patterns and Economic Strategies in South China, 1860–1930.* Stanford: Stanford UP, 1989.

HILDEGARD OF BINGEN *(1098–1179)*

The Light Speaks

Hildegard of Bingen was one of the most accomplished and influential women of her time. A powerful abbess, she was known not only as a healer, theologian, and woman of science, but also as a musician and poet. Her major written contribution to the theological and metaphysical discussions of her time consists in large part of a trilogy that was composed over a period of thirty years; her other written works include biographies of St. Disibode and St. Rupert, treatises on healing and natural science, and a commentary on the Rule of St. Benedict. Critical and academic interest in the life, writings, and music of Hildegard of Bingen has recently intensified; her opera, *Ordo Virtutum,* continues to be performed and, more recently, recorded. In this section, she stands as an example of a woman who used her prominent position within the institutional hierarchy of medieval Catholicism in order to effect change both in her own circumstances and in those of the women in her charge.

Hildegard of Bingen was the last of ten children. In 1106, still a young girl, she was placed under the care and tutelage of Jutta of Spanheim, a religious woman who became the leader of the women's cloister attached to the monastery of Disibodenberg in 1112. This monastery, located near the Rhine River, had a long and somewhat complex history; the site was originally the dwelling-place of St. Disibode, a Celtic monk who lived there as a hermit in the seventh century. The women's community was present when the construction of the monastic buildings was officially begun in the first half of the twelfth century. After the death of Jutta in 1136, Hildegard was chosen as the head of the cloister. Significantly, more and more women joined the community as Hildegard's fame as a thinker and spiritual leader spread.

In 1147 Hildegard and her sisters left Disibodenberg. Four years later they formed a new cloister in Rupertsberg (near contemporary Bingen). This controversial move was partly the result of the institutional tension occasioned by the rapid growth and increasing wealth of the women's cloister at Disibodenberg. In the first letter we reprint here, Hildegard defends her community's right not only to take possession of the new site at Rupertsberg but also to retain control of the substantial real estate and financial assets that had become attached to the cloister in the form of dowries held by the sisters and religious donations offered to the community. It is clear from Hildegard's letter that the departure of the women from Disibodenberg involved a substantial transfer of worldly possessions out of the control of the monks. Hildegard retained her position as abbess at Rupertsberg until the end of her life; as a writer and a preacher, she was an influential figure in the German Church and a respected social and religious critic.

In both of the letters we have included below, Hildegard writes of the spiritual visions that serve not only as favorable confirmation of her virtuous intentions but as supreme justifications for her exercise of religious authority. In the first, it is the "bright streaming light" that justifies her resolution to demand "the freedom of the place and the possessions of [her] daughters." In the second, Hildegard discusses the ban that was placed on her community following the sisters' refusal to exhume the body of a man buried in their cemetery. (The sisters, who argued that the previously excommunicated man had reconciled with the church before his death, were ultimately vindicated.) Here, it is the "words in [her] soul" that urge Hildegard to persist in her decision not to unearth the corpse and remove it from the cemetery. In both of the letters, Hildegard identifies herself with an authority emanating directly from God; her ability to assert the independence of her community from within the institutional structure of the Church might be seen as the result of this connection forged between her own worldly authority and the mystical power of the Divine Will.

NM

FROM HILDEGARD OF BINGEN'S LETTERS[§]

Letter Twelve

Hildegard to her spiritual daughters O daughters, who out of your love for charity are following the footsteps of Christ, and who for the sake of spiritual improvement have chosen me, poor creature that I am, in humble submissiveness to be your mother, I have something to say to you from my maternal heart, something that doesn't originate with me but comes from godly vision: this spot, the resting place for the earthly remains of the holy confessor Rupert, to whose patronage you have taken refuge, is the site I have recognized according to God's will and with the evidence of miracles as a place for the sacrifice of praise. I came here with the approval of my superiors and with God's aid I have freely taken possession of it for myself and all of those who follow me. After that I went back by God's direction to Disibodenberg, the community I had left with permission, and I presented before all who lived there this proposal—namely, that not only our place of residence, but all the real estate added to it as gifts, should not be attached to them but should be released. But in all of this practical business I had nothing else in mind but the salvation of souls alone and concern for the discipline commanded in our rule.

I then shared with the Abbot [Kuno], the superior at this site, what I had received in a true vision: "The bright streaming light speaks, 'You should be the father over the provost [Volmar] and over the spiritual care of this mystical plant-nursery for my daughters. The gifts made to them belong neither to you nor to your brothers. On the contrary, your monastery should be their shelter.' But if you want to grow stubborn in your opposition and gnash your teeth against us, you will be like the hated Amalekites in the Bible and like Antiochus, of whom it is written that he robbed the temple of the Lord. (I Maccabees 1:21) Some of you have said in your unworthiness, 'We want to diminish your possession.' Here is the response of the Divine: 'You are the worst thieves! But if you should try to take away the shepherd of the sisters' spiritual healing [Provost Volmar], then I further say to you: You are like the sons of Belial and you don't have the justice of God before your eyes. Therefore, God's judgement will destroy you!'"

§ Reprinted by permission of publisher from *Hildegard of Bingen's Book of Divine Works with Letters and Songs* by Hildegard of Bingen. Edited by Matthew Fox. Published Santa Fe: Bear & Company, Copyright © 1987. Reprinted from pages 294–296, 354–355.

When in these words, I, poor creature that I am, demanded from the abbot named above the freedom of the place and the possessions of my daughters (as I explained above), all these things were granted to me through a written contract in a legal codex. All who saw, heard, and perceived these things, great and lowly alike, took a favorable view of them, so that it was surely God's will that this was all pinned down in writing. And all who depend on God, experience God, and listen to God's word, should favorably certify, enforce, and defend this legal transaction, so that they might receive that blessing which God gave to Jacob and Israel. . . .

Letter Forty-One

Hildegard to the prelates of Mainz In the vision which was impressed upon my soul before its birth from the Creator, I see myself compelled to write something relating to the ban placed on us by our spiritual superiors. It deals with a dead man, whose transferral and burial in our cemetery through his priest took place without opposition. When our superiors ordered us a few days after the burial to remove him from our cemetery, I was overcome with no insignificant alarm and, as I usually do, I looked to the true light and with open eyes I saw the following words in my soul: If we were to follow your instruction and dig up the body of this dead man, then through that removal a great danger would threaten our locale and would beset us like the black cloud which serves to point out coming storms and bad weather. Therefore, we do not presume to dig up the body of the deceased, since he went to confession, received anointing and communion, and was buried without opposition. Also, we agree neither with the counsel nor the instruction of those who told and ordered us to do this. It is not as though we do not lay proper store on the counsel of proven men or the instruction of our prelates. But we only want to avoid the appearance that the sacrament of Christ, with which the man was strengthened in his body, should be brought to disgrace through distraught women. But lest we appear to be disobedient, we have followed the ban and have suspended the singing of the divine office and our reception of the Lord's Body, which we were accustomed to receive monthly. All my sisters and myself have experienced great sorrow because of this. Finally, almost overwhelmed from such a heavy burden, I received the following words in my vision: It is not good for you, because of the words of human beings, to forego the mysteries of my Word clothed in human nature and born as your salvation in the spotless womb of the Virgin Mary. And so you must ask your prelates to release you from this ban they have placed on you.

WORKS CONSULTED

Dronke, Peter. *Women Writers of the Middle Ages.* Cambridge: Cambridge UP, 1984.

Fox, Matthew. Introduction. *Hildegard of Bingen's Book of Divine Works with Letters and Songs.* Ed. Matthew Fox. Santa Fe: Bear and Company, 1987.

Kraft, Kent. "The German Visionary: Hildegard of Bingen." *Medieval Women Writers.* Ed. Katharina M. Wilson. Athens: U of Georgia P, 1984: 109–130.

BEE MILES *(early 20th century)*

"They Say I'm Insane"

Bee Miles "became legendary in Sydney for stridently transgressing bourgeois mores and manners" according to Kay Daniels and Mary Murname, who compiled a collection of documents on women in Australia (Daniels and Murname 71). Educated and with some private income, Miles wrote about her experiences of homelessness and incarceration in mental asylums. "She had a capacity to distance herself from her immediate situation and analyze it . . . not bewildered by and submissive to authority. . ." (71). In this excerpt from her unpublished writings, she records her views of society matrons, doctors, other patients and herself as they all interact in the world of the psychiatric hospital. Miles relays what literally millions of women have experienced and what only in the 1970s came to be analyzed from a feminist perspective.

In an essay that set the stage for many later developments, Naomi Weisstein criticized the way psychology had ignored empirical evidence and created twentieth-century Western women in an image that served its own ends: "How are women characterized in our culture and in psychology? They are inconsistent, emotionally unstable, lacking in a strong conscience or superego, weaker, nurturant rather than productive, intuitive rather than intelligent, and, if they are at all 'normal,' suited to the home and the family. In short, the list adds up to a typical minority-group stereotype of inferiority" (221). Weisstein's analysis laid the groundwork for feminists to wrestle with this monolithic image of women, stripped of their cultural and ethnic diversity and based more in myth than lived realities.

Phyllis Chesler applied similar insights to the study of mental illness, arguing that sex-role stereotypes are at the heart of much of what is called mental illness. She asserted that, beginning in the sixteenth century, the range of behaviors for which women receive psychiatric care or are committed to mental asylums reflects a double standard for the normal or healthy individual. Women who are independent, creative, or assertive are deemed abnormal and "treated" while men with the same characteristics are praised and rewarded. Ehrenreich and English furthered this argument when they looked at the history of the relationships among women, medicine, and mental health. They demonstrated the intertwined developments of women seeking more and more advice from the medical, psychological, and helping professions while at the same time receiving assistance that was more and more distant from their own experiences. Since Weisstein, Chesler, Ehrenreich and English, and their colleagues first put psychiatric practice and psychology under a feminist lens in the 1970s, there has been a virtual explosion in analyzing and resisting the ways in which women are viewed by, and view, these professions.

The women's health movement is further evidence of this revolution. In 1969, a small group of women in the Boston area came together to talk about health, seeking answers to the questions that were unattended as they sought professional help. Their discussions led to the formation of the Boston Women's Health Collective and the publication of *Our Bodies, Ourselves* in 1971, the first women's health handbook available for the popular market. Millions of copies have been sold and the handbook is now in its fourth edition (1992). The original handbook included specific medical advice on common women's health problems, statements from women about their health issues and how they resolved them, and common remedies that allowed women to practice preventive health care. Unlike most of the medical advice books available at the time, *Our Bodies, Ourselves* placed women's health issues in a socio-political context and encouraged women not only to seek help but to do so on terms that worked for them and to reject stereotypes that did not match their own realities.

From the beginning, the women's health movement made connections between women's physical and mental health on the one hand and the options and restrictions they experienced as women in culture and society on the other. The empirical work in the medical sciences, the theoretical underpinnings provided by feminist scholars, and the practical assistance that women's clinics and publications provided, combined to create a movement that has challenged the status quo. By the 1980s, many mental health professionals took a very different stance toward their female clients and understood that the problems they presented had a socio-cultural context as well as an individual basis. While the situation has changed dramatically since Bee Miles wrote in the early part of this century, health-care activists still contend there is a long road to travel before women are seen as "normal" human beings. Bee Miles starts us on that journey for she, without the help that has developed in the decades since then, understood much of what was happening to her and resisted.

JFO

FROM AN UNPUBLISHED MANUSCRIPT BY BEE MILES [§]

This is the afternoon for the Board Ladies to make their sacred and silent appearance. They tiptoe—metaphorically speaking—through the refractory wards with fear on their faces. Sister and a couple of nurses form their bodyguard. I have not yet found out the actual use of these women but I wish Mrs Larkins would go for one of them. They're so respectable that a good savaging might make them a bit more human. I think they are here to see that no person is wrongfully incarcerated but, as they are in the hands of Super who just falls short of telling them what they must think, where are we!

. . . Am just in time to see Mrs Dawson give Walker a kick in the tummy despite the fact that Mrs Dawson is in a straight jacket and is strapped to a seat. Walker calls for aid and three of the attendants belt into the patient and leave her very subdued. Feeling nauseated I stroll back to our landing and open an onesided discussion (my side) with Gertrude on the evils of Mental Hospitals. These are many from the stupidity and ignorance of the Doctors and their unholy conceit to the ignorance and stupidity of the nurses and their disgusting cruelty. I state loudly that there is no cure. "We read," I say, "that insane people

[§] Reprinted by permission of publisher from *Australia's Women: A Documentary History* edited by Kay Daniels and Mary Murname. Copyright © 1980 by the University of Queensland Press, Queensland, Australia. Material excerpted from pages 71–72.

used to be thrashed. They're not treated any less cruelly now. I saw Watkins strangling the other day with her fingers, and what price the grazes on Mattie's throat from the stocking that Taylor twisted round it? We could tell Super but what on earth is the use? When the nurse denied it he'd put us down as delusioned . . . Besides when we do tell him Charge locks us up and tells him we have been violent to justify herself." To which Gertie answers with a hearty "it's true what you say."

. . . It is very sad when a devoted and good mother becomes insane. Kate, in one of her periods of insanity, was weeping for her babies. She had apparently been told by her husband that she would find peace and rest in the hospital (the usual foul lie told by those who want their relatives to go quietly). But the ward she is in is the noisiest here and poor Kate is irritated and upset all day . . .

. . . Today there's some bad news for me. I am to be transferred to another hospital. The reason for this is, I think, that the doctors here do not feel they are making any headway with me and they wish to give another lot of medicos the opportunity to try and make an impression. The poor half wits. They say I'm insane but won't admit there's no cure for it. If a person returns to sanity in these hospitals he does so not because of any treatment he has received but as a rule in spite of the doctors and attendants. Any treatment he may be given is almost invariably irrational. . . . I feel very depressed and weep loudly. I have come to love many of the patients. Still I'd better be philosophic about it because I cannot alter Super's decision. I have been here long enough to realize that the wishes and happiness of a patient are rarely considered. At the least the short trip in a car to my new home will be a break in the general monotony. I have been a mental patient for about a year and a month and there doesn't seem any chance of leaving these prisons alive.

. . . after a year's observation of myself I have come to the conclusion that I am not mad and am beginning to long very heartily for my liberty.

. . . I am off again. This time, with the very sensible help of some friends. I am successful in remaining away for twenty eight days after which, according to the laws of this state, one automatically becomes free.

WORKS CONSULTED

Boston Women's Health Collective. *Our Bodies, Ourselves.* 4th ed. New York: Simon and Schuster, 1992.

Chesler, Phyllis. *Women and Madness.* New York: Doubleday, 1972.

Daniels, Kay and Mary Murname. *Australia's Women: A Documentary History.* Queensland: U of Queensland Press, 1980.

Ehrenreich, Barbara and Deirdre English. *For Her Own Good: 150 Years of the Experts' Advice to Women.* New York: Doubleday, 1978.

Weisstein, Naomi. "Psychology Constructs the Female." *Woman in Sexist Society: Studies in Power and Powerlessness.* Ed. Vivian Gornick and Barbara K. Moran. New York: Basic Books, 1971.

OLYMPIAS *(late 4th/early 5th century CE)*

"Unsuited for the Conjugal Life"

Olympias lived during the late 4th and early 5th centuries CE in Constantinople, the eastern capital of the Roman Empire. Constantine the Great had declared Christianity the official state religion in 312, when he won a crucial battle under the sign of the Cross. After his conversion, he quickly sought to Christianize the Empire, and so opened the possibility for great social influence and rapid upward mobility among fourth-century Christian families in his newly-founded capital (Coon 28). This was the type of family into which Olympias was born.

Her grandfather, though not of aristocratic birth, had risen to a high position within the government, and so when Olympias was orphaned at an early age, the prefect (a title roughly equivalent to that of mayor) of Constantinople became her guardian. She was raised for the purpose of making a desirable match with a high-level government official, which is exactly what happened in 386, when she married Nebridius, who was appointed prefect of the city one year later. Soon after, however, he died, leaving a huge fortune to Olympias. The wealth she then commanded was something that most readers would find unimaginable; one estimate places her resources at over 900 million dollars (in present-day U. S. dollars) in addition to sizable amounts of property.

In the wake of her husband's death, Olympias decided that she wanted to adopt a life of Christian asceticism which would have left her without a husband to control the dispensation of her fortune. At this point, however, she had entered a realm of socio-economic influence so formidable that the highest official in the government, the Emperor Theodosius the First, attempted to force Olympias into a marriage with one of his own relatives. The excerpt which follows is an account of Olympias' appeal to Theodosius to respect her decision to remain unmarried. Her appeal was successful, and Theodosius allowed her to be ordained as a deaconess of Constantinople. From that point on, she used her wealth to support Nectarius, the Bishop of Constantinople, to fund the operations of the church of Constantinople during the reign of John Chrysostom (she and Chrysostom were close friends), and to build and assume the leadership of a monastery for 250 women.

As with other Christian ascetics discussed in this anthology (including Margery Kempe, Perpetua, and Rebecca Cox Jackson), Olympias was able to utilize an extreme form of religious devotion in order to free herself from constraints (specifically those associated with marriage) that often hindered women's public activities. As Ross S. Kraemer has argued, "As long as Christian belief and practice advocated ascetic control of the body, a tension would exist between traditional male social control over women and the relative autonomy and freedom inherent for women in such asceticism" (196). Nonetheless, it would take many decades, and even centuries, before the Roman Empire would become fully Christianized (Kraemer 197). Thus, Olympias' ability to circumvent the wishes of the Roman Emperor was also rooted in the complex religious and social traditions of the eastern Empire.

Constantine the Great's rather sudden conversion to Christianity resulted in rapid changes in a few major urban areas. Still, older religious traditions, namely "paganism" and Judaism, persisted in this eastern region of the Empire (a profoundly multi-cultural locale) despite Christianity being declared the official religion. This was attested to by Chrysostom's frequent and virulent sermonizing against Christians who continued to partake in Jewish and "pagan" festivals and practices (Kraemer 102–3, 108–9, 124). These older religions also had more subtle and pervasive effects which continued to persist; certain beliefs about women's role in religion stemming from these more ancient traditions were widely-held and still influenced the behavior of even the most devout of recently converted Christians. In the Judaic and "pagan" religious forms of the Mediterranean world, women were recognized as possessing rights and responsibilities within a sphere of religious activity quite separate from that of men (Kraemer 3–21). In some locations "women's religion" was mocked as superstitious, excessive, and inferior to men's religions; in others it was considered of equal value and essential to the well-being of the state. In any case, a tradition of women's religious leadership and autonomy was familiar in this world. Olympias' story thus reminds us that there has never been a single Christian "experience" and that historical continuity, as well as change, can result in women's ability to act independently of custom and established authority.

KKF

FROM *THE LIFE OF OLYMPIAS*[§]

. . . The pious Olympias, however, explained her position to the emperor Theodosius: "If my King, the Lord Jesus Christ, wanted me to be joined with a man, he would not have taken away my first husband immediately. Since he knew that I was unsuited for the conjugal life and was not able to please a man, he freed him, Nebridius, from the bond and delivered me of this very burdensome yoke and servitude to a husband, having placed upon my mind the happy yoke of continence."

She clarified these things to the emperor Theodosius in this manner. . . . The emperor, when he had heard the testimony against the pious Olympias, commanded the man then prefect of the city, Clementius, to keep her possessions under guard until she reached her thirtieth year, that is, her physical prime. And the prefect, having received the guardianship from the emperor, oppressed her to such a degree at Elpidius' urging (she did not have the right either to meet with the notable bishops nor to come near the church) so that groaning under the strain, she would meekly bear the option of marriage. But she, even more grateful to God, responded to these events by proclaiming, "You have shown toward my

§ Reprinted from *Maenads, Martyrs, Matrons, Monastics: A Sourcebook on Women's Religions in the Greco-Roman World,* edited by Ross S. Kraemer. Copyright © 1988 Fortress Press. Reproduced by permission of Augsburg Fortress Publishers. Material excerpted from pages 196–197.

humble person, O sovereign master, a goodness befitting a king and suited to a bishop, when you commanded my very heavy burden to be put under careful guard, for the administration of it caused me anxiety. But you will do even better if you order that it be distributed to the poor and to the churches, for I prayed much to avoid the vainglory arising from the apportionment, lest I neglect true riches for those pertaining to material things."

The emperor, upon his return from the battle against Maximus, gave the order that she could exercise control over her own possessions, since he had heard of the intensity of her ascetic discipline. But she distributed all of her unlimited and immense wealth and assisted everyone, simply and without distinction. . . .

Then by the divine will she was ordained deaconess of this holy cathedral of God and she built a monastery at an angle south of it. . . .

WORKS CONSULTED

Coon, Lynda L., et al., eds. *That Gentle Strength: Historical Perspectives on Women in Christianity.* Charlottesville: U of Virginia Press, 1990.

Kraemer, Ross S. *Her Share of the Blessings: Women's Religions Among Pagans, Jews and Christians in the Greco-Roman World.* New York: Oxford UP, 1992.

HÉLOÏSE *(c. 1100–c. 1163)*

"The Name of Mistress"

Héloïse was born in 1100 or 1101 and was brought up in the Convent of Sainte Marie of Argenteuil, six miles northeast of Paris.[1] Nothing is known of her parents (it has been conjectured that she was of illegitimate birth), though her uncle was Fulbert, one of the canons of Notre Dame Cathedral. At the age of 17, Héloïse went to live in Paris with Fulbert. During the early years of her life, she received educational training by the Benedictine nuns of Sainte Marie and through her uncle's efforts. During this time, her remarkable intellectual gifts became apparent. This made Héloïse unusual in a number of ways. Most women outside of the nobility received little or no education during this period; among them only a minute number achieved renown for their intellectual powers. Even more rare were those who publicly expressed ideas that challenged conventional thinking. Héloïse, like Grazida Lizier, chose to assert her own notions of female sexuality, even though they would have been deemed sacrilegious or dishonorable by church and secular authorities of the time.

To further Héloïse's education, Fulbert hired the well-known teacher and philosopher Peter Abelard to tutor Héloïse in his home. According to Abelard's autobiography, *Story of His Misfortunes,*[2] Héloïse was well-known in Paris for her high degree of learning; because of her good looks and intellect, he decided to make her his lover. In his mid-thirties at the time, director of the Cloister School of Notre Dame, and a member of the minor nobility, Abelard claims to have set about confidently scheming to win Héloïse's love by proposing a tutorial to Fulbert and then, after he agreed, seducing Héloïse while they studied. Abelard claims that Héloïse was a willing lover and that they often spent more time love-making than studying. His own work began to suffer noticeably, and news of their affair spread. It was not until Héloïse became pregnant, however, that the affair was revealed to Fulbert, who reacted by trying to separate the lovers.

Although Abelard tried to appease Fulbert's anger and proposed to protect Fulbert's family's honor by marrying Héloïse, he could not be satisfied. Abelard eventually had to remove Héloïse to his family's estate in Brittany, where she bore their son Astralabe.[3] During this time, Héloïse and Abelard fiercely debated his proposed marriage: she argued strenuously against it, but in the end Abelard prevailed. They left the child with Abelard's sister, returned to Paris, married secretly, and then separated. Abelard also persuaded Héloïse, again against her wishes, to return to the convent at Argenteuil, and to assume a habit. This time was punctuated by furtive meetings, during which Abelard recalled they sacrilegiously made love in holy places, and by angry confrontations with Fulbert. In an act of revenge, Fulbert had his servants break into Abelard's chambers and castrate him. After this event, which appears in Abelard's autobiography as both a tragedy and an act of saving grace, he and Héloïse would separate for many years, each assuming a monastic life, and each eventually coming to prominence as religious authority figures. They were the respective heads of a monastery and convent that were linked as brother and sister institutions.

The excerpt which follows is part of a letter that Héloïse wrote to Abelard sometime after 1132, when he wrote the first version of his autobiography.[4] This appears to have been around nine years after Abelard was castrated and Héloïse took vows to enter monastic life (Heloise was nineteen when she took her vows, and so would have been twenty-eight when she wrote this letter). Abelard's autobiography, which was written in the form of a letter to a friend, was somehow given to Héloïse, who responded to it as if it were indeed a letter that she happened to intercept. This was perhaps the first correspondence between them since their separation. In it, Héloïse reopens the subject of their tumultuous affair, expressing her sexual frustration and inability to stop thinking of their happiness together as lovers (Radice 96).[5]

In this letter, Héloïse reveals much of the philosophical and social content of her past relationship with Abelard, as well as much about the changing ideals of love and gender relations in Romanesque, or early medieval, France. Héloïse's objections to their marriage were based on their shared ideal of the philosopher as a man existing above human ties. This ideal was based on classical Greek and Roman authors (for example, Cicero, Theophrastus, Socrates, Seneca) rather than on Christian concepts, although Héloïse and Abelard did illustrate this principle with the lives of Jewish and Christian mystics. According to these classical notions, for the philosopher to become embroiled in domestic life would be inimicable to the pursuit of philosophical truth. More importantly though, the only form of love that would be in keeping with true philosophical ideals was that of *gratia,* (derived from Cicero's *De amicitia*), a true friendship of disinterested love, in which love given freely and pure intentions were of the utmost importance. Marriage, linked as it was in Heloïse's opinion to financial and social scheming, was incompatible with *gratia.* For this reason she claims that "the name of mistress would be dearer . . . and more honorable for me" (Radice 92).

These opinions place Héloïse at the forefront of what medievalists have termed the emerging "secular culture of Romanesque France" (Bond). Based in a marginal yet powerful group of lettered and leisured persons associated with royal courts and religious academic institutions, this culture was characterized by new styles of dress, manners, language, and ideology. The precursors of later proponents of "courtly love," these secular intellectuals developed new ideals of personality, based especially on the writings of Cicero, that were intricately bound up with new ideas about love—a term which in Romanesque writings covered a wide range of meaning from desire, to friendship, to peace.

These new ideas about love, however, were also connected to redefinitions of gender roles, and through this redefinition, desire and eloquence became crucial elements in an emerging ideal of romantic, sexual love. At the same time, a new form of essentializing, a notion of "woman" that excluded women as *subjects* of desire, laid the groundwork for important and contradictory ideas about love and personhood that would dominate Western philosophical thought for centuries. Héloïse's letter is a fascinating reflection on the conflicts and ambiguities that figured in the formation of this ideological matrix.

KKF

LETTER TO ABELARD[§]

You know, beloved, as the whole world knows, how much I have lost in you, how at one wretched stroke of fortune that supreme act of flagrant treachery robbed me of my very self in robbing me of you; and how my sorrow for my loss is nothing compared with what I feel for the manner in which I lost you. Surely the greater the cause for grief the greater the need for the help of consolation, and this no one can bring but you; you are the sole cause of my sorrow, and you alone can grant me the grace of consolation. You alone have the power to make me sad, to bring me happiness or comfort; you alone have so great a debt to repay me, particularly now when I have carried out all your orders so implicitly that when I was powerless to oppose you in anything, I found strength at your command to destroy myself. I did more, strange to say—my love rose to such heights of madness that it robbed itself of what it most desired beyond hope of recovery, when immediately at your bidding I changed my clothing along with my mind, in order to prove you the sole possessor of my body and my will alike. God knows I never sought anything in you except yourself; I wanted simply you, nothing of yours. I looked for no marriage-bond, no marriage portion, and it was not my own pleasure and wishes I sought to gratify, as you well know, but yours. The name of wife may seem more sacred or more binding, but sweeter for me will always be the word mistress, or, if you will permit me, that of concubine or whore. I believed that the more I humbled myself on your account, the more gratitude I should win from you, and also the less damage I should do to the brightness of your reputation.

You yourself on your own account did not altogether forget this in the letter of consolation I have spoken of which you wrote to a friend;[6] there you thought fit to set out some of the reasons I give in trying to dissuade you from binding us together in an ill-starred marriage. But you kept silent about most of my arguments for preferring love to wedlock and freedom to chains. God is my witness that if Augustus, Emperor of the whole world, thought fit to honour me with marriage and conferred all the earth on me to possess for ever, it would be dearer and more honourable to me to be called not his Empress but your whore.

For a man's worth does not rest on his wealth or power; these depend on fortune, but worth on his merits. And a woman should realize that if she marries a rich man more readily than a poor one, and desires her husband more for his possessions than for himself, she is offering herself for sale. Certainly any woman who comes to marry through desires of this kind deserves wages, not gratitude, for clearly her mind is on the man's property, not himself, and she would be ready to prostitute herself to a richer man, if she could. This is evident from the argument put forward in the dialogue of Aeschines Socraticus[7] by the learned Aspasia to Xenophon and his wife. When she had expounded it in an effort to bring about a reconciliation between them, she ended with these words: 'Unless you come to believe that there is no better man nor worthier woman on earth you will always still be looking for what you judge the best thing of all—to be the husband of the best of wives and the wife of the best of husbands.'

[§] Reprinted from *The Letters of Abelard and Héloïse,* translated by Betty Radice. (Penguin Classics, 1974). Material excerpted from pages 113–118.

These are saintly words which are more than philosophic; indeed, they deserve the name of wisdom, not philosophy. It is a holy error and a blessed delusion between man and wife, when perfect love can keep the ties of marriage unbroken not so much through bodily continence as chastity of spirit. But what error permitted other women, plain truth permitted me, and what they thought of their husbands, the world in general believed, or rather, knew to be true of yourself; so that my love for you was the more genuine for being further removed from error. What king or philosopher could match your fame? What district, town or village did not long to see you? When you appeared in public, who did not hurry to catch a glimpse of you, or crane his neck and strain his eyes to follow your departure? Every wife, every young girl desired you in absence and was on fire in your presence; queens and great ladies envied me my joys and my bed. . . .

Remember, I implore you, what I have done, and think how much you owe me. While I enjoyed you with the pleasures of the flesh, many were uncertain whether I was prompted by love or lust; but now the end is proof of the beginning. I have finally denied myself every pleasure in obedience to your will, kept nothing for myself except to prove that now, even more, I am yours. Consider then your injustice, if when I desire more you give me less, or rather, nothing at all, especially when it is a small thing I ask of you and one you could so easily grant. And so, in the name of God to whom you have dedicated yourself, I beg you to restore your presence to me in the way you can—by writing me some word of comfort, so that in this at least I may find increased strength and readiness to serve God. When in the past you sought me out for sinful pleasures your letters came to me thick and fast, and your many songs put your Héloïse on everyone's lips, so that every street and house echoed with my name. Is it not far better now to summon me to God than it was then to satisfy our lust? I beg you, think what you owe me, give ear to my pleas, and I will finish a long letter with a brief ending: farewell, my only love.

NOTES

[1] Biographical information has been taken from Betty Radice's article entitled "Héloïse: The French Scholar-Lover," in *Medieval Women Writers.*

[2] This work has been translated by J.T. Muckle as *The Story of Abelard's Adversities* (Toronto: Pontifical Institute of Medieval Studies, 1954).

[3] There seems to have been no subsequent contact between Astralabe and his parents. Héloïse knew of his location when he was around 26 years of age, and asked Abelard to assist him in attaining some money or land from the church. In addition, Abelard wrote his son several letters of what Radice calls "platitudinous advice." Beyond these two instances, nothing more is known of possible contacts between parents and son (Radice 99).

[4] Based on Radice's introduction, it would seem that the only writings of Héloïse's that have survived are her letters to Abelard. Beyond that, information about her has been garnered from Abelard's letters, treatises and autobiography.

[5] In subsequent correspondence, they came to a reconciliation of their past through their new

lives in Christ, and began to associate on a professional basis about their monastic lives and difficulties, Abelard going to great lengths to raise funds for Héloïse's abbey.

[6] This suggests that, unless she is writing ironically, Héloïse believed the *Historia calamitatum* to be a genuine letter to a real person, and not an example of a conversational epistolatory genre. [Radice]

[7] Aeschines Socraticus, a pupil of Socrates, wrote several dialogues of which fragments survive. This is, however, no proof that Héloïse knew Greek, as the passage was well-known in the Middle Ages from Cicero's translation of it in *De inventione,* I.31. [Radice]

WORKS CONSULTED

Bond, Gerald A. *The Loving Subject: Desire, Eloquence, and Power in Romanesque France.* Philadelphia: U of Pennsylvania Press, 1995.

Muckle, J. T. *The Story of Abelard's Adversities.* Toronto: Pontifical Institute of Medieval Studies, 1954.

Radice, Betty. "Héloïse: The French Scholar-Lover." *Medieval Women Writers.* Ed. Katharina M. Wilson. Athens, Georgia: U of Georgia Press, 1984.

NING LAO T'AI-T'AI *(1867–?)*

Walking Out the Gate

As described in the headnote introducing the Canton Delta marriage resisters, Cantonese women modified the traditional Confucian marriage system in a variety of ways. Some women adjusted the timing of the marriage process; others rejected marriage altogether. However, outside of this atypical region, only more subtle forms of resistance could be undertaken. One example comes from the autobiography of Ning Lao T'ai-T'ai, as it was told to the American Ida Pruitt in the mid-1930s. Born in 1867, Ning Lao T'ai-T'ai was of roughly the same generation as those Cantonese women who worked in the silk trades and practiced delayed transfer marriage. Ning Lao T'ai-T'ai, though, never had at her disposal the resources they commanded, nor did she possess the same degree of economic and social value to her larger community. After learning to overcome the passivity that nearly brought about her demise in her marriage, Ning Lao T'ai-T'ai then began to support herself by various means, from peddling to begging and working as a servant for a variety of religious groups (Buddhists, Muslims, Christian missionaries). The part of her account that has been excerpted here concerns her and her sister's extremely strict upbringing by their father, and the mental and emotional collapse of her sister during her abusive, traditional marriage. Ning Lao T'ai-T'ai's story tells us about the burdens and survival strategies of women *within* the traditional patriarchal family—and about the great deviation of traditional familial and marital practices from Confucian ideals.

The relationship between mother-in-law and daughter-in-law is infamous in Chinese culture. The tradition of patriarchal and patrilocal marriage that has prevailed throughout most of China relied upon structural relationships that set the interests of these two women in direct conflict, fostering and even requiring fierce competition between them. Traditionally, daughters were relocated into their husbands' families upon marriage. For these women, integration into a new family meant that their labor and resources would be appropriated while they were subjugated completely. By contrast, the arrival of a daughter-in-law was the first real opportunity for the mother-in-law to exercise authority and command another individual's obedience and services, with the full weight of patriarchal sanction behind her. Moreover, because her own status was dependent on that of her son, a mother-in-law was motivated to force her new daughter-in-law to conform to the highest standards of conduct (usually extremely oppressive standards insofar as women were concerned) in order to gain the greatest respect and prestige for the marital family (Stacey 42–43, 54–56).

Ning Lao T'ai-T'ai describes the emotionally and physically violent behavior of her sister's husband and mother-in-law, as well as the only form of resistance that her sister was able to exercise—psychologically withdrawing from the here-and-now. As a "crazy woman," she removed herself from the confines of a highly structured and oppressive life.

Anger was another unofficial weapon available to women, for an outright quarrel between women who were not related by blood was considered a bad omen for a family. Moreover, according to a 1938 study, Chinese village residents attributed "familiar outbursts of mental disorder" in women to anger at their husbands (Stacey 46). In the case of Ning Lao T'ai-T'ai's sister, her illness gave her the freedom (unconscious though it may have been) to leave her abusive marriage behind and return to the women of her natal family.

Ning Lao T'ai-T'ai's father was the embodiment of stern, unbending patriarchal conservatism, refusing to allow his daughters to wear or say anything that diverged from total austerity. Both before and after marriage, Ning Lao T'ai-T'ai and her sister spent most of their lives indoors, highly segregated from the outside world. Because of her father's strictness and repression, and because of all that she was denied, Ning Lao T'ai-T'ai became a keen observer of physical style and fashion and their symbolic meanings. Most strikingly, she gives a fascinating account of hair as an intricate register of a woman's place in her life cycle, and in Chinese society more generally. She illustrates the depths of her sister's mental illness and resistance to her oppressive marriage when she reports that someone, or some spirit, has cut off the marriage knot in her hair, thus loosing her from the bonds which had previously held her.

KKF

FROM AN AUTOBIOGRAPHICAL ACCOUNT BY NING LAO T'AI-T'AI[§]

When I was thirteen my parents stopped shaving the hair from around the patch of long hair left on my crown. I was no longer a little girl. My hair was allowed to grow and was gathered into a braid at the back of my head. It was braided in a wide loose plait which spread fanlike above and below the knot that held the hair at the nape of the neck. It was like a great butterfly. Girls do not wear their hair that way now. Part of the hair was separated and braided into a little plait down my back. When the little braid was gathered into the big braid I was a woman and not allowed out of the gate. So we have a saying that the girl with the full head of hair is not as free as the one with a bare head, that is, partly shaved. And at the age of thirteen I was taught to cook and sew.

My father was a very strict man. We were not allowed, my sister and I, on the street after we were thirteen. People in P'englai were that way in those days. When a family wanted to know more about a girl who had been suggested for a daughter-in-law and asked what kind of girl she was, the neighbors would answer, "We do not know. We have never seen her." And that was praise. . . .

My sister was married when she was fifteen, and I was married when I was fifteen. I was eight when my sister was married.

[§] Reprinted from *A Daughter of Han: The Autobiography of a Chinese Working Woman*, edited by Ida Pruitt. Originally published by Yale University Press in the 1930s; Copyright © Yale University Press. Reprinted by permission of Yale University Press. Material excerpted from pages 29–32 in an edition published in 1967 by Stanford University Press.

My sister's match was considered a very suitable one. Her husband was only three or four years older than she and he had a trade. He was a barber. And the father-in-law was still young enough to work also. But my sister was a child, with the ways of a child and the heart of a child. She had not become used to housework. She did not know how to mix wheat bread or corn bread. She got the batter too thick or too thin, and so her mother-in-law would scold. She had no experience and could not plan meals. At one meal she would cook too much and at the next not enough. This also made her mother-in-law angry and she would scold. Though my sister had not learned to work she had learned to smoke. This also made her mother-in-law angry. She would say that my sister was not good for work but only for luxury. So there was bitterness.

Her mother-in-law forbade her to smoke. She took her pipe and broke it into many pieces. My sister made herself a pipe from a reed and smoked when there was no one around. One day her mother-in-law came suddenly into the room. My sister hid the pipe under her clothes as she sat on the k'ang. The lighted pipe set the wheat chaff under the bed matting afire, and her mother-in-law beat her. When her husband came home his mother told him the story and he also beat my sister. There was a great quarrel and her mother-in-law reviled her with many words that were too hard to bear.

She said, "In the path around the mill does one not look for the hairs of the mule?" She meant to call my sister a mule and also to say that there were no signs of a daughter-in-law where such signs should be—there was no work done. She went out of the house to find her husband, saying that she would show my sister when she came back what real anger was like. My sister went crazy.

In P'englai it is the custom for the women to stand in their gateways in the evenings to watch whatever may be passing by. When my sister went to the gate that evening she did not stop and watch as is the custom, but went out of the gate and walked south. She walked until she reached the South Gate of the city, and she walked out of the gate. She walked three li to the village of the Three Li Bridge. All the people came out to see the crazy woman. The cry went out for all to come and see the crazy woman. We lived near the North Gate of the city, but we had an aunt who lived outside the South Gate at the village of the Three Li Bridge. She too came out to see the crazy woman, and she said, "Is this not Yintze, the daughter of my sister? Come with me." And she took my sister home with her.

That very evening my brother went to my sister's mother-in-law's home to fetch my sister and bring her back to our home for a visit. When he got there she was gone and no one knew where she was. All that night he searched for her, and her husband and father-in-law searched, but they could not find her. The next day my aunt sent her son to tell us where my sister was, and we sent and fetched her home. But her mother-in-law claimed that we had hidden her and that she had left home that night for a bad purpose. So she stayed with us for six months.

And she was not right for all those six months. She had come crying and combing her hair with her fingers, so that her hair was in all directions and we would not comb it out. Then one day we found that her hair was cut, and we never knew who had cut it. Straight off it was cut, between the knot, into which a woman's hair is bound at marriage, and the head. Later we found the hair hanging on a bramble bush in the court of the Chou Wang Temple. It must have been cut off by the demon who was troubling her. . . .

WORK CONSULTED

Stacey, Judith. *Patriarchy and Socialist Revolution in China.* Berkeley: U of California Press, 1983.

RUBY THOMPSON *(1884–1970)*

"Things That I Shouldn't Write"

Ruby Thompson was born in London, England, to a solidly middle-class family.[1] Throughout the 1890s, London was a city awash in new ideas and concerns about urban poverty, factory labor, women's rights, children's welfare, and education. Women were prominent leaders in many of these reform movements, and these years marked the beginning of one of the strongest periods (extending until the start of World War I) of egalitarian, political feminist activism in Britain. Pursuing the goal of complete equality between men and women, these activities encouraged education for both middle-class and elite women, and called for the lifting of social, political and legal restrictions on women.

Ruby was educated at a private girl's school until the age of fifteen, spent one year at a business school, and then began to work for the London General Post Office. Additionally, along with her father and friends, she explored London's radical social, religious, and political ideas. She attended lectures, concerts, and plays with her father, and he introduced her to the classics and popular books of the turn of the century. She also joined the Fabians, a group which supported such goals as the equality of women, universal education, and international disarmament. Through her participation in these activities Ruby met such literary and social luminaries as William Butler Yeats, William Morris, and George Bernard Shaw.

She was also to meet her husband through the Fabian magazine, the *Clarion,* where in 1904 a letter to the editor that was written by Ruby appeared, praising the skills and talents of women workers in the Post Office. Ted Thompson, an Englishman working in New York, read this letter and believed its author to be so "full of life" that he arranged to meet her in London. A courtship ensued, and although Ruby's parents did not approve of the match, within a year Ruby had moved to the United States and married Ted. Their early relationship was colored by radical thought and social idealism: they considered moving to a socialist colony in Paraguay, discussed American society, and critiqued mainstream religion: Ted was an atheist and Ruby, an agnostic.

Within a number of years however, this situation had changed dramatically. No longer working outside the home, Ruby bore two sons in her first three years of marriage. Then, while she and the children were away in London for a family visit in 1908, Ted converted to Catholicism, apparently the first step in a move toward a social conservatism that would become more pronounced over the years. Such sudden and significant changes in the couple's lifestyle and attitudes revealed underlying complexities in their social beliefs. Ruby's reactions to these changes in Ted, and her ongoing analysis of his behavior and its impact on her life, make up the bulk of a journal (actually forty-two handwritten books) that she started in 1909 and continued through the late 1960s. The segments of her journal collected in this selection focus on the years before and after the First World War.

Her journal entries, in their focus on her dissatisfactions with her husband and her marriage, and her concern with personal and sexual intimacy in her marriage, might lead one to see Ruby as an insular and isolated woman. In fact, she was well aware of then-current social and literary trends (she recorded the titles of thousands of books she had read) and her understanding of her own life and relationships was undergirded by assumptions held in this period by many Anglo-Americans, including Anglo-American feminists. Just as Ted seems to have become more traditional with regard to marriage, gender, and religion as he aged, Ruby's journal entries reveal that she held a similar, though distinct, conservatism as well. Still, this conversation coexisted uneasily in her writings with more radical notions about such issues as sexuality, egalitarianism, and women's self-fulfillment.

While Ruby describes in detail the exhausting and oppressive aspects of pregnancy and childbirth, frequently despairing of the latest of her seven pregnancies, she also craves the affection and sensual contact of an infant. While she complains passionately of her husband's unjustified and excessive criticisms, his spiteful grudges and ignorance of her difficulties (indicating a desire for distance), she often wishes that she could get rid of her long-term houseguests, so that she could have her man and her home to herself. While she repeatedly gives evidence of her love of reading and desire to write a novel, she questions the desirability of women's education, cynically noting how education only serves to heighten the frustration and suffering of women trapped in domestic drudgery. Still Ruby expressed her support for many of the more radical planks of feminism, such as birth control, free love, and equal career opportunities and equal pay for working women. Although Ruby's status as an immigrant may have limited her contacts with larger groups of women, these contradictions are not simply personal idiosyncrasy, but correspond to ambivalences embedded in the white, middle-class, Western feminism of the 1910s and 1920s.

Susan Kingsley Kent and Barbara Epstein have shown that, especially after World War I, many U. S. and British feminists' responses to traditional beliefs about women and gender were ambiguous and even contradictory. Many Western feminists of this period abandoned the more straightforward egalitarian appeals of the prewar period and, perhaps in defensive reaction to the hostility of returning solders, were willing to accept and promote a modified version of the Victorian ideal of "separate spheres." Although many Anglo-American feminists argued that "masculinity" and "femininity" were cultural constructs, they also slipped into asserting that the aggressiveness of men had caused the war, and that only the political ascendancy of women and their peaceful "natures" could save the world from another war. Although many Anglo-American feminists argued for women's control of their own bodies and affirmed the need for women's sexual satisfaction in marriage, they also promoted a sexual ideal that valued chastity and purity, and the rational channeling and control of all sexual impulses.

Such waverings and contradictions open up interesting questions about the very nature of feminist thought and analysis. Just as there is no monolithic, trans-historical category of "woman," there is also no single or clear-cut category of "feminism." What does it mean when the feminists of one place and time disagree with each other and even contradict themselves? What does it mean that many elements of current feminist thought can also be seen in writings that predate the nineteenth-century initiation of feminism as a social movement? The ways in which Ruby's ideals for sexual intimacy, marriage, and gender relations both dovetail with and diverge from those of earlier writers, such as Grazida Lizier, Susan B. Anthony, and Héloïse, reveal the ways in which such concerns and ideals have long historical roots, and yet vary considerably from period to period, not following any trajectory of "progress," but rather reappearing in new guises as social, cultural, and economic contexts shift.

KKF

FROM THE DIARIES OF RUBY THOMPSON[§]

Friday, July 25th. [1913]

Last night Ted and I had one of our periodic differences about money and about diet. He wound up the evening's dispute by saying that I hadn't said a single sensible thing and I was a perfect fool about the whole thing. Consequently I went to bed to cry and to feel hurt. I still feel hurt and I shed a few tears about it this morning. I do try hard and think hard about the whole domestic problem, and I can't help feeling deeply hurt when he says he thinks me such an idiot about it.

Last night I showed Ted the monthly bills and asked him to look after them. He won't. Or rather, he said he would settle them another time and that I ought to try, even if it was hard, to manage on my monthly hundred dollars. How can I? If there were any luxuries, I could cut them out but there are none. The children must be fed sufficiently and this is where Ted provokes me so. His solution is to cut out meat. I say that is no economy because the articles which take its place, eggs, milk, cheese, and butter, are more expensive than meat. Twenty-five cents' worth of eggs won't go as far as twenty-five cents' worth of meat, as any housewife knows. Ted maintains that meat does not require any substitute, which is nonsense. Protein has to be supplied in the diet somewhere. No. His plan is to live on all that monotonous insipid, unappetizing stuff: rice, prunes, cornmeal, porridge, and macaroni. I don't see why we should. We are not peasants, used and compelled to live on pulse and grains. I detest this vegetarianism idea of his.

What makes me so furious is that he attributes my misfortunes about my head and my feet to my wrong feeding. Such nonsense makes me speechless. My cancer was no more explainable than anybody else's cancer and as for my feet, it is ceaseless childbearing and child tending that wears them out. When I haven't the weight of a child within to carry, I have one on my arm. I feel I have no sympathy at all for all the pain and the labor. Here is the fifth child stirring within me and because I have not the energy of an athletic girl of twenty, Ted is sure there is something wrong with my diet, with my manner of living.

Ted also accuses me of buying unnecessary things and mentions the two dollars' worth of books I bought whilst he was away. That is what galls me and has all my married life. It is so humiliating to feel I have never any money of my own. No money for books, flow-

[§] Selections reprinted from *Ruby: An Ordinary Woman* edited by Bonnie Thompson Glaser and Ann Martin Worster. Copyright © 1995 by Bonnie Thompson Glaser and Ann Martin Worster. Reprinted by permission of Faber and Faber Publishers, Inc. Material excerpted from pages 26–27, 39, 93, 131, 139, 231.

ers, fallals, sweetmeats, or any of the pleasurable things of life. If I should indulge in chocolates, I feel I am wasting his money. If I spend half a dollar for a book, I feel ashamed of myself, almost a criminal. Why should I feel so? I am surely entitled to something. I can't believe it. Whenever I do spend money for such things I always feel guilty.

If only I had some money of my own which I could throw down the sewer if I wanted to. Ted is certainly one of the best of men and I know he loves me but he is also one of the most unsympathetic and uncomfortable. See how he makes me grumble. I am so heartsore today. I am always conscientiously trying to do my best and then I am told I am always wrong; a fool. That hurts.

Four-thirty P.M. I have to smile. I have just received this telegram: JUST ARRIVED PHILA BUSINESS IF NOT HOME TONIGHT DONT WORRY GROUCHO.

"Groucho" is right, though.

Friday, July 2nd. [1915]

When I can only find time to make an entry here once a month, so much seems to have happened.

I was ill the whole of June. I had been feeling poorly for two or three weeks and, on the tenth of June, I collapsed with a miscarriage. It was a dreadful mess and I really thought I was dying. It was far worse than any of the births except the awful first one. I have been around for a couple of weeks now but feel anything but strong. What is there in marriage for a woman besides children, children, and perpetual suffering? Five births and a miscarriage in ten years is too much for me.

With all this to suffer still Ted will not sleep with me. He does not give me that intimacy and companionship of the night. That one sexual act of love is not the whole of loving. I hate it when he only comes to my room for a casual hour or a casual night and then leaves me alone for weeks. It is a torment to me and hurts my pride. I think he does not care for me but only for that. I have begged him so often to sleep regularly with me but he won't. He says he cannot sleep properly unless he sleeps alone. Why do I write all these things that I shouldn't write? Yet whom can I speak to except this blank page?. . .

Tuesday, November 26th. [1918]

Miserable and full of trouble. Things happen, words are said, and I will not record them here, because I think they were not meant, or will be forgotten. Ted wounds me deeply. I despair. I suppose part of the trouble is that I am essentially a modern woman, whilst Ted becomes more of an old-fashioned man every day.

Last Sunday the argument began with Mrs. Thomlinson halting him when he made some expression about the husband being the head of the house. She wouldn't allow it, insisting that marriage was an equal partnership, and that neither party should be head over the other. Neither yielded and somehow the discussion passed on to religion. I kept quiet.

Last night Ted began by saying how well Mrs. Thomlinson argued "for a woman," but of course she was wrong, though she tried to be logical. Then he went on to say that I agreed with her. He could tell by the look I had had on my face and that my bad disposition and philosophy was stamped on my countenance and made me look disagreeable and ugly, and what a disagreeable person I am, and how everybody knows it. I didn't answer.

I made no defense. Then he scolded me for a long time about religion and belief and how foolish and bad I was, and so on. I looked down at my hideous figure, my swollen ankles and I broke up. There isn't a characteristic I possess, either physical, mental, moral, spiritual, or social, that suits him. There isn't a thing I can do or be that he will approve. He seems to have made up his mind that he has a thoroughly bad bargain, but he is going to be sensible and abide it. As a Catholic, he cannot think of divorce. He must keep his wife in respectable condition and decent order, the same as the rest of his worldly belongings.

The wife must be obedient. She must succumb to the bodily possession whenever lust sweeps him. That is what galls. That is the degradation. He will score me up like this, tear me to pieces like an old circular, breaking my heart, and not care at all. But any night he wishes, he may walk into my room without a knock or a by-your-leave and work his will with my body. That is what I *hate*. It is humiliating. It hurts.

Friday, December 23rd. [1921]

. . . I want a letter from Dad. I am thinking of him often, of the times when I was a little child and he must have been a young man, of him taking me walking the tracks to his cottage office. On our way we went to scores of places and met all sorts of different people. I am listing them in my mind. And as I look back I see how fond he must have been of me. He never took any of his other children about as he took me, never talked to them as he talked to me. Dear old Dad, passionate, selfish, a most un-model-like husband and father. And yet how much he gave me. He showed me the historical world I lived in and he showed me the way into the imaginary world that has no end. I wish I could make a story of it all. I think of Mother, passionate too but passionate about persons and personalities. Dad was only passionate about the impersonal things, intangible things like art and literature, actors, and politics. They are another pair who could never understand each other, another pair dissatisfied, unsatisfied. What is wrong with marriage that so few people can find it tolerable? Common courtesy will make daily living tolerable. But what heart is satisfied with courtesy any more than justice?

Thursday, April 27th. [1922]

. . . In the last twenty or thirty years women have changed fundamentally. We are not like our mothers. We do not look at life as they did and we will not accept it as they did. Our men have not changed. They are just like their forebears and they can't understand us. We hurt them in their vanities and sensibilities and then they hurt us back again. It is tragic. Yet how do we alter it? I can't see any way except in giving new ideas to our sons. Perhaps the youngsters will find out the proper way to change marriage.

Today women have a sense of separateness that is new to the sex. We regard ourselves as individuals, not as simply wives or mothers, not possessions. Men hate that. They call it disloyalty and that is the unforgivable Judas sin. We can't change that. The men must change their ideas.

Thursday, February 27th. [1936]

I am in a bad way. My head and my womb are creepy with desire and I have an inner trembling I cannot still. All my morning work is done, but no work wears away this misery.

Last night I was thrust into anger by a rebuff. At the bottom of half my troubles lies unappeased eroticism. Ted spends his passion and his romantic imagination on religion and the Church, whilst I consume myself. He gushes a devotion to Mary, the Mother of God; but for Ruby, the mother of his children, there is no devotion, only depreciation of her motherhood. If I were a frigid woman I might appreciate his "chastity" and "purity." I might even be thankful he was like that. I am not a frigid woman. I am ardent and full blooded, and I require both affection and passion to live happily. Ted's neglect chafes me, whilst his passion for religion enrages me. His piety, his sanctimoniousness, his perfect self-satisfiedness, and his occasional cold lust infuriate me.

Since 1920 there have come times when in desperation of my physical unease I have been driven to secret masturbation. This should not be, I know but it has been the only way in which I could ease myself. I should have taken a lover. I didn't. The regret of my life, now that it is too late, is that I never did so. Life has been a constant warfare: with him, with myself. I am trying to presume the appearances of graciousness. God help me.

NOTE

[1] Biographical information is from *Ruby: An Ordinary Woman,* edited by Bonnie Thompson Glaser and Ann Martin Worster.

WORKS CONSULTED

Epstein, Barbara. "Family, Sexual Morality, and Popular Movements in Turn-of-the-Century America." *Powers of Desire: The Politics of Sexuality.* Ed. Ann Snitow et al. New York: Monthly Review Press, 1983.

Glazer, Bonnie Thompson, and Ann Martin Worster, eds. *Ruby: An Ordinary Woman.* New York: Faber and Faber, 1995.

Kent, Susan Kingsley. *Making Peace: The Reconstruction of Gender in Interwar Britain.* Princeton: Princeton UP, 1993.

SUSAN B. ANTHONY *(1820–1906)*

The Ideal Man

> I never met a man whom I thought I loved well enough to live with all my life, and for that matter, I never met one whom I thought loved me well enough to live with me all his life. That marriage proposition has two sides. Probably I'd have been very trying to live with.
>
> *Susan B. Anthony, 1896*

Cultural historian William Leach has argued that a concern with "love" played a crucial role in the ideological work of some mid- to late nineteenth-century U. S. feminists. Rejecting a narrow equation between feminism and "suffragism," Leach examines these men's and women's struggles to "forge a new union based on what they often referred to as true love" (3). For these feminists, true love meant "rational" love. The basis of rational love was to be found in personal and social equality between heterosexual partners, including equal access to sexual and scientific truths, to educational and economic opportunities, and to equally functional public dress. Even more, rational love was a complex ideological position which rejected two other dominant tropes of "love" in the mid-nineteenth century, sentimental love and romantic love.

Although both sentimental and romantic love have long roots in western thought (see the headnote on Héloïse in this section), each re-emerges at certain historical junctures for specific social and cultural reasons. In the United States, sentimental love had its roots in the appearance of a sexual division of labor in the nineteenth-century economy, and in the rise of a more gentle, fluid, "feminized," and democratic evangelism, in the place of a grim and static eighteenth-century Calvinism. Sentimental love was based on a glorification of sexual difference in which women were held to be the idealized objects of men's affection as well as the passive recipients of that affection. The ideal woman in the sentimental mindset was selfless, benevolent, domesticated, and pure, most frequently embodied in the image of the ever-giving, self-sacrificing mother. In exchange for this sacrifice, women were granted a certain authority over the private lives of their husband and children in the form of a redemptive moral power.

Romantic love stems from the ideas of the French Revolution and the larger Enlightenment project, and in the rise of economic individualism in the U. S. in the late eighteenth and early nineteenth centuries. Romantic love was based on extreme passion and on the uncertain and potentially painful process of "falling in love" by possessing or being possessed by an Other. In romantic love, the object of passion was often cloaked in a magical aura, and could be alternately idealized and vilified. Moreover, romance required resistance, tension, and conflict. The romantic lover (usually represented as male) takes a jealous attitude toward the beloved (usually represented as female), hoping at once to "save" her from oppression, and yet also fearful of dangers (betrayal of some sort) that she posed to him. Eighteenth- and nineteenth-century observers often linked romanticism to social and political radicalism and revolution that followed from the acting out of the extremes of sexual difference that were part of the ideology of these movements.

These nineteenth-century feminist writers attacked both sentimental and romantic love for what they saw as their oppressiveness insofar as women were concerned. Sentimental love was regarded as the justification for the unhealthy segregation of the sexes and for the oppressive and dysfunctional ideal of "separate spheres" which shackled women to the household; the ideology of "separate spheres" both upheld and obscured the status quo. Moreover, the sentimentalization of love was believed to constantly threaten sexual and personal disaster by making women sexually unapproachable and undermining male self-confidence, thus encouraging the abuse and brutalization of women by men. Romantic love was attacked for the way in which it perpetuated ignorance, shallow sexual infatuation, vanity, infantile fantasies, unreasonable expectations, and unhealthy desires. Seen as blinding and dangerous, romantic love was charged with severely undermining any sort of stable relationship.

In distinction to these notions, these feminists created and promoted a version of love which would provide stability and equal authority to women in the marital relationship. Rejecting fantasy and passion, which could place women in vulnerable and dependent positions, proponents of rational love emphasized self-control, balance, moderation, and a rational calculation of mutual interests by those entering into marriage. Also, harmonious and healthy sexual relations were promised through an equal knowledge by both sexes of the science and physiology of sex. Rational love would be based upon an entirely new process of gender socialization, in which boys and girls were not separated, but were educated together, shared the same foods and the same functional clothing, and developed mutual interests from the start. This ideal, according to Leach, embodies the fact that most middle-class feminists had no desire to further "endanger" sexual relations between men and women, that they were neither "anarchists nor radical individualists," but instead wanted to reconstruct gender relations on a more secure basis by rejecting sentimentalism and romanticism in favor of rationalism (123).

Nonetheless, Leach notes that in many ways, the nineteenth-century feminists he describes would slip into sentimentalism and romanticism, because these alternatives were not without their benefits to women. Sentimentalism was frequently called upon to justify women's efforts in public reform, by positing the moral improvement that women would bring to men in a public setting,[1] while romantic individualism would often emerge in feminists' calls for individual freedom and self-fulfillment, exemplified in divorce reform and "free love" debates. Rational love, then, had as its foundation the individual relationship, just as sentimental and romantic love did. By so carefully and intricately outlining the ideal love relationship, and by describing such clear-cut yet often unattainable conditions by which it was to be enjoyed, these activists created a situation in which great expectations for rational love, and thus the possibility for great disappointment, existed.

Such expectations and disappointments are clearly manifest in the private writings of

Ruby Thompson from the early twentieth century. They are also manifest in the public proclamations of Susan B. Anthony about ideal relationships. The excerpts which follow were written by Anthony in 1896 and 1901, towards the end of her life. During this period, Anthony was president of the National American Woman Suffrage Association, the group formed by the reunited factions of the women's suffrage movement, which had split in the 1870s (Kugler). In this position, Anthony was compelled to account for her choice to remain single. Even when not speaking to the question of her single status directly, Anthony addressed this issue every time she spoke of gender relations. Her search for an ideal partnership, partially achieved through her career-long collaboration with Elizabeth Cady Stanton, reveals the depth and complexity of feminist concerns during this period, as well as the importance of love ideals and the complex relationship between notions of love and gender in the thought of the time.

KKF

FROM THE WRITINGS OF SUSAN B. ANTHONY[§]

From a Letter to the Editor, 1896

Men want for wives the intelligent, educated and in every way well-developed woman, and at the same time they want to keep her the same, old-fashioned, meek, submissive, willing reflection of the man who marries her. The two cannot be combined. The woman of the past, who was but an echo of her husband's wish and will, can be duplicated in the woman of the present only by keeping her ignorant and dependent.

As a matter of fact the modern, progressive man would not be satisfied with the old-style wife: she would pall upon him—he would be ashamed of her. The college-bred man of to-day wants an educated, up-to-date wife, who can "hold her own" in conversation with his friends, who belongs to a good club, who is a recognized influence in the community. He will have to learn, however, that the very qualifications which fit her for all this make it impossible for her to take a subordinate place in the household, and that her equality must be recognized. But he will find, also, that this education, this discipline, this knowledge of the world will render her a much more capable housekeeper and an infinitely better mother. . . .

This new order of womanhood will finally result in a superior type of manhood. This modern woman will not be averse to marriage, but she will insist upon a manhood which will be worthy of woman, her love and respect, and she never will rest until she brings men up to her standard. We then will have not only a better motherhood, but a nobler fatherhood.

[§] Reprinted from *Failure is Impossible: Susan B. Anthony in Her Own Words*, edited by Lynn Sherr. Copyright © 1995 by Lynn Sherr. Reprinted by permission of Times Books, a division of Random House, Inc. Material excerpted from pages 11–12.

From a Newspaper Article, "The Ideal Husband," 1901

The ideal husband is the one who does not take advantage of the power which the law confers upon him. . . .

Our foremothers kept no record of their ideal man, not even on the faded pages of their little worn dairies. Whenever their brief, practical entries go beyond the details of the household expenses and the family illnesses, into the realm of aspiration, it is always in regard to the heavenly life. The conditions of this one they considered beyond remedy. But, understanding the nature of woman, and knowing that her dearest hopes, her fondest desires, are concentrated in the future of her children, we may well believe that these old-time mothers did dream of an ideal husband for their daughters and that, if interpreted, it would have read: "A man who will lift women up to a plane with himself."

For the past two generations men have been approaching this ideal. . . .

The man of to-day does not find his equanimity very rudely disturbed when his blushing bride declines to promise at the altar "to obey." He has rather more respect for her for not doing it. The old attitude of sovereignty on one hand and obedience on the other has largely disappeared. Enlightened men no longer marry for the purpose of getting a housekeeper or with the sole object of raising a family of children, but through the desire of congenial companionship and with the intention of stimulating the development of the wife along the lines for which she is best fitted. Thus far we have the ideal husband, not universally, but in sufficient numbers to offer much hope for the future.

An ideal husband will not come into the presence of wife and children exhaling the odor of liquor and tobacco. In olden times it is doubtful if women would have dared form such an ideal as this, but already it is partly reached. Then, liquor was on every sideboard and ladies withdrew from the dinner table in order that gentlemen (!) might get drunk. Now the gentleman who gets drunk carefully conceals that fact from the ladies of his acquaintance. Where formerly the woman endured the intemperate husband as her inevitable lot, the law now steps in and sets her free. The abolition of the tobacco habit forms a part of the future ideal.

The woman of to-day has a moral ideal. She dreams of a time when there shall be but one standard of virtue for the two sexes. . . . The attitude of society toward the immoral man is gradually changing. Like the drunkard he is beginning to cover his tracks. His lapses are no longer a matter of pride. The new self-respect of women is protesting against man's defiance of the moral code and he is commencing to feel the effects of social ostracism, which will increase as women grow stronger in self-reliance. And here again the revised statutes come to the rescue of the wife and relieve her from that body of living death—a husband who is unfaithful to his marriage vows.

NOTE

[1] This was an important aspect of the funding of coeducational institutions in the nineteenth century, as described by Lori Ginzberg in "The 'Joint Education of the Sexes': Oberlin's

Original Vision," from *Educating Men and Women Together: Coeducation in a Changing World.*

WORKS CONSULTED

Ginzberg, Lori. "The 'Joint Education of the Sexes': Oberlin's Original Vision." *Educating Men and Women Together: Coeducation in a Changing World.* Ed. Carol Lasser. Urbana: U Illinois Press, 1987.

Kugler, Israel. *From Ladies to Women: The Organized Struggle for Women's Rights in the Reconstruction Era.* Westport, CT: Greenwood Press, 1987.

Leach, William. *True Love and Perfect Union: The Feminist Reform of Sex and Society.* New York: Basic Books, 1980.

CHINESE WOMAN *(20th century)*

"Justice for Single Women"

> There are three things which are unfilial, and the greatest of them is to have no posterity.
>
> *Mencius (c. 370–334 BCE)*[1]

Mencius was a philosopher and advisor to provincial kings of the Chinese Empire who provided in his writings perhaps the most thorough and widely-read account of Confucian values. In the Confucian system, a protocol for the proper form of social and familial life (see headnote for Canton Delta Marriage Resisters), the basis of both civilization and of virtue was filial piety—the loyalty and obedience of children to the customs and wishes of their father.[2] Throughout the roughly one-thousand-year period of the Chinese Empire, the preservation of the family as the unit of social and economic security and respectability was the foremost concern of a Chinese patriarch. There were moreover highly specific means by which posterity was to be continued. Patrilocal marriage, wherein the bride left her natal home to be incorporated into her husband's home, was the most prestigious form of marriage, and only under unusual circumstances, such as prevailed in the sericulture (silk-producing) regions of Canton, were alternatives accepted. Those who challenged the dominant expectations of familial participation were thus subject to the strongest criticism and estrangement by the dominant ethical system in China for millennia.

This ethical system, along with the importance of "filial piety" in shaping the lives of millions, was shaken as China entered the twentieth century and the age of Empire came to a close in 1911. As communist agitation spread throughout China (especially during the 1920s, as the Chinese Republic was faltering and social chaos prevailed), the nation began to experience a "family revolution," just as had happened in Russia approximately a decade earlier (Stacey 3). Leaders in the vanguard of social change attempted to restructure gender and generational hierarchies as part of a larger social transformation. The Chinese Communist Party (CCP) was never as radical in its attack on the traditional family as the Bolsheviks (the CCP advocated neither "free love" nor the "withering away" of the family). Nonetheless, antipatriarchal family reforms were a prominent part of revolutionary process in China during the late 1940s. The first law passed by the Chinese Communist Party upon assuming power in 1950 was a Marriage Law that explicitly attacked the patriarchal family by making divorce equally accessible to men and women, and making the government, rather than prominent local families, the arbiter of family disputes (Stacey 176–182).

By 1953 however, the CCP began to abandon this activist approach to family reform in part because of stiff resistance from the peasantry. Divorce rights, communal kitchens, and day-care programs were all targets of resentment from many involved in rural and semirural agriculture and industry. The CCP began an alternate process of strengthening the traditional patriarchal family, albeit with certain reforms, which in turn strengthened peasant support for and cooperation with the revolution. Peasant resistance during the Great Leap Forward nearly brought the Communist Party to its knees, and it learned that peasant cooperation was crucial to the continuation of the People's Republic. The CCP thus reverted to a stance which has been dubbed patriarchal socialism—in effect a democratization of the patriarchal ideal so that it became a reality for many millions more than it could have become under the old Imperial system (Stacey 115–135).

This autobiographical account by a contemporary Chinese teacher[3] shows that a strong bias against unmarried people still prevails even among the most educated strata of society. The popular distaste that scholars have noted towards all types of alternative marriage practices in China (for example, the demonization of "girls' houses" and "sworn spinsters" as sites or persons devoted to profligacy or homosexuality) survived the antipatriarchal reforms of the Chinese Communist Party, while the demands of filial piety have maintained their hegemony. Despite recent concern and attempts by the government to curb population growth, foremost among these traditional demands is the responsibility to bear children and preserve a patriarchal line (Stacey 268–280). This unmarried contemporary Chinese woman came of age during the cultural revolution of the 1960s, a time when women were first being exposed to opportunities for higher education. But despite the degree to which she was educated, in her small home town (near the Sanggan river), traditional marriage and family life have prevailed as more important to social success than an advanced education.

KKF

FROM A CONTEMPORARY INTERVIEW WITH A CHINESE TEACHER[§]

It's no crime not to marry. In general I get on well with my colleagues but because I'm not married they always make me feel the odd one out, different from the rest. Lots of students come to see me here and that's okay, but male colleagues couldn't. Gossip is a terrible thing.

I live among the students. I like teaching them. What chance do country children have of broadening their experience except by getting an education? All that most of them have to look forward to is going home to work the land. So they're really keen to learn. If a student is prepared to make an effort, I'll do anything I can to help, whether it's a matter of coaching, finding some money or fixing something up. Country children are honest. It's the students who keep me going. . . .

§ Reprinted from *Chinese Lives: An Oral History of Contemporary China* by Zhang Xinxin and Sang Ye, translated and edited by W. J. F. Jenner and Delia Davin. Copyright © 1987 by W. J. F. Jenner and Delia Davin. Reprinted by permission of Pantheon Books, a division of Random House, Inc. Material excerpted from pages 203–208.

This is my home town. I was thirty-one when they started holding college entrance exams again in 1978. Another year and I would have been over the age limit. I didn't dare apply for university, so I put down Hebei Teachers' College. I was the only woman in the whole county to get in anywhere that year. My family all thought I would go far but I ended up back here. . . .

After my mother's death I simply went to pieces. In 1974 I came down with hepatitis and neurasthenia. I also had a stomach hemorrhage and myocarditis. As soon as I was taken off the drip, I went straight back to my classes. Immediately I felt my life was still worth something. I kept at my books all the time I was ill: I told myself that if I wasn't going to be an educated woman, I could at least be an educated ghost.

Now I was alone I lived in the dormitory by the main gate. . . . It was very lonely being the only person there in the holidays. I asked the principal to let me have a little room in the back courtyard where the teachers' families lived. "Nobody's stopping you getting married," was his reply. "The rules say that single people have to live in collective accommodation." Collective indeed! I was living all by myself. What harm was I doing to anyone? Why should single people be refused their own rooms? So I did as my students suggested and moved into an empty room in the back courtyard.

The school authorities were furious. They swore at me and I lost my temper and told them I'd die before I moved. They took the case to the county education department and someone came to sort it out. He was quite sympathetic and said that as I'd already settled in, I shouldn't be asked to move. The principal felt let down and threatened to resign if I wouldn't give up the room. Then he cancelled my classes. I told him he had no right to do this and deprive my students of their lessons. It wasn't even a good room, just a storeroom, dirty and full of rubbish.

All I want is justice for us single women. Only children are doing fine these days, so why should women who are on their own be given such a hard time? We're not distracted by housework, we don't take maternity leave and we don't have to miss work because of sick children. Some mothers take it very easy at work, as if they deserved some reward. That's not fair at all. In other countries people are eager to employ single women. Now that we're adopting so many other things from abroad, why don't we take up that one? . . .

My students often ask why I never married. I tell them it's simple. I was eighteen when the Cultural Revolution began, and it went on until my mother died when I was twenty-six. Then my health collapsed. By the time I'd finished college I was nearly thirty-seven. People don't understand. They think I set my sights too high, or that I'm cranky, or have had some infection I'm ashamed to reveal. At least it's better than during the Cultural Revolution when unmarried people were accused of being secret agents sending off messages in the middle of the night. . . .

I talk to men and boys a lot in my work. Frankly I think a lot of men are pettier than women. Marriage can be just a series of trivial quarrels. Marriage for its own sake is stupid. It's tiring enough being out at work all day, without having to be on your guard against someone at home and sharing your bed with a virtual stranger. What's more I don't understand at all why loose women get on so well, unlike us serious women. I can't fathom this "sexual liberation". Marriage is a serious matter. I could never switch from one man to another. Why do women always let men deceive them? It's not as if we were any less intelligent than them. . . .

I'm sure I'm not the only single woman to feel the way I do. I want to appeal for equal rights for us. I wrote a letter to *New Outlook* and they published about a third of it. Perhaps they thought it got too complicated. Extracts were reprinted in various papers. Then I really did have problems. I got dozens of letters every day, sometimes as many as a hundred. Some supported me or poured out their woes—these were from women. Others told me what to do. I tried to reply to all of this group. The other 90 per cent were proposals of marriage. They thought I'd been advertising for a husband!. . . Some letters were really obscene. But I don't want to marry . . .

I never thought that the leadership would take any notice of my letter in *New Outlook*. But they did. They said I'd implied they neglected me. In the staff appraisal at the end of the year I'm always put in the bottom 5 per cent. I complained about being in the lowest group when my class had the best marks. "As you're so good at writing, put it in the papers," was the principal's reply. And I know I'll have more trouble now we're going to have our professional gradings fixed. Letters to the county education department and visits from higher officials are no use in the end. As soon as the high-ups leave he says: "Don't you forget I'm the principal."

My only fault is that I'm different from other people because I haven't married.

NOTES

[1] Cited in Ch'u Chai and Winberg Chai, *The Changing Society of China*. New York: New American Library, 1962: 81 n3.

[2] "This obedience was of a part with the obedience due to a sovereign from his subject, to a husband from his wife, and to an elder brother from the younger. These were the relationships identified by Confucian scholars as most important in the social system" (Stacey 30).

[3] The oral history in which this account appears does not provide her name. [Eds.]

WORKS CONSULTED

Ch'u Chai and Winberg Chai. *The Changing Society of China*. New York: New American Library, 1962.

Stacey, Judith. *Patriarchy and Socialist Revolution in China*. Berkeley: U of California P, 1983.

HORTENSIA *(1st century BCE)*

Taxation Without Representation

> . . . what has nature wanted to be more dear to us than our daughters?
>
> *Cicero, 70 BCE*[1]

Unlike ancient Athenians (see Hipparchia in **Work and Education**), Romans maintained no radical separation of women from men in the arenas of politics, culture, and social life. In both Roman history and legend, gatherings of women for political purposes were frequent and notable. The historian Livy in particular recounted several stories about honorable Roman women congregating at critical moments and performing actions which insured the safety of the state (Pomeroy 176). Women in Rome were not permitted any formal role in the government, but through their central role in elite families (as well as the central role of elite families in Roman politics), they were able to exert great influence on political, economic, and social matters. The family position which afforded Roman women the most influence was not mother or wife, but daughter.[2]

The power of all family members, including daughters, was ultimately derived from the father or *paterfamilias,* the most powerful figure in Roman society. Fathers were granted extensive rights over all their family members, including the right to kill disobedient children or sell them into slavery, even as adults. Roman fathers and sons were thought to be (and often were) in fierce political competition with one another, while the presumed closeness between mothers and sons was based on the idea that mothers pursued their political ambitions through their sons. Conversely, the father-daughter bond was supposed to be removed from that competition. A daughter was expected to be deferential and dependent on her father throughout her life. Her allegiance to her father was assumed to supersede that to her husband, but in return she gained a support and prominence that would serve as cultural currency allowing her as an adult to behave assertively in public and private.

The distinctiveness of the bond between Roman fathers and daughters is highlighted when compared to Athenian and Etruscan societies, in which daughters were devalued; in these cultures it was acceptable to routinely "expose" infant girls—to abandon them to die—or to sell them into prostitution or slavery. Also, unlike the Etruscans in particular, Romans did not particularly value the husband-wife bond, but made the father-daughter bond the heterosexual family bond of primary importance (Hallett 32, 219).

Hortensia was the daughter of Quintus Hortensius, a distinguished orator who died in 50 BCE, eight years before the incident described in our selection. Certainly Hortensia's success, as well as her subsequent praise by Roman historians, was due to the ways in which she manifested the positive bond between herself and her father by reviving his eloquence, as well as his republican traditionalism through her anti-triumvir stance. According to the first-century CE historian Valerius Maximus, when Hortensia spoke in the Forum, "Quintus Hortensius lived again in the female line and breathed through his daughter's words. If any of her male descendants had wished to follow her strength, the great heritage of Hortensian eloquence would not have ended with a woman's action" (qtd. in Lefkowitz and Fant 152). Maximus' comments attest to the honor that elite daughters, as well as sons, could gain by embodying and carrying on the virtues of their esteemed fathers.

We have very few sources from the ancient world written by women themselves, but Hortensia's speech was apparently recorded and later retold (in similar versions) by many male historians. This version was written by Appian in the 2nd century CE, from his account of the civil wars that began in Rome in 44 BCE with the assassination of Julius Caesar and the seizure of power by the second triumvirate of Anthony, Octavian, and Lepidus. Hortensia's speech makes it clear that elite women in late Republican Rome not only had control over substantial amounts of property—property that could play a crucial role in affairs of state—but also that these women had a very firm understanding of their rights and responsibilities with regard to the government, and felt confident to judge what constituted legitimate political authority. This highlights the long-standing tie between family connections and political activism—a tie that has had particular impact on the processes by which women gain access to political power.

KKF

FROM *HORTENSIA'S SPEECH, ROME, 42 BC* [§]

> Since Appian wrote in Greek during the second century AD, what follows is his own version of what Hortensia said, though it is known . . . that her speech was preserved and read many years after it was delivered. When the triumvirs Octavian, Antony and Lepidus were unable to raise enough money by selling the property of the people they had proscribed (or condemned to death by judicial process for political revenge or financial expediency), they decided to pass an edict demanding evaluations of the property of the 1,400 wealthiest women, in order to collect money from them. The speech had an effect: the next day the triumvirs reduced considerably the number of women to be taxed, and instead decreed that men worth 100,000 sesterces or more were required to make substantial contributions (Lefkowitz and Fant, 149).

[The historian Appian] [These] women decided to ask the wives of the triumvirs for help.[3] They were not disappointed by Octavian's sister or by Antony's mother, but when Antony's wife Fulvia threw them out of the house, they did not put up with the insult and pushed their way into the forum onto the tribunal of the triumvirs, while the people and

the guards stood aside for them. This is what they said, through Hortensia who was selected as their spokesman:

'As was appropriate for women like ourselves when addressing a petition to you, we rushed to your womenfolk. But we did not get the treatment we were entitled to from Fulvia, and have been driven by her into the Forum. You have already stolen from us our fathers and sons and husbands and brothers by your proscriptions, on the grounds that they had wronged you. But if you also steal from us our property, you will set us into a state unworthy of our family and manners and our female sex. If you claim that you have in any way been wronged by us, as you were by our husbands, proscribe us as you did them. But if we women have not voted any of you public enemies, if we did not demolish your houses or destroy your army or lead another army against you; if we have not kept you from public office or honour, why should we share the penalties if we have no part in the wrongdoing?

Why should we pay taxes when we have no part in public office or honours or commands or government in general, an evil you have fought over with such disastrous results? Because, you say, this is a time of war? And when have there not been wars? And when have women paid taxes? By nature of their sex women are absolved from paying taxes among all mankind. Our mothers on one occasion long ago were superior to their sex and paid taxes, when your whole government was threatened and the city itself, when the Carthaginians were pressuring you. They gave willingly, not from their land or their fields or their dowry or their households, without which life would be unlivable for free women, but only from their own jewellery, and not with a fixed price set on it, nor under threat of informers and accusers or by force, but they gave as much as they themselves chose. Why are you now so anxious about the government or the country? But if there should be a war against the Celts or Parthians, we will not be less eager for our country's welfare than our mothers. But we will never pay taxes for civil wars, and we will not cooperate with you against each other. We did not pay taxes to Caesar or to Pompey, nor did Marius ask us for contributions, nor Cinna nor Sulla, even though he was a tyrant over this country. And you say that you are re-establishing the Republic!'

After Hortensia made this speech, the triumvirs were angry that women had the nerve to hold a public meeting while the men were silent, and that women demanded an accounting from the triumvirs, and that they would not supply the money while the men were serving in the army. They ordered the lictors to drive them away from the tribunal, until the lictors were stopped by the shouts of the crowd outside and the triumvirs postponed the proceedings till the next day.

NOTES

[1] Quoted and translated by Judith P. Hallett in *Fathers and Daughters in Roman Society: Women and the Elite Family.* Princeton: Princeton UP, 1984: 62–3.

[2] This is Hallett's argument, which she advances most fully in chapters 1 and 3.

[3] Such petitions to the ruler's womenfolk became standard practice in the Empire [Lefkowitz and Fant].

WORKS CONSULTED

Hallett, Judith P. *Fathers and Daughters in Roman Society: Women and the Elite Family.* Princeton: Princeton UP, 1984.

Lefkowitz, Mary R., and Maureen B. Fant. *Women's Life in Greece and Rome: A Source Book in Translation.* 2nd ed. Baltimore: Johns Hopkins UP, 1992.

Pomeroy, Sarah B. *Goddesses, Whores, Wives, and Slaves: Women in Classical Antiquity.* New York: Schocken Books, 1975.

KUSUNOSE KITA *(1833–1920)* **AND MITSUI MARIKO** *(20th century)*

Feminist Agendas in Japan

Historian Ellen DuBois has written on woman suffrage around the world, arguing for the necessity to recognize the "internationalism of these movements, the co-operation among women of various nations, the influence that actions of women in one country have had on those in another, and the way that women's international co-operation gave them resources to combat their marginalisation in the politics of their own nations. Woman suffrage can be usefully conceptualized as an international protest movement. . . ." (DuBois 254). Our selections on Japanese women resisters, the writings by Kusunose Kita and Mitsui Mariko excerpted here, and those by Hiratsuka Raicho in **Representing Women**, illustrate this general context for the suffrage movement and evoke the specific issues faced by the women who have worked to build a feminist political agenda in Japan.

DuBois identifies three phases in the internationalism of suffrage. The first is the tie between women's temperance and woman suffrage: "The first international suffrage movement, much overlooked, was the World's Women's Christian Temperance Union. The WCTU, formed in the United States in 1874, began as a conventional Protestant women's organization with a narrow moral reform focus, but soon became an amazingly ambitious, politically aggressive women's organization" (256). A world representative of the WCTU visited Japan in 1886 and helped found the first branch in Tokyo. Like their counterparts around the world, these women pushed for temperance and high moral standards; in Japan, they also pushed the newly emergent state as it was setting up its structures and formulating its gender ideology.

The second phase linked suffrage with socialism: "What really distinguished socialist women's suffragism from the bourgeois variant was the link they made between women workers and political equality. The distinctively socialist argument for woman suffrage rested on the recognition that the increasingly public character of women's labour had to be matched with an equally public political role" (262). A popular rights movement emerged in Japan at this historical moment and found a number of female leaders. Hiratsuka Raicho, whose work we present in the third section, was one such activist who claimed that without women's participation, public policy on women's issues would be misguided; for her, women's voices made an important contribution to political debate. A century later, Mitsui Mariko, a Socialist Party member, would amplify this tradition, addressing the educational and employment issues of women in the late twentieth century.

The third phase was militant suffragism, most evident after 1890, that made a "contribution to the revival of suffragism by linking it to a fundamental challenge to gender definitions and relations, and adding a whole new level of tactical radicalism to suffrage agitation" (265). The history of Japanese suffrage is protracted, beginning with the debates on modernism in the 1860s, continuing through the ban on women's political participation from 1890 to 1922, entering a period of modified access to decision-making from 1922 until, finally, universal suffrage was granted with the new constitution of 1945. These three elements, the influence of Western ideas of morality, the changing status of women and work, and the shifting ideas about gender, provide an outline for the story of why women wanted the vote, the stages in their acquisition of it, and the results of having it.

After 1868, the beginning of the Meiji period in which Japan was rushed into contact with the rest of the world, Japanese women began to reflect on their experiences and to interpret them in light of what they were learning about women in other countries, and in contrast to the opportunities being given to men with modernization (Pharr 15–41). The Japanese debates over women's place in politics were particularly focused on two questions: should men and women enter the new era with similar opportunities or did women have a special character (sometimes understood positively, sometimes negatively) that meant they needed a separate status? (Sievers 10–25). The rise and evolution of feminist movements in Japan revolve around these two sets of questions and within the overlapping phases that DuBois outlined.

In the early 1870s, debates raged over how to have "modernity" without losing a grounding in tradition. For example, the government banned short hair for women, a tactic many women had taken up to show their enthusiasm for what they understood as the new ways. As Yukiko Matsukawa and Kaoru Tachi point out, "the state found it hard to manage selective Westernisation and the Japanese women's movement was galvanized in response to its attempts to do so" (173). The movement for women's rights was stymied in 1890 when the government banned women's participation in the political process (Sievers 100). The response of women throughout the country, like that of their counterparts in other parts of the world who were continually denied access to the vote, was to engage in reform societies and exert pressure on the government from outside rather than from within.

We include one excerpt that captures the essence of that debate here. In 1878, at a regional prefectural meeting in Hiroshima, a motion to extend voting rights to women who were property owners and taxpayers failed. The discussion spread to other prefectures and in September of that year, Kusunose Kita, a forty-five year old woman from Shikoku "who had assumed the property and tax liability for her husband after his death in 1872, raised angry questions about the links between property, voting rights, and gender" (Sievers 29). Her speech, part of which we include here, was reprinted in newspapers throughout the country and she became "an overnight celebrity in the nation and in the popular rights movement" (Sievers 29). Kusunose Kita remained an important symbol for Japanese women during the years in which massive shifts in ideas about women's roles took place and some women went public with their concerns.

Like Hortensia before her, Kusunose Kita links participation in decision-making with the power to resist circumstances. Hortensia rejected being taxed without being consulted; Kusunose Kita makes an additional claim, demanding that her rights match her responsibilities. The official ban on women's political participation was lifted in 1922. The next two decades witnessed continual agitation for suffrage against a national political agenda with alternate priorities. It was not until 1945, with the new constitution set up at the end of World War II, that the legal status for women's voting rights was ensured.

The attainment of suffrage, as feminists around the world came to understand by the middle of the twentieth century, was no guarantee that the political process would produce outcomes that changed the status of women. A key question for the women's movement internationally has been whether equality of access to political power is a sufficient basis for altering the status of women or whether policy outcomes that achieve equity or positively alter women's circumstances provide the grounds on which to base judgments about the change in women's status. The second excerpt reprinted here takes up this question.

Mitsui Mariko was elected to the Tokyo Metropolitan Assembly in 1987 as a member of the Socialist Party in Japan and "has gained a reputation as one of the most vocal and energetic representatives and one who gives top priority to women's issues" (Kaya 384). Long involved in women's groups during and after her university years, she worked both as an "office lady" (one of the women in business corporations whose professional duties include not only the expertise for which they have been trained but the traditional female tea-pouring ceremonies for colleagues) and as a school teacher before running for office. During these years, she visited the United States and followed the developments of the United Nations International Decade for Women (1975–85), observing the women's movement from a comparative perspective. She served as an assemblywoman from 1987 to 1993 when, citing its lack of commitment to feminist issues, she left the Socialist Party, and made an unsuccessful bid as an independent candidate for the national Diet. She helped to found the National Federation of Feminist Legislators in 1992, a nonpartisan group of males and females dedicated to increasing the participation of women in politics and to bringing a feminist agenda to the assemblies where they sit. We reprint the excerpts from her speech that are included in a biographical article on her, written in 1993. These arguments demonstrate her understanding that the right to vote and the right to hold electoral office are but the first steps in building a feminist agenda in any political arena. Kusunose Kita and Mitsui Mariko, a century apart, illuminate for us how women's resistance both reflects the varying contexts within which women work and maintains a steady eye on improving women's circumstances through whatever means they believe will be effective.

JFO

KUSUNOSE KITA[§]

From a Letter to the Governmental Authorities

We women who are heads of households must respond to the demands of the government just as other ordinary heads of household, but because we are women, we do not enjoy equal rights. We have the right neither to vote for district assembly representatives nor to act as legal guarantors in matters of property, even though we hold legal instruments for that purpose. This is an enormous infringement of our rights! . . .

[§] Excerpted from *Flowers In Salt: The Beginnings Of Feminist Consciousness In Modern Japan* by Sharon L. Sievers, with the permission of the publishers, Stanford University Press. Copyright © 1983 by the Board of Trustees of the Leland Stanford Junior University. Material excerpted from page 29.

If it is reasonable to assume that rights and duties go together, then we should make that widely held assumption that they are in fact corresponding responsibilities a reality. . . . I do not have the right to vote. I do not have the right to act as guarantor. My rights, compared with those of male heads of household, are totally ignored. Most reprehensible of all, the only equality I share with men who are heads of their households is the onerous duty of paying taxes. . . .

Officials to whom I complained tell me that men have greater rights than women because they bear the additional burden of military service . . . but my protest stands, since it is well known that men are routinely excused from military service precisely because they are heads of their households!

MITSUI MARIKO[§]

From a Speech before the Tokyo Metropolitan Assembly

Please imagine the following, everyone, that all the directors sitting on this side of the podium were women, except for one man, and that 118 of the 127 people sitting in the assembly were women and only nine were men. You would certainly think it was strange if all the members of the highest deliberative bodies with decision-making power in the government of Tokyo were women. Yet this strange phenomenon exists within the present assembly, only the situation is exactly the reverse. . . .

The place of learning is where equality should be carried through more than anywhere else. How on earth, then, can the Tokyo government allow public high school to discriminate against girls through the practice of setting recruitment quotas for girls? Because the so-called "numbered schools" (i.e., prestigious high schools which used to be boys' middle schools before the war) have a quota on girls that is about one-third that of boys, even girls who score the same as boys or higher on the entrance examinations end up not getting admitted. . . .

From "The Day Women Launched into Politics"

We are faced with the reality in which women's naked bodies are used for advertisement posters of many companies, and the government of Tokyo is no exception. An example was a poster for Tokyo's Bureau of Transportation which featured a woman in bikini. . . . Also, the subway posters showing only legs in high-heeled shoes were terrible. Our protest led to the Bureau of Citizens and Cultural Affairs issuing a warning, though it was not in writing, to all departments of the metropolitan government that in advertisement posters the female body or its parts should never be used as objects or simply to attract attention. . . .

[§] The two excerpts from Mitsui Mariko appear in the article by Emiko Kaya, "Mitsui Mariko: An Avowed Feminist Assemblywoman," included in *Japanese Women: New Feminist Perspectives on the Past, Present, and Future,* edited by Kumiko Fujimura-Fanselow and Atsuko Kameda; and published in 1995 by The Feminist Press at The City University of New York. Our material is excerpted from pages 385–390. Mitsui Mariko's speech originally appeared in the Minutes of the Tokyo Metropolitan Assembly, July 3, 1987; her article, "The Day Women Launched into Politics," first appeared in the *Bulletin of the Japan Women's Forum,* no. 49 (March).

When politicians talk about their achievements in the assembly, male politicians will usually talk about having sponsored the building of a hall, a bridge, or a subway, which cost some hundreds of millions of yen. My accomplishments are totally different from those of traditional politicians, but if there existed a newspaper devoted to the cause of advocating gender equality, I'm sure I would appear on the front page. Most people, other than those who are committed to the women's movement, do not consider the kinds of things I have been doing as having much importance. . . . Traditional politics has neglected issues pertaining to culture, social welfare, education, and equality, and spent most of our tax money on buildings and subways. However, I will stick to my position to give top priority to human rights and equality issues in politics. . . .

WORKS CONSULTED

DuBois, Ellen. "Woman Suffrage Around the World: Three Phases of Suffragist Internationalism." *Suffrage and Beyond: International Feminist Perspectives.* Ed. Caroline Daley and Melanie Nolan. New York: New York UP, 1994. 252–274.

Kaya, Emiko. "Mitsui Mariko: An Avowed Feminist Assemblywoman." *Japanese Women: New Feminist Perspectives on the Past, Present, and Future.* Ed. Kumiko Fujimura-Fanselow and Atsuko Kameda. New York: Feminist Press at CUNY, 1995.

Matsukawa, Yukiko, and Kaoru Tachi. "Woman's Suffrage and Gender Politics in Japan." *Suffrage and Beyond: International Feminist Perspectives.* Ed. Caroline Daley and Melanie Nolan. New York: New York UP, 1994.

Pharr, Susan. *Political Women in Japan: The Search for a Place in Political Life.* Berkeley: U of California P, 1981.

Sievers, Sharon L. *Flowers in Salt: The Beginnings of Feminist Consciousness in Modern Japan.* Stanford: Stanford UP, 1983.

THÉROIGNE DE MÉRICOURT *(1762–1808)*

Citizenship and Women's Right to Bear Arms

Théroigne de Méricourt was born the same year that Rousseau's famous pedagogical (and anti-feminist) text *Emile* was published (see headnote for Mary Wollstonecraft in **Vision and Transformation**). She has become one of the legendary female figures of the French Revolution, despite (and partly because of) the fact that she was horribly maligned by both the royalist and the revolutionary press during her lifetime. As a young woman during the period before the French Revolution, Théroigne made her living as the mistress of a number of European nobles and led the somewhat bohemian life of a *femme entretenue* (kept woman). Typically, even when she became a feminist activist and "amazon" later in her life, stories of her sexual past were consistently used against her as a form of reproach. Both her detractors and admirers make constant reference to her sexual charms and supposed availability. True to form, the famous French historian Michelet depicts her as "the heroic beauty who enchanted the hearts of our fathers and who caused them to see in a woman the very image of Liberty." Nevertheless, Théroigne was also the organizer of a *salon,* a frequent public speaker, and a participant in the capture of the Tuileries on August 10, 1792 (after which the King was provisionally relieved of his functions). She was the daughter of a family of well-to-do peasant farmers and spent her early years in Marcourt, a town in the Low Countries which was under Austro-Hungarian rule at the time. As a political figure, she often spoke out in favor of a French war with Austria as a means of liberating this area from imperial control. Théroigne spent the last decade of her life in confinement (she was officially "declared mad" in 1794) and died in La Salpêtrière asylum. Interestingly, the name by which she is known today was an invention of the royalist press; she was born Anne-Josèphe Terwagne.[1] She remains one of the most controversial personalities of the French Revolution.

Théroigne was ardently in favor of the right of French women to bear arms, which she linked to the attainment of women's social and political equality with men. Legend has it that she often dressed as an "amazon" on public occasions.[2] Feminist scholar Elisabeth Roudinesco, in her study of Théroigne de Méricourt, sees her as exemplifying what Roudinesco calls the second stage of French revolutionary feminist thought: namely, a "warrior feminism" that began to emerge in 1792. In contrast to the earlier trend of "theoretical feminism" (which focused on legal arguments in favor of civil and political rights for women), warrior feminism highlights the image of "amazon legions" and calls on women to participate in the French battle against foreign enemy powers. According to Roudinesco, this second stage of feminist activism is less elitist in its orientation than the first. It is the third stage of revolutionary feminism, however, that is primarily associated with street demonstrations and public rioting by working-class women, phenomena that became more frequent toward 1793 (a year that bore witness to the beginning of the most politically extreme phase of the

Revolution). Théroigne, who was a sympathizer with the more moderate and bourgeois Girondin politicians, was in fact vilified (in addition to being publicly whipped and then arrested) during this third period, both for her opposition to the political techniques of the Terror and for her support of women's participation in the public arena.[3]

Roudinesco describes Théroigne as the first revolutionary feminist to raise the issue of women's right to bear arms. Unlike the militarism of other activists such as Pauline Léon and Claire Lacombe, who wanted to organize "amazon legions" to combat an enemy which they saw as residing within France, Théroigne's militarism was partly a result of her desire to liberate her homeland from aristocratic oppression. In the speech which follows, Théroigne does not explicitly demand political equality for women. However, she does draw a connection between women's right to defend their country and the emergence of French women from "their shameful nullity, where the ignorance, pride and injustice of men had kept them enslaved for so long a time." She poses the questions, "Fellow women citizens, why should we not enter into rivalry with the men? Do they alone lay claim to have rights to glory . . ." Military action becomes a key component in this image of "glory" and "honor" which is inclusive of women. For Théroigne,"female citizens" must be defined by their rights not only to "[debate] in the public Assemblies "but to [fight] side by side with their husbands." In fact, it is because Théroigne's notion of citizenship is imbued with militarism that her vision of "amazon legions" is essentially a feminist one; her feminism reflects the critical role played by military power in the formation of modern nation-states. She remained firm in her support of "amazonian" intervention during her entire public career. Moreover, at a banquet held the evening after her speech to the Société Fraternelle des Minimes, Théroigne de Méricourt appeared once again in the costume of an amazon.

NM

FROM A SPEECH BEFORE THE *SOCIÉTÉ FRATERNELLE DES MINIMES* 25 MARCH 1792[§]

Women citizens, let us not forget that we owe ourselves wholly to the Fatherland; that it is our most sacred duty to strengthen between us the bonds of union, of confraternity, and to spread the principles of a calm energy, in order to prepare ourselves with as much wisdom as courage to repulse the attacks of the enemy. Women citizens, we may, through our generous devotion, break the thread of these intrigues. Let us arm ourselves; this is our right, by nature and even by the law; let us show the men that we are not inferior to them, either in virtues or in courage: let us show Europe that French women know their rights, and are capable of rising to the heights of the illuminists of the eighteenth century; let us despise prejudices, which, through the simple fact of being prejudices, are absurd, and often immoral, in that they make even our virtues seem a crime. The attempts that the executive might make

[§] Reprinted from *Théroigne de Méricourt: A Melancholic Woman during the French Revolution,* by Elisabeth Roudinesco. Translated by Martin Thom. Published 1991 by Verso, London. Material excerpted from pages 96–97.

subsequently in order to win back the confidence of the public will merely be snares which we should mistrust: for so long as our mores are not in accord with our laws, it will not give up hope of profiting from our vices in order to put us in chains again. It is perfectly simple, and you should even be forewarned against it, they will marshall the carpers and the hired hacks in an attempt to keep us back, using the weapons of ridicule and calumny, and all the ignoble means that base men employ in order to stifle the impulses of patriotism in feeble souls. However, fellow Frenchwomen, now that the spread of Enlightenment calls upon you to reflect, compare what we are in the social order with what we should be. In order to know our rights and duties, we must take reason as our arbiter, and, guided by her, we shall distinguish the just from the unjust. What consideration might then hold us back? . . . We shall take up arms, because it is reasonable to take steps to defend our rights and our hearths, and because we would be failing both ourselves and the Fatherland if the pusillanimity which we have suffered in our condition of slavery had still sufficient sway over us to prevent us from redoubling our efforts. In all respects, you surely can have no doubts that the example of our devotion will arouse in the souls of men the public virtues and the all-engulfing passions of the love of glory and of the Fatherland. We shall thus preserve liberty through emulation and through the social perfection arising out of this felicitous rivalry. Fellow Frenchwomen! I would urge you yet again: let us raise ourselves to the height of our destinies; let us break our chains; at last the time is ripe for Women to emerge from their shameful nullity, where the ignorance, pride and injustice of men had kept them enslaved for so long a time; let us return to those times when our Mothers, the Gauls and the proud Germans, debated in the public Assemblies, fought side by side with their husbands and repulsed the enemies of Liberty. Fellow Frenchwomen, the same blood still flows in our veins; what we did at Beauvais, and at Versailles, on 5 and 6 October, and in several other important and crucial circumstances, proves that we are not unfamiliar with generous sentiments. Let us then summon up our energy; for if we wish to preserve our liberty, we must prepare ourselves to do the most sublime things. . . . Fellow women citizens, why should we not enter into rivalry with the men? Do they alone lay claim to have rights to glory; no, no. . . . And we too would wish to earn a civic crown, and court the honour of dying for a liberty which is dearer perhaps to us than it is to them, since the effects of despotism weigh still more heavily upon our heads than upon theirs. Yes . . . generous fellow women citizens, all of you who hear me, let us take up arms, let us go and drill two or three times a week on the Champs Elysées, or on the Champ de la Fédération; let us open a list of French Amazons; and let all those who truly love their Fatherland write their names there; we shall then meet and agree as to the means by which we may organize a Regiment, after the fashion of the pupils of the Fatherland, the Old Men or of the sacred Regiment of Thebes. To finish, I hope that I may be allowed to present a *tricolore* flag to the women citizens of the faubourg Saint-Antoine.

NOTES

[1] Compare Zitkala-Ša and Olympe de Gouges, whose proper names were entirely self-invented.

[2] The Amazons, in classical mythology, were a tribe of warrior women of great military prowess who lived apart from men. Details of Théroigne's version of amazon costume are ambiguous: an anonymous portrait shows her in feminine attire with one breast exposed, echoing the classical Greek image from which the name amazon ("without a breast") was derived; a more famous engraving by Auguste Raffet shows her in more modest but extremely mannish skirt and jacket, with pistols at her side and a sword in her hand. Roudinesco suggests that both images are more "romantic fable" than fact; such contradictory images, however, exemplify the scandalous combination of sexuality and power embodied in Théroigne's "warrior woman" persona.

[3] It is important to note that Olympe de Gouges was executed in 1793. The feminism of this period tended to support the association of women with private life and thus condemned women like Olympe and Théroigne for their public activities.

WORKS CONSULTED

Michelet, Jules. *Les Femmes de la Révolution.* Ed. Françoise Giroud. Paris: Carrère, 1988.

Roudinesco, Elisabeth. *Théroigne de Méricourt: Une femme mélancolique sous la Révolution.* Paris: Editions du Seuil, 1989.

Soprani, Anne. *La Révolution et les Femmes de 1789 à 1796.* Paris: MA Editions, 1988.

AMADA PINEDA *(c. 1943–)*

"We Fought All the Harder"

The testimony of Amada Pineda, a Nicaraguan woman who was part of the revolutionary struggle against her government in the 1970s, confronts us with issues at the heart of accounts of many women who resist the political conditions of their times. How do gender dynamics play out in revolutionary movements? Is a focus on women central to attempts to change other oppressive systems or is it a facet of oppression that can be attended to at a later stage, after a movement for social change has attained some successes? What role do women play in such struggles? Do they provide domestic support for men as they traditionally do in peacetime? Do they fill in the economic and political vacuums created by men's departure to participate in these movements? Do they assume leadership positions during times of crises that are different from those that they hold otherwise? Are they attacked by their enemies in ways specific to their sex? How do men understand women's experiences in these struggles? Why are women in some countries and cultures able to sustain political resistance against military oppression when others are not? These are just some of the questions that arise from the brief but horrifying account that Pineda gives us of her torture by government forces.

Nicaragua has a long history of political conflict. Originally conquered by the Spanish in the sixteenth century, land was taken from the Indian peasants and consolidated into plantations where the indigenous populations were put under a system of slavery. Violence was the cornerstone of these relationships between colonizers and colonized and the seventeenth and eighteenth centuries were characterized by revolts and massive deaths among the Indian populations. Nicaragua became a republic in 1821 as the Spanish empire disintegrated. The United States began an active and interventionist relationship with this Central American country shortly thereafter, occasionally placing military occupation forces there.

The basis of the political struggles in Nicaragua has been economic. As the Spaniards departed, they left in place an elite that was in control of land, the military, economic resources, and political power. That elite was continually challenged by peasant armies, foremost among them one led by Augusto Cesar Sandino in the 1930s. In 1962, the FSLN (Sandinista Front for National Liberation) was formed, "a national liberation organization . . . with the aim of reviving Sandino's bid for sovereignty free of US domination" (Collinson 4). In 1979, the Sandinistas overthrew the Somoza dictatorship in power. But this formal success did not usher in the period of change anticipated by the revolutionary leadership. Rather, supported by international economic interests and assisted by the United States, armies known as the *contras* carried on a guerilla war that attempted to destabilize the new government. While the multiple international actors were confronting one another, Nicaraguan women were forming their own organizations and asking themselves and their countrymen fundamental questions about gender and the political process. It was in this context that Amada Pineda told her story to Margaret Randall.

Amada Pineda's torture was not unique: it was the experience of many of the women who joined in the revolutionary struggle. Margaret Randall, an activist and author who has written extensively on Nicaraguan women's lives over the past two decades, points out that "the advent of the feminist movement and the new theoretical and psychological breakthroughs it has engendered" (*Sandino's Daughters* 31) have enabled many women like Amada Pineda to survive their experiences of trauma and come out as active political resisters. Randall continues:

> But Nicaraguan women, despite these pressures and perhaps in some strange way because of their unrelenting intensity, have reacted in ways not seen before. And because the vast majority of Nicaraguan feminists have come to their feminism through years of political struggle, the other side of this reality may be that when they tell their stories and listen to each other, they are together able to move through an amazing spectrum of consciousness, healing and vision—with impressive speed and extraordinary potential for clarity. (33)

JFO

FROM AN INTERVIEW WITH AMADA PINEDA[§]

They used different kinds of approaches. Sometimes they used torture—they would beat me. Sometimes it was soft talk. I had to be careful not to contradict myself. Once they asked me how far I'd gotten in school, if I'd finished grade school or high school. I told them no, that we peasants never could go to school at all. When I was a child the nearest school was a three days' walk. I said I'd only been to second grade. "You aren't so dumb," the officer said. "You understand more than you let on. You know a lot more than you've told us." They asked about the "subversive activities" that took place in the union. "I don't know what you mean by subversive," I said. "Who is Sandino?" they asked. "Sandino," I said. "I never knew Sandino. I never even saw him."

When they came to rape me, after a while it was just. . . . unbearable. I wasn't going to take it anymore and I told the officer, "What do you men think I am? A prostitute? Someone they picked up in some market place? I'm a married woman, and even if my husband and I are separated now, I have children and they're all by him. And so do me a favour and tell your guards to leave me alone. Not to come near me anymore. I can't stand them." I was a prisoner but I think I made an impression on him because after that they just locked us all in that room and the guards didn't rape me anymore. But they'd already destroyed me. Raped me seventeen times. The first thing I asked for, later, when they let me go and I

[§] Reprinted from *Sandino's Daughters: Testimonies of Nicaraguan Women in Struggle,* by Margaret Randall. Copyright © 1994 by Margaret Randall. Published by Rutgers University Press. Reprinted by permission of Margaret Randall. Material reprinted from pages 87–89.

came to Managua, was to see a doctor. I didn't want to be pregnant, I didn't want to have a baby by one of them. Even if it wasn't the baby's fault.

Toward the end, they said they were going to take me up in a helicopter and drop me from the sky. "Okay," I said, "I've never been in an airplane or a helicopter either. It's fine by me if I have to go up in one to die. If you are going to do it let's get it over with." But they didn't. Instead, they took the other prisoners and tortured them in front of me. They beat them. They burned them. They half-buried them in ant hills.

After six or seven days of that, they let me go. Four officers from Managua came with the papers ordering my release. They told me to bathe and wash my clothes. I had to wash my clothes and put them right back on again, wet. They gave me a comb for my hair because it looked like a bird had built its nest there. They gave me soap, powder, deodorant. Imagine, all of a sudden they were the "nice guys." After all they'd done to me! My belly was still black and blue, and I was in constant pain. I had bruises all over my body. They even had the nerve to ask if I wanted to stay there with them, to cook for them and things like that. "No thank you," I said. "I think I'll just go home."

All this time my husband was in the Soviet Union. By chance he found out I had been captured. He read about it in *Granma,*[1] there in the Soviet Union. Once he knew what was happening to me he couldn't go on studying so he asked to be sent home. As soon as he got to the Nicaraguan border they picked him up. That's when they told me I wasn't a peasant; I was the wife of a "subversive element." They tortured my husband terribly. They strung him up for nine days, they beat him to a pulp, and they left him for dead in an empty cell. And they tortured him psychologically too. They told him about me, how all of them had "had" me, and that I'd enjoyed it.

When finally we could get together again, I was afraid. I knew the kinds of things they'd said to him, that they'd tried to set him against me. I thought he was going to reject me, that he wouldn't be able to stand me anymore. But no. He told me, "Don't worry. That can happen to any woman who fights, or whose husband is involved in the struggle. Look at what happened to Doris Tijerino, and lots of others sisters, too. I don't know why you feel so ashamed." But I did feel ashamed, for everything I'd been through. It was terribly traumatic. I felt like I smelled bad, and I couldn't get rid of the smell. But my husband was understanding; he helped me a lot.

I think the peasant men did understand what their wives went through. At least all the ones I knew. The wives and husbands continued living together and afterwards they fought on with even more courage. The National Guard thought that by torturing people they would force us to abandon the struggle. They thought the peasants would go home and not take part anymore. It wasn't true. All that we suffered made us fight with more determination. When they burned houses—often with children inside—we fought all the harder. . . .

NOTE

[1] The Cuban Communist Party Central Committee's daily paper [Randall].

WORKS CONSULTED

Collinson, Helen, ed. *Women and the Revolution in Nicaragua.* London: Zed Books Ltd., 1990.

Randall, Margaret. *Sandino's Daughters: Testimonies of Nicaraguan Women in Struggle.* New Brunswick: Rutgers UP, 1994.

—. *Sandino's Daughters Revisited: Feminism in Nicaragua.* New Brunswick: Rutgers UP, 1995.

IDA B. WELLS BARNETT *(1862–1931)*

"To Tell the Truth Freely"

Erased for many years from histories of reform, Ida B. Wells Barnett is remembered today as one of the outstanding investigative journalists in the history of the United States. It was she who amassed the details that proved lynchings of African Americans to be retaliations for economic success rather than punishments for rape, and she conducted a vigorous one-woman campaign for legal justice. Her arguments were fact-filled and relentlessly logical. They were also scathing, impassioned exposés of the ways in which the authority system she was attacking mystified the real power relations at issue: power relations based on race, class, and gender subordination. In her challenge to dominant white stereotypes of African-American and white womanhood and African-American manhood, Wells was literally staking her life in the cause of justice for African Americans.

Such activism placed Wells in the new category of "Afro-American agitator," a term used proudly by the National Afro-American League as an indicator of their militant insistence on claiming their Constitutional rights (Thompson 20). Wells' career as an agitator began on a train in Tennessee in 1884, not long after the repeal of the Civil Rights Bill had paved the way for a retrenchment of white power in the South. A conductor told Wells, a young schoolteacher, to leave the ladies' car where she had always sat before. She refused, he tried to drag her out, and she fastened her teeth in his arm, bracing herself between the seats. After he and two other men succeeded in ejecting her to the applause of white passengers, Wells sued the railroad company and won $500 damages in a decision that was quickly reversed by the supreme court of Tennessee.

Wells' account of the experience for a church newspaper launched her career in journalism, which became her livelihood after one of her editorials in the *Memphis Free Speech* caused the school board to fire her. When a close friend was lynched for what was obviously the "crime" of competing successfully with a white man in the grocery business, Wells used the paper, of which she was co-publisher, to organize mass westward emigration and a streetcar boycott. Her extremely successful work as an agitator culminated in an editorial that put her life in jeopardy. Wells declared, ". . . Nobody in this section believes the old thread-bare lie that Negro men assault white women. If Southern white men are not careful they will over-reach themselves and a conclusion will be reached which will be very damaging to the moral reputation of their women" (*Crusade* 65–66). A white paper countered with an editorial that fortunately appeared when Wells was out of town, and resulted in her "exile" in the North: "The black wretch who had written that foul lie should be tied to a stake at the corner of Main and Madison Streets, a pair of tailor's shears used on him and he should then be burned at a stake" (qtd. in *Crusade* 66).

The virulence of this editorial showed that Wells' suggestion, documented in her extensive research, had been accurate: the publicizing of "rape" as the reason for lynchings was merely a cover. First, it was a cover for economic motives—"An excuse to get rid of Negroes who were acquiring wealth and property and thus keep the race terrorized . . . " (*Crusade* 64). Second, although less often, it was a cover for consenting sexual relations between white women and African-American men. A white woman found in the cabin of her lover thus became, in newspaper reports, a seven-year old girl "raped" by an African-American man (*Crusade* 66); another man was lynched with letters from his white lover in his pocket; and so on. In reading the excerpt reprinted here, it is important to realize that Wells shared the ethical and religious consensus of her society—including the white men who defended the honor of "their" women in the editorial calling for Memphis citizens to lynch her—that any sexual relationship between people who were not married to each other was morally wrong, "illicit." Hence her comments on the damage the truth would do to white women's "reputation" and her reference to the moral "weakness" of African-American men who succumbed to sexual temptation, which she contrasts with the "crime" of which they were actually accused.

After the incident of the Memphis editorial, Wells searched for a forum that would enable her to change white people's minds about the causes of lynching. Finding most white organizations inaccessible, she took her campaign to Britain in two difficult, but highly successful, tours that aroused a public outcry against lynch law in the U.S. and opened a number of doors when she returned. Although in much of her work Wells felt that she was, as she once said, "treading the wine press alone," she quickly became a vital part of a network of political and social activists. A fund-raising event organized by prominent African-American women for Wells' anti-lynching work was the catalyst for the founding of the African-American women's club movement, one of the most influential forces in the social, educational, cultural, and political transformation of African Americans' lives in the late nineteenth and early twentieth centuries. Wells herself organized such a club in Chicago and was active in the National Association of Colored Women.

The pace of her activism is indicated in her account of her marriage to Frederick Lee Barnett, a fellow agitator, which had to be postponed three times due to new speaking engagements (*Autobiography* 241). Wells' decision to marry was a source of distress to her friend Susan B. Anthony and to many African Americans, who assumed she would be compromising her work. In this they were mistaken, although balancing motherhood with activism was difficult. By the time her second child was born she had concluded "that the duties of wife and mother were a profession in themselves and it was hopeless to expect to carry on public work" (*Autobiography* 249). But reports of lynchings brought her out on the road again even before her second baby was weaned. She remained active in public work for the rest of her life, promoting women's suffrage (see Hendricks), founding a kindergarten and an African-American settlement house, investigating and protesting racial violence after World War I, and running for state senate in Illinois in 1930, the year before she died.

In much of her work Wells had to play a double role as agitator, resisting authority systems side by side with white allies at the same time she was resisting her allies' racism, which brought those same authority systems into the very organizations designed to fight them. In 1913, for example, the predominantly white leadership of the suffrage movement informed her that to appease Southern women, she and the members of her Alpha Suffrage Club must march in a segregated contingent at the back of a demonstration. Wells' response was typical. Entering the all-white section of the march unexpectedly from the sidelines (Giddings 128), she insisted on her rightful place as a matter of course, just as she had on the train in 1884.

ECD

FROM "TO TELL THE TRUTH FREELY"[§]

Having lost my paper, had a price put on my life, and been made an exile from home for hinting at the truth, I felt that I owed it to myself and to my race to tell the whole truth now that I was where I could do so freely. Accordingly, the fourth week in June the *New York Age* had a seven-column article on the front page giving names, dates, and places of many lynchings for alleged rape. This article showed conclusively that my editorial in the *Free Speech* was based on facts of illicit association between black men and white women.

Such relationships between white men and colored women were notorious, and had been as long as the two races had lived together in the South. This was so much a fact that such unions had bleached a large percentage of the Negro race, and filled it with the offsprings of these unions. These children were and are known as mulattoes, quadroons, and octoroons.

Many stories of the antebellum South were based upon such relationships. It has been frequently charged in narratives of slave times that these white fathers often sold their mulatto children into slavery. It was also well known that many other such white fathers and masters brought their mulatto and quadroon children to the North and gave them freedom and established homes for them, thus making them independent.

All my life I had known that such conditions were accepted as a matter of course. I found that this rape of helpless Negro girls and women, which began in slavery days, still continued without let or hindrance, check or reproof from church, state, or press until there had been created this race within a race—and all designated by the inclusive term of "colored."

I also found that what the white man of the South practiced as all right for himself, he assumed to be unthinkable in white women. They could and did fall in love with the pretty mulatto and quadroon girls as well as black ones, but they professed an inability to imagine white women doing the same thing with Negro and mulatto men. Whenever they did so and were found out, the cry of rape was raised, and the lowest element of the white South was turned loose to wreak its fiendish cruelty on those too weak to help themselves.

No torture of helpless victims by heathen savages or cruel red Indians ever exceeded the cold-blooded savagery of white devils under lynch law. None of the hideous murders by

---

[§] Reprinted by permission of publisher from *Crusade for Justice: The Autobiography of Ida B. Wells,* edited by Alfreda M. Duster. Copyright © 1970 by The University of Chicago Press. Material reprinted from pages 69–71.

butchers of Nero to make a Roman holiday exceeded these burnings alive of black human beings. This was done by white men who controlled all the forces of law and order in their communities and who could have legally punished rapists and murderers, especially black men who had neither political power nor financial strength with which to evade any justly deserved fate.

The more I studied the situation, the more I was convinced that the Southerner had never gotten over his resentment that the Negro was no longer his plaything, his servant, and his source of income. The federal laws for Negro protection passed during Reconstruction times had been made a mockery by the white South where it had not secured their repeal. This same white South had secured political control of its several states, and as soon as white southerners came into power they began to make playthings of Negro lives and property. This still seemed not enough to "keep the nigger down."

Hence came lynch law to stifle Negro manhood which defended itself, the burning alive of Negroes who were weak enough to accept favors from white women. The many unspeakable and unprintable tortures to which Negro rapists (?) of white women were subjected were for the purpose of striking terror into the hearts of other Negroes who might be thinking of consorting with willing white women.

I found that in order to justify these horrible atrocities to the world, the Negro was being branded as a race of rapists, who were especially mad after white women. I found that white men who had created a race of mulattoes by raping and consorting with Negro women were still doing so wherever they could, these same white men lynched, burned and tortured Negro men for doing the same thing with white women; even when the white women were willing victims.

It seemed horrible to me that death in its most terrible form should be meted out to the Negro who was weak enough to take chances when accepting the invitations of these white women; but that the entire race should be branded as moral monsters and despoilers of white womanhood and childhood was bound to rob us of all the friends we had and silence any protests that they might make for us.

For all these reasons it seemed a stern duty to give the facts I had collected to the world. The Negro race should be ever grateful to T. Thomas Fortune and Jerome B. Peterson of the *New York Age* that they helped me give to the world the first inside story of Negro lynching. These men printed ten thousand copies of that issue of the *Age* and broadcast them throughout the country and the South. One thousand copies were sold in the streets of Memphis alone. . . .

WORKS CONSULTED

Giddings, Paula. *When and Where I Enter: The Impact of Black Women on Race and Sex in America.* New York: Bantam, 1984.

Hendricks, Wanda. "Ida B. Wells-Barnett and the Alpha Suffrage Club of Chicago." *One Woman, One Vote: Rediscovering The Woman Suffrage Movement.* Ed. Marjorie Spruill Wheeler. Troutdale, OR: New Sage Press, 1995. 263–76.

Thompson, Mildred I. *Ida B. Wells-Barnett: An Exploratory Study of an American Black Woman, 1893–1930*. Black Women in United States History, a Carlson Publishing Series. Ed. Darlene Clark Hine. Brooklyn, NY: Carlson, 1990.

Wells, Ida B. *Crusade for Justice: The Autobiography of Ida B. Wells*. Ed. Alfreda M. Duster. Chicago: U of Chicago Press, 1970.

—. *On Lynchings: Southern Horrors [1892], A Red Record [1895], Mob Rule in New Orleans [1900]*. New York: Arno/New York Times, 1969.

HARRIET MARTINEAU *(1802–1876)*

"Brutality to Women"

Millions of women worldwide fall victim to domestic violence each year. Compared to males, females experience approximately 10 times as many incidents of violence by an intimate partner. These numbers reveal why the fight against domestic violence has been a prime objective of the women's movement during the last 25 years. Through the efforts of feminist activists, domestic violence has entered the public awareness and is beginning to be recognized as a substantial social problem. Opposition against various forms of violence has a long history, and it has often unified women from diverse backgrounds, as the agenda of the Beijing Conference (reprinted in **Vision and Transformation**) demonstrates. Harriet Martineau's piece, entitled "Brutality to Women," offers a historical perspective in an analysis of domestic violence that emphasizes the social embeddedness of spousal abuse and its connection to gender inequality. She provides us with a careful description of abused women's personal and social situations and their difficulties in escaping destructive relationships. Read against Abigail Abbot Bailey's personal testimony of her desperation in the face of domestic violence in her own family (see excerpt in **Representing Women**), Martineau increases our understanding of the social complexity of domestic violence.

Harriet Martineau, born in England in 1802, was keenly aware of the unequal distribution of power between the sexes. A life-long advocate of women's rights, her motivation to become a writer was nurtured by her desire to gain influence: "I want to be doing something with the pen, since no other means of action in politics are in a woman's power" (qtd. in Yates 1). Martineau managed to support herself all her life through writing; she published more than 100 separate titles and produced over 1,600 newspaper editorials. Her work spans a wide range of topics and genres. We find travel accounts, theoretical pieces, translations, and novels among her writings. Her astute observations and the analytic quality of many texts established her as an important social critic. In fact, her travels in America and her subsequent analyses of American society stand alongside the better known writings of Alexander de Tocqueville and are considered by some to be of greater value although less widely read and cited. Today she is recognized as one of the founders of modern sociology, because she spelled out her methods of social observation and delineated principles for describing society.

She was born into a middle-class family, yet the education she and her sisters received extended well beyond the standards for girls at that time. Her first published works, in which she popularized the economic theories of Adam Smith and John Stuart Mill, among others, were an instant success, and they enabled her to enter literary circles in London. Her fiancé died at that time, and thereafter Martineau resolved to remain single, since she viewed her character and her professional life as best suited for living alone. In her autobiography, she concludes, "I am probably the happiest single woman in England" (133). Nonetheless, she, like the American Susan B. Anthony a few decades later, was concerned with the institution of marriage and women's inferior status within it.

In 1853, when Martineau wrote the editorial "Brutality to Women" for the liberal *London Daily News,* a married woman basically had no rights of her own. In the words of a standard legal commentary by Blackstone, "the very being, or legal existence of a woman is suspended during marriage. . . ." (qtd. in Perking 1). Wives were not allowed to own property, and husbands had the right to use physical force in order to discipline their spouses. Men had direct control over women's bodies. In Martineau's graphic description of domestic violence in working-class circles it becomes painfully clear how limited the possibilities of married women were for escaping abusive relationships.

Martineau errs in perceiving male violent behavior as an exclusively working-class phenomenon, a point of view held by many members of the middle class in Victorian England. While she is wrong about who suffers domestic violence, she is on target with a broader critique of the inferior position of wives. She challenges the authority of legal and religious systems that deny women the possibility of divorce. In her editorial, Martineau criticizes a report of the Commission on the Law of Divorce, appointed in 1853, for favoring husbands' rights over these wives. The report suggested that divorce should only be allowed on grounds of adultery; thus, if a batterer had not committed adultery, the wife could not secure a divorce. It was not until 1857 that civil divorce was introduced in England.

Martineau emphasized the reform of divorce laws as a way of fighting widespread domestic abuse; however, she did not suggest any broader societal changes that could have led to a decrease in domestic violence. Access to legal separation gave women the possibility of regaining control over their lives and bodies, but it did not eliminate the complex causes of domestic violence. Almost 150 years and numerous reformed divorce laws later, the battle against spousal abuse is ongoing and we now have multiple vantage points on the fight against domestic violence and the cultures which produce it.

KV

FROM "BRUTALITY TO WOMEN" [§]

One domestic subject is again exciting universal remark and must surely lead to action of one kind or another. Everyone is talking about the continued revelation of the brutality with which women of the working classes are treated, as disclosed by the reports of the police courts. . . .

What must be done?

We may turn first to the Commission on the Law of Divorce, whose Report was pre-

[§] Reprinted from *Harriet Martineau On Women* edited by Gayle Graham Yates, Copyright © 1985 by Rutgers, The State University. Reprinted by permission of Rutgers University Press. Material excerpted from pages 221–224.

sented to Parliament early in the late session. From that report we learn, first, that it is proposed to refuse divorce to women (in England) altogether, except in cases of such rare atrocity as to constitute, practically, no exception at all; and next, that in Scotland, there were 95 cases of successful suit for a divorce in five years, —the parties being almost all of the labouring classes, under favour of the smallness of the cost; one-third of these divorces were at the suit of the wife. Such is the state of the law beyond the Tweed, while, on this side of it, the expense of a divorce rises from 500£ to several thousands, and, as we said, the wife is, practically speaking, excluded from release altogether. The Commissioners propose various and considerable relaxations; but all in favour of the husband, and their strange doctrine is that such facilities are good for the husband, while yet the impossibility of divorce is good for the wife. Such a view will not be sanctioned by the sense and feeling of the English people, if fairly brought before their judgement; and the present disclosures of the liabilities of wives will infuse new animation into that sense and feeling on behalf of the weaker party. It had need be so; for in this case only one party is represented. The husbands are the law makers; and the wife is dumb before the law, and Parliament, and the Commission which is to decide upon her interests. The case of divorce is proposed to be transferred from the jurisdiction of Parliament to that of a common law court, from being a matter of exceptional legislation to a position within the domain of common law. Divorce is to be obtainable by the laws of the country, which now interdict it. This is good, as far as it goes; that is, it is good for the husband. But the wife gains nothing by it. Another important benefit will be that pauper suits will be admissible in this, as in other cases, under the law of the land. But here again the wife gains nothing. Legal separation is to be made more attainable by both parties; and in this there is so much of good that we are anxious to obtain it without delay. But there will be no permanent settlement of the question till English and Scotch wives are placed on the same footing. Nobody pretends that the Scotch law is profligate: and if it is not, it follows that the English law is cruel. That cruelty must be abolished, and soon, or the cruelty of husbands, at which society now stands aghast, may, within a certain space of the social area, overbear marriage altogether.

One more appeal must be made—to the Catholic clergy, especially in London. It is observable that the great majority of brutal husbands sentenced in the police courts are Irishmen. We commend this fact to the notice of the priests of their religion. The Catholic doctrine is that marriage is indissoluble, and the more imperative is the obligation on the clergy of that faith to see that the institution is preserved from abuse. They have more influence over the conscience and conduct of the poor and ignorant than any other clergy; and it is unavoidable, therefore, that any class of offenses which particularly distinguishes their flocks should be imputed to some imperfection in their discharge of their office. We appeal to them to look seriously into this matter, and to try whether they cannot preserve the sanctity of marriage by procuring better conduct among those whom they have admitted to that sacrament. In proportion to their dread and dislike of all relaxation of the bond should be their care to prevent its becoming unendurable. They can, if they will, restrain the brutality of men whom they hold in their spiritual charge; and they cannot be blind to the nature and extent of the consequences if they neglect the duty.

WORKS CONSULTED

Doggett, Maeve E. *Marriage, Wife-Beating and the Law in Victorian England.* Columbia: U of South Carolina P, 1993.

Martineau, Harriet. *Autobiography.* London: Virago, 1983.

Perking, Joan. *Women and Marriage in Nineteenth-Century England.* Chicago: Lyceum, 1989.

Pichanick, Valerie Kossew. *Harriet Martineau: The Women and Her Work.* Ann Arbor: U of Michigan P, 1980.

Thomas, Gillian. *Harriet Martineau.* Boston: Twayne, 1985.

Yates, Gayle Graham, ed. *Harriet Martineau on Women.* New Brunswick: Rutgers UP, 1985.

MARGARET SANGER *(1879–1966)*

"Woman Alone Can Free Herself"

In 1917 Margaret Sanger stood trial in New York for violating the state's obscenity statutes that banned passing out "contraceptive information to anyone for any reason" (*Autobiography* 211). Sanger had distributed educational material on birth control and contraceptives to women at her private clinic in Brooklyn. The court offered her immunity from prosecution if she would promise not to violate the law again. She refused the offer, declaring, "I cannot promise to obey a law I do not respect." Margaret Sanger was sentenced to 30 days in prison where she lectured her fellow inmates on sex and birth control. For almost fifty subsequent years, she never shied away from civil disobedience in order to continue her relentless struggle for women's right to reproductive freedom.

For many women in the late twentieth century, the ability to control their fertility presents an integral component of their individual rights. More than a hundred years ago, however, a broad alliance of women's rights advocates had to introduce the term "voluntary Motherhood" into the public consciousness and establish the concept, along with other claims such as the vote and access to legal divorce, as a basic right for women. The suffragists who supported "voluntary motherhood" in the 1870s and 1880s emphasized women's right to refuse sexual intercourse. Control of fertility was to be reached through abstinence, not through the use of contraceptives. These early birth control supporters overwhelmingly came from white middle-class backgrounds and wanted to guarantee women's emancipation within marriage and the family; they did not challenge the Victorian middle-class ideology of two distinct and gendered spheres. Margaret Sanger's generation of reproductive rights activists was the first to address the possibility of separating sexuality from reproduction. Margaret Sanger believed that women's unrestricted right to control their fertility and to enjoy sexuality was the most crucial component of their emancipation. The two excerpts we have included here are vivid examples of the extent to which she valued access to birth control over other social measures in achieving women's emancipation and alleviating social injustice.

In order to understand why Margaret Sanger often regarded birth control as a panacea for all social ills, it is important to keep her family background in mind. Sanger was born in 1879, the sixth child of a poor Irish family. Her mother died around the age of fifty, exhausted after giving birth to eleven children. Like her father, Sanger sympathized with socialism, but turned away from it later to invest her energies solely in the birth control movement. She trained as a nurse, and opened a private, non-profit birth control clinic, the first in the country, in Brooklyn in 1916. Through the clinic, she was able to put into practice her powerful claim for women's right to know and to control their bodies.

In the second piece included here, taken from Sanger's first book, *Woman and the New Race,* published in 1920, she discusses women's right to reproductive freedom along with their responsibility toward "the future of the race." As Angela Davis (see excerpt in this section) and a number of historians have pointed out, Sanger and many other proponents of birth control supported eugenic ideas, believing that the human race could be improved through "controlled breeding." Advocates of eugenics split society into "fit" and "unfit" members and wanted to discourage "unfit" members from reproducing. Eugenic discourses often had racist and classist undertones: the members of society they designated as "unfit" were often members of ethnic minorities and the working class. Sanger's writings raise the question of how a woman's reproductive autonomy can be reconciled with her duty "towards the future of the race." The conflict between individual rights and social obligations inherent in eugenicist discourse exists as an unresolved tension in Sanger's thought.

While we now acknowledge the role played by eugenics in the history of the birth control movement, Sanger's and her colleagues' accomplishments cannot be ignored. She tirelessly fought for the legalization of contraception and established a successful voluntary social organization that provided women with contraceptives (mainly condoms and diaphragms), sex education, and preventive gynecology. She headed an association of birth control supporters that would later develop into Planned Parenthood. When Margaret Sanger died in 1966 she had prepared the ground for legal access to birth control.

KV

FROM *MY FIGHT FOR BIRTH CONTROL*[§]

But as the hour of my departure came nearer, her anxiety increased, and finally with trembling voice she said: "Another baby will finish me, I suppose."

"It's too early to talk about that," I said, and resolved that I would turn the question over to the doctor for his advice. When he came I said: "Mrs. Sacks is worried about having another baby."

"She well might be," replied the doctor, and then he stood before her and said: "Any more such capers, young woman, and there will be no need to call me."

"Yes, yes—I know, Doctor," said the patient with trembling voice, "but," and she hesitated as if it took all of her courage to say it, "*what* can I do to prevent getting this way again?"

"Oh ho!" laughed the doctor good naturedly, "You want your cake while you eat it too, do you? Well, it can't be done." Then, familiarly slapping her on the back and picking up his hat and bag to depart, he said: "I'll tell you the only sure thing to do. Tell Jake to sleep on the roof!"

With these words he closed the door and went down the stairs, leaving us both petrified and stunned.

[§] Reprinted from *The Feminist Papers: From Adams To De Beauvoir,* edited, with a new preface, by Alice S. Rossi. Copyright 1973 by Alice S. Rossi. Reprinted with the permission of Northeastern University Press from pages 524–528.

Tears sprang to my eyes, and a lump came in my throat as I looked at that face before me. It was stamped with sheer horror. I thought for a moment she might have gone insane, and she conquered her feelings, whatever they may have been, and turning to me in desperation said: "He can't understand, can he?—he's a man after all—but you do, don't you? You're a woman and you'll tell me the secret and I'll never tell it to a soul."

She clasped her hands as if in prayer, and she leaned over and looked straight into my eyes and beseechingly implored me to tell her something—something *I really did not know.* It was like being on a rack and tortured for a crime one had not committed. To plead guilty would stop the agony; otherwise the rack kept turning. . . .

The intelligent reasoning of that young mother—how to *prevent* getting that way again—how sensible, how just she had been—yes, I promised myself I'd go back and have a long talk with her and tell her more, and perhaps she would not laugh but would believe that those methods were all that were really known.

But time flew past, and weeks rolled into months. That wistful, appealing face haunted me day and night. I could not banish from my mind memories of that trembling voice begging so humbly for knowledge she had a right to have. I was about to retire one night three months later when the telephone rang and an agitated man's voice begged me to come at once to help his wife who was sick again. It was the husband of Mrs. Sacks, and I intuitively knew before I left the telephone that it was almost useless to go.

. . . She died within ten minutes after my arrival. It was the same result, the same story told a thousand times before—death from abortion. She had become pregnant, had used drugs, had then consulted a five-dollar professional abortionist, and death followed. . . .

The Revolution came—but not as it has been pictured nor as history relates that revolutions have come. It came in my own life. It began in my very being as I walked home that night after I had closed the eyes and covered with a sheet the body of that little helpless mother whose life had been sacrificed to ignorance. . . .

It was like an illumination. I could not see clearly the various social strata of our life; all its mass problems seemed to be centered around uncontrolled breeding. There was only one thing to be done: call out, start the alarm, set the heather on fire! Awaken the womanhood of America to free the womanhood of the world! I released from my almost paralyzed hand the nursing bag which unconsciously I had clutched, threw it across the room, tore the uniform from my body, flung it into a corner, and renounced all palliative work forever.

I would never go back again to nurse women's ailing bodies while their miseries were as vast as the stars. I was now finished with superficial cures, with doctors and nurses and social workers who were brought face to face with this overwhelming truth of women's needs and yet turned to pass on the other side. They must be made to see these facts. I resolved that women should have knowledge of contraception. They have every right to know about their own bodies. I would strike out—I would scream from the housetops. I would tell the world what was going on in the lives of these poor women. I *would* be heard. No matter what it should cost. *I would be heard. . . .*

FROM "BIRTH CONTROL—A PARENTS' PROBLEM OR WOMAN'S?" [§]

The problem of birth control has arisen directly from the effort of the feminine spirit to free itself from bondage. Woman herself has wrought that bondage through her reproductive powers and while enslaving herself has enslaved the world. The physical suffering to be relieved is chiefly woman's. Hers, too, is the love life that dies first under the blight of too prolific breeding. Within her is wrapped up the future of the race—it is hers to make or mar. All of these considerations point unmistakably to one fact—it is woman's duty as well as her privilege to lay hold of the means of freedom. Whatever men may do, she cannot escape the responsibility. For ages she has been deprived of the opportunity to meet this obligation. She is now emerging from her helplessness. Even as no one can share the suffering of the overburdened mother, so no one can do this work for her. Others may help, but she and she alone can free herself.

The basic freedom of the world is woman's freedom. A free race cannot be born of slave mothers. A woman enchained cannot choose but give a measure of that bondage to her sons and daughters. No woman can call herself free who does not own and control her body. No woman can call herself free until she can choose consciously whether she will or will not be a mother. . . .

Woman must not accept; she must challenge. She must not be awed by that which has been built up around her; she must reverence that within her which struggles for expression. Her eyes must be less upon what is and more clearly upon what should be. She must listen only with a frankly questioning attitude to the dogmatized opinions of man-made society. When she chooses her new, free course of action, it must be in the light of her own opinion—of her own intuition. Only so can she give play to the feminine spirit. Only thus can she free her mate from the bondage which he wrought for himself when he wrought hers. Only thus can she restore to him that of which he robbed himself in restricting her. Only thus can she remake the world. . . .

WORKS CONSULTED

Chesler, Ellen. *Woman of Valor: Margaret Sanger and the Birth Control Movement in America.* New York: Simon and Schuster, 1992.

Gordon, Linda. *Woman's Body, Woman's Right: Birth Control in America.* Revised ed. New York: Penguin, 1990.

Sanger, Margaret. *An Autobiography.* New York: Dover, 1971.

—. *Woman and the New Race.* New York: Brentano's Publishers, 1920.

[§] Reprinted from *Woman and the New Race* by Margaret Sanger. Copyright © 1920 by Brentano's Publishers, New York. Material reprinted from pages 93–99.

ANGELA DAVIS *(1944–)*

"Racism, Birth Control, and Reproductive Rights"

Angela Davis's essay "Racism, Birth Control, and Reproductive Rights," written in 1981 and published in her book *Women, Race and Class,* presents a crucial contribution to our understanding of the complexity of the reproductive rights question. Davis, a powerful voice in the fight against racism and social injustice, provides a perspective on the birth control movement that addresses its racist and classist aspects and that calls for a careful and differentiated treatment of reproductive rights issues. Often activists of the birth control movement have failed to see the influence of class, race, ethnicity, and sexual orientation on their demands for women's reproductive rights. In her sharp analysis, Davis guides us through several instances in which a general claim for women's need to freely control their reproductive capacity nevertheless excluded particular groups of women.

In the headnote to Margaret Sanger's excerpt (see this section), we made a connection between birth control activists and the eugenics movement in the first decades of this century. Eugenic discourses turned a woman's right to control her fertility into a "duty" if she was considered "unfit." Angela Davis exposes the continuity of these practices when she investigates the abuse of sterilization that particularly affects African-American women and other women of color. Davis observes that the existence of an abstract "right" to birth control does not guarantee women's freedom to choose how to make use of that right. Unlike Sanger, who focused on women's access to contraception as an avenue to emancipation, Davis documents the interconnectedness of different systems of oppression, arguing convincingly that feminists cannot afford to ignore the links between race, class, and gender.

In her own life, Davis has fought multiple forms of discrimination and inequality. In her writings, speeches, and protests she advocates the rights of African Americans, women, and groups affected by political and economic oppression. Born in 1944 into a middle-class family in Birmingham, Alabama, she early discovered Marxism as a political tool in her struggle for social change. After graduating with honors from Brandeis University, she studied in Germany and at the University of California, San Diego. She joined the Communist Party in 1968. A year later, her affiliation with the Che-Lumumba Club, the Black Communist Party Unit in Los Angeles, and her involvement in militant demonstrations and protests led to her dismissal from the faculty of the University of California, Los Angeles. She resumed her position after a court order, although UCLA did not renew her contract. In the same year, Davis, through her personal contact with a prisoner, was connected to an attempted prison-break that resulted in a shoot-out. In a case that made her famous all over the world, Angela Davis was charged with kidnapping, conspiracy, and murder, and spent two years in prison, but was later acquitted. Davis now teaches philosophy, aesthetics, and women's studies at San Francisco State University and continues her work as writer and lecturer. Among her current topics of investigation is the system she calls "the prison-industrial complex." Focusing especially on women's experience in prisons, she argues for the abolition of the present U. S. prison system and its replacement by effective, rehabilitating alternatives capable of addressing drug addiction and other social and economic problems.

Besides her involvement in the Communist party, Davis has been politically active in numerous organizations, among them the National Alliance Against Racist and Political Repression, the National Black Women's Health Project, and the Black Panthers. The lectures she has given around the world, and her numerous non-fiction publications, including an autobiography, are inseparable from her political struggle to empower the disenfranchised. This multifaceted approach notwithstanding, Davis, like Jo Carrillo (see selection in **Representing Women**), cautions feminists against hastily forming broad coalitions because such efforts often result in misrepresentation of, or discrimination against, marginalized groups. Angela Davis's astute analyses and reflections force feminists to ponder the question of how women can work together effectively without denying difference.

KV

FROM "RACISM, BIRTH CONTROL, AND REPRODUCTIVE RIGHTS" [§]

Birth control—individual choice, safe contraceptive methods, as well as abortions when necessary—is a fundamental prerequisite for the emancipation of women. Since the right of birth control is obviously advantageous to women of all classes and races, it would appear that even vastly dissimilar women's groups would have attempted to unite around the issue. In reality, however, the birth control movement has seldom succeeded in uniting women of different social backgrounds, and rarely have the movement's leaders popularized the genuine concerns of working-class women. Moreover, arguments advanced by birth control advocates have sometimes been based on blatantly racist premises. The progressive potential of birth control remains indisputable. But in actuality, the historical record of this movement leaves much to be desired in the realm of challenges to racism and class exploitation. . . .

During the early abortion rights campaign it was too frequently assumed that legal abortions provided a viable alternative to the myriad problems posed by poverty. As if having fewer children could create more jobs, higher wages, better schools, etc., etc. This assumption reflected the tendency to blur the distinction between *abortion rights* and the general advocacy of *abortions*. The campaign often failed to provide a voice for women who wanted the *right* to legal abortions while deploring the social conditions that prohibited them from bearing more children. . . .

It was not a coincidence that women's consciousness of their reproductive rights was born within the organized movement for women's political equality. Indeed, if women remained forever burdened by incessant childbirths and frequent miscarriages, they would

[§] Reprinted from *Women, Race and Class,* by Angela Davis. Copyright © 1981 by Angela Davis. Reprinted by Permission of Random House, Inc. Material excerpted from pages 202–221.

hardly be able to exercise the political rights they might win. Moreover, women's new dreams of pursuing careers and other paths of self-development outside marriage and motherhood could only be realized if they could limit and plan their pregnancies. In this sense, the slogan "voluntary motherhood" contained a new and genuinely progressive vision of womanhood. At the same time, however, this vision was rigidly bound to the lifestyle enjoyed by the middle classes and the bourgeoisie. The aspirations underlying the demand for "voluntary motherhood" did not reflect the conditions of working-class women, engaged as they were in a far more fundamental fight for economic survival. Since this first call for birth control was associated with goals which could only be achieved by women possessing material wealth, vast numbers of poor and working-class women would find it rather difficult to identify with the embryonic birth control movement. . . .

When Margaret Sanger embarked upon her lifelong crusade for birth control—a term she coined and popularized—it appeared as though the racist and anti-working-class overtones of the previous period might possibly be overcome. For Margaret Higgens Sanger came from a working-class background herself and was well acquainted with the devastating pressures of poverty. When her mother died, at the age of forty-eight, she had borne no less than eleven children. Sanger's later memories of her own family's troubles would confirm her belief that working-class women had a special need for the right to plan and space their pregnancies autonomously. Her affiliation, as an adult, with the Socialist movement was a further cause for hope that the birth control campaign would move in a more progressive direction. . . .

During the first phase of Sanger's birth control crusade, she maintained her affiliation with the Socialist party—and the campaign itself was closely associated with the rising militancy of the working-class. . . .

Unfortunately, the alliance between the birth control campaign and the radical labor movement did not enjoy a long life. While Socialists and other working-class activists continued to support the demand for birth control, it did not occupy a central place in their overall strategy. And Sanger herself began to underestimate the centrality of capitalist exploitation in her analysis of poverty, arguing that too many children caused workers to fall into their miserable predicament. Moreover, " . . . women were inadvertently perpetuating the exploitation of the working-class," she believed, "by continually flooding the labor market with new workers." Ironically, Sanger may have been encouraged to adopt this position by the neo-Malthusian ideas embraced in some socialist circles. . . .

When Margaret Sanger severed her ties with the Socialist party for the purpose of building an independent birth control campaign, she and her followers became more susceptible than ever before to the anti-Black and anti-immigrant propaganda of the times. Like their predecessors, who had been deceived by the "race suicide" propaganda, the advocates of birth control began to embrace the prevailing racist ideology. The fatal influence of the eugenics movement would soon destroy the progressive potential of the birth control campaign. . . .

The abortion rights activists of the early 1970s should have examined the history of their movement. Had they done so, they might have understood why so many of their Black sisters adopted a posture of suspicion toward their cause. They might have understood how important it was to undo the racist deeds of their predecessors, who had advocated birth control as well as compulsory sterilization as a means of eliminating the "unfit" sectors of the population. Consequently, the young white feminists might have been more receptive to the suggestion that their campaign for abortion rights include a vigorous condemnation of sterilization abuse, which had become more widespread than ever.

It was not until the media decided that the casual sterilization of two Black girls in Montgomery, Alabama, was a scandal worth reporting that the Pandora's box of sterilization abuse was finally flung open. But by the time the case of the Relf sisters broke, it was practically too late to influence the politics of the abortion rights movement. It was the summer of 1973 and the Supreme Court decision legalizing abortions had already been announced in January. Nevertheless, the urgent need for mass opposition to sterilization abuse became tragically clear. The facts surrounding the Relf sisters' story were horrifyingly simple. Minnie Lee, who was twelve years old, and Mary Alice, who was fourteen, had been unsuspectingly carted into an operating room, where surgeons irrevocably robbed them of their capacity to bear children. The surgery had been ordered by the HEW-funded Montgomery Community Action Committee after it discovered that Depo-Provera, a drug previously administered to the girls as a birth control measure, caused cancer in test animals.

After the Southern Poverty Law Center filed suit on behalf of the Relf sisters, the girls' mother revealed that she had unknowingly "consented" to the operation, having been deceived by the social workers who handled her daughters' case. They had asked Mrs. Relf, who was unable to read, to put her "X" on a document, the contents of which were not described to her. She assumed, she said, that it authorized the continued Depo-Provera injections. As she subsequently learned, she had authorized the surgical sterilization of her daughters. . . .

Over the last decade the struggle against sterilization abuse has been waged primarily by Puerto Rican, Black, Chicana and Native American women. Their cause has not yet been embraced by the women's movement as a whole. Within organizations representing the interests of middle-class white women, there has been a certain reluctance to support the demands of the campaign against sterilization abuse, for these women are often denied their individual rights to be sterilized, when they desire to take this step. While women of color are urged, at every turn, to become permanently infertile, white women enjoying prosperous economic conditions are urged by the same forces, to reproduce themselves. They therefore sometimes consider the "waiting period" and other details of the demand for "informed consent" to sterilization as further inconveniences for women like themselves. Yet whatever the inconveniences for white middle-class women, a fundamental reproductive right of racially oppressed and poor women is at stake. Sterilization abuse must be ended.

WORKS CONSULTED

"Angela Davis." *Contemporary Literary Criticism.* Vol. 77. Ed. James P. Draper. Detroit: Gale Research, 1993.

Committee for Abortion Rights and Against Sterilization Abuse. *Women Under Attack: Victories, Backlash and the Fight for Reproductive Freedom.* Ed. Susan E. Davis. Boston: South End Press, 1988.

Davis, Angela. *An Autobiography.* New York: Random House, 1974.

Gordon, Linda. *Woman's Body, Woman's Right: Birth Control in America.* New York: Penguin, 1990.

Nadelson, Regina. *Who is Angela Davis? The Biography of a Revolutionary.* New York: Peter H. Wyden, 1972.

ELIZABETH CADY STANTON *(1815–1902)* **AND SUSAN B. ANTHONY** *(1820–1906)*

A Life-Long Friendship

The names of Elizabeth Cady Stanton and Susan B. Anthony are virtually synonymous with feminism in popular culture in the United States. Famous in their own era for their long term leadership of the suffrage movement, they became famous again in the 1970s when women's historians began recovering foremothers and fostering a more comprehensive picture of the U.S. political process. For fifty years, these two women had a major influence on the development of women's rights.

Stanton's involvement with women's rights began in 1840 when she went with her husband, Henry, to the World Anti-Slavery Convention in London. He was a delegate; since women were not allowed to be delegates, she found herself in the visitor's gallery. There she discussed the circumstances with abolitionist Lucretia Mott; their conversations over the next few years led to the organization of the world's first women's rights convention in Seneca Falls, New York, in 1848. Some one hundred women and men attended, signing a *Declaration of Sentiments* that called for "higher education and professional opportunities for women, for married women's property rights, the right to divorce, and the right to custody of children; its most radical demand was for the women's right to vote" (Crumpacker 845). By 1852, when she met Susan B. Anthony in the course of her work, she was the mother of seven children.

Susan B. Anthony was born into a Quaker family that participated in a variety of reform movements. She taught school for a few years and then settled into a life of reform work, drawing on her family's financial and moral support for her endeavors. She worked for temperance, for abolition, and then exclusively for women's rights.

The Stanton-Anthony collaboration was a distinctive one. Stanton, with family responsibilities, tended to be the one who remained at home; Anthony traveled and lectured more, becoming a well-known figure in a black dress and red shawl. Stanton was the one who researched and wrote; Anthony became a highly effective public speaker in an era when women's public lectures were rare. Together, they founded organizations that fought for suffrage, led campaigns and petition drives too numerous to count, and wrote thousands of letters, editorials, and articles on behalf of women's rights. They worked together on the first four volumes of the *History of Women's Suffrage* (1881–2).

As the years wore on and the goal of women's suffrage continued to prove elusive, the pair sought a variety of different tactics and alliances to achieve their goals. They split with some of their fellow reformers, built coalitions that angered some of their supporters, and, according to many critics, failed to link women's concerns effectively with racial concerns. Whatever the tasks and tensions at hand, these two friends supported one another. The support did not always come easily. And they followed individual paths at many points. Elizabeth Cady Stanton grew more radical as she grew older and published the *Woman's*

Bible in 1895, offering feminist interpretations that many would find startling even in the late 20th century. Susan B. Anthony became increasingly involved in the international suffrage movement and served for many as the symbol of an independent woman.

Yet it was their political partnership, their respect for their individual strengths, and their mutual commitment to reform, that has inspired many feminists of the current era. The excerpt we have included here is from a set of speeches the two gave. They understood that neither could have accomplished as much without the other. Their personal collaboration and their determination to forge organizations that involved other women serve as a model of women's collective action. While they did not see women gain the right to vote in their time and while they have been accurately criticized by subsequent generations for their failure to fully engage race issues, their ability to sustain friendship, to draw out the best in one another, and to work for social justice together has left a legacy that many continue to admire.

JFO

FROM A SPEECH BY ELIZABETH CADY STANTON, 1890[§]

If there is one part of my life that gives me more satisfaction than any other, it is my friendship of forty years' standing with Susan B. Anthony. Her heroism, faithfulness and conscientious devotion to what she thinks her duty has been a constant stimulus to me to thought and action. Ours has been indeed a friendship of hard work and self denial. . . . *Sub rosa,* dear friends, I have had no peace for forty years. . . . She has kept me on the war-path at the point of the bayonet, so long that I have often wished my untiring coadjutor might, like Elijah, be translated, a few years before I was summoned, that I might spend the sunset of my life in some quiet chimney corner, and lay superfluous on the stage no longer.

SUSAN B. ANTHONY RESPONDED IN KIND, 1890[§]

The one thought I wish to express is how little my friend and I could accomplish alone. What she has said is true; I have been a thorn in her side, and in that of her family, too, I fear. Mr. Stanton was never jealous of any one but Susan, and I think my going to that home many times robbed the children of their rights. But I used to take their little wagon and draw them around the garden while Mrs. Stanton wrote speeches, resolutions, petitions, etc., and I never expect to know any joy in this world equal to that of going up and down, getting good editorials written, engaging halls and advertising Mrs. Stanton's speeches. After that is through with, I don't expect any more joy. If I have ever had any inspiration she has given it to me. I want you to understand that I never could have done the work I have if I had not had that woman at my right hand.

[§] Reprinted from *Failure Is Impossible: Susan B. Anthony In Her Own Words,* by Lynn Sherr. Copyright © 1995 by Lynn Sherr. Reprinted by permission of Times Books, a division of Random House, Inc. Material excerpted from pages 173–174.

WORKS CONSULTED

Barry, Kathleen. *Susan B. Anthony: A Biography of a Singular Feminist.* New York: New York UP, 1988.

Crumpacker, Laurie. "Stanton, Elizabeth Cady." *The Oxford Companion to Women's Writing in the United States.* Cathy N. Davidson and Linda Wagner-Martin. New York: Oxford UP, 1995. 845–6.

DuBois, Ellen Carol, ed. *Feminism and Suffrage: The Emergence of an Independent Women's Movement in America, 1848–1869.* Ithaca: Cornell UP, 1978.

Griffith, Elisabeth. *In Her Own Right: The Life of Elizabeth Cady Stanton.* New York: Oxford UP, 1984.

Kleitz, Katherine. "Anthony, Susan Brownell." *The Oxford Companion to Women's Writing in the United States.* Ed. Cathy N. Davidson and Linda Wagner-Martin. New York: Oxford UP, 1995. 54.

Rossi, Alice S., ed. *The Feminist Papers: From Adams to de Beauvoir.* Boston: Northeastern UP, 1988.

VISION AND TRANSFORMATION

Eugenia C. DeLamotte

In the preceding section we asked how women learn to resist and transform the particular circumstances of their lives and those of others. We addressed the question: where do women gain the knowledge that inspires and enables them to enact change? This final section views the same question from a wider angle. This time we ask how women have discovered, created, and transmitted the kinds of knowledge that can provide a basis for *systemic* social transformation. What do women need to know in order to change their world? How can they know it?

One answer that presents itself with increasing urgency is that women must know each other's lives and experiences. In order to effect meaningful systemic change—change at the level of ideological, political, and economic systems that fundamentally shape women's lives—women must reach across all kinds of cultural, ethnic, racial, and national barriers. As Gerda Lerner has said, patriarchal systems use "deviant out-groups" to construct each other. For that reason, gaining knowledge of each other's lives means that women must not only learn but unlearn, working to discern ways in which their self-conceptions and conceptions of others may derive from oppressive ideologies. This process of seeing clearly takes place within individual women as well as among them, since all women are taught, in a myriad of ways that reproduce systems of hierarchical dominance, to misapprehend their multiple identities. Such systems teach women—often through the voices and examples of other women—to value or devalue aspects of themselves, to exaggerate some parts as salient, and to ignore others as inconsequent. The first two sets of readings in this section involve these issues of knowing-across-difference, in the context of distinguishing not only the differences among women but also the differences women experience within themselves.

Thinking about such forms of knowledge raises questions about women and the act of knowing more generally. Thus a third group of readings asks, What kinds of knowing do women engage in? What kinds of authority are they able to claim for their knowledge? And what positions do they take toward the established authority of other forms of knowledge, whether embodied in laws or holy texts or social conventions? Such knowledge often assumes the form of so-called definitive information about women; thus a fourth and final group of readings revolves around women's constructions and reconstructions of knowledge about themselves.

The topic of constructions of knowledge about women leads back around to the topic of women's efforts to understand each other's experiences and needs. All four groups of readings reveal that such efforts lead inevitably to an investigation of women's history. For many of the writers here, that project involves reclaiming stories from the past that can provide an authority for resistance in the present. From Christine de Pizan to Margaret Fell, who use praise for great women of the past as a means of justifying their own speaking positions, to Mọlara Ogundipẹ-Leslie, who looks for indigenous forms of women's resistance in the history of Africa, to Paula Gunn Allen, who insists that feminists should know who their "mothers" really are, such efforts to know one's legacy are a constant in women's studies, and a motivating principle behind our choice of these final selections.

KNOWLEDGE ACROSS DIFFERENCE

The first two groups of selections address the questions of how women come to understand each other across lines of difference, and how they come to understand themselves, individually, across corresponding *internal* lines of difference. We begin with a group of writers who confront explicitly the problems created when differences disrupt the potential for solidarity. The first of these, Sayyida Salme (Emily Ruete), a woman from nineteenth-century Zanzibar (now Tanzania), deplores false inferences about the supposedly debased status of women in her culture, inferences that appear in Western analyses and arise out of superficial observations made from a far different cultural perspective. The issue she raises was a crucial one in the nineteenth century, when colonizing nations of the West made women and the family a locus for structural transformations of whole societies. Deploring women's debased status all over the world—except in the West—became a staple of imperial ideology, part of the transmission of a supposedly superior culture to benighted peoples, of whom women were regarded as the most pathetically ignorant and benighted of all.[1] Suppositions about women's inferior status in these cultures, expressed in Western travel literature and Western orientalist theory, worked to mystify the violent economic assault on those cultures—an assault, ironically, of which women tended disproportionately to be the victims. Salme resists the potentially oppressive qualities of her role as an Arabian princess not by glorifying the position of the "European Lady," but by redefining the notion of "Eastern woman" for a Western audience. At the same time she works to demystify Western notions of the superiority of "Christian wedlock." Her writing is a reminder of the long history behind contemporary Muslim women's protests against Western feminists' misreadings of their lives and needs.[2]

In contrast to Salme's complaint, the stories of Kitty Smith, a Native Yukon elder, represent one of the many ways in which women can work cross-culturally to create and preserve information about women's lives. Through her stories, Smith articulates her knowledge about women in her society, and works with a woman from a different culture to translate this information into a form her grandchildren will be able to read. In this collaboration both parties are aware of the potential dangers arising from ignorance of each other's culture, and both work to avoid misperceptions in order that succeeding generations can participate knowledgeably in the continuing transformation of a vital cultural heritage.

The excerpts from Anna Julia Cooper, Domitila Barrios de Chungara, and Paula Gunn Allen reveal the importance of women's knowledge about each other to achieving the solidarity necessary for resistance at the systemic level. Each offers a systemic analysis of women's oppression; each criticizes a mainstream, predominantly white and middle-class women's movement for failing to understand what she regards as the crucial issues. In the case of Cooper, a former slave, writing in the late nineteenth century, the starting point is a white feminist's speech, "Woman vs. the Indian," which presupposes a competition among oppressed groups instead of seeing that oppressions based on race, class, and gender are all implicated in each other. Cooper sets her criticism of this speech in the context of a larger argument about the kinds of knowledge to which women have special access, a subject that links her writings to those in our third group, as well as to those included here.

For Domitila Barrios de Chungara, the starting point is an international women's meeting at which, as a Bolivian miner's wife who has spent years risking her life for social change, she feels herself completely alienated by the dominant conversations. She sees a vast chasm between her and the white bourgeois women she perceives as "fighting [against] men" instead of struggling in solidarity with men for the political and economic changes that will bring about a better life.

Just as Chungara sees almost overwhelming differences between her vision for the future and that of women who, as she says, can afford to wear a different outfit every day, Paula Gunn Allen sees differences between her vision of the past and that of white feminists who are unaware of their "red roots" in Native American women's history. Clearly, knowing other women's experience involves learning their past and unlearning distorted versions of it. Allen shows that the Laguna Pueblo question, "Who is Your Mother?" is a crucial question for all feminists, and that the dangers of forgetting what the past can teach us are not merely theoretical but play themselves out in women's experience: "The root of oppression is loss of memory."

The selections discussed thus far involve knowledge-across-difference among women. The second group of selections addresses the question of knowledge-across-difference within women. Sui Sin Far, Cherríe Moraga, and Mab Segrest consider the problem of "knowing who you are" within a dominant culture that defines at least some parts of one's identity as inferior to other parts. Sui Sin Far, a turn-of-the century journalist, searches for knowledge of what it means to be "Chinese" in Canadian and U. S. society. She turns for clues to a family that offers only ambiguous answers and to a culture that teaches lessons of racial inferiority. Her writing provides an extraordinarily subtle account of what it means to learn a multiple identity—to learn who you are within a social construction that presupposes knowledge about you: knowledge to which, initially, you have no access. In particular, she analyzes what it is like to live as a working person in a system of multiple identities.

Cherríe Moraga, in contrast, grew up in a family that did give her directions for interpreting her multiple identities, urging her to claim her status as "la güera," fair-skinned, and to deny her Mexican heritage. Moraga discusses her struggle to encompass all of her identities in the same circle of meaning, and she links that struggle with struggles for solidarity in the feminist movement. Her focus is on women's self-knowledge and knowledge of each other; she concludes that the oppressor's greatest fear is the fear of knowing oneself to be deeply connected with those who seem safely distant as Others. She sees this dynamic at work not only among women, but within women as they confront an internalized oppressor.

Mab Segrest, too, received a great deal of instruction from her family, who gave her the sense that her membership in privileged racial, class, and religious groups made her Somebody: a belief she experienced as dissonant with her sense of belonging to the unprivileged category of lesbian. As she works to unlearn this false knowledge about herself—deconstructing her social construction as white, Christian, a person with Background—she is also exploring the problem of unlearning what she had been taught about other women.

WOMEN AND THE SOURCES OF KNOWING

As women struggle to know each other and themselves across barriers of difference, the question often arises of *how* we know: is experiential knowledge better than theoretical knowledge? do women know in ways different from (inferior to, superior to) the ways men know? do women have radically different bases for their knowledge? do they theorize in different ways? do certain kinds of privilege (for example, upper-class, white, male, heterosexual) irrevocably preclude certain kinds of knowledge? In one sense, these are epistemological questions—questions not just of how we know, but of how we know that we know. And they are by no means confined to abstract academic discussions. The question of how we know something emerges often concretely and painfully in conversations at the work place, in the classroom, or over family meals. Inevitably it animates the experience of reading and discussing an anthology such as this one.

Two of the selections included here address the question of knowing at this level. Anna Julia Cooper, who calls for women to bring to light the "feminine side to truth," has already been mentioned; the fact that this call establishes the context for her vision of women's solidarity across class and racial lines shows that she, at least, did not regard as merely abstract the question of "how women know." Mọlara Ogundipẹ-Leslie, a contemporary Nigerian feminist, directly addresses the question of women's knowledge, especially women's knowledge about women, as a crucial point of debate with male social and political activists who criticize her for being ignorant of what so-called real African women want. These men say Ogundipẹ-Leslie is too educated, too Westernized; ordinary women do not want change. Is this so, she demands? What do research and analysis tell us? As a member of a women's group devoted to just such research, she can answer that women's resistance is not exclusively Western but has taken many indigenous forms throughout Africa. Further, she challenges two assumptions: first, the "myth" that there is no "sex" to intellect (women "know" better, she says), and second, the notion that reading the work of a Western male, Karl Marx for example, is admirable, but reading Western feminist literature is not (208). Ogundipẹ-Leslie exemplifies a mode of knowing that draws on multiple sources: experience (what women know about their own ways of knowing); research (the compilation of data); and a careful consideration of such revered sources of knowledge as the Bible and the Koran. How are we to read these texts, she asks? "Should culture be placed in a museum of minds or should we take authority over culture as a product of human intelligence and consciousness to be used to improve our existential conditions?" (224).

The question of what sources women draw on for knowledge, and what authority they invoke for knowing, is at issue as well in the next group of writings, those of Glückel of Hameln, Margaret Fell, and Soma. Glückel's story represents women's intuition, a kind of knowledge with which women have often been credited, or discredited, and which they have variously claimed or rejected in their resistance to assumptions that their intelligence was inferior to men's. She reports her initial distrust of her own intuition of her baby's needs, followed by her vindication when, contrary to received opinion, her baby did indeed need exactly the food she had craved in pregnancy. In this case, her claim for the superior access of woman's intuition to truth is a relatively limited act of resistance on the basis of gender. Hers is not a systemic challenge to patriarchy, but a kind of challenge without which such systemic challenges would not be possible. Her claim to intuitive knowledge is an important claim—one many women have made and continue to make in patriarchal contexts they may seem to contest in few other ways. It bespeaks a tradition of women's resistance based on "trusting what we know": a crucial, fundamental form of resistance without which, in some version or other, there could be no meaningful change in the conditions of women's lives.

Glückel defied received opinion to get what she needed for her child. Margaret Fell argues with equal confidence against received opinion, when she reads the Christian Bible from a pro-woman perspective. Like Ogundipẹ-Leslie, although in the quite different framework of seventeenth-century Quakerism, she asks what research and analysis tell us. Does the Bible in fact support the kinds of knowledge about women it has been used to support—the judgment that they are properly inferior to men as religious teachers and speakers? Fell analyzes all the most problematic passages, demanding that they be seen afresh, apart from mere prejudice that women should keep silence. She concludes that the scriptures not only do not prohibit, but fully justify a woman's call to voice true spiritual knowledge. Her writings resonate strikingly with analyses made by many feminist theologians today. In particular, her discussion of the woman who poured perfume over Jesus's feet anticipates María Clara Bingemer (see headnote in **Sexuality, Spirituality, and Power**), who uses that incident as a metaphor for what happens when women pour out their spiritual knowledge in settings where that knowledge seems to others disturbingly unfamiliar—an intrusion.

Margaret Fell's approach to gaining knowledge from a holy text—and the unorthodox conclusions she draws—is grounded in her assumption that knowledge of ultimate Truth is ultimately unmediated. If that is so, she argues, experiential knowledge must be the basis even for the reading of holy texts. Otherwise, "We are all thieves" who "have taken the Scriptures in words and know nothing of them in ourselves" (qtd. in Ross 11). Fell's effort to "know" the Scriptures experientially "in herself" clearly involved faith in her knowledge, also gained experientially, of gender issues in seventeenth-century England.

One barrier to women's knowledge is precisely the many pressures against trusting such knowledge, pressures that devalue women's ability to know. Thus we include here a brief poem from the *Therigatha,* by the first Buddhist nuns of the 6th century BCE. In this poem, the nun Soma describes a temptation which, if yielded to, would have kept her from enlightenment. Mara, the enticing agent of death and destruction, tries to lure her into thinking that her intelligence, like that of all women, is no bigger than the width of two fingers, just enough to measure rice, not enough to attain nirvana. What Soma tells Mara, essentially, is to look elsewhere for a dupe—someone with intelligence small enough to pose such questions about women.

CONSTRUCTING AND RECONSTRUCTING KNOWLEDGE ABOUT WOMEN

All of the writers examined thus far place a high value on women's ability to know, whether through intuition, experience, research, divine revelation, or some other means. Historically, such valuing of women's ability to know has often involved women in the process of constructing, or re-constructing, knowledge *about women.* Among the writers who have engaged in this process are those in the next group: Christine de Pizan, Mary Wollstonecraft, two nineteenth-century Boston teenagers (Ednah Dow Littlehale and Caroline Wells Healy), and Tarabai Shinde. Christine de Pizan asks two interesting questions: what intellectual contributions have women made that have not been attributed to them (she answers with a long list), and why do women generally know less than men do? She answers that it is all a matter of their education. "Without the slightest doubt, it is because they are not involved in many different things, but stay at home. . . ." Furthermore, women know more than men think; indeed, men need to be educated about women's historical contributions to men's knowledge. The form of the excerpt, a dialogue with "Lady

Reason," comprises an interesting aspect of its argument: reason is allegorized as an external authority—female, as such allegories usually were presented, but with the difference that here, the sex of the allegorical figure is part of the point. Reason is indeed a woman, and she corrects "Christine's" ignorance of women's true intellectual worth, including Christine's own. In one sense Christine's intellectual capacity is of course identical with the intellectual worth of Lady Reason, an externalization of the author's faculty of analysis. In another sense, Lady Reason validates Christine's ideas about women with an authority that transcends the capacity of any individual reasoner, whether female or male.

Three centuries later, Mary Wollstonecraft poses a similar question—why do women know so little about their world?—and answers with yet another precursor of contemporary social constructionist views of gender. The education of girls, based on the idea that they are inferior, is precisely what makes them inferior: a self-fulfilling prophecy. If you don't teach a girl anything significant, she will not know anything significant. And Wollstonecraft goes further, maintaining that focusing a girl's attention on trivial matters such as dolls, clothes, and gossip, in the belief that these are what interest girls, insures that women will focus on trivial matters.

By the time Ednah Dow Littlehale and Caroline Wells Healy are writing letters to each other about the proper place of woman, "the woman question" is clearly at the forefront of much debate. These girls are very much aware of the transformation of knowledge about women, women's nature, and women's potential. We see them responding to new ideas; trying to sort out what sources of knowledge they should use in thinking about this issue; and creating, defending, and recreating their own knowledge about women.

In Tarabai Shinde, writing at the end of the same century in India, we see two important strategies in the new construction of knowledge about women. First, she explicitly positions woman as the knowing subject rather than the object of men's knowledge. Responding to criticisms of women from the outside, she asks what women know, from the inside—not only about their own characteristics, so slandered by men, but about men's supposedly superior characteristics. Furthermore, she seeks knowledge of both women and men, and gender relations, by reversing the positions. From woman's point of view, what are men like? How can we compare their actions to stereotypical female actions? Behind her analysis is her assumption that the knowledge of women claimed by the particular men she talks about is not created in a vacuum, but is part of the fabric of British imperialist ideology.

The next group of writers connects the new knowledge about women with the exhortation to alternative thinking that is part of revolutionary movement. In the writings by the women of the French Third Estate, by Qiu Jin, and by Luisa Capetillo, we see three versions of political activism in which revolts against gender subordination are linked to revolutionary analyses of oppressive systems. The women of the Third Estate who petitioned the French monarch in 1789 were part of the more general ferment of the French Revolution in which women exercised a crucial role. In their demand that respect be paid to women's social and economic productivity, they challenge traditional assumptions about gender, even as they rely on some of those assumptions when distancing themselves from immodest or sexual women who are not employed "honestly."

Qiu Jin and Luisa Capetillo belong to another revolutionary context, that of late nineteenth-century revolts all over the world against imperialism and economic inequality. In China, Qiu Jin belonged to a group of intellectuals who seized on the revolutionary potential of a new, universal, transcendent concept of woman. She represents a crucial conceptual transformation that is linked to the spread of Western ideas through nineteenth-century imperialism,[3] even as this new "category" of woman, in the thought of such revolutionaries as Qiu Jin, becomes part of revolt against imperialism. Qiu Jin sees gender subordination as inevitably tied to other kinds of political subordination; in her view, women are not only the objects of her own sometimes lonely revolutionary efforts to liberate them, but crucial initiators of a broader liberation that will free working people from economic domination and China from Western domination. Similarly, Luisa Capetillo, writing in Puerto Rico during the same time period, draws women's rights and workers' rights together in her fervent call for revolution. Even more than Qiu Jin, she sees women in the vanguard of revolution, inevitably casting off gender oppression in the act of fighting for social and political transformation of their world.

In the last part of the twentieth century, questions about the relationship between social and political systems in general, and women's oppression in particular, have been at the center of women's efforts to collaborate globally for change in the conditions of their lives. We conclude this anthology with one example of such cooperation: a selection from the Platform for Action that emerged from the 1995 United Nations Fourth World Conference on Women in Beijing. The most recent in a series of conferences (Mexico City in 1975, Copenhagen in 1980, and Nairobi in 1985), this one was devoted, like the others, to producing knowledge about women that could be used effectively all over the world as a basis for transforming women's lives. As at the other conferences, the difficulty for women of producing such knowledge, without knowing each other's experience and concerns, was evident everywhere. At the same time, it became clear that all over the world women are working actively for change in women's lives, and that global coalitions, focused on specific issues and tasks, are emerging out of the new possibilities for formulating knowledge about women's needs and desires. Among these possibilities is something not available to previous generations of women: the global amassing of evidence through new information technologies that allow women to share the burgeoning research on women's lives. The project of getting women's rights on the international agenda can benefit immeasurably from the knowledge these technologies can provide, but it is only one resource. At the most basic level, women's knowledge about each other, created and recreated through the process of resistance, is the surest foundation for action.

NOTES

[1] For a contemporary discussion of these issues, see Anne McClintock's *Imperial Leather: Race, Gender and Sexuality in the Colonial Conquest.*

[2] Feminist scholars of Muslim women have produced a large body of literature dealing with the relationship between Western colonialism and feminist discourse in Islamic cultures

(some of which has already been cited in this anthology). See Deniz Kandiyoti's introduction to *Women, Islam and the State* as well as her article entitled "Islam and Patriarchy: A Comparative Perspective" in *Women in Middle Eastern History: Shifting Boundaries in Sex and Gender;* see also Fatima Mernissi's preface to *Beyond the Veil: Male-Female Dynamics in Modern Muslim Society.* For a discussion of Middle Eastern women's history, see Leila Ahmed's *Women and Gender in Islam: Historical Roots of a Modern Debate.*

[3] The emergence of this category is analyzed by Tani Barlow in her essay "Theorizing Woman," which shows how indigenous, traditional ideas about women were transformed, in China, under colonialism and modernization. Barlow's central argument is that "sex-identity grounded in anatomical difference did not hold a central place in Chinese constituting discourses before the early twentieth century" (147). Thereafter, a "transcendent category" referring to the "masses of Chinese women" (157) emerged as the new intellectual elite associated with the "imperialist semicolonization of China" began to employ ideas derived from the West and impose them on Chinese practices (138).

WORKS CONSULTED

Ahmed, Leila. *Women and Gender in Islam: Historical Roots of a Modern Debate.* New Haven: Yale UP, 1992.

Barlow, Tani. "Theorizing Woman: Funu, Gujia, and Jiating [Chinese Women, Chinese State, Chinese Family]." *Genders* 10 (Spring 1991): 132–160.

Kandiyoti, Deniz. Introduction. *Women, Islam and the State.* Ed. Deniz Kandiyoti. Philadelphia: Temple UP, 1991.

—. "Islam and Patriarchy: A Comparative Perspective." *Women in Middle Eastern History: Shifting Boundaries in Sex and Gender.* Ed. Nikki R. Keddie and Beth Baron. New Haven: Yale UP, 1991.

McClintock, Anne. *Imperial Leather: Race, Gender and Sexuality in the Colonial Conquest.* New York: Routledge, 1995.

Ogundipẹ-Leslie, Mọlara. *Re-Creating Ourselves: African Women and Critical Transformations.* Trenton, NJ: Africa World Press, 1994.

Ross, Isabel. *Margaret Fell, Mother of Quakerism.* York, England: Ebor Press, 1984.

SAYYIDA SALME BINT SA'ID IBN SULTAN (EMILY RUETE) *(1844–1924)*

"She, Too, Was an Eastern Woman!"

Sayyida (Princess) Salme, the daughter of Omani ruler Sa'id ibn Sultan and a Circassian concubine, was born on the island of Zanzibar in the Indian Ocean off the coast of what is now Tanzania. At the time of her birth, Omani-inspired trade in Zanzibar was in the midst of a period of intense development; in 1840, Salme's father had transferred the capital of his sultanate from Muscat, the traditional stronghold of Omani power, to Zanzibar, located on the outskirts of the far-ranging Omani territories.[1] Prior to the removal of the court from Muscat, the Omani Sultanate had maintained authority on the island through a series of appointed governors and—later on—military occupation. The cosmopolitan Omani "state" was not organized around a centralized system of government, however, but rather according to a loosely maintained tribal structure in which communities often settled their own disputes and chose their own local leaders. Throughout the nineteenth century, Salme's father and brothers were involved in not only a series of conflicts with African coastal communities but also increasingly difficult negotiations with the British imperialist presence in India and East Africa.[2]

In the seventeenth century, Zanzibar had been the last of Portugal's allies in East Africa to come under Omani rule. However, Omani communities had an extremely long history of settlement on the East African coast as well as close ties to the Indian merchants who were key participants in the development of international trading networks centered on Zanzibar (Bhacker). Paradoxically, the island was given an economic boost by the suppression of the European slave trade, since surplus slave labor could be exploited in order to meet the increasing international demand for products such as ivory and dates. Zanzibar, as a center of commercial expansion for the Omani economy, soon became to be perceived by the British as a threat to their trading activities in the Indian Ocean. In fact, the European presence on the island and in East African trade in general was to play a significant role in Salme's life history.

Salme began working on her memoir as a gift to her children, who were never able to get to know their Eastern family. Patricia Romero suggests that "Salme may have been the only woman of her generation on [Zanzibar] who could both read and write, and is certainly the only one to have left a personal memoir" (vi), although it is true that many women living in the centers of Islamic culture at the time were highly educated. As a child, Salme and her sisters learned to ride horses, engaged in outdoor activities, and had close relationships with their father. In the excerpt from her memoirs which we include here, Salme makes the point that Middle Eastern women—especially from the elite classes—have often had much more power over their lives than Western visitors assumed; this was certainly the case for Sayyida Salme during her childhood.

A major turning point in the Princess' life occurred when, still unmarried and in her twenties, Salme began an affair with a German merchant named Rudolph Heinrich Ruete whose home was in the vicinity of her own. Salme feared for her life when the rumor began to spread that she was pregnant with Ruete's child; she hurriedly made arrangements to sell off as much of her property as she could before making her escape to Germany. She waited in Aden (contemporary Yemen) for Heinrich to join her; there her child was born and died in 1866. In 1867 she was baptized Emily and married to Heinrich Ruete shortly before their journey to Hamburg. The two daughters and one son to whom she gave birth in the following years were brought up as Christians in Germany.

Heinrich Ruete died in 1870, leaving Emily Ruete alone and in straitened financial circumstances. After her illegitimate pregnancy, conversion, and marriage, Emily Ruete's relations with her brother Barghash, who had succeeded her father as Sultan of Zanzibar, were extremely strained to say the least; nevertheless, she was often filled with nostalgia for her home and culture. As she writes in her *Memoirs,* "I had left my home a complete Arab and a good Muslim, and what am I now [in 1886]? A bad Christian, and somewhat more than half a German" (qtd. in Van Donzel 32). Van Donzel remarks in an introduction to Ruete's *Memoirs* that "The separation between religion and culture, brought about by baptism—itself the result of her love for her future husband more than of an inner conversion—was probably the greatest problem which Frau Ruete had to face" (32).

Emily Ruete made repeated attempts over the next two decades to reconcile with her brother Barghash and to gain access to the inheritance which she had abandoned in Zanzibar. She was never to succeed in either of these efforts, both because Muslim law denies the right of a "renegade of Islam"—as Ruete calls herself—to inherit and because the British government eventually intervened to cut off contact between the siblings. Emily Ruete's connections with high-level German government officials may have worked to her disadvantage given the nature of British influence in Zanzibar. Ruete spent much of the remaining years of her life in Beirut; she never did gain access to her heritage, although she was awarded an allowance from the Zanzibar government in 1923, a year before her death.

In the excerpt which follows, Emily Ruete attempts, with her description of "woman's position" in the Middle East, to dispel many of the Western prejudices concerning Muslim women's unhappy and degraded status. In the original chapter in her *Memoirs,* Ruete ends her discussion with the story of her aunt Aashe's military and political exploits. Perhaps not unlike her niece, this aunt "did not care what the world might have to find fault with . . . but went her way, unperturbed, with skill and energy" (277). Most importantly, as Ruete proclaims in the chapter's final sentence, "She, too, was an Eastern woman!"

NM

FROM *MEMOIRS OF AN ARABIAN PRINCESS*[§]

. . . I will turn at once to the most momentous of all these questions, to the description of woman's position in the East. I find it rather difficult to speak of this matter. I am

[§] Reprinted from *Memoirs Of An Arabian Princess* by Emily Ruete [Sayyida Salme bint Sa'id ibn Sultan] published London: East-West Publications, 1981. Material excerpted from pages 143–145, 147, 152–153, 235.

convinced that, as a woman born in the East, people will be apt to think me partial, and I fear I shall not succeed in eradicating altogether the false and preposterous views existing in Europe, and especially in Germany, on the position of the Arab wife in relation to her husband. In spite of the easier ways of communication in these days, the East is too much considered the land of fairy-tales, about which all sorts of stories may be told with impunity. A traveller making a few weeks' tour to Constantinople, to Syria, Egypt, Tunis, or Morocco, sets about at once to write a big book on the life and the customs of the East. He has been able to judge only quite superficially of these, and has seen absolutely nothing of domestic life. He contents himself with setting down the distorted stories and second-hand accounts of the French or German waiters at his hotel, or from sailors and donkey boys, and considers these sources of information perfectly reliable and trustworthy. But even from these there is not much to learn, and accordingly he throws the reins over the neck of his imagination, and gallops away into fable-land. The only necessary merits of his book are, he thinks, amusement and entertainment, which are the sugar-plums between the pages, and lure the reader on, and his production is pronounced "such a success!"

My own experience, I admit, was somewhat similar—for I myself judged things in Europe at first by their outward appearance only. When I first met in European society faces beaming all over with smiles, I was, of course, led to believe that the condition of husband and wife must be much better regulated, and that connubial happiness was a thing much more frequently met here than in the Mahometan East. When, however, my children had outgrown the age when a mother's continual presence is more desirable than her absence, and I was able to go more into society, I soon perceived that I had completely misjudged men as well as the general state of affairs. I have watched many cases of what is called "wedded life," in which the parties seemed to be chained together expressly to make each other suffer excruciating torments. I have seen too many of such unhappy cases to make me believe that Christian wedlock stands on a higher level or renders people much happier than the Mahometan. To my mind married life, in the first instance, cannot be made more or less happy by any particular religion, or by existing views or habits alone; matrimonial happiness can depend alone upon real congeniality and harmony between husband and wife. Where these exist, happiness and peace will always predominate, and from them will spring in time that harmonious sympathy which wedlock truly ought, and is intended, to be. . . .

In the first instance, it is quite a fallacy to think that woman in the East is placed socially on a lower level than man. The legitimate wife—the purchased Sarari are of course to be excepted—stands in all respects on a par with her husband, and she always retains her rank, and all rights and titles emanating from it, to their full extent. . . .

It is true that a single woman is an object deserving pity. Shut out completely by precept and custom from any intercourse with men, and without any protection, her position frequently becomes a painful one. As she is not allowed to see or speak to her own officials and managers, if these be Arabs, she is often robbed by them; and I am myself acquainted with several ladies who only married to save themselves from being at the mercy of these frauds and impostures. This proves that the seclusion of women has its unmistakable drawbacks, and that this also is carried too far. There is, on the other hand, a great deal of sentimental pity wasted on the Eastern woman. She is perfectly unaware that any constraint is put upon her, and habit makes the greatest inconveniences bearable after a time. . . .

In the East there are, of course, women too who know how to take care of themselves; who first take the precaution to inquire whether the suitor to their hand has a wife already, and who stipulate the clause of a formal promise in the marriage-contract that he will wed no other wife or purchase a Surīe. . . .

If foreigners had more frequent opportunities to observe the cheerfulness, the exuberance of spirits, even, of Eastern women, they would soon and more easily be convinced of the untruth of all those stories afloat about the degraded, oppressed, and listless state of their life. It is impossible to gain a true insight into the actual domesticity in a few moments' visit. And the conversation carried on on those formal occasions hardly deserves that name; there is barely more than the exchange of a few commonplace remarks—and it is questionable if even these have been correctly interpreted.

Notwithstanding his innate hospitality, the Arab has the greatest possible objection to having his home pried into by those of another land and creed. Whenever therefore, a European lady called upon us, the enormous circumference of her hoops (which were the fashion then, and took up the entire width of the stairs) was the first thing to strike us dumb with wonder; after which the very meagre conversation generally confined itself on both sides to the mysteries of the different costumes; and the lady retired as wise as she was when she came, after having been sprinkled over by the Eunuchs with attar of roses, and being the richer for some parting presents. It is true, she had been to and entered a Harem, she had seen the much-pitied oriental ladies (though only through their veils), she had with her own eyes seen our dresses, our jewellery, the nimbleness with which we sat down on the floor—and that was all. She could not boast of having seen more than any other foreign lady who had called before her. She is conducted upstairs and downstairs again by the Eunuchs, and is watched all the time. Rarely does she see more than the reception room, and more rarely still can she guess or find out who the veiled lady is with whom she conversed. In short, she has had no opportunity whatsoever of learning anything of the domestic life or the position of Eastern women. . . .

NOTES

[1] According to M. Reda Bhacker's study of trade and colonialism in nineteenth-century Muscat and Zanzibar, ". . . commercial prosperity was to reach its zenith [in Zanzibar] during the late 1870s and early 1880s" (195).

[2] "Said's increasing dependence on the British may have resulted from his realisation that the tribal/dynastic structures of Oman were no longer adequate in holding the far-flung empire together" (Sheriff 208).

WORKS CONSULTED

Bhacker, M. Reda. *Trade and Empire in Muscat and Zanzibar: Roots of British Domination.* London: Routledge, 1992.

Romero, Patricia W. Introduction. *Memoirs of an Arabian Princess from Zanzibar.* By Emily Ruete. New York: Marcus Wiener Publishing, 1989.

Sheriff, Abdul. *Slaves, Spices and Ivory in Zanzibar: Integration of an East African Commercial Empire into the World Economy, 1770–1873.* London: James Currey, 1987.

Van Donzel, E. Introduction. *An Arabian Princess Between Two Worlds.* By Sayyida Salme/Emily Ruete. Ed. E. Van Donzel. Leiden: E.J. Brill, 1993.

KITTY SMITH *(1880–1989)*

A Resourceful Woman

> "This is a story about a woman alone,
> She's so smart she didn't need a husband!"
>
> *Kitty Smith*[1]

Kitty Smith was one of the oldest living native women in the Yukon at the time when she was recounting the story reprinted here. She was born just before the Klondike gold rush; her father was Tlingit and her mother Tagish Athapaskan.[2] Because she was left an orphan at a young age, her father's Tlingit family—particularly her paternal grandmother—took the responsibility of raising her and cultivating her high status within the tribe. Nevertheless, Kitty Smith went to live with her maternal relatives shortly after separating from her first husband. Julie Cruikshank, the anthropologist who collaborated with Kitty Smith in publishing her stories, states that "Although [Smith] does not discuss the implications of her decision to leave, such an act must have flown in the face of clan arrangements backing up the alliance" (161). Besides being a woman of a seemingly highly independent turn of mind, Kitty Smith was also extremely successful as a trapper. She was married a second time to a man who acted as her equal partner in contributing to the maintenance of the family. When this husband also died, however, she decided not to remarry, affirming that "Should be you're on your own. Nobody can boss you around then. You do what you want. My grandchild can look after me" (Cruikshank 173).

Smith, who died in June 1989, published several booklets of stories in addition to a booklet of family history in collaboration with Julie Cruikshank, a U. S. anthropologist. Her stories function not only to transmit the knowledge of past generations to younger people, but also as a key explanatory framework for living. Story-telling, in this tradition, is one of the ways in which information about women's lives is preserved and perpetuated. It is also a means of understanding the relationship of individual lives to larger cultural traditions and important historical events. Julie Cruikshank explains that, ". . . Mrs. Smith seems to use events from her own experience as the framework for presenting the relevance of her stories" (165). From this perspective, story-telling is the means by which accounts of individual experience are given a meaning; it is in recounting stories that ideas about the world are constituted and reshaped. Smith's stories do not necessarily conform to Western expectations about autobiographical accounts. She not only uses story-telling to comment on individual experience but also considers her life and her stories as interwoven—mutually constitutive of one another. It is important to add that these stories should not be seen as reflections of a way of life which is vanishing or somehow "in transition." Smith's stories interpret events from the past in order to pass them on to succeeding generations and show a commitment to maintaining cultural forms against sometimes enormous odds. We have included a sample from one of her tales as an striking example of a woman formulating, interpreting, and transmitting cultural knowledge about women's place in society.

In her stories, Kitty Smith emphasizes women's independent experience. According to Cruikshank, "She focuses on her travels, her observations, her remarkable success as a trapper, her economic independence, and her friendships with other women" (174). In the excerpt we present here, she explores one woman's life as a hunter and trapper who works alone as well as in collaboration with her grandmother. (Relationships between grandmothers and grandchildren are particularly important in Smith's accounts.) Kitty Smith hoped that recording these stories on paper would one day benefit young Native women and serve as a link between the oral tradition in which she was educated and more recently developed print-based forms of knowledge.

NM

FROM "MOUNTAIN MAN" §

There was one lady.
She walked around—young lady, you know.
They say she was stealing some kind of cache—nobody likes that.

One lady loved her, though—
Her auntie or half-sister, I'm not sure.
She gave her lots of things—
Snare, some knife, sewing things, rabbit snare—
She gave it, you know, everything.

"They're going to throw away you!
You're going to go by yourself.
They talk about you all the time.
You steal, they say that you steal," she tells her.

"It's all right.
I'm going to try to live by myself anyhow.
Sometime somebody is going to find me, marry me," she says to that woman.

And they cut fish; she cut fish, too.
Then she packs them.
She went someplace.
People don't call her: used to be they call people when they're going to hunt.

§ Reprinted from *Life Lived Like a Story: Life Stories of Three Yukon Native Elders* by Julie Cruikshank [in collaboration with Angela Sidney, Kitty Smith, and Annie Ned] by permission of the University of Nebraska Press. Copyright © 1990 by the University of Nebraska Press. Material reprinted from pages 233–236.

"You're going to come with us?" they used to say.
But that time they don't say anything—just everybody gone.

But that woman told her,
"They're going to leave you right there."

"That's right."

And one man, just like a chief, said to her,
"What for you steal all the time?
Everything, you steal.
You can go anyplace you want to from here.
They're not going to take you anymore," that chief said.
He gives her matches, you know, that stone [flint]
He throws it to her.

"You keep this one."
And some kind of knife, don't know what kind of knife.

"Thank you."

That fish, they take it all away, I guess.

She catches some fish now—oh, she's got cache.
And she goes now herself.
She puts snare, catches gopher.
Strong woman.

One time she saw fire down there, on a lake.
She knows that's Indians, so thinks she'll go there.
One old lady is getting water.

She's coming to the shore, that [young] lady.
That old lady sees her.
"Ahh . . . Where comes from that person who comes here?"

Her husband is coming, too.
"Where you come from?"
"Oh, I walk around—people left me.
I walk around. Anyplace I can die."
She says that.

"Well, come on. We're Indians. We're good.
Our son, used to be he killed game for us.
Bear killed him."
That's what they said.
"We're living now ourself. We do fishing here."

Lake fishing, I guess—little creek comes down—
Some kind of thing they put in the water:
The fish come in.
"One month ago our son got killed. Bear killed him.
We're just the same as you, too.
We pretty near die, us here."

He had bow and arrow, that young man.
They've got them:
"This one our son owned, look!"
They show that young lady.
"But he can't do it, your grandpa; he can't aim it."

"I'm going to try it, Grandma," she tells them.
Gee, it went a long way!

They go gopher hunting—that lady came with her.
Aha! Bull caribou walks around.
"I'm going to try it, Grandma."

"Yes, I'm going to watch you from here."

She sneaks up, that lady.
Just close, gee, that caribou jumps.
Another one comes same place—she aimed at that one, too.
That one falls down there. She runs there.

"Grandma!" she said.
That old lady runs there. Gee, both two.
"What are we going to do, Grandma?"
They take off guts.

"We're going to see Grandpa. Show him!
That grandchild, she's got two!"
He's surprised at that.

They make dry meat there and then they give her that bow and arrow.
"Keep it, Grandchild. Keep it."

She carries it around all the time—she's got sack, you know.
She hunts around all the time.
She sees some kind of game—xaas, they call it [buffalo].
She goes there, just close.
She shoots him with bow and copper arrow.
That thing is going just that way till he falls down.
My . . .

They've got all winter grub now. . . .

NOTES

[1] Qtd. in Cruikshank 233.

[2] The Tlingit are an important coastal people who participated in extensive trading with both Native and European groups. The Tagish Athapaskan tribe is established further inland. Kitty Smith's parents met as a result of trading activities between the two.

WORK CONSULTED

Cruikshank, Julie in collaboration with Angela Sidney, Kitty Smith, and Annie Ned. *Life Lived Like a Story: Life Stories of Three Yukon Native Elders.* Lincoln: U of Nebraska P, 1990.

DOMITILA BARRIOS DE CHUNGARA *(1937–)*

"But For Us It Isn't That Way"

See also **Work and Education**

Domitila Barrios de Chungara's visibility in Bolivian miners' struggles resulted in her invitation to attend the International Women's Year Tribunal in Mexico in 1975 as a representative of her Housewives' Committee. Afterwards, as a way of completing her work there, she collaborated with Moema Viezzer in the oral history of her life and ideas which became the book *Let Me Speak!*

In an interview printed in the English edition, she responds to critics who charged that the book implies socialism will solve all the problems of women. Calling socialism "the tool which will create the conditions for women to reach their level," she argues that fighting "alongside the men" for "liberation of our people" has to come first. This is not to accept *machismo*. "But I think that *machismo* is a weapon of imperialism just like feminism is. Therefore, I think that the basic fight isn't between the sexes; it's a struggle of the couple. And when I say couple, I also include children and grandchildren. . ." (234).

This primary commitment to the "struggle of the couple" underlies her first words at the conference—"I'm the wife of a mine worker from Bolivia"—whose connotations to many of her more privileged listeners were worlds apart from their context in her own experience. Underlying all of her disagreements with First-World women was more than a decade of suffering, "alongside the men," as a political activist in Bolivia. Two stories can stand as examples. Once, when in prison, she was told her children would be killed because she had not signed a certain document; only much later did she learn they were alive. And once when she was pregnant she fought back as her torturer punched her in the stomach, after which his father beat her again in retaliation. He stamped on her hands while shouting, "Those hands will never again leave their mark on my son's face! Neither his mother nor I have ever touched him. . ." (147). When he left she delivered her baby squatting in a corner of her cell, waking from unconsciousness to find it dead beside her (147–49).

Such incidents are the context in which Domitila Barrios de Chungara left her family to take her first plane trip, to the Tribunal in Mexico. Just before she boarded, a government official approached her with congratulations and best wishes for her forthcoming journey. And then the official concluded, "Ay, but señora, your return to the country depends a lot on what you say there. So it's not a question of talking about any old thing. . . . Above all, you've got to think of your children who you're leaving behind. I'm giving you good advice. Have a good time" (196).

ECD

FROM *LET ME SPEAK!*[§]

It was my first experience and I imagined I'd hear things that would make me get ahead in life, in the struggle, in my work.

Well, at that moment a *gringa* went over to the microphone with her blonde hair and with some things around her neck and her hands in her pockets, and she said to the assembly:

"I've asked for the microphone so I can tell you about my experience. Men should give us a thousand and one medals because we, the prostitutes, have the courage to go to bed with so many men."

A lot of women shouted "Bravo!" and applauded.

Well, my friend and I left because there were hundreds of prostitutes in there talking about their problems. And we went into another room. There were the lesbians. And there, also, their discussion was about how "they feel happy and proud to love another woman . . . that they should fight for their rights. . . ." Like that.

Those weren't my interests. And for me it was incomprehensible that so much money should be spent to discuss those things in the Tribunal. Because I'd left my compañero with the seven kids and him having to work in the mine every day. I'd left my country to let people know what my homeland's like, how it suffers, how in Bolivia the charter of the United Nations isn't upheld. I wanted to tell people all that and hear what they would say to me about other exploited countries and the other groups that have already liberated themselves. And to run into those other kinds of problems . . . I felt a bit lost. In other rooms, some women stood up and said: men are the enemy . . . men create wars, men create nuclear weapons, men beat women . . . and so what's the first battle to be carried out to get equal rights for women? First you have to declare war against men. If a man has ten mistresses, well, the woman should have ten lovers also. If a man spends all his money at the bar, partying, the women have to do the same. And when we've reached that level, then men and women can link arms and start struggling for the liberation of their country, to improve the living conditions in their country.

That was the mentality and the concern of several groups, and for me it was a really rude shock. We spoke very different languages, no? And that made it difficult to work in the Tribunal. Also, there was a lot of control over the microphone.

So a group of Latin American women got together and we changed all that. And we made our common problems known, what we thought women's progress was all about, how the majority of women live. We also said that for us the first and main task isn't to fight against our compañeros, but with them to change the system we live in for another, in which men and women will have the right to live, to work, to organize. . . .

In the Tribunal I learned a lot also. In the first place, I learned to value the wisdom of

---

§ Reprinted from *Let Me Speak! Testimony of Domitila, a Woman of the Bolivian Mines* by Domitila Barrios de Chungara in collaboration with Moema Viezzer. Translated by Victoria Ortiz. Copyright © 1978 by Monthly Review Press. Reprinted by permission of Monthly Review Foundation. Material excerpted from pages 198–204.

my people even more. There, everyone who went up to the microphone said: "I'm a professional person, I represent such and such organization. . . ." And bla-bla-bla, she gave her speech. "I'm a teacher," "I'm a lawyer," "I'm a journalist," said the others. And bla-bla-bla, they'd begin to give their opinion.

Then I'd say to myself: "Here there are professionals, lawyers, teachers, journalists who are going to speak. And me . . . what am I doing in this?" And I felt a bit insecure, unsure of myself. I couldn't work up the guts to speak. When I went up to the microphone for the first time, standing before so many "titled" people, I introduced myself, feeling like a nothing, and said: "Well, I'm the wife of a mine worker from Bolivia." I was still afraid, see?

I worked up the courage to tell them about the problems that were being discussed there. Because that was my obligation. And I stated my ideas so that everyone in the world could hear us, through the Tribunal.

That led to my having a discussion with Betty Friedan, who is the great feminist leader in the United States. She and her group had proposed some points to amend the "World Plan of Action." But these were mainly feminist points and we didn't agree with them because they didn't touch on some problems that are basic for Latin American women.

Betty Friedan invited us to join them. She asked us to stop our "warlike activity" and said that we were being "manipulated by men," that "we only thought about politics," and that we'd completely ignored women's problems, "like the Bolivian delegation does, for example," she said.

So I asked for the floor. But they wouldn't give it to me. And so I stood up and said:

"Please forgive me for turning this Tribunal into a marketplace. But I was mentioned and I have to defend myself. I was invited to the Tribunal to talk about women's rights and in the invitation they sent me there was also the document approved by the United Nations which is its charter, where women's right to participate, to organize, is recognized. And Bolivia signed that charter, but in reality it's only applied there to the bourgeoisie."

I went on speaking that way. And a lady, who was the president of the Mexican delegation, came up to me. She wanted to give me her own interpretation of the International Women's Year Tribunal's slogan, which was "equality, development, and peace." And she said:

"Let's speak about us, señora. We're women. Look, señora, forget the suffering of your people. For a moment, forget the massacres. We've talked enough about that. We've heard you enough. Let's talk about us . . . about you and me . . . well, about women."

So I said:

"All right, let's talk about the two of us. But if you'll let me, I'll begin. Señora, I've known you for a week. Every morning you show up in a different outfit and on the other hand, I don't. Every day you show up all made up and combed like someone who has time to spend in an elegant beauty parlor and who can spend money on that, and yet I don't. I see that each afternoon you have a chauffeur in a car waiting at the door of this place to take you home, and yet I don't. And in order to show up here like you do, I'm sure you live in a really elegant home, in an elegant neighborhood, no? And yet we miners' wives only have a small house on loan to us, and when our husbands die or get sick or are fired from the company, we have ninety days to leave the house and then we're in the street.

"Now, señora, tell me: is your situation at all similar to mine? Is my situation at all similar to yours? So what equality are we going to speak of between the two of us? If you and I aren't alike, if you and I are so different? We can't, at this moment, be equal, even as women, don't you think?" . . .

In the end they said to me:

"Well, you think you're so important. Get up there and speak."

So, I went up and spoke. I made them see that they don't live in our world. I made them see that in Bolivia human rights aren't respected and they apply what we call "the law of the funnel": broad for some, narrow for others. That those ladies who got together to play canasta and applaud the government have full guarantees, full support. But women like us, housewives, who get organized to better our people, well, they beat us up and persecute us. They couldn't see all those things. They couldn't see the suffering of my people, they couldn't see how our compañeros are vomiting their lungs bit by bit, in pools of blood. They didn't see how underfed our children are. And, of course, they didn't know, as we do, what it's like to get up at four in the morning and go to bed at eleven or twelve at night, just to be able to get all the housework done, because of the lousy conditions we live in.

"You," I said, "what can you possibly understand about all that? For you, the solution is fighting with men.[1] And that's it. But for us it isn't that way, that isn't the basic solution.". . .

NOTE

[1] That is, *against* men. [Eds.]

WORK CONSULTED

Barrios de Chungara, Domitila. *Let Me Speak! Testimony of Domitila, a Woman of the Bolivian Mines.* With Moema Viezzer. Trans. Victoria Ortiz. New York: *Monthly Review Press,* 1978.

ANNA JULIA COOPER *(c. 1858–1964)*

A Feminine Side to Truth

In the more than one hundred years of her life Anna Julia Cooper saw the U.S. move from slavery to Emancipation, from Reconstruction to the disfranchisement of African Americans and the rise of the Ku Klux Klan, from segregation to the Civil Rights movement. Her activism as an African-American feminist educator spanned the whole period between the Supreme Court decision of 1896 supporting "separate but equal" schools and the reversal of that decision with *Brown v. Board of Education* in 1954. Her personal history encompassed equally dramatic changes. Born a slave at a time when slaves were forbidden even to learn the alphabet, she graduated from Oberlin College in 1884, became a moving force in the African-American women's club movement and a delegate to the first Pan African Congress, was admitted as an exception to the all-male Negro Academy, published books in French as well as English,[1] and at the age of age 67 earned a doctorate from the Sorbonne.

As a child in Raleigh, North Carolina, at the end of the Civil War, Cooper was one of the first students to enter St. Augustine's, a new school for African Americans. Here she won the first of many battles against gender discrimination by gaining admission to a Greek class reserved for boys. A few years later, after a two-year marriage that ended with her husband's death, she enrolled in Oberlin, gained her B.A., turned down a position at St. Augustine's when an offered professorship shrank insultingly to the post of "teacher in charge of girls" (Hutchinson 39), taught briefly at Wilberforce College, then accepted positions first as teacher and subsequently as principal of the African-American high school in Washington, D.C.

This career embroiled Cooper in some of the major conflicts associated with the question of African-American education after the Civil War. As funds dwindled (Hutchinson 45–50) and the question of how and why African Americans should be educated was more and more hotly debated, Cooper maintained an aggressive, effective commitment to developing her predominantly working-class students' full range of intellectual potential, whether they were headed for trades or college. Her white superior's distaste for her educational philosophy was undoubtedly at the root of a complicated controversy that eventually led to her non-renewal as principal (Hutchinson 67–76). Even so she returned to the school as a teacher after a brief absence.

Cooper's long career there encompassed her hard-won attainment of a Ph.D. despite bureaucratic obstacles and the unexpected burden of raising her brother's five grandchildren after their mother died. In 1930 she retired from the school and became president of the innovative Frelinghuysen University, which provided higher education for African-American working people. To this institution she dedicated her life into her nineties, spending, as she said in her will, her "entire earnings in this service" and asking at the end only to be remembered as "'Somebody's old Teacher on Vacation now!' Resting a while, getting ready for the next opening of a Higher School" (Hutchinson 173).

Today she is remembered as much more: a pioneer theorist of African-American feminism whose important work *A Voice from the South* (1892) provided a far-reaching analysis of the cultural, social, and political systems linking U.S. imperialism in the Third World, race and gender subordination in the U.S., and the self-contradictions of the mainstream white women's movement. As Hazel Carby has said, "By linking imperialism to internal colonization, Cooper . . . provided black women intellectuals with the basis for an analysis of how patriarchal power establishes and sustains gendered and racialized social formations." Although white feminists were implicated in the racialization of these formations, Cooper nonetheless "placed her hopes for change on the possibility of a transformed woman's movement. She wanted to expand the rubric defining the concerns of women to encompass an ideal and practice that could inspire a movement for the liberation of all oppressed peoples. . ." (306–307).

From *A Voice from the South* we reprint two selections, one on women and knowledge and the other on the women's movement as an avenue of social, cultural, and political transformation. The two subjects are elaborately interwoven throughout Cooper's argument in ways that are not fully evident in either selection; thus it is helpful to review briefly the context in which they are set. Cooper was an educator, and a large part of her arguments in this book have to do with women's knowledge, which she approaches from two related angles: the question of what kind of knowledge women might contribute to the world if allowed to do so, and the question of how girls should be educated. In the first excerpt reprinted here, Cooper insists on the hitherto neglected "feminine side of truth," which she sees as the basis for a transformation of the world, too long under influence of masculine brawn, brutality, and respect for "power" instead of womanly sympathy for "weakness." She talks about the importance of educating girls, criticizing male African-American educators for excluding them from funding and other kinds of encouragement. Grounding her argument in the importance of African-American women to the "uplift" of the race as a whole, she demolishes various arguments against girls' education, including the concern that it might render them unfit for marriage. A woman, she says, need no longer ask, "How shall I so cramp, stunt, simplify and nullify myself as to make me eligible to the honor of being swallowed up into some little man?" Rather, the man must strive to "reach the ideal of a generation of women who demand the noblest, grandest and best achievements of which he is capable" (70–71).

Clearly, Cooper emphasizes the transformative influence—on all of society, not just the individual woman—of both women's education and women's special knowledge, the "feminine side to truth." Her consistent emphasis on both of these points suggests a question. What does she see as the relationship between the "feminine side of truth" and the education of girls—that is, the kind of formal education in the traditionally male curriculum of which her own learned prose is such an impressive showcase? At the heart of this issue is a larger one: what exactly is the relationship between nature and nurture (or, in contemporary terms, between what is essential and what is socially constructed) in Cooper's vision of women's relation to knowledge?

The second selection comes from the chapter entitled "Woman vs. the Indian," a reference to a speech by Rev. Anna Shaw, a white leader of the movement for woman suffrage. The criticism of Shaw here, however, comes only after a long preparation. The chapter begins with praise for Shaw's and Susan B. Anthony's refusal to tolerate an African-American woman's exclusion from club named "Wimodaughsis" (Wives, Mothers, Daughters, and Sisters), which Cooper sarcastically suggests might better be named "Whimodaughsis"—white mothers, daughters and sisters, with the reference to "wives" omitted for the sake of euphony. "Whiwimodaughsis might be a little startling," she says, "and on the whole wives would better yield to white; since clearly all women are not wives, while surely all wives are daughters" (81–82). This is an elaborate joke about exclusion and inclusion, typical of Cooper's subtle analogies. Having noted that the club secretary did not know "there were any wives, mothers, daughters, and sisters, except white ones" (81), she renders the dilemma of who must be left out, and of what categories might include or exclude other categories, as an absurd quandary. Should we exclude whites, or wives?

After praising Shaw and Anthony for being above such petty questions, Cooper moves away from the question of racism in the predominantly white women's movement for a time, strategically re-approaching it from another direction. Proving that "the American woman" (that is, the upper-class white American woman) holds sway over the "manners" of the nation, she moves into a description of white men's "manners" to African-American women travelling alone. The ironic understatement by which she reduces racism, even racial violence, to a question of manners becomes more and more apparent as the argument proceeds. It culminates with her description of being threatened on a train by a tobacco-chewing "great burly six feet of masculinity," who growls "over the paper I am reading, 'Here gurl,' (I am past thirty) 'you better git out 'n dis kyar 'f yer don't I'll put yer out." To his threat she makes what she describes as a "mental annotation . . . *Here's an American citizen who has been badly trained. He is sadly lacking in both 'sweetness' and 'light'* . . ." (95).

The passage shows Cooper in a typical strategy, using class as a defense against racism.[2] The sense of class "superiority" that Cooper pits against the man's sense of racial "superiority" is closely identified with education: by the fact that the (working-class) white man must look "over" her reading material to condescend to her, and by the "mental annotation" she makes on him, as if she were already writing him up into yet more reading matter. She quotes disapprovingly his non-Standard English, embedding it in her own most erudite discourse. What follows next, however, should forestall any too-easy criticism of her use of class as a source of dignity in what was clearly a dangerous situation. For, in an equally typical move, she modulates deftly from this personal encounter into an incident that sets her individual experience of racism in the context of a larger economic and judicial system. At this systemic level of her analysis, class is decidedly a source of oppression linked to race, and both are interwoven with gender: ". . . and when in the same section of our enlightened and progressive country, I see from the car window, working on private estates, convicts from the state penitentiary, among them squads of boys from fourteen to eighteen years of age in a chain-gang, their feet chained together and heavy blocks attached . . . I make a note on the flyleaf of my memorandum, *The women in this section should organize a Society for the Prevention of Cruelty to Human Beings, and disseminate civilizing tracts, and send throughout the region apostles of anti-barbarism . . .*" (96). The women she refers to, of course, are the wives, daughters, mothers, and sisters who live on those private estates, and Cooper's reader well knows the chances that those women will use their privilege to organize against cruelty to the impoverished African-American youths whose labor sustains that privilege. Further, the word "barbarism" links their behavior to the masculine version of brute power which Cooper deplored early in the book, and which she had criticized the white feminist Mary Livermore for approving against the grain of her "real self" (55).

It is against this background of the discussion of white women's power to civilize white men out of their racism—and their failure, because of class and race privilege, to use that power—that Cooper finally returns to the question of Anna Shaw's talk with the "unfortunately worded" title of "Woman vs. the Indian." This is the point at which we pick up her argument, in the passage reprinted as the second excerpt below. Her analysis in this passage of the interconnections among different kinds of oppression has been subtly prepared by the long preceding analysis of masculine and feminine truth, of the role of women's knowledge in social transformation, and of the necessity for white women to be true to a womanly self that knows, with a special knowledge, the dangers of all systems whereby the strong oppress the weak. It is this vision of oppression as systemic—and of women's knowledge as capable at once of analyzing the system and healing it if women do not allow themselves to be divided from each other and from other oppressed groups—that makes her seem so modern. In this vision she anticipates such late twentieth-century African-American feminists as bell hooks, Patricia Hill Collins, the Combahee River Collective, Angela Davis, Audre Lorde, Barbara Smith, Patricia J. Williams, and many others who have worked to bring the question of interlocking oppressions to the center of feminist discourse and feminist action for change.

ECD

FROM "THE HIGHER EDUCATION OF WOMEN"[§]

Since the idea of order and subordination succumbed to barbarian brawn and brutality in the fifth century, the civilized world has been like a child brought up by his father. It has needed the great mother heart to teach it to be pitiful, to love mercy, to succor the weak and care for the lowly.

Whence came this apotheosis of greed and cruelty? Whence this sneaking admiration we all have for bullies and prize-fighters? Whence the self-congratulation of "dominant" races, as if "dominant" meant "righteous" and carried with it a title to inherit the earth? Whence the scorn of so-called weak or unwarlike races and individuals, and the very comfortable assurance that it is their manifest destiny to be wiped out as vermin before this advancing civilization? As if the possession of the Christian graces of meekness, non-resistance and forgiveness, were incompatible with a civilization professedly based on Christianity, the religion of love! . . .

Says one, "The Chinaman is not popular with us, and we do not like the Negro. It is not that the eyes of the one are set bias, and the other is dark-skinned; but the Chinaman, the Negro is weak—and *Anglo Saxons don't like weakness.*"

The world of thought under the predominant man-influence, unmollified and unrestrained by its complementary force, would become like Daniel's fourth beast: "dreadful and terrible, and *strong* exceedingly;" "it had great iron teeth; it devoured and brake in pieces, and stamped the residue with the feet of it;" and the most independent of us find ourselves ready at times to fall down and worship this incarnation of power.

Mrs. Mary A. Livermore, a woman whom I can mention only to admire, came near shaking my faith a few weeks ago in my theory of the thinking woman's mission to put in the tender and sympathetic chord in nature's grand symphony, and counteract, or better, harmonize the diapason of mere strength and might.

She was dwelling on the Anglo-Saxon genius for power and his contempt for weakness, and described a scene in San Francisco which she had witnessed.

The incorrigible animal known as the American small-boy, had pounced upon a simple, unoffending Chinaman who was taking home his work, and had emptied the beautifully laundried contents of his basket into the ditch. "And," said she, "when that great man stood there and blubbered before that crowd of lawless urchins, to any one of whom he might have taught a lesson with his two fists, *I didn't much care.* ["]

This is said like a man! It grates harshly. It smacks of the worship of the beast. It is contempt for weakness, and taken out of its setting it seems to contradict my theory. It either shows that one of the highest exponents of the Higher Education can be at times untrue to the instincts I have ascribed to the thinking woman and to the contribution she is to add to the civilized world, or else the influence she wields upon our civilization may be potent without being necessarily and always direct and conscious. The latter is the case. Her voice may strike a false note, but her whole being is musical with the vibrations of human suffering. Her tongue may parrot over the cold conceits that some man has taught her, but her heart is aglow with sympathy and loving kindness, and she cannot be true to her real self without giving out these elements into the forces of the world. . . .

. . . You will not find theology consigning infants to lakes of unquenchable fire long after women have had a chance to grasp, master, and wield its dogmas. You will not find science annihilating personality from the government of the Universe and making of God an ungovernable, unintelligible, blind, often destructive physical force; you will not find jurisprudence formulating as an axiom the absurdity that man and wife are one, and that one the man—that the married woman may not hold or bequeath her own property save as subject to her husband's direction; you will not find political economists declaring that the only possible adjustment between laborers and capitalists is that of selfishness and rapacity—that each must get all he can and keep all that he gets, while the world cries *laissez faire* and the lawyers explain, "it is the beautiful working of the law of supply and demand;" in fine, you will not find the law of love shut out from the affairs of men after the feminine half of the world's truth is completed. . . .

Now please understand me. I do not ask you to admit that these benefactions and virtues are the exclusive possession of women, or even that women are their chief and only advocates. It may be a man who formulates and makes them vocal. It may be, and often is, a man who weeps over the wrongs and struggles for the amelioration: but that man has imbibed those impulses from a mother rather than from a father and is simply materializing and giving back to the world in tangible form the ideal love and tenderness, devotion and care that have cherished and nourished the helpless period of his own existence.

All I claim is that there is a feminine as well as a masculine side to truth; that these are related not as inferior and superior, not as better and worse, not as weaker and stronger, but as complements—complements in one necessary and symmetric whole. That as the man is more noble in reason, so the woman is more quick in sympathy. . . .

FROM "WOMAN VERSUS THE INDIAN"§

The philosophic mind sees that its own "rights" are the rights of humanity. . . .

The cause of freedom is not the cause of a race or a sect, a party or a class, —it is the cause of humankind, the very birthright of humanity. Now unless we are greatly mistaken the Reform of our day, known as the Woman's Movement, is essentially such an embodiment, if its pioneers could only realize it, of the universal good. And specially important is it that there be no confusion of ideas among its leaders as to its scope and universality. All mists must be cleared from the eyes of woman if she is to be a teacher of morals and manners: the former strikes its roots in the individual and its training and pruning may be accomplished by classes; but the latter is to lubricate the joints and minimize the friction of society, and it is important and fundamental that there be no chromatic or other aberration when the teacher is settling the point, "Who is my neighbor?"

It is not the intelligent woman vs. the ignorant woman; nor the white woman vs. the black, the brown, and the red,—it is not even the cause of woman vs. man. Nay, 'tis woman's strongest vindication for speaking that *the world needs to hear her voice.* It would be subversive of every human interest that the cry of one-half the human family be stifled. Woman in stepping from the pedestal of statue-like inactivity in the domestic shrine, and daring to think and move and speak,—to undertake to help shape, mold, and direct the thought of her age, is merely completing the circle of the world's vision. Hers is every interest that has lacked an interpreter and a defender. Her cause is linked with that of every agony that has been dumb—every wrong that needs a voice.

It is no fault of man's that he has not been able to see truth from her standpoint. It does credit both to his head and heart that no greater mistakes have been committed or even wrongs perpetrated while she sat making tatting and snipping paper flowers. . . . The world has had to limp along with the wobbling gait and one-sided hesitancy of a man with one eye. Suddenly the bandage is removed from the other eye and the whole body is filled

§ Reprinted from *A Voice From The South* by Anna Julia Cooper. Copyright © 1990 by Anna Julia Cooper. Used by permission of Oxford University Press, Inc. Material reprinted from pages 118–126.

with light. It sees a circle where before it saw a segment. The darkened eye restored, every member rejoices with it.

What a travesty of its case for this eye to become plaintiff in a suit, *Eye vs. Foot.* "There is that dull clod, the foot, allowed to roam at will, free and untrammeled, while I, the source and medium of light, brilliant and beautiful, am fettered in darkness and doomed to desuetude." The great burly black man, ignorant and gross and depraved, is allowed to vote; while the franchise is withheld from the intelligent and refined, the pure-minded and lofty-souled white woman. Even the untamed and untamable Indian of the prairie, who can answer nothing but "ugh" to great economic and civic questions is thought by some worthy to wield the ballot which is still denied the Puritan maid and the first lady of Virginia.[3]

Is not this hitching our wagon to something much lower than a star? Is not woman's cause broader, and deeper, and grander, than a blue stocking debate or an aristocratic pink tea? Why should woman become plaintiff in a suit versus the Indian, or the Negro or any other race or class who have been crushed under the iron heel of Anglo-Saxon power and selfishness? If the Indian has been wronged and cheated by the puissance of this American government, it is woman's mission to plead with her country to cease to do evil and to pay its honest debts. If the Negro has been deceitfully cajoled or inhumanly cuffed according to selfish expediency or capricious antipathy, let it be woman's mission to plead that he be met as a man and honestly given half the road. If woman's own happiness has been ignored or misunderstood in our country's legislating for bread winners, for rum sellers, for property holders, for the family relations, for any or all the interests that touch her vitally, let her rest her plea, not on Indian inferiority, nor on Negro depravity, but on the obligation of legislators to do for her as they would have others do for them were relations reversed. Let her try to teach her country that every interest in this world is entitled at least to a respectful hearing, that every sentiency is worthy of its own gratification, that a helpless cause should not be trampled down, nor a bruised reed broken; and when the right of the individual is made sacred, when the image of God in human form, whether in marble or in clay, whether in alabaster or in ebony, is consecrated and inviolable, when men have been taught to look beneath the rags and grime, the pomp and pageantry of mere circumstance and have regard unto the celestial kernel uncontaminated at the core,—when race, color, sex, condition, are realized to be the accidents, not the substance of life, and consequently as not obscuring or modifying the inalienable title to life, liberty, and pursuit of happiness,—then is mastered the science of politeness, the art of courteous contact, which is naught but the practical application of the principal of benevolence, the back bone and marrow of all religion; then woman's lesson is taught and woman's cause is won—not the white woman nor the black woman nor the red woman, but the cause of every man or woman who has writhed silently under a mighty wrong. The pleading of the American woman for the right and the opportunity to employ the American method of influencing the disposal to be made of herself, her property, her children in civil, economic, or domestic relations is thus seen to be based on a principle as broad as the human race and as old as human society. Her wrongs are thus indissolubly linked with all undefended woe, all helpless suffering, and the plenitude of her "rights" will mean the final triumph of all right over might, the supremacy of the moral forces of reason and justice and love in the government of the nation.

God hasten the day.

NOTES

[1] For a full listing of works by Anna Julia Cooper see Jean Fagan Yellin and Cynthia D. Bond, compilers of *The Pen is Ours: A Listing of Writings by and about African-American Women before 1910 With Secondary Bibliography to the Present.* New York: Oxford UP, 1991.

[2] On the complexities of class and race in works by African-American women in the late nineteenth and early twentieth century, see Hazel Carby's *Reconstructing Womanhood.*

[3] Cooper is summarizing here some common arguments for suffrage made by many middle-class white feminists who were her contemporaries. [Eds.]

WORKS CONSULTED

Carby, Hazel V. "'On the Threshold of Woman's Era': Lynching, Empire, and Sexuality in Black Feminist Theory." *Critical Inquiry* (Autumn 1985): 262–77. Rpt. in *"Race," Writing, and Difference.* Ed. Henry Louis Gates, Jr. Chicago: U of Chicago P, 1986.

—. *Reconstructing Womanhood: The Emergence of the Afro-American Woman Novelist.* New York: Oxford UP, 1987.

Cooper, Anna Julia. *A Voice from the South.* 1892. Rpt. Schomburg Library of Nineteenth-Century Black Women Writers. New York: Oxford UP, 1988.

Hutchinson, Louisa Daniel. *Anna J. Cooper: A Voice from the South.* Washington, DC: Anacostia Neighborhood Museum of the Smithsonian Institution, by the Smithsonian Institution Press, 1981.

Sterling, Dorothy. *We Are Your Sisters: Black Women in the Nineteenth Century.* New York: W.W. Norton, 1984.

Washington, Mary Helen. Introduction. *A Voice from the South.* By Cooper.

PAULA GUNN ALLEN *(b. 1939)*

"A Feminist Heroine"

"Native writers write out of tribal traditions, and into them," Paula Gunn Allen says in the introduction to *Spider Woman's Granddaughters* (4). Her own work as a writer of fiction, literary criticism, and theory is an excellent example. She shapes the form and content of her writing in creative interaction with oral traditions of storytelling, even as she grounds her feminist values in Native American traditions. Among these she includes "a belief in the central importance of female energies, autonomy of individuals, cooperation, human dignity, human freedom, and egalitarian distribution of status, goods, and services." She includes, as well, "Respect for others, reverence for life, . . . pacifism as a way of life; . . . kinship ties; a sense of the sacredness and mystery of existence; balance and harmony in relationships both sacred and secular" (*Sacred Hoop* 211–212). Her feminist articulation of these values is to be found in her collections of poems, including *The Blind Lion* (1974), *Coyote's Daylight Trip* (1978), *Star Child* (1981), *Shadow Country* (1982), *A Cannon Between My Knees* (1983), and *Skins and Bones* (1988); her novel, *The Woman Who Owned the Shadows* (1983); her edited volumes of Native American works, including *Studies in American Indian Literature* (1983) and *Spider Woman's Granddaughters;* and her many essays, including those in the volume from which the following excerpt comes, *The Sacred Hoop: Recovering the Feminine in American Indian Traditions* (1986).

Born in New Mexico into a culturally diverse family, Allen has emphasized the multiplicity of her own roots (Lebanese/Laguna/Sioux/Scottish) even as she writes out of a primary affiliation with her Native American origins. After receiving her B.A. and M.F.A. from the University of Oregon at Eugene and her Ph.D. in American Studies from the University of New Mexico in 1975, she taught at San Francisco State University, the University of New Mexico, Fort Lewis College in Colorado, the University of California at Berkeley, and most recently at UCLA. While she has won prizes both for her poetry and fiction, she is equally renowned for her interdisciplinary critical essays on U. S. history, culture, and literature (Coltelli 6–8).

The essay from which which the following excerpt comes incorporates some central aspects of that critical work. It begins with the importance, for the people of Laguna Pueblo, of the question "Who is your mother?" In this gynocratic society, she says, "your mother's identity is the key to your own identity" (209); not to know who your mother was means alienation from your own life, self-estrangement (210). Yet U. S. society, with its multiple patriarchal oppressions, is based on forgetting history—especially, the origins of that society "in the matrix and context of Native America" (211). Such forgetting is dangerous; indeed, Allen insists, "the root of oppression is loss of memory" (213).

Most specifically in this essay, she calls on white feminists to remember their Native American mother or matrix. She alludes, for example, to the fact that the famous Seneca

Falls Convention for women's rights in 1848 took place, unbeknownst to its organizers, at almost the same site as a successful Native American women's rebellion in 1600. In that rebellion, Iroquois women declared a moratorium on sexual relations until men granted them the power of declaring war or peace. "The price the feminist community must pay because it is not aware of the recent presence of gynarchical societies on this continent," Allen warns, "is unnecessary confusion, division, and much lost time" (213).

Paula Gunn Allen works to keep alive such knowledge of our "mothers," not from "nostalgia" but from a sense that such knowledge is crucial to the very survival of oppressed peoples. Her writing "out of tribal traditions, and into them" is a vital affirmation of that knowledge, part of its own continuing vitality.

ECD

FROM "WHO IS YOUR MOTHER? RED ROOTS OF WHITE FEMINISM"[§]

A Feminist Heroine

Early in the women's suffrage movement, Eva Emery Dye, an Oregon suffragette, went looking for a heroine to embody her vision of feminism. She wanted a historical figure whose life would symbolize the strengthened power of women. She found Sacagawea (or Sacajawea) buried in the journals of Lewis and Clark. The Shoshoni teenager had traveled with the Lewis and Clark expedition, carrying her infant son, and on a small number of occasions acted as translator.[1]

Dye declared that Sacagawea, whose name is thought to mean Bird Woman, had been a guide to the historic expedition, and through Dye's work Sacagawea became enshrined in American memory as a moving force and friend of the whites, leading them in the settlement of western North America.[2]

But Native American roots of white feminism reach back beyond Sacagawea. The earliest white women on this continent were well acquainted with tribal women. They were neighbors to a number of tribes and often shared food, information, child care, and health care. Of course little is made of these encounters in official histories of colonial America, the period from the Revolution to the Civil War, or on the ever-moving frontier. Nor, to my knowledge, has either the significance or incidence of intermarriage between Indian and white or between Indian and Black been explored. By and large, the study of Indian-white relations has been focused on government and treaty relations, warfare, missionization, and education. It has been almost entirely documented in terms of formal white Christian patriarchal impacts and assaults on Native Americans, though they are not often characterized as assaults but as "civilizing the savages." Particularly in organs of popular culture and miseducation, the focus has been on what whites imagine to be degradation of Indian women ("squaws"), their equally imagined love of white government and white conquest

[§] Reprinted from *The Sacred Hoop: Recovering the Feminine in American Indian Tradition* by Paula Gunn Allen. Copyright © 1986, 1992 by Paula Gunn Allen. Reprinted by permission of Beacon Press, Boston. Material reprinted from pages 215–217.

("princesses"), and the horrifyingly misleading, fanciful tales of "bloodthirsty, backward primitives" assaulting white Christian settlers who were looking for life, liberty, and happiness in their chosen land.

But, regardless of official versions of relations between Indians and whites or other segments of the American population, the fact remains that great numbers of apparently "white" or "Black" Americans carry notable degrees of Indian blood. With that blood has come the culture of the Indian, informing the lifestyles, attitudes, and values of their descendants. Somewhere along the line—and often quite recently—an Indian woman was giving birth to and raising the children of a family both officially and informally designated as white or Black—not Indian. In view of this, it should be evident that one of the major enterprises of Indian woman in America has been the transfer of Indian values and culture to as large and influential a segment of American immigrant populations as possible. Their success in this endeavor is amply demonstrated in the Indian values and social styles that increasingly characterize American life. Among these must be included "permissive" childbearing practices, for as noted in an earlier chapter ("When Women Throw Down Bundles"), imprisoning, torturing, caning, strapping, starving, or verbally abusing children was considered outrageous behavior. Native Americans did not believe that physical or psychological abuse of children would result in their edification. They did not believe that children are born in sin, are congenitally predisposed to evil, or that a good parent who wishes the child to gain salvation, achieve success, or earn the respect of her or his fellows can be helped to those ends by physical or emotional torture.

The early Americans saw the strongly protective attitude of the Indian people as a mark of their "savagery"—as they saw the Indian's habit of bathing frequently, their sexual openness, their liking for scant clothing, their raucous laughter at most things, their suspicion and derision of authoritarian structures, their quick pride, their genuine courtesy, their willingness to share what they had with others less fortunate than they, their egalitarianism, their ability to act as if various lifestyles were a normal part of living, and their granting that women were of equal or, in individual cases, of greater value than men.

Yet the very qualities that marked Indian life in the sixteenth century have over the centuries since contact between the two worlds occurred, come to mark much of the contemporary American life. And those qualities, which I believe have passed into white culture from Indian culture, are the very ones that fundamentalists, immigrants from Europe, the Middle East, and Asia often find the most reprehensible. Third- and fourth-generation Americans indulge in growing nudity, informality in social relations, egalitarianism, and the rearing of women who value autonomy, strength, freedom, and personal dignity—and who are often derided by European, Asian, and Middle Eastern men for those qualities. Contemporary Americans value leisure almost as much as tribal people do. They find themselves increasingly unable to accept child abuse as a reasonable way to nurture. They bathe more often than any other industrial people on earth—much to the scorn of their white cousins across the Atlantic, and they sometimes enjoy a good laugh even at their own expense (though they still have a less developed sense of the ridiculous than one might wish).

Contemporary Americans find themselves more and more likely to adopt a "live and let live" attitude in matters of personal sexual and social styles. Two-thirds of their diet and a large share of their medications and medical treatments mirror or are directly derived from

Native American sources. Indianization is not a simple concept, to be sure, and it is one that Americans often find themselves resisting; but it is a process that has taken place, regardless of American resistance to recognizing the source of many if not most of American's vaunted freedoms in our personal, family, social, and political arenas.

NOTES

[1] Ella E. Clark and Margot Evans, *Sacagawea of the Lewis and Clark Expedition* (Berkeley: University of California Press, 1979), pp. 93–98. Clark details the fascinating, infuriating, and very funny scholarly escapade of how our suffragette foremothers created a feminist hero from the scant references to the teenage Shoshoni wife of the expedition's official translator, Pierre Charbonneau. [Allen]

[2] The implications of this maneuver did not go unnoticed by either whites or Indians, for the statues of the idealized Shoshoni woman, the Native American matron Sacagawea, suggest that American tenure on American land, indeed, the rights to be on this land, is given to whites by her. While that implication is not overt, it certainly is suggested in the image of her that the sculptor chose: a tall, heavy woman, standing erect, nobly pointing the way westward with upraised hand. The impression is furthered by the habit of media and scholar of referring to her as "the guide." Largely because of the popularization of the circumstances of Sacagawea's participation in the famed Lewis and Clark expeditions, Indian people have viewed her as a traitor to her people, likening her to Malinalli (La Malinche, who acted as interpreter for Cortés and bore him a son) and Pocahontas, that unhappy girl who married John Rolfe (not John Smith) and died in England after bearing him a son. Actually none of these women engaged in traitorous behavior. Sacagawea led a long life, was called Porivo (Chief Woman) by the Commanches, among whom she lived for more than twenty years, and in her old age engaged her considerable skill at speaking and manipulating white bureaucracy to help in assuring her Shoshoni people decent reservation holdings.

A full discussion is impossible here but an examination of American childrearing practices, societal attitudes toward women and exhibited by women (when compared to the same in Old World cultures) as well as foodstuffs, medicinal materials, countercultural and alternative cultural systems, and the deeply Indian values these reflect should demonstrate the truth about informal acculturation and cross-cultural connections in the Americas. [Allen]

WORKS CONSULTED

Allen, Paula Gunn. *The Sacred Hoop: Recovering the Feminine in American Indian Traditions.* Boston: Beacon, 1986.

—, Ed. *Spider Woman's Granddaughters: Traditional Tales and Contemporary Writing by Native American Women.* Boston: Beacon, 1989.

Coltelli, Laura. "Paula Gunn Allen." *Native American Women: A Biographical Dictionary.* Ed. Gretchen M. Bataille. New York and London: Garland, 1993. 6–8.

SUI SIN FAR *(1865–1914)*

"Individuality Is More Than Nationality"

Sui Sin Far was the first Asian–North American fiction writer, and the first writer to sympathetically portray the experience of Chinese communities in the United States and Canada. Born Edith Maude Eaton in Macclesfield, England, she experienced the complex interrelationships of nationality, race, and class throughout her life. Her father, an English merchant, and her mother, a Chinese woman educated in England and trained as a missionary, met and married in Shanghai and eventually migrated to Montreal, Canada, where Edith and her thirteen siblings grew up. Her father's rejection of a business career in favor of art left the family impoverished; Edith left school at age ten to care for her younger siblings and to earn money by selling her father's paintings and her own lace work in the streets (White-Parks 9–20). The racism experienced by the children of this biracial family and the strategies they developed to resist it are poignantly described in the first passages of this excerpt from "Leaves from the Mental Portfolio of an Eurasian," an autobiographical article published in 1909.

For the "Eurasian" daughter of British-identified parents—a woman who did not speak Chinese and who had had little contact with the Montreal Chinese community before the age of eighteen—constructing an individual, national, and racial identity was no simple task. The Eaton children's European features made it possible for them to "pass," and most of them chose as adults to assimilate and marry into white communities (White-Parks 30–31). Her sister Winifred cultivated a more exotic "Japanese" identity and became a successful writer under the pen name Onoto Watanna. Edith, in contrast, embraced her Chinese heritage and devoted herself to learning more about the people in whom her interest had been "keen and perpetual ever since the day I learned that I was of their race" (Sui Sin Far 234).

This was a difficult and courageous decision. The late nineteenth and early twentieth centuries were a period of intense hostility toward Chinese immigrants in the U. S. and Canada, as those countries attempted to exclude the same Chinese workers whom they had previously invited to help in the building of the transcontinental railroads and other industries. Laws such as the U.S. Chinese Exclusion Act of 1882 suspended further immigration and prohibited Chinese Americans from becoming citizens. Moreover, in many areas Chinese Americans faced economic discrimination, segregation, and even violent attacks and lynchings (White-Parks 105–106). In the second passage of the excerpt, we can see the struggle she faces as she must choose whether to endure racism silently or to risk the persecution then directed at "[her] mother's countrymen."

From 1888 to 1913, she published fiction, articles, and editorials on a wide variety of Chinese-American issues under the name Sui Sin Far (a childhood nickname). She began as a reporter for the small but growing Montreal Chinese community and later lived and worked in the much larger and more established "Chinatowns" of San Francisco, Los

Angeles, Seattle, and Boston. Her writing includes heated arguments against racism and passionate defenses of the contributions of "Chinese Americans" (a term she is believed to have coined) to North American culture.

In both her fiction and her journalism, Sui Sin Far counters stereotypes of Chinese people as passive, emotionless, and inscrutable. Arguing that "there is no type of white person who cannot find his or her counterpart in some Chinese" (235), Sui Sin Far portrays Chinese characters with a wide variety of personalities and illuminates the complex emotional and intellectual struggles underlying their behavior. She also turns the tables on European-Americans, submitting them to an equally searching gaze. The title character of her only published collection of stories, *Mrs. Spring Fragrance* (1912), echoes the author's conviction that Chinese people have a far better critical perspective on Americans than vice versa. Observing that white women are constantly writing books about the Chinese, Mrs. Spring Fragrance decides to do the reverse: "Ah, these Americans! These mysterious, inscrutable Americans! Had I the divine right of learning I would put them into an immortal book!" (33). Her efforts to understand the complicated romantic troubles of her neighbors reveal that the Chinese are far from being the only people whose behavior seems perplexing, contradictory, or hypocritical.

Sui Sin Far's focus on women and children disrupts the traditional notion of North American Chinatowns as "bachelor societies." Although the vast majority of Chinese immigrants at this time were men, Sui Sin Far's stories and articles show the vital and diverse social roles held by women in Chinese-American communities as wives, mothers, and workers.[1] Many of her stories show the strength of Chinese-American women in the face of racist oppression or oppressive marriage and family conditions. Other stories and articles explore the issues of interracial marriage ("Her Chinese Husband") and the difficulties faced by "Half-Chinese Children." Her story "The Americanization of Pau Tsu" explores the tension between assimilation and women's emancipation as a husband attempts to make his Chinese bride become more like his American woman friend. This story suggests the ways in which women from different cultures can learn from and support one another: the bride leaves her husband, and the American woman condemns his behavior and applauds his wife's resistance.

Sui Sin Far viewed such communities of women as an important context for negotiating the issues of individual and national identity central to her life and work. In a 1912 interview, she discussed how she learned from the Chinese American women who welcomed their "Eurasian" sister into their communities: "I also formed friendships with women who braced and enlightened me, women to whom the things of the mind and the heart appealed; who were individuals, not merely the daughters of their parents, the wives of their husbands; women who taught me that nationality was no bar to friendship with those whose friendship was worthwhile" (294). In this excerpt, she envisions herself as the "connecting link" between the cultures that together constitute her individual identity. Her commitment to an identity that embraces multiple cultures while respecting the value of each, anticipates the models of plural or hybrid identity envisioned by many of the writers in this section.

JP

FROM "LEAVES FROM THE MENTAL PORTFOLIO OF AN EURASIAN"[§] 1909

The scene of my life shifts to Eastern Canada. The sleigh which has carried us from the station stops in front of a little French Canadian hotel. Immediately we are surrounded by a number of villagers, who stare curiously at my mother as my father assists her to alight from the sleigh. Their curiosity, however, is tempered with kindness, as they watch, one after another, the little black heads of my brothers and sisters and myself emerge out of the buffalo robe, which is part of the sleigh's outfit. There are six of us, four girls and two boys; the eldest, my brother, being only seven years of age. My father and mother are still in their twenties. "Les pauvres enfants," the inhabitants murmur, as they help to carry us into the hotel. Then in lower tones: "Chinoise, Chinoise."

For some time after our arrival, whenever we children are sent for a walk, our footsteps are dogged by a number of young French and English Canadians, who amuse themselves with speculations as to whether, we being Chinese, are susceptible to pinches and hair pulling, while older persons pause and gaze upon us, very much in the same way that I have seen people gaze upon strange animals in a menagerie. Now and then we are stopt and plied with questions as to what we eat and drink, how we go to sleep, if my mother understands what my father says to her, if we sit on chairs or squat on floors, etc., etc., etc.

There are many pitched battles, of course, and we seldom leave the house without being armed for conflict. My mother takes a great interest in our battles, and usually cheers us on, tho I doubt whether she understands the depth of the troubled waters thru which her little children wade. As to my father, peace is his motto, and he deems it wisest to be blind and deaf to many things.

School days are short, but memorable. I am in the same class with my brother, my sister next to me in the class below. The little girl whose desk my sister shares shrinks close against the wall as my sister takes her place. In a little while she raises her hand.

"Please, teacher!"

"Yes, Annie."

"May I change my seat?"

"No you may not!"

The little girl sobs. "Why should she have to sit beside a ———"

Happily my sister does not seem to hear, and before long the two little girls become great friends. I have many such experiences. . . .

I am living in a little town away off on the north shore of a big lake. Next to me at the dinner table is the man for whom I work as a stenographer. There are also a couple of business men, a young girl and her mother.

[§] First appeared in the *Independent* 21 January 1909. Reprinted from *Mrs. Spring Fragrance and Other Writings* by Sui Sin Far, edited by Amy Ling and Annette White-Parks. Published 1995 by the University of Illinois Press. Excerpted from pages 220–230.

Someone makes a remark about the cars full of Chinamen that past that morning. A transcontinental railway runs thru the town.

My employer shakes his rugged head. "Somehow or other," says he, "I cannot reconcile myself to the thought that the Chinese are humans like ourselves. They may have immortal souls, but their faces seem to be so utterly devoid of expression that I cannot help but doubt."

"Souls," echoes the town clerk. "Their bodies are enough for me. A Chinaman is, in my eyes, more repulsive than a nigger."

"They always give me such a creepy feeling," puts in the young girl with a laugh.

"I wouldn't have one in my house," declares my landlady.

"Now, the Japanese are different altogether. There is something bright and likable about those men," continues Mr. K.

A miserable, cowardly feeling keeps me silent. I am in a Middle West town. If I declare what I am, every person in the place will hear about it the next day. The population is in the main made up of working folks with strong prejudices against my mother's countrymen. The prospect before me is not an enviable one—if I speak. I have no longer an ambition to die at the stake for the sake of demonstrating the greatness and nobleness of the Chinese people.

Mr. K. turns to me with a kindly smile.

"What makes Miss Far so quiet?" he asks.

"I don't suppose she finds the 'washee washee men' particularly interesting subjects of conversation," volunteers the young manager of the local bank.

With a great effort I raise my eyes from my plate. "Mr. K.," I say, addressing my employer, "the Chinese people may have no souls, no expression on their faces, be altogether beyond the pale of civilization, but whatever they are, I want you to understand that I am—I am a Chinese."

There is silence in the room for a few minutes. Then Mr. K. pushes back his plate and standing up beside me, says:

"I should not have spoken as I did. I know nothing whatever about the Chinese. It was pure prejudice. Forgive me!"

I admire Mr. K.'s moral courage in apologizing to me; he is a conscientious Christian man, but I do not remain much longer in the little town. . . .

I secure transportation to many California points. I meet some literary people, chief among whom is the editor of the magazine who took my first Chinese stories. He and his wife give me a warm welcome to their ranch. They are broadminded people, whose interest in me is sincere and intelligent, not affected and vulgar. I also meet some people who advise me to "trade" upon my nationality. They tell me that if I wish to succeed in literature in America I should dress in Chinese costume, carry a fan in my hand, wear a pair of scarlet beaded slippers, live in New York, and come of high birth. Instead of making myself familiar with the Chinese Americans around me, I should discourse on my spirit acquaintance with Chinese ancestors and quote in between the "Good mornings" and "How d'ye dos" of editors.

"Confucius, Confucius, how great is Confucius, Before Confucius, there never was Confucius. After Confucius, there never came Confucius," etc., etc., etc., or something like that, both illuminating and obscuring, don't you know. They forget, or perhaps they are not aware that the old Chinese sage taught "The way of sincerity is the way of heaven."

My experiences as an Eurasian never cease; but people are not now as prejudiced as they have been. In the West, too, my friends are more advanced in all lines of thought than those whom I knew in Eastern Canada—more genuine, more sincere, with less of the form of religion, but more of its spirit.

So I roam backward and forward across the continent. When I am East, my heart is West. When I am West, my heart is East. Before long I hope to be in China. As my life began in my father's country it may end in my mother's.

After all I have no nationality and am not anxious to claim any. Individuality is more than nationality. "You are you and I am I," says Confucius. I give my right hand to the Occidentals and my left to the Orientals, hoping that between them they will not utterly destroy the insignificant "connecting link." And that's all.

NOTE

[1] Ninety percent of Chinese immigrants to the U.S. between 1849 and 1882 were male (Daniels 9). However, as Annette White-Parks argues in her biography of Sui Sin Far, reducing these numbers to ratios does not fully convey the population of women as a whole: for example, the 1920 Los Angeles Census counted only 120 women and 3,089 men, but 120 women taken together form a quite significant group (White-Parks 106).

WORKS CONSULTED

Daniels, Roger. *Asian America: Chinese and Japanese in the United States since 1850.* Seattle: U of Washington P, 1988.

Sui Sin Far. *Mrs. Spring Fragrance and Other Writings.* Ed. Amy Ling and Annette White-Parks. Urbana: U of Illinois P, 1995.

White-Parks, Annette. *Sui Sin Far/Edith Maude Eaton: A Literary Biography.* Urbana: U of Illinois P, 1995.

MAB SEGREST *(1949–)*

"Race and Class, A Personal Accounting"

See also **Work and Education**

The following selection comes from Segrest's essay "Mama, Granny, Carrie, Bell: Race and Class, A Personal Accounting" in her book *My Mama's Dead Squirrel,* which examines the racist heritage both of herself and her mother. "I wrote many parts of the book in a furious attempt to understand, hoping it would save us both," she has explained. "And then I sent her what I had written to say, 'This is how I am and am not you' and to know what parts of her to keep alive in me and what I had to bury" (*Memoir of a Race Traitor* 101).

Segrest has made it clear that her writings are always at some level attempts to heal her self-divisions, which she sees as internal enactments of external divisions based on hate in the world around her: racism, homophobia, class prejudice, religious persecution. Just as all the "deviant outgroups" who are the targets of that hate are used to construct each other,[1] Segrest's strategies for psychological and political transformation make bridges out of difference in order to deconstruct the kinds of privilege that might open her to complicity with oppression. Thus she works to make connections across the lines of deviance, using her lesbianism, for example, as a link to African-American experience that will help dismantle the foundations of her identity as a white Christian upper-class Southerner.

For these reasons, Segrest's writings bridge, as she says, "Race and family, the intimate and the historic, action and reflection. . ." (*Memoir* 4). Her work of self-healing is therefore at the same time a call to political action. She experiences both as urgent necessities. When she first began talking to reporters about her organizing against the Ku Klux Klan, she says, they would often ask why she does this work. "As the years progressed, it was all I could do not to grab the mike and shoot back into the camera's eye, 'Why doesn't everybody?'" (*Memoir* 20).

ECD

FROM "MAMA, GRANNY, CARRIE, BELL: RACE AND CLASS, A PERSONAL ACCOUNTING"[§]

Introduction

Several summers ago I agreed to try to write a piece on the traditional relationships between my white mother and grandmother and the two Black women who worked for them

[§] Reprinted from *My Mama's Dead Squirrel: Lesbian Essays on Southern Culture* by Mab Segrest. Copyright © 1985 by Mab Segrest. Reprinted by permission of Firebrand Books, Ithaca, New York. Material excerpted from pages 146–173.

as nurses, maids, and—in my grandmother's words—"beloved friends." Back then I wrote:

> I want to try to untangle some of the painful, complex relationships among white and Black women in the South. I am afraid. I do not know if I can discern genuine love from racist sentimentality. I do not know if I even dare use the word *love* about relationships so bound up in the white supremacist South. As a white Southerner I have grown up in such a system of lies and delusions that I fear I will not ever be able to recognize the truth. But I am a lesbian, and relationships between women matter to me more than anything else in my life. I must take a hard look at the ways race and class have benefitted me, and the ways—by their false power—they have thwarted my need for wholeness. I must look at the ways my mother and grandmother betrayed women they said they loved, and ways my own life furthers those betrayals.

I did not finish the article then. I knew that if I could not say something different as a white woman, I should remain silent. I knew that I must write not only to my mother and grandmother and the Black women Carrie Nichols and Bell Lewis,[2] but also to those working-class white women and women of color of my generation who are more open about their anger and their pain. . . . I was also afraid that whatever I wrote attempting to understand race and class in my life would betray my racism and my class pretensions—I would unconsciously illustrate what I was trying to criticize. So notes and drafts lay in piles on my desk, then under it, for months. . . .

I have waited and worked for all these issues to feel resolved by the last page of this essay. I'm not sure that will happen. But over the last three years I do know that I have had to change my life to get near the end of this version of the story.

Mabelle and Carrie: "Nothing . . . Separate from the Thought of Her"

My grandmother Mabelle was born in Alabama in the mid-1800's, the daughter of the president of a small women's college. Carrie Nichols was born around 1870, the first generation of Black Southerners born after emancipation. . . .

In 1932 my grandmother gave one of the addresses at the fiftieth anniversary of Tuskegee Institute's founding. She was invited because her father had been president of a white women's college in Tuskegee while Booker Washington was building the Institute. . . . [M]y grandmother spoke of Carrie Nichols:

> The world thinks—and it's a funny old world, it thinks so straight about some things and gets so mixed up on others—the world thinks that its great men have made it possible, easy, pleasant and profitable for two races so unlike to live so close together. The great men have tried, and have helped some, but what every woman knows who has been a baby, a child, or a young mother in the cotton belt of The South, is that the laurels belong to the Carries.

During this speech, my grandmother articulated the importance of Carrie to her emotional life:

> I must have gotten off on the wrong foot, for the infant wails increased in volume and intensity until my parents were beside themselves. Finally in desperation my mother went into the country and brought back a little colored girl. Her name was Carrie, and as far as the eye could see she was about twelve years of age. As soon as she took me in her arms the wailing suddenly ceased. On my part, it was love at first sight, a love that has grown deeper, and stronger, and fuller for fifty-one years. . . . There is father, mother, Carrie: life, marriage, death, Carrie. There is nothing in my life that I can separate from the thought of [her].

I do not know if Carrie was in the audience to hear these remarks.

My grandmother's speech was a success. I have known about it since I was little. Then I interpreted it to mean that my grandmother was good. She did not say "nigger" or support the Ku Klux Klan. And, by my mother's account, she had been brave to go and talk. Later, after I came out as a lesbian and became a feminist, I thought my grandmother's speech was woman-identified. She was valuing women's relationships over her relationships with men. But lately I have read other messages in her text.

She said: "Will the time come when I will say to Carrie, 'I am the mistress and you are the maid; my place is here, yours there?' Not as long as God rules in Heaven!" But she did not have to say it when the whole structure of their society acknowledged it as true. . . . How much choice, economically or physically, did the twelve-year-old Carrie have when white people went "into the country" and brought her back? There were truths about the effects of racism and poverty on Carrie Nichols' life that my grandmother did not have to know because she did not have to experience them. . . .

At the end of her speech my grandmother called on the audience to "go from this room today and tell other people up and down the length and breadth of this fair Southland there daily walk such goodly things as honor, justice, mutual regard, sincerity, peace, joy, love and brotherhood." Every time I read this passage I want to think my grandmother meant that the audience should go forth and *work* for justice, brotherhood, etcetera. But I'm afraid that's not it. At no point in the speech—or in my other memories of her, or stories I've told about her—does she clearly name the white dishonor, injustice, racial hatred, hypocrisy, and the inflicting of violence and pain rampant in Alabama during her lifetime.

The extent of her distortion became apparent to me when I realized that the very next year the U.S. Public Health Service began its study on syphilis in Macon County (Tuskegee is its county seat), using 399 Black men, withholding treatment to determine scientifically if untreated syphilis progressed differently in Blacks than in whites. No white men were used as a control group. Although this study was not exposed until the 1970s, it indicates the extent to which racist attitudes sapped Black people's lives at the time my grandmother made her pronouncements about mutual regard. "Each man's color line depends on where he stands and how he looks at life," Mabelle had said, completely without irony. Also my grandmother did not see that for Black women like Carrie Nichols to have made "possible, easy, pleasant and profitable for two races so unlike to live so close together" was to say that they carried in their arms—were expected to *nurture*—the entire racist system of the South.

In addition to this speech, I have a more private token of my grandmother's feelings for Carrie Nichols: her Bible. . . . Inside the cover she pasted several items. One is a picture of a one-year-old baby—me, I think—sitting on a swing in our backyard and held by an old Black woman who is thin, neat, her face impassive as she looks down at the child. Next to the picture is a newspaper clipping headed "Carrie is Dead; Beloved Negro Passes." It quotes a letter my grandmother wrote to the alumnae of the women's college where her father had been president and Carrie a servant for thirty years. It told that Carrie Nichols had died "as peacefully and unselfishly as she lived.". . .

On an envelope back is written in my grandmother's hand: "Father, we thank thee for the dear and faithful dead who make Heaven a home for us." Opposite this page is a card with a baby's head on the front and a lullaby, also in my grandmother's handwriting, inside. Only a few years ago, I happened to find in the lullaby card a note my grandmother had written to me on my first birthday in 1950: "I am proud that you and I bear the same name. Take it for what it is worth. Wipe off the stains and heal the scars of seventy years. Use to the best of your ability whatever God gives you of strength and grace." She signed the card, "The Other Mab."

Then, and often since, I have stared at the Bible trying to decipher the message. "Wipe off the stains." Does she really mean it? Is the message "Be true to my friend Carrie," or am I to continue the tradition of "service to others" (*noblesse oblige*) and being served by people darker and poorer than me? What am I to do with the knowledge that now jumps at me from her Bible: she did not see the terrible irony in her words, "the dear and faithful dead who make Heaven a home for us"; she expected Carrie to be her maid in Heaven too. In my grandmother's imagination, could this "beloved" friend *never* be free?. . .

If my grandmother did not see how Carrie Nichols was expected to nurture the "pleasant and profitable" racist system that oppressed her as a Black woman, she also did not recognize the extent to which she as a white woman was "made" by and for white men to do the same. . . .

These men of my great-grandfather's generation—the College President, the Banker, the State Circuit Judge—were part of the ruling class of their town and state, practitioners of a lethal goodness. . . . These patriarchs operated on the assumption that the whole world was—or should be—as Christian as they were. Christianity was part of what gave them their right to rule. These men were Mabelle's connection to power and money, but more than that, to feeling she was Somebody. She hung her father's portrait in the front hall, where he looked down like a combination of Moses and Napoleon. Long before I knew what *patriarch* meant, I despised his humorless self-righteousness and the way he must have basked in female adoration. Yet I was ambivalent. Because he somehow made me Somebody, too. Mother would explain how we had Background, which I came to understand made us better than and responsible for even other white people. "You are Somebody," she would say. . . .

This class identity got me things I never would have gotten merely as a woman, even a white woman; certainly never as a lesbian. I got it because my grandmother "kept in her heart an inner shrine where she worshipped the memory of the man who gave himself and all he had in an effort to raise the ideals of Southern womanhood." I think it was this being Somebody from worshipping at the shrine of God-her-Father that caused her to fail the dark woman she called beloved. Her love for Carrie Nichols let her go a certain way, but she could not go further without reconceiving who she was. I never talked to her about this, but the *her* in *me* tells me it was too huge, too risky, to much to lose.

If I am not to fail Carrie Nichols, too, I have to find a way to be Somebody that does not make other people into Nobody. . . .

In my work for my own liberation from many various roles as oppressor, I often find myself caught in contradictions. One good example occurred at Women in Print, a meeting of feminist publishers, bookstores, and printers in 1981.

Four women, including myself, are facilitating a workshop on race and class in women's publications, presses, bookstores, and lives. I have agreed to talk briefly about white women's racism. Three of us met several times during the conference to prepare for the session, without having made solid contact with the other facilitator. The first remarks of the only Black woman in our group of three made me feel safer: "We don't want to throw the white girls up against the wall." Relief. "Throw the white girls up against the wall." I wondered if that was where I would be.

In an earlier workshop another Black woman had remarked that she considered white people experts on racism—that we could use our expertise to explain a lot. She wanted to hear how racism hurt white people too. I knew I knew a lot about that. I wanted to be clear and concise, to say what I have learned about myself without wallowing in it, to present it in a positive, hopeful context. I was afraid I would not say everything "right." I fantasized being interrupted and having to deal with my bigotries in front of everyone.

C began the session explaining what we hoped to accomplish. When I started to talk I had to start over; I was speaking too softly. When I finally found my voice, I said something like this: "What white women—and class-privileged women and Christian women—who are working on their privilege have to do is find a new basis for our identities because the sense of self we have been taught is based on lies. This is at first a very disorienting process, and what we have to do is support each other in this disorientation. I have found that for me and friends who work together this process has four stages. First, I am so racist, class privileged, Christian that I don't even realize it but assume that I am naturally wonderful and superior. Then I begin to see the false status that I get from my race and class and Christian privilege. And as soon as I do, I begin to see lies everywhere and everywhere my own responsibility, my own complicity. As I begin to feel what slavery did to Black people, I look up and see—God, we killed the Indians too. Then I hit the third stage of intense self-hatred which is the reality beneath the false self-love all along. I think the reason why white women avoid their racism so much and can act so weird around women of color is because deep down we are afraid that this third level is all that there is. That we will end up stuck in despair and self-hatred and suicide. But I believe that underneath there is another level, a self that longs for wholeness and connection." I sat down relieved, feeling I'd done ok. . . .

When I got back home I tried to sort through the contradictions. I experienced the relief of articulating for myself forces I'd felt trapped in my whole life. I felt freer, safer, because of the feedback that I had not sounded crazy, that I was on the right track. I felt proud of making a good showing, then confused about that. I was in the middle of writing the first parts of this paper, and I had to ask myself: How was I being like my grandmother, making speeches about race relations, with four generations of literacy behind me and practice in talking out loud from ten years of college teaching? Part of the zap I'd felt after the session wasn't pure liberation; it was feeling like Somebody. My stock had gone up. I am in a movement working on liberation, but it is easy for me to feel the old competitiveness, the wanting recognition and success. Part of me still wants to be Somebody in a way that gets its power comparing itself to other people, feeling good when I see myself "ahead" and wretched when I feel "behind." On the other hand, this liberating work of real self-love is daily work that takes a lifetime. In its process I often find myself caught in its contradictions—between the world that I want to leave behind and the world I want to help create in front of me. . . .

Lillian Smith . . . wrote of the need to find "the hour when faith in the future becomes knowledge of the past." That is the hour I have searched for in this writing—the hours, days, months, when knowledge of the past becomes faith in the future, when activity in the present helps create something not yet proved. In this search I carry within me many women—not only Mabelle and Frances, but also Carrie and Bell. And all of them, the hers-in-me, tell me: the future is nothing if not what we love in the past, set free.

1980–1983

NOTES

[1] As Gerda Lerner argues in her seminars on "The Construction of Deviance."

[2] Bell Lewis worked for Segrest's mother Frances for many years. Their relationship is discussed in a section of the essay not reprinted here. [Eds.]

WORKS CONSULTED

Segrest, Mab. *Memoirs of a Race Traitor.* Boston: South End, 1994.

—. *My Mama's Dead Squirrel: Lesbian Essays on Southern Culture.* Ithaca, NY: Firebrand, 1983.

CHERRÍE MORAGA *(1952–)*

"La Güera"

"A political commitment to women does not equate with lesbianism. As a Chicana lesbian, I write of the connection my own feminism has had with my sexual desire for women. . . . What is true, however, is that a political commitment to women must involve, by definition, a political commitment to lesbians. To refuse to allow the Chicana lesbian the right to free expression of her sexuality, and her politicization of it, is in the deepest sense to deny one's self the right to the same" (*Loving In the War Years* 139).

This passage from Cherríe Moraga highlights the issues of lesbianism and sexuality as two prevalent themes in her writing because being a lesbian has created the space for her to identify multiple and intersecting forms of oppression. Specifically, her lesbianism has taught her what it means to be silenced and oppressed. The passage also exemplifies the connections that she sees as possible between and among various political alliances such as lesbians, feminists, and Chicanas. Moraga's writing, and her commitment to it, serves as her means of expressing, confronting, problematizing, and coping with her identity as a Chicana lesbian feminist.

Moraga is a writer, poet, playwright, and activist. She also teaches drama at Stanford University. As a playwright, she says that she writes tragedies "because I believe that by naming the wound, by naming the ill, that's when you call attention to it and there's the hope of transformation and the hope of healing" (qtd. in Marquez). In addition to her plays, she has written two books, *Loving In the War Years* (1983) and *The Last Generation* (1993), and co-edited *This Bridge Called My Back* (1981) with Gloria Anzaldúa.

Each of Moraga's books contains its own specific purpose, based in part on where Moraga locates herself within the time the text was written. Thus, in her first book, Moraga states, "It is the daughters who are my audience" (vii). *Loving* is an autobiography that "seeks to define for Chicanas a conceptual space that is not a priori enmeshed in the ideological systems denotated by white patriarchal culture, by the white feminist opposition to that culture, by the Chicano male resistance to Anglo hegemony, or even by heterosexual Chicana feminists" (Saldívar 187). Her second book is written "out of a sense of urgency that Chicanos are a disappearing tribe" (*Last Generation* 2) and to reconstitute ideas of making *familia* [family]. More specifically, Sternbach writes, "Moraga uses the act of writing as a process of concientización in order to reclaim Chicanismo" (51). In other words, Moraga's writing signals the way in which she defines and articulates herself.

In reading Moraga's work, there are two issues to bear in mind which inform her writing: first, the concept of her shifting/fragmented identity as a Chicana lesbian feminist; and second, the way in which this identity informs her writing and use of language. First, Moraga's subject position emanates from her identity—Chicana lesbian feminist—wherein all three identities are inextricably linked. She has written that it is impossible to write about one part of her identity without addressing other aspects, since each fragmented identity (Chicana, lesbian, feminist) constantly affects and informs her politics and her sense of community. Moraga's choice to identify as a Chicana writer, rather than Mexican-American or Hispanic, is based on a politic that resists assimilation into the dominant society. Historically, the label *Chicana* connotes cultural and political self-assertion. In contrast, Moraga has declared in an interview, "Hispanic . . . has no political bite" (qtd. in Marquez).

Moraga's identification with Chicanas, and more broadly with women, involves her in challenging and resisting racist politics within the women's movement, which, she argues, has not created spaces for women of color to identify as feminists. Similarly, identifying as a lesbian causes Moraga to confront how lesbianism affects her feminism and feminist politics, in that her struggle towards freedom is based on her love for women. Moraga writes in *Loving In the War Years* that while acknowledging that sexuality has been used as a source of oppression towards women, gays, and lesbians, it can and must be used as a tool to liberate all individuals.

Thus, acknowledging the location of Moraga's identity provides a way of understanding how it undergirds her writing. Her commitment to writing opens the space for her to address and challenge forms of oppression and domination that she sees prevailing in society, such as racism, classism, (hetero)sexism, assimilation, and hierarchies based on gradations of skin color. But her writing also demonstrates her commitment to maintain her native tongue, Spanish. In *Loving In the War Years* she writes that relearning Spanish scares her because it is a part of herself that has been subverted in assimilation into a dominant culture. Simultaneously, she recognizes the deficiencies in expressing ideas only in English because there are some things deep within her that call for being expressed in her native tongue. Hence, in *The Last Generation* she code-switches between English and Spanish more heavily than in her earlier works and in so doing she affirms the Chicana part of her identity.

In both her books, Moraga articulates her visions of the future. First, she posits that, individually, we must struggle with the multiple "ism's" that exist in society; anything short of that "will only isolate us in our own oppression" (*Loving* 53). Second, her vision culminates in an essay entitled "Queer Aztlan: the Re-formation of Chicano Tribe." She redefines and reclaims the male-oriented and nationalistic vision of Aztlan (the mythical homeland of Chicana/os). The re-formation of Queer Aztlan requires a radical transformation of consciousness and would include a spectrum of racial/ethnic diversities, sexualities, and genders. "The whole purpose of Queer Aztlan," states Moraga, "is to try and get everybody out of their multi-issue-isms and so that notion of Queer Aztlan would be something that combines all that" (qtd. in Marquez).

Finally, in reading the trajectory of Cherríe Moraga's work we witness the personal transformations and growth she experiences; simultaneously, we partake in her transformation. Therefore, in reading her work there are two possibilities of individual introspection that emanate for her readers. First, readers can maintain a passive and detached reading in which we read Moraga's work and (attempt to) transpose her ideas and experiences onto our individual lives (which consequently may result in a lack of identification with Moraga's work). Or, second, we can view Moraga's work as igniting us, her readers, to reflect on our individual lives and make our own personal transformations.

MAH

FROM "LA GÜERA"[§]

> It requires something more than personal experience to gain a philosophy or point of view from any specific event. It is the quality of our response to the event and our capacity to enter into the lives of others that help us to make their lives and experiences our own.
>
> *Emma Goldman*[1]

I am the very well-educated daughter of a woman who, by the standards of this country, would be considered largely illiterate. My mother was born in Santa Paula, Southern California, at a time when much of the central valley there was still farm land. Nearly thirty-five years later, in 1948, she was the only daughter of six to marry an anglo, my father.

I remember all of my mother's stories, probably much better than she realizes. She is a fine story-teller, recalling every event of her life with the vividness of the present, noting each detail right down to the cut and color of her dress. I remember stories of her being pulled out of school at the ages of five, seven, nine, and eleven to work in the fields, along with her brothers and sisters; stories of her father drinking away whatever small profit she was able to make for the family; of her going the long way home to avoid meeting him on the street, staggering toward the same destination. I remember stories of my mother lying about her age in order to get a job as a hat-check girl at Agua Caliente Racetrack in Tijuana. At fourteen, she was the main support of the family. I can still see her walking home alone at 3 a.m., only to turn all of her salary and tips over to her mother, who was pregnant again.

The stories continue through the war years and on: walnut-cracking factories, the Voit Rubber factory, and then the computer boom. I remember my mother doing piecework for the electronics plant in our neighborhood. In the late evening, she would sit in front of the T.V. set, wrapping copper wires into the backs of circuit boards, talking about "keeping up with the younger girls." By that time she was already in her mid-fifties.

Meanwhile, I was college-prep in school. After classes, I would go with my mother to fill out job applications for her, or write checks for her at the supermarket. We would have the scenario all worked out ahead of time. My mother would sign the check before we'd get to the store. Then, as we'd approach the checkstand, she would say—within earshot of the cashier—"oh honey, you go 'head and make out the check," as if she couldn't be bothered with such an insignificant detail. No one asked any questions.

I was educated, and wore it with a keen sense of pride and satisfaction, my head

[§] Reprinted from *Loving in the War Years* by Cherríe Moraga. Copyright © 1983 by Cherríe Moraga. Used by permission of Cherrie Moraga. Published by South End Press, Institute for Social and Cultural Change, Boston. Excerpted from pages 50–59.

propped up with the knowledge, from my mother, that my life would be easier than hers. I was educated; but more than this, I was "la güera"—fair-skinned. Born with the features of my Chicana mother, but the skin of my Anglo father, I had it made.

No one ever quite told me this (that light was right), but I knew that being light was something valued in my family (who were all Chicano, with the exception of my father). In fact, everything about my upbringing (at least what occurred on a conscious level) attempted to bleach me of what color I did have. Although my mother was fluent in it, I was never taught much Spanish at home. I picked up what I learned from school and from over-heard snatches of conversation among my relatives and mother. She often called other lower-income Mexicans "braceros," or "wet-backs," referring to herself and family as "a different class of people." And yet, the real story was that my family, too, had been poor (some still are) and farmworkers. My mother can remember this in her blood as if it were yesterday. But this is something she would like to forget (and rightfully), for to her, on a basic economic level, being Chicana meant being "less." It was through my mother's desire to protect her children from poverty and illiteracy that we became "anglocized"; the more effectively we could pass in the white world, the better guaranteed our future.

From all of this, I experience, daily, a huge disparity between what I was born into and what I was to grow up to become. Because, (as Goldman suggests) these stories my mother told me crept under my "güera" skin. I had no choice but to enter into the life of my mother. *I had no choice.* I took her life into my heart, but managed to keep a lid on it as long as I feigned being the happy, upwardly mobile heterosexual.

When I finally lifted the lid to my lesbianism, a profound connection with my mother reawakened in me. It wasn't until I acknowledged and confronted my own lesbianism in the flesh, that my heartfelt identification with and empathy for my mother's oppression—due to being poor, uneducated, and Chicana—was realized. My lesbianism is the avenue through which I learned the most about silence and oppression, and it continues to be the most tactile reminder to me that we are not free human beings.

You see, one follows the other. I had known for years that I was a lesbian, had felt it in my bones, had ached with the knowledge, gone crazed with the knowledge, wallowed in the silence of it. Silence *is* like starvation. Don't be fooled. It's nothing short of that, and felt most sharply when one has had a full belly most of her life. When we are not physically starving, we have the luxury to realize psychic and emotional starvation. It is from this starvation that other starvations can be recognized—if one is willing to take the risk of making the connection. For me, the connection is an inevitable one.

What I am saying is that the joys of looking like a white girl ain't so great since I realized I could be beaten on the street for being a dyke. If my sister's being beaten because she's Black, it's pretty much the same principle. We're both getting beaten any way you look at it. The connection is blatant; and in the case of my own family, the difference in the privileges attached to looking white instead of brown are merely a generation apart.

In this country, lesbianism is a poverty—as is being brown, as is being a woman, as is being just plain poor. The danger lies in ranking the oppressions. *The danger lies in failing to acknowledge the specificity of the oppression.* The danger lies in attempting to deal with oppression purely from a theoretical base. Without an emotional, heartfelt grappling with the source of our own oppression, without naming the enemy within ourselves and outside of us, no authentic, non-hierarchical connection among oppressed groups can take place. . . .

But at the age of twenty-seven, it is frightening to acknowledge that I have internalized a racism and classism, where the object of oppression is not only someone *outside* my skin, but the someone *inside* my skin. In fact, to a large degree, the real battle with such oppression, for all of us, begins under the skin. I have had to confront the fact that much of what I value about being Chicana, about my family, has been subverted by anglo culture and my own cooperation with it. This realization did not occur to me overnight. For example, it wasn't until long after my graduation from the private college I'd attended in Los Angeles, that I realized the major reason for my total alienation from and fear of my classmates was rooted in class and culture. . . .

But it is not really difference the oppressor fears so much as similarity. He fears he will discover in himself the same aches, the same longings as those of the people he has shitted on. He fears the immobilization threatened by his own incipient guilt. He fears he will have to change his life once he has seen himself in the bodies of the people he has called different. He fears the hatred, anger, and vengeance of those he has hurt.

This is the oppressor's nightmare, but it is not exclusive to him. We women have a similar nightmare, for each of us in some way has been both oppressed and oppressor. We are afraid to look at how we have failed each other. We are afraid to see how we have taken the values of our oppressor into our hearts and turned them against ourselves and one another. We are afraid to admit how deeply "the man's" words have been ingrained in us.

To assess the damage is a dangerous act. I think of how, even as a feminist lesbian, I have so wanted to ignore my own homophobia, my own hatred of myself for being queer. I have not wanted to admit that my deepest personal sense of myself has not quite "caught up" with my own "woman-identified" politics. I have been afraid to criticize lesbian writers who choose to "skip over" these issues in the name of feminism. In 1979, we talk of "old gay" and "butch and femme" roles as if they were ancient history. We toss them aside as merely patriarchal notions. And yet, the truth of the matter is that I have sometimes taken society's fear and hatred of lesbians to bed with me. I have sometimes hated my lover for loving me. I have sometimes felt "not woman enough" for her. I have sometimes felt "not man enough." For a lesbian trying to survive in a heterosexist society, there is no easy way around these emotions. Similarly, in a white-dominated world, there is little getting around racism and our own internalization of it. It's always there, embodied in someone we least expect to rub up against. . . .

But one voice is not enough, nor two, although this is where dialogue begins. It is essential that feminists confront their fear of and resistance to each other, because without this, there *will* be no bread on the table. Simply, we will not survive. If we could make this connection in our heart of hearts, that if we are serious about a revolution—better—if we seriously believe there should be joy in our lives (real joy, not just "good times"), then we need one another. We women need each other. Because my/your solitary, self-asserting "go-for-the-throat-of-fear" power is not enough. The real power, as you and I well know, is collective. I can't afford to be afraid of you, nor you of me. If it takes head-on collisions, let's do it. This polite timidity is killing us.

As Lorde suggests . . . , it is looking to the nightmare that the dream is found. There, the survivor emerges to insist on a future, a vision, yes, born out of what is dark and female. The feminist movement must be a movement of such survivors, a movement with a future.

NOTE

[1] Alix Kates Shulman, "Was My Life Worth Living?" *Red Emma Speaks.* (New York: Random House, 1972), p. 388. [Moraga]

WORKS CONSULTED

Marquez, M. T. Interview with Cherríe Moraga. CHICLE [On-line], 1–4. Available: CHICLE@UNMVA.UNM.EDU.

Moraga, Cherríe. *The Last Generation.* Boston: South End, 1993.

—. *Loving in the War Years.* Boston: South End, 1983.

Moraga, Cherríe, and Gloria Anzaldúa, eds. *This Bridge Called My Back: Writings By Radical Women of Color.* New York: Kitchen Table Press, 1981.

Saldívar, Ramón. *Chicano Narrative: The Dialectics of Difference.* Madison: U of Wisconsin P, 1990.

Sternbach, N. S. "'A Deep Racial Memory': The Chicana Feminism of Cherríe Moraga." *Breaking Boundaries: Latina Writing and Critical Readings.* Eds. Asunción Horno-Delgado, et al. Amherst: U of Massachusetts P, 1989. 48–61.

MỌLARA OGUNDIPẸ-LESLIE *(late 20th century)*

"Stiwanism: Feminism in an African Context"

Mọlara Ogundipẹ-Leslie is a poet, scholar, feminist theorist, and global activist on women's issues. She has been a professor at the University of Ibadan and head of the English Department at Ogun State University, Nigeria; she has also lectured internationally on subjects ranging from literature to African women in economics. In 1977 she was one of the founders of AAWORD, the Association of African Women in Research and Development, created by African women doing research on women "from an African perspective" (Davies 217). An example of AAWORD's work, and of Ogundipẹ-Leslie's characteristically local/global focus, was their "Statement on Genital Mutilation." AAWORD condemned Western campaigns against genital mutilation for their sensationalist insensitivity "to the dignity of the very women they want to 'save.'" They also condemned genital mutilation unconditionally, together with "all other practices. . . which oppress women and justify exploiting them economically or socially," and called for African women's unequivocal resistance to such practices. At the same time they urged feminists from developed countries to see genital mutilation in the broader context of all these practices, and to "avoid ill-timed interference, maternalism, ethnocentrism and misuse of power" in addressing the issue (218–19).

In 1982 Ogundipẹ-Leslie helped found WIN, Women in Nigeria, to gain for Nigerian women "full social, economic, and political rights . . . in the family, in the workplace and in society in general" (*Re-creating Ourselves* 128). Its work has included documenting women's disadvantages in every area of life, making policy recommendations, and researching "indigenous forms of feminist resistance" in response to criticisms that African feminism is merely an imitation of Western ideas (126). WIN is unique, she says, in its double attack on both class and gender oppression (127).

WIN's insistence on the importance of both class and gender oppression comes out of a debate within African Marxism over the proper relationship between work toward women's liberation and work toward national liberation. This debate, which is also in the background of the excerpt reprinted here, has been of urgent concern to women in many liberation movements all over the world. Ogundipẹ-Leslie stated her position on the issue in her essay "African Marxists, Women and a Critique of Everyday Life," which called on men in particular to recognize that socialist economic and social change "does not automatically entail changes in actual persons" (150). Emphasizing male Marxists' "insensitivity" on women's issues (152), she posed the question, "How liberated are our individual psyches for the process of revolutionary practice?" (146). In opposition to the view that class oppression precedes and subsumes all others—and that therefore women's issues should wait—she said that oppressions on the basis of sex, gender, and race "compound" class oppression but also "exist independently and have to be fought independently" (150). In a subsequent essay, "Mobilizing the Mobilizers," she proposes a list of questions that political organizers, both men and women, should ask themselves, "somewhat like the Rotary club":

(i) Have I thought of both men and women in this project?
(ii) Have I asked and looked for women to play leadership roles in this?
(iii) Am I thinking and acting in terms of the truth about women?
(iv) Is this fair to all concerned i.e. to both men and women? (157–158)

Although she has been a blunt and forthright critic of sexism among her male co-workers for political change, Ogundipẹ-Leslie's feminism is grounded firmly in a broad political context of solidarity with progressive men. She places herself among those African feminists and women—the majority, she says—who "are 'womanist' in Alice Walker's sense of being committed to survival and wholeness of entire peoples, male and female; being not in any way separatist or adversarial to men" (12–13). In order, she says, "to deflect energies from constantly having to respond to charges of imitating Western feminism" and to conserve them for concentration on "the real issue of the conditions of women in Africa," she terms her version of feminism "Stiwanism": *Social Transformation Including Women in Africa* (229).

The excerpt below, from Ogundipẹ-Leslie's recent collection of essays on African women, is one of her calls for the "survival and wholeness" at the heart of her Stiwanist vision. The essay itself models many ways of seeing things whole. She insists on both the psyche and the family as crucial sites of social and political change. She makes an important connection between African women's resistance to sexist oppression and African men's and women's resistance to dominance by developed nations. She insists that progressive men link their political vision to personal transformation in the area of gender relations. And finally, the complete essay mingles poetry and analytical prose, bringing aesthetic pleasure into a feminist manifesto. In this, the essay exemplifies one of the powers for which she calls in the foreword to the book—the "power to collapse all screens which threaten to obscure our women's eyes from the beauties of the world."

ECD

FROM "STIWANISM: FEMINISM IN AN AFRICAN CONTEXT"§

. . . Often the argument is that feminism is not necessary in Africa because gender was balanced in an idyllic African past, which is their own creation. African feminists are said to be merely the parrots of Western women. Race and nationalism are used in bad faith to attack gender. Sometimes race, nationalism, and class are brought together to attack gender politics. Feminist concerns are said to be the predilections of Westernized women like myself or Ifi Amadiume or Filomina Steady, for example.[1] Feminist concerns are, then, not those of the great rural and faithful African women who are "the true African women" who are

§ Reprinted from *Re-Creating Ourselves: African Women and Critical Transformations* by Mọlara Ogundipẹ-Leslie. Copyright 1994 by Mọlara Ogundipẹ-Leslie. Reprinted by permission of the Africa World Press, Lawrenceville, New Jersey. Material excerpted from pages 222–226.

happy as they are and have always been. But what do research and analysis tell us about these newly discovered and glamorized creatures; "the rural women of Africa?" Certainly not that "rural," poor women are happy with the status quo and desire no change.

Feminism can be defined by its etymological roots. Femina is "woman" in Latin. Feminism, an ideology of woman; any body of social philosophy about women. This definition of feminism gives us enough leeway to encompass various types of feminisms: right-wing, left-wing, centrist, left of center, right of center, reformist, separatist, liberal, socialist, Marxist, nonaligned, Islamic, indigenous, etc. Believe me, all these feminisms exist. Nawal el Saadawi is an Islamic socialist feminist. So, one question could be, "What is feminism for you." What is your feminism? Do you, in fact, have an ideology of women in society and life? Is your feminism about the rights of women in society? What is the total conception of women as agents in human society—her conditions, roles and statuses—her recognition and acknowledgement? Generally, feminism, however, must always have a political and activist spine to its form. If we take feminism to imply all these, is the African woman on the African continent, in an African context without problems in all these areas?

For those who say that feminism is not relevant to Africa, can they truthfully say that the African woman is all right in all these areas of her being and therefore does not need an ideology that addresses her reality, hopefully and preferably, to ameliorate that reality? When they argue that feminism is foreign, are these opponents able to support the idea that African women or cultures did not have ideologies which propounded or theorized woman's being and provided avenues and channels for women's oppositions and resistance to injustice within their societies? Certainly, these channels existed. Are the opponents of feminism willing to argue that indigenous African societies did not have avenues and strategies for correcting gender imbalance and injustice? Will they argue that these aspects of social engineering could only have come from white or Euro-American women? Are they saying that African women cannot see their own situations and demand change without guidance from white women? Nationalism and race pride, I know, will make our men beat a retreat at this question and they had better beat that retreat. The issue is that there were indigenous feminisms. There were indigenous patterns within traditional African societies for addressing the oppressions and injustices to women.

So, what kind of feminism exists in an African context? In view of all I have said above, in view of all I have argued as well as the realities of Africa, we should more correctly say: What *feminisms* exist in Africa? Indeed, there are many feminisms, depending on the center from which one is speaking or theorizing. These feminisms have to be theorized around the junctures of race, class, caste and gender; nation, culture and ethnicity; age, status, role and sexual orientation. Certainly more research is needed to discover what African women themselves, particularly, the working classes and the peasantry think about themselves as women, what ideology they possess and what agenda they have for themselves, daily and historically.

Once we agree that an ideology of women and about women is necessary and has always existed in Africa, we can proceed to ask if these existent ideologies remain relevant or need to be changed. Our opportunistic and irredentist compatriots who argue culture and heritage when it serves their interests, should consider whether our inherited cultures should be taken hook, line and sinker, or should be subjected to change where necessary.

Should we, when necessary, change the notion that man is always superior to woman, hence, boys should go to school and girls should only go when they can, when there is money to "waste" and no work to be done at home or in the farms and markets? Should we apply the sexist ideas in the Bible, without criticism, with preference for Old Testament ideas and the Pauline section of the New Testament, stressing only the verses on male dominance? Should we adapt Koranic ideas to modern times or continue to beat the recalcitrant woman lightly as said in the fourth Sura of the Koran. (If your woman does not listen, first admonish her then, sexually withdraw from her and finally beat her "lightly.") How light is light? Is not the issue the proprietary right to beat her in the first place? Should culture be placed in a museum of minds or should we take authority over culture as a product of human intelligence and consciousness to be used to improve our existential conditions? Should we preach cultural fidelity only when it does not affect us negatively, which is usually the position of African men who wish to keep only those aspects of culture which keep them dominant?

For the rest of this essay, I shall try to indicate what some of the outspoken African women are saying about feminism in Africa. Some quite outstanding women like Buchi Emecheta, say they are not feminists without saying why. Others like the Nigerian writer, Flora Nwapa, say that they are not feminists, but they are "womanists." There are still other views: the great and late South African writer, Bessie Head, says in her posthumous essays collected under the title *A Woman Alone,* that in the world of the intellect where she functions as a writer and an intellectual, feminism is not necessary because the world of the intellect is neither male nor female.[2] I think she is deceived or perhaps deluded on this point by the post-romantic and Victorian patriarchal notion and myth about the world of the intellect being sexless. This, women know to be a myth, although it has been sold to all the women of the world. We know how male sexism actually functions in the world of the intellect or in the world of "the life of the mind" as they say. Bessie Head, in my view, expresses a false consciousness often expressed by successful middle-class women of all cultures (including African women who proudly and aggressively announce that their achievement has taken place outside their identity as women). "I am just a writer, not a woman writer," "I am a professor of physics," "an astronaut," "a prime minister, not a woman" and I wonder what is that? What is that neuter thing? But notice that only women engage in that kind of rhetoric. It speaks volumes that only women make that kind of statement. Have you ever heard a man say, "I'm just a professor, not a man." "I'm just a professor," "a mathematician," "a tycoon," "a president of the United States, but not a man, not a man at all." Perhaps we need to deconstruct that formulation elsewhere.

Let us now, however, consider the theories of some of the most visible African women who hold that feminism is relevant to the African context. A summary of their positions indicates some common denominators:

1. That feminism need not be oppositional to men. It is not about adversarial gender politics.
2. That women need not neglect their biological roles.
3. That motherhood is idealized and claimed as a strength by African women and

seen as having a special manifestation in Africa. Davies has asked whether African women have specially cornered motherhood.[3]

4. That the total configuration of the conditions of women should be addressed rather than obsessing with sexual issues.
5. That certain aspects of women's reproductive rights take priority over others.
6. That women's conditions in Africa need to be addressed in the context of the total production and reproduction of their society and that scenario also involves men and children. Hence, there has always been an emphasis on economic fulfillment and independence in African feminist thinking.
7. That the ideology of women has to be cast in the context of the race and class struggles which bedevil the continent of Africa today; that is, in the context of the liberation of the total continent.

It is this generally holistic attitude of African women to feminism which often separates them from their Western sisters. . . .

NOTES

[1] Ifi Amadiume, *Male Daughters, Female Husbands* (London: Zed Press, 1987) and Filomena Steady, *The Black Woman Cross-Culturally* (Cambridge, MA: Schenkman, 1981) . . . Steady, "African Feminism, a Worldwide Perspective," *Women in Africa and the African Diaspora,* eds., Harley, Rushing and Terbog-Penn (Washington, D.C.: Howard University Press, 1987). [Ogundipẹ-Leslie]

[2] Bessie Head, A Woman Alone: Autobiographical Writings (London: Heinemann, 1990) 95. [Ogundipẹ-Leslie]

[3] Carole Boyce Davies, "Motherhood in the Works of Male and Female Igbo Writers," *Ngambika: Studies of Women in African Literature* (Lawrenceville, NJ: Africa World Press, 1986), 241-256. See also the introduction to the book. [Ogundipẹ-Leslie]

WORKS CONSULTED

AAWORD. "A Statement on Genital Mutilation." *Third World—Second Sex : Women's Struggles and National Liberation. Third World Women Speak Out.* Comp. Miranda Davies. London: Zed Books, 1983.

Ogundipẹ-Leslie, Mọlara. *Sew the Old Days and Other Poems.* 1985.

—. *Re-Creating Ourselves: African Women and Critical Transformations.* Lawrenceville, NJ: Africa World Press, 1994.

—. "Not Spinning on the Axis of Maleness." *Sisterhood Is Global.* Ed. Robin Morgan. London: Doubleday, 1984.

— and Carole Boyce Davies, eds. *Moving Beyond Boundaries.* International Dimensions of Black Women's Writing 1. London: Pluto, 1995.

GLÜCKEL OF HAMELN *(1646–1724)*

A Pregnant Woman's Craving

See headnote in **Sexuality, Spirituality, and Power.**

FROM THE MEMOIRS OF GLÜCKEL OF HAMELN[§]

Here, my dear children, I will write of an incident that is true. If young, pregnant women at any time, anywhere, see fruit or anything tasty which they fancy, they should not go away but should first sample it, and not listen to their own silly heads which say, 'Ay, it cannot harm you!' and go away. For it can, God forbid, be a matter of life and death to them, as well as to the unborn child, as I found to my cost. I used always to laugh and make merry when I heard that a pregnant woman had longings after anything and suffered any harm by not indulging in her fancy. I would not believe it. On the contrary, many times when I was pregnant and went to market and saw some nice fruit which I fancied, if it was too dear I would not buy. And in truth, I never suffered any ill effects. But not all times are the same: this I discovered when I was in the ninth month with my son Joseph.

My mother had some business to transact with an advocate who lived in the Horse Market. She asked me to go with her. Although it was far from my house, and the time for evening prayers was approaching, it was the beginning of the month of Kislev,[1] I could not refuse her. I was in fine health then. We went together to the gentile quarter. Opposite the advocate's house there lived a woman who sold medlars. I was always very fond of medlars and ate them with relish. I said to my mother, 'Mumma, do not forget, when we come back, I want to buy some medlars.' We went to the advocate and there accomplished our business. It was very late when we were finished and nearly night. We walked homewards and both of us forget the medlars; I remembered them only when I got indoors. I felt sorry that I had not bought any and gave no further thought to them, just as one thinks of food one likes, but which is not immediately to hand. I went to sleep, feeling as well as usual, but after midnight, my pains commenced. The midwives were summoned and my son was born.

The news was immediately conveyed to my husband, who was overjoyed that he now had his father's name. But I noticed that the women who were with me put their heads together and whispered among themselves. I wanted to know what was the matter and insisted that they must tell me. At length they informed me that the baby had brown spots over his head and body. They had to bring a candle to the bed so that I could see for myself. I saw that not only was he covered with spots but that he lay like a lump of clay, not moving an arm or leg, just as though, God forbid, his soul had departed. He would not suckle or open his mouth. My husband, too, saw this and was very much upset. This was on Wednesday night and the circumcision was to be celebrated on Thursday week.

[§] Reprinted from *The Life Of Glückel Of Hameln 1646–1724; Written By Herself*. Translated and edited by Beth-Zion Abrahams. Copyright © 1963 Thomas Yoseloff Publishers, New York. Material reprinted from pages 100–103.

There was no improvement during the week, and he grew weaker day by day. Sabbath came, we celebrated *Shalom Zochor.*[2] But still there was no improvement in the child. At the close of Sabbath, while my husband was reciting the *Habdalah,*[3] I said to my mother who was with me, 'I beg you, send the *shabbos-goya*[4] to me. I want to send her somewhere.' My mother enquired where to? I answered, 'I have been puzzling all the time why the baby should have these spots, and why he has grown so much weaker. I wonder whether the cause is that on the night I was brought to bed I had a longing for those medlars and did not have any? I want to send the woman to get me a few schilling's worth. I will squeeze a little into the baby's mouth. Perhaps God in His mercy will help, so that the child will get better.'

My mother was very cross with me and cried, 'You've always got such nonsense in your head! The weather is as bad as if heaven and earth were joining, and the woman won't want to go out in it. It is all a lot of foolishness.' But I persisted, 'My dear mother, do me but this favour. Send the woman. I will give her as much as she wants, as long as I get the medlars; otherwise my heart will not be at rest.' So we called the woman and sent her to get the medlars. It was a long distance. She ran all the way. It was wretched weather, not fit to send a dog out in. The time passed very slowly until her return, as is natural when one waits impatiently for anything. Each second seemed as long as an hour. At length the woman returned with the medlars. Everyone knows that medlars, being sourish, are not food for such a young child. I called the nurse to unbind the baby and seat herself with him in front of the oven and squeeze a little of the medlar into his mouth. Although everyone laughed at what they called my foolishness, I insisted on this, and it had to be done. When she squeezed a little of the medlar between the baby's lips, he opened his little mouth so eagerly, as though he wanted to swallow it whole, and sucked away all the soft part. Before this he had not opened his mouth wide enough to take a drop of milk or sugar-pap such as one gives to babies. The nurse handed him to me in bed, to see if he would suck. As soon as he felt the breast, he began to suck with the strength of a three-month babe, and from then till the day of his circumcision there remained no spot on his face or body, save one on his side, as large as a broad lentil. The child was fine grown and hale at the time of his circumcision. The ceremony was performed, praised be God, at the right time. There was a great celebration on his initiation into the Jewish covenant, the like of which Hamburg had not seen for a long time. Though we lost 1000 marks banco the same day through the bankruptcy of a Portuguese Jew Isaac Vas, my husband did not take it to heart because of the joy he had in his son. So you see, dear children, women's longings are not all folly and should not be despised.

NOTES

1 Either the end of November or the beginning of December. [Abrahams]

2 A feast on the first Sabbath evening after the birth of a son, in celebration of the event. [Abrahams]

3 A prayer recited at the close of the Sabbath. [Abrahams]

4 A gentile woman employed in Jewish homes on the Sabbath to perform small duties forbidden by Jewish law. [Abrahams]

MARGARET FELL *(1614–1702)*

Women's Speaking Justified

A justice before whom Margaret Fell[1] was tried in 1664 described her as having an everlasting tongue (Trevett 55)—a fitting description of the woman who would soon write from prison a book entitled *Women's Speaking Justified.* Fell's talent for speaking was evident from the beginning of her conversion to Quakerism in 1652. On the way home from a business trip in the summer of that year, her husband, a well-to-do judge, was met by a group of neighbors who warned him that a travelling preacher had "bewitched" his wife, children, and servants in his absence. When he entered the house, Margaret related later, "any may think what a condition I was like to be in, that either I must displease my husband, or offend God" (qtd. in Ross 15). But at dinner, "seized" suddenly by "the power of the Lord," she explained her new religious doctrines so eloquently that "he was struck with amazement, and knew not what to think" (qtd. in Ross 15).

Although she never fully converted her husband to her views as a member of the Religious Society of Friends, or Quakers, Fell seems to have persuaded him at least to use his influence to protect her and many of her friends from religious persecution until his death in 1658. As an outspoken adherent of the new religion itself she used her eloquence—and her power as a member of the very small landholding class[2]—to help shape its doctrines and organization internally and articulate them to the outside world. Her power in early Quaker circles was enhanced by her marriage in 1669 to George Fox, founder of the movement, to whose itinerant preaching she had responded so strongly in 1652. As Susan Mosher Stuard says, "Over the next twenty years . . . the guiding hand of Margaret Fell may be found in the established practices of Quakerism" (15).

The rise of Quakerism, a religion focused on a belief in the primacy of an "Inner Light" or "Teacher Within" as the source of spiritual knowledge, occurred during the period of civil and religious upheaval in England that the historian Christopher Hill has described as "The World Turned Upside Down." In general this tumultuous era was characterized by the flourishing of a number of new Protestant sects, of which the Religious Society of Friends is one of the few that still remains. Many of these sects, in their emphasis on experiential religion completely or substantially unmediated by priests or church hierarchies, provided unusual opportunities for women to escape gender restrictions. Phyllis Mack has identified over three hundred "visionary women" who wrote and/or prophesied in England during the period from 1642 to 1660; of them, she says, over two thirds were Quakers (1). As she points out, "Women as prophets enjoyed virtually the only taste of public authority they would ever know" (5); on the other hand, it is important to avoid the simple conclusion "that visionary women were pursuing a covert strategy of self-assertion. . . . For the ground of women's authority as spiritual leaders was their achievement of complete self-transcendence, surely a very different subjective experience from that of the modern social activist or career woman" (5).

Whatever its different meanings, Fell can be seen as having had a long and influential "career" as a Quaker. For many years her role within Quakerism was described in images of her as "secretary" or "helpmeet" to Fox, or "nursing mother" to the sect as a whole. More recently, in contrast, Bonnelyn Young Kunze has documented Fell's role as a primary shaper, alongside such other figures as George Fox and William Penn, of important aspects of Quaker practice and theory. Within the Society of Friends itself, Fell was the first woman to publish a defense of women's public ministry (Kunze 5). At the organizational level she was especially influential in initiating a system of separate women's meetings for business (Kunze 143–168). Together with doctrines about women's spiritual role that Fell, among others, helped to articulate, these meetings gave generations of Quaker women administrative, financial, and organizational skills that have been seen as contributing significantly to the extraordinarily high proportion of Quakers involved in the nineteenth and twentieth-century feminist and peace movements.[3]

Outside the Society of Friends, Fell's career as a public activist for Quakerism included a "Declaration" to the King and Houses of Parliament in 1660 explaining Quaker opposition to war and violence—the first such published testimony. She also wrote letters and made visits to King Charles II and other powerful individuals to urge religious toleration for Quakers in general and freedom for specific Quakers, including George Fox during his various imprisonments. Although her approaches to those in authority bespeak a certain amount of class and economic power in her own right as an heir to Judge Fell, she herself was at one time in danger of having her whole estate confiscated and was twice imprisoned. Indeed the work from which the following excerpt was taken, *Women's Speaking Justified* (1666), was one of the four books that Fell wrote while imprisoned in Lancaster Castle from 1665 to 1668. Although arguments similar to Fell's had been made before (see Trevett 44–48 and 54), this book has been described as the most comprehensively argued piece of Quaker writing about women's ministry, unusual for its "thoroughness" in citing Biblical precedent, for its critical stance toward the church and clergy, and for its optimism that although men have made "a mountain" of certain Biblical passages apparently prohibiting women's ministry, "the Lord is removing all this" (Trevett 54).

There is much to suggest that the spiritual equality Fell advocated in this book had its counterpart in her relationship with George Fox, a man of a considerably lower class than hers, whom she married in a newly invented Quaker procedure that she had done much to shape. Before the ceremony, Fox—who had himself written two books on the spiritual equality of men and women (Ross 201)—requested the approval of her children and drew up a document renouncing any claim to her property and income, to which he would have been entitled as her husband under English law. The ceremony was preceded by several meetings in which Fell, Fox, and others present testified to their sense of the marriage as being "of the Lord"; the ceremony itself consisted of a meeting for worship at which the woman and man stood up to declare their marriage to each other, without a presiding minister or priest, "in the presence of God and these our friends" (Bacon 16). Also in keeping with Quaker views of the time on the proper relationship between marriage and responsibility to the "leadings" of the spirit, Fell and Fox spent most of their married life apart from each other doing the religious work each felt called to do, which required extensive travelling. Both insisted, in general, "that spouses leave each other free to do God's work" (Mack 228).

Although Fell's writings are little known today, her influence on middle-class feminism in Britain and the United States has been substantial if indirect. The effect of the women's meetings has already been mentioned. In addition, the effect of her uncompromising stance on women's authority as speakers no doubt helped sustain the Quaker recognition of female ministers—an authority, in turn, that gave courage to such eloquent feminist speakers as Lucretia Mott, Angelina Grimké, and Susan B. Anthony. Indeed Anthony often appealed directly to that authority in her speeches, citing the precedent of Quaker women ministers (Bacon 118). Through such spiritual descendants, the woman with the "everlasting tongue" continues to have her say.

ECD

FROM *WOMEN'S SPEAKING JUSTIFIED* [§]

Whereas it hath been an Objection in the minds of many, and several times hath been objected by the Clergy, or Ministers, and others, against Womens speaking in the Church; and so consequently may be taken, that they are condemned for meddling in the things of God; the ground of which Objection, is taken from the Apostles words, which he writ in his first Epistle to the *Corinthians,* chap. 14., vers. 34, 35. And also what he writ to *Timothy* in the first Epistle; chap. 2, vers. 11, 12. But how far they wrong the Apostles intentions in these Scriptures, we shall shew clearly when we come to them in their course and order. But first let me lay down how God himself hath manifested his Will and Mind concerning women, and unto women.

And first, when *God created Man in his own Image: in the Image of God created he them, Male and Female: and God blessed them, and God said unto them, Be fruitful, and multiply: And God said, Behold, I have given you of every Herb, &c.* Gen. I. Here God joyns them together in his own Image, and makes no such distinctions and differences as men do; for though they be weak, he is strong; and as he said to the Apostle, *His Grace is sufficient, and his strength is made manifest in weakness,* 2 Cor. 12. 9. And such hath the Lord chosen, even *the weak things of the world, to confound the things which are mighty; and things which are despised, hath God chosen, to bring to nought things that are,* I Cor. I. And God hath put no such difference between the Male and Female as men would make.

It is true, *The Serpent that was more subtile than any* other *Beast of the Field,* came unto the Woman, with his Temptations, and with a lie: his subtilty discerning her to be more inclinable to hearken to him, when he said, *If ye eat, your eyes shall be opened:* and the woman saw that *the Fruit was good to make one wise,* there the temptation got into her, *and she did eat, and give to her Husband, and he did eat* also; and so they were both tempted into the transgression and disobedience; and therefore God said unto *Adam,* when that he hid himself when he heard his voice, *Hast thou eaten of the Tree which I*

[§] Reprinted from *Women's Speaking Justified* by Margaret Fell Fox. Augustan Reprint Society Edition, published 1979 by the William Andrews Clark Memorial Library, Los Angeles. Material excerpted from pages 3–12. Original text and literary rights owned by the Henry E. Huntington Library. Used by permission.

commanded thee that thou shouldest not eat? And *Adam* said, *The Woman which thou gavest me, she gave me of the Tree, and I did eat. And the Lord said unto the Woman, What is this that thou hast done?* and the Woman said, *The Serpent beguiled me, and I did eat.* Here the Woman spoke the truth unto the Lord: See what the Lord saith, vers. 15. after he had pronounced Sentence on the Serpent; *I will put enmity between thee and the Woman, and between thy Seed and her Seed; it shall bruise thy head, and thou shalt bruise his heel,* Gen. 3.

Let this Word of the Lord, which was from the beginning, stop the mouths of all that oppose Womens Speaking in the Power of the Lord; for he hath put enmity between the Woman and the Serpent; and if the Seed of the Woman speak not, the Seed of the Serpent speaks; for God hath put enmity between the two Seeds, and it is manifest, that those that speak against the woman and her Seeds Speaking, speak out of the enmity of the old Serpents Seed; and God hath fulfilled his Word and his Promise, *When the fulness of time was come, he hath sent forth his son, made of a woman, made under the Law, that we might receive the adoption of Sons,* Gal. 4. 4, 5. . . .

Thus much may prove that the Church of Christ is a woman, and those that speak against the womans speaking, speak against the Church of Christ, and the Seed of the woman, which Seed is Christ; that is to say, Those that speak against the Power of the Lord, and the Spirit of the Lord speaking in a woman, simply, by reason of her Sex, or because she is a Woman, not regarding the Seed, and Spirit, and Power that speaks in her; such speak against Christ, and his Church, and are of the Seed of the Serpent, wherein lodgeth the enmity. And as God the Father made no such difference in the first Creation, nor never since between the Male and the Female, but alwayes out of his Mercy and loving kindness, had regard unto the weak. . . .

Also that Woman that came unto Jesus with an Alabaster Box of very precious Oyntment, and poured it on his Head, as he sat at meat; it's manifested that this Woman knew more of the secret Power and Wisdom of God, then his Disciples did, that were filled with indignation against her; and therefore Jesus saith, *Why do ye trouble the Woman? for she hath wrought a good work upon me; Verily, I say unto you, Wheresoever this Gospel shall be preached in the whole World, there shall also this that this Woman hath done, be told for a memorial of her,* Matt. 26, Mark 14. 3. *Luke* saith further, *She was a sinner,* and that *she stood at his feet behind him weeping, and began to wash his feet with her tears and did wipe them with the hair of her head, and kissed his feet, and annointed them with Oyntment.* And when Jesus saw the Heart of the *Pharisee* that hath bidden him to his house, he took occasion to speak unto *Simon,* as you may read in Luke 7. and he turned to the woman, and said, *Simon, seeth thou this Woman? Thou gavest me no water to my feet, but she hath washed my feet with tears, and wiped them with the hair of her head: Thou gavest me no kiss, but this woman, since I came in, hath not ceased to kiss my Feet: My Head with Oyl thou didst not annoint, but this Woman hath annointed my Feet with Oyntment: Wherefore I say unto thee, her sins, which are many, are forgiven her, for she hath loved much,* Luke 7. 37, to the end. . . .

Thus we see that Jesus owned the Love and Grace that appeared in Women, and did not despise it, and by what is recorded in the Scriptures, he received as much love, kindness, compassion, and tender dealing towards him from women, as he did from any others, both in his life time, and also after they had exercised their cruelty upon him, for *Mary Magdalene,* and *Mary* the Mother of *James,* beheld where he was laid: *And when the Sabbath was past,* Mary Magdalen, *and* Mary *the Mother of* James, *and* Salom, *had brought sweet spices that they might annoint him: And very early in the morning, the first day of the week, they came unto the Sepulchre at the rising of the Sun, And they said among themselves who shall roll us away the stone from the door of the Sepulchre? And when they looked, the stone was rolled away for it was very great:* Mark 16. I, 2, 3, 4. Luke 24. I, 2. *and they went down into the Sepulchre,* and as *Matthew* saith, *The Angel rolled away the stone, and he said unto the Women, Fear not, I know whom ye seek, Jesus which was Crucified: he is not here, he is risen,* Mat. 28. Now *Luke* saith thus that there stood two men by them in shining apparel, and as they were perplexed and afraid, the men said unto them, He is not here; remember how he said unto you when he was in Galilee, That the Son of Man must be delivered into the hands of sinful men, and be crucified, and the third day rise again, and they remembred his words, and returned from the Sepulchre, and told all these things to the eleven, and to all the rest.

It was *Mary Magdalene,* and *Joanna,* and *Mary* the Mother of *James,* and the other Women that were with them, which told these things to the Apostles, *And their words seemed unto them as idle tales, and they believed them not.* Mark this, ye despisers of the weakness of Women, and look upon yourselves to be so wise, but Christ Jesus doth not so, for he makes use of the weak. . . .

Mark this, you that despise and oppose the Message of the Lord God that he sends by women, what had become of the Redemption of the whole Body of Mankind, if they had not believed the Message that the Lord Jesus sent by these women, of and concerning his Resurrection? And if these women had not thus, out of their tenderness and bowels of love, who had received Mercy, and Grace, and forgiveness of sins, and Virtue, and Healing from him, which many men also had received the like, if their hearts had not been so united and knit unto him in love, that they could not depart as the men did, but sat watching, and waiting, and weeping about the Sepulchre untill the time of his Resurrection, and so were ready to carry his Message, as is manifested, else how should his Disciples have known, who were not there?. . .

And now to the Apostles words, which is the ground of the great Objection against Womens speaking: And first, I Cor. 14. let the Reader seriously read that Chapter, and see the end and drift of the Apostle in speaking these words: for the Apostle is their exhorting the *Corinthians* unto charity, and to desire Spiritual gifts, and not to speak in an unknown tongue, and not to be Children in understanding, but to be Children in malice, but in understanding to be men; and that the Spirits of the Prophets should be subject to the Prophets, for God is not the Author of Confusion, but of Peace: And then he saith, *Let your Women keep silence in the Church, &c.*

Where it doth plainly appear that the women, as well as others, that were among them, were in confusion, for he saith, *How is it Brethren? when ye come together, every one of you hath a Psalm, hath a Doctrine, hath a Tongue, hath a Revelation, hath an Interpretation? let all things be done to edifying.* Here was no edifying, but all was in confusion speaking together: Therefore he saith, *If any man speak in an unknown Tongue, let it be by two, or at most by three, and that by course, and let one Interpret, but if there be no Interpreter, let him keep silence in the Church.* Here the Man is commanded to keep silence as well as the woman, when they are in confusion and out of order.

But the Apostle saith further, *They are commanded to be in Obedience, as also saith the Law; and if they will learn anything, let them ask their Husbands at home, for it is a shame for a Woman to speak in the Church.*

Here the Apostle clearly manifests his intent; for he speaks of women that were under the Law, and in that Transgression as *Eve* was, and such as were to learn, and not to speak publickly, but they must first ask their Husbands at home, and it was a shame for such to speak in the Church. . . .

And what is all this to Womens Speaking? that have the Everlasting Gospel to preach, and upon whom the Promise of the Lord is fulfilled, and his Spirit poured upon them according to his word, *Acts* 2. 16, 17, 18. And if the Apostle would have stopped such as had the Spirit of the Lord poured upon them, why did he say just before, *If any thing be revealed to another that sitteth by, let the first hold his peace?* and *you may all prophesie one by one.* Here he did not say that such Women should not Prophesie as had the Revelation and Spirit of God poured upon them, but their Women that were under the Law, and in the Transgression, and were in strife, confusion and malice in their speaking. . . .

And what is all this to such as have the Power and Spirit of the Lord Jesus poured upon them, and have the Message of the Lord Jesus given unto them? must not they speak the Word of the Lord because of these undecent and unreverent Women that the Apostle speaks of, and to, in these two Scriptures? And how are the men of this Generation blinded, that bring these Scriptures, and pervert the Apostles Words, and corrupt his intent in speaking of them? and by these Scriptures, endeavour to stop the Message and Word of the Lord God in Women, by contemning and despising of them. If the Apostle would have had Womens speaking stopt, and did not allow of them, why did he entreat his true Yoak-fellow to help those Women who laboured with him in the Gospel? *Phil.* 4. 3. And why did the Apostles joyn together in Prayer and Supplication with the Women, and *Mary* the Mother of Jesus, and with his Brethren, *Acts* I. 14. if they had not allowed, and had union and fellowship with the Spirit of God, wherever it was revealed in Women as well as others?. . .

And so let this serve to stop that opposing spirit that would limit the Power and Spirit of the Lord Jesus, whose Spirit is poured upon all flesh, both Sons and Daughters, now in his Resurrection; and since that the Lord God in the Creation, when he made man in his own Image, he made them *male* and *female;* and since that Christ Jesus, as the Apostle saith, was made of a Woman, and the power of the Highest overshadowed her, and the holy Ghost came upon her, and the holy thing that was born of her, was called the *Son of God,* and when he was upon the Earth, he manifested his *love,* and his *will,* and his *mind,* both to the Woman of *Samaria,* and *Martha,* and *Mary* her Sister, and several others, as hath been shewed; and after his Resurrection also manifested himself unto them first of all, even before he ascended unto his Father. *Now when Jesus was risen, the first day of the week, he appeared first unto Mary Magdalene,* Mark 16. 9. And thus the Lord Jesus hath manifested himself and his Power, without respect of Persons, and so let all mouths be stopt that would limit him, whose Power and Spirit is infinite, that is pouring it upon all flesh.

And thus much in answer to these two Scriptures, which have been such a stumbling block, that the ministers of Darkness have made such a mountain of; But the Lord is removing all this, and taking it out of the way. M.F.

NOTES

[1] It is customary to refer to refer to Margaret Askew Fell Fox by her first married name.

[2] Two percent of the population (Trevett 55, citing R.A. Houlbrooke, *The English Family 1450–1700*. London 1983, 23.)

[3] See Bacon 42, and her discussion of Quaker women as "Mothers of Feminism" in general. Susan B. Anthony, Lucretia Mott, Elizabeth Comstock, Sarah and Angelina Grimké, Helen Hunt Jackson, Jane Addams, Alice Paul, and many other feminist organizers were all Quakers or closely connected with Quakerism; more recently, Audre Lorde considered herself for a time to be a Quaker before identifying herself with animism (Steif interview 33).

WORKS CONSULTED

Bacon, Margaret Hope. *Mothers of Feminism: The Story of Quaker Women in America*. San Francisco: Harper and Row, 1986.

Hill, Christopher. *The World Turned Upside Down: Radical Ideas During the English Revolution*. New York: Viking, 1972.

Kunze, Bonnelyn Young. *Margaret Fell and the Rise of Quakerism*. Houndmills, Basingstoke, Hampshire, and London: Macmillan, 1994.

Lorde, Audre. "I'm Angry About the Pretenses of America." Interview with William Steif. *The Progressive* 55.1 (1 Jan. 1991): 32–33.

Mack, Phyllis. *Visionary Women: Ecstatic Prophecy in Seventeenth-Century England*. Berkeley, Los Angeles, and Oxford: U of California P, 1992.

Ross, Isabel. *Margaret Fell: Mother of Quakerism*. York, England: William Sessions Book Trust/Ebor Press, 1984.

Stuard, Susan Mosher. "Women's Witnessing: A New Departure." *In Witnesses for Change: Quaker Women over Three Centuries*. Ed. Elisabeth Potts Brown and Susan Mosher Stuard. New Brunswick and London: Rutgers UP, 1989. 3–25.

Trevett, Christine. *Women and Quakerism in the 17th Century*. York, England: Sessions Book Trust, Ebor Press, 1991.

SOMA *(6th Century BCE)*

On Woman's "Two-Finger Intelligence"

Soma was one of the most famous of the group of early Buddhist nuns that included Sumangalamata, Nanduttara, and Vimala, whose poems from the *Therigatha* are reprinted in **Sexuality, Spirituality, and Power.** Like theirs, her poem focuses on the process of enlightenment, but it addresses specifically the question of women's fitness for that religious goal. This is not to say that she presents *herself* as posing the question. On the contrary, as Rita Gross has said, whatever doubts male writers may express about the nuns' abilities, and whatever moments of discouragement the nuns describe in their accounts of their spiritual journeys, the nuns do not themselves describe their struggles in terms of despair or agony over whether *gender* unfits them for spiritual attainment (52). On the contrary, Soma presents the *idea* of woman's inferiority as a temptation to be overcome. In this her view is consonant with the Buddha's teaching, as Alan Sponberg points out, citing a metaphor in which the Buddha pictures women's spiritual capacity as identical to men's: "And be it woman, or be it man for whom / Such chariot doth wait, by that same car / Into Nirvana's presence shall they come" (9). As Sponberg says, "the crucial point in such passages is not that sex and gender differences do not exist, but rather that they are soteriologically insignificant. . . ." (9).

Whether significant or not in the context of spiritual goals, such differences were quite significant in the gender stratification of early Buddhist hierarchy as well of the surrounding society (see headnote for Sumangalamata, et al., and Sponberg 11–12). It is in this double context that the following excerpt should be read. It consists of Soma's response to Mara, the mythical Buddhist tempter (Gross 62), of whom the Buddhist text *Samyutta Nikaya* tells the following story: "Mara the evil one, desirous of arousing fear, wavering, and dread in her, desirous of making her desist from concentrated thought, went up to her and addressed her in verse: 'That vantage point the sages may attain / Is hard to win. With her two-finger wit, / That may no woman ever hope to achieve'" (qtd. in Sponberg 9). The two-finger wit or two-finger intellligence with which Mara taunts Soma apparently refers to the idea that women know whether rice is cooked only by testing it between two fingers (Sponberg 30, n7).

In a strategy that many women since Soma have found useful, she refuses to let the tempter set the terms of the debate. She eludes entrapment in his paradigm by posing a question that re-frames the issue completely: "How should the woman's nature hinder us?" or, as another translation puts it, "What should the woman's nature signify / When consciousness is taut and firmly set. . . ?" (Sponberg 9). Mara is not fit to talk to *her,* she concludes, but only to someone who regards gender as a category relevant to enlightenment—that is, to one who asks the wrong question. Only to someone who would think of asking, "With regard to spiritual issues, am I a woman, or a man, or what?" is Mara fit to talk. For those who do not ask such questions—who speak out of a different set of assumptions—Mara's temptation does not count. For women who resist, "framing the question" in their own terms has been crucial for centuries to successful transformation at all levels, whether spiritual, psychological, or political.

ECD

FROM THE *THERIGATHA*[§]

How should the woman's nature hinder us?
Whose hearts are firmly set, who ever move
With growing knowledge onward in the Path?
What can that signify to one in whom
Insight doth truly comprehend the Norm?
To one for whom the question doth arise:
Am I a woman in these matters, or
Am I a man, or what not am I then?
To such a one are you, Sir, fit to talk!

WORKS CONSULTED

Sponberg, Alan. "Attitudes toward Women and the Feminine in Early Buddhism." In *Buddhism, Sexuality, and Gender.* Ed. Josee Ignacio Cabezón. Albany, NY: State U of New York P, 1992. 3–36.

Gross, Rita M. *Buddhism After Patriarchy: A Feminist History, Analysis, and Reconstruction of Buddhism.* Albany, NY: State U of New York P, 1993.

[§] Reprinted from *Buddhism After Patriarchy: A Feminist History, Analysis, and Reconstruction of Buddhism,* by Rita M. Gross. Published 1993 by the State University of New York Press, Albany. Material reprinted from page 52.

CHRISTINE DE PIZAN *(c. 1365–c. 1430)*

"To Ennoble the Mind of Woman"

See also **Representing Women**

The excerpt which follows is taken from Christine de Pizan's *The Book of the City of Ladies,* written around 1405. In this unusual work—a universal history of women from a woman's point of view—Christine de Pizan provides a further development of the arguments that she had begun to formulate in her contribution to the *querelle* surrounding *The Romance of the Rose* (a selection from which appears earlier in this anthology). According to Earl Jeffrey Richards, "Christine's task in *The Book of the City of Ladies* is to transform her own erudition into an emblem of women's potential for erudition. . . . She cites tradition in order to remold the same tradition to meet her own needs in writing a history from the point of view of women, a radical break with all previous historiography" (xxviii). The title of the book is a direct allusion to Augustine's *City of God,* a reference that suggests Christine de Pizan understood her work as figuring within a Christian religious/intellectual tradition of political and moral thought. Moreover, *The Book of the City of Ladies* is also partly a rewriting of Boccaccio's earlier *De mulieribus claris,* a treatise on illustrious or "notorious" women. Christine de Pizan's approach differs radically from Boccaccio's, however, in that her work—a paean to women's past and present accomplishments—might be considered both as a feminist intervention in the domain of public discourse about the social role of women[1] and as an invitation to women of all classes to realize their own dignity and worthiness as women. After completing *The Book of the City of Ladies,* Christine de Pizan wrote *The Book of the Three Virtues*—a discussion of women's roles in contemporary society—as a companion piece. Together the two works make up *The Treasury of the City of Ladies.*

In *The Book of the City of Ladies,* Christine de Pizan describes an allegorial city, ruled over by the three virtues Justice, Reason, and Discretion,[2] and inhabited by women who had made important intellectual, military, political, cultural, and religious contributions to society. The work itself is written in the form of an exchange between the author and the virtues. In *The Book of the Three Virtues,* Christine de Pizan outlines further the ways in which women from all walks of life might strive to enter the City through their achievements. Richards suggests that, by naming this domain the City of Ladies rather than the City of Women, Christine de Pizan "transposes the dignity afforded to noble women in the late medieval French class structure to women who have proven their worthiness through their achievements" (xxx). Christine de Pizan's outlook remains a religious and hierarchical one, yet her defense of women's learning and abilities still constitutes an important commentary on the gendered construction of knowledge as well as a call to the women of her day to exercise their intellectual potential. Notably, her work was widely read by a whole generation of women leaders, including such figures as Marguerite of Navarre (Queen of Navarre and author of the *Heptaméron*), Louise of Savoy (the regent of France),

Anne of Brittany (queen of France), and Marguerite of Austria and Mary of Hungary (both governors of the Netherlands). As Charity Cannon Willard has pointed out, "The multiplicity of paper copies which exist along with the handsome illuminated manuscripts, as well as the repeated printings, attest to the fact that these works were also read by more ordinary women" ("Christine de Pizan" 140). Christine de Pizan's contributions both to women's history and the Renaissance debate surrounding the social role of women mark her as one of the most notable—as well as one of the first—French women of letters.

NM

FROM *THE BOOK OF THE CITY OF LADIES* §

Christine asks Reason whether god has ever wished to ennoble the mind of woman with the loftiness of the sciences; and Reason's answer.

After hearing these things, I replied to the lady who spoke infallibly: "My lady, truly has God revealed great wonders in the strength of these women whom you describe. But please enlighten me again, whether it has ever pleased this God, who has bestowed so many favors on women, to honor the feminine sex with the privilege of the virtue of high understanding and great learning, and whether women ever have a clever enough mind for this. I wish very much to know this because men maintain that the mind of women can learn only a little."

She answered, "My daughter, since I told you before, you know quite well that the opposite of their opinion is true, and to show you this even more clearly, I will give you proof through examples. I tell you again—and don't fear a contradiction—if it were customary to send daughters to schools like sons, and if they were then taught the natural sciences, they would learn as thoroughly and understand the subtleties of all the arts and sciences as well as sons. And by chance there happen to be such women, for, as I touched on before, just as women have more delicate bodies than men, weaker and less able to perform many tasks, so do they have minds that are freer and sharper whenever they apply themselves."

"My lady, what are you saying? With all due respect, could you dwell longer on this point, please. Certainly men would never admit this answer is true, unless it is explained more plainly, for they believe that one normally sees that men know more than women do."

She answered, "Do you know why women know less?"

"Not unless you tell me, my lady."

"Without the slightest doubt, it is because they are not involved in many different things, but stay at home, where it is enough for them to run the household, and there is nothing which so instructs a reasonable creature as the exercise and experience of many different things."

§ Reprinted from *The Book of the City of Ladies* by Christine de Pizan, translated by Earl Jeffrey Richards, copyright © 1982 by Persea Books, Inc. Reprinted by permission of Persea Books, Inc. Excerpted from pages 62–81.

"My lady, since they have minds skilled in conceptualizing and learning, just like men, why don't women learn more?"

She replied, "Because, my daughter, the public does not require them to get involved in the affairs which men are commissioned to execute, just as I told you before. It is enough for women to perform the usual duties to which they are ordained. As for judging from experience, since one sees that women usually know less than men, that therefore their capacity for understanding is less, look at men who farm the flatlands or who live in the mountains. You will find that in many countries they seem completely savage because they are so simple-minded. All the same, there is no doubt that Nature provided them with the qualities of body and mind found in the wisest and most learned men. All of this stems from a failure to learn, though, just as I told you, among men and women, some possess better minds than others. Let me tell you about women who have possessed great learning and profound understanding and treat the question of the similarity of women's minds to men's."...

Then I said to her, "Now, my lady, I indeed understand more than before why you spoke of the enormous ingratitude, not to say ignorance, of these men who malign women, for although it seems to me that the fact that the mother of every man is a woman is reason enough to attack them, not to mention the other good deeds which one can clearly see that women do for men, truly, one can see here the many benefits afforded by women with the greatest generosity to men which they have accepted and continue to accept. Henceforth, let all writers be silent who speak badly of women, let all of them be silent—those who have attacked women and who still attack them in their books and poems, and all their accomplices and supporters too—let them lower their eyes, ashamed for having dared to speak so badly, in view of the truth which runs counter to their poems: this noble lady, Carmentis, through the profundity of her understanding taught them like a schoolmistress—nor can they deny it—the lesson thanks to which they consider themselves so lofty and honored, that is, she taught them the Latin alphabet!

"But what did all the many nobles and knights say, who generally slander women with such false remarks? From now on let them keep their mouths shut and remember that the customs of bearings arms, of dividing armies into battalions, and of fighting in ordered ranks—a vocation upon which they so pride themselves and for which they consider themselves so great—came to them from a woman and were given to them by a woman. Would men who live on bread, or who live civilly in cities following the order of law, or who cultivate the fields, have any good reason to slander and rebuff women so much, as many do, if they only thought of all the benefits? Certainly not, because thanks to women, that is, Minerva, Ceres, and Iris, so many beneficial things have come to men, through which they can lead honorable lives and from which they live and will live always. Ought not these things be considered?"

"Doubtless, my lady. It seems to me that neither in the teaching of Aristotle, which has been of great profit to human intelligence and which is so highly esteemed and with good reason, nor in that of all the other philosophers who have ever lived, could an equal benefit for the world be found as that which has been accrued and still accrues through the works accomplished by virtue of the knowledge possessed by these ladies."...

NOTES

[1] For a detailed discussion of the significance of Christine de Pizan's position on the social effects of the defamation of women, see Helen Solterer's *The Master and Minerva: Disputing Women in French Medieval Culture.*

[2] These virtues were customarily gendered female in the intellectual tradition within which Christine de Pizan was writing.

WORKS CONSULTED

"Christine de Pizan." *Great Women Writers.* Frank N. Magill, ed. New York: Holt, 1994.

Richards, Earl Jeffrey. Introduction. *The Book of the City of Ladies.* By Christine de Pizan. New York: Persea, 1982.

Solterer, Helen. *The Master and Minerva: Disputing Women in French Medieval Culture.* Berkeley: U of California P, 1995.

Willard, Charity Cannon. "The Franco-Italian Professional Writer: Christine de Pizan." In *Medieval Women Writers.* Ed. Katharina M. Wilson. Athens: U of Georgia P, 1984. 333–342.

—. Introduction. *The Writings of Christine de Pizan.* New York: Persea, 1994.

MARY WOLLSTONECRAFT *(1759–1797)*

"It Is Time to Effect a Revolution in Female Manners"

> "Woman and man are made for one another, but their mutual dependence is not equal; men depend on women by virtue of their desires; women depend on men by virtue of their desires and their needs; we could exist without them but not they without us."
>
> *Jean-Jacques Rousseau, Emile V, 538*

Mary Wollstonecraft is one of the most traditionally canonical writers—from the U. S. and Western European points of view—included in this anthology. Her best-known feminist work, *A Vindication of the Rights of Woman,* continues to be an important reference for any understanding of feminist thought and activism at the end of the eighteenth century. While her oeuvre might be read in a certain sense as highly representative of Enlightenment bourgeois feminist thought, *A Vindication of the Rights of Woman,* as a complex piece of social philosophy, also reveals how the specificity and subtlety of any given work is often elided by means of such generic categories as "Enlightenment thought" or "bourgeois feminism." Although Mary Wollstonecraft certainly places great emphasis on a progressivist vision of the social role of "reason" and "natural freedom"—concepts which have been extensively critiqued by many contemporary feminist scholars, a closer analysis of the way in which these categories function in her work remains worthwhile. To a certain extent, Mary Wollstonecraft's *Vindication* is a reflection on the interaction between feminist and philosophical thought (see Michèle Le Doeuff in **Representing Women**); this essay also functions as a remarkable intervention in a field of intellectual debate dominated at the time almost entirely by men.

Before becoming a professional writer, Wollstonecraft had supported herself as did many "respectable" but impoverished middle-class women of her day: as a governess, companion, and schoolteacher (Kelly 352). Her subsequent work as a writer and philosopher continued to center upon issues of women's education. Her first book, *Thoughts on the Education of Daughters* (1787), was followed by novels and stories that illustrated both her own principles of education and the often tragic consequences of women's (mis)education as it was more commonly practiced in her day. Her most famous work, *A Vindication of the Rights of Woman,* is in large part structured as a response to several works on women's education and female conduct written by men during the latter half of the eighteenth century. Of these, the best-known and most influential for future generations of readers is probably Jean-Jacques Rousseau's *Emile or On Education* (1762), to which the excerpt included here explicitly refers.

Emile, divided into five books, is a highly detailed treatment of the pedgogical, philosophical, and religious principles governing the education of a fictional male figure, Emile.

When Emile nears the end of his adolescence, however, it becomes clear that, as Rousseau writes, "Emile is a man; we promised him a female companion, we must give him one. This companion is Sophie" (*Emile* V 528). Book Five, then, contains a treatment of the education of Sophie, who is to become Emile's wife. Her upbringing, which complements that of her future husband, is nevertheless completely dissimilar to his. As Rousseau puts it, "In the union of the sexes each strives for a common object, but not in the same fashion . . . One should be active and strong, the other passive and weak; one must necessarily desire and act, the other need only resist a little" (*Emile* V 529). It is to this philosophy of the social function of gender and female sexuality that Mary Wollstonecraft provides an impassioned response.

In *A Vindication of the Rights of Woman,* Wollstonecraft writes against a conception of women and femininity as defined primarily by the ability to evoke male sexual desire. This fact should be kept in mind in any consideration of Wollstonecraft's views on active female sexuality, which are regarded as deeply ambivalent. Her vision of women's emancipation "from the slavery to which the pride and sensuality of man and their short-sighted desire . . . has subjected them" hinges on a notion of "natural freedom." From Wollstonecraft's perspective, were women to be "governed by reasonable laws" rather than the "despotism" that has characterized men's treatment of them, they might accede to that state of liberty and moral dignity which has so often been denied to them. Thus, she is harshly critical of the intense sexualization of femininity that she sees Rousseau—among others—as undertaking, for it is this association of women with bodily dependence that prevents them, according to Wollstonecraft, from acquiring "vigour of intellect" and rational thought.

Wollstonecraft's analysis of gender relations is based on a critique of the way in which women's social roles are culturally constructed to hinder their ability to become fully rational and autonomous moral individuals. *A Vindication of the Rights of Woman* takes a historicist perspective on female education and what might be termed a universalist approach to social theory. Finally, Wollstonecraft demands that men grant women the possibility to prove themselves as individuals blessed with the qualities of reason and independent thought. As she puts it, "It is time to effect a revolution in female manners—time to restore to them their lost dignity—and make them, as a part of the human species, labour by reforming themselves to reform the world."

NM and *JP*

FROM *A VINDICATION OF THE RIGHTS OF WOMAN*[§]

Let us examine this question. Rousseau declares that a woman should never for a moment feel herself independent, that she should be governed by fear to exercise her natural cunning, and made a coquettish slave in order to render her a more alluring object of desire,

[§] Reprinted from *A Vindication of the Rights of Woman* by Mary Wollstonecraft. Edited by Miriam Brody. Published 1992 London: Penguin Books. Material excerpted from pages 108–134.

a sweeter companion to man, whenever he chose to relax himself. He carries the arguments, which he pretends to draw from the indications of nature, still further, and insinuates that truth and fortitude, the corner-stones of all human virtue, should be cultivated with certain restrictions, because, with respect to the female character, obedience is the grand lesson which ought to be impressed with unrelenting rigour.

What nonsense! When will a great man arise with sufficient strength of mind to puff away the fumes which pride and sensuality have thus spread over the subject? If women are by nature inferior to men, their virtue must be the same in quality, if not in degree, or virtue is a relative idea; consequently their conduct should be founded on the same principles, and have the same aim.

Connected with man as daughters, wives, and mothers, their moral character may be estimated by their manner of fulfilling those simple duties; but the end, the grand end, of their exertions should be to unfold their own faculties, and acquire the dignity of conscious virtue. . . .

But avoiding, as I have hitherto done, any direct comparison of the two sexes collectively, or frankly acknowledging the inferiority of woman, according to the present appearance of things, I shall only insist that men have increased that inferiority till women are almost sunk below the standard of rational creatures. Let their faculties have room to unfold, and their virtues to gain strength, and then determine where the whole sex must stand in the intellectual scale. Yet let it be remembered that for a small number of distinguished women I do not ask a place.

It is difficult for us purblind mortals to say to what height human discoveries and improvements may arrive, when the gloom of despotism subsides, which makes us stumble at every step; but, when morality shall be settled on a more solid basis, then, without being gifted with a prophetic spirit, I will venture to predict that woman will be either the friend or slave of man. . . .

These may be termed Utopian dreams. Thanks to that Being who impressed them on my soul, and gave me sufficient strength of mind to dare to exert my own reason, till, becoming dependent only on Him for the support of my virtue, I view, with indignation, the mistaken notions that enslave my sex.

I love man as my fellow; but his sceptre, real or usurped, extends not to me, unless the reason of an individual demands my homage; and even then the submission is to reason, and not to man. In fact, the conduct of an accountable being must be regulated by the operations of its own reason; or on what foundation rests the throne of God?

It appears to me necessary to dwell on these obvious truths, because females have been insulated, as it were; and while they have been stripped of the virtues that should clothe humanity, they have been decked with artificial graces that enable them to exercise a short-lived tyranny. Love, in their bosoms, taking place of every nobler passion, their sole ambition is to be fair, to raise emotion instead of inspiring respect; and this ignoble desire, like the servility in absolute monarchies, destroys all strength of character. Liberty is the mother of virtue, and if women be, by their very constitution, slaves, and not allowed to breathe the sharp invigorating air of freedom, they must ever languish like exotics, and be reckoned beautiful flaws in nature. Let it also be remembered, that they are the only flaw.

As to the argument respecting the subjection in which the sex has ever been held, it retorts on man. The many have always been enthralled by the few; and monsters, who scarcely have shown any discernment of human excellence, have tyrannized over thousands of their fellow-creatures. . . .

I have, probably, had an opportunity of observing more girls in their infancy than J. J. Rousseau. I can recollect my own feelings, and I have looked steadily around me; yet, so far from coinciding with him in opinion respecting the first dawn of the female character, I will venture to affirm, that a girl, whose spirits have not been damped by inactivity, or innocence tainted by false shame, will always be a romp, and the doll will never excite attention unless confinement allows her no alternative. Girls and boys, in short, would play harmlessly together, if the distinction of sex was not inculcated long before nature makes any difference. I will go further, and affirm, as an indisputable fact, that most of the women, in the circle of my observation, who have acted like rational creatures, or shown any vigour of intellect, have accidentally been allowed to run wild, as some of the elegant formers of the fair sex would insinuate.

The baneful consequences which flow from inattention to health during infancy and youth, extend further than is supposed—dependence of body naturally produces dependence of mind; and how can she be a good wife or mother, the greater part of whose time is employed to guard against or endure sickness? Nor can it be expected that a woman will resolutely endeavor to strengthen her constitution and abstain from enervating indulgences, if artificial notions of beauty, and false descriptions of sensibility, have been early entangled with her motives of action. Most men are sometimes obliged to bear with bodily inconveniences, and to endure, occasionally, the inclemency of the elements; but genteel women are, literally speaking, slaves to their bodies, and glory in their subjection. . . .

Women are everywhere, in this deplorable state; for, in order to preserve their innocence, as ignorance is courteously termed, truth is hidden from them, and they are made to assume an artificial character before their faculties have acquired any strength. Taught from their infancy that beauty is women's sceptre, the mind shapes itself to the body, and roaming round its gilt cage, only seeks to adore its prison. Men have various employments and pursuits which engage their attention, and give a character to the open mind; but women, confined to one, and having their thoughts constantly directed to the most insignificant part of themselves, seldom extend their views beyond the triumph of the hour. But were their understanding once emancipated from the slavery to which the pride and sensuality of man and their short-sighted desire, like that of dominion in tyrants, of present sway, has subjected them, we should probably read of their weakness with surprise. . . .

Let not men then in the pride of power, use the same arguments that tyrannic kings and venal ministers have used, and fallaciously assert that woman ought to be subjected because she has always been so. But, when man, governed by reasonable laws, enjoys his natural freedom, let him despise woman, if she do not share it with him; and, till that glorious period arrives, in descanting on the folly of the sex, let him not overlook his own.

Women, it is true, obtaining power by unjust means, by practicing or fostering vice, evidently lose the rank which reason would assign them, and they become either abject slaves or capricious tyrants. They lose all simplicity, all dignity of mind, in acquiring power, and act as men are observed to act when they have been exalted by the same means.

It is time to effect a revolution in female manners—time to restore to them their lost dignity—and make them, as a part of the human species, labour by reforming themselves to reform the world. It is time to separate unchangeable morals from local manners. If men be demi-gods, why let us serve them! And if the dignity of the female soul be as disputable as that of animals—if their reason does not afford sufficient light to direct their conduct whilst unerring instinct is denied—they are surely of all creatures the most miserable! and, bent beneath the iron hand of destiny, must submit to be a fair defect in creation. But to justify the ways of Providence respecting them, by pointing out some irrefragable reason for thus making such a large portion of mankind accountable and not accountable, would puzzle the subtilest casuist. . . .

WORKS CONSULTED

Flexner, Eleanor. *Mary Wollstonecraft: A Biography.* New York: Coward, McCann and Geoghegan, 1972.

Kelly, Gary. "Mary Wollstonecraft." *Dictionary of Literary Biography.* Vol. 104. *British Prose Writers, 1660–1800.* Ed. Donald T. Siebert. Detroit: Gale Research, 1991.

Rousseau, Jean-Jacques. *Emile ou De l'education.* Paris: Editions Gallimard, 1969.

EDNAH DOW LITTLEHALE AND CAROLINE WELLS HEALY *(19th century)*

"The Faithful Support of *Your* Argument"

The two letters which follow are part of a four-letter debate which took place in 1837 and 1838 between Ednah Dow Littlehale (later Cheney) and Caroline Wells Healy (later Dall), when they were thirteen and fifteen years old, respectively. The teenagers were both from liberal religious families in Boston, and they both went to school at Joseph Hale Abbot's private women's academy, where the pedagogical practices were grounded in a notion of "Republican motherhood." According to this set of beliefs, the education of girls was critical to the shaping of the new nation because women played the unique and crucial role of educating children in the home.[1] As adults, Ednah and Caroline became part of the northeastern urban intellectual milieu in the mid-nineteenth century—a setting in which discussions were dominated by debates over slavery and abolition and, later, the question of women's rights. Both women would go on to play prominent roles in the Boston women's rights and social reform movements in the later 19th century; Ednah became a reformer and organizer, while Caroline became a noted public speaker and journalist. Both participated in the famed "Conversations" held by Margaret Fuller in the 1840s. Throughout their careers, they retained the basic core of beliefs expressed in these early letters, although each developed her argument further.

Margaret McFadden, who first edited and introduced these letters in the journal *Signs,* maintains that each of these teenagers' arguments encapsulates one of the two major positions in the women's rights debates of the time—namely, the minimizer and the maximizer positions (836–8). Ednah argues for the more egalitarian, Enlightenment-derived opinion that men and women are equals, and minimizes any differences between the genders. Accordingly, she concludes that men and women should be given completely equal treatment in the civic realm. Caroline on the other hand is in favor of a gynocentric or "separate spheres" position that maximizes perceived differences between the genders in order to maintain that women deserve equal treatment and special privileges by right of their special abilities and responsibilities (centering around childrearing, domestic work, and religious duties). McFadden adds that these letters are important because they demonstrate that "the key argumentative themes that structured the debate about women for the next 150 years were present and accessible quite early in the nineteenth century. [They] also [reveal] in a striking way how such themes had a dramatic impact on adolescent schoolgirls" (833). Proof of McFadden's assertion can be found in the work of many recent feminist historians.

For example William Chafe's analysis of second-wave feminism of the 1970s identifies three competing versions of Euro-American feminist thought (liberal, radical and socialist) that nonetheless were all derived from the nineteenth-century egalitarian-gynocentric discourses (202–213). Liberal feminism can be identified as the closest continuation of

Ednah's egalitarianism, focusing as it does on the reformation of existing social and political systems so that women as individuals can be accepted or assimilated into such systems on a completely equal basis with men. The eradication of any sort of "separate spheres" ideology was seen as a precursor to the success of egalitarian reform.

Radical and socialist feminists both contested the individualistic focus of liberal feminism. They rejected the assimilation of women into existing social structures. Radical feminists insisted that the patriarchal system be overthrown and that most men acted consistently to uphold this system; for many of these women, a separatist ideology was part of the strategy for achieving feminist revolution. By advocating this rejection of male-dominated institutions in favor of "woman-identified" values and groups (such as "consciousness-raising" groups), radical feminists were in fact re-fashioning a "separate spheres" or gynocentric position.

For the most part, socialist feminists rejected this primary focus on all-female groups and values in order to promote cross-racial and cross-class alliances between men and women who would fight together to overthrow capitalist patriarchy. Although they advocated revolution rather than reform, socialist feminists did share with liberal reformers the ideal of a world in which gender was irrelevant. This overview of more contemporary forms of feminist discourse testifies to the continuity of the ideological frameworks outlined in the Ednah-Caroline correspondence, as well as to the wide variety of uses to which a common core of beliefs can be put.

KKF

FROM "BOSTON TEENAGERS DEBATE THE WOMAN QUESTION, 1837–1838" [§]

To Caroline Healey from Ednah Dow Littlehale, Nov. 14th, 1837

I am going to begin in critic's style, now Caroline, and have got all the marks made in the beginning. First, as to your feeling ashamed that's all wrong, you know you felt dreadful proud to think you knew So much more than I did; if you did not, you had a right to. You say there is much sense, & much nonsense, now what you call the sense I call the nonsense, & and what you call the nonsense I call the Sense. You never will be happy do not think so.

Do you know Caroline you commit Sin in saying so, you doubt the power of your Heavenly Father, unless you have committed some great crime, there is no earthly reason for your never being happy, and if you have, you have a Saviour to whom you can go for pardon, and he will grant you peace. Perhaps I am presumptuous to tell you so, & I would not dare to, were it not that I think much of you. Peace is destroyed by this idea. Your affections have been blighted, who have you ever been in love with? For I*[2] do not know what else you mean. You advise me not to seek fame; you throw away your ink, time and

[§] Documents 3 and 4 reprinted from "Boston Teenagers Debate the Woman Question, 1837–1838," edited by Margaret McFadden for *Signs: Journal of Women in Culture and Society* 15.11 (1990): pages 844–847. Published by the University of Chicago Press.

advice, when you say so, for I shall not follow your advice. "I have a heart at ease," good gracious, deliver me from those that have not then. Caroline, you think you see right through me, but you cannot; you don't know half as much about me as you think you do. You refer me to F. Hemans. Unfortunately she is dead, and if she were alive I do not think she would honor me with her acquaintance: political—what do I mean by the rights of women!!! *mean,* I mean what I say—we have as good a right to rule men as they have to rule us. And to go to Caucus as they have; If we don't have a hand in making laws, I don't think we ought to obey them & if I could break a law without committing a moral wrong I should not scruple to do it. You ask me if I am a friend of H. Martineau's *No, No;* if there is a woman I despise and dislike it is H. Martineau and you need never fear, I shall become a disciple of hers. As I never intend to be married, (because I shall never have a chance) I shall not have any husband or children to take care of. I know what I am saying, I am equal to the men, and not superior to them. I am a slave until I am free, & I am not free yet. You may call me a *ninny,* but I call myself Ednah. I do not know what book Lucy Aikins is, but if you will lend it to me I shall be happy to read it. If you thought as I do, when at my age, you were wiser than you are now, & if you keep on growing silly as fast as you have done, I hope I shan't have to live with you, when you are fifty. If you don't think women have as good a right to vote as men you ought to be ducked in the *frog pond.*

E. D. Littlehale

To Ednah Dow Littlehale from Caroline Healy, Feb. 10th, 1838

For the Casket

The Rights of Woman My subject has been nearly exhausted by the ridiculous efforts of many writers to prove that woman has and should exercise the right of legislation and public speaking. "Why then do I select it?" Simply that I may add my share to the modicum of absurdity. I am a woman and have the right to speak; gentlemen, you are bound to listen.

I do not deny that women may have the right to vote; the right of legislation, for I am very tenacious of my sex's privileges, and am not prepared to argue, as I could wish, to the contrary:—but what *lady* would claim the right?

Truly, when I see a woman, arguing with grace and skill, and more than this, with ardor and earnestness upon this subject, I am inclined to believe her a fanatic; or a candidate for Bedlam. Neither am I one, who will attempt to prove that woman is inferior to her helpmeet; for I believe and I know, that the sexes are equal in mental, though *not* in bodily strength; and that the latter difference is induced by Education and not caused by Nature!

God, Our Benefactor and Creator, has formed men and women for different purposes. To woman as a sex, he has given superior delicacy and suppleness of form—angelic beauty of feature: To her belong the finer susceptibilities and the tenderer, stronger affections of the heart. To her belongs gentle decision and submissive firmness, and to her in many, in most, instances the higher qualities of intellect, are vouchsafed; but in no way does she so visibly betray her weakness, as in vindicating what *she* calls her rights.

To man, he has given a firmer mould of body, a stronger cast of mind. His are the closer powers of reasoning; his, the more logical, and mathematically exact, habits of thought. His affections are more fickle, his sentiments more coarse, but his powers of apprehension are in general more ready.

A Hemans and a Bacon, an Edgeworth[3] and a Scott, are good illustrations of the two sexes. Few *men* die of broken hearts, *many women* do! I have explained what I consider, the radical differences, between man and woman. In the former, the brain presides, in the latter, the heart! Education may have much to do with this.

To return to my subject. It has been agreed, I think in all ages, and among all nations (is a very important branch) (that division of labor) of Economy.[4] To women belong the gentler, the sweeter duties, of the fireside; man's proper element is the bustle of political or commercial action.

As soon as these great parties interfere with each other, everything returns to it's original chaos. True, one wife exclaims: "*I* only wish to vote, and go to Caucus." and so do I, exclaims another, and another, and another. Very well! good people, coax your husbands, to nurse your children, cook your dinner, and superintend the domestic ménage—and you *may* go to Caucuses.

Things would only return to their original condition if the experiment should succeed; women would be the iron; men the water of the human race. But the former class, for want of education would make sad work, at the caucus, or in the senate; while men would learn by instinct many feminine duties. "But I don't want my husband to do all this," I hear someone say, "I can do this and go to Caucus too." No! You cannot, as soon as you become accustomed to it, political and public life will be exciting and necessary to you; and your homes and your children?—would be left to the care of Heaven, and your husbands! I am too young to argue well on this subject but if I could express myself as readily as I can think, the matter should be settled at once!

Thank Heaven! the bonds of habit are not easily broken, and women are in no danger of rendering themselves more ridiculous than they are at present. Content yourselves, my companions, with things as they are ordered by Beneficent and All-seeing Providence, and believe that *thus* is best. Listen not to the specious arguments of those who would persuade you to the contrary; listen to the pleadings of your own hearts!

My young friends, if this subject were argued among you, the minority might prevail, and the majority be left without an argument. I will tell you why. Not because your cause is the *wrong* cause! Do not be disheartened, though your adversary have the most words, if *you* have the most ideas.

You are not old enough to perceive to perceive [*sic*] the relation between man and woman, taken in this view. You are not old enough to understand the beautiful, the glorious economy of nature, and you cannot now perceive or if you can perceive, you cannot avail yourselves of the fallacious logic and weak arguments of your opponent. You are not old enough to take a full and comprehensive view of the arguments you have a right to use. Much talent, much knowledge of the world, much readiness of pen, and much humorous tact, is necessary to the task you have undertaken, is necessary to the faithful support of *your* argument!

It is easy to make *assertions,* but it is difficult to produce *facts.*

Farewell then, let me hope that if the jewel I have added to your Casket, do not prove a *Gem,* that it's modest lustre, may not be *entirely* dimmed by the superior brilliancy of it's companions.[5]

NOTES

[1] For more on this concept, see the important article by Linda Kerber, "The Republican Mother: Women and the Enlightenment—An American Perspective."

[2] Asterisk in manuscript. At bottom of page, "*You dont know much, C." in Caroline Healey Dall's hand [McFadden].

[3] Maria Edgeworth (1767–1849). Anglo-Irish Gothic novelist [McFadden].

[4] Sentence incomplete in manuscript [McFadden].

[5] Part of a discussion on Suffrage with E.D. (Cheney)—age 15 1/2 by C. H. (Dall) [in Dall's hand] {McFadden}.

WORKS CONSULTED

Chafe, William H. *The Paradox of Change: American Women in the 20th Century.* New York: Oxford UP, 1991.

Kerber, Linda. "The Republican Mother: Women and the Enlightenment—An American Perspective." *American Quarterly* 28 (Summer 1976).

McFadden, Margaret. "Boston Teenagers Debate the Woman Question, 1837–1838." *Signs: Journal of Women in Culture and Society* 15.11 (1990): 836–8.

TARABAI SHINDE *(c. 1850–1910)*

"Why Blame Women?"

The death-sentence of a woman in late nineteenth-century India, either for abortion or infanticide, together with the publication of a hostile response to the woman's action, were the motivating factors behind Tarabai Shinde's "A Comparison of Men and Women," published as a forty-page book in 1882.[1] "I cannot restrain myself from writing in such fiery language," she says (qtd. in Tharu and Lalita 222), and her language is searing indeed—full of references to her opponents as "dastardly, perfidious, treacherous" (224), "learned asses" who "organize big meetings every day, deliver impressive speeches, offer unwanted advice to all and sundry, and do a hundred other such stupid things" (235). In opposition to such stupidity, she presents her own views on men, turning the tables on those who complained about modern women's "'new' loose morals" (221).

Somewhat like Soma many centuries before her, Tarabai Shinde works to reframe the terms of the debate as they have been set by her opponents. The strategy she uses is a forecast of much more to come in the next century, as she works toward knowledge of gender arrangements and gender relations by means of a process of reversal. What happens if we ask, not (as Wollstonecraft did) what is wrong with women, but rather what is wrong with men? And, in looking at what is wrong with women, what if we look for the causes at the site where the most power lies—with men? By means of this strategy, she responds to misogynist charges without ever falling into the trap of asserting women's intelligence, integrity, and virtue from a purely defensive position. Instead, she lays each of the charges against women at men's own door.

Her style, according to critic and translator Maya Pandit, is "racy and absolutely full of fire. She uses many idiomatic expressions and phrases that occur particularly in the language of women" (qtd. in Tharu and Lalita 222). Tharu and Lalita call attention to what sets Tarabai apart from other writers on women's issues in India "at a time when intellectuals and activists alike were primarily concerned with the hardship of a Hindu widow's life and other easily identifiable atrocities . . . ." Moving beyond them, she "was able to broaden the scope of the analysis to include the ideological fabric of patriarchal society. Women everywhere, she implies, are similarly oppressed" (222).

Of the woman who wrote this remarkable analysis, little is known. In the essay, she describes herself as a "powerless dull woman, prisoner within a Maratha household" (qtd. in Tharu and Lalita 222). Tharu and Lalita cite S. G. Malshe's use of evidence from oral history for opinions that she was high-caste, an only child, married young to a man she "soon lost regard for," and without children (221). Beyond that, "There are stories, perhaps apocryphal, that speak of her as a fiercely independent and self-confident person who rode a horse and wielded a sword as well as most soldiers could" (221). If those stories are true, she resembles Qiu Jin and other women of the period who defied gender conventions flamboyantly. If not, it is nonetheless clear that she defied those conventions vigorously in print, at least once, in the only essay that has been attributed to her.

ECD

FROM "A COMPARISON OF MEN AND WOMEN"[§]

Let me ask you something, Gods! You are supposed to be omnipotent and freely accessible to all. You are said to be completely impartial. What does that mean? That you have never been known to be partial. But wasn't it you who created both men and women? Then why did you grant happiness only to men and brand women with nothing but agony? Your will was done! But the poor women have had to suffer for it down the ages.

One comes across several charges against women both in the written literature and in everyday discourse. But do men not suffer from the same flaws that women are supposed to have? . . .

First, if, as you claim, a woman has more power than a device for witchcraft or black magic, let me ask you, you who are endowed with an intellect far more powerful than hers, what have you not achieved with your intellect? You who have made possible what was believed to be impossible, of what worth can a woman's power be before your valiant deeds? Of none.

Second, it may be true that women are a whirlpool of suspicion. But that is because they are uneducated and all kinds of doubts inhabit their minds. But even then, it must be borne in mind that their suspicions are usually and necessarily about their own relationships. But if one casts just a fleeting glance at the webs of doubt in your minds, one's eyes will surely be dazed. Your minds are full of all kinds of treacherous plans. "Let's bluff this moneylender and pocket a thousand rupees from him.". . . Or, "Let's lie to that officer about that particular case and change his judgment in X's favor." Or, "That woman Y, what a coquette she really is! What airs she gives herself! Must corner her one of these days, and see whether some affair with her can be managed. My current affair has begun to bore me. This is the chance to end it once and for all and begin a new one." Such disgusting thoughts never enter a woman's mind. This is, of course, not to say that all the women in the world are as luminous as the sun and as pure as the waters of the Holy Ganges. But even if one takes into account the entire female community in the world, it would be difficult to come across more than 10 percent of them who, like you, are caught in the whirlwind of such insidious perfidies, though not a single one of you is free of them.

Third, women are called the acme of impudence. But does your own species lack this quality in any measure? A judicious comparison would reveal the balance weighted far heavier on your side in this respect. Fourth, women are considered a megapolis of inad-

[§] Tarabai Shinde, excerpt from *Stri Purush Tulana* (A Comparison of Men and Women), translated by Maya Pandit. Reprinted by permission of The Feminist Press at the City University of New York, from Susie Tharu and K. Lalita, *Women Writing in India: Volume I: 600 B.C. to the Early Twentieth Century,* edited by Susie Tharu and K. Lalita. Copyright 1991 by Susie Tharu and K. Lalita. Material excerpted from pages 223–233.

vertent acts. But what about you, the dastardly, perfidious, treacherous people that you are? You, who would not hesitate even for a moment in cutting somebody's throat immediately after winning his confidence. . . . On top of all this, you have the audacity to call yourselves judicious! What can anyone say?

Granted, women are as stupid as buffaloes in the cow pen! They are ignorant and do not know how to read or to write. But does that mean God did not grant them even an iota of intelligence? Thoughtless and rash they may sometimes be, but even then they are far preferable to you. Yes! To you who are the bastions of erudition and wisdom! Why, one has only to visit a prison to get a proof of this! The prisons are packed to capacity with such people. . . .

Furthermore, we need to ask, what is the greatest crime that women commit? Adultery. That is the highest peak of their criminal ventures. They behave recklessly only because of such inclinations. But then, who takes the first step of sowing the seed of such designs in their minds? Who else but you? . . .

Another charge against women is that they are extremely mean minded and shallow. But they are never obsessed by such thoughts as "How will I get promoted to a higher office? How will I get more money? When will I rise to dizzy heights in public esteem? When will people address me as 'Sir' or 'Sahib' and speak humbly and meekly to me?" Women never waste their lives as you do, trying to achieve such impossible things. Then why do you pretend all these things are absolutely unknown to you and charge women with being the sole proprietors of "reckless vanity"?

The fifth charge against women is that they are the treasure houses of transgressions. But in fact, it is you who fit that description best. It's you who cause women to transgress. Let me substantiate this. Many fathers give away their beautiful and very young daughters, who are hardly ten or eleven years old, to men who are eighty or ninety in exchange for a purse of gold. They do it with an eye only on his wealth. Their reasoning is, "Even if the husband dies, there's no need to worry. She will be rolling in money. She will be able to get the best of things to eat, and be able to wear nice clothes—at least for a few days. She will have nothing to worry about. So what if she doesn't have a husband?" That is what they think. So without any scruples, they give their daughters away to such old men as lambs to a tiger. But once he who is her love, her real happiness, passes away, what meaning does life hold for her? The only man to delight in her new clothes, admire her, and consider her more precious than his life is her husband. Without him her life is like a desert. Then why would she hanker after those dry festivities? It might seem far better in the past when women used to burn themselves on their husbands' funeral pyres.[2] At least when one was reduced to a heap of ashes along with the husband, there was nothing left to worry about. . . .

. . . Let me remind you of something. When you are young and your parents are very poor, they are greatly worried about your marriage. At that time, they borrow heavily and somehow manage to marry you off. In such circumstances you can hardly expect to get a beautiful girl for a wife. At that time, even a wife who is as ugly as an owl seems like a Venus to you. But later on, when you are blessed by the goddess Saraswati, and have become "learned" and educated, when you get promoted in your job, you are ashamed of this first wife. Because you are wealthy now, you consider her to be worthless. She is nothing more to you than a servant or a cook whom you can hire to keep house for you for a few small coins. For you, she is just a slave you have bought for a thousand rupees. Perhaps you love even your dog or your horse more than your wife. A wife is nothing but a dark corner or a heap of rubbish in the house. Who cares for her? But why would a rich man care for his wife? For him wives come a dime a dozen. The rich are ready to be bridegrooms any day—indeed every day. It is only because Yama, the God of Death, doesn't have time to carry off their wives so fast. Otherwise they wouldn't mind tying the knot thrice a day. . . . Now tell me, do women ever behave in this fashion? Whether in prosperity or in poverty, they always behave obediently, according to your commands. Have you ever heard of a woman running off with another man just because her husband is ugly or poor? Now who deserves to be blamed? Women or men?

The sixth argument against women is that a woman is enveloped in a hundred guises of fraud and deceit. My friends, as far as these particular merits are concerned, the honor of the first rank undoubtedly goes to you. How can I describe your deceit? . . .You smear your body with the so-called holy ash, grow your hair long into a mass of matted locks, proclaim that you have renounced the world, and roam all over cheating and deceiving people with your beguiling tricks. . . . Somebody just has to say "Look at his virtues! They defy any description! He's wonderful. Besides, he is free from all worldly desires. He has great magical power," and so on. That is enough of an introduction for a credulous public! Then the fake sadhu goes on prolonging his stay, putting on grander and grander pretensions. He gorges himself with rich, sweet food like a fat tomcat, and then begins his "worship." That is, reposing in a corner, he closely eyes all the women who come for an audience with him, and selects a few beautiful ones whose names he reiterates on his rosary. That's the end! All gods are forgotten promptly and forever. And these "goddesses," in the form of beautiful women, occupy that place. In his eyes, their lovely, smiling faces and in his heart a burning desire for money. . . .

In short, it is you who are vice incarnate. Why blame women? . . .

NOTES

[1] All biographical information comes from Tharu and Lalita's introduction (221–223). [Eds.]

[2] What a great service the Sarvajanik Sabha in Pune has rendered to women! In their journal, or whatever it is that they publish annually or biannually, they very pompously declared, "It would be better if the government allowed women to burn themselves on the funeral pyres of their husbands." But tell me, if you want women to do that, why don't you propose the same plan for yourselves? Why do you want to survive your wives? To knead cow dung and pat it into cakes for your own cremation? Why shouldn't you burn yourselves on the pyres of your wives? Better you than her. Because her passing away proves to be far more detrimental than yours. Do you want to know how? Well, she is always survived by her young children. Who would look after them for her?

There is a proverb, "Let a prosperous father die but even a pauper of a mother should never die." If the father dies, the mother will endure any amount of grief and sorrow but maintain her children. But what do you do in such circumstances? If your wife dies today, you rush to bring another the very next day and render your children homeless. Don't you? Admit it now! Already there is a great outcry about this! In fact it's you who should be thrown into that pyre before your wives [Tarabai Shinde].

WORKS CONSULTED

Shinde, Tarabai. "A Comparison of Men and Women." 1882. Excerpted in Tharu and Lalita. 223–235.

Tharu, Susie, and K. Lalita. "Tarabai Shinde." *Women Writing in India 600 B.C. to the Present.* Vol. 1. 221–223.

WOMEN OF THE THIRD ESTATE *(18th century)*

Working Women Petition the King

Women played an increasingly important public role in the early days of the French Revolution. French working-class women in particular exercised their political influence through mass protest and collective action; during the famous October days of 1789 the women of Paris marched to Versailles and demanded an audience with the King in order to discuss the subsistence problems which had been plaguing the inhabitants of Paris. Louis XVI and his family then accompanied the demonstrators back to the capital in a triumphal procession intended to consecrate this instance of unprecedented popular—and female—activism. On the one hand, this march may be considered a remarkable moment within a long-standing tradition of French women's protest; the women did address the King in the terms of the paternalist discourse of the *ancien régime* and (to a certain extent) reaffirmed the legitimacy of the monarch within his role as benevolent protector of the people. On the other, this event served to lay the foundations for the continued development of both French popular republicanism and working-class women's collective protest during the revolutionary period. Siméon-Prosper Hardy, an observer of the march, claimed on this occasion that "These women said publicly that 'men didn't understand anything about the matter and that they wanted to play a role in affairs.'"[1] (For further discussions of the culture and politics of eighteenth-century France, see the entries on Olympe de Gouges in **Representing Women** and Théroigne de Méricourt in **Identifying Sources of Resistance.**)

This "Petition of the Women of the Third Estate to the King" was presented to the monarch on January 1, 1789, months before the revolutionary merging of the Three Estates (clergy, nobility, and commoners) into a unicameral National Assembly and the drafting of the "Declaration of the Rights of Man and the Citizen." Nevertheless, many of the political assumptions (feminist, royalist, and populist simultaneously) which came into sharp focus with the famous October march of the women on Versailles are present in this earlier document. This petition was drawn up after Louis XVI, in August 1788, had asked the people of France to meet together in order to compile lists of grievances and demands; more than sixty thousand of the resulting lists, known as *cahiers de doléances,* still exist. Although this petition is not itself an official *cahier de doléances,* it does form a part of the general outpouring of public speech which occurred during the months following the King's request. Moreover, this document should be considered in the context of women's frequent participation in political protest during subsistence crises. As Joan Landes points out in *Women and the Public Sphere in the Age of the French Revolution,* the women of *ancien régime* France were not necessarily strangers to the political arena. In fact, women had traditionally held the right to vote and be elected to office, although few made use of the privilege. Accordingly, some of the delegates to the Estates General[2] had been selected with the help of women's votes, although no women participated in the assembly itself. The political transformations of the French Revolution did bring about unparalleled changes in the social role of women. According to Landes, "... all women were affected by the dramatic alteration of public space which transformed the political geography of power in the French nation" (107).

During the early period of the French Revolution, then, women exercised a sometimes crucial political influence. They joined revolutionary clubs and societies (the best-known women's society of the time was the Parisian *Citoyennes Républicaines Révolutionnaires* [Revolutionary Republican Citizens]), rioted, published, made speeches, and petitioned both the King and, later on, the National Assembly. The "Petition of the Women of the Third Estate to the King" is only one of a number of similar documents which were created around this time period by women such as the flower sellers and the fishwives of Paris. In this particular petition, the women of the Third Estate "make their voice heard" by addressing the King directly. In this way, the social context of the *ancien régime* allows these women a dual status as subjects: they are both subject to the King's authority and the subjects of speech in this particular instance.

The women's concerns are to some extent traditionally corporate; they ask that men "not be allowed, under any pretext, to exercise trades that are the prerogative of women—such as seamstress, embroiderer, *marchande de mode* [seller of fashion]." However, they also demand a respect for women as workers and productive members of society; they distinguish sharply between women who are employed and educated—who engage in "honest work"—and women who depend upon their sexual charms for sustenance. The ideological separation which is at play here (that which separates the pure women of the public from the sensual and immodest public women or prostitutes) is similar to that discussed by Mary Wollstonecraft (see excerpt in this section) and might be shown to signify a desire to valorize the social role of women on other than sexual terms. Importantly, female purity as it is represented in this petition is not necessarily linked to domesticity or to the private sphere (as Rousseau might have it). The women of the Third Estate, from within a discourse which remains paternalist throughout, call for the right to reappropriate their "reputations" and their good names. Finally, they resist assimilating a concept of the sensual body to that of "natural" woman; they demand recognition for women as a gender on the basis of their social and economic productivity.

NM

PETITION OF WOMEN OF THE THIRD ESTATE TO THE KING[§]

Sire,

At a time when the various orders of the state are busy with their interests, when everyone is trying to assert his titles and his rights, when some people are worrying about recalling centuries of servitude and anarchy, when others

[§] Reprinted from *Women in Revolutionary Paris 1789–1795, Selected Documents,* edited and translated by Darline Gay Levy, Harriet Branson Applewhite, and Mary Durham Johnson. Copyright © 1979 by the Board of Trustees of the University of Illinois. Used with the permission of the University of Illinois Press. Material reprinted from pages 18–21.

are making every effort to shake off the last links which still bind them to the imperious remains of the feudal system, women—continual objects of the admiration and scorn of men—women, wouldn't it be possible for them also to make their voice heard amidst this general agitation?

Excluded from the national assemblies by laws too well consolidated for them to hope to break, they do not ask, Sire, for your permission to send their deputies to the Estates General; they know too well how great a role interest would play in an election and how easy it would be for the representatives [*les élus*] We prefer, Sire, to place our cause at your feet; not wishing to obtain anything except from your heart, we address our complaints and confide our miseries to it.

The women of the Third Estate are almost all born without fortune; their education is very neglected or very defective: it consists in their being sent to schools at the house of a teacher who himself does not know the first word of the language he is teaching. They continue going there until they are able to read the service of the Mass in French and Vespers in Latin. Having fulfilled the first duties of religion, they are taught to work; having reached the age of fifteen or sixteen, they can make five or six *sous* a day. If nature has refused them beauty, they get married without dowry to unfortunate artisans, lead aimless, difficult lives stuck away in the provinces, and give birth to children they are incapable of raising. If, on the contrary, they are born pretty, without culture, without principles, without any idea of morals, they become the prey of the first seducer, commit a first sin, come to Paris to bury their shame, end by losing it altogether, and die victims of licentious ways.

Today, when the difficulty of subsisting forces thousands of them to put themselves up for auction, when men find it easier to buy them for a spell than to win them over forever, those whom a happy penchant inclines to virtue, who are consumed by the desire to learn, who feel themselves led by a natural taste, who have overcome the deficiencies of their education and know a little of everything without having learned anything, those, to conclude, whom a haughty soul, a noble heart, a pride of sentiment cause to be called *prudish,* are forced to throw themselves into cloisters where only a modest dowry is required, or forced to hire themselves out when they do not have enough courage, enough heroism, to share the generous devotion of the daughters of Vincent de Paul.

Also, several, solely because they are born girls, are disdained by their parents, who refuse to set them up, preferring to concentrate their fortune on the head of a son whom they designate to carry on their name in the capital; for it is good that Your Majesty understands that we also have names to keep up. Or, if old age finds them spinsters, they spend it in tears and see themselves the object of the scorn of their nearest relatives.

To prevent so many ills, Sire, we ask that men not be allowed, under any pretext, to exercise trades that are the prerogative of women—such as seamstress, embroider, *marchande de mode,* etc., etc.; if we are left at least with the needle and the spindle, we promise never to handle the compass or the square.

We ask, Sire, that your benevolence provide us with the means of putting to use the talents with which nature will have furnished us, notwithstanding the impediments which are forever being placed on our education.

May you assign us positions, which we alone will be able to fill, which we will occupy only after having passed a strict examination, after trustworthy inquiries concerning the purity of our morals.

We ask to be enlightened, to have work, not in order to usurp men's authority, but in order to be better esteemed by them, so that we might have the means of living out of the way of misfortune and so that poverty does not force the weakest among us, who are blinded by luxury and swept along by example, to join the crowd of unfortunate beings who overpopulate the streets and whose debauched audacity is a disgrace to our sex and to the men who keep them company.

We would want this class of women to wear a mark of identification. Today, when they go so far as to adopt the modesty of our dress, when they mingle everywhere in all kinds of clothing, we often find ourselves taken for them; some men are mistaken and make us blush because of their scorn. It would be necessary that under pain of having to work in the public workshops for the benefit of the poor (it is known that work is the greatest punishment that can be inflicted on them), they never be able to remove this mark. . . . .[*sic*] However, it occurs to us that the empire of fashion would be destroyed and one would run the risk of seeing many too many women dressed in the same color.

We implore you, Sire, to set up free schools where we could learn our language on the basis of principles [and] religion and ethics. May one and the other be offered to us in all their grandeur, entirely stripped of the petty applications which attenuate their majesty; may our hearts be formed there; may we be taught above all to practice the virtues of our sex: gentleness, modesty, patience, charity; as for the arts that please, women learn them without teachers. Sciences? . . . they serve only to inspire us with a stupid pride, lead us to pedantry, go against the desires of nature, make of us mixed beings who are rarely faithful wives and still more rarely good mothers of families.

We ask to come out of the state of ignorance, to be able to give our children a sound and reasonable education so as to make of them subjects worthy of serving you. We will teach them to cherish the beautiful name of Frenchmen; we will transmit to them the love we have for Your Majesty, for we are willing to leave valor and genius to men, but we will challenge them over the dangerous and precious gift of sensitivity; we defy them to love you better than we; they run to Versailles, most of them for their interests, and when we, Sire, see you there, with difficulty and with pounding hearts, and are able to gaze for an instant upon your August Person, tears flow from our eyes. The idea of Majesty, of Sovereign, vanishes, and we see in you only a tender Father, for whom we would sacrifice our lives a thousand times.

NOTES

[1] Cited in Levy, Applewhite, and Johnson, eds. *Women in Revolutionary Paris,* p. 35.

[2] The Estates General might be thought of as a kind of representative body within the political system of the ancien régime. It was composed of the three Estates mentioned above and had not met since 1614. The members of the Estates General voted by order rather than by head, and it was thus assumed that the first two Estates (clergy and nobility) would consistently nullify whatever the more numerous Third Estate might propose.

WORKS CONSULTED

Desan, Suzanne. "Women's Experience of the French Revolution: An Historical Overview." *Literate Women and the French Revolution of 1789.* Ed. Catherine R. Montfort. Birmingham, Alabama: Summa Publications, 1994.

Hufton, Olwen H. *Women and the Limits of Citizenship in the French Revolution.* Toronto: U of Toronto, 1992.

Landes, Joan B. *Women and the Public Sphere in the Age of the French Revolution.* Ithaca: Cornell UP, 1988.

Levy, Darline Gay, Harriet Branson Applewhite, and Mary Durham Johnson, eds. and trans. *Women in Revolutionary Paris 1789–1795, Selected Documents.* Urbana, IL: U of Illinois, 1979.

Soprani, Anne. *La Révolution et les Femmes de 1789 à 1796.* Paris: MA Editions, 1988.

QIU JIN (CH'IU CHIN) *(1877–1907)*

"Promoting Women's Rights"

Executed in 1907 for her role in a plot to overthrow the Manchu rulers of China, Qiu Jin spent her brief adult life in passionate political engagement on behalf of women's rights and revolution. Daughter of a successful civil servant and scholar who had her educated with his son, she engaged in such unconventional behavior as martial arts, horseback riding, drinking, and cross-dressing. She spent her formative years in Hunan, one of the centers of the Western-influenced Reform Movement, which emphasized education, including women's education, and opposed footbinding. In 1903 she moved to the capital with her husband. There he frequented prostitutes and became increasingly abusive, while she became increasingly involved with revolutionary ideas in the wake of the failed Boxer Uprising against foreign influence in China.

Combining her political and domestic rebellion, Qiu left her husband and children to study in Japan, where there was a burgeoning feminist movement. Here she added two names to hers, one meaning "heroine of Ch'ien Lake" (near her home), the other meaning "challenger of men" or "emulate male bravery" (Rankin 52). With her man's dress and sword, she became a memorable figure in revolutionary circles, committing herself tirelessly to political action. She wrote feminist and revolutionary articles, learned to make explosives, recruited for the Revolutionary Alliance against foreign control of China, and founded a magazine dedicated to the democratic revolution and feminism. Here she issued a manifesto to "Fellow Women Citizens of China," beginning, "We, the two hundred million women of China, are the most unfairly treated objects on this earth" (Spence 50). It deplored discrimination against girls, footbinding, domestic seclusion, arranged marriage, obedience, and the double standard (Tao, "Inception" 141). In her feminist agitation she emphasized education for girls, especially so that they could support themselves financially and expand their social world beyond the home. The treatment of women in China created for them, she said, a "black prison" of "darkness and ignorance" in which most were divorced from reality and all were robbed of the will and capacity to resist (Rankin 57).

Returning to China in 1905, Qiu became an important local leader of the Revolutionary Alliance and principal of a school where she trained the girls as a women's army. When her role in planning an uprising was discovered, she was arrested, tortured, and executed.

Qiu's legacy to feminism was her call to women to be in the vanguard of cultural and political change, based on a view that resistance to oppressive political systems was logically intertwined with resistance to cultural systems that subordinated women. She often used poetry as the means to express her commitments, finding in its form a way to describe a situation incisively, envision alternatives, and stir her audience to action. Of the poems that follow, the first was written in Japan when Qiu was making feminist speeches publicly and working privately for individual women's self-liberation. She raised money, for example, to enable a fellow revolutionary's concubines to leave him; she called a women's meeting to persuade one woman to defy her father's plan of making her a concubine (Tao, "Inception" 141). The famous second poem was written around the time when Qiu founded the short-lived *Chinese Women's Journal* in the hope of organizing readers around feminist issues. The third, with its references to "my heart . . . more heroic than a man's," evokes a theme central to her life and work. She has in fact been remembered—in biographies, works of fiction, and folk legend—as the heroic figure she aspired to be.

ECD

RANDOM FEELINGS[§]

Written in Japan

The sun and moon lusterless, heaven and earth grow dark;
Submerged womankind—who will rescue them?
Barrette and bracelet pawned to travel across the sea,
Parting from kith and kin, I left my homeland.
Freeing my bound feet, I washed away the poison of a thousand years,
And, with agitated heart, awakened the souls of all the flowers.
Alas, I have only a binding cloth woven of mermaid's silk,
Half stained with blood, half with tears.

A SONG: PROMOTING WOMEN'S RIGHTS

Our generation yearns to be free;
To all who struggle: one more cup of the Wine of Freedom!
Male and female equality was by Heaven endowed,
So why should women lag behind?
Let's struggle to pull ourselves up,
To wash away the filth and shame of former days.
United we can work together,
And restore this land with our soft white hands.

Most humiliating is the old custom,
Of treating women no better than cows and horses.

[§] Three poems by Qiu Jin (Ch'iu Chin), translated by Pao Chia-lin, reprinted from *Waiting for the Unicorn: Poems and Lyrics of China's Last Dynasty, 1644–1911*, edited by Irving Yucheng Lo and William Schultz. Reprinted by permission of publisher, Indiana University Press, 1986. Material reprinted from pages 400–403.

When the light of dawn shines on our civilization,
We must rise to head the list.
Let's tear out the roots of servitude,
Gain knowledge, learning, and practice what we know.
Take responsibility on our shoulders,
Never to fail or disappoint, our citizen heroines!

TUNE: *MAN CHIANG HUNG* (FULL RIVER RED)

In the capital for a short stay,
And again it is the splendid Mid-Autumn Festival,
Along the fence, chrysanthemums are everywhere in bloom;
The face of autumn shines as if wiped clean.
All around us our enemies sing of our defeat;
For eight years I have missed the flavor of my native land.
How I resent being taken for a reluctant female;
I hardly deserve that fame!

My sex disqualifies me
For the role of male,
But my heart
Is more heroic than a man's.
I guess I'm headstrong, full of daring,
One who warms up when people are around.
Among those of common mind, who can know me?
A heroine at road's end is bound to meet frustration.
In this vulgar world of red dust, where can I find someone
Who truly appreciates me?
Tears wet my dress.

WORKS CONSULTED

Kazuko, Ono. *Chinese Women in a Century of Revolution, 1850–1950.* Tokyo, 1978. Ed. Joshua A. Fogel. Trans. Kathryn Bernhardt, Timothy Brook, Joshua A. Fogel, Jonathan Lipman, Susan Mann, and Laurel Rhodes. Stanford: Stanford UP, 1989.

Rankin, Mary Backus. "The Emergence of Women at the End of the Ch'ing: The Case of Ch'iu Chin." *Women in Chinese Society.* Ed. Margery Wolf and Roxane Witke. Stanford: Stanford UP, 1975.

Snow, Helen Foster. *Women in Modern China.* The Hague: Mouton, 1967.

Spence, Jonathan D. *The Gate of Heavenly Peace: The Chinese and Their Revolution, 1895–1980.* New York: Viking, 1981.

Tao, Chia-lin Pao. "Ch'iu Chin's Revolutionary Career." *Chinese Studies in History: A Journal of Translations* (Summer 1992).

—. "The Inception of the Women's Movement in China: Ch'iu Chin and Her Family." *Families: East and West.* Vol. 1. Ed. Phylis Lan Lin et. al. Indianapolis: U of Indianapolis Press, 1992.

—. "Ch'iu Chin." *Waiting for the Unicorn: Poems and Lyrics of China's Last Dynasty 1644–1911.* Ed. Irving Yucheng Lo and William Schultz. Bloomington: Indiana UP, 1986.

LUISA CAPETILLO *(1879–1922)*

"To Put It into Practice"

Luisa Capetillo was born to an unconventional couple who emigrated to Puerto Rico from France and Spain, bringing with them an admiration for the French feminist novelist and cross-dresser George Sand and revolutionary ideas about politics as well as love. Although her father had come from a wealthy aristocratic family in Spain and her mother began by working as a governess, both became working-class. Except for a brief period at a private school, Luisa received her education primarily from her parents and from her job as a reader in a cigar factory (Romero-Cesareo 777).[1]

This position, which Capetillo may have held again in a New York cigar factory around 1920 (Ramos 66), was inaugurated in the 1860s and made illegal in Puerto Rico and most of the U.S. by the 1930s. It was of critical importance in sustaining the vigorous union activity of the tobacco workers and informing their political philosophy. While workers performed their tasks, the reader read aloud from a "moveable, clandestine library" that included such writers as Marx, Nietzsche, Tolstoy, Kropotkin, Bakunin, Sorel, Malatesta, and various socialist newspapers that included pieces by, or discussions of, socialist feminists such as Clara Zetkin and Rosa Luxemburg (Romero-Cesareo 778–779). Workers discussed the issues after the readings. No doubt this experience affirmed Capetillo's belief in the transformative power of education as a foundation for resistance: "Education is the basis for the happiness of the people. . . . tear away the veil of ignorance. . . . Ignorance is the cause of the greatest crimes and injustices" (*Ensayos libertarios* 89, qtd. in Romero-Cesareo 779).

Capetillo's own resistance involved both theorizing and working actively in the trade union movement. Sylvia P. Apodaca says that "Her skill was in the way she managed to relate and interweave the issues of the private world (such as the family, single motherhood, and women's rights in general) with those of the public world (such as politics, wages, and education)" (72). Her publications included *Ensayos libertarios* [Libertarian Essays] (1907), *La humanidad en el futuro* [Humanity in the future] (1910), *Mi opinión sobre las libertades, derechos y deberes de la mujer como compañera, madre y ser independiente* [My opinion about the liberties, rights, and duties of woman as comrade, mother, and independent being] (1911), and a play, *Influencias de las ideas modernas* [Influences of Modern Ideas] (1916), about "a thinly-disguised Luisa Capetillo" (Romero-Cesareo 776).

Mi opinión is Capetillo's most famous and influential work. Written in what Asunción Lavrin terms an often hasty and unpolished style, it calls on women to assume responsibility for changing history in spite of the slavery to which they were subjected (Romero-Cesareo 777). Arguing for sex education, free love, and political engagement on the part of women, it nonetheless condemns masturbation and homosexuality and assigns men the leading action in terms of marriage. In this, Lavrin points out, the book bestrides two worlds, reaching for modernity even as it is infused with traditional ideas.[2]

If Capetillo was in certain ways traditional, she also expressed her nontraditional ideas dramatically, in all her works picturing "herself and her life as a spectacle from which to learn" (Romero-Cesareo 776). For several years beginning in 1912 she lived in the U.S., first in New York and then in Tampa, Florida, an important center of anarchist and socialist workers' activity centered around the tobacco industry. In 1914 she left for Cuba, where she was arrested for wearing trousers in public and deported for her work with an anarcho-syndicalist workers' movement. Returning to Puerto Rico, she was active in agricultural organizing. 1919 found her back in New York, publishing in the workers' press and continuing her labor activism. She died in Río Piedras in 1922.

Throughout her life Capetillo was a controversial figure. Her cross-dressing, in particular, drew a great deal of attention. As Romero-Cesareo says, "She often attracted large crowds . . . because of her outlandish outfits: trousers, culottes, or men's clothing from head to toe. She had a strong sense of her body as a signifying body; whether it was through her clothing, her expressions and poses in photographs, or her demeanor as she rode a horse through the crowds, she carried a banner that spelled out her contestatory stance. Her visualization of herself as the heroine of a spectacle—a spectacle for herself and for others—enabled her to pursue her political projects and, rather than merely theorize about them, to live them. She tried to be living proof of the fact that certain things can be achieved without waiting for conditions to be ideal" (776).

ECD

FROM *MY OPINION* [§]

From the Preface to *My Opinion*

There is nothing more prejudicial to the success of a cause than timidity, shyness, doubt. Only idle people have that type of cowardice. I believe nothing impossible; I do not wonder about any moment or discovery; that is why I do not find any idea utopian. The essential thing is to put it into practice. To begin! The rest is weakness and a mistaken concept of human power.

On Man and Woman

I cannot explain to myself why man always believes himself to have rights over woman. For example, a young man, regardless of age, always aspires to marry a young virgin without any knowledge of life. Even though he has tasted and enjoyed all pleasures, and known all the vices, he still believes that it is very natural to aspire to marry a moderate and honest young woman.

This has been permitted by social customs. Rather, we women have tolerated it on account of the supposed weakness that we have always been accused of having.

§ Reprinted from *Amor y anarquía: los escritos de Luisa Capetillo* [Love and Anarchy: The Writings of Luisa Capetillo] edited by Julio Ramos. Material for this anthology translated by Asunción Lavrin from pages 74, 198–201, 194–195. Published 1992 by Ediciones Huracán, Río Piedras, Puerto Rico. Used by permission.

Whenever I have the opportunity to observe a young man courting a young woman and observe their faces, I become astonished, and protest the fact that this man dares to pretend to her although he is not equal to her in morality. He is withered and even spent; she is beautiful, evocative, and chaste. Even so, she finds that he does her a great favor in marrying her.

We must change this system; we must transform this custom. No woman should accept a man who is not in the same condition; if men do not want to abandon their habits, they must agree to let us share them.

It is ridiculous and stupid that two people in love cannot belong to each other because, according to old conventions, this is immoral. And on leaving each other he goes to satisfy his repressed passion with another woman, while she masturbates or has sexual "relations" with another woman, thus atrophying her brain and damaging her beauty. That is criminal, hateful, embarrassing, and unnatural, and parents are to blame for it. The natural thing is that man and woman complement each other using the rights that nature has granted them without stupid fears.

Man should not make use of his sexual needs until he achieves his full development and then should look for a woman to love, to make a home and form a family.

Following this practice we should have a healthy, strong, robust, and happy generation.

No man should belong to any other woman except for the one with whom he has chosen to form a family. Then we could talk about good customs and morality, but the way we are, we are all prostituted; to talk about morality is ironic, stupid, and useless.

If we practice this system we will take love to its truest condition. This is the free love that is being defined and libeled as immoral, when immorality, disorder, and vice is what we have right now. Man today believes it is correct and decent to engage in sexual acts with a woman who does not belong to him alone, and then assume the right to court a chaste woman—or one who looks chaste. He is sure of that. What I see is that he does not look for a woman in the same condition he is. No, he must seek the virgin, and within that inequality he dares to speak about goodness. And woman today, who has rights equal to men, must in the name of honesty deprive herself of belonging to her fiancee, only to hurt herself, to become sick, destroying her body, atrophying her brain, becoming prematurely old, suffering thousands of sicknesses, dizziness, hysteria—laughing and crying without reason. And all of this because woman ignores her rights and does not know what would make her happy, which is to belong without fears to the man she loves. Her lover must not be deprived of the right of enjoying the first offerings of her love. And man, in many cases, wanting to avoid contagion or not wanting to be in the arms of a woman he does not love, engages in acts against nature. Who is to be blamed for such aberrations?

The moralizers should speak out!

Who has made of the most beautiful and sublime act in which two people who love each other should engage, a mere pastime with no consequences for human reproduction?

The celibate "priesthood" should speak out . . .

Who is to be blamed for the fact that a man and woman who love each other refrain from having children because they cannot afford to sustain them and resort to conjugal fraud? There is in nature enough to feed humanity, without exploitation, frauds, and misery.

The egotist and exploiters should speak out.

On sex education for women

How can woman achieve true knowledge if she cannot see things as they are? For her all is hidden behind a veil of mystery that does not allow her to see reality; if she is in a dance, or in the theater, or at home, all deceive her and she does not even realize this. She is the eternal blind guided, generally, by a libertine who continuously tells her: "Do as I tell you and not as I do." And she continues to believe this spiteful person without realizing that she is being cheated. And she lives cheated, and is educated and perverted with such deceits and she does not notice it. When she was a girl they told her: "girls should not do this or that because girls must believe this and that" and she begins her role of victim of her parents' conventionalities, and later of social fancy, and later, or at the same time, of the eccentricities of her fiancee, and later of the tyranny of her husband. . . .

How deluded is everybody!

Eventually woman realizes the vile and infamous comedy played to cheat her, and how people have perverted themselves using her. But when she assumes her freedom, there are no pretexts, or reasoning, or anything that can stop her. Then, what is the use of deceiving her? To enslave her on the pretext of stupid egoisms of the flesh.

After such parental precautions to keep her ignorant of everything she should know (which is the procedure man has adopted toward woman since ancient times, and how he has used her, and the vices he has taught her), she must enter into her new home to become the victim of her ignorance. A woman instructed in all that concerns her sex, before and after she becomes one with her rightful (or not) husband, has to know how to defend herself. And if she does not defend herself because she is blind, knowing that she does not know is already a benefit, because even if she becomes her husband's accomplice, she will always have the opportunity of thinking about her acts and she will end by rejecting them. It is convenient for a woman to be educated scientifically. All single and married women should read *The Hygiene of Marriage*. I cannot advise this without thinking of those enemies of women who want women to remain ignorant of their own existence or to unknowingly learn obscene practices, taught to them by those who are always criticizing the women, who are their disciples. I believe that in the same manner that a male obstetrician may be present and facilitate a difficult birth based on his title, a woman should be able to study men's vices and diseases to prevent her from acquiring obscene and indecent habits. As for those who may dare to consider this immoral, it is really because they are guilty and fear being discovered by their wives. This needs a strong and fearless correction. Women of all social classes, defend yourselves! The enemy is formidable, but do not fear him, because his cowardice knows no measure!

NOTES

[1] I would like to thank Elizabeth Waters and Asunción Lavrin for their contributions to the information and ideas in this headnote.

[2] For the broader context of Capetillo's ideas, see Lavrin's *Ideology of Feminism* and *Women, Feminism, and Social Change.*

WORKS CONSULTED

Apodaca, Sylvia P. "Luisa Capetillo." *Notable Hispanic Women.* Ed. Diane Telgen and Jim Kamp. Detroit: Gale Research, 1993. 72–73.

Capetillo, Luisa. *Amor y anarquía: los escritos de Luisa Capetillo.* Ed. Julio Ramos. Río Piedras, Puerto Rico: Ediciones Huracán, 1992.

Ferrer, Norma Valle. *Luisa Capetillo: Historia de una mujer proscrita.* Río Piedras: Editorial Cultural, 1990.

Lavrin, Asunción. Conversations with Eugenia DeLamotte October 18, 1996 and October 21, 1996.

—. *The Ideology of Feminism in the Southern Cone 1900–1940.*Washington, D.C.: Latin American Program, The Wilson Center, 1986.

—. *Women, Feminism, and Social Change in Argentina, Chile, and Uruguay, 1890–1940.* Lincoln: U of Nebraska P, 1995.

Romero-Cesareo, Ivette. "Whose Legacy? Voicing Women's Rights from the 1870s to the 1930s." *Callaloo* 17.3 (1994): 770–789.

UNITED NATIONS FOURTH WORLD CONFERENCE ON WOMEN, BEIJING, CHINA *(1995)*

"Global Framework" of the *Platform for Action*

Beijing 1995—the phrase has become an important marker for those seeking ways to improve the conditions of women's lives. Our exploration, in this anthology, of the multiple approaches that women have used to examine themselves and their societies concludes with a section of the *Platform for Action* that emerged from the UN Fourth World Conference on Women. This international gathering of women to envision the future at the close of the twentieth century represents a significant event in the long history of resistance.

The United Nations Charter, adopted at the close of World War II, called for equality between women and men. Over the next three decades, female officials at the United Nations as well as leaders of women's movements around the world pushed for action on the principles of the charter. In 1975, the official world body declared the decade 1975–1985 the "Decade of Women." The formal discussions began with a World Conference on Women in Mexico City, Mexico, in 1975. (See selections from Domitila Barrios de Chungara in **Work and Education.**) Governments appointed official representatives; organizations from around the world sent members to the non-governmental agencies forum. The women leaders at that conference were struck with the lack of research on women. They subsequently organized two conferences, one at Wingspread, Wisconsin, and a second at the Center for Research on Women at Wellesley College in Massachussetts (Wellesley Editorial Committee). Although both conferences were held in the United States of America, participants from around the world who had been in Mexico City attended and the emphasis was on developing information that would allow the Decade of Women to move forward.

Midway through the decade in 1980, a second World Conference was held in Copenhagen, Denmark. The conference was characterized by the availability of a growing body of research on women but also by troubling political divisions. Despite the emerging efforts by feminist leaders to articulate how women's issues were human rights issues, the nationalist politics of many countries participating threatened to hamper the future of such conferences and of the Decade.

The experiences of Copenhagen served to energize both the government offices that had sent delegates to the official forum and the women's organizations worldwide that had participated in the non-governmental organizations forum. The next five years witnessed the pouring of energy into discussions, meetings, and plans for celebrating the Decade's end with a vision for the future. Meeting in Nairobi, Kenya, in 1985, more than 15,000 women and men addressed issues of equality, development, and peace. While there were ongoing divisions among and within the delegations—over the relationship between political revolution and change in women's position, whether issues of sexuality should have the same degree of importance as issues of subsistence, the ways in which class and race intersect with gender to determine women's status, and many other issues—Nairobi marked an important turning point in conversations among women worldwide. More women from more diverse backgrounds attended. With more information available and more experience in addressing women's issues at local, national, and international levels, women in both the official and non-governmental forums found themselves agreeing on goals and spending more time talking about strategies for change.

The Fourth World Conference on Women was held in Beijing, China, in September 1995, marking two decades of attention to women's issues by national governments and organizations as well as international agencies. Beijing was different. The delegates to both forums—governmental and non-governmental—benefitted from twenty years of active organizing. They had before them almost two decades of scholarship, policy documents, and legislative experiences. They knew of the thousands of efforts at organizing women around all of the issues that touched their lives. They had come to understand and to insist that the world community recognize that issues of women and gender must be at the heart of all political endeavors for social change.

While the meeting in China was by no means without rancor, the consensus that emerged across remarkable differences in class, race, ethnicity, religion, sexual orientation, political stance, and many other variables was a twelve-point plan for action for delegates to "bring home from Beijing." The emphasis had shifted in this fourth conference from what many viewed as first world women telling other women what women's problems were and what needed to be done about them, to a broad spectrum of women identifying the issues that restricted their lives and debating how they might effect social change in their particular contexts.

The twelve points of the Beijing *Platform for Action* were widely summarized in the popular press. They include:

- The persistent and increasing burden of poverty on women
- Inequalities and inadequacies in and unequal access to education and training
- Inequalities and inadequacies in and unequal access to health care and related services
- Violence against women
- The effects of armed or other kinds of conflict on women, including those living under foreign occupation
- Inequality in economic structures and policies, in all forms of productive activities and in access to resources
- Inequality between men and women in the sharing of power and decision-making at all levels
- Insufficient mechanisms at all levels to promote the advancement of women
- Lack of respect for and inadequate promotion and protection of the human rights of women
- Stereotyping of women and inequality in women's access to and participation in all communication systems, especially in the media

- Gender inequalities in the management of natural resources and in the safeguarding of the environment
- Persistent discrimination against and violation of the rights of the girl-child (Platform for Action 34)

These issues, framed locally, were to serve as the basis for discussion in follow-up meetings around the world as delegates returned to their home countries to decide "what next?" The global awareness engendered in Beijing is at once tangible and elusive. In many organizations, churches, educational institutions, and in legislative bodies throughout the world, programs that describe what women want have been presented, debated, and sometimes acted on. Nonetheless, the goals remain elusive: the changes called for in the *Platform for Action* require fundamental shifts in social and cultural institutions that will certainly meet opposition. And yet the consensus on targets for action that drove the delegates in Beijing suggests that a new vision informs the desire for transformation in women's lives.

We reprint here the section of the *Platform for Action* called the "Global Framework," a set of principles hammered out by the official delegates (and largely endorsed by the non-governmental organizations forum) that illustrates the thinking of women and men who came together to reflect on the past and envision the future.

JFO

FROM THE "GLOBAL FRAMEWORK" [§]

The Fourth World Conference on Women is taking place as the world stands poised on the threshold of a new millennium. . . .

The objective of the Platform for Action, which is in full conformity with the purposes and principles of the Charter of the United Nations and international law, is the empowerment of all women. The full realization of all human rights and fundamental freedoms of all women is essential for the empowerment of women. While the significance of national and regional particularities and various historical, cultural and religious backgrounds must be borne in mind, it is the duty of States, regardless of their political, economic and cultural systems, to promote and protect all human rights and fundamental freedoms. . . .

. . . The universal nature of these rights and freedoms is beyond question. . . .

The maintenance of peace and security at the global, regional and local levels, together with the prevention of policies of aggression and ethnic cleansing and the resolution of armed conflict, is crucial for the protection of the human rights of women and girl-children, as well as for the elimination of all forms of violence against them and of their use as a weapon of war.

[§] Reprinted from *The Beijing Declaration and The Platform for Action.* United Nations Fourth World Conference on Women, Beijing, China, 4–15 September 1995, by permission of the United Nations Department of Public Information, New York. Copyright © 1996 by the United Nations. All United Nations rights reserved. Material reprinted from pages 21–30.

Excessive military expenditures, including global military expenditures and arms trade or trafficking, and investments of arms production and acquisition have reduced the resources available for social development. . . .

In this context, the social dimension of development should be emphasized. Accelerated economic growth, although necessary for social development, does not by itself improve the quality of life of the population. In some cases, conditions can arise which can aggravate social inequality and marginalization. Hence, it is indispensable to search for new alternatives that ensure that all members of society benefit from economic growth based on a holistic approach to all aspects of development: growth, equality between men and women, social justice, conservation and protection of the environment, sustainability, solidarity, participation, peace and respect for human rights. . . .

Absolute poverty and the feminization of poverty, unemployment, the increasing fragility of the environment, continued violence against women and the widespread exclusion of half of humanity from institutions of power and governance underscore the need to continue the search for development, peace and security and for ways of assuring people-centered sustainable development. The participation and leadership of the half of humanity that is female is essential to the success of that search. Therefore, only a new era of international cooperation among Governments and peoples based on a spirit of partnership, an equitable, international social and economic environment, and a radical transformation of the relationship between women and men to one of full and equal partnership will enable the world to meet the challenges of the twenty-first century.

Recent international economic developments have had in many cases a disproportionate impact on women and children, the majority of whom live in developing countries. For those States that have carried a large burden of foreign debt, structural adjustment programmes and measures, though beneficial in the long term, have led to a reduction in social expenditures, thereby adversely affecting women, particularly in Africa and the least developed countries. This is exacerbated when responsibilities for basic social services have shifted from Governments to women.

Economic recession in many developed and developing countries, as well as ongoing restructuring in countries with economies in transition, have had a disproportionately negative impact on women's employment. Women often have no choice but to take employment that lacks long-term job security or involves dangerous working conditions, to work in unprotected home-based production or to be unemployed. Many women enter the labour market in under-remunerated and undervalued jobs, seeking to improve their household income; others decide to migrate for the same purpose. Without any reduction in their other responsibilities, this has increased the total burden of work for women.

Macro- and microeconomic policies and programmes, including structural adjustment, have not always been designed to take account of their impact on women and girl-children, especially those living in poverty. Poverty has increased in both absolute and relative terms, and the number of women living in poverty has increased in most regions. There are many urban women living in poverty; however, the plight of women living in rural and remote areas deserves special attention given the stagnation of development in such areas. In developing countries, even those in which national indicators have shown improvement, the majority of rural women continue to live in conditions of economic underdevelopment and social marginalization.

Women are key contributors to the economy and to combating poverty through both remunerated and unremunerated work at home, in the community and in the workplace. Growing numbers of women have achieved economic independence through gainful employment.

One fourth of all households worldwide are headed by women and many other households are dependent on female income even where men are present. Female-maintained households are very often among the poorest because of wage discrimination, occupational segregation patterns in the labour market and other gender-based barriers. Family disintegration, population movements between urban and rural areas within countries, international migration, war and internal displacements are factors contributing to the rise of female-headed households.

Recognizing that the achievement and maintenance of peace and security are a precondition for economic and social progress, women are increasingly establishing themselves as central actors in a variety of capacities in the movement of humanity for peace. Their full participation in decision-making, conflict prevention and resolution and all other peace initiatives is essential to the realization of lasting peace.

Religion, spirituality and belief play a central role in the lives of millions of women and men, in the way they live and in the aspirations they have for the future. The right to freedom of thought, conscience and religion is inalienable and must be universally enjoyed. This right includes the freedom to have or to adopt the religion or belief of their choice either individually or in community with others, in public or in private, and to manifest their religion or belief in worship, observance, practice and teaching. In order to realize equality, development and peace, there is a need to respect these rights and freedoms fully. Religion, thought, conscience and belief may, and can, contribute to fulfilling women's and men's moral, ethical and spiritual needs and to realizing their full potential in society. However, it is acknowledged that any form of extremism may have a negative impact on women and can lead to violence and discrimination. . . .

The growing strength of the non-governmental sector, particularly women's organizations and feminist groups, has become a driving force for change. Non-governmental organizations have played an important advocacy role in advancing legislation or mechanisms to ensure the promotion of women. They have also become catalysts for new approaches to development. Many Governments have increasingly recognized the important role that non-governmental organizations play and the importance of working with them for progress. Yet, in some countries, Governments continue to restrict the ability of non-governmental organizations to operate freely. Women, through non-governmental organizations, have participated in and strongly influenced community, national, regional and global forums and international debates.

Since 1975, knowledge of the status of women and men, respectively, has increased and is contributing to further actions aimed at promoting equality between women and men. In several countries, there have been important changes in the relationships between women and men, especially where there have been major advances in education for women and significant increases in their participation in the paid labour force. The boundaries of the gender division of labour between productive and reproductive roles are gradually being crossed as women have started to enter formerly male-dominated areas of work and men have started to accept greater responsibility for domestic tasks, including child care. However, changes in women's roles have been greater and much more rapid than changes in men's roles. In many countries, the differences between women's and men's achievements and activities are still not recognized as the consequences of socially constructed gender roles rather than immutable biological differences.

Moreover, 10 years after the Nairobi Conference, equality between women and men has still not been achieved. On average, women represent a mere 10 per cent of all elected legislators worldwide and in most national and international administrative structures, both public and private, they remain underrepresented. The United Nations is no exception. Fifty years after its creation, the United Nations is continuing to deny itself the benefits of women's leadership by their underrepresentation at decision-making levels within the Secretariat and the specialized agencies.

Women play a critical role in the family. The Family is the basic unit of society and as such should be strengthened. It is entitled to receive comprehensive protection and support. In different cultural, political and social systems, various forms of the family exist. The rights, capabilities and responsibilities of family members must be respected. Women make a great contribution to the welfare of the family and to the development of society, which is still not recognized or considered in its full importance. The social significance of maternity, motherhood and the role of the parents in the family and in the upbringing of children should be acknowledged. The upbringing of children requires shared responsibility of parents, women and men and society as a whole. Maternity, motherhood, parenting and the role of women in procreation must not be a basis for discrimination nor restrict the full participation of women in society. Recognition should also be given to the important role often played by women in many countries in caring for other members of their family. . . .

. . . Care of children, the sick and the elderly is a responsibility that falls disproportionately on women, owing to lack of equality and the unbalanced distribution of remunerated and unremunerated work between women and men. . . .

Many women face particular barriers because of various diverse factors in addition to their gender. Often these diverse factors isolate or marginalize such women. They are, *inter alia,* denied their human rights, they lack access or are denied access to education and vocational training, employment, housing and economic self-sufficiency and they are excluded from decision-making processes. Such women are often denied the opportunity to contribute to their communities as part of the mainstream.

The past decade has also witnessed a growing recognition of the distinct interests and concerns of indigenous women, whose identity, cultural traditions and forms of social organization enhance and strengthen the communities in which they live. Indigenous women often face barriers both as women and as members of indigenous communities.

The continuing environmental degradation that affects all human lives often has a more direct impact on women. Women's health and their livelihood are threatened by pollution and toxic wastes, large-scale deforestation, desertification, drought and depletion of the soil and of coastal and marine resources, with a rising incidence of environmentally related health problems and even death reported among women and girls. Those most affected are rural and indigenous women, whose livelihood and daily subsistence depends directly on sustainable ecosystems.

Poverty and environmental degradation are closely interrelated. While poverty results in certain kinds of environmental stress, the major cause of the continued deterioration of the global environment is the unsustainable patterns of consumption and production, particularly in industrialized countries, which are a matter of grave concern and aggravate poverty and imbalances.

Global trends have brought profound changes in family survival strategies and structures. Rural to urban migration has increased substantially in all regions. The global urban population is projected to reach 47 per cent of the total population by the year 2000. An estimated 125 million people are migrants, refugees and displaced persons, half of whom live in developing countries. These massive movements of people have profound consequences for family structures and well-being and have unequal consequences for women and men, including in many cases the sexual exploitation of women.

Since 1975, significant knowledge and information have been generated about the status of women and the conditions in which they live. Throughout their entire life cycle, women's daily existence and long-term aspirations are restricted by discriminatory attitudes, unjust social and economic structures, and a lack of resources in most countries that prevent their full and equal participation. In a number of countries, the practice of prenatal sex selection, higher rates of mortality among very young girls and lower rates of school enrollment for girls as compared with boys suggest that son preference is curtailing the access of girl-children to food, education and health care and even life itself. Discrimination against women begins at the earliest stages of life and must therefore be addressed from then onwards.

The girl-child of today is the woman of tomorrow. The skills, ideas and energy of the girl-child are vital for full attainment of the goals of equality, development and peace. For the girl-child to develop her full potential she needs to be nurtured in an enabling environment, where her spiritual, intellectual and material needs for survival, protection and development are met and her equal rights safeguarded. If women are to be equal partners with men, in every aspect of life and development, now is the time to recognize the human dignity and worth of the girl-child and to ensure the full enjoyment of her human rights and fundamental freedoms, including the rights assured by the Convention on the Rights of the Child, universal ratification of which is strongly urged. Yet there exists worldwide evidence that discrimination and violence against girls begin at the earliest stages of life and continue unabated throughout their lives. They often have less access to nutrition, physical and mental health care and education and enjoy fewer rights, opportunities and benefits of childhood and adolescence than do boys. They are often subjected to various forms of sexual and economic exploitation, pedophilia, forced prostitution and possibly the sale of their organs and tissues, violence and harmful practices such as female infanticide and prenatal sex selection, incest, female genital mutilation and early marriage, including child marriage.

Half the world's population is under the age of 25 and most of the world's youth—more than 85 per cent—live in developing countries. Policy makers must recognize the implications of these demographic factors. Special measures must be taken to ensure that young women have the life skills necessary for active and effective participation in all levels of social, cultural, political and economic leadership. It will be critical for the international community to demonstrate a new commitment to the future—a commitment to inspiring a new generation of women and men to work together for a more just society. This new generation of leaders must accept and promote a world in which every child is free from injustice, oppression and inequality and free to develop her/his own potential. The principle of equality of women and men must therefore be integral to the socialization process.

WORKS CONSULTED

Women's Bureau, U.S. Department of Labor, and the President's Interagency Council on Women, The White House. *Bringing Beijing Home.* Jan. 1996.

President's Interagency Council on Women. *U.S. Follow-Up to the U.N. Fourth World Conference on Women.* U.S. Government Printing Office, 1996.

United Nations Fourth World Conference on Women, Beijing, China, 4–15 September 1995. *The Beijing Declaration and The Platform for Action.* New York: United Nations Department of Public Information, 1996.

Wellesley Editorial Committee, eds. *Women and National Development: The Complexities of Change.* Chicago: U of Chicago P, 1977.

SUBJECT INDEX

NAME INDEX